DICTIONARY OF BANKING AND FINANCIAL SERVICES

DICTIONARY OF BANKING AND FINANCIAL SERVICES

Jerry M. Rosenberg, Ph.D.

Professor, Graduate School of Management
Chairman, Department of Business Administration
Faculty of Arts and Sciences
Rutgers University
Newark, New Jersey

SECOND EDITION

JOHN WILEY & SONS

New York • Chichester • Brisbane • Toronto • Singapore

Library of Congress Cataloging in Publication Data:
Rosenberg, Jerry Martin.
   Dictionary of banking and financial services.

   Rev. ed. of: Dictionary of banking and finance.
c1982.
   Includes index.
   1. Finance—Dictionaries.   2. Banks and banking—
Dictionaries.   I. Rosenberg, Jerry Martin.   Dictionary
of banking and finance.   II. Title.
HG151.R67 1985   332′.03′21   85-12461
ISBN 0-471-83088-7
ISBN 0-471-83133-6 (pbk.)

Printed in the United States of America

10 9 8 7 6 5 4 3 2 1

To Lauren

with love

FOREWORD

David Rockefeller
Chase Manhattan Bank, N.A.
Chairman and Chief
Executive Officer (retired)

As I look back over nearly 35 years as a banker, I cannot help noting how much more complex banking is now than when I began my career. It has indeed been a business of change, with the rate of change itself continually increasing.

From all indications, this rapid change in the banking business is not likely to abate. Rather, all indicators suggest that it is likely to increase geometrically in the days ahead. Increasingly responsive communications and increasingly diverse and demanding market forces have led to more complex arrangements for lending, funding, money transfers, and other bank services. At the same time, increased competition has made it necessary for financial institutions to market their products and services more vigorously and effectively.

New international financial structures which have emerged in past decades have themselves induced other changes in banking—and it is likely that more structural changes will be created in the future to serve international financial needs and markets.

Meanwhile, on the domestic scene, crumbling statutory and regulatory barriers between banks and other kinds of financial institutions, in conjunction with long overdue trends toward reduced regulation, have added new competition for commercial banks. New and more innovative competitive responses will no doubt be required.

New markets, new products, new regulatory constraints, new participants, and new competitors in the financial marketplace—all these represent challenges to clear understanding and communications in an increasingly complex and evolving business.

In this challenging atmosphere of transition and turmoil in the financial industry, effective communication—clear understanding among people and financial institutions—is absolutely fundamental to business effectiveness. Simply put, we must know how to express precisely what we mean, and we must be able to discern correctly the intended meaning of what is being said to us. The changes in our financial community, domestically and internationally, and the need to communicate more clearly make it essential that we use terminology accurately, and that we agree on the full meaning of the terms we use in our business affairs. This clarity of meaning is as important in our letters to associates and statements to the public as it is in our highly structured financial communications, letters of credit, and loan agreements.

Thus, as we face a changing business and financial environment and recognize the need to communicate more clearly, I am confident that Professor Rosenberg's dictionary of terms in banking and finance will be welcomed by the community it seeks to serve. I am particularly pleased that it reaches to the periphery of banking and financial services so that relevant terms in such areas as computer systems, organization, and manpower can be understood in their banking and financial contexts.

August 1980

PREFACE

The growth of the financial services industry, encompassing insurance companies, banks, and securities firms, has been one of the major developments of the 1980s. As these corporations move beyond their traditional activities, they are not only offering additional products but also encroaching on other segments of this industry and testing the boundaries of government regulations.

In addition, with all these changes, lexicographic excellence demands a vision to fine-tune what is unique to U.S. systems and where foreign concepts affect usage. Spurred by a spreading free-market ideology by advances in global communications, and by the dismantling of financial regulations, we are witnessing a rush toward the internationalization of markets, with domestic banking and financial opportunities being opened to foreigners. In this edition, I have attempted to intertwine these subtleties and bridge the gap to include phrases of interest here and abroad.

The end product is a totally new work, with numerous terms deleted or revised and thousands more added. By receiving authorization to incorporate entries from the American Bankers Association's *Banking Terminology*, this second edition of approximately 15,000 terms emerges as the most complete dictionary available in the areas of banking and financial services.

One significant difference between the first and second editions is the change of title to reflect the fading differences between banks and other financial institutions. Another is the removal of all appendices. Realizing that these entries quickly became obsolete, I encourage readers wishing detailed reference tables of statistical data to seek out appropriate current sources.

Stephen Kippur, executive publisher, and John Mahaney, my new editor, both of John Wiley & Sons, have been enlightened professional supporters for this revision.

My colleague at Rutgers University, Paul Nadler, Professor of Banking, was most helpful in his thorough review and critique of the first edition.

Ellen, my wife, and daughters Lauren and Elizabeth continue to be my inspiration. Time away from them, whether spent researching an article or struggling with a complex term, is more than compensated by their affection.

Finally, to my reader—the ultimate jurist—I continue to seek your critical comments and urge you to bring errors and suggestions to my attention.

JERRY M. ROSENBERG, PH.D.

New York
September, 1985

A revolution among financial institutions is under way. Differences between them are fading, arbitrary barriers to nationwide retail banking are threatened, and the dividing line between banking and securities is challenged.

Sweeping legislation passed in 1980—the Depository Institutions Deregulation and Monetary Control Act—ratified and extended innovation and price competition in the financial marketplace, and over the course of the next few years these changes will bring about a rationalization of the industry via interstate banking.

As the shape of financial institutions is transformed, savings and loan associations are going to take on more qualities usually attributed to commercial banks, and they will have to manage their assets and liabilities more like commercial banks.

In sum, with deregulation in banking and finance, change is bound to create a combination of threats and challenges, requiring a better awareness of the full range of strategies, options, and meanings open to all.

This dictionary is a practical guide and reference tool for proper handling of the many banking and financial problems and questions that arise in business every day. It provides a deeper understanding of operations, methods, and practices in the rapidly changing fields of banking and finance.

This work of approximately 10,000 entries has been prepared with the hope that awareness of the accepted meanings of terms may enhance the process of sharing information and ideas. Though it cannot eliminate the need for the user to determine how a writer or speaker treats a word, such a dictionary shows what usages exist. It should reduce arguments about words and assist in stabilizing terminology. Most important, it should aid people in saying and writing just what they intend with greater clarity.

A word can take on different meanings in different contexts. There may be as many meanings as there are areas of specialty. A goal of this dictionary is to be broad and to establish core definitions that represent the variety of individual meanings. My purpose is to enhance parsimony and clearness in the communication process within the banking and financial fields.

Many terms are used in different ways. I have tried to unite them without bias of giving one advantage or dominance over another. Whenever possible (without creating a controversy), I have stated the connection among multiple usages.

Commonly used symbols, acronyms, and abbreviations are given. Foreign words and phrases are included only if they have become an integral part of our English vocabulary.

Other dictionaries that deal with a similar subject tend to define their task rather narrowly, whereas this work purports to reach throughout all departments within banks and financial institutions by acknowledging that the sum of an organization is greater than any of its individual parts—the result, an all-inclusive dictionary of banking and financial terms.

The broad base in the banking and financial fields necessitated inclusion of terms within this dictionary from accounting, banking, brokerage, capital structure, capitalization, collections, commercial banking, commodities markets, computer systems, credit, credit unions, financial institutions, financial law, financial management, financial planning, financial reports, foreign trade, funding, government regulations and agencies, import-export, insurance, investments, lending, methods of financing, manpower and human resources, money concepts, mortgages, organization, personal finance, public finance, savings and loan associations, savings banks, securities markets, services, sources of bank and financial information, systems, transfers, and trusts.

ORGANIZATION

This is a defining work rather than a compilation of facts. The line is not easy to draw because in the final analysis meanings are based on facts. Consequently, factual information is used where necessary to make a term more easily understood.

All terms are presented in the language of those who use them. Obviously, the level of complexity needed for a definition will vary with the user; one person's complexity is another's precise and parsimonious statement. Several meanings are sometimes given—relatively simple for the layman, more developed and technical for the specialist.

I have organized the dictionary to provide information easily and rapidly. Keeping in mind two categories of user—the experienced person who demands precise information about a particular word, and the newcomer, support member, teacher, or student who seeks general explanations—I have in most cases supplied both general and specialized entries. This combination of "umbrella" entries and specialized definitions should make this dictionary an unusually useful reference source.

FORMAT

Alphabetization. Words are presented alphabetically. Compound terms are placed where the reader is most likely to look for them. They are entered under their most distinctive component, usually nouns, which tend to be more distinctive than are adjectives. Should you fail to locate a word where you initially look for it, turn to a variant spelling, a synonym, or another, differing word of the compound term.

Entries containing mutual concepts are usually grouped for comparison. They are then given in inverted order; that is, the expected order of words is reversed to allow the major word of the phrase to appear at the beginning of the term. These entries precede those that are given in the expected order. The terms are alphabetized up to the first comma and then by words following the comma, thus establishing clusters of related terms.

Headings. The currently popular term is usually given as the principal entry, with other terms cross-referenced to it. Some terms have been included for historical significance, even though they are not presently in common usage.

Cross-References. The rule followed for cross-references calls for going from the general to the specific. Occasionally, "see" references from the specific to the general are used to inform the user of words related to particular entries. "See" references to presently accepted terminology are made wherever possible. The use of "Cf." suggests words to be compared with the original entry.

Synonyms. The word "synonymous" following a definition does not imply that the term is exactly equivalent to the principal entry under which it appears. Usually the term only approximates the primary sense of the original entry.

Disciplines. Many words are given multiple definitions based on their utilization in various fields of activity. The definition with the widest application is then given first, with the remaining definitions listed by area of specialty (identified in boldface italic type). Since the areas may overlap, the reader should examine all multiple definitions of a term.

ACKNOWLEDGMENTS

No dictionary can be the exclusive product of one person's effort. Even when written by one individual, such a work requires the tapping of many sources, which is especially true of this book. By the very nature of the fields included, I have had to rely on the able and extensive efforts of others, especially the members of the Advisory Board.

When I have quoted a definition from another copyrighted source, a number in brackets appears at the end of the definition. This number indicates the primary reference used in defining the term which is identified in Appendix K of the dictionary. When no reference source is shown following a term, this suggests that I have not deliberately quoted the definition from any copyrighted source. Any apparent similarity to existing, unreleased definitions in these cases is purely accidental and the result of the limitations of language.

Much assistance has come indirectly from authors of books, journal articles, and reference materials. They are too numerous to be named here. Various organizations have aided me directly by providing informative source materials. Some government agencies and not-for-profit associations have provided a considerable amount of usable information.

On a more personal level, I thank the various individuals whom I used as a sounding board to clarify my ideas and approach; they offered valuable suggestions and encouraged me to go on with the project. Stephen Kippur, my editor, of John Wiley & Sons, had the foresight to initiate this book, and with sensitivity and creativity followed it through to publication. And I thank, once again, my wife Ellen and my daughters Lauren and Elizabeth, who showed understanding and offered full support during the preparation of this book.

FEEDBACK

The definitions given here have been reviewed by bank and finance specialists, and educators. However I am solely responsible for choosing the terms to be included. The vast range of material makes it inevitable that definitions may vary based on perspective, background, and connotation. I welcome critical comments bringing errors to my attention, to make it possible to correct them in later editions, thus evolving a greater conformity of meaning for all.

JERRY M. ROSENBERG, PH.D.

New York
January, 1982

CONTENTS

DICTIONARY OF BANKING AND FINANCIAL SERVICES

A:
- (1) see *account*.
- (2) Class "A" or Series "A."
- (3) the total average dollar inventory.

A1: the highest class rating.

AA:
- (1) see *active account*.
- (2) see *active assets*.

AAA
- (1) *finance:* the Standard & Poor's bond rating, given "only to bonds of the highest quality." Moody's grants a parallel AAA rating.
- (2) *government:* Agricultural Adjustment Act; a 1933 federal law intended to aid farmers by raising the prices of crops and livestock through controlling their production. The 1933 law was declared unconstitutional, but a 1938 revised law is constitutional. It provides for soil conservation, research laboratories, parity prices, marketing quotas, and loans by the Commodity Credit Corporation.

AAD: at a discount.

AB: see *bond adjustment*.

ABA:
- (1) see *American Bankers Association*.
- (2) see *American Bankers Association number*.

abandonment
- (1) *general:* giving up a facility without the intention of regaining possession at some later time.
- (2) *finance:* the elimination from use of a fixed asset. The total retirement of a fixed asset from service, following salvage or other reclaiming of removable parts.
- (3) *law:* with a patent, trademark, or copyright, the cession of rights by the owner, wherein his or her invention, design, or name falls into the public domain.

abandt: see *abandonment*.

abatement
- (1) *finance:* the cancellation of part or all of an expenditure.
- (2) *finance:* the cancellation or reduction of an assessed tax.
- (3) *law:* a reduction or pulling down, as with a nuisance.

abator: one who gains illegal posses-

1

sion of an estate, thus preventing the rightful heirs from obtaining possession.

ABA Transit Code: see *American Bankers Association number.*

ABC Agreement: when buying a New York Stock Exchange seat, the applicant's membership can be bought by a member firm for his or her use with monies advanced by the member firm.

Abe's cabe: slang, a $5 bill.

abeyance

(1) *banking:* a temporary suspension of title to property before the correct owner is determined. see *cloud on title.*

(2) *law:* the state of not having been settled.

ability: skill, aptitude, and other factors essential in job performance. It is measured by work records, performance measures, and other ratings designed to identify an employee's day-to-day handling of his or her work.

ability test: a test of performance, prepared to reveal a level of present ability (e.g., a bank teller test or a typing test).

ability to pay

(1) *general:* the ability of the bank or financial organization's management to meet the financial demands of a union. This capacity depends on the financial condition of the institution and is often disputed.

(2) *general:* also used regarding a borrower—that is, capacity to pay back.

(3) *finance:* a criterion used to ascertain who shall bear the cost of government programs; the rationale for taxing individuals in the form of a progressive income tax.

ab initio: "from the beginning" (Latin).

For example, an individual who enters the land of another person by permission and thereafter abuses that right becomes a trespasser ab initio—that is, becomes a trespasser from the first time he or she walked on the property.

ABL: see *accepted batch listing.*

above par (value): the price of a stock or bond, higher than its face amount.

abrasion: weight loss in coins that results from wear in circulation.

abrogation of agreement: the cancellation or setting aside of a contract or any portion of it.

absence: an employee's temporary unavailability for work lasting for one or more days or shifts.

absenteeism: being absent from work, especially when deliberate or habitual.

absenteeism, chronic: the constant recurrence of absences.

absolute address: synonymous with *machine address, specific address.*

absolute advantage: an advantage of one nation or area over another in the costs of manufacturing an item in terms of used resources.

absolute code: coding designed so that all instructions are described in basic machine language. Synonymous with *specific coding.*

absolute error

(1) *computers:* a form of error in which the magnitude of error is determined without regard for the algebraic sign or direction.

(2) *statistics:* the amount of error expressed in the same units as the quantity holding the error.

absolute gift: a gift of property by will that carries with it possession of and complete dominion over the property, opposed to a *conditional gift.* [105]

absolute ownership: where the interest or exclusive right of possession of the insured is so free from limitations, restrictions, or qualifications that it cannot be taken from the insured without his or her consent. [56]

absolute priority rule: the concept that creditors' rights must be satisfied prior to stockholders' equities following liquidations or corporate reorganizations.

absolute title: a title without any conditions. An absolute title is usually critical to the granting of a mortage by a bank.

absorb

(1) *general:* to merge by transfer all or portions of an account with another account, resulting in the loss of identity of the first account.

(2) *finance:* to include pertinent actual costs in determining a price or standard cost.

(3) *investments:* to assimilate sell orders of stock with offsetting requests to buy.

absorbed: designates a security, no longer in the hands of an underwriter, and now with a shareholder.

absorption: the total demand of an economy for internal and external resources; emphasizing the importance of the identity equating the balance of trade with national income less national absorption. [82]

absorption account: see *adjunct account.*

absorption point: the point at which the securities market rejects further offerings unaccompanied by price concessions. see *digested securities, undigested securities.*

abstinence concept: a theory according to which a postponement in the use of an item involves a cost that should be reimbursed by a payment such as interest.

abstract: a brief summary of a potential employee's background, interests, and other relevant information.

abstraction of bank funds: laws dealing with criminal offenses in the banking field. For example, embezzlement, abstraction, or willful misapplication of bank funds are misdemeanors and punishable by fine up to $5,000 and/or imprisonment for five years.

abstract of title: an attorney's prepared statement tracing the history of the ownership of real property to determine the present title. see *deed, encumbrance, search, title deed, title insurance.*

abutting: joining or adjacent; contiguous to another property. This variable is clearly identified in the granting of a bank mortgage.

AC

(1) see *account current.*

(2) see *active capital.*

A/C: see *account.*

ACB: see *Associated Credit Bureaus of America, Inc.*

Acc.

(1) accept.

(2) accepted.

(3) see *account.*

Accelerated Cost Recovery System: see *ACRS.*

accelerated depreciation: depreciation at a larger than expected rate; makes the depreciation allowance, therefore the tax allowance, available sooner, resulting in a benefit to the owner.

accelerated remainder: property that passes to the remainderman through the failure of the income or preceding beneficiary. [105]

accelerating premium pay: a wage incentive system under which the bonus or premium is progressively higher as the production standard is exceeded.

acceleration: by law, when an installment obligation goes into default, all remaining installments become immediately due and payable; thus suit can be brought for the entire unpaid balance. see *recomputation.* [55]

acceleration clause

(1) *banking:* the statement that a debt must be paid in total in the event of default of any of its covenants.

(2) *law:* a clause included in the body of a contract, stipulating that the entire balance shall become due immediately and payable in the event of a breach of certain other conditions of the contract, such as insolvency or the debtor's failure to pay taxes on the mortgaged property.

acceleration premium: the increasing rate of pay permitted workers with increasing production.

accelerator: see *marginal propensity to invest.*

acceptability: an attitude toward money resulting in its acceptance as a medium of exchange in the marketplace. see *eligible paper, rediscount.*

acceptance: a time draft (bill of exchange) on the face of which the drawee has written "accepted" over his signature. The date and place payable are also indicated. The person accepting the draft is known as the *acceptor.* see *bank acceptance, draft, trade acceptance.*

acceptance credit: commercial banks and foreign banking institutions are able to participate in the acceptance practice to assist in financing import-export and domestic transactions by establishing an acceptance credit with a bank. see *bank acceptance, letter of credit.*

acceptance for honor: the receiving of a draft or bill of exchange by another party when collection has been rejected by the drawee and protest for nonacceptance has been claimed. cf. *notice of dishonor.*

acceptance house: an organization that specializes in lending funds on the security of bills of exchange or offers its name as an endorser to a bill drawn on another party.

acceptance liability: a bank's full liability that has been accepted in handling bills drawn on it by customers for financing domestic, import, or export business. Banks are required by law to keep a record of the total of the liability by such acceptances in an account called liability on account of acceptances. see *acceptance credit, acceptance line, letter of credit.*

acceptance liability ledger: a ledger listing the bills accepted for each bank customer entered under an account containing his name, including name and address of customer, line, date, letter of credit number, acceptance number, expiration date, bill amount, total amount accepted or expired, and payment date. see *acceptance liability.*

acceptance line: the maximum limit in monies that a bank commits itself to accept for a single client.

acceptance maturity tickler: an accounting where acceptances are listed in order of maturity dates so that the amount of daily maturities can be grasped quickly. One page is usually given to the maturities for each day. see *tickler.*

acceptance register: a record containing details on all bills accepted by a bank for its depositors. Listed by date, these entries include date of acceptance, bank's acceptance number, name of bank representative giving authorization, signature of representative, customer's number of bill, date, tenor, maturity, drawee, payee, amount, list of document collected, affixed original or duplicates, number, and credit date.

acceptance supra protest: following a protest, the payment of a bill to preserve the reputation or credit of the drawer or endorser.

accepted batch listing (ABL): an itemized listing of each dollar amount entry that has been accepted by a computer system for any particular day. [105]

accepted bill: see *acceptance*.

accepted credit card: any credit card that the cardholder has requested or applied for and received, or has signed, used, or authorized another person to use for the purpose of obtaining money, property, labor, or services on credit. [105]

accepted debit card (or other means of access): a card, code, or other means to a consumer's account to initiate electronic fund transfers (e.g., transfer money between accounts or obtaining money, property, labor, or services). [105]

accepting house: a member of the London Accepting House Committee; there are 17 such firms, normally regarded as the most prestigious of the merchant banks.

acceptor: the drawee of a note for acceptance, who upon signing the form, agrees to pay a draft or bill when due.

access: the process or act of putting financial data into computer storage or retrieving data from the computer.

accession
(1) *general:* the hiring of a new employee or the rehiring of a former worker.
(2) *banking:* elevation to a higher office within the bank.
(3) *law:* the doctrine that the property owner is entitled to all that is added or affixed to the property.

accession rates: the average number of persons added to a payroll in a given period per 100 employees. see *turnover*.

accessorial services: the service in addition to actual transportation which a carrier furnishes as part of the applicable rate (e.g., sorting, packing, precooling, etc.).

access right: the right of an owner of property or another person with the owner's approval to enter, enjoy, or leave the property without obstruction. If the property abuts on a public way, this is called a direct access right. If there is other property intervening between the owned property and the public way, the right is known as an *easement right*.

access time
(1) *computers:* the time interval between the instant at which data are requested from a storage device and the moment delivery begins.
(2) *computers:* the time interval between the moment data become ready for storage and the instant storage is terminated.

accidental death benefit: a benefit in addition to the face amount of a life insurance policy, payable if the insured dies as the result of an accident. Sometimes referred to as *double indemnity*. [58]

accident severity: a measure of the amount of time lost as the result of an accident.

accommodation: historically, the lending of currency by a person who has it to another who has need of it, without collateral. More popularly, the lending of a person's honor or credit, without any consideration, to enable another to obtain borrowed money.

accommodation bill (of lading): a bill of lading issued by a common carrier before receipt of items for shipment. see *bill of lading*.

accommodation charge: a single purchase when credit is arranged on a temporary basis without the need to open a regular credit account. synonymous with *this transaction only*.

accommodation check: a check drawn by an association on its account with a bank, payable to a third party named by the saver making the withdrawal. [59]

accommodation endorsement: the signature or endorsement of a note or draft solely for the purpose of inducing a bank to lend money to a borrower whose personal credit is not substantial enough to warrant a loan.

accommodation endorser: a person who endorses a negotiable instrument for the accommodation of another person or parties, having no ownership right but simply guaranteeing the fulfillment of the contract to subsequent holders of the instrument. see *endorsement, endorser*.

accommodation note: any note that has received an accommodation endorsement.

accommodation paper: a promissory note, endorsed by an individual(s), allowing the original signer of the note to receive bank credit; thus the second or other signer(s) accept the guarantee of credit.

accommodation party: one who signs a note as maker, drawer, acceptor, or endorser without receiving value, although remaining totally liable for the purpose of lending the credit worthiness of his or her name to another person. see *accommodation paper*.

accord and satisfaction: an agreement between two people, one of whom has a right of action against the other, that the latter should do or give, and that the former accepts, something in satisfaction of the right of action that is different from, and often less than, what might be enforced by law.

account: a record of all the transactions and the date of each, affecting a particular phase of a bank or financial institution, expressed in debits and credits, evaluated in money, and showing the current balance, if any. see *bank account*.

accountabilities: assets, liabilities, items held in trust, and the like, for which an individual, organization, or other legal entity renders an accounting. For example, when bank officials give an accounting of the disbursed funds entrusted to their care, the items are referred to as accountabilities.

accountability: the management process by which a person is evaluated on the basis of end results.

account activity: all transactions on individual or group accounts, including, for example, debts, credits, and status changes.

account analysis: the process of determining and explaining the profit or loss on any account by means of systematic procedures.

account and risk: based on a relationship between a customer and his broker. Serving as the customer's agent, the broker will execute, buy, and sell orders at the risk of the customer.

accountant: an individual engaged in accounting work. cf. *certified public accountant.*

accountant's certificate: a report prepared by an independent accountant or auditor addressed to stockholders, directors, or owners of the firm that has been audited. The form and scope of the audit is stated and an expression of the fairness of the appended financial statement is given.

account asset: a record of additions and subtractions from the properties owned by a business enterprise or individual. These properties usually include cash, supplies, stock-in-trade, real estate, machinery, furniture, and fixtures, as well as intangible assets. [105]

account balance: the net debit or net credit amount in a specific account in the ledger. An excess of total debits over total credits results in a debit balance, whereas an excess of total credits over total debits results in a credit balance.

account conversion: changing a person's account from one bank card plan to another (e.g., from a merchant's to a bank card plan or from one bank to another). [105]

account current: a statement posting the debits and credits of a depositor and the balance at the end of the accounting period or cycle billing time.

account day: the day identified by stock and commodity exchanges for the settlement of accounts between members. synonymous with *settlement day.*

account debtor: an individual who is obligated on an account, contract right, or general intangible.

account error: see *billing error.*

account executive: see *registered representative.*

account history: the payment history of an account over a specified period of time, including the number of times the account was past due or over limit. [105]

account hold: a warning placed on a savings, loan, or other account to indicate the need for special handling. [59]

account in balance: an account where the debit and credit footings are equal.

accounting: the art, science, interpretation, and organized method of recording all transactions affecting the financial condition of a given business or organization.

accounting control: a component of internal controls, which comprises the plan of organization, procedures, and records that are concerned with the safeguarding of assets and with the reliability of financial records. [105]

accounting cycle: the series of accounting activities that occur from the commencement of an accounting period to the end of that period. The cycle begins with the determination of the account balance at the beginning of the period; then the effects of transactions occurring during the period are recorded, the records are closed, and financial statements for the period are prepared.

accounting equation: the basic identity of double-entry bookkeeping, which reflects the relationship among assets, liabilities, and equity. In its simplest form: assets = liabilities + equity. [105]

accounting period: the 12-month period used for keeping a taxpayer's records. When the accounting period ends other than in the month of December, a fiscal year is established. For income tax purposes a special 52–53–week accounting period is also acknowledged. cf. *fiscal year.*

accounting processes: the classification of accounts, accounting records, forms, procedures and controls through which changes in asset, liability, reserves, capital, income, and expense account transactions are generally recorded and controlled. [59]

accounting rate of return: income for a period divided by the average investment that has occurred during that period.

accounting system: the total structure of records and procedures that discover, record, classify, and report information on the financial position and operations of a governmental unit or any of its funds, balanced account groups, and organizational components. [49]

account inquiry: used to identify the capability of accessing account information for such matters as demand deposit account, savings account, NOW account, line-of-credit, credit card, or other personal accounts. Often with this capability there is the ability to update temporarily or "memo post" the account balance and status. [105]

account in trust: an account opened by an individual to be held in trust and maintained for the benefit of another. In the absence of a legally constituted trust fund, withdrawals from the account are subject to the approval of the individual who has established the account. see *Totten trust.*

account number: the numerical identification given to an account in a given institution or business, such numerical identification being a part of and in direct harmony with the whole system of numerical description given to the accounts as a whole that exist in that institution or business. cf. *American Bankers Association number.*

account reconciliation plan (ARP): a program using the auxiliary On-Us field on MICR checks to give high–volume accounts a list and the sum of paid and/or outstanding checks in numerical serial sequence and to assist in the balance of the bank's statement to the customer's check register.

account sales: a record prepared by a broker, consignee, or other agent, indicating the proceeds of goods or securities purchased for the account of the owner.

accounts payable: a current liability representing the amount owed by an individual or a business to a creditor for merchandise or services purchased on an open account or short-term credit. see *accounts payable account.*

accounts payable account: an account in the general ledger showing the full amount owed to creditors for items bought on account; the title of the general ledger controlling account that affects the accounts payable ledger and that indicates the sum owed to creditors on account.

accounts receivable: money owed a business enterprise for merchandise bought on open account. see *accounts receivable account.*

accounts receivable account: the title of the general ledger controlling account that affects the accounts receivable ledger and indicates the sum to be collected on account from all of the firm's customers.

accounts receivable financing: the securing of working capital by borrowing with accounts receivable as collateral, or by selling accounts receivable outright. The latter is referred to as *factoring.*

accounts receivable turnover: in determining credit risks; the determination of how rapidly accounts receivables are turned over—that is, when credit conditions are met as indicated by collections.

account reconcilement: a bookkeeping service offered to some bank service customers to aid them in balancing their accounts. This service includes numerical sorting of checks, itemization of outstanding checks, and/or the actual balancing of the account. [105]

account representative: an individual responsible for resolving mail and telephone inquiries for bank card customers (or others). [105]

accounts current: see *account current.*

accounts receivable acquisition: the taking over by the bank of outstanding balances on charge accounts formerly carried by a merchant or other financing agency. [105]

account stated: the understanding and liability of a debtor that an account or bill presented is valid if it has not been questioned by the debtor within a reasonable time period.

account status report: listing of all cardholder accounts on which there has been activity within a specified period of time. [105]

account transfer: see *account conversion.*

Accrd. Int.: see *accrued interest.*

Accred.: accredited.

accredited list: a list of customers to whom the public warehouse official can make distribution of spot stock without further authority from the storer.

accretion: addition of principal or interest to a fund over a period of time resulting from a plan of accumulation. cf. *amortization.*

accretion account: a record of the increase between the acquisition value and the face value of bonds purchased at a discount.

accretion of discount: a straight-line accumulation of capital gains on discount bonds in anticipation of being paid par at maturity. [105]

accrual basis: the basis of accounting under which revenues are recorded when earned and expenditures are recorded as soon as they result in liabilities for benefits received, notwithstanding that the receipt of the revenue or the payment of the expenditure may take place, in whole or in part, in another accounting period. see *accrue(d), levy.* [49]

accrual method of accounting: see *cash method of accounting.*

accrual of discount: the yearly addition to book value of bonds that have been bought below par. see *amortization.*

accrual system: a method of recording and apportioning expense and income for the period in which each is involved, regardless of the date of payment or collection.

accrue(d)

(1) *general:* to gain or profit by.

(2) *finance:* to accumulate, grow, or add in an orderly fashion (e.g., interest accrues on invested funds).

(3) *law:* to become eligible for a right or claim.

accrued assets: interest, commission, services offered, and items of revenue neither received nor past due but earned (e.g., accrued dividends).

accrued charges: charges that though known are not yet due (e.g., margin payment).

accrued depreciation: depreciation, or loss in value, that has occurred during a specified period. [59]

accrued dividend: the customary, regular dividend considered to be earned but not declared or payable on legally issued stock or other instruments of part ownership of a legally organized business or financial institution.

accrued expenses: expenses that are recognized by a firm prior to that firm's disbursement of cash. Accrued expenses arise when a company has used goods or services before it has paid for them.

accrued income: income earned (e.g., commissions or interest on notes receivable) but not received.

accurred income receivable: income earned but not yet received. [105]

accrued interest: a bond's accumulated interest made since the last interest payment. The purchaser of the bond pays the market price plus accrued interest. Bonds that are in default and income bonds are exceptions. see *flat.*

accrued interest payable: interest accumulated on an indebtedness (e.g., time deposits or borrowed money) but not yet paid.

accrued interest receivable: interest earned by a bank but not yet collected.

accrued liabilities: liabilities arising from expenses that have been incurred but have not yet been paid. Accrued liabilities are the counterpart of *prepaid expenses.*

accrued taxes and interest: money set aside to pay taxes and interest incurred but not yet paid. [105]

accuring: the allocation of income and/or expense, which has been earned or incurred but not yet collected or paid out, to the acounting period in which the income is earned or the expense incurred. cf. *deferring.*

accumulate: a purchase by traders who hope to retain the contracts for a more or less extended period.

accumulate at interest: increasing the principal by the amount of interest due, thereby forming a new basis for calculating interest.

accumulated: added onto what had previously been in existence.

accumulated dividend: a dividend not paid when due. The dividend is expected to be paid at a later time, but it becomes a business liability until payment.

accumulated earnings tax: a tax on earnings accumulated beyond the business requirement of the frm. By design, it attempts to tax corporations on earnings that have been kept for no apparent business purpose.

accumulated income: that portion of

the income from a trust which is retained in the account. [105]

accumulated interest: unpaid interest payments that are past due.

accumulated profit tax: a tax penalty directed at corporations that avoid announcing dividends to reduce stockholders' declarations of additional income.

accumulated surplus: a corporation's excess of profits that are either reinvested or held.

accumulation

(1) *banking:* the opposite of *amortization*; a percentage added to life insurance benefits as a form of reward for continuous renewal.

(2) *finance:* adding income from dividends, interest, and other sources to the principal amount of a fund, and the treatment of such additions as capital.

(3) *investments:* the deliberate, well-controlled assembling of blocks of stock without necessarily bidding up prices.

(4) *investments:* profits that are not distributed to stockholders as dividends but instead are transferred to a capital account.

accumulation bond: see *bond, accumulation*.

accumulation distribution: the amount of income earned by a trust in a previous year which is distributed to a beneficiary and is subject to the income tax throwback rules. [105]

accumulation plan: a schedule that permits an investor to buy mutual fund shares on a regular basis in differing amounts, with provisions for the investment of income dividends and the acceptance of capital gains distribution

in additional shares. Such plans can be either voluntary or contractual.

accumulative: see *cumulative.*

accumulative dividend: see *cumulative dividends.*

accumulator

(1) *computers:* a device in which the result of an arithmetic or logic operation is determined.

(2) *computers:* a register that stores a quantity. When a second quantity is entered, it arithmetically combines the quantity and stores the result in the location of the register.

ACE

(1) see *Amex Commodities Exchange.*

(2) slang, a one-dollar bill.

ACH: see *automated clearinghouse.*

achievement battery: a collection of tests designed to measure a level of skill or knowledge attained in several areas.

achievement test: a measure of proficiency level determined by testing performance displayed in a particular field. It is designed to determine the relative excellence of an individual's past learning.

acid test ratio: a credit barometer used by lending institutions; indicates the ability of a business enterprise to meet its current obligations. The formula used to determine the ratio is

$$\frac{\text{cash} + \text{receivables} + \text{marketable securities}}{\text{current liabilities}}$$

Usually a 1 : 1 ratio is considered to be satisfactory.

Ack.

(1) acknowledge.

(2) see *acknowledgment.*

acknowledgment

(1) *general:* on a document, a signature that has received certification from an authorized person.

(2) *banking:* a written notification that an item, now received, is available for its immediate payment.

(3) *law:* a statement that a proper document has been submitted.

Ac. Pay.: see *accounts payable.*

Acpt.

(1) accept.

(2) see *acceptance.*

Acq.: see *exchange acquisition.*

acquired surplus

(1) the surplus of an enterprise existing at the date of its acquisition by another enterprise.

(2) the initial surplus of a successor enterprise where there has been a pooling of interests and no full capitalization of surplus. The initial surplus may be paid-in surplus or retained earnings or both, depending on the nature of the predecessor. [43]

acquiring bank: a bank, in interchange, which maintains the merchant relationship and receives all transactions. [105]

acquisition: a general term for the taking over of one company by another. see *amalgamation, merger.*

acquisition cost

(1) *banking:* monies paid in order to obtain property title prior to the granting of a mortgage.

(2) *finance:* the cost to a company of securing business; primarily commissions to agents and brokers.

acquisition program: advertising campaign, solicitation, or promotion designed to attract consumers to apply for a bank card. [105]

acquittance: a document giving written evidence of the discharge of, or freedom from, a debt or financial obligation.

Acrd.: see *accrue(d).*

Ac. Rec.: see *accounts receivable.*

acronym: a word formed from the first letter or letters of words in a term, title, or proper name (e.g., COBOL for common business-oriented language).

across the board

(1) *general:* applying to all, in a uniform fashion.

(2) *investments:* the unified price activity of the daily securities market, as when described as being weak, slow, strong, or active across the board.

across-the-board increase: a general pay increase affecting equally all or most of the employees covered by a contract. May be expressed as a percentage or in cents per hour.

ACRS: Accelerated Cost Recovery System; the depreciation method introduced in the 1981 tax act.

Acs. Pay.: see *accounts payable.*

Acs. Rec.: see *accounts receivable.*

action

(1) *investments:* the performance by a stock with respect to trading volume and price trend.

(2) *investments:* in France, a share of stock.

(3) *law:* the legal demand for rights as asked of a court.

action ex contractu: an action at law to receive damages for breach of a responsibility specified in a contract. The action can arise out of contract (ex contractu) or out of tort (ex delicto). cf. *action ex delicto.*

action ex delicto: an action at law to receive damages arising out of an infraction of a civil or criminal law (e.g., receiving damages for personal injury created by negligent use of a car). Tort, or wrong, is the reason for the action. cf. *action ex contractu.*

action to quiet title: the legal process by which any person claiming an interest or estate in real property not in the actual possession of another may maintain a suit in equity against another who claims an adverse interest or estate therein for determining such conflicting or adverse claims, interests, or estates. [105]

activation program: advertising campaign or solicitation program designed to activate inactive accounts. [105]

active account
(1) *banking:* an account in which bank deposits or withdrawals are frequent.
(2) *investments:* an account handled by one broker who makes frequent purchases and sales.

active assets: company assets that are used for daily operations of the firm.

active bad debt account: an account charged off but judged to be collectible at a later date. see *inactive bad debt account.* [55]

active capital: capital that is continuously used in profit-making activities.

active corporation: an organization that maintains a system for operating property or administering its financial affairs.

active crowd: the New York Stock Exchange's Bond Department for the trading of active bonds. These bonds are usually convertible bonds and are only a small percentage of the total bonds traded. see *cabinet crowd.* synonymous with *free crowd.*

active market: characterized by nu-merous transactions in securities trading. see *New York Stock Exchange.*

active money: currency in circulation.

active partner: a partner of an organization who participates actively in the firm's operations for the benefit of all associates.

active securities: stocks and bonds that are actively traded each day and where quotations on these transactions are available to the public.

active stock: a specific stock issue that has a continuous broad market and is sold and purchased with ease.

active trade balance: a balance of trade that is favorable.

active trust: a trust where the trustee has a specific role to perform, as contrasted with a passive, bare, dry, or naked trust. see *trust.*

activity
(1) *banking:* a sign that a record in a bank's file has moved or has been referred to.
(2) *banking:* any data resulting in use or modification of the data in a bank or financial institution's master file.
(3) *computers:* indicating the percentage of records in a file that are processed.

activity charge: a service charge imposed on checking account depositors by banks for check or deposit activity, where the average balances maintained are not enough to compensate for the cost of handling the items. see *checking account.*

activity file: a listing of the most recent transactions in a terminal, group of terminals, or system containing sufficient information to permit detection of fraudulent repetitive transactions. [105]

activity ratio: the number of active accounts expressed as a percentage of total accounts. Calculated by dividing the number of active accounts by the number of total accounts in the cardholder file. [105]

activity status report: see *account status report.*

acts of bankruptcy: any act listed under Section 3 of the National Bankruptcy Act, the most common being the inability to settle debts of not less than $1000 as they mature and voluntarily appearing in a bankruptcy court or undergoing involuntary bankruptcy where unpaid creditors petition the bankruptcy court. see *bankruptcy.*

Act to Regulate Commerce of 1887: federal legislation regulating the practices, rates, and rules of firms engaged in transportation in interstate commerce. Known in its current amended state as the *Interstate Commerce Act.*

actual: any physical commodity.

actual cash value: the cost of repairing or replacing damaged property with other of like kind and quality in the same physical condition; commonly defined as replacement cost less depreciation.

actually outstanding: securities that have actually been issued and not reacquired by or for the issuing corporation.

actuals: an actual physical commodity; as distinguished from *futures.*

actual total loss: in marine insurance, where the subject matter is completely destroyed or where the subject matter ceases to be a thing of the kind insured, or where the assured is irretrievably deprived of the subject matter.

actual value: the price that property

commands when sold on the open market.

actuarial: related to a bank's insurance mathematics and the application of statistics.

actuary: an individual, often holding a professional degree, whose primary functions include determining rates and rating systems, determining reserves against future liabilities for corporate and rate-making purposes, and designing and interpreting experience systems. see *insurance.*

Act. Val.: see *actual value.*

ACUs: see *Asian Currency Units.*

ACV: see *actual cash value.*

AD

(1) see *accrued dividend.*

(2) see *after date.*

(3) anno Domini (in the year of our Lord).

(4) ante diem (before the day).

(5) see *availability date.*

ADA: see *Airlines Deregulation Act.*

ADB

(1) see *African Development Bank.*

(2) see *Asian Development Bank.*

ad damnum clause: a clause in a plaintiff's complaint or statement that makes the demand for damages and declares the monies involved.

added-value tax: see *value-added tax.*

addendum: "thing added" (Latin). An addition to an agreement, contract, or written statement.

additional insured: a person, other than the one identified as the insured in a policy, who is also protected, either by being listed as an additional insured, or by definition, according to the terms of the policy.

additions: any supplemental fixed asset that yields greater capacity without replacing existing capacity. The addition of a wing to an existing structure is an example of an addition.

add-on charge: a method, no longer permissible, of advertising an interest rate on installment loans that understates the true interest rate. [78]

add-on clause: a provision allowing additional purchases on an existing installment credit agreement, normally stating that default in making payments on the additional purchases constitutes default on all purchases. [78]

add-on interest: a method of calculating interest payments where a percentage of the desired principal is used to calculate the interest cost. Interest cost is then added to the principal to calculate the total amount to be repaid by the borrower. [105]

add-on minimum tax: see *alternative minimum tax.*

add-on purchase: combining a new purchase with an older one, adding it to an existing installment contract. [28]

add-on rate: an installment finance technique where the rate is computed on the advance. The factor for each maturity is pro rata per annum of the rate. Five percent add-on means $5 per $100 for one year, $10 per $100 for two years, and so on, on monthly and seasonal contracts.

add-ons: additional cash or remittance letters prepared to be included with letters previously sent on the same business day. Each add-on contains the total of its letter and the grand total of all items sent. Preparing and sending several letters during the day reduces the work load at the end of the day. see *cash letter, remittance letter.* [10]

address
(1) *general:* the location of a customer.
(2) *banking:* the location of a mortgaged structure or property.
(3) *computers:* an identification, as represented by a name, label, or number for a location or any other data source.

addresser: equipment used in connection with a chargeplate to imprint a customer's name, address, and other pertinent information, on the sales check.

address of record: the official or primary location for an individual, company, or other organization.

address register: a register in which an address is stored in a computer.

adequate notice: a printed notice to a cardholder which sets forth the facts clearly and conspicuously, so that a person against whom it is to operate could reasonably be expected to have noticed it and understood its meaning. [105]

ad hoc: "for this" (Latin). Refers to a specific situation; for one purpose only.

ad idem: "to the same point or effect" (Latin).

Adj.: see *adjustment.*

adjacent property: property near to or in the immediate vicinity of the insured property which may increase the hazard of loss. [56]

adjoining property: property that touches in some part the insured property. As distinguished from *adjacent property.* [56]

adjudicate: to carry out judicial authority by hearing, trying, and identifying the claims of litigants at court.

adjudication: the resolution of a dispute by a court or tribunal. Specifically, the act of a court's declaring a person bankrupt.

adjunct account: an account that adds to another existing account, represented by transfers from another account (e.g., the balances of related accounts are combined when preparing a financial statement). synonymous with *absorption account.*

adjustable life insurance: insurance that allows the insured to switch the type of protection, raise or lower the face amount of the policy, increase or decrease the premium, and lengthen or shorten the protection period. [58]

adjustable mortgage rate: see *variable-rate mortgages.*

adjustable peg: a system permitting changes in the par rate of foreign exchange after a country has had long-run disequilibrium in its balance of payments. It also allows for short-run variations within a narrow range of a few percentage points around the par value.

adjustable-rate mortgages (ARMs): variable-rate instruments, with initial rates below conventional fixed-rate loans.

adjusted capital funds: used in determining a bank's capital adequacy ratios—the change in book total of capital funds indicating more precise availability of capital cushion to risk assets—for establishing the risk asset ratio.

adjusted credit proxy: see *credit proxy.*

adjusted gross estate: the value of an estate after all allowable deductions have reduced the gross estate, but before federal estate taxes. [34]

adjusted gross income: an individual's gross income minus business expenses, deductions for income-producing property, some property losses, self-employment expenses, and moving expenses. Used primarily in federal income tax returns.

adjusted monetary base (AMB): a measure that is intended to isolate the effects of Federal Reserve actions that affect the money stock in a single summary measure. see *reserve adjustment magnitude.* [79]

adjusted trial balance: the merger of the trial balance columns of the work sheet with the adjustment columns. This balance represents the trial balance that could be obtained if it were prepared right after the adjusting entries are posted.

adjuster: an individual who reviews a bank customer's complaint concerning service or accuracy, with the authority to find an appropriate remedy.

adjusting entries: bookkeeping entries that are made after the trial balance has been prepared, but before the closing entries. The adjusting entries are necessary to make the income and expense accounts consistent with the accrual method of accounting. [105]

adjustment: a change in an account to correct an incorrect entry or for some other sound reason.

adjustment bond: see *bond, reorganization.*

adjustment mortgage: any mortgage that has been released out of a reorganization.

adjustment of debt of an individual with regular income plan: see *wage earner plan.*

adjustment preferred securities: preferred stock that has resulted from an adjustment of claims in a restructuring of the company.

adjustments: deductions made to charge off losses, as with bad debts or the sale of commodities.

ad litem: for purposes of a suit; for a suit's duration. see *guardian ad litem*.

administered price: the price established under situations of imbalanced competition wherein one business has some degree of control.

administration

(1) *general:* designates those who determine purpose and policy in an organization.

(2) *law:* the management and settling of the estate of an intestate person, under a commission from a proper authority.

administration board: a retirement board or retirement committee charged with the policy direction of a retirement system. The board may consist of representatives of the employer and employees, and sometimes pensioners. An administrative board is also frequently referred to as the pension board or retirement board. [2]

administrative control: a segment of internal controls that is concerned with the decision processes leading to management's authorization of transactions. [105]

administrative expenses: expenses chargeable to the managerial and policymaking phases of a business. cf. *cost.*

administrative law: laws emanating from regulations of a government agency that is responsible for carrying out statute law. Administrative law is distinguished from common law or statute law.

administrative protection: the use of regulations relating to customs procedure, sometimes in a harassing man-

ner, so as to control imports. Delays in assessing customs duties, high valuation, meticulous enforcement of documentary rules, and so on, may be so used.

administrative provisions: provisions in a will or trust agreement setting forth the duties and powers of the executor or the trustee regarding the care and management of the property; to be distinguished from *dispositive provisions.* [37]

administrative revenues: revenues obtained by the various departments and agencies of public administration in the course of performing their functions or services.

administrator:

(1) *general:* a key executive in an organization.

(2) *banking:* a qualified individual or bank appointed by a court of law to manage and distribute the estate of a person who died intestate (without leaving a will) or leaving a will that fails to name an executor. see *executor, letter of administration.*

administrator ad colligendum: an administrator appointed to collect foreign assets. [37]

administrator ad litem: an administrator appointed by the court to supply a party to an action at law or in equity in which the decedent or his or her representative was, or is, a necessary party. [37]

administrator cum testamento annexo (administrator with the will annexed): An individual or a trust institution appointed by a court to settle the estate of a deceased person in accordance with the terms of his or her will when no executor has been named in the will or when the one named has failed to qualify. [37]

administrator cum testamento annexo de bonis non (administrator with the will annexed as to property not yet distributed): an individual or a trust institution appointed by a court to complete the settlement of the estate of a deceased person in accordance with the terms of his or her will when the executor or the administrator with the will annexed has failed to continue in office. [37]

administrator de bonis non (administrator as to property not yet distributed): an individual or a trust institution appointed by a court to complete the settlement of the estate of a person who has died without leaving a valid will when the administrator originally appointed has failed to continue in office. [37]

administrator de son tort: an individual or corporation charged with the duties and liabilities of an administrator, although not appointed one, because of his or its own wrongdoing with respect to assets in his or its possession. [37]

administrator durante absentia: an administrator appointed by the court to serve during the absence of the executor or administrator. [37]

administrator pendente lite: an individual or a trust institution appointed by a court to take over and safeguard an estate during a suit over an alleged will, or over the right of appointment of an executor or administrator. [37]

administrator's deed: see *deed, administrator's*.

administrator with the will annexed: an individual or a trust institution appointed by a court to settle the estate of a deceased person in accordance with the terms of his or her will when no executor has been named in the will or when the one named has failed to qualify. [37]

administratrix: the feminine form of *administrator*.

admission by investment: the addition to a partnership of a new partner who contributes more cash to the business, thus increasing the assets and the number of owners of the firm.

admission temporaire: the free entry of goods normally dutiable for the purpose of processing items for export.

admitted assets: when reporting claims with the state's insurance departments, those assets that can be identified under the rules and regulations of the state's insurance laws.

admitted to dealings: following approval by the SEC, a security can be officially listed and traded on an exchange.

ADP

(1) *computers:* automatic data processing; used to describe equipment.

(2) *computers:* processing of information by a system of electro-mechanical interacting to minimize the intervention of human beings.

(3) synonymous with *integrated data processing (IDP)*.

ADR: see *American depositary receipt*.

ad referendum: indicating that even though a contract has been signed, specific issues remain to be considered.

Ad. Val.: see *ad valorem*.

ad valorem: according to value. Rates or duty on a percentage of the invoice value, not on weight or quantity. see *tariff.*

ad valorem taxes: real estate taxes determined by the value of the property. see *land tax.*

advance
(1) *general:* a price increase.
(2) *banking:* a loan.
(3) *finance:* a payment on account made prior to the due date.
(4) *finance:* a rise in value or cost.
(5) *investments:* an increase in the price of stocks.

advance bill: a bill of exchange drawn prior to the shipment of goods.

advance commitment
(1) *investment:* an agreement by a private buyer to take up a bond issue at some future date.
(2) *real estate:* a written contract calling for the sale of a specified amount of mortgages (or mortgage-backed securities) at a given price or yield within a specified time. [105]

advance-decline index: a leading indicator, showing the cumulative net difference between stock price advances and declines. [105]

advance-decline line: the index of comparison between the general market and the Dow Jones Industrial Average.

advanced optical character reader (AOCR): a new generation of optical character readers capable of storing approximately 90 fonts of typewritten addresses.

advance funding: a method for making contributions to a pension plan in advance of the date when the funds are actually required to meet payments for benefits. Actuarial reserve financed pension plans imply advance funding. [52]

advancement
(1) *general:* a promotion.
(2) *finance:* money paid in advance.
(3) *law:* a gift made to a child of a portion of what will ultimately be that individual's share of an intestate's estate.

advance premium: payment made at the beginning of the period covered by an insurance policy. [56]

advance refunding: used in public debt refinancing. Possessors of a government security maturing soon are able to exchange their securities ahead of the due date for others that mature at a later time. By this process, the national debt is extended.

advancing market: the state of a market where stock prices are generally rising.

advantage: favorable state or circumstances; superiority over a competitor.

adventure
(1) *finance:* a speculative undertaking involving the sale of goods overseas at the best available price.
(2) *investments:* a security flotation by a syndicate; a joint venture.
(3) see entries under *venture.*

adverse action
(1) the refusal to grant credit in the amount or under the terms requested.
(2) the termination of an account.
(3) the refusal to increase the amount of an existing credit line when the applicant requested it in accordance with the creditor's procedures.
(4) an unfavorable change in terms that affects only some of the debtors. [78]

adverse claim: as applied to a bank account, a claim to ownership by a person other than the one in whose name the account has been entered. [39]

adverse possession: acquiring of property by a person who does not have title, or who has a defective title to it.

advice: information on a shipment of an item or some other matter pertaining to a business.

advice book: a statement of incoming and outgoing advices. see *advices.*

advice department: a department within the bank that processes advices. see *advices.*

advice fate item: see *wire fate item.*

advices: connotes several types of forms used in the banking field. Generally speaking, an advice is a form of letter that relates or acknowledges a certain activity or result with regard to a depositor's relations with a bank. Examples include credit advice, debit advice, advice of payment, and advice of execution. In commercial transactions, information on a business transaction such as a shipment of goods. [10]

adviser: the organization employed by a mutual fund to give professional advice on its investments and management of its assets. [23]

advisory funds: funds placed with a bank to invest at its own discretion on the customer's behalf.

AE: see *accommodation endorsement.*

A&F: August and February (semiannual interest payments).

affairs, statement of: a declaration indicating the estimated results of liquidating a financially depressed firm, frequently prepared for creditors or for a receiver or court of bankruptcy.

affiant: one who makes an affidavit.

affidavit: a written, notarized, dated, and sworn statement of the facts pertaining to a financial transaction or civil event. Such a statement must show the name and address of the affiant, be signed by that person, and bear the signature of the attesting official (e.g., a notary).

affidavit of claim: the form required when filing a claim. In general, it contains the information on which the claim is based.

Affil.: see *affiliate.*

affiliate: a legal term described in the Banking Act of 1933, pertaining to any organization which a bank owns or controls by stock holdings, or which the bank's shareholders possess, or whose officers are also directors of the bank. see *subsidiary.*

affiliated company: under the Investment Company Act, a company in which there is any direct or indirect ownership of 5 percent or more of the outstanding voting securities. [30]

affiliation

(1) *general:* adoption as a member or branch.

(2) *labor relations:* the association of a local or international union with a larger group (e.g., of a state, national, or international labor union federation).

affinity: relationship by marriage; to be distinguished from consanguinity, which is relationship by blood. [37]

affirmative action: positive steps taken by banks and other financial organizations to remedy imbalances in their employment of members of minority groups. see *Federal Contract Compliance Office.*

affluent society: popularized by John Kenneth Galbraith to describe a wealthy nation, most of whose citizens enjoy an abundance of material items.

affreightment: an agreement for chartering a carrier for the movement of goods.

afghani: monetary unit of Afghanistan.

AFH: see *acceptance for honor.*

AFL: see *American Federation of Labor.*

AFL-CIO: see *American Federation of Labor–Congress of Industrial Organizations.*

a fortiori: "by a stronger reason" (Latin). Since conclusions are made from stated and accepted facts, there are other facts that logically follow to make the conclusion even stronger.

African Development Bank (ADB): formed in 1964 with an objective to help provide development capital for Africa. The headquarters is at Abidjan, Ivory Coast.

AFT: see *automatic fund transfers.*

after-acquired clause: a section of the mortgage stating that any additional property which the mortgagor acquires after the mortgage is drawn will also be used as security for the loan.

after-acquired property: property acquired by a corporation subsequent to the execution of a mortgage or by a testator subsequent to the making of his or her will. [37]

after-born child: a child born after the execution of the parent's will. [37]

after date: in bills of exchange and notes, the stated maturity of the instrument.

after market: the market that automatically exists once a corporation's securities have been offered for sale to the public. see *go public.*

after sight: used in a bill to determine the due date of payment and meaning "after the bill is given to the drawee for acceptance."

AG: silver (from *argentum*).

against actuals: see *exchange of spot.*

against the box: in a short sale of stock, a person selling against the box actually owns the security sold short but prefers not to or cannot deliver the stock to the buyer. The result is that, through a broker, he or she borrows the stock in order to make delivery. see *short sale.*

age change: the date halfway between natural birthdays when the age of an individual, for the purposes of life insurance rating, changes to the next higher age.

Age Discrimination in Employment Act of 1967: federal legislation that bans employers of 20 or more workers from firing or refusing to hire an individual 40 to 65 years of age simply because of age—unless age is a bona fide qualification; forbids employment agencies to refuse to refer a job applicant because of age and to indulge in other discriminatory practices. Violators of the law face penalties. Amended in 1978, it raised from 65 to 70 the age at which an employer can require workers to retire involuntarily.

agency: used to describe certain types of accounts in trust institutions. The main distinguishing characteristic of an agency is that the title to the property does not pass to the trust institution but remains in the name of the owner of the property, who is known as the principal. [32]

agency bill: bills drawn on, and accepted by, the London branches of banks whose headquarters are located in other countries.

agency bond: see *bond, agency.*

agency coupled with an interest: an agency in which the agent has a legal interest in the subject matter. Such an agency is not terminated, as are other agencies, by the death of the principal but continues in effect until the agent can realize upon his legal interest. [37]

Agency for International Development (AID): agency in the U.S. Department of State charged with coordinating overseas economic assistance.

agency issues: debt issued by a government agency. [105]

agency security: security issued by federal agencies. [105]

agency shop: the result of a provision of collective agreement stating that nonunion employees in the bargaining unit must pay the union a sum equal to union fees and dues as a condition of continuing employment. Nonunion workers are not required to join the union, however. The agency shop is the most commonly encountered union security measure in the public sector.

agenda: a listing of activities to be carried out during a meeting.

agent: an individual authorized by a bank or financial institution to act in behalf of another person, the principal. Banks are also appointed by individuals to act as their agents.

agent bank
(1) a bank acting for a foreign bank.
(2) in the Eurocredit market, a bank appointed by other banks within the syndicate to handle the administration of the loan. The agent is usually a lead bank, but the agent functions starts with the signing of the loan when the lead bank function terminates. [83]

agent de change: a member of the Paris Bourse (stock exchange).

agent middleman: one who negotiates purchases or sales between producers and retailers without taking title to the goods.

aggregate: any total (e.g., the gross national product; the sum of monthly sales).

aggregate balance: the calculated accumulation of account balances during the statement period. Used to determine the *average daily balance.* [31]

aggregate contractual liability: the total amount of money which an insurance company will pay under the terms of liability policy for claims that arise as a result of liability assumed by the insured under contracts. [56]

aggregate corporation: an incorporated venture having more than one stockholder.

aggregate demand: the total of personal consumption expenditures, business investments, and government spending.

aggregate economics: see *macroeconomics.*

aggregate of intermediates clause: the clause of the Interstate Commerce Act (Sec. 4, Part 1) that prohibits a through rate higher than the sum of intermediate rates except by its Commission order.

aggregate risk: full exposure of a bank to a customer for both spot and forward contracts. cf. *marginal risk.*

aggregate supply: the capacity of a country's total resources to produce real goods and services.

aggressive growth fund: a mutual fund whose investment objective is capital appreciation. Most investments are in common stocks of higher growth potential and risk.

aggressive portfolio: a securities portfolio held for appreciation rather than defensive quality or yield opportunity.

aggrevative index number: there are different types, but the common characteristic is the ratio of the summation of the actual prices of different products in the later period divided by the summation of the actual prices of the same products in the base period. The ratio is then multiplied by 100.

AGI: see *adjusted gross income.*

aging of receivables: an accounting check that analyzes the time interval between the date of sale and the current date; used to evaluate the adequacy of a firm's allowance for uncollectable accounts. see *accounts receivable turnover.*

aging report: see *delinquent activity report.*

aging schedule: a listing of accounts receivable showing amounts and length of time outstanding.

agio

(1) *finance:* a premium paid for the exchange of one nation's currency for that of another's. cf. *disagio.*

(2) *finance:* the sum given above a nominal value, as in "the agio of exchange."

(3) *finance:* the rate of exchange among differing countries.

agreement: a mutual understanding between two or more persons, requiring a consideration.

agreement, collective bargaining: a written agreement (contract) arrived at as the result of negotiation between an employer or a group of employers and a union, which sets the conditions of employment and the procedure to be used in settling disputes that may arise during the term of the contract.

agreement among underwriters: a legal document binding an underwriting group into a syndicate. In the United States, the agreement is between a borrower and all underwriters of an issue. In Great Britain and in Eurobond markets, it is usually confined to an agreement among managing underwriters, and the latter proceeds to make a subunderwriting agreement with other underwriters.

agreement corporation: a state-chartered corporation organized under Section 25 of the Federal Reserve Act to engage in international banking and finance. [105]

agreement for deed: a contract describing additional property payments and conditions; the deed will be delivered and title will pass after fulfillment of these terms.

agribusiness: the activity of farming as a major force of the economy. California has the largest agribusiness in the United States.

Agricultural Adjustment Act of 1933: federal legislation originally intended to provide emergency assistance to agriculture during the Depression years; also contains "omnibus" provisions regarding farm mortgage aid and price stimulation. Also referred to as *AAA Farm Relief Act.*

agricultural cooperative: a form of cooperative selling. The organizations formed are chiefly for the purpose of effecting the unified sales of a product produced by small farmers.

agricultural loans: loans to farmers not secured by real estate. [40]

agricultural paper: notes and acceptances resulting from transactions dealing with farming and ranching, as distinguished from traditional commercial or industrial activities. see *Federal Intermediate Credit Banks, Federal Loan Bank.*

Agt.:
(1) see *agent.*
(2) see *agreement.*

Agy.: agency.

AI:
(1) see *accrued interest.*
(2) see *accumulated interest.*

AIB: see *American Institute of Banking.*

AIBD: see *Association of International Bond Dealers.*

AID: see *Agency for International Development.*

Airlines Deregulation Act: federal legislation signed on October 28, 1978. Designed as an anti-inflation tool, the act enabled many new carriers to enter new routes and permitted operators to change flight schedules and their fares.

air-mail transfer: see *transfer.*

air pocket: noticeably extreme weakness in a specific stock.

air rights: the right to use open space above a property, or conversely, the right to control the air space by not constructing to ensure that light and air will not be blocked out.

air waybill: a document having prima facie evidence of a contract between a consignor and a carrier to transport items by air.

Aj.: see *adjustment.*

AJOJ: April, July, October, January, (quarterly interest payments or dividends).

a/k/a: "also known as" (e.g., John Doe a/k/a J. Doe).

AL: see *accrued liabilities.*

ALALC: see *Latin American Free Trade Area.*

Aldrich-Vreeland Act: a forerunner of the Federal Reserve Act. Congress in 1908 passed legislation as a temporary relief measure until such time as new banking rules could be formulated.

ALGOL: algorithmic language. Primarily a means of expressing computer programs by algorithms or problem-solving formulas for machine analysis. see *general purpose computer, linear programming, program.*

alienate: the transfer of title to property.

alienation: the transfer of interest and property title to another person or organization. see *involuntary alienation, voluntary alienation.*

alienation clause: a form of acceleration clause that requires full payment of the mortgage note upon the transfer of title of the mortgaged property either through sale or some other means. [105]

alien company: an incorporated company formed and operating under the regulations of a foreign nation.

all-commodity index: a measure of changes in the averages of the wholesale prices of commodities. The U.S. Bureau of Labor Statistics releases such an index.

all-commodity rate: a transportation rate (usually a carload rate) applicable regardless of the nature of the commodities shipped.

Alliance for Progress: a cooperative effort begun in 1961 by 20 countries to improve the economic and social conditions in Latin America. see *Inter-American Development Bank.*

allied members: voting shareholders or partners in a stock exchange member organization who are permitted to carry out business on the trading floor of the exchange.

all-inclusive concept: a form of income statement presentation incorporating all items of revenue and expense in the computation of net income for an accounting period. This concept makes no distinction between items related to the current operations of the entity and those that are unusual and infrequent.

all-in-one program: a bank's program in which the customer, if approved, is set up with a checking account, bank card account, instant cash, courtesy card, free personal checks, and traveler's checks. A monthly fee is charged. [105]

allocated expense: proportioned expense, usually by company or function. [12]

allocation: assigning one or more items of cost or revenue to one or more segments of an organization according to benefits received, responsibilities, or other logical measure of use.

allonge: a paper affixed to a bill on which further endorsements are written.

all or any part: used in discretionary accounts by brokers when representing their clients. It authorizes the securities broker to execute all or any part of an order as he or she deems appropriate, but only at the customer's specified price limit.

all or none order
(1) *investments:* a stipulation that

a request to purchase or sell a security must be achieved in total or not at all.
(2) *investments:* all securities sold by a broker or underwriter of a new issue become final only when the entire issue is purchased within a stated time period.

allot: to divide an appropriation into amounts for certain periods or for specific purposes. [49]

allotment
(1) *general:* an assignment of pay for the benefit of dependents.
(2) *finance:* the separation of anticipated revenues among specific classes of expenditures.
(3) *investments:* the part of a stock issue apportioned or assigned by an investment firm to a purchaser or subscriber.

allotment ledger: a subsidiary ledger that contains an account for each allotment, showing the amount allotted, expenditures, encumbrances, the net balance, and other related information. see *appropriation ledger.* [49]

allotment notice: a document completed by an investment banker or syndicate manager which states the amount and related information or price and time of payment for securities and which is transmitted to the subscriber. It can be for the full amount of securities asked for by the subscriber, or less.

allottee: the firm or person that has subscribed to buy securities and has been assigned a share or allotment.

allowable depreciation: the amount of depreciation that could have been claimed on a capital asset, but which was not claimed during a particular reporting period. This amount is added to the value of the asset. [105]

allowance: a reserve, or money set aside, for bad debts or for depreciation.

allowance for bad debts: an account showing the estimated loss on uncollectable debts as an offset against the value shown for accounting receivables. synonymous with *reserve for bad debts.*

allowed depreciation: the amount of depreciation that the Internal Revenue Service allows to be subtracted from normal income for normal replacement of capital equipment. [105]

alloy: base metal or metals combined with gold or silver to create a coin with superior durability. Today most coins are base-metal coins.

all-purpose computer: a computer combining the benefits previously assigned solely to general-purpose or special-purpose computers. synonymous with *general-purpose computer.*

all-risk insurance: a policy insuring against loss caused by all perils except those specifically excluded, in contrast to the ordinary policy, which names the perils covered.

All-Savers certificates: a tax break under the Economic Recovery Tax Act of 1981 to encourage savings, the law created this instrument designed basically to benefit savings and loan associations rather than investors. Under the act, thrift institutions were able to offer a new, one-year Treasury note yield for a little more than 10 percent at current interest rates. What made the new certificate attractive was that interest income up to $1000 ($2000 on a joint return) was exempt from federal income tax. Now defunct.

Alot: see *allotment.*

Alotm.: see *allotment.*

alpha cardholder file: record of all cardholder accounts with names arranged in alphabetical order. Minimum data content: name, address, and account number. [105]

alpha cross-reference file: record of all cardholder accounts with names arranged in alphabetical order. Minimum data content: name, address, and account number. [105]

alphameric: see *alphanumeric.*

alphanumeric
(1) *computers:* describes characters that may be letters of the alphabet, numerals, or symbols.
(2) *computers:* pertains to a character set that contains letters, digits, and other characters (e.g., punctuation marks).
(3) synonymous with *alphameric.*

ALTA: see *American Land Title Association.*

alteration: any change involving an erasure or rewriting in the date, amount, or payee of a check or other negotiable instrument. In accounting records, necessary alterations are best made by crossing out the unwanted figure, leaving it legible, and writing the correct one above or below the original.

altered check: check on which the date, payee, or amount has been changed or erased. A bank is responsible for paying a check only as it is originally drawn; consequently, it may refuse to pay a check that has been altered.

altered sales draft: a sales draft in which the dollar amount was changed to read something other than what the cardholder actually agreed to and signed. [105]

alternate account: an account in the name of two or more persons, any of whom may draw against the account without further authority from the others. see *joint account; survivorship account.* [50]

alternate depositors: holders of a joint account; a deposit account made out in the names of husband and wife or of two partners which is payable to either or to the survivor is a joint account.

alternative minimum tax (AMT): requires some payments from every taxpayer with substantial income, even if part or all of such income would not ordinary be taxable, as in the case of long-term capital gains. AMT was established by the 1978 tax act as one of two additional taxes designed to raise more revenue for the federal government. The other was a 15 percent surtax known as an *add-on minimum tax,* which affected certain tax preferences, such as those for accelerated depreciation of real estate or oil-depletion allowances. The 1982 tax law eliminated the add-on tax for individuals, placed most of its preferences under the alternative minimum tax, and changed some other elements of the AMT.

alternative mortgage instruments (AMIs): one of three alternatives to the traditional fixed-rate mortgage. see *graduated-payment mortgages, reverse-annuity mortgage, variable-rate mortgage.*

alternative mortgages: see *flexible loan insurance plan, graduated-payment mortgages, shared-appreciation mortgage.*

alternative payee: one of two parties to whom an account or negotiable instrument, other bill, or draft is payable. Payment to either removes the payor

of that extent of obligation to both or either. In a joint account in the name of a spouse, the financial organization may pay either as holder of the draft, passbook, or other financial instrument.

alternative pricing: when a borrower is given a choice of getting a loan tied to the prime, or some spread over the rate on the lender's certificates of deposit.

alternative rate: the lower of two of more transportation rates applicable to the same shipment.

AM:
(1) see *active market.*
(2) see *after market.*
(3) ante meridiem (before noon).

amalgamation
(1) *general:* the joining together of businesses for the mutual advantage of all.
(2) *finance:* a combination under a single title of all or a portion of the assets and liabilities of two or more business units by either merger or consolidation. It may take the form of a merger, where one company absorbs another, or a consolidation, in which the original companies form a new one. see *consolidation, merger.*

AMB: see *adjusted monetary base.*

amendment: an addition, deletion, or change in a legal document. [37]

American Arbitration Association: a private not-for-profit organization formed in 1926 to encourage the use of arbitration in the settlement of disputes.

American Bankers Association (ABA): the national organization of banking formed in 1875 to "promote the general welfare and usefulness of banks and financial institutions." The association consists of 35 working groups, 4 divisions, 7 commissions, and a number of councils and committees.

American Bankers Association (ABA) number: a unit in the numerical coding system originated by the American Bankers Association for the easy identification of banks and to aid in sorting checks for their proper and ultimate destinations. Used principally on checks, the ABA number is usually placed in the upper right-hand corner of the check after the drawee bank's name.

American depository receipt: a form similar to a stock certificate which is registered in the holder's name. The certificate represents a certain number of shares in an alien corporation. Such shares are held by an alien bank that serves as the agent for a domestic commercial bank which has released the depository receipt.

American Federation of Labor (AFL): organized in 1881 as a federation of craft unions. Originally called the Federation of Organized Trade and Labor Unions of the United States and Canada, the name "American Federation of Labor" was adopted in 1886. In 1955 the AFL merged with the Congress of Industrial Organizations (CIO), which had been expelled from the AFL in 1937, to form the AFL-CIO.

American Federation of Labor–Congress of Industrial Organizations (AFL-CIO): a federation of craft and industrial unions, as well as unions of mixed structure. Created in 1955 by the merger of the AFL and the CIO, the AFL-CIO is not itself a bargaining agent. Its primary functions are education, lobbying, and furnishing organizational aid to constituent unions.

American Institute of Banking (AIB): the educational section of the American Bankers Association, organized in 1900 to provide educational opportunity in banking for bank people. The institute's activities are carried on through numerous chapters and study groups in many cities and towns. In addition to its regular classes, the institute conducts correspondence courses. Membership is open only to employees and officers of ABA member institutions. [10]

American Land Title Association (ALTA): an organization composed of title insurance companies, abstracts, and attorneys specializing in real property law, which has adopted certain insurance policy forms to standardize coverage on a national basis. [105]

American National Standards Institute (ANSI): a nonprofit organization engaged in the development of national standards. Membership comes from industry, trade associations, and the federal government. Special committees within ANSI deal with standards for bank cards and the financial communications network. [105]

American option: an option that can be exercised any time up to maturity. [106]

American parity: in foreign exchange, showing the equivalent in U.S. funds of the foreign price of securities traded overseas.

Americans: the expression used on the London Stock Exchange for U.S. securities.

American Savings and Loan Institute: see *Institute of Financial Education.*

American selling price: the price charged by U.S. producers for goods, used to determine the duty to be paid on a similar item brought into the United States, rather than determining the duty on the actual cost of the item to an importer.

American Stock Exchange (Amex): the second largest securities exchange in the country; called the Little Board or the Curb Exchange, from the market's origin on a a street in downtown Manhattan. Amex began listing stock options in 1975. see *Commodity Exchange, MC.*; cf. *Big Board.*

American terms: an exchange rate expressed as a number of currency units per dollar. [106]

Amex: see *American Stock Exchange.*

Amex Commodities Exchange (ACE): a commodity exchange launched by the American Stock Exchange in 1977 to offer its member firms a broader range of products. ACE functions as an independent exchange, sharing facilities and services with the Amex by contract. Merged in 1980 with the New York Futures Exchange. see *New York Futures Exchange.*

AMIs: see *alternative mortgage instruments.*

amortisement: synonymous with *amortization.*

amortization
(1) *banking:* the gradual reduction of a debt by means of equal periodic payments sufficient to meet current interest and to liquidate the debt at maturity. When the debt involves real property, the periodic payments often include a sum sufficient to pay taxes and insurance on the property.
(2) *finance:* an attempt to liquidate a future obligation slowly by making charges against a capital account or by adding monies to cover the debt.

amortization fund: the sum of money accumulated periodically for the payment of a debt.

amortization loan: long-term loan permitted by the Federal Farm Loan Act where the principal is eliminated or amortized during the time the loan is made. see *amortized mortgage loan.*

amortization of debt discount: noncash expenditures charged on a company's income statement to offset, over the life of a bond issue, the difference between the proceeds of bonds sold at a discount and the par value payable at maturity. [105]

amortization of discount on funded debt: a charge to income each fiscal period for a proportion of the discount and expense on funded debt obligations applicable to that period. The proportion is determined according to a rule, the uniform application of which through the interval between the date of sale and date of maturity will extinguish the discount and expense on funded debt. However, the accounting company may, at its option, charge to profit and loss all or any portion of discount and expense remaining unextinguished at any time. [18]

amortization of premium: charges made against the interest received on bonds in order to offset any premium paid for the bonds above their par value or call price. The premium may be gradually amortized over the life of the bond issue or paid off at one time. [105]

amortization payments: synonymous with *installment payments.*

amortization quota: the funds currently removed from income to provide for amortization.

amortization reserve: a balance sheet account in which are recorded the net accumulated provisions for the extinguishment of an asset at the end of a predetermined period. [3]

amortization schedule: a table showing the amounts of principal and interest due at regular intervals and the unpaid principal balance of the loan after each payment is made. [105]

amortize

(1) *general:* to write off a portion or all of the cost of an asset; to retire debt over a period of time.

(2) *banking:* to discharge a debt in periodic payments until the total, including the interest, has been paid.

amortized mortgage loan: a mortgage loan that provides for repayment within a specified time by means of regular payments at stated intervals (usually monthly, quarterly, or semiannually) to reduce the principal amount of the loan and to cover interest as it is due. [44]

amortized value: the investment value of a security determined by the process of amortization. This value is appropriate for use in connection with bonds that are fully secured, and are not in default as to either principal or interest. see *amortization. [12]*

amount: the value or quantity of a transaction. [105]

amount at interest: principal sum deposited for the purpose of earning interest. [12]

amount financed: the amount lent or financed exclusive of finance charges; total of payments less the finance charge. [55]

Amstel Club: finance houses from 15 European nations which make reciprocal arrangements for trade finance.

AMT: see *alternative minimum tax.*

Amt.: amount.

AMW: see *average monthly wage.*

AN: see *account number.*

analog(ue) computer: a machine that performs arithmetical functions upon numbers where the numbers are represented by a physical quantity. An analog computer accepts data continuously and performs operations of addition, subtraction, multiplication, division, integration, and so on. The result may be a graph, a marking on a electron tube, or a signal to be used as a control of some machine or process. Analog computers, unlike digital computers, cannot store large quantities of financial data.

analysis, multivariate: any of a number of methods or techniques used to identify, or show the effect of, many variables when interacting. cf. *MAPS.*

analysis, sequential: a procedure in which a certain set of calculations is performed after each observation, and on the basis of that calculation it is decided whether the hypothesis is acceptable or, the alternative, to withhold judgment until more data are found.

analysis department: the statistical unit of a financial institution dealing with the interpretation and preparation of operating data and cost accounting.

analysis files: in bank examination terms, those files containing the papers of examiners during the general examination. Upon completion of the examination, materials of continuing interest are transferred to a permanent file. [105]

analysis history record: a statement that contains the profits or losses and other historical conditions concerning the account over a period of time, usually month by month. [31]

analysis of covariance: an extension of methods used in the analysis of variance to include two or more related variables.

analysis of variance: a method for determining whether the differences found in a dependent variable, when it is exposed to the influence of one or more experimental variables, exceed what may be expected by chance.

analysis paper: paper used to analyze the trial balance and to gather information for the profit and loss statement and the balance sheet.

analyst: a specialist in a brokerage firm or other investment organization who is primarily responsible for determing the assets and liabilities of a new or existing corporation for purposes of making a recommendation to the sales representatives of his organization. Analysts are also found in banks.

analyst, program: a person who creates sets of instructions for computers in addition to analyzing problems, systems, and specific specialties as requested. The instructions are used by the computer as numerical codes for analysis of financial data. see *programming.*

anarchism

(1) *general:* the concept that formal government is unnecessary and wrong in purpose. Elimination of the government is often intended to be achieved by riot or revolt.

(2) *finance:* the elimination of ownership or private property by coercive government.

ancestor: one who precedes another in the line of descent. In common law the term *ancestor* is applied only to a

person in direct line of ascent (father, grandfather, or other forebear), but by statute it has been broadened to apply also to a person of collateral relationship (uncle or aunt, for example) from whom property has been acquired. [32]

ancillary: designating or pertaining to a document, proceeding, officer, office, and so on, that is subordinate to, or in aid of, another primary or principal one; that is, an ancillary attachment, bill, or suit presupposes the existence of another principal proceeding. [62]

ancillary administration: see *domiciliary administration.*

ancillary letters testamentary: letters subordinate or auxiliary to letters testamentary, as, for example, those issued in one jurisdiction for probate of property owned by a nonresident decedent. [37]

ancillary receiver: a person appointed to assist a receiver. Usually, the receiver is handling a foreign corporation (one located outside the state) and the ancillary receiver aids in the liquidation and handles the claims within his or her own domestic state reporting to and taking guidance from the receiver who is in the foreign state. see *receiver, receivership.*

ancillary trustee: see *domiciliary trustee.*

Andean Group: founded in 1969 under the Cartagena agreement to aid economic integration between the nations of Bolivia, Colombia, Chile (until 1977), Ecuador, Peru, and Venezuela.

and interest: a bond quotation term to show that accrued interest is to be added to the price; that is, the price quoted is exclusive of interest. see *accrued interest.*

ANFM: August, November, February, May (quarterly interest payments or dividends).

Ann.

(1) annual.

(2) see *annuity.*

annual balanced budget: a concept holding that total revenues and expenditures in a government's budget should be balanced or brought into equality each year.

annual basis: statistical shifting of data that are for a period less than 12 months in order to estimate the full results for an entire year. To be accurate, the processing should consider the effect of the seasonal variation.

annual earnings: the total of all monies received during a year; income less expenses during a year.

annual investment accumulation tables: see *tables, annual investment accumulation.*

annualize: translation of statistics that apply to a short period of time into the statistics that would apply for a full year. [105]

annual percentage rate (APR): the cost of credit on a yearly basis expressed as a percentage. synonymous with *true annual rate of interest.* [1]

annual report: a report of financial and organizational conditions prepared by corporate management at yearly intervals. In most cases, the Securities Exchange Commission requires an annual report for publicly held firms. see *annual statement.*

annual return: see *yield.*

annual statement: the annual report made by a company at the close of the fiscal year, stating the company's receipts and disbursements, assets and liabilities. Such a statement usually includes an account of the progress made by the company during the year. see *annual report.* [54]

annual wage: a guaranteed minimum income for total number of hours of employment during a year. see *guaranteed annual wage.*

annual yield: the percentage of return or income in dividends or interest that an investment yields each year.

annuitant: an individual to whom an annuity is payable, the person usually to receive the annuity during his or her lifetime. see *variable annuity.*

annuity

(1) *general:* a scheduled payment to a retired person.

(2) *finance:* a series of equal payments at fixed intervals.

annuity, installment refund: a life annuity with an agreement that the insurer will, on the death of the annuitant, continue payments to a beneficiary until the total of the payments to annuitant and beneficiary equals the consideration paid to the insurer. [53]

annuity, joint and survivor: an annuity payable as long as any one of two or more persons survives. [53]

annuity, life: an annuity payable as long as the annuitant or annuitants live. [53]

annuity, retirement: a deferred annuity for which the premiums, less loading, are accumulated at interest and are used to purchase an annuity at a specified age. Prior to that age, the annuitant is entitled to a cash surrender value. In case of death, the surrender value is paid to his beneficiary. [53]

annuity, survivorship: an annuity payable to the annuitant for the period during which he survives the insured. [53]

annuity bond: see *bond, perpetual.*

annuity certain: an annuity payable for a particular period of time, regardless of the time of the death of the annuitant.

annuity certain and life: an annuity payable for a specified time period and for as long thereafter as the annuitant lives.

annuity deferred: an annuity, beginning more than one year from the payment of a lump sum, or from the beginning of periodic payments, to the insurer.

annuity due: an annuity where the initial payment is made at the beginning of each period (i.e., month, quarter) rather than at the end.

annuity insurance: an insurance contract providing for payment of a stipulated sum annually or periodically to a party called the annuitant for life or for a stated period.

annuity method of depreciation: taking the initial cost of a capital asset, deducting the expected salvage value at the time it is discarded, and assuming a rate of interest, the straight-line portion of cost plus interest in the undepreciated balance is charged to each period.

annuity plan: a type of retirement insurance whereby, after having made payment for a specified number of years, a person receives income for a given period (or for life). [105]

annuity reserve: a monetary sum equal to the actuarial value of future payments to be made on account of an annuity. [52]

annuity reserve fund: an amount or sum set aside in a reserve to provide for the payment of annuities. Usually derived from the members' accumulated contributions, or contributions by the members and the employer. [52]

annuity table: a listing of the present values of $1 per year or month payable for life, or for a term of years at specified ages for each sex, computed on the basis of assumed rates or mortality and interest. [52]

annulment: a judicial decree that a marriage was void from the beginning. [76]

annunciator boards: large boards on a stock exchange wall were a telephone clerk seeks the attention of the firm's floor broker. Each broker is assigned a number that is flashed on the board to call the broker or a messenger to the firm's booth on the rim of the trading floor.

ANSI: see *American National Standards Institute.*

antecedents: used in making credit inquiries to determine if the corporation has been controlled by the existing employer(s) for a short or long time period and how often the firm has changed ownership.

antedated check: a check that is dated prior to the date on which it is issued— that is, delivered or mailed to the payee. For example, if a check dated August 12 is not issued until August 17, it is an *antedated check.*

anticipated acceptance: an acceptance that has been paid prior to the specified terms of payment.

anticipated balance: the bank account balance projected through the end of the interest or dividend period, assuming that no additional deposit or withdrawal transactions occur.

anticipated interest: the amount of interest projected as earnings on bank accounts, assuming that no deposits or withdrawals occur before the end of the current interest period. This figure is updated after each deposit or withdrawal activity.

anticipation

(1) *banking:* payment of an account before the actual due date, thus permitting a discount.

(2) *finance:* assigning or making charges against income or profit before such gain is actually realized.

(3) *law:* describing a situation in which a claimed invention is known to others regardless of whether the anticipating invention has been patented.

anticipation, right of: the privilege given the mortgagor, by a provision in the mortgage instruments, to pay all or any portion of the outstanding balance of the obligation prior to its due date without penalty. [44]

anticipation and intentions data: provide information on the plans of businessmen and consumers regarding their economic activities in the near future. These plans are considered valuable aids to economic forecasting, either directly or as an indication of the state of confidence concerning the economic outlook. [73]

anticipation rate: the rate allowed in addition to the cash discount for payment in advance of the cash discount date or the rate allowed for payment before the due date where no cash discount is stated.

anticipation warrant: a short-term promise to pay, usually issued by a government in anticipation of later revenue.

anticipatory breach: the informing of the seller by a buyer before the closing of title that the buyer plans to terminate any involvement in the transaction.

Antidumping Act of 1974: legislation designed to prevent the sale of goods at a lower price than exists in the goods' country or origin. The Treasury Department determines whether imported products are being sold at "less than fair value" in this country. Should it be determined that the domestic industry is harmed by the imports, extra duties can be imposed.

antidumping duty: a tariff designed to prevent imports of goods for sale at a price in the importing country lower than the price in the country of origin of the goods.

Antikickback Law: see *Copeland Act of 1934.*

Antiracketeering Law: the Hobbs Act of 1934, making it a felony to interfere with commerce by robbery or extortion, by conspiracy, or by threat of violence.

antitrust: describing an action of the courts taken to curb monopolistic tendencies or to limit power stemming from monopolies.

antitrust acts: see *Celler Antimerger Act, Clayton Antitrust Act of 1914, Robinson-Patman Act of 1936, Sherman Antitrust Act of 1890.*

any-quantity rate: a transportation rate applicable to any quantity of a commodity shipped.

A&O: April and October (semiannual interest payments).

AO

(1) account of.

(2) see *average out.*

AOCR: see *advanced optical character reader.*

AP: see *authority to purchase.*

appellant: the party who makes a motion for an appeal from one jurisdiction or court to another.

appellee: the individual or stated party in a cause against whom an appeal is made.

applicant: any person who requests, or who has received, an extension of credit from a creditor. However, the term may also include any person who is or may be contractually liable regarding an extension of credit. [105]

application

(1) *computers:* the problem or business situation in relation to which a computer is used.

(2) *law:* any offer to purchase something or to enter into some form of contract.

application for guaranteed loan: bank's application to FmHA requestion an FmHA loan guarantee. [105]

application-for-loan form: a printed form used by most financial institutions which contains a prospective borrower's request for a loan. [51]

application holder: container placed at the point of sale or throughout bank lobbies to display cardholder application (e.g., "Take One" box). [105]

application of funds statement: constructed from balance sheets to two periods, the statement allows an analysis of the changes that have evolved during the period that was chosen.

applied proceeds swap: the sale of a block of bonds, the proceeds of which are applied to purchasing another block of bonds.

apportion: to assign a cost factor to a person, unit, product, or order.

apportioned tax: a tax whose proceeds are distributed to different units of government.

apportionment

(1) *general:* dividing a unit into proportionate parts; the proper allocation of receipts and expenses between income and principal.

(2) *banking:* involves the question of how much each of two or more insurance policies will contribute to the loss sustained by a covered risk. The decision of distribution is the apportionment.

appraisal: the setting of a value or evaluation of a specific piece of personal or real property, or the property of another as a whole. see *Baltimore method, Bernard rule, cost approach to value.*

appraisal fee: a charge for estimating the value of collateral being offered as security. [78]

appraisal of business: an examination to decide how much a business is worth. [61]

appraisal report: a written report of the factors considered in arriving at a valuation of a particular piece of property. [61]

appraisal rights of minority stockholders: the statutory rights for the protection of dissenting minority stockholders during a shift in shares at the time of a merger or consolidation.

appraisal surplus: the excess of appraised values over book values. [62]

appraise: to determine the cost, quality, or value of an item (e.g., to appraise the value of one's house). Also used to appraise the adequacy and effectiveness of systems and procedures.

appraised value: an estimate of property value reached by an appraiser. [105]

appraiser: a person who makes appraisals.

appraising: synonymous with *valuation.*

appreciation: the increase in the value of an asset in excess of its depreciable cost which is due to economic and other conditions; the increase of present value over the listed book value. see *capital gain.*

appreciation rate: the index figure used against the actual or estimated cost of property in computing its cost of reproduction, new as of a different date or under different conditions of a higher price level. [62]

appreciation surplus: the addition to net worth appearing in surplus as the result of a revaluation upward of the value at which assets are shown on the books of an enterprise.

appropriated retained earnings: see *retained earnings, appropriated.*

appropriate surplus: that part of the surplus of a corporation which has been set aside by the board of directors for a specific purpose other than to recognize an existing liability. The appropriation can be reversed by the board.

appropriation: an authorized sum of money set aside to pay certain known or anticipated costs of a given item or service.

appropriation ledger: a subsidiary ledger containing an account with each appropriation. Each account usually shows the amount originally appropriated, transfers to or from the appropriation charged against the appropriation, the net balance, and other related information. If allotments are made and a separate ledger is maintained for them, each account in the appropriation ledger usually shows the amount appropriated, transfers to or from the appropriation, the amount allotted, and the unallotted balance. see also *allotment ledger.* [49]

appropriation of income or surplus: action taken by a board of directors, setting aside amounts for specific use, such as payment of dividends, allotments to sinking funds, and additional investment.

approval ratio: number of cardholder applications approved, expressed as a percentage of total applications received; calculated by dividing the number of approved applications for a specified time period by the total number of applications processed within the same time period. [105]

approved bond: see *bond, approved.*

approved list: a list, statutory or otherwise, which contains the authorized investments that a fiduciary may acquire. [37]

approved plan: a plan that has been accepted by the Internal Revenue Service for tax deduction of contributions thereunder. [52]

appurtenances: rights and interest that attach to and pass with the land.

APR: see *annual percentage rate.*

a priori: a general, first-impression statement based on presuppositions, not facts.

Aprx.: approximately.

A&R: see *account and risk.*

AR:
(1) see *accounts receivable.*
(2) see *annual report.*
(3) see *annual return.*

Arab Bank for Economic Development in Africa: headquartered in Khartoum, Sudan; founded in 1973.

Arab Fund for Economic and Social Development: formed in 1968 to finance joint Arab programs in Arab nations which may be of general Arab interest; headquartered in Kuwait.

Arab League: founded in 1945 with headquarters in Egypt.

Arab Monetary Fund: created in 1977 and headquartered in Abu Dhabi.

arbitrage
(1) *finance:* simultaneous purchasing and selling of the identical item in different markets in order to yield profits. The result is that the price of an item becomes equal in all markets.
(2) *finance:* the purchase of foreign exchange, stocks, bonds, silver, gold, or other commodities in one market for sale in another market at a profit.
(3) *banking:* the simultaneous purchase and sale of mortgages, future contracts, or mortgage-backed securities in different markets to profit from price differences.

arbitrage house: a financial institution, such as a foreign exchange dealer or private banker, conducting business in arbitrage. see *arbitrage.*

arbitrager (arbitrageur): an individual who engages in the activity of arbitrage. see *arbitrage.*

arbitragist: synonymous with *arbitrager.*

arbitration of exchange: when prices of bills of exchange payable in foreign currency vary throughout financial centers in the world. Consequently, an individual from country A may find it profitable to purchase a bill of exchange from country B for payment in still another country.

archmonetarist: a supporter of Milton Friedman's monetary theory that changes in growth of money supply operate on the economy with such a long time lag that it is impossible for the authorities to know at any one moment what policy should be. cf. *balanced budget exercises, compensatory fiscal policy, New Economics.*

Arcru: a unit of account first used in 1974; based on the movement of 12 Arab currencies against the U.S. dollar.

Area Redevelopment Program: a federal program under the Area Redevelopment Act of 1961 to stimulate employment and business growth in depressed locales.

arguendo: Latin, referring to the case by way of argument or within an argument.

ARIEL: Automated Real-time Investments Exchange. Established in 1974, ARIEL is a computerized system for dealing in large blocks of securities. cf. *NASDAQ.*

arithmetic mean: the sum of all items divided by the number of items added.

ARMs: see *adjustable-rate mortgages.*

arm's-length transaction: one negotiated by unrelated parties, each acting in his or her own self-interest. The basis for a fair market value determination. [105]

around: used in quoting forward premium/discount (e.g., five-five around means five points on either side of pan).

ARQ: answer-return query.

arrange for the extension of credit (or for a lease of personal property): to provide or offer to provide consumer credit or a lease that is or will be extended by another person under a business or other relationship pursuant to which the person arranging such credit or lease (1) receives or will receive a fee, compensation, or other consideration for such service; or (2) has knowledge of the credit or lease terms and participates in the preparation of the contract documents required in connection with the extension of credit or the lease. [105]

array: an arrangement of single observations or times in ranked order, from the least to the most, or the reverse.

arrearages on preferred securities: the accumulation of unpaid dividends. A statement that such dividends for cumulative preferred stock must be paid prior to payment on the firm's common stock.

arrears

(1) a real or contingent obligation remaining unpaid at the date of maturity. Frequently used in connection with installment notes, mortgages, rent, and other obligations due and payable on a certain specified date.

(2) monies due but unpaid.

arrival draft: a draft accompanying shipping documents that is payable when the goods arrive as described in the papers. The arrival draft is presented upon receipt to the drawee as a means of preparing him or her to pay when the goods have arrived. see *draft.*

Article 4—Uniform Commercial Code: governs checks and other negotiable instruments during bank collection and payment. [105]

articles of agreement: any contract between two or more people that is reduced to a written instrument.

articles of association: any instrument that is similar to a corporate certificate; usually used with non-stock corporations (e.g., charitable organizations).

articles of copartnership: the written agreement by which a partnership is formed.

articles of incorporation: a document filed with an appropriate state agency by persons establishing a corporation. Upon return accompanied by a certificate of incorporation, the document becomes the firm's charter.

articles of partnership: a written agreement between business partners that outlines the provisions of their business arrangement. [105]

Article 3—Uniform Commercial Code: governs the rights and duties of parties to commercial paper. [105]

AS:

(1) see *accumulated surplus.*

(2) see *active securities.*

(3) see *assented securities.*

(4) see *assessable stock.*

ASAP: as soon as possible.

Asd.: assented.

ASE: see *American Stock Exchange.*

ASEAN: see *Association of South-East Asian Nations.*

as earned: describes the basis of income of a customer who is not paid on a regular basis—that is, business-for-self. [55]

Asian Clearing Union: a joint arrangement for settling international payments imbalances between Bangladesh, Burma, India, Iran, Nepal, Pakistan, and Sri Lanka.

Asian Currency Units (ACUs): the separate accounting entities by which the Asiadollar deposit market was created. The market emerged from a Bank of America proposal. ACUs totaled over $42 billion in early 1980.

Asian Development Bank (ADB): established in 1966 to help provide development capital for Asia. Head-quartered in Manila.

Asian dollars: U.S. dollar bank deposits traded outside the United States.

ask: an offer to sell at a designated price.

asked: see *bid and asked.*

asked (asking) price

(1) *general:* the price that is officially offered in a sale.

(2) *investments:* the price at which a stock is offered for sale. In open-end shares, the price at which the purchaser may buy stock from the investment firm. In closed-end shares, the lowest price at which the stock is then offered for sale in the public market.

ASKI system: an exchange control system under which payment for imported goods is made in marked funds usable only to purchase goods of the importing country. The term is the abbreviation of the German for "foreigners' special accounts for domestic payments.

ASP: see *American selling price.*

as per advice: words on a bill of exchange showing that the drawee has been notified that the bill has been drawn on him or her.

assay: a test of content, composition, and purity, often carried out in an assayer's office, on metals, usually gold and silver.

assay office: a location designated for the testing of ore, commodities, and bullion in addition to foreign coin.

assay office bar: assayed by an assay office and made at a mint, a bar of pure or near pure gold or silver.

assemblage: the act of bringing two or more individuals or things to form an aggregate whole; specifically, the cost or estimated cost of assembling two or more parcels of land under a single ownership and unit of utility over the normal cost or current market prices of the parcels held individually. [62]

assembling: the activities involved in concentrating supplies or assortments of goods or services to facilitate sale or purchase. [48]

assembling land: the combining of nearby or contiguous properties to form one tract.

assented securities: securities whose owners agree to some change in status, usually in case of corporate restructuring, when an assessment is made or the amount of securities is reduced according to some logical plan.

assess: to determine the value of something, or to fix its value for tax purposes.

assessable insurance: an insurance contract in which the policyholder is liable for an additional premium payment if losses are unexpectedly large.

assessable stock: security that is subject to an assessment order resulting from a corporation's reorganization or insolvency.

assessed value: the official record of a tax assessed and collected; the tax roll value assigned to property.

assessment

(1) *banking:* a charge made against property for the purpose of levying a tax. see *nonassessable stock.*

(2) *finance:* any levy on members of a corporation for purposes of raising capital.

assessment insurance: a form of mutual insurance where the policyholders are assessed whenever there is a loss.

assessment ratio: the ratio of the assessed value of property to the full or true property value. Full value may be defined as fair market value at the bid side of the market, less a reasonable allowance for sales and other expenses. [105]

assessment roll

(1) in the case of real property the official list containing the legal description of each parcel of property and its assessed valuation. The name and address of the last known owner are also usually shown.

(2) in the case of personal property, the assessment roll is the official list containing the name and address of the owner, a description of the personal property, and its assessed value. [49]

assessor: a designated public official who makes the official estimate of value.

asset:

(1) *general:* anything owned by an individual or business that has commercial or exchange value. Assets may consist of specific property or claims against others, in contract to obligations due others. see *balance sheet, current assets to current debt, fixed assets, intangible asset, tangible assets.*

(2) *banking:* uses of bank funds—cash, security investments, loans, and fixed assets. [105]

asset, capital: see *capital assets.*

asset, contingent: see *contingent asset.*

asset, current: see *current assets to current debt.*

asset, dead: see *dead asset.*

asset, deferred: see *deferred asset.*

asset, fixed: see *fixed assets.*

asset, fixed register: see *fixed register asset.*

asset, fixed test: see *fixed test asset.*

asset, fixed to tangible net worth: see *fixed-to-tangible-net-worth asset.*

asset, floating: see *floating assets.*

asset, fluid: see *current assets.*

asset, frozen: see *frozen asset.*

asset, gross: see *gross asset.*

asset, hypothecated: see *hypothecated asset.*

asset, inactive: see *inactive asset.*

asset, intangible: see *intangible asset.*

asset, ledger: see *ledger asset.*

asset, liquid: see *liquid assets.*

asset, minus: see *minus asset.*

asset, net: see *net assets.*

asset, net value: see *net asset value.*

asset, nominal: see *nominal asset.*

asset, nonaccrual: see *nonaccrual asset.*

asset, nonledger: see *nonledger asset.*

asset, ordinary: see *ordinary asset.*

asset, original: see *original asset.*

asset, permanent: see *permanent asset.*

asset, personal: see *personal asset.*

asset, physical: see *tangible assets.*

asset, pledged: see *pledged assets.*

asset, quick: see *quick assets.*

asset, tangible: see *tangible assets.*

asset, value: see *value asset.*

asset, wasting: see *wasting assets.*

asset, working: see *working asset.*

asset and liability statement: a balance sheet.

asset card: synonymous with *debit card.*

asset coverage: *direct*—the extent to which net assets (after all prior claims) cover a specific senior obligation, whether bank loans, debentures, or preferred stock. It may be expressed in either dollar, percentage, or ratio terms. *Overall*—the ratio of total assets to the sum of all prior obligations including that of the specific issue under consideration taken at liquidating value. [30]

asset currency: bank notes that are not secured by any particular assets but by the general assets of the issuing bank. Some countries have such characteristics. Today, more popularly referred to as *general asset currency.* see also *Baltimore method.*

asset enter mains: used in the transactions of executors or trustees, showing an asset available to fulfill immediate obligations.

assets, total: see *total assets.*

assign: to transfer to another. A person to whom property is assigned. [76]

assignability: the capacity of property to be transferred to another person or organization.

assignat: paper currency issue during the French Revolution backed by land that was confiscated from the church and aristocracy. The money was later repudiated.

assigned account: an account, usually receivable, which has been assigned to a bank as security for a loan by a borrower. In theory, the bank takes possession of the account pledged. In actual practice, however, so as not to jeopardize the relationship between the borrower and his customer (whose account has been pledged), the bank will allow the account to be paid by the customer in the normal manner, and will rely upon the integrity of the borrower to apply this payment against the loan balance. [31]

assigned book account: see *assigned account.*

assigned expense: expense incurred by a particular function. [12]

assigned in blank: the space on a transfer-of-ownership document for placing the new owner's name. Often street certificates are assigned in blank where no name appears on the certificate.

assignee
(1) *general:* one to whom an assignment is granted.
(2) *law:* an individual to whom property or rights have been transferred for the benefit of self or others. see *assignment, assignment in blank, assignor.*

assignment
(1) *banking:* the transfer in writing by one individual to another of title of property.
(2) *investments:* the transfer of title of stocks.
(3) *law:* a transfer in writing of the legal right in a policy to another party. see *assignment in blank, good delivery, stop order.*

assignment, lease: transferring leasehold interest to another person or group.

assignment, mortgage: transferring a mortgage to another person or group.

assignment for the benefit of creditors: a person or firm's action to transfer legal title to property to a trustee who has been authorized to administer and liquidate the property and make a distribution to creditors. see also *National Bankruptcy Act of 1898.*

assignment in blank: see *assigned in blank.*

assignment of leases: additional security often taken in connection with mortgages of commercial properties. [22]

assignment of mortgage: the written instrument evidencing an association's transfer of a loan obligation from the original borrower to a third person. [59]

assignment of rents: a written document that transfers to a mortgagee on default the owner's right to collect rents. [59]

assignment separate from certificate: a detached assignment or stock (bond) power. The certificate is the same as the rear portion of the security and includes a complete description of the security. This permits the holder to transfer the certificate safely by sending the unsigned certificate and properly filled out stock power under separate cover. One without the other has no value, so little damage would result if it is lost or stolen.

assignment to creditors: the transfer of property in trust or for the benefit of creditors. [76]

assignor: an individual who assigns or transfers a claim, right, or property. see *assigned in blank, assignment, assignment for the benefit of creditors.*

assimilation: the completed distribution of new shares of securities to the public by the issue's underwriters and syndicate members.

assistance and subsidies: cash contributions and subsidies to persons and foreign governments, not in payment for goods or services or for claims against the government. Includes direct cash assistance to public welfare recipients; veterans bonuses; direct cash grants for tuition, scholarship, and aid to nonpublic educational institutions; and payments for agricultural support programs and foreign aid.

Assmt.: see *assessment.*

Assn.: see *association.*

associated banks: banks that are associated through membership in a clearinghouse association.

Associated Credit Bureaus of America, Inc.: membership organization of credit bureaus and collection service departments throughout the nation. Facilitates interbureau credit reporting by means of a *coupon system.* [41]

associate member: a bank that participates in a credit plan administered by another bank or group of banks. [105]

association: a grouping of people for mutually beneficial purposes or for the furtherance of some goal. An unincorporated group, not formed for profit. see *voluntary association.*

Association Cambiste Internationale: the international organization of foreign exchange dealers, consisting of national Forex clubs affiliated throughout the world; headquartered in Paris.

association (ABA) number: a numerical coding system originated by the ABA to facilitate the sorting and processing of checks. Each bank is assigned a unique identifying number, made of two parts separated by a hyphen. The first part of the number identifies the state, city, or territory in which the bank is located, and the second part identifies the bank itself. [105]

Association of International Bond Dealers (AIBD): headquartered in Zurich; dealers' professional organization that recommends procedures and policies.

Association of South-East Asian Nations (ASEAN): created in 1967 and headquartered in Indonesia.

Asst. Cash.: assistant cashier.

assumable mortgage: a home mortgage where the buyer takes over the seller's original, below-market-rate mortgage.

assumed bond: see *bond, assumed.*

assumed liability: an obligation for payment accepted by another person.

assumpsit
(1) a common law action alleging that damages have been incurred.
(2) a common law action to recover damages for breach of contract.

assumption: bank loan payments accepted by a party other than the original maker.

assumption of debt: taking on another's debt. [61]

assumption of mortgage: accepting a property title that has an existing mortgage with personal liability for all payments by another.

assurance: commonly used in England. Similar to *insurance*, but differs in that assurance does not depend on a possibility: it is a payment of a premium at regular periods for a stated sum that becomes payable at a given time.

Astd.: assented.

AT: see *absolute title.*

at a discount: a security selling in the marketplace below its par value.

at a premium: a security selling in the marketplace above its par value.

ATB: see *across the board.*

at best: an instruction given to a dealer to buy or sell currency or securities at the best rate that he or she can obtain.

at call: any transaction occurring in the call money market. see *call money, call money market.*

ATM:
(1) see *at the market.*
(2) see *automated teller machine.*

at market: see *at the market.*

ATO: see *at the opening.*

at or better: when placing a purchase order for securities, to buy at the price specified or under; in a selling request, to sell at the price given or above.

ATP: see *authority to purchase.*

at par: designating a bond or share of preferred stock issued or selling at its face amount.

ATS: see *automatic transfer service accounts.*

at seller's option: see *seller's option.*

at sight: in the body of negotiable instruments indicating that payment is due upon presentation or demand.

attached account: an account against which a court order has been issued, permitting disbursement of the balance only with the consent of the court. see *frozen account.*

attached ledger: the book or ledger in which records of attached accounts are segregated and kept.

attachment: the legal proceeding following a court's action whereby a plaintiff acquires a lien on a defendant's property as security for payment of a judgment that the plaintiff can recover. cf. *judgment lien.*

attachment ledger: see *attached ledger.*

attention party: in EFTS, the person or department within the receiving bank whose attention should be drawn to the message. [105]

attest: to bear witness to; as, to attest a will or other document. [32]

attestation: the act of bearing witness or giving authenticity to a document by signing as a witness to the signature of another. see *notary public.*

attestation clause: the clause of a document containing the formal declaration of the act of witnessing; in the case of a will, the clause immediately following the signature of the testator and usually beginning "Signed, sealed, published, and declared by the said. . . ." [105]

attested wills: prepared in writing or typewritten and signed by the testator or by someone for him and acknowledged by him. His signature has to be witnessed by two or more adults at the time of execution. Attested wills are the most popular form of will.

attesting witness: one who testifies to the authenticity of a document, as the attesting witness to a will; to be distinguished from *subscribing witness*. [37]

at the close: an order to be executed at the best price attainable at the close of the market on the day it is entered. Rule 130 of the American Stock Exchange does not permit this arrangement.

at the market: an order that the broker has executed at the best price available after it was received by the broker on the floor of the exchange. synonymous with *market order*. see *limit order*.

at the opening: a securities order that is either executed immediately following the opening of the exchange or canceled entirely. see *odd lot*.

at thirty days sight: where the drawee is permitted 30 days' time on a time draft from the date of acceptance in which to pay the paper.

attorney-at-law: a person who has a state license giving the privilege to practice law.

attorney-in-fact: a person who has the written authorization of another to carry out business for his or her principal out of court.

attorney of record: the lawyer whose name is entered in the records of the court as the representative of a party in a legal action or suit.

Atty.: attorney.

AU: gold (from *arum*).

auction: a unique trading market in which there is one seller and many potential buyers. see also *Dutch auction*.

auction market: the system of trading securities through brokers or agents on an exchange such as the New York Stock Exchange. Buyers compete with other sellers for the most advantageous price. Most transactions are executed with public customers on both sides since the specialist buys or sells for his own account primarily to offset imbalances in public supply and demand. see *dealer, quotation, specialist*. [20]

Aud.
(1) see *audit*.
(2) see *auditor*.

audit
(1) *general:* inspection of a firm's books; a final statement of account.
(2) *finance:* periodic or continuous verification of the stated assets and liabilities of a company or other organization. see *bank examination*.

audit comment: a situation that is noted by the auditors and reported to the department manager but which may not be reported to the senior management of the bank. [105]

audit committee: a committee appointed by a board of directors or president to validate and report on the accuracy of the treasurer's records.

audited voucher: a voucher that has been examined and approved for payment. see *accounts payable*. [49]

audit function: periodic or continuous verification of the bank's assets and liabilities. This function is performed by the auditor. The auditor is appointed by the board of directors and is responsible for the carrying out of this verification. Among the assets and liabilities more regularly verified are cash, loans, collateral for loans, and savings and checking accounts. Verification may consist of a physical count of the assets as reflected by the general ledger or a listing of the balances, as shown on each savings or checking account, with a proof of the total as shown on the general ledger. Direct verification may also be made with borrowers or depositors. [10]

auditing department: a unit within a bank or other financial organization, responsible for bookkeeping, accounting and auditing activities. Daily control of all transactions is the primary goal of this department, usually headed by an auditor.

auditor: a person qualified to conduct an audit. Qualification is defined by each state. see *audit, auditing department, bank examiner, certified public accountant.*

auditor's certificate: a statement signed by an auditor in which the auditor states that he or she has examined the financial statements, the system of internal control, the accounting records, and supporting evidence in accordance with generally accepted auditing standards and in which the auditor expresses his or her opinion, based on such examination, regarding the financial condition of a unit or any of its enterprises, the results from operations, and any facts that he or she has investigated in his or her professional capacity.

audit program: a detailed outline of work to be done and the procedure to be followed in any given audit. [49]

audit report: the report prepared by an auditor covering the audit or investigation made by him or her. As a rule, the report should include a statement of the scope of the audit, a summary of findings, recommendations, a certificate, financial statements, and, sometimes, statistical tables. [49]

audit trail: a printed record of transaction listings created as a by-product of data-processing runs or manual or mechanized accounting operations.

audit trail number: a 10-digit number recorded on the top right-hand corner of a payment for tracing purposes. [105]

au jour le jour: the rate for money lent from day to day on the French money market. Rates vary according to whether the loan is made against the security of Treasury or private bills.

austerity program: a governmental policy reducing the level of living of the people so as to accomplish desired ends, such as a balanced budget, payment of external national debt, and so on.

austral: monetary unit of the Argentines.

autarky: an attempt to minimize a nation's dependence on other countries by substituting national manufacturing imports of goods.

Auth.: authority.

authenticated copy: a copy of an instrument on which an attestation is made in the manner required by law by an official authorized to make such certification, as by the certification and seal of a specified public official. [37]

authentication

(1) *investments:* the signing of a certificate on a bond by a trustee in order to identify it as having been issued under a specific indenture, thereby validating the bond.

(2) *law:* the verification of a document as truthful, genuine, or valid.

authority bond: see *bond, authority.*

authenticator: in EFTS, the code in a message between the sender and the receiver used to validate the source and the full text of the message. [105]

authority to purchase: used in Far Eastern trade, a substitute for a commercial *letter of credit*; this instrument permits the bank to which it is directed to purchase drafts drawn on an importer rather than on a bank. see *letter of credit.*

authorization: the issuance of approval, by or on behalf of the card issuer, to complete a transaction for a merchant or another affiliate. [105]

authorization center: a credit-card centralized office that has records of the cardholder's account with an issuer bank. If sufficient credit is there, the purchase is authorized.

authorization code: number assigned by the bank to a merchant sale or cash advance which has received specific approval. The code is used as proof that the transaction has been properly authorized. [105]

authorization department: department responsible for providing telephone approval for purchases and cash advances. [105]

authorization index: listing of credit customers by name and address, credit limits, and other instructions or restrictions. Can be arranged alpha-betically or geographically. In the latter case the street number is the primary key to the index. [41]

authorization in float: see *authorization outstanding.*

authorization number: see *authorization code.*

authorization outstanding: describes a situation where a transaction has been authorized, but the sales draft representing that transaction has not yet been received and posted by the bank. [105]

authorization request: a request for approval, by or on behalf of the card issuer, for a financial transaction. [105]

authorization reversal: a nonmonetary transaction issued to reverse a previous authorization and which increases the account's available credit by the amount of the authorization. [105]

authorized capital stock: the full amount of stock that a corporation is permitted by its charter to issue.

authorized dealer: banks allowed by their regulating body to deal in foreign exchange. [84]

authorized depositary: in Great Britain, people authorized by an order of H.M. Treasury to receive securities into deposit in accordance with the terms of the Exchange Control Act of 1947. [84].

authorized investment: an investment that is authorized by the trust instrument; to be distinguished from *legal investment.* [37]

authorized issue

(1) the total number of shares of capital stock that a charter permits a corporation to sell.

(2) the total number of bonds that may be sold under a given mortgage.

authorized settlement bank: a bank in the United States that clears cash items, either directly or indirectly, through the U.S. Federal Reserve System; and which has been empowered by a Visa International Clearing Member to prepare and/or honor clearing drafts for the settlement of interchange. [105]

authorized stock: the maximum number of all classes of securities that can be issued by a corporation. see *capital stock.*

authorizing member: a member providing authorization facilities for its merchants and other members. [105]

authorizor: the person in a credit office designated to approve or disapprove requests for purchases to be charged to credit accounts. [41]

automated clearinghouse (ACH): a computerized facility used by member depository institutions to process (i.e., combine, sort, and distribute) payment orders in machine-readable form (computer tapes or punched cards).

automated teller: see *unattended banking terminal.*

automated teller machine (ATM): a machine capable of processing a variety of transactions between a depository institution and its customers. These functions might include accepting deposits, providing withdrawals, transferring funds between accounts, and accepting instructions to pay third parties in the transaction. An ATM may or may not be on-line to a computer system and may be located on or off the premises of a depository institution. Placement in certain locations may permit customer access 7 days a week, 24 hours a day. see *Bellevue Project, cash dispenser,*

debit card, Customer-Bank Communication Terminal.

automated transit: the basic transit functions are reading, calculating, accumulating, printing, and sorting of all out-of-city MCR-encoded items. When automated, these functions are performed on MICR sorters/readers, high-speed check listers, and computers. [10]

automatic bill payment: payment by one check to a number of creditors or direct payment by the bank for specified recurring bills. [105]

automatic charge back: a transaction that does not meet the conditions for acceptance by the banks as set forth in the merchant agreement. [105]

automatic currency: see *elasticity.*

automatic data processing: see *ADP.*

automatic deposit plan: a savings account deposit plan whereby the customer arranges for checks, such as Social Security payments and stock dividends, to be sent directly to his association for deposit to his savings account. [59]

automatic fiscal stabilizers: nondiscretionary approaches that automatically cushion recession by assisting in creating a budget deficit and curb inflation by helping to create a budget surplus.

automatic fund transfer: a regulation by the Federal Reserve Board and the Federal Deposit Insurance Corporation permitting a financial institution to move funds from a depositor's savings account to his checking account upon specific request.

automatic guarantee: a provision of the Veterans Administration under which it will guarantee with prior approval a mortgage loan made by a supervised lender. [59]

automatic premium loan: a provision in a life insurance policy that any premium not paid by the end of the grace period (usually 31 days) be automatically paid by a policy loan if there is sufficient cash value.

automatic reinvestment: a service, often associated with mutual funds, enabling the investor to automatically put income dividends or capital gains distributions back into the fund to buy new shares and thereby build up new holdings.

automatic stabilizer: a tool of economics and finance used to compensate for shifts in the business cycle without the involvement of a government official.

automatic standard: a monetary standard (the best example is gold standard) where the amount and value of money is consciously managed but is the result of the working of demand and supply for the precious metal or foreign currency that follows upon differences in trading volume between nations.

automatic transfer between accounts: a deposit service that authorizes periodic transfer of funds between accounts. [105]

automatic transfer of funds: movement of funds between accounts at prearranged times, according to a prespecified agreement between a bank and a customer.

automatic transfer service (ATS) accounts: effective November 1, 1978, commercial banks began offering interest-paying checking accounts. Automatic transfer service accounts allow a bank saver to keep funds in a 5 percent passbook account, allowing the bank to shift a predetermined amount into a checking account periodically. see *negotiable order of withdrawal.*

automation: conversion to the use of automatic machines or devices designed to control various processes. Originally coined in 1935 by D. S. Harder of the Ford Motor Company and popularized by John Diebold. In banks and financial institutions, this term usually refers to the use of electronic equipment and computers.

autonomous investment: new investment caused by events independent of changes in the interest rate or the level of consumption or national income.

autonomous tariff system: tariff duties where rates are created by legislative action exclusively, and not wholly or partly by commercial treaties. cf. *conventional tariff system.*

autonomous transactions: transactions among nations that arise from factors unrelated to the balance of payments as such. The primary classes are merchandise trade and services and long-term capital movements as well as unilateral transfers.

auxiliary account: a contra, offset, or adjunct account that is related to the principal account.

auxiliary operation: an operation performed by equipment off-line or not under continuous control of the central processor. A supplemental function to be combined with others to complete a major transaction. [10]

auxiliary storage: a storage device used to supplement the main internal storage of a computer (e.g., magnetic tape, disk, or drum). Such devices are used to store software; master files, such as savings and demand deposit accounts and records; and so on. see *software*. [10]

Av.: see *average*.

AV

(1) see *actual value*.

(2) see *ad valorem*.

avail: the amount remaining following a discount or expense deduction.

availability clause: see *currency availability clause*.

availability date: the date on which checks payable at out-of-town banks are considered to be collected and available for customers withdrawal; determined by the geographical location of the drawee bank, in relation to time and distance from the sending bank. Recently, local banks were included, and volume is replacing distance.

availability schedule: a list indicating the time that must elapse before deposited checks can be considered to be converted into usable funds. [105]

available assets: a person's or firm's assets that may be readily sold to meet a need. Such assets would usually not be mortgaged or pledged.

available balance: the book balance less any hold, uncollected funds, and restrictions against an account. [31]

available credit: the difference between the credit limit assigned to a cardholder account and the present balance, including authorization outstanding, of that account. see *open to buy*. [105]

available fund: the amount of cash or demand deposits obtainable by a person or organization to fulfill a need. Such assets would usually not be pledged. Also, the collected balance

less the reserve requirement available for investment.

available time

(1) *general:* time other than maintenance time.

(2) *computers:* time when the computer's power is turned on and the device is ready for use.

avails: the proceeds from a discounted note. see *net avails*.

aval: payment of a bill of exchange or promissory note that has been guaranted by the signature of a third person appearing on the bill. Used extensively in Europe.

average

(1) *general:* a measure of central tendency.

(2) *investments:* to buy or sell more shares, items, or whatever with the goal of receiving a better average price.

average adjustor: the person who prepares claims made under the average clause in insurance contracts.

average annual bill per customer: annual revenue (exclusive of discounts and penalties) from a class of service divided by the average annual number of customers for that class of service. [3]

average balance

(1) *general:* the sum of the daily balances in an account during a month divided by the number of days in that month.

(2) *banking:* a high average balance for an account, indicating a more profitable account than another with a lower average balance.

average bond: see *bond, average*.

average book: lender's record, as in a bank, showing differing averages, such as the average balance or average loan, by each customer, which are posted and often entered into the computer to aid management in future planning.

average collected balance: the average collected balance of a depositor's account is usually determined on a monthly basis. It is arrived at by adding the daily balances of the account, and deducting the sum of the float, or uncollected items, from the formal total, and dividing the remainder by the number of days in the month. [10]

average collection period: the ratio of (1) the total accounts receivable at any date multiplied by 365 to (2) net credit sales for the year. Tests the quality of accounts receivable.

average cost: the sum of all output costs divided by the quantity of production.

average daily balance: the average amount of money that a customer keeps on deposit; determined by adding the daily balances of an account for a given length of time and dividing the total by the number of days covered.

average daily float: that portion of a customer's balance said to consist of deposited checks that are in the process of collection. The average daily float is deducted from the average book balance for purposes of account analysis. [105]

average draft size: the average amount of sales drafts received by a bank during a specific period of time. [105]

average due date: the average date when several payments, coming due at differing times, can be paid.

average fixed cost: the total of those costs of a business that do not vary with the amount of business done, di-

vided by the number of units produced at the point under consideration.

average hourly earnings: the amount of money actually received by an employee per hour of work during a pay period.

average life: the average maturity of a borrowing after taking into account repayments or sinking-fund provisions.

average loan file: see *average book.*

average monthly wage: the average rate of remuneration per month, computed as prescribed by law.

average number of customers: the average of the number of customers counted regularly once in each of 12 consecutive months. [3]

average out: to conclude a buy or sell transaction without any loss, and hopefully with a profit, by the process of averaging. see *averaging.*

average outstanding balance: the averaged balance outstanding on all cardholder accounts within a specified time period; calculated by dividing the total outstanding by the number of accounts with balances. [105]

average price: the mean, or average, price of a security obtained in the purchase or sale of a security by a process of averaging.

average revenue: the amount received from all sales divided by the number of items that have been sold.

averages: various ways of measuring the trend of securities prices; one of the most popular is the Dow Jones average of 30 industrial stocks listed on the New York Stock Exchange. Formulas—some very elaborate—have been devised to compensate for stock splits and stock dividends and thus given continuity to the average. In the case of the Dow Jones industrial average, the prices of the 30 stocks are totaled and then divided by a divisor which is intended to compensate for past stock splits and stock dividends and which is changed from time to time. As a result, point changes in the average have only the vaguest relationship to dollar price changes in stocks included in the average. see *NYSE Common Stock Index, points, split*. [20]

average straight-time hourly earnings: the actual earnings per straight-time hour, excluding shift differentials and overtime pay but including incentive and merit payments.

average ticket, average sale: the averaged dollar amount of sales drafts received by a bank during a specific period; can be calculated by adding the dollar totals of all sales drafts received (within a specified time period) and dividing the total by the number of sales drafts received (within the same period). Cash advances can be so identified also. [105]

average variable cost: the total of those costs of a business that vary with the amount of business done, divided by the number of units produced at the point under consideration.

average weekly benefit: as prescribed by law, the amount payable per week to compensate for disability or death. It is usually a percentage of the average weekly wage, subject to a minimum and a maximum amount. In worker's compensation insurance, this is referred to as weekly compensation. The benefit is paid by an insurance carrier of the institution.

average weekly wage: the average rate of remuneration per week, computed as prescribed by law.

average yield: in Great Britain, the av-erage of all the yields implied by the prices bid for U.S. Treasury bills at the Bank of England tender.

averaging
(1) *federal income taxes:* a benefit allowing individuals to average taxable income for four preceding years over a five-year period.
(2) *investments:* the methods used in an attempt to improve the average price paid or received for securities.

averaging up: in the stock market, the practice of selling short the same dollar amount of shares as the market price is rising so that prices can fall only partway back toward the original starting price and there will be a net profit if the shares are brought to cover before the original prices are reached again.

Avg.: see *average.*

avoirdupois
(1) *general:* French term meaning having weight.
(2) *finance:* commodities sold by weight.

AVT:
(1) see *ad valorem taxes.*
(2) see *value-added tax.*

avulsion: any shift of land from one property to another caused by forces of nature without change in ownership.

award
(1) *finance:* the acceptance of a bid or the assigning of a project on the basis of a made offer. see *competitive bid.*
(2) *investments:* the acceptance by a borrower of a competitive bid for a security issue in the form of notification to the high-bidder investment banker or syndicate.
(3) *labor relations:* the final deci-

sion of an arbitrator, binding on both parties to the dispute.

(4) *law:* the findings of a competent court or board on a matter to be settled by such a body in favor of one of the parties to the case.

axia: unchartered, voluntary form of credit union found only in large cities and limited to a single foreign-born group. Indorsed notes and shares are used as security for loans.

AY: see *annual yield.*

B
- (1) the monetary base.
- (2) see *bid*.

B&A: see *bid and asked.*

BA: see *bank acceptance.*

baby bond: see *bond, baby.*

Baby Wagner Acts: state and territorial labor laws based on the Wagner-Connery Act. which deal with representation procedures and unfair labor and management practices.

back: to finance, sponsor, or endorse (e.g., to back a plan to add a wing to the plant).

Back.: see *backwardation.*

backdating: placing on a statement a date prior to the date on which it was drawn up.

back door: another name for the U.S. Treasury.

backdoor financing: the practice enabling a government agency to borrow from the U.S. Treasury instead of relying on congressional appropriations. synonymous with *public debt transaction.*

backdoor listing: a company's practice of making itself eligible for listing on an exchange by acquiring a listed firm and merging itself into acquisition, after failing to fulfill the listing requirements of an exchange on its own.

back-end processing: a bank with an EFT network, perhaps an ATM network, that has each device attached directly to its proprietary data processing facility. At the same time, the bank participates in a shared ATM network with other banks where their customers can access other ATMs. The distinction is how those ATMs may be attached in the network environment. For transaction activity all on-us items, or items conducted by the owning bank at their ATM by their customer, will be processed at their data center. This is back-end processing for the network. Their customers accessing other ATMs in shared network would receive authorization from the same bank data center but through machines that could be attached at the front end. The back-end arrangement involves proprietary authorization of proprietary activity without passing the data through the shared network. Thus a back-end processor looks at and authorizes its own customers for its own customers at its own ATMs while participating in a large network. [105]

backer: an individual who supports with money a project or person.

back freight: freight payable when delivery is not taken within a reasonable period at the discharge point; the executive in charge deals with the items at the owner's expense.

backlog: the existence and accumulation of unfilled requests on a firm's books.

back office crunch (crush)
(1) *general:* a delay in daily operations, often resulting from a pileup of unprocessed work.
(2) *investments:* an operational failure, where brokerage houses are deficient in processing a heavier than normal volume of transactions.

back order: part of an original order that was not filled in the first shipment, to be sent when ready, without obliging the customer to reorder the item(s).

back pay: wages due an employee because of employer violation of minimum wage laws, layoff or discharge in violation of a collective agreement, or adjustment of piece rate following the settlement of a grievance.

back spread: exists when the price for identical items in two markets is less than the normal difference (e.g., a stock is selling for $50 on a New York stock exchange and for the equivalent of $55 on the London Stock Exchange, the difference being due to shipping costs, insurance, and other factors).

back-to-back
(1) operations where a loan is made in one currency in one nation against a loan in another currency in another nation.

(2) credit opened by a bank on the strength of another credit. [85]

back-to-back letters of credit: two letters of credit with identical documentary requirements, except for a difference in the price of merchandise as shown by the invoice and the draft. [105]

backtracking: using seniority rights to displace junior workers when business conditions warrant layoffs. see *bump.*

backwardation: a basic pricing system in commodity futures trading. A price structure in which the nearer deliveries of a commodity cost more than contracts that are due to mature many months in the future. A backwardation price pattern occurs mainly because the demand for supplies in the near future is greater than the demand for supplies at some more distant time.

Bacon-Davis Act: a federal law of 1931 providing that the Secretary of Labor can set wage rates on public construction projects to conform to rates currently paid for similar work in the area.

bad debt: amount due on an open account that has been proved to be uncollectible; any uncollectible receivable.

bad debt expense: the cost of uncollectible accounts receivable. In most companies, bad debt expense is debited for the estimated amount uncollectible, and allowance for uncollectible accounts is credited.

bad debt recovery: money collected on a bad debt account. [55]

bad debts collected: amounts earlier written off as uncollectable that are subsequently collected.

bad debts ratio: the ratio of bad debt(s) to sales outstanding. [105]

bad debt writeoff: a customer's account that is removed from the books when payment appears unlikely.

bad delivery

(1) *general:* a delivered item not conforming to the original terms of agreement.

(2) *investments:* an improperly prepared or transferred security or certificate.

bad faith: the intent to mislead or deceive (mala fides). It does not include misleading by an honest, inadvertent, or uncalled-for misstatement. see *fraud.*

bad money: see *good money.*

bad news: slang, any bill for money owed.

baht: monetary unit of Thailand.

BAI: see *Bank Administration Institute.*

bail

(1) *as a noun:* a bond given by another in his or her behalf, for the payment of money in the event that the accused fails to appear in court on a specific day. see *bond, penal.*

(2) *as a verb:* to release an arrested or imprisoned individual.

bail bond: see *bond, bail.*

bailee: a person who acts as a receiver for personal property.

bailee receipt: the receipt presented to a bank holding title to goods by a bailee, a customer of the bank who is allowed to sell them for the amount of the owning bank.

bailment

(1) *general:* the providing of bail for an arrested person.

(2) *law:* delivery of personal property to another person for a specific purpose.

bailor: an individual who delivers personal property for possession to another.

bailout: the use of corporate monies to provide to shareholders payments that are taxable at desirable capital gains rates. The Securities Exchange Commission has ruled the bailout illegal.

Bal.: see *balance.*

balance: the amount standing to the credit of a customer's account, representing the amount he is entitled to withdraw. The difference between total debits and credits, whether against or in favor of a bank at the clearinghouse. [31]

balance as a whole: a form of proof method employed in banks, usually in the bookkeeping department. A control total is established for several books or ledgers. Each bookkeeper processes work by posting to his or her accounts. At the end of the posting run, several bookkeepers will add their combined totals, and will *balance as a whole* to the control total for their group of ledgers. [10]

balance commerciale: French term for *balance of trade* in merchandise.

balanced budget: a budget in which forward expenditures for a set period are matched by expected revenues for the same period.

balanced budget exercises: government spending that keeps the size of the budget deficit the same by simultaneously increasing and decreasing various taxes. cf. *archmonetarist.*

balanced budget multiplier: the concept that when the budget of a government is balanced, taxes result in reduction of consumption by less than the tax (since not all of the money would have been spent). Thus when the taxes are spent by the government, more is spent than would have been spent had there been no tax.

balanced economy: a condition of national finances in which imports and exports are equal.

balance des paiements courants: French term for *current account* of the balance of payments.

balanced fund: a mutual fund which has an investment policy of *balancing* its portfolio, generally by including bonds, preferred stocks, and common stocks. [23]

balance due: the total amount needed to equalize the debit and credit sum of an account; the amount you owe.

balance of account: the net amount of the total debits and total credits posted to a given account. Balances are of three types: *zero balance,* indicating that total debits and total credits are equal; *debit balance,* indicating an excess of total debits over total credits; and *credit balance,* indicating an excess of total credits over debits, at a given time.

balance of payments (b.o.p.): a statement identifying all financial transaction of a country and its population with the other nations of the world. cf. *dollar shortage.*

balance-of-payments table: a summary of transactions (loans, investments, repayments, donations, and other transfer of funds) in a given time period, published by the Department of Commerce. [105]

balance of trade: the difference between a country's imports and exports over a set period.

balance on goods and services: the algebraic sum of exports and imports of goods and services. It includes merchandise trade (exports and imports of goods) and the so-called invisible items: shipping charges, income on investments, rents, royalties, payments for insurance, donations, and travel. A surplus balance on goods and services is compatible with an export of capital or an accumulation of foreign exchange reserves. On the other hand, a deficit balance on goods and services must be financed by an import of capital or a drawing down of foreign exchange reserves. [73]

balance on goods, services, and unilateral transfer: the balance on goods, services, and unilateral transfers represents the balance on current account which—except for errors and omissions—must be counterbalanced by capital movements, a change in official reserves, or both. All transactions involving transfers of goods and services are included in the current account, with the exception of monetary gold transactions, which are recorded as a component part of U.S. official reserve assets. The balance on goods, services, and unilateral transfers is net foreign investment by the United States. [73]

balance owing: the amount outstanding. [105]

balance sheet: an itemized statement listing the total assets and the total liabilities of a given business to portray its net worth at a given moment in time.

balance sheet audit: an examination of a statement of financial condition as of a given date, usually at the end of the normal accounting period. [49]

balance sheet equation: the equation stating that the total of assets equals the total of liabilities plus net worth (ownership).

balance sheet tests: the application of

ratio and statement analysis to a company's balance sheet.

balance slip: an itemized list made daily of coin and paper money to verify the correctness of a cash register audit tape strip.

balances with domestic banks: the total amounts that reporting member banks have on deposit in other commercial banks. [40]

balance transfer: the process of forwarding the balance from an old to a new ledger sheet. All or part of the old ledger becomes a statement of account which will be sent to a customer. [31]

balancing: the ultimate act of bringing two sets of related figures into agreement. As in proof work—the total of deposits being in agreement with the totals of all items making up the deposits—this is "balance" in banking parlance. All work in banks must be in balance, all debits equaling all credits. Minor errors that develop from large volumes are carried into "difference" or "suspense" accounts until uncovered by audits or until customers' discrepancies are reported and located. Adjustments are then made, and the difference account properly adjusted. [10]

balancing the account: determining the balance of an account, writing it on the smaller side, totaling and ruling the account, and bringing the balance into the new section of the account below the double lines.

balboa: monetary unit of Panama.

balloon: a lump-sum payment a home borrower owes after expiration of a home loan payable to the loaning bank. See *buy down, roll over.*

ballooning: price manipulation used to send prices beyond safe or real values.

balloon loan: a loan on which small payments are made during the term of the obligation.

balloon maturity: a bond issue having a substantially larger dollar amount of bonds falling due in the later maturity dates. [105]

balloon mortgage: a mortgage that allows for payments that do not completely amortize the loan at the time of termination. As a result, the final payment is larger than any single payment made previously.

balloon note: a promissory note requiring only a small payment during the initial loan period, which is then offset by larger payments made before the date of maturity.

balloon payment: a large extra payment that may be charged at the end of a loan or lease. [1]

Baltic Exchange: headquartered in London; has the major responsibility for matching cargoes to ships, and vice versa.

Baltimore method: a formula for appraising corner lots in which the lot is determined to be worth the value of the inside lots on each of its sides.

Baltimore Stock Exchange: see *Philadelphia-Baltimore-Washington Stock Exchange.*

band: under the Bretton Woods agreement, the range within which a currency is permitted to move.

banded currency: paper money that has been sorted, counted, and banded in separate denominations. [59]

bank: an organization, normally a corporation, chartered by the state or federal government, the principal functions of which are: (a) to receive demand and time deposits, honor instruments drawn against them, and pay interest on them as permitted by law; (b) to discount notes, make loans, and invest in government or other securities; (c) to collect checks, drafts, notes, and so on; (d) to issue drafts and cashier's checks; (e) to certify depositor's checks; and (f) when authorized by a chartering government, to act in a fiduciary capacity. see *branch banking, commercial bank, correspondent bank, country bank, drive-in banking, Federal Reserve Bank, group banking, independent bank, industrial bank, insured bank, investment banking, member bank, mortgage banker, multiple banking, mutual savings bank, national bank, private bank, savings bank, state bank, trust company.*

bankable bill: a document that can be discounted at a bank.

bankable paper: paper that meets the credit standards for acceptance or endorsement by a bank. This paper is called *bank paper.* see also *bankable bill.*

bank acceptance: signed by a bank, any accepted bill of exchange or draft.

bank accommodation: a short-term bank loan to a customer, either on the individual's own note or on the endorsement of another's note owed to him or her.

bank account: a financial relationship created in the name of a business or individual. There are a variety of such accounts, including time accounts; demand accounts; and single name, multiname, joint, or trustee accounts. Minimum balance and payment of interest will vary. see specific types of accounts.

Bank Act, Canada: passed in December, 1980 in Toronto, Canada, the size of any foreign-owned banking operation was limited to 8 percent of the domestic assets of all banks. The act automatically terminates in 10 years unless revised or extended.

Bank Administration Institute (BAI): an organization of bank officials, the purpose of which is to formulate and encourage the use of standard auditing and operating procedures for the common good of all banks. BAI, founded in 1924, was previously called the National Association of Bank Auditors and Comptroller (NABAC). [105]

BankAmericard Service Exchange: see *BASE.*

bank balance: the funds in a depositor's account after all deposits have been added to the previous balance and the depositor's checks and services charges have been subtracted.

bank bill: see *bank note.*

bank book: a passbook used by banks to list entries such as interest, deposits, and withdrawals for a customer. In ordinary situations, the customer retains the book as a permanent record.

bankbooks: a bank's records of the status of other banks' deposits with it and vice versa. The term *bankbook* is sometimes used in lieu of *passbook.* [31]

bank branch: an office that is physically separated from a bank's main office, but which offers banking services. [105]

bank by mail: a banking service offered by most institutions, where a customer can perform his or her transactions through the mail. [105]

bank call: a request for a bank's balance sheet for a specified date, made by government statement.

bank card: see *bank credit card.*

bank card association: a group of banks formed either for the purpose of sponsoring a single identity (i.e., Visa or MasterCard); or a group of banks formed to jointly operate a credit or debit card plan through common processing and administrative facilities. [105]

bank certificate of deposit: see *certificate of deposit.*

bank charge plans: a relatively new and important development in the general field of consumer credit. Usually a copyrighted plan brought to a community by a bank or private organization under charter or franchise for providing a complete credit service, including credit authorization, billing, and collection of 30-day accounts for representative stores. Most banks charge 5 percent or less of total credit sales for their service. [41]

bank charter: a document of incorporation issued by the state or federal government giving a group of individuals the right to establish a bank.

bank check: a check drawn by a bank on itself and signed by an authorized officer. Savings banks do not usually draw such checks. synonymous with *cashier's check, officer's check, treasurer's check.* [39]

bank clearing

(1) *banking:* bank items sent by member banks to a local clearinghouse for collection.

(2) *finance:* the total volume of dollars on all items that are exchanged among members of a local clearinghouse(s).

bank clubs: to cope with possible bankruptcies and near-failures, lending institutions are attempting, through the formation of a group of creditors, to administer the orderly liquidation or rehabilitation of their shakiest borrowers.

bank credit: credit created by commercial banks through the media of loans and discounts granted with or without collateral. The amount of credit so extended is controlled in part by the rediscount rates established by the Federal Reserve Board.

bank credit card: a credit card issued by a bank, enabling the borrower to buy goods and services or obtain a cash loan from banks honoring that card. [78]

bank credit proxy: an average deposit liability (including demand and time deposits and individuals, businesses, and agencies) of member banks. The information is available each day to the Federal Reserve Banks and is used as a relative correlation of the loans and investments of member banks. The latter figure is not available daily.

bank currency: see *bank note.*

bank debits: the sum total of all debits drawn against deposited funds of individuals, partnerships, corporations, and other legal entities during a given period—usually reported by banks daily.

bank deposit: the placing of valuables, including money, in a bank for safekeeping.

Bank Deposit Insurance Act of 1934: federal legislation, to protect depositors, extended to June 1935 for bank deposit insurance originally established by the Banking Act of 1933. This act eventually led to the creation of a permanent deposit insurance program in 1935.

bank deregulation: see *Depository Institutions Deregulation Committee*

bank directors: selected by the stockholders of a bank from among their own number, directors are responsible to the stockholders for profitable management and to government supervisory authority for operation of the bank according to law and sound banking principles. [50]

bank discount: a charge, often expressed as a percent of the face amount of the commercial paper or personal note, which is imposed by a bank for payment prior to the note's maturity.

bank draft: a check drawn by one bank against funds deposited to its account in another bank.

bank-eligible issues: issues of U.S. Treasury obligations eligible for immediate purchase by commercial banks—mainly those due or callable within 10 years. [67]

bank endorsement: an endorsement stamped on the back of items passing through the bank. This endorsement is stamped either by a hand stamp or by endorsing machines. Banks either endorse or identify all items taken in through the teller's window or deposited through the mail, except "on us" checks cashed or items coming into the bank from clearinghouse exchanges or in cash letters. Banks in larger cities may use endorsing equipment whereby they can delete a portion of the bank endorsement, and show only the date and ABA transit number of the bank sending in the item. In this way, these banks can identify any item as to the bank which sent it to them. Bank endorsements contain the following legend: "Pay to the order of any bank, banker, or trust company. All prior endorsements guaranteed."

The endorsement will show the date, the bank's name in full, and the bank's transit number, usually in two places. Bank endorsements are very important to all bankers, in that they provide a means of tracing items through the collection channels of the banking system. see *examine for bank endorsement, return item.* [10]

banker's acceptance: bill of exchange drawn on or accepted by a bank to pay specific bills for one of its customers when the bills become due.

banker's bank: a central bank. In the United States, one of the 12 Federal Reserve District Banks. They are:

1st	District	Boston
2nd	District	New York
3rd	District	Philadelphia
4th	District	Cleveland
5th	District	Richmond
6th	District	Atlanta
7th	District	Chicago
8th	District	St. Louis
9th	District	Minneapolis
10th	District	Kansas City
11th	District	Dallas
12th	District	San Francisco

banker's bill: a bill of exchange drawn by an exporter on the importer's bank. [105]

banker's blanket bond: see *bond, banker's blanket.*

banker's draft: a draft payable on demand and drawn by or on behalf of a bank upon itself. [85]

banker's payment: an order or draft drawn by one bank in favor of another bank.

banker's pool: a combination of prominent financial and banking interests during the 1929 market break to support key issues. It failed in its effort to stabilize the market.

banker's shares: shares issued to an investment banker which frequently in the past could control or manipulate the firm because of voting features which the banker's shares had compared to the lack of vote or fractional vote of other shares, such as Class A stock.

bank examination: an examination made by representatives of a federal or state bank supervisory authority to make certain that a bank is solvent and is operating in conformity with banking laws and sound banking principles. [50]

bank examiner: a person who, as the representative of a federal or state bank supervisory authority, examines the banks under its jurisdiction with respect to their financial condition, management, and policies. [31]

bank exchanges: checks, notes, drafts, and so on, that are collected through a clearinghouse system.

bank failure: the closing of a bank, either temporarily or permanently, resulting from financial difficulties.

bank for cooperatives: see *Farm Credit Administration.*

Bank for International Settlements (BIS): established in 1930, this organization was designed to foster cooperation among world central banks, to seek opportunities for development of financial activity among governments, and to serve as an agent involving the transfer of payments. BIS is located in Basel, Switzerland.

bank-guaranteed bond funds: portfolios of bonds unconditionally guaranteed against default by a major bank because the bank has agreed to buy any of the underlying securities in the portfolio at face value on six days' notice.

bank holding company: in general usage, any company that owns or controls one or more banks. However, a bank holding company as defined in the Bank Holding Company Act of 1956 is one that controls two or more banks. Such companies must register with the Board of Governors of the Federal Reserve System and are commonly referred to as registered bank holding companies. see entries under *Bank Holding Company Act.*

Bank Holding Company Act of 1956: applied to any corporation controlling 25 percent or more of the voting shares of at least two banks, or otherwise controlling the election of a majority of the directors of two or more banks. The law formulated standards for the formation of bank holding companies. These companies were strictly limited to the business of banking, managing banks, and providing services to affiliated banks. see *Bank Holding Company Act Amendments of 1966, 1970.* [64]

Bank Holding Company Act Amendments of 1966: established uniform standards for bank agencies and the court in evaluating the legality of bank holding company acquisitions. see *Bank Holding Company Act of 1956, Bank Holding Company Act Amendments of 1970.* [64]

Bank Holding Company Act Amendments of 1970: ended the exemption from the Bank Holding Company Act that one-bank holding companies had enjoyed since 1956. This last amendment clearly regulated the ownership of bank shares and limited bank holding company entries into activities related only to the business of banking. see *Bank Holding Company Act of 1956, Bank Holding Company Act Amendments of 1966.* [64]

bank holiday: a day on which banks are closed.

bank identification: a series of digits used to identify a particular bank. [105]

Bank Identification Number (BIN): a series or group of digits used to identify card-issuing banks, bank card associations, or interchange groups. [105]

Banking Act of 1933: the first major piece of banking legislation during the Roosevelt administration; it led to significant changes in banking laws (see, e.g., *bank credit, branch banking, insurance*). see also *Federal Deposit Insurance Corporation.*

Banking Act of 1935: federal legislation amending the Banking Act of 1933, the Federal Reserve Act, and other banking regulations, to make these laws more specific.

banking business: primarily the business of receiving funds on deposit and making loans. [10]

banking department (government): that part of a federal or state agency concerned with the enforcement of the respective banking code.

banking house: a structure used by a bank in its regular functions of banking.

banking power: the strength of investing possessed by a bank as determined by the bank's excess reserves.

"banking school" principle: a principle developed in England in the nineteenth century; maintains that under a purely metallic currency a gain or loss of gold from abroad would not automatically result in a corresponding increase or decrease of currency in circulation and thus influence the price level, but might instead change the amount of gold in hoards. The banking school also maintained that under a mixed currency of gold and convertible paper notes, the amount of paper notes in circulation was adequately adjusted to the needs of business by the processes of competitive banking. cf. *"currency school"* principle.

banking syndicate: a group of banks created for the purpose of underwriting and selling of an issue of securities.

banking system: the type, structure, and method of operation of a state or country's banks.

bank insolvency: where a bank's capital is impaired and the appropriate authorities decide to close and/or liquidate the bank.

bank loan: any money borrowed from a bank for the purposes of business investment.

Bank Merger Act: federal legislation of 1960, amended in 1966, identifying the legal responsibilities resulting from bank mergers. see also entries under *Bank Holding Company Act.*

bank money: deposits (promises by a bank to pay) created by a bank when it is required to have on hand in reserves only a fraction of its total deposits.

bank money order: see *money order.*

bank note: a promissory note released by an authorized bank that is payable on demand to the bearer and can be used as cash. Such notes, as established by law, are redeemable as money and are considered to be full legal tender. synonymous with *bank bill* or *bank currency.*

bank number: see *American Bankers Association number.*

bank of circulation: see *bank of issue.*

bank of deposit: usually associated

with commercial banks that accept deposits subject to demand check withdrawal.

bank of discount: banks, usually commercial, that offer credit on acceptances, bills of exchange, and notes. When Federal Reserve Banks engage in discounting, it is properly called *rediscounting* because the notes have already been discounted by the borrowing commercial bank.

bank of issue: any bank that is legally permitted to issue money (e.g., bank notes).

Bank of the United States: now defunct, a quasi-public bank, formed under a congressional charter, which through a central office and various branches issued bank notes and served as a depositary for federal funds and as a fiduciary agent for the government.

bank overdraft: an amount owed to a bank by a customer on his or her account, resulting from payment of checks for an amount in excess of the drawer's balance. The bank levies a charge based on the amount overdrawn and calculated on a day-to-day basis, establishing a fixed limit that the customer may withdraw.

bank paper: paper showing acceptance or endorsement by a bank; paper that meets the credit standards for acceptance or bank endorsement.

bank passbook: a small book given to the customer by a bank to record deposits and withdrawals.

bank post remittance: the conversion into cash or a money form of a foreign bill of exchange, and subsequent mailing of the latter to the payee.

bank premises: book value of building and equipment. [40]

bank rate
(1) the rate of discount established by the national bank of a country for rediscounting of eligible paper.
(2) the rate charged by the national bank of a country on advances on specific collateral to banks.

bank reconcilliation: see *reconciliation.*

bank reference: the name of the bank with which a firm has an account, presented to another firm as a reference so that its credit position can be assessed.

bank release: a document from a bank after it has been paid or given an acceptance on a bill of exchange, thereby permitting the purchaser of items involved to take delivery, although the rights of other parties may need to be satisfied before the items are released for delivery, and in any case customs clearance must be arranged in due course.

bank reserves: commercial banks that are members of the Federal Reserve System are required to hold a proportion of their deposit liabilities in the form of reserves with the Federal Reserve District Bank or till cash. Nonmember state banks only have to fulfill the requirements of their state's banking laws.

bank return: a statement of a check clearinghouse.

bankroll: slang, to support with money any project managed by others.

bank run: a series of unusually large withdrawals made on a bank out of fear that the bank may run out of funds.

bankrupt: a person, corporation, or other legal entity which, being unable to meet its financial obligations, has been declared by a decree of the court to be insolvent, and whose property becomes liable to administration under the Bankruptcy Reform Act of 1978. see *insolvent.*

bankruptcy: the conditions under which the financial position of an individual, corporation, or other legal entity are such as to cause actual or legal insolvency. Two types are: (a) *involuntary bankruptcy*—one or more creditors of an insolvent debtor file a petition having the debtor declared a bankrupt; and (b) *voluntary bankruptcy*—the debtor files a petition claiming inability to meet debts and willingness to be declared a bankrupt. A court adjudges and declares a debtor a bankrupt. see *Bankruptcy Reform Act of 1978. insolvency, National Bankruptcy Act of 1898.*

Bankruptcy Act: see *National Bankruptcy Act of 1898.*

Bankruptcy Reform Act of 1978: taking effect on October 1, 1978, the first complete overhaul of bankruptcy statutes in 75 years. Some major provisions are: (a) a consolidation of the three sections of the old law that dealt with business reorganizations—in effect, a restructuring to permit a company to return to fiscal soundness—into a new, streamlined Chapter 11; (b) various new tactical weapons for business creditors, one of which may allow them, in certain instances, to file their own reorganization plans for a company; (c) new federal exemptions for consumers that may allow them to keep more property after bankruptcy than they could under state laws unless the states take contrary action; and (d) a new procedure that will allow small businesses to pay off their debts

gradually under a proceeding similar to a reorganization. see *bankruptcy.*

Bankruptcy Tax Act of 1980: federal legislation that went into effect on January 1, 1981. In part, the law says that a company that buys back its own bonds at a discount price must pay income tax on the spread between the face value of the bonds, or the original sales price, and the discount repurchase price. see also *solvent debtor section.*

Bank Secrecy Act of 1970: federal legislation compelling banks to keep records of all customer transactions and to report any financial dealings involving more than $10,000 to the U.S. Treasury Department. The government contends that the records are the bank's business records and are not owned by the depositor.

bank securities: commercial bank offerings include convertible or nonconvertible capital debentures, convertible or nonconvertible preferred stock, and common stock.

bank service charge: a monthly charge made by a bank when the depositor's balance is less than a fixed sum in order to conpensate the bank for the cost of handling a small account.

Banks for Cooperatives: a system of 12 banks scattered over the United States under the supervision of the Farm Credit Administration (FCA) to extend credit to farmer cooperatives.

bank stamp: a bank's endorsement placed on the back side of a check, note, or other negotiable instrument with an endorsement machine or rubber stamp.

bank statement
(1) *banking:* a statement of a cus-

tomer's account periodically rendered by the bank. It shows all deposits made and all checks paid and other debits posted during the period, usually one month, as well as the current balance; the customer's canceled checks may or may not be enclosed.

(2) *banking:* a bank's financial statement.

bank term loan: a loan terminating in a year or more. At times used instead of a long-term bond isue, especially during periods of high interest rates.

bank-to-bank information: in EFTS, miscellaneous information pertaining to the transfer, including information specifying for which bank(s) the information is intended. [105]

Bank Wire System: a private, computerized message system administered for and by participating banks, through the facilities of Western Union. The system links about 250 banks in about 75 cities. Like the Fedwire, the Bank Wire transmits funds and transfers information, but also relays data concerning loan participations, bond closings, payment for securities, borrowing of federal funds, and balances in company accounts.

banque d'affaires: a French bank involved in long-term financing and in the ownership of companies, usually industrial firms. synonymous with *merchant bank.*

Banque de France: the central bank of France, created by Napoleon Bonaparte in 1800.

BANs: see *bond anticipation notes.*

Ban Ser Corp: formed in 1974 to service insurance plans offered by savings banks to their employees, depositors, and/or mortgagors. Ban Ser does not handle general lines of insurance or service claims. Rather, it acts as liaison between savings banking and the insurance industry in developing new insurance plans to meet savings banks' changing needs and in monitoring existing plans for pricing, service, and standards of coverage. Ban Ser offers a complete insurance consulting service for thrift institutions. [8]

bar chart: a chart showing the price action of a security; used to aid in shaping opinion about future movements.

bareboat charter: charting a ship without the crew. cf. *demise charterparty.*

bargain counter: describing stocks offered for sale at prices below their intrinsic value.

bargain hunter

(1) *general:* an individual who seeks out the store selling items at the lowest possible price.

(2) *investments:* a speculator or investor who waits until stocks are on the bargain counter.

bargaining agent: the formally designated agency, usually a labor union, that represents employees seeking or having a collective bargaining agreement (contract). Its rights and obligations are defined by federal law (e.g., National Labor Relations Act).

bargaining creep: progress made in collective bargaining that is slow, with minimal compromise.

bargaining rights

(1) *general:* the legal rights of workers to bargain collectively with their employers.

(2) *labor relations:* the right of a specific union to represent its members in collective bargaining.

bargaining unit: the group of employees, usually defined by the National Labor Relations Board after a hearing, which a union may seek to represent as bargaining agent on wages, hours, and working conditions. see *collective bargaining.*

bar graph: a graph having solid bars showing the comparisons of two or more amounts.

"barometers": business measurements used to determine the condition of a market or economy (e.g., Consumer Price Index, housing starts, gross national product, new plant expenditures).

barometer securities: stocks that move in the same direction as the market and are considered to be representative of the market.

barracudas: synonymous with *guerrillas.*

barratry
(1) *foreign trade:* any unlawful dealing with a vessel or its cargo by the master or crew.
(2) *law:* inciting quarrels or litigation.

barrel: in the oil industry, 42 gallons. That is the way oil is measured, even though an actual barrel, or drum, holds 50 gallons.

barren money: currency that does not earn interest or other forms of income.

Barron's: a weekly publication of financial and investment matters by Dow Jones & Company.

Barron's Confidence Index: the ratio of Barron's highest-grade corporate bond yield average to the Dow Jones composite bond yield average (including lower-grade bonds). This index changes with corresponding changes in these yields.

barter: the direct exchange of one item for another without the transfer of money.

barter agreement: an agreement between two nations providing for the exchange of given quantities or values of specified commodities.

BAS: see *block automation system.*

BASE (BankAmericard Service Exchange): the national authorization and electronic draft interchange network used to process BankAmericard credit transactions. [36]

base
(1) *general:* a reference value.
(2) *computers:* the number of characters of use in the digital positions of a numbering system.
(3) *finance:* metal, coin, or bullion that is adulterated, containing inferior of less valuable metal. They have little value when compared to precious metals of gold and silver.
(4) *statistics:* a number that is multiplied by itself.

BASE central: the Visa U.S.A. operations center, which provides BASE I and II and central computer services. [105]

Basel Agreement: signed in 1967 between Great Britian and the major nations of the West, this agreement determined the repayment of advances for funds given to the United Kingdom during its sterling crisis. The agreement is important since it represents the first time that a nation agreed to a dollar guarantee on its debt to other nations.

BASE I: a data processing network of Visa U.S.A. capable of providing message processing, authorization services, and file services. [105]

BASE I activity file: a file, maintained at BASE central, containing a record of account numbers that have had authorization approval responses generated by BASE I within a four-day period. [105]

BASE I exception file: a file, maintained at BASE central, which contains those cardholder account numbers for which authorization responses have been predetermined by the issuer. [105]

BASE I user: an authorizing member who, through a terminal or computer device, connects to BASE I for authorization and other services. (BASE I users include those affiliates who are so identified on their interchange data forms and all U.S. affiliates.) [105]

base pay: the regular rate of pay for an identified time period, excluding overtime, bonuses, and other premiums. see *basic wages.*

base period

(1) *finance:* a chosen date from the past used in measuring the price index.

(2) *personnel:* the period during which an employee fulfills the length of employment required to receive state unemployment insurance benefits.

base price: the price used as a starting point. To this price additions may be made for freight, extra services, packaging, and so on, or deductions may be made.

base rate: the regular rate of pay, excluding overtime, bonuses, and premiums.

base stock method of inventory: valuing the relatively fixed and permanent quantity of inventory at a fixed price (usually a historically low point) with the remainder of the inventory valued by another method.

base surplus plan: a pricing scheme (where the product is capable of several uses with each use commanding a different price) giving the producer a

fixed price for the amount produced in a base period and a lower price for any surplus.

base time: the established time for the normal performance of work by an average employee, excluding time allowed for rest, mechanical failures, and other delays.

BASE II: an electronic draft data transmission system owned by Visa U.S.A. for the exchange of draft data by Visa U.S.A. and Visa International Clearing Members, including all BASE II equipment, software, processes, techniques, programs, and information provided by Visa U.S.A. and used in connection with the system. [105]

BASE II request: a request sent through BASE II for a copy of a specific sales draft retained at another bank card center. [105]

BASE II sales draft: purchase identified by a reference number which begins with "4." [105]

base-year analysis: a method of analysis of financial statements, whereby the figures for each of a series of years are compared to those of a common base year. [105]

basic balance: the sum of the balance-of-payments current account plus long-term capital movements.

basic crops: clearly identified farm items subject to government price support, including wheat, corn, cotton, rice, and peanuts.

basic IS-LM Model: see *IS-LM model.*

basic piece rate: part of a wage incentive plan allowing for payment to be made as a direct proportion to the production yield.

basic rating: standard classification under the numerical system for selection of risks. [12]

basic wages: payment received by employees for work performed, based on time or output. see *base pay.*

basic yield: a concept similar to pure interest, that is, the annual rate of return in percent on a risk-free investment such as a long-term U.S. government bond. see also *pure interest.*

basing point: an approach for quoting prices of products. A purchaser determines his or her delivered cost from a geographic point used as the base even though the product is not necessarily shipped from there.

basis
(1) *finance:* the yield to maturity of bonds at a given price, as shown by bond tables.
(2) *taxation:* in calculating capital gains or losses, the value employed as the original property cost, which may or may not be the true cost.
(3) *investments:* the difference between the cash price of a money market instrument that is hedged and a futures contract.

basis book: a book of mathematical tables used to convert bond yields-to-maturity to equivalent dollar prices at various rates of interest. [105]

basis point: $1/100$ of 1 percent, a minimal measure in finance and trade.

basis price: the price expressed in yields or in net return on an investment. [105]

basis quote: the sale or offer of a cash commodity measured as the difference less than or more than a futures price.

basis value: the value of a security considered as an investment, and, with bonds, as bearing interest, if held to maturity.

basket purchase: the purchase of a group of assets for one price. So that the items can be recorded individually in the accounts, however, a cost is assigned to each asset.

batch: a group of deposits, or a group of other items, which are proved in one operation. synonymous with *block.* [39]

batch number: a number assigned to a batch of items processed in the proof department. The number is placed in the account number field of the batch ticket and on the rear of the remainder of the items in the batch.

batch processing
(1) *computers:* the technique of executing a set of computer programs such that each is completed before the next program of the set is begun.
(2) *systems:* a sequential processing procedure that uses an accumulation or set of units.

batch proof: a system for proving deposits, usually performed in the following sequence: (a) deposits are assembled in groups of various sizes; (b) deposit tickets are sorted into one group; (c) checks are sorted into several classifications, such as clearings, transit, and bookkeeping; (d) cash release tickets are sorted according to teller; (e) deposit tickets, checks, and cash release tickets are listed on a "batch" or "block" sheet in their respective columns; and (f) the total of the deposit and other credits should equal the recapitulation of the checks and debits. [10]

batch sheet: a proof sheet used in the batch proof system. The batch sheet is arranged in columns for deposits, various classifications of checks and other debits, and cash release tickets. After sorting, all items in the batch are listed in their respective columns, the totals recapped and proved. The batch sheet then becomes a permanent record of the bank, and is used by bank auditors to check any errors arising from transactions. [10]

batch system: see *batch proof.*

batch ticket: when used in an MICR system, the batch ticket is a control document encoded with the total amount of a batch and identified by a special transaction code. The batch ticket can also contain such encoded information as batch number, source number, and/or proof machine number. This ticket accompanies the items from the proof department to the document processing center. [31]

bathtub theorem: using the analogy of a bathtub, the total stock of goods (water in the tub) is equal to production (faucet flow) less consumption (drain flow). The rate of accumulation is the excess of inflow or outflow.

batten: to grow wealthy at another's expense.

bay: space on a selling floor between four columns; a recess or opening in walls. [63]

BB
(1) see *Big Board.*
(2) see *bond, baby.*
(3) see *bond, bearer.*
(4) see *buy back.*

BC: see *blue chip.*

BD
(1) see *bad delivery.*
(2) see *bill discounted.*

Bd.
(1) see *board.*
(2) see *bond.*

BDO: see *bottom dropped out.*

BDR: see *bearer depositary receipt.*

B/E: see *bill of exchange.*

bear: a person who thinks security prices will fall. A bear market is one that goes down over a period of time. see *bears.* [68]

bear account: any short account.

bear campaign: the practice of selling securities short to lower prices, and then attempting to close out the short sales at a significant profit. synonymous with *bearing a market* and *bear raiding.*

bear clique: a group of people or orgainizations that attempt to depress the price of stocks and commodities by selling short. The formation of a bear clique for this manipulative objective is outlawed. see *bear raid, short sale.*

bear covering: the purchase by bears of the stock, commodity, or currency which they have sold.

bearer: any person holding a negotiable instrument.

bearer bond: see *bond, bearer.*

bearer certificate: a certificate that is not filled out in the name of a particular person. Since these certificates are negotiable without endorsement, they should always be kept in a safe place.

bearer check: a check payable to cash or to the bearer rather than to a specific party. [59]

bearer depositary receipt (BDR): a depositary receipt made out in bearer form; used to assist in the trading of foreign corporations. [86]

bearer form: in a form payable to bearer, the security having no registered owner. [67]

bearer instrument: a negotiable instrument payable on demand to the individual who holds the instrument. Title passes by delivery without endorsement.

bearer paper: in dealing with negotiable instruments, an instrument is called *bearer paper* when it is payable to bearer (i.e., the person having possession of it). Ownership of such a document is transferred by delivery, no indorsement being needed. If the person who originally issued the paper placed it in bearer form, it cannot thereafter receive a special indorsement. cf. *order paper*.

bearer security: securities whose owners are not registered with the borrower; the securities are owned by those who possess them. The 1982 tax law requires the registration of all securities issued in the United States, with only a few exceptions.

bearer stock: capital stock evidenced by certificates that are not registered in any name. They are negotiable without endorsement and transferable by delivery. They carry numbered or dated dividend coupons. [105]

bear hug: an unnegotiated corporate takeover proposal, made privately or publicly to directors. The major goal is to force a board into a decision.

bearing a market: synonymous with *bear campaign*.

bearish and bullish: when conditions suggest lower prices, a bearish situation is said to exist. If higher prices appear warranted, the situation is said to be bullish. [2]

bear market: a declining stock market. [20]

bear panic (squeeze): a condition resulting when securities advance in price, rather than declining, to the disappointment of the bears, thus forcing the bears to close out their positions at a loss.

bear pool: now prohibited, a type of manipulation consisting of a formally organized fund contributed by operators who desire prices to be forced downward.

bear position: stance taken by a person who expects the market to fall. As a consequence, he or she sells securities short, hoping that the market will move downward.

bear raid: attempts to depress the price of a security or item by heavy selling.

bear raiding: synonymous with *bear campaign*.

bears: speculators who anticipate that prices are going to drop. see *bear, hammering the market*.

bear squeeze: a strategy by central banks which know that uncovered bears have sold their currency short. By temporarily bidding up the currency until the time comes for the bears to deliver the currency they had contracted to sell, the central bank forces the bears to take a loss.

beat down: slang, to bargain to lower the cost of an item.

beating the gun: prohibited by the SEC, the practice of accepting customer orders for a new stock, and/or releasing significant data on a new offering, prior to the registration statement of the security's becoming effective.

beewy: slang, money, especially coins.

beggar-my-neighbor policy: an attempt to discourage imports by increasing tariffs or using other effective means.

Bellevue Project: a banking program of study and implementation leading to the Bellevue Exchange, an automated teller facility in Bellevue, Washington, available to the customers of a group of cooperating thrift institutions on a shared basis and has become a model for other banks.

bellwether stock: any security used as a measure of the stock market's movement. In most cases, these are stocks that indicate the direction of the general market about two or three weeks before other securities follow a similar pattern.

below par: at a discount; less than face amount.

below the line: the classification applied to an out-of-the-ordinary revenue or expense, or an extraordinary and material nonrecurring item that requires a separate grouping in a company's balance sheet or income statement. [105]

below the market: at a price lower than the prevailing level at which a security is currently quoted or traded. [105]

benchmark reserves: reserve funds, representing a specified percentage of savings deposits, that all savings association members of the Federal Savings and Loan Insurance Corporation must hold. [59]

benchmark statistics: detailed information used as a basis for evolving adjusting interim estimates made from sample data.

Benef.: see *beneficiary*.

beneficial interest (owner): an individual, not the true owner of property, who enjoys all or part of the benefits to it, by reason of a trust or private arrangement.

beneficiary
(1) *general:* a person beneficially interested in a trust or estate.
(2) *banking:* the person(s) to whom the proceeds of a life insurance contract are payable at the death of the insured.

(3) *law:* the person for whose benefit a trust, policy, will, or contract promise is made. synonymous with *cestui que trust.*

beneficiary, change of: process of altering the beneficiary endorsement to provide for payment to one other than originally named, or to provide for payment in a different manner. [12]

beneficiary, contingent: a beneficiary who is entitled to benefits only after the death of a primary beneficiary. [53]

beneficiary, endorsement: an endorsement placed on (or attached to in rider form) the policy setting forth the names of the beneficiaries, relationship to the insured, manner in which policy proceeds are to be paid, and conditions upon which each beneficiary's right to receive such payment is based. [12]

beneficiary, irrevocable: a beneficiary for whom another may not be substituted by the insured. [53]

beneficiary, primary: synonymous with *immediate beneficiary.*

beneficiary advice charges: information specifying who to charge for advising the beneficiary and how to apply those charges. [105]

beneficiary advice identifier: information used on contacting the beneficiary in order to send an advice (e.g., phone number, cable address). [105]

beneficiary advice instructions: additional information that pertains to notification of the beneficiary (e.g., person's name, hours of availability). [105]

beneficiary advice method: a code that specifies the method to be used to notify the beneficiary that his or her account has been credited or that funds are available (e.g., phone, letter, wire). [105]

beneficiary identifier: a code that uniquely identifies the beneficiary to the beneficiary's bank. [105]

beneficiary identifier type: a code that specifies the type of beneficiary identifier used. [105]

beneficiary method of payment: specifies how payment is to be made to the beneficiary. [105]

beneficiary name and address: identifies the beneficiary by name and, optionally, the beneficiary's postal address. [105]

beneficiary's bank: a bank that acts as the financial agent for the beneficiary of a transfer. [105]

beneficiary's bank advice charges: information specifying who to charge for advising the beneficiary's bank and how to apply those charges. [105]

beneficiary's bank advice identifier: information used in contacting the beneficiary's bank in order to send an advice (e.g., phone number, cable address). [105]

beneficiary's bank advice instruction: additional information which pertains to notification of the beneficiary's bank (e.g., bank's name, hours of availability). [105]

beneficiary's bank advice method: a code that specifies the method to be used to notify the beneficiary's bank that the account has been credited or that the funds are available (e.g., phone, letter, wire). [105]

beneficiary's bank identifier: a code that uniquely identifies the beneficiary's bank. [105]

beneficiary's bank identifier type: a code that specifies the type of identifier used for the beneficiary's bank. [105]

beneficiary's bank name and address: identifies the beneficiary's bank by name and optionally, the beneficiary's bank's postal address. [105]

beneficiary type: a code that specifies whether the beneficiary is a bank or a nonbank. [105]

benefit

(1) *general:* a gain or advantage received by an individual; that which fulfills a need.

(2) *banking:* the amount of indemnity to be regularly paid.

benefit formula: a formula for computing the amount of annuity, pension, or other benefit payable under a retirement plan, usually based upon salary, or wages, length of service, and age. [52]

benefit principle of taxation: the rationale for taxation based on the benefits received from the government by the taxpayer.

Benelux: a cooperative organization formed by Belgium, the Netherlands, and Luxembourg to encourage economic activity among the three nations.

bequeath: to offer personal property in a will.

bequest: a gift of personal property made by a testator. see *legacy.*

Bernard rule: a rule for appraising a corner lot. First, the property is appraised as if it were an inside lot fronting on a side street; it is then taken as an inside lot on the main street. The value placed on the corner lot is the total of the two appraisals.

Berne Union: established in 1934, with 26 member nations, works for "the international acceptance of sound principles of export credit and investment insurance."

best bid: the highest price a person is

willing to pay for something offered for sale. This bid is the relevant one used in determining the market for a security.

best effort: a new issue not underwritten nor purchased as a whole from the issuer but sold by securities dealers on a "sell what can be sold" basis. [87]

Beta: a measure of a stock's sensitivity to the movement of the general market (S&P 500), in either direction over the last five years. A Beta of 1.6 means that over the past five years, the stock has moved 60 percent greater than the S&P 500, both up and down. [68]

Better Business Bureau: a voluntary agency of business executives created to improve business practices and to define fair standards and ethics in the conduct of business activity. The movement to better conditions began in 1921, when Vigilance Committees for Truth in Advertising first appeared in local advertising clubs.

betterment: an improvement made to property that increases its value more than would ordinary repair or maintence work.

BF: see *backdoor financing.*

Bfcy.: see *beneficiary.*

Bgt.: bought.

BH: see *bank holiday.*

biannual: occurring twice a year [61]

bid: an offering of money in exchange for property (items, goods, etc.) put up for sale. Types of bids are: *best bid—* not necessarily the lowest or highest, but good for the organization seeking a bid; *competitive bid—*a bid secured from a public announcement of the competition; and *sealed bid—*a bid that is not disclosed until a specified time, when all other bids are revealed and compared. (This approach pur-

ports to guarantee the independence of bidders.)

bid ahead: used to explain to a prospective purchaser of securities that bids at the same price or at a higher price arrived on the trading floor before his or her's and therefore have priority for the same issue.

bid and asked: synonymous with *quotation.* cf. *bids and offers.*

bid bond: see *bond, bid.*

bidding

(1) *general:* the application by an employee for consideration for a job open in a plant or office. In most contracts, assuming all qualifications to be equal, first preference is given to the applicant with the most seniority. see *posting.*

(2) *finance:* the act of offering money as an exchange for an item or service.

bidding up: the activity of raising the price bid for a security, for fear of failing to have an order executed before an upswing begins.

bid price: in the case of open-end shares, the price at which the holder may redeem his shares; in most cases, it is the current net asset value per share. In the case of closed-end shares, the highest price then offered for stock in the public market. [30]

bids and offers: a "bid" is the quotation of a prospective buyer for the purchase; and an "offer" is the quotation of a seller for the sale of a trading unit or other specified amount of a security. Some of the established methods of trading in securities are: *for cash—*delivery and payment must be made on the same day; *regular way delivery—* securities must be delivered and paid for on the third full business day after sale; and *seller's option*—the seller has the right to deliver the securities within a period of not less than 4 nor more than 60 days. [10]

bid wanted: a request by the seller of a stock or commodity who wishes to locate a purchaser for it.

big bath accounting: the practice not only of writing off segments of a business that are obviously doing poorly, but of getting rid of marginal operations as well. The value of the item being written down is reduced by a one-time subtraction from the asset side of the balance sheet, and income is reduced accordingly. But lowering the values of plant and equipment also means lower depreciation costs in the future; and a smaller depreciation expense—which is subtracted from gross sales—means higher earnings.

Big Board: the New York Stock Exchange, Inc. cf. *Little Board.*

Big Eight: the eight largest public accounting firms.

big figure: used by foreign exchange dealers to denote the first three digits of an exchange rate.

Big Five

(1) the five largest credit card companies: American Express, Carte Blanche, Diners Club, MasterCard, and Visa (BankAmericard).

(2) the five largest commercial banks of the United Kingdom: Midland Bank Ltd., Barclay's Bank Ltd., Lloyd's Bank Ltd., National Provincial Bank Ltd., and Westminster Bank Ltd.

big George: slang, a quarter (25 cents).

big one: slang, $1000, usually a $1000 bill.

Big Steel: the United States Steel Corporation. Sometimes the term is used to include the other large manufacturers of steel: Bethlehem, Republic, National, Armco, Jones Laughlin, Inland Steel, and Youngstown Sheet and Tube. see *Little Steel.*

Big Three: the three largest automobile manufacturers in the United States: General Motors Corporation, the Ford Motor Company, and the Chrysler Corporation.

big ticket: slang, the selling of an expensive item to a customer.

bilateral agreement: an agreement made between two persons or two groups.

bilateral clearing: an international trade system to economize on the use of scarce foreign exchange by routing all payments through a central bank instead of with foreign trade banks or their equivalent demanding that the nations involved be required exactly to balance their mutual trade every year.

bilateral contract: an agreement containing promises, with each party serving as a promisor or promisee.

bilateralism: an international policy having as its object the achievement of particular balances of trade between two nations by means of discriminatory tariff, exchange, or other controls. The initiative is usually taken by the country having an "unfavorable" balance of trade. Extensive bilateralism results in a shift of international trade away from channels that would result from the principle of comparative advantage.

bilateral monopoly: exists when there is only one purchaser for an item or service and the creation of the supply is controlled by one seller.

bilateral payments agreement: an agreement between two countries or their central banks to channel all or specified settlements between themselves through special accounts, normally subject to a reciprocal credit margin (swing). Arrangements of this nature usually imply that the use of convertible foreign currencies or gold between the partner countries is avoided except when the credit margin is exceeded or net balances are settled. [42]

bill

(1) *general:* an invoice of charges for services or a product.

(2) *finance:* paper currency.

(3) *law:* the instrument of formal issuance of a complaint before a court; a court's formal statement reporting its findings.

bill adjuster: a person employed in a credit office. Receives and investigates complaints made by customers of errors on bills. [41]

bill adjustment: action taken either to correct a billing error on a cardholder account or to satisfy a cardholder complaint. [105]

bill book: synonymous with *liability ledger.*

bill broker: any financial dealer in bills of exchange.

bill check: a payment system in which a debtor, on receipt of an invoice or statement, authorizes the creditor to obtain payment directly from the debtor's deposit account.

bill discounted: a promissory note or bill of exchange from which a bank deducts its interest in advance.

billed escrow: the amount of escrow payment that represents a total of the regular escrow payment plus arrears or minus prepaid escrow amounts.

billed principal: the amount of principal payment that represents a total of the normal principal amount plus any arrears.

biller: a person trained in operation of bookkeeping or billing machines and responsible for posting all debit and credit transactions to a group of individual customers' accounts. [41]

bill for payment: an instrument given to a debtor or representative for the purpose of being paid, as differentiated from one that was presented for acceptance.

billing: the process of submitting invoices or bills.

billing cycle: time interval, often a month, between regular periodic billing statement dates. [78]

billing date: the month, day, and year when a periodic or monthly statement is generated, and when calculations for appropriate finance charges, minimum payment due, and new balance have been performed. [105]

billing error: a mistake in a periodic statement due to a charge made by someone not authorized by the cardholder, an error in arithmetic, failure to reflect a credit, a charge for which the cardholder requests clarification, or other instances defined by the Fair Credit Billing Act and Regulation Z. [78]

billing-only account: a bank card account set up with no cards being issued on the account. [105]

bill of credit

(1) *banking:* an individual's written request to a bank asking for the delivery of money to the bearer on the credit or account of the writer.

(2) *finance:* used as if it were a state's currency. Article 1 of the U.S. Constitution forbids the states to issue their own currency.

bill of exchange: instructions from one

party to another party to pay a third party following completion of an assignment. see *commercial set.*

bill of lading: a statement whereby the carrier acknowledges receipt of freight, identifies the freight, and sets forth a contract of carriage. see *commercial set.* cf. *accommodation, clean, straight, through bill of lading.*

bill of materials: a specification of the quantities of direct materials allowed for manufacturing a given quantity of output.

bill of sale

(1) *general:* a written agreement by whose terms the ownership of goods is transferred or assigned to another person.

(2) *banking:* a formal written agreement by which one person transfers to another his or her rights, interest, and title in specified property. It is considered to be sufficient warranty of the seller's title to the property and his or her right to sell; it need not be recorded as a deed for real property.

bill of sight: a temporary entry permit, authorized by a customs official, for imported items, allowing the goods to be unloaded from a carrier to permit examination by a customs agent to identify their true character.

bill payment: checkless system for paying recurring bills through one authorization statement to a financial institution. Automated clearinghouses are used by financial institutions to make necessary debits and credits. [105]

bills discounted: bills of exchange, notes, and acceptances that a bank has discounted for its customers.

bills discounted overdue: bills, notes

acceptances, and similar obligations that have passed their due date or matured and are as yet unpaid. Representing past due accounts of doubtful value, they are segregated from other assets.

bills of credit: an obsolete term found in the U.S. Constitution for paper money issued by the government.

bills payable

(1) *general:* a comprehensive term that includes all notes and trade acceptances that are owed by a business to trade creditors and must be paid by the business at maturity.

(2) *banking:* the sum of money that a member bank has borrowed, on its own collateral note, from a Federal Reserve Bank.

bills receivable: a comprehensive term that includes the total of all notes and trade acceptances given by customers, usually in payment of merchandise, which the debtors must pay at maturity.

bimetallism: a double standard of metals used in coins. The ratio of content and weight must be specified in terms of, for example, gold and silver. cf. *monometallism, parallel standard, real money.*

BIN: see *Bank Identification Number.*

binary

(1) *general:* pertaining to a characteristic or property involving a selection, choice, or condition in which there are two possibilities.

(2) *computers:* a numbering system based on 2's rather than 10's that uses only the digits 0 and 1 when written.

binary card: a standard data-processing card on which information is punched in binary form.

bind: when a country agrees not to increase its tariff; used during trade negotiations.

binder

(1) *banking:* a legal agreement issued either by an agent or by a company, to provide temporary insurance until a policy can be written. It usually contains a definite time limit, is in writing, and clearly designates the company in which the risk is bound the amount, the perils insured against, and the type of insurance.

(2) *banking:* an initially written agreement, with a valuable consideration given as evidence of good faith by the offerer to purchase property.

(3) *law:* any temporary agreement obligating the several parties to the contract.

binding signature: a legally acceptable signature. One which when affixed to a legal document makes that document valid and enforceable. [55]

bind the bargain: see *earnest money*.

BIR: Bureau of Internal Revenue. The division of the Treasury Department of the federal government which collects all internal taxes, including excise and income taxes.

bird-dog: to seek data to assist in studying a firm's position and potential earnings.

birr: monetary unit of Ethiopia.

BIS: see *Bank for International Settlements*.

bit

(1) *computers:* a binary digit (acronym).

(2) *computers:* a single character in a binary number.

Bk.: see *bank*.

Bkg.: banking.

Bkr.: see *broker*.

Bks.: see *book(s)*.

B&L ASSN: see *building and loan association*.

B/L: see *bill of lading*.

blackboard trading: the practice of selling commodities from a blackboard on a wall of a commodity exchange.

black box: a projected working model of a wholly electronic stock exchange that some predict will eventually replace the traditional stock exchanges.

black capitalism: an attempt to increase business ownership among the blacks.

Black Friday: September 24, 1869: the day of a business panic resulting from an attempt by financiers to corner the gold market. A depression followed. Coincidentally, the financial panics of 1873 and 1929 also first became serious on Fridays, hence the term, indicating a day of evil or calamity.

black light: a signature verification method whereby an ultraviolet ink signature is placed on a depositor's passbook. The signature of the customer can be verified on other items by comparing it to the ultraviolet signature, which shows up when placed under black light. [105]

black list: in international trade, a list of individuals and firms of another country with whom the domestic nation forbids commerce by its nationals.

black market: buying or selling of products and commodities, or engaging in exchange of foreign currencies in violation of government restrictions. cf. *gray market*.

black money: slang, for income that is not reported for tax purposes because of its illegal origin.

black work: slang, for tax-evading labor that people do outside their regular jobs. Black work induces some workers to demand cuts in normal working hours so that they will have more time for outside jobs, where they attempt to escape mandatory Social Security contributions. see *moonlight.*

Bland-Allison Act: federal legislation of 1878 authorizing limited governmental purchase and coinage of silver; also permitted the issuance of silver certificates secured by silver in amounts equal to the face value of the certificates.

blank bill: a bill of exchange with the payee's name not appearing.

blank check: a bank form that has been signed, although the amount payable or the name of the payee has been left out.

blank endorsement: the signature or endorsement of a person or firm on an instrument such as a note or check making it payable to the bearer and therefore negotiable without restrictions.

blanket agreement: a collective bargaining agreement based on an industrywide negotiation or large geographic areas within an industry, as established by the Norris-LaGuardia Act (the Anti-Injunction Act). see *Anti-Injunction Act of 1932, injunction.*

blanket bond: see *bond, blanket.*

blanket fidelity bond: see *bond, blanket.*

blanket loan: a loan made to a developer or contractor for a number of individual properties. [59]

blanket mortgage: a mortgage covering all the property of a corporation and given to secure a single debt.

blanket order: a preseason order to meet expected buyer demand.

blanket rate
(1) a rate that applies from and/or to a group of points, (e.g., if the same rate applied to all shipments of a given good from all points on the Atlantic coast to all points on the Pacific coast).
(2) a special rate for several different articles moving in one shipment.

blanket rate increase: a uniform and all-inclusive increase applicable to a large group of items; usually expressed as a percentage. [105]

blank indorsement: the placing of one's name on a negotiable instrument without any qualification. synonymous with *general indorsement.*

blank stock: stock whose terms need not be set forth in the articles of incorporation but may be established by the board of directors at the time of issue.

blasted: slang, a person without money.

blended credit: financial credit extended on the basis of more than one source of funding.

blighted area: an area in a community or neighborhood that is about to become a slum.

blind entry: a bookkeeping entry stating only the accounts and the amounts debited and credited, but not giving other data or accounting factors essential to an accurate record.

blind pool: a speculative device used in financial markets where a group of speculators allow one of their members to handle the operation of their obligated funds. The pool's composition, aside from the chosen member, is concealed from the public. see *bobtail pool.*

blip: slang, a nickel (5 cents).

block
(1) *banking:* a bundle of checks

deposited for credit with a bank, along with their relative deposit slips.

(2) *computers:* a group of words or characters considered or transported as a unit, particularly with reference to input and output.

(3) *investments:* a large holding or transaction of stock popularly considered to be 10,000 shares or more. [20]

blockade: the act of preventing commercial exchange with a country or port, usually during wartime, by physically preventing carriers from entering a specific port or nation. see *embargo, navicert;* cf. *preclusive purchasing.*

blockage: designating the administration of an account as subject to U.S. Treasury control because of enemy or suspected enemy interest. A discount from the established market for which a large block of stock of a single corporation would have to be sold if the entire holding were placed on the market at a given date (a term used in connection with federal estate tax). [37]

block automation system: initiated in 1970 by the New York Stock Exchange, a computerized communications network to aid in large-block transactions by institutional investors. This approach enables such investors to identify buyers and sellers rapidly when they are considering a trade.

block busting: the unethical real estate practice of creating fear by renting or selling units in a neighborhood to families of a religion or race different from that of the current residents, thus exploiting the prejudices and emotions of property owners so that they will sell their homes at reduced prices.

blocked accounts: in time of war the president of the United States issues directives to financial institutions to suspend payment of the accounts of enemy nationals of or individuals inhabiting occupied countries in the sphere of enemy influence. These funds may be released only by executive order, or by license under certain conditions. This action was taken in 1979 during the Iranian crisis.

blocked currency: currency, the conversion of which into another foreign currency is prohibited by law. [105]

block positioner: a firm that acquires stock in blocks so as to facilitate the handling of customer orders.

block sale: the sale of a significant number of shares, with a buying price of usually more than $100,000.

block system: see *batch proof.*

blood bath: slang, a tremendous loss suffered by investors when the stock market declines sharply.

blotter: a book of accounts or a journal used for entering the first or temporary list of transactions or occurrences. cf. *daily reports.*

blowing off: a temporary purchasing peak, often along with heavy trading volume and occurring after an extended advance.

BLS: see *Bureau of Labor Statistics.*

blue chip: a corporation maintaining a good dividend return and having sound management and good growth potential. see also *gilt-edged bond, seasoned issues, seasoned security.*

blue-collar workers: production and maintenance workers, as contrasted with office and professional personnel. The force of blue-collar workers is declining numerically, and by 1980 there were more white-collar workers.

blue law: any state or local law restricting business activity on Sunday. Blue laws have been contested as an infringement of individual and free enterprise rights.

blue list: the trade offering sheets of bond dealers, listing dealers' offerings of municipal bonds for sale all over the country. A composite list published five days a week by The Blue List Publishing Company, New York City, showing current municipal bond offerings by banks and municipal bond houses all over the country. [67]

blue sky law: name given to certain laws enacted by the various states to regulate the sale and issuance of securities, specifically, attempting to prevent fraud in their sale and disposition. cf. *SEC.*

Blumenthal bond: see *bond, Carter.*

BM
(1) see *bear market.*
(2) see *buyers' market.*

BN: see *bank note.*

BO
(1) see *back order.*
(2) see *buy order.*

boa: a proposed system of jointly floated currencies whose exchange rates are allowed to fluctuate against each other within limits that are wider than in the snake. see *snake system.*

board: a standing committee of high rank or importance (e.g., a board of directors).

board lot: the unit of trading for stocks on an exchange; the unit of trading in stocks on the New York Stock Exchange is 100 shares. see *even lots.*

board of directors: people chosen by stockholders of a corporation to manage the enterprise.

Board of Governors: the seven-member governing body of the Federal Reserve System.

board of managers: in some states, the board of trustees of a mutual savings bank. [39]

board of trade: business executives who operate a local commodities exchange or a member of commerce.

board of trustees: the body in a mutual savings bank which manages the institution, establishes the policies under which it is to be operated, appoints the officers, and the like. [39]

boardroom
(1) *finance:* a room set aside for use by the board of directors of a business.
(2) *investments:* a room for registered representatives and customers in a broker's office, where opening, high, low, and last prices of leading stocks used to be posted on a board throughout the market day. Today such price displays are normally electronically controlled, although most board rooms have replaced the board with the ticker and/or individual quotation machines. [20]

bobtail pool: speculators acting independently of each other having a common goal and arrangement in mind. Commitments made by each member are his or her own responsibility. see *blind pool.*

bobtail statement: an abbreviated statement prepared for holders of demand deposit accounts. [105]

BOC
(1) see *back office crunch.*
(2) see *breach of contract.*

BOD: see *board of directors.*

"body": see *corpus.*

Boerse: Dutch and German for stock exchange.

boffo: slang, $1.

boff out: slang, to lose one's money.

BOG: see *Board of Governors.*

bogey: efforts by employees to restrict output by setting up an informal standard (bogey), which the employees do exceed.

bogus: false, counterfeit, nonexistent, or fraudulent. Bogus money is counterfeit currency; a bogus check is written on nonexistent account or bank.

"boilerplate": slang, standard legal language used in motions, wills, closings, and so on.

"boilerplate" legends: long stereotyped provisions contained in a document, such as a deposit slip or contract, usually in very small print. [105]

boiler room tactic: selling of very speculative and often worthless securities through the use of high-pressured and misleading literature. see also *dynamiter.*

bolivar: monetary unit of Venezuela.

boliviano: monetary unit of Bolivia.

bolsa: Spanish, for *stock exchange.*

BOM: see *buying on margin.*

bona fide: "in good faith" (Latin); with honest intent. cf. *mala fides.*

bona fide purchaser: an individual who buys property in good faith, without notice of any defect in the title, and for a valuable consideration.

bonanza
(1) *general:* an enormously successful business venture.
(2) *investments:* a highly profitable investment resulting in sudden wealth for the owner.

bona vacentia: describing property of which there is no apparent owner nor claimant (e.g., property in the hands of a liquidator after a firm has been dissolved).

bond
(1) *general:* an interest-bearing certificate of debt, usually issued in series, by which the issuer obligates itself to pay the principal amount at a specified time, usually five years or more after date of issue, and to pay interest periodically, usually semiannually. Bonds may be distinguished from promissory notes or other evidences of debt because of their formal execution under seal, and because a bank has certified that their issue has been authorized by the board of directors of a corporation or other governing body. Corporate bonds are usually secured by a lien against certain specified property.
(2) *banking:* an instrument used as proof of a debt, usually secured by a mortgage. see other entries under *bond.* [5]
(3) *finance:* a promise, under seal (i.e., closed from view by the public) to pay money.
(4) *finance:* the obligation to answer for the debt of another person.

bond, accumulation: a bond that is sold at a discount. If held to maturity, interest is realized up to the difference between the face value and the original purchase price. If sold before maturity, interest is the difference between the purchase and sale price. [105]

bond, adjustment: see *bond, reorganization.*

bond, agency: a bond issued by U.S. agencies and corporations to cover their own debt. These agency securities rank just below Treasury paper.

bond, annuity: see *bond, perpetual.*

bond, approved: in the preparation for fiduciaries, *legal lists* are determined in some states. The bonds named in the *legal list* are approved bonds. see *legal list.*

bond, assumed: a bond of one corporation whose liability is taken on by another corporation. see *bond, guaranteed.*

bond, authority: a bond payable from the revenues of a specific authority. Since such authorities usually have no revenue other than charges for services, their bonds are ordinarily revenue bonds. [49]

bond, average: a bond given by an individual in receipt of freight, stating that the recipient will contribute to any standard claim.

bond, baby: a bond with a face value usually of $100 or less.

bond, bail: a bond guaranteeing the appearance in court of the principal named in the bond. [53]

bond, banker's blanket: business insurance coverage guaranteeing banks against loss due to dishonest, fraudulent, or employee criminal activity. This bond insures against loss resulting from robbery, larceny, burglary, theft, holdup, misplacement, and other unexplained disappearances.

bond, bearer: a bond payable to the holder that does not have the owner's name registered on the books of the issuing company.

bond, bid: a guarantee that the contractor will enter into a contract, if it is awarded to him, and will furnish such contract bond (sometimes called performance bond) as is required by the terms of the bond. [54]

bond, blanket: a form of broad-coverage protection carried by financial institutions to cover losses from robbery, burglary, or employee dishonesty.

bond, bonus
(1) a security issued to war veterans, given in addition to their rated pay.

(2) a rare device in bond form given as with bonus stock. see *bonus stock.*

bond, borrowed: to meet specific requirements, banks and other financial institutions borrow bonds. Banks borrow bonds to comply with collateral requirements of governmental agencies, whereas brokers borrow bonds to make delivery on short sales.

bond, bridge: securities issued for bridge construction.

bond, callable: a bond issue, all of part of which may be redeemed by the issuing corporation under definite conditions, before the issue reaches maturity.

bond, called: a bond that the debtor has declared to be due and payable on a certain date, prior to maturity, in accordance with the provisions of an issue to be redeemed; the bonds to be retired are usually drawn by loss. [37]

bond, Carter: a medium-term foreign currency obligation issued by the United States to government during President Carter's administration as a way of achieving foreign currency balances.

bond, circular: a complete description of a bond offering used to publicize the relevant facts about the issue. A circular is traditionally released by an underwriter and given to interested parties.

bond, city: see *bond, municipal.*

bond, civil: a bond circulated by any governmental agency.

bond, classified: a debt security that receives a designation such as "Series A" or "Series B" to differentiate it from another bond of the same debtor. The series differ as to maturity date and interest.

bond, clean: a bond of the coupon type that has not been changed by any endorsement or rephrasing of the original contract. see *stamped security*.

bond, collateral: further security for a loan.

bond, collateral trust: an issue of bonds for which collateral has been pledged to guarantee repayment of the principal. This type of bond usually arises out of intercompany transactions in which the parent company issues bonds with securities of a subsidiary as the underlying collateral.

bond, combination: a bond issued by a governmental unit which is payable from the revenues of a governmental enterprise but which is also backed by the full faith and credit of the governmental unit. [49]

bond, commercial blanket: a bond issued for a stated amount on all regular workers of the covered firm, insuring against loss from an employee's dishonest acts. see also *bond, banker's blanket*.

bond, completion: a bond guaranteeing the construction for an improvement in connection with which, and prior to the completion of which, a mortgagee or other lender advances funds to an owner.

bond, consolidated: a debt instrument issued to replace two or more bonds issued earlier, often done to simplify a debt structure or to benefit from a lower prevailing rate of interest.

bond, construction: business insurance coverage protecting the insured from traditional risks associated with construction.

bond, continued: a debt instrument that need not be redeemed at maturity but can continue to earn interest.

bond, contract: a guarantee of the faithful performance of a construction contract and the payment of all labor and materials bills incident thereto. In those situations where two bonds are required—one to cover performance and the other to cover payment of labor and material—the former is known as a *performance bond* and the latter as a *payment bond*. [54]

bond, convertible: a bond that gives to its owner the privilege of exchanging it for other securities of the issuing corporation on a preferred basis at some future date or under certain conditions.

bond, corporate: an obligation of a corporation. see *bond, long-term corporate*.

bond, cost: a bond that guarantees the payment of costs in any legal action. [105]

bond, coupon: a bond with interest coupons attached. The coupons are clipped as they come due and are presented by the holder for payment of interest. see *talon*. [20]

bond, court: all bonds and mortgages required of litigants to enable them to pursue certain remedies of the courts. [54]

bond, currency: in 1934 the U.S. Supreme Court decided that all bonds, even those with gold clauses, were henceforth to be paid in lawful currency.

bond, cushion: a high-interest-rate bond of top quality that sells at a premium level above par and that usually results in a higher yield to maturity.

bond, customhouse: a bond required by the federal government in connection with the payment of duties or to produce bills of lading.

bond, debenture: a bond for which there is no specific security set aside or allocated for repayment of the principal.

bond, deferred: see *bond, extended.*

bond, deferred serial: a serial bond in which the first installment does not fall due for two or more years from the date of issue. [49]

bond, definitive: any bond issued in final form; used particularly with reference to permanent bonds for which temporary bonds or interim certificates were issued.

bond, depository: a bond guaranteeing payment of funds to depositors in accordance with the terms of a deposit in a bank. [53]

bond, divisional: a bond secured by a lien on a branch or division of a railroad, not on the main line or the entire mileage. [105]

bond, dollar: a bond quoted and traded in dollars rather than on a yield basis. [105]

bond, drawn: a bond that has been called for redemption by lot. see *bond, called.*

bond, endorsed: a bond that has been extraneously signed permitting it to be considered for normal delivery according to the regulations of the exchange and which therefore must be sold.

bond, equipment trust: a bond used to finance the purchase of equipment, such as railroad rolling stock. [105]

bond, escrow: bond held in escrow. see *escrow.*

bond, estate tax: a certain designated government bond redeemable at par less accrued interest for federal estate taxes to the extent that the entire proceeds are applied to such taxes due, providing the securities were owned by the decedent at the time of death. [52]

bond, extended: a bond that has matured and on which the debtor has not yet paid the principal but has agreed to extend or continue to pay the principal at a later time. Upon the creditor's accepting the extension, the bonds are stamped to show such agreement. synonymous with *deferred bond.*

bond, external: a bond issued by a country or firm for purchase outside that nation, usually denominated in the currency of the purchaser.

bond, federal: the promissory note of a central government. [28]

bond, fidelity: insurance for an employer (the insured) for loss sustained by him or her because of any dishonest act by an employee covered by the insurance. Blanket fidelity bonds cover groups of employees. see *fidelity insurance.*

bond, fiduciary: a bond, in behalf of a person appointed by a court to a position of trust, as executor of an estate. [12]

bond, flat income: the price at which a bond is traded includes consideration for all unpaid accruals of interest. Bonds that are in default of interest or principal are traded flat. Income bonds, which pay interest only to the extent earned, are usually traded flat. All other bonds are usually dealt in *and interest*, which means that the buyer pays to the seller the market price plus interest accrued since the last payment date. [20]

bond, floating-rate: a bond on which the interest payable is variable.

bond, flower: a U.S. government bond. Until the Tax Reform Act of 1976, flower bonds sold at a substantial premium in relation to other bonds issued at similarly low interest rates because the Treasury accepted them for estate tax payments at 100 cents on the dollar, whatever their cost at the time of purchase. Now this benefit is in part taxable as a capital gain.

bond, forgery: insurance against loss due to forgery or alteration of, on, or in checks or other instruments. [53]

bond, fraud: business insurance protection against fraud losses.

bond, free: an unpledged bond; any bond disposable immediately.

bond, funding: a bond issued to retire outstanding floating debt and to eliminate deficits. [49]

bond, general mortgage: a bond secured by a blanket mortgage upon property already subject to prior mortgages.

bond, general obligation: a bond secured by the pledge of the issuer's full faith and credit, usually including unlimited taxing power. [105]

bond, gilt-edged: a high-grade bond issued by a company that has demonstrated its ability to earn a comfortable profit over a period of years and to pay its bondholders their interest without interruption. see also *blue chip.*

bond, gold: a debt instrument giving the legal holder an option of being paid principal and/or interest in gold. Since 1935 these bonds are paid in legal currency instead of gold.

bond, government: an obligation of the U.S. government, regarded as the highest-grade issues in existence. see *Treasury bills; Treasury notes.* [20]

bond, guaranteed: a bond on which the principal or income or both are guaranteed by another corporation or parent company in case of default by the issuing corporation.

bond, honor: a consumer-size certificate of deposit with denominations as low as $5.00, many banks promoted

these bonds and told purchasers that they were merely honor-bound to report the interest on their tax returns. The Internal Revenue Service moved swiftly to eliminate this irregularity.

bond, improvement: any bond issued by a municipality to finance a public improvement.

bond, improvement mortgage: a bond issued for financing improvements of the debtor business that are secured by a general mortgage.

bond, inactive: see *inactive stock (bond).*

bond, income: a type of bond on which interest is paid when and only when earned by the issuing corporation.

bond, indemnity: a bond that protects the obligee (the party for whom the applicant for bond, the *principal*, has undertaken to perform specified duties) against losses resulting from the principal's failure to fulfill his obligations. Examples of miscellaneous indemnity bonds are warehouse, lost instrument, and lien.

bond, indenture: a written agreement under which bonds are issued, setting forth maturity date, interest rate, and other terms.

bond, indexed: a bond where the values of the principal and the payout rise with inflation or the value of the underlying commodity. cf. *bond, nonindexed.*

bond, industrial revenue: a revenue bond deriving its earnings from an industrial facility.

bond, installment: synonymous with the *serial bond.*

bond, insular: a bond issued by a unit of the United States (e.g., Alaska, New York). synonymous with *territorial bond.*

bond, interchangeable: a bond in either a registered or coupon form that can be converted to the other form or its original form at the request of the holder. A service charge is often made for such a conversion.

bond, interim: sometimes used before the issuance of permanent bonds to raise funds needed only temporarily. synonymous with *temporary bond.* see *bond, temporary.*

bond, intermediate: a callable bond bearing no date of maturity. The call aspect usually is not effective until some stated time period has passed.

bond, interminate: a callable bond having no set maturity date. The call feature is usually not effective until some stated period has passed. see *bond, callable.*

bond, internal: a bond issued by a country payable in its own currency; to be distinguished from an external bond, which is a bond issued by one country and sold in another country and payable in the currency of that other country. [37]

bond, internal revenue: a bond required by the U.S. government which guarantees payment of federal taxes and compliance with government regulations. [54]

bond, irredeemable: a bond issued which contains no provisions for being "called" or redeemed prior to maturity date. [10]

bond, jeopardy assessment: a bond remaining in jeopardy assessment pending appeal. This bond is required to guarantee payment of federal taxes due or claimed to be due.

bond, joint and several: any debt instrument where the holder seeks payment from more than one corporation

up to the full face amount of the security.

bond, joint control: a bond needed prior to transfer of the assets of an estate to the custody of the principal.

bond, judgment: bond issued to fund judgments. see *funding.* [49]

bond, junior: those bonds that are not senior; they are subordinate or secondary to another issue which in the event of liquidation, would have prior claim to the junior bond.

bond, junk: basement-rated and bargain-priced securities.

bond, legal: a bond that federal and state laws identify as an acceptable and legal investment for fiduciary institutions.

bond, license and permit: a bond guaranteeing proper compliance with statutory requirements and municipal ordinances. It is generally required by governmental bodies of such persons as pawnbrokers, plumbers, and electricians. [105]

bond, limited tax: a bond that is secured by a tax that is limited as to amount and rate.

bond, long-term corporate: a debt of industrial corporations, finance companies, utilities, and telephone companies. Maturities range from 10 to 40 years, with intermediates running from 4 to 10 years. They are rated AAA and AA for high quality, A and BBB for medium quality. The face denomination for corporate bonds is $1000, but new issues are often marketed above or below par to adjust to current yields. Older bonds with lower interest coupons sell at discounts.

bond, lost-instrument: a bond that indemnifies the issuer of a document of consequences that may arise from possession of the document by others than the recognized owner. [105]

bond, maintenance: a bond guaranteeing against defects in workmanship or materials for a stated time after the acceptance of work.

bond, mortgage: a bond that has as an underlying security a mortgage on all properties of the issuing corporation.

bond, municipal: a bond issued by a state or a political subdivision (county, city, town, village, etc.). Also, a bond issued by a state agency or authority. In general, interest paid on municipal bonds is exempt from federal income taxes and state and local taxes in the state of issue.

bond, municipal revenue: banks now may underwrite a few kinds of revenue bonds, which are obligations backed not by city or state tax revenues, but by revenue produced by the facilities that are financed—for example, a housing project. Banks want to be permitted to underwrite more kinds of revenue bonds. In addition, the Comptroller of the Currency is seeking to determine the legality of municipal revenue bonds underwriting, under which banks offer, in effect, to repurchase the bonds at par within five years. This recent activity in banking is testing the Glass-Steagall Act. see *Glass-Steagall Act.*

bond, named schedule: a fidelity bond that covers several employees of a firm, by listing their names on an attached schedule. [105]

bond, new housing authority: a bond issued by a local public housing authority to finance public housing. It is backed by federal funds and the pledge of the U.S. government. [105]

bond, noncallable: a bond that cannot, under the terms of the issue, be called by the obligor (the corporation) for redemption or conversion. [37]

bond, nonindexed: a bond wherein inflation erodes the value of the principal because the investor will be paid back in dollars that are worth less. The value of the bond declines further as inflation also drives up interest rates, since bond prices move inversely with interest rates. cf. *bond, indexed.*

bond, obligation: a bond authorized by a mortgagor that is larger than the original mortgage amount. A personal obligation is created to safeguard the lender against any costs that may develop over the amount of the mortgage.

bond, open-end: a mortgage bond of an issue that has no limit on the number or quantity of bonds that can be issued under the mortgage. However, some relationship is often required of the number and quantity of bonds to the value of the property that has been mortgaged.

bond, optional: see *bond, callable.*

bond, optional payment: a bond that gives the holder the choice to receive payment of interest or principal or both in the currency of one or more foreign countries, as well as in domestic funds. [37]

bond, overlying: a junior bond, subject to the claim of a senior underlying bond having priority of claim.

bond, par: a bond selling at par, in line with prevailing new issues or estimated going yield rates.

bond, participating: a bond which, following the receipt of a fixed rate of periodic interest, also receives some of the profit held by the issuing business. A form of profit sharing, this bond is rarely used today.

bond, passive: a bond that does not carry any interest. Often these bonds are issued following a reorganization.

bond, payment: see *bond, contract*.

bond, penal: a bond given by an accused, or by another in his or her behalf, for the repayment of money in the event that the accused fails to appear in court on a specific day. see also *bond, surety*.

bond, performance: see *bond, contract*.

bond, permit: a bond guaranteeing that the person to whom a permit is, or is to be, issued will comply with the law or ordinance regulating the privilege for which the permit is issued. [53]

bond, perpetual: any bond having no maturity date; rarely issued in the United States.

bond, petitioning on creditors': a bond providing that, if a petition in bankruptcy filed by creditors against a debtor is dismissed, the bonding company will pay to the debtor all expenses, costs, and damages. [105]

bond, plain: any debenture. see *certificates of debt*.

bond, position-schedule: a fidelity bond that covers any employee of a business firm who occupies the position named in the schedule attached to the bond. [105]

bond, preference: any income or adjustment bond.

bond, premium: in the United States, a bond that is selling above its face value. In Europe, a bond having a lottery feature. When called, as distinguished from regular maturity, a premium bond generally pays substan-

tially more than the face amount. Also, the excess of the price at which a bond is acquired or sold, over its face value. The price does not include accrued interest at the date of acquisition or sale. [49]

bond, prior-lien: a bond holding precedence over other bonds issued by the same corporation.

bond, privileged: a convertible bond that has attached warrants.

bond, profit-sharing: a bond that participates in the issuing company's profits as well as receiving a guaranteed interest rate. [105]

bond, public: any bond issued by a governmental agency, domestic or foreign.

bond, public official: a fidelity bond that provides coverage against loss due to dishonesty or mishandling of public funds by a public official. [105]

bond, purchase-money: a bond having as security a purchase-money mortgage. see *purchase-money mortgage*.

bond, real estate: a bond secured by a mortgage or trust conveyance of real estate.

bond, redeemable: any callable bond. see *bond, callable*.

bond, redemption: a *refunding bond*. see *redemption*.

bond, redemption value: guaranteed face amount of a bond payable at maturity. [12]

bond, refunding: a bond issued to retire a bond already outstanding. Refunding bonds may be sold for cash and outstanding bonds redeemed in cash, or they may be exchanged with holders of outstanding bonds. [49]

bond, registered: a bond in which the name of the owner is designated, and the proceeds are payable only to him or her. Bonds may be registered as to principal and interest, or principal only. Interest on a bond registered as to both principal and interest is paid to the owner by check as it becomes due. Bonds registered as to principal only have coupons attached which are detached and collected as the interest becomes due. [10]

bond, regular serial: serial bond in which all periodic instalments of principal repayment are equal in amount. [49].

bond, reorganization: a debt security issued in the recapitalization of a firm in financial difficulty; an *adjustment bond*.

bond, revenue: a bond whose principal and interest are to be paid solely from earnings; such bonds are usually issued by a municipally owned utility or other public service enterprise the revenues and possibly the properties of which are pledged for this purpose. [49]

Bond, Savings (U.S.): Series EE, introduced at the start of 1980, replaced the highly popular Series E bonds. These new bonds are available in face-value denominations of $50, $75, up to $10,000, and are sold at one-half their face value. EE bonds pay varying interest rates—as much as one percent at six-month intervals if market conditions warrant. Presently, the maturity on Series EE bonds is eight years, down from nine years, effectively boosting the rate on those bonds to 9 percent. The rate on HH bonds is 8.5 percent. HH bonds are bought at face value, pay interest semiannually, and mature in 10 years. In 1982 a variable-interest-rate U.S. Savings Bond was approved.

The investment yield on these bonds was increased to a level equal to 85 percent of the yield on five-year Treasury securities when held five years.

bond, schedule: a bond listing the names and positions of employees included as principals. see *bond, fidelity.* [12]

bond, school: a municipal bond to help finance the building and equipment purchases for a school.

bond, second-mortgage: a bond issued on property that already has a first mortgage outstanding on it.

bond, secured: a bond secured by the pledge of assets (plant or equipment), the title to which is transferred to bondholders in case of foreclosure.

bond, self-liquidating: a bond serviced from the earnings of a municipally owned enterprise, usually a utility. The earnings must be sufficient to cover the debt service with a reasonable margin of protection if the bonds are to be regarded as entirely self-liquidating. [105]

bond, senior: those bonds having prior claim to the assets of the debtor upon liquidation.

bond, serial: an issue of bonds in which a certain proportion of the bonds is retired at regular intervals, issued when the security depreciates through use or obsolescence. These issues usually provide that the bonds outstanding shall not exceed the vaue of the security.

bond, serial annuity: a serial bond in which the annual installments of the bond prinicpal are so arranged that the payments for principal and interest combined are approximately the same each year. [49]

bond, sheriff idemnity: a bond providing for the reimbursement of a sheriff who undertakes a seizure of goods, in the event that he or she is held liable for damages in an action brought against him or her for unlawful seizure. [105]

bond, sinking fund: a bond secured by the deposit of specified amounts. The issuing corporation makes these deposits to secure the principal of the bonds, and it is sometimes required that the funds be invested in other securities.

bond, special assessment: a bond payable from the proceeds of special assessments. The bond is payable only from the proceeds of special asessments levied against the properties presumed to be benefited by such improvements or services. [49]

bond, special assistance: a bond payable from levies on the properties presumably benefited by the improvement being financed. The issuing government agrees to make the assessments and earmarks the proceeds for debt service on these bonds. [105]

bond, special district: a bond issue of a local taxing district which has been organized for a special purpose, such as road, sewer, fire, drainage, irrigation, and levee districts. [49]

bond, special lien: a special assessment bond that acts as a lien against a particular piece (or pieces) of property. [49]

bond, special tax: a bond secured by a special tax, such as a gasoline tax. [105]

bond, stamped: when a debtor fears default on a bond, should he receive approval from the holder, the maturity date and/or rate of interest can be altered and a stamp affixed to the bond to signify the holder's acceptance of the terms.

bond, state: a division of municipal bonds, or the promissory note of a state. [28]

bond, sterling: a bond denominated in British pounds sterling as distinguished from a bond denominated in another currency unit (i.e., U.S. dollar).

bond, straight serial: a serial bond in which the annual installments of bond principal are approximately equal. [49]

bond, strip: where traders clip the coupons off a fixed-interest bond or note and then sell the principal and interest parts separately to two groups of investors. Those seeking current income buy the strip of coupons and those wanting a lump sum at maturity, and a capital gain, buy the principal or "corpus" portion. Because each portion is worth less than its whole before taxes, both are sold at a deep discount from their face values.

bond, surety: an agreement providing for monetary compensation in the event of failure to perform specified acts within a stated period. The firm that is the surety company, for example, becomes responsible for fulfillment of a contract if the contractor defaults. see also *bond, penal.*

bond, tax anticipation: any short-term, interest-bearing bond created to be bought by businesses with money assembled as a reserve in order to pay taxes.

bond, tax-exempt: any security of a state, city, or other public authority specified under federal law, the interest on which is either wholly or partly exempt from federal income taxes. see *bond, municipal.* [20]

bond, temporary: similar to a definitive

bond except that it has been printed rather than engraved. see *bond, definitive.*

bond, term: bonds of the same issue usually maturing all at one time and ordinarily to be retired from sinking funds. Sometimes a term bond has more than one maturity date—for example, a serial issue having postponed maturities in only a few late years of its term. [49].

bond, terminable: any bond having a stated maturity.

bond, terminal: bonds secured by property in the form of railroad or grain terminals.

bond, territorial: see *bond, insular.*

bond, treasury: a U.S. government long-term security, sold to the public and having a maturity longer than five years.

bond, underlying: a bond that has a senior lien where subsequently claims exist.

bond, unified: see *bond, consolidated.*

bond, unlimited tax: a bond secured by pledge of taxes which may be levied by the issuer in unlimited rate or amount. [52]

bond, unsecured: a bond backed up by the faith and credit of the issuer instead of the pledge of assets.

Bond, U.S. Savings: see *Bond, Savings (U.S.)*

bond, warehouse customs: bonds given only on statements prescribed by the U.S. Treasury Department that are required by federal regulations in connection with the importation of items that carry a duty.

bond, zero-coupon: a security sold at a deep discount from its face value and redeemed at the full amount at maturity. The difference between the cost of the bond and its value when redeemed is the investor's return. These notes provide no interest payments to holders.

bond amortization: indicating the premium over par that has been paid for a bond.

bond anticipation notes (BANs): short-term notes of a municipality sold in anticipation of bond issuance which are full faith and credit obligations of the governmental unit and are to be retired from the proceeds of the bonds to be issued. see *interim borrowing.* *[49].*

bond averages: calculations of the mean price of selected bonds over a specific period of time. A series of such calculations reflects the general trend of the bond market. [105]

bond buy-backs: as prices for corporate bonds drop, often a result of soaring interest rates, the buying up of a firm's outstanding bonds at discounts creates yields of 15 to 20 percent, thus exceeding those on most other short-term investments. In addition, corporate buyers save interest while they get ahead of their required sinking fund payments and clean up their balance sheets. see *buy back, sinking fund.*

bond buyer: a trade publication that describes upcoming municipal bond sales, posts the results of those sales, and carries news items of special interest to the municipal bond industry. [105]

bond circular: a full description of a bond offering used to communicate the major facts of the issue. The circular is prepared by the underwriters and distributed to interested persons and firms.

bond crowd: brokers working in the securities markets who specialize in the trading of bonds.

bond discount: the amount below the face or par amount of a bond at which the bond is purchased.

bonded

(1) *general:* protected or secured by a pledge of property or by a bond.

(2) *finance:* describing a messenger who delivers valuables.

(3) *finance:* a bond posted as security that a tax or tariff will be paid on time.

(4) *government:* describing goods in a government-supervised storage facility, where items are stored without the payment of duties or taxes until they are removed.

bonded debt: that amount of the debt of a company or government which is represented by bonds. If there are sinking fund bonds, this term should be replaced by *gross bonded debt* and *net bonded debt*. [49]

bonded goods: items kept in a bonded warehouse. The owner of the goods has deposited a bond with the government that guarantees that a duty or tax on the items will be paid upon withdrawal of the goods.

bonded indebtedness: see *bonded debt.* [49]

bonded items: items stored in a bonded warehouse to guarantee the government that the tax or duty on the merchandise will be paid upon withdrawal of the items.

bonded (state) warehouse: see *warehouse, state bonded; warehouse, U.S. Customs bonded.*

bond equivalent yield: calculating the return on original-issue discount securities, such as U.S. Treasury bills, so that it can be compared to returns on long-term debt securities.

bond fund

(1) a fund established to receive and disburse the proceeds of a governmental bond issue. [49]

(2) an investment company, the portfolio of which consists primarily of bonds. [23]

bondholder: one who owns bonds and therefore is a creditor of the issuer. [50]

bond house: a financial organization whose major activity is the selling of bonds.

bond immunization: approaches that attempt to match up investment income with future liabilities—the lack of certainty that they will always be able to reinvest a bond's coupon income at high enough rates.

bonding company: an organization whose business is the forming of contracts of surety and the providing of bonds.

bond interest: interest on bonds, often paid twice a year, as determined by the conditions of the bonds. Should the bond be registered, it might take the form of a check. If it is a bearer bond, the interest may be paid with a coupon.

bond market

(1) the place where bonds are sold. Most are sold over the counter; others, in large amounts, are sold on an exchange.

(2) financial institutions that buy bonds (e.g., trust funds, banks, insurance firms).

bond of indemnity: an indemnity agreement used in filing a claim when the claimant, unable to show the freight bill or bill of lading, is given relief from liability for any action for which a carrier would have otherwise been liable.

bond ordinance (or resolution): an ordinance or resolution authorizing a bond issue. [49]

bond power: a form of assignment executed by the owner of registered bonds which contains an irrevocable appointment of an attorney-in-fact to make the actual transfer on the books of the corporation. see *power of attorney, stock power.* [37]

bond premium: the excess of the price at which a bond is acquired or sold over its face value. [49]

bond puts: see *put bond option.*

bond quality ratings: symbolic ratings to various levels of investment qualities of bonds, measured according to their investment risk.

bond rating: appraising and rating, by a recognized financial organization (e.g., Moody's Investors Service) of the worth of a bond as a sound investment. Ratings are based on the reputation of the organization, its record of interest payments, its profitability, and the like. A triple A (AAA) bond is the most secure, followed by AA, A, B, and so on.

bond ratio: the total face value of bonds of a corporation divided by the total face value of bonds, preferred stock, common stock, reserve, and surplus.

bond register: a book of original entry, in bound or loose-leaf form, in which are recorded the details relative to the purchase and sale of bonds for the firm's own investment account. [10]

bond resolution: a legal order or contract by the appropriate body of a governmental unit authorizing a bond issue. The rights of the bondholders and the obligations of the issuer are carefully detailed in this resolution. [105]

bonds authorized and unissued: bonds that have been legally authorized but have not been issued and which can be issued and sold without further authorization. [49]

bonds issued: bonds sold. [49]

bonds payable, matured: bonds that have reached or passed their maturity date but remain unpaid. [49]

bond swap: the simultaneous sale of one issue and the purchase of another. Ideally, a swap should consist of, in effect, trading a shorter maturity for a longer one because longer maturities tend to sell for less than shorter ones in today's market and have a greater potential for appreciation should interest rates drop.

bond value tables: tables of bond yields to bond values used to compute bond yields to maturity or to determine the price of a bond necessary to afford a given yield to a given maturity.

bond yield: the rate of return on bonds. [37]

bond yield to maturity: the calculation of the precise return paid by a bond upon maturation, as a function of purchase price. [105]

bonification

(1) *general:* rendering of an advantage or benefit.

(2) *finance:* said to be achieved when certain items that are made for export relieve the manufacturer of paying an excise tax on such items.

(3) *taxation:* the return or exclusion of a tax.

bonus: an additional dividend paid to savers who have met all the requirements of a special savings account contract.

bonus account: a savings account that earns interest at a bonus rate if the customer makes regular deposits to the account, leaves a specified amount on deposit for a specified term, or fulfills other conditons of the account contract. [59]

bonus bond: see *bond, bonus*.

bonus futures: a recently uncovered means for increasing executive bonuses. For example, an executive hedges his expectations of a substandard year-end bonus from the company by selling a future to a colleague. The purchaser agrees to guarantee the seller an amount equivalent to, say, 10 percent of the seller's annual salary. If the company at year-end grants a bonus of more than 10 percent, the futures buyer gets the excess and makes a nice profit. On the other hand, if the company gives out a disappointing bonus of 9 percent, the futures speculator suffers a loss.

bonus stock: securities given most often to top management and other employees as a bonus.

boodle
(1) money received through corruption in public activities.
(2) counterfeit money.

book: a notebook the specialist in a stock exchange uses to keep a record of the buy and sell orders at specified prices, in strict sequence of receipt, which are left with him or her by other brokers. [20]

book account: synonymous with *open account*.

book cost: the amount at which property is recorded in plant accounts without deduction of related reserves or other accounts.

book credit: items shown on a ledger accounts representing commitments of firms and individuals which are not secured by notes or other security.

book crowd: synonymous with *cabinet crowd*.

book depreciation: the amount that can be deducted for depreciation purposes from the cost of an asset of the property owner.

book-entry security: an issued security, not in the form of a certificate, but merely as an entry in an account at a bank. Eighty percent of marketable Treasury securities are held in book-entry form. [88]

bookkeeper: a person who makes entries on the general ledger of a business.

bookkeeping: the art, practice, or labor involved in the systematic recording of the transactions affecting a business.

bookkeeping cycle: the full bookkeeping process discharged in a fiscal period, including journalizing, posting, preparing a trial balance, and preparing financial statements.

bookkeeping department: a department of a bank where the records of all depositors' checking accounts are posted and kept. In the larger banks, there may be found several bookkeeping departments, such as commercial, corporation accounts, special checking, general ledger, bank ledger, foreign accounts, stock transfer, and trust bookkeeping. [10]

bookkeeping equation: a one-line summary of a balance sheet. The basic equation is assets = liabilities + proprietorship.

book liability: the amount at which securities issued or assumed by the carrier and other liability items are recorded in the accounts of the carrier. [18]

book of final entry: a book to which information is transferred from a book of original entry.

book of original entry: the record in which transactions are formally recorded for the first time, such as the cash journal, check register, or general journal. Where machine bookkeeping is used, it may happen that one transaction is recorded simultaneously in several records, one of which may be regarded as the book of original entry. [49]

book of secondary entry: ledger; not books of original entry (i.e., journals).

book profit: the increase in the value of a stock that has not been sold. For example, a stock is bought at $50 and its price climbs to $60, but it is not sold, leading to a book profit of $10. cf. *realized profit.*

books
(1) journals, ledgers, or other records containing a firm's accounts.
(2) the record kept by a specialist in a particular security of all orders that were not executed because they were limited to a price other than the one prevailing in the market.

books (close): the date the transfer agent closes the transfer books of a corporation and checks the stockholder list to determine eligibility to vote or receive dividends. see also *books (open).*

books (open): the date the transfer agent opens the transfer books of a corporation to commence transferring stocks after they had been closed to check the list of stockholders. see also *book (close).*

bookshares: a modern share-recording system which eliminates the need for mutual fund share certificates but gives the fund shareowner a record of his holdings. [23]

book sort: a method of sorting checks and deposits into the books within the bookkeeping department's alphabetical breakdown by a rough sort (i.e., all items going to the A-B-C-D book or ledger are rough-sorted into this four-letter breakdown).

book transfer: a transfer of funds between two accounts, both on the books of the bank executing the transaction. [105]

book value
(1) *general:* the amount of an asset found in the company's records, not necessarily that which it could bring in the open market. see *depreciated cost.*
(2) *investments:* determined from a company's records by adding all assets, then deducting all debts and other liabilities, plus the liquidation price of any preferred issues. The sum arrived at is divided by the number of common shares outstanding, and the result is "book value per common share." [20]

boom
(1) *general:* a period of rapidly rising prices and an increased demand for goods and services, usually accompanied by full employment.
(2) *investments:* when business expands and the value of commodities and securities increases.

boomerang: an international program to minimize the practice of goods dumping, by returning such items duty free and exempt of quantity restrictions.

boot: payments by or to the U.S. Treasury that may be necessary in an advance refunding in order to align more closely the respective values of the eligible issues and the issues offered. [71]

booth: the areas on the outside rim of an exchange trading floor occupied by a member firm; used to transmit orders from the firm's offices to the trading floor.

bootlegging: traffic in goods which is prohibited by law or which attempts to avoid payment of taxes on the items.

boot money: money used as an additional compensation by one of the parties to a bargain.

bootstrap
(1) *general:* a technique designed to bring about a desired state by internally generated means.
(2) *computers:* a method for getting the first few instructions into memory when a routine is loaded.

bop: see *balance of payments.*

borax: slang, cheap or low-grade items.

bordereau: particularly in insurance, a digest of the transactions between an agent and his or her company or an insurer and the reinsurer.

borrow: to receive something from another, with the understanding that the item is to be returned.

borrowed bond: see *bond, borrowed.*

borrowed funds: all direct or indirect nondeposit liabilities. Borrowings may be accomplished through the use of promissory notes, purchase of federal funds, bills payable, mortgages payable, due bills, securities borrowed, customer paper rediscounted, and assets sold with the bank's endorsement. [105]

borrowed reserves: discounts and advances from Federal Reserve Banks; mainly advances secured by U.S. government securities or eligible paper. [72]

borrowed stock: the security a broker borrows to complete the obligation of a short selling contract held by his client. see *loan stock.*

borrower: one who borrows cash or buys something on time.

borrowing power: the ability to secure a loan from an individual or firm such as a bank.

borrowings: the amount borrowed by reporting member banks; the breakdown shows the amounts borrowed from the Federal Reserve Banks, and from others—mostly other commercial banks. [40]

Boston bookkeeping (or ledger): a single-entry system that is progressive.

Boston interest: ordinary interest computed by using a 30-day month rather than the exact number of days in a month. cf. *New York interest.*

Boston Stock Exchange: organized on October 13, 1834, this stock exchange has but once failed to perform its operations, when it closed from July 30, 1913 to December 10, 1914 during the frantic period at the beginning of World War I.

Boston trustee: an individual who undertakes to act as a professional trustee.

BOT: see *board of trustees.*

Bot.: bought.

bottom: a phase of a projection of a time series found on a chart where the lowest point of the series appears; usually associated with a depression phase of a cycle.

bottom dropped out: a situation of sharply falling prices occurring when the market is well liquidated, thus establishing a panic atmosphere.

bottom-fishing: buying stocks in countries whose currencies are lowest against the U.S. dollar.

bottom out: the condition in which a time series that has been graphically plotted after reaching a low point shows signs of improving or rising.

bottom price: the lowest price for a stock or commodity for a period of time, such as a day, week, year, or cyclical period.

bottomry: a loan secured by a lien on a vessel. The contract of bottomry is in the nature of a mortgage. If the carrier is lost, the debt is canceled.

bounce: slang, the failure of a check to fulfill payment for an item or service.

bounty: added payments offered by a government as an incentive for a specific industry or the export of certain items.

bourse: French for *stock exchange*.

box: short for *safe deposit box* where valuables are kept.

boxcar discovery: slang, request for every remotely relevant document.

boycott
(1) *finance:* an attempt to prevent the carrying on of a business by urging people not to buy from the firm being boycotted. Frequently used on the international scene for political or economic reasons; illustrated by appeals, threats, and so on, to secure redress of a grievance.
(2) *labor relations:* collective pressure against an employer to discourage public acceptance of his products or services. A *primary boycott* involves one employer and his employees only; a *secondary boycott* involves a third

party, and in many cases is forbidden by law.

BP
(1) see *bills payable.*
(2) see *book profit.*

BQ: see *basis quote.*

BR
(1) see *bills receivable.*
(2) see *bond rating.*
(3) depository institutions' borrowing from the Federal Reserve. [81]

Br.: see *branch.*

BRA: see *Bankruptcy Reform Act of 1978.*

bracket: groupings determined by underwriting amounts in a new issue or loan.

bracket creep: a reaction when taxpayers receive raises to offset the ravages of inflation. In this situation, they are taxed more heavily on some or all of their added income under a system that levies at a progressively higher rate. see *Economic Recovery Tax Act of 1981.*

brain storm: slang, a rapidly arrived-at solution to a problem; a good, spontaneous idea.

branch
(1) *computers:* a set of instructions in a program consisting of a series of changes from the normal sequence of steps.
(2) *systems:* a point in a routine at which one of two or more alternatives is selected, under control of the routine.

branch banking: any banking system where there are few parent institutions, each having branches operating over a large geographic area. Some states have authorized the concept of branch banking under strict regulation. Federal control is maintained by the Board of Governors of the Federal Reserve System and the Office of Comptroller of the Currency.

branch clearing account: a general ledger account that reflects the flow of debit and credit items between community offices or administrative units. [105]

branch expense: cost of activities performed by bank branches on behalf of the bank credit card operation, such as receiving payments and merchant deposits and issuing cash advances. [105]

branch pickup: method of distributing new bank cards to cardholders whereby cardholders are notified that their new bank cards are being held for them at a specified branch and asked to visit that branch to obtain their new cards. [105]

brand: a name, term, sign, symbol, or design, or a combination of these which is intended to identify the goods or services of one seller or group of sellers and to differentiate them from those of its competitors. [48]

Brannan plan: a proposal made in 1949 by U.S. Secretary of Agriculture Charles F. Brannan to eliminate parity payments to farmers and give them direct payments instead. cf. *price support.*

brassage: the charge made by a government for producing coins from bullion. see *seignorage.*

brazen law of wages: see *iron law of wages.*

breach of contract: not fulfilling one's part in an agreement; breaking a promise to carry out one's contractual responsibility.

breach of trust: violation of a duty of a trustee to a beneficiary. [37]

breach of warranty: when a warranty made by a seller is found to be false, the warranty is said to be breached.

bread: slang, money.

break
(1) *general:* a second chance or another opportunity.
(2) *finance:* a discount.
(3) *investments:* an unexpected drop in the price of stocks and commodities.
(4) in a Eurocredit, a clause which passes on to a borrower the risk that certain events may curtail the lender's activity or close the Eurocurrency market. cf. *disaster clause.*

breakage
(1) *general:* an allowance for losses resulting from breakage of merchandise.
(2) *finance:* the fractional pennies due either party resulting from percentage calculations (e.g., when the decimal shows itself to be 0.5 or more, an added point is entered).

breakdown: an itemized listing of all activity occurring on an individual cardholder account. [105]

break-even point: the point of activity at which the company earns zero profit. It is reached when total revenue equals total expense. see *margin of safety.*

breaking bulk: the practice of some middlemen to take the large, economical shipment from a manufacturer and divide it into smaller units for sale for greater profit.

break in the market: an unusually sharp drop in the price for a product.

breakout: when a specific security climbs above a level where strong selling resistance exists, or drops below a level of strong purchasing support.

breakup value: in an investment fund

or an issue of a holding firm, the value of the assets available for the issue, taking all marketable securities at their market price.

B. Rec.: see *bills receivable.*

Bretton Woods Agreement of 1944: articles of agreement adopted by the international monetary conference of 44 nations which met at Bretton Woods, New Hampshire. The International Monetary Fund and the International Bank for Reconstruction and Development were created. The fund's major responsibility is to maintain orderly currency practices in international trade, while the bank's function is to facilitate extension of long-term investments for productive purposes. Periodic meetings are held at Bretton Woods to amend the original agreement.

bribe: a payment resulting in the payer's receiving some right, benefit, or preference to which he has no legal right and which he would not have obtained except with the payment of the money. A *bribe* is a criminal offense.

brick: a package of new currency which is banded with steel straps, the straps being sealed at the joining points. New currency is shipped from the Federal Reserve Bank by this method of packaging. [10]

bridge bond: see *bond, bridge.*

bridge financing: emergency financing whereby a short- or medium-term loan is secured to meet a debt obligation or to await favorable conditions for a longer-term loan.

bridge loan: synonymous with *swing loan.*

bridge supplement: a supplement amending an effective tariff and an issued but not yet effective tariff which is to succeed the effective tariff.

bridging loan: see *swing loan.*

bring out: the offering to the public of a new security issue by one or more underwriters.

broadcast system: syndicating Eurocredits whereby a bank (or banks) receive a mandate to provide the funds and then offer participation in the loan, more or less indiscriminately, to other banks, by letter or telex.

broad market: describing a time of considerable volume in the buying and selling of stocks and bonds.

broad tape: slang, the Dow Jones news ticker displayed in brokerage houses as a large rectangular screen on which lines of copy roll upward.

Brok.: see *broker, brokerage.*

broke: slang, without funds.

broken lot: an odd lot, usually less than 100 shares of a stock.

broken period: a forward foreign exchange arrangement which is not for a standard maturity period.

broken time: work schedule or shift where the employee works for a certain length of time, then is off duty, then returns for another period of work.

broker

(1) *general:* a person who prepares contracts with third parties on behalf of the broker's principal.

(2) *banking:* a specialist who represents buyers of property and liability insurance and deals with either agents or companies in arranging for the coverage required by the customer. The broker is licensed by the state or states in which he or she conducts business.

(3) *banking:* a state-licensed individual who acts as middleman in prop-

erty transactions between a buyer and seller.

(4) **investments:** a member of a stock exchange firm or any exchange member who handles orders to buy and sell securities and commodities for a commission. cf. *street broker;* see also *floor broker.*

brokerage: the business of a broker. [62]

brokerage account: a client's account managed by a broker subject to the client's order. The broker purchases and sells securities or commodities either on margin or for cash.

broker-dealer: a firm that retails mutual fund shares and other securities to the public. [23]

brokering: slang, when an attorney gives a case to another lawyer for a forwarding fee. It is considered by the legal profession as an unethical way of making money.

broker's broker: a dealer, that is, one who buys or sells for his or her own account.

broker's free credit balance: the idle amount of funds in brokerage accounts reported by the New York Stock Exchange on a monthly basis.

broker's loan: a loan made to a stockbroker and secured by stock exchange collateral.

broker's market: exists when the investing public is generally inactive at the same time that brokers are trading quite heavily with their own accounts.

broker's ticket: a written statement of all buy and sell orders executed by a broker, giving the date, name, and amount of the security traded, the price, the customer's name, the broker's name, and so on.

brown Abe: slang, a penny.

BS
(1) see *back spread.*
(2) see *balance sheet.*
(3) see *bellwether stock.*
(4) see *bill of sale.*
(5) see *block sale.*
(6) see *butterfly spread.*

Bs.L.: see *bill of lading.*

Bt.: bought.

BTG: see *beating the gun.*

BTM: see *bulling the market.*

bubble: an unwise business venture in which the price of the item has little or no relationship to the value of the asset.

bubble company: a firm that never had any true business or did not intend to be honest, or a firm created to defraud the public.

buck: slang, one dollar.

bucketeer: a person associated with a bucket shop.

bucketing: activity of a broker who executes a customer's order for his or her own account instead of on the market, with the expectation of profiting from a balancing transaction at a future time. This activity is forbidden by the SEC.

bucket shop
(1) **general:** slang, an institution engaged in securities dealings of doubtful legality.
(2) **investments:** an unlicensed, dishonest business; customers place bets on the increase or decrease of stock prices on the regular exchange. No orders are filled, but profits and losses are based on the actual price movement on the exchange, with a commission going to the broker. The SEC has declared the maintenance of a bucket shop illegal.

bucking the trend: going contrary to "the crowd," that is, buying long in a declining market or selling short in a rising market.

Buck Rogers: stocks that enjoy a sudden rise in a short period of time.

budget

(1) *general:* an itemized listing, and frequently the allotment, of the amount of all estimated revenue a given business anticipates receiving; and the listing, and frequently the segregation, of the amount of all estimated costs and expenses that will be incurred in obtaining the revenue during a stated period of time. see also *cash, flexible budget.*

(2) *government:* an annual statement of the probable revenues (see estimated revenues) and expenditures of a nation for the following year. see *federal budget expenditures, federal budget receipts, general control expenditures, planning-programming-budgeting, zero-base budgeting.*

budget, cash: see *cash budget.*

budget, flexible: see *flexible budget.*

budget account: see *charge account.*

budgetary accounts: those accounts necessary to reflect budget operations and conditions, such as estimated revenues, appropriations, and encumbrances, as distinguished from *proprietary accounts.* [49]

budgetary control: a plan to control all operations in order to secure maximum profit from a minimum capital investment. This is accomplished by setting standards against which actual performance can be measured. An efficient budgetary control program not only detects inefficiencies but also definitely fixes responsibility upon the proper person or persons. [38]

budget calendar: the step-by-step listing of the component requirements of a complete budget together with the specified date on which each of the component parts are to be completed.

budget deficit: excess of expenditures over revenues.

budget document: the instrument used by the budget-making authority to present a comprehensive financial program to the appropriate body. [49]

budget loan: a mortgage loan that requires a proportionate amount of tax, insurance, and assessment to be held in escrow, in addition to interest and principal payments.

budget plan: a system of buying or making expenditures in divided equal payments over a period of time. [28]

budget surplus: excess of revenues over expenditures.

buffering: a fraud scheme for bank cards containing usage information. It consists of copying and storing magnetic stripe information, using the card, and restoring the original information. synonymous with *refreshing.*

bug

(1) *computers:* a mistake or malfunction. cf. *debug.*

(2) *computers:* any electrical or mechanical defect that interferes with the operation of the computer.

building and loan association: a cooperative or stock society for the saving, accumulation, and lending of money. Deposits in an institution of this kind may be represented by shares issued in the name of the depositor. [31]

building loan: a mortgage loan made to finance the construction of a building. It is advanced in stages as the construction work progresses. see *construction loan.* [39]

building societies: a British term for *public deposits* where a high interest rate is given to attract funds to finance home loans and property purchases. Similar to savings and loan associations in the United States.

built-in stabilizers: countercyclical factors that come into play automatically when the business cycle rises or falls (e.g., the income tax). When the cycle is rising, the volume of taxes collected rises (even though tax rates stay the same) and has a deterrent effect of further price rises; vice versa when prices fall.

bulge: a temporary, though sudden climb in the price of a stock or commodity.

bulk cargo: cargo that consists entirely of one commodity.

bulk cash: rolled or bagged coins or banded currency. [105]

bulk discount: a reduced charge for quantity or multiple purchases.

bulk filing: the filing of canceled customer checks and/or debit/credit transactions in a bulk of mass file and not by individual account number. Such items filed in a bulk manner are not returned to the customer at the time the account statement is rendered. Items are retrieved only upon request. [105]

bulk-line costs or pricing: setting prices high enough to draw forth the bulk of the production desired from the industry.

bulk sales: the sale of all or substantially all of the assets of a business. Such a sale has required procedures for the protection of the creditors of the seller.

bulk transfer: the transfer of more than 50 accounts from one branch office to one or more other branch offices in a one-week period. [55]

bulk zoning: division of an area by the

size and number of buildings, their shape, and other characteristics.

bull: a person who believes security prices will rise. [68]

bull account
(1) the total amount of securities held for anticipated appreciation.
(2) that portion of the market which believes that prices will rise.

bull campaign: an informal concentrated effort by financial interests or market operators to push security prices upward. see *bull clique.*

bull clique: an informal group of people or interests that carry out a bull campaign. see *bull campaign.*

"bullet": a borrowing that is not to be repaid gradually but in a lump sum at the end of its term. [89]

bulletproof: slang, any document with no loopholes.

bulling the market: speculator trading purporting to force the level of prices upward. Techniques include spreading rumors and entering price orders at levels somewhat above the prevailing price.

bullion: usually gold or silver, formed in ingots or bars, for use as a coin.

bullion broker: a company or person dealing in precious metals.

bullionism
(1) the monetary policy of mercantilism that called for direct regulation of transactions in foreign exchange and in precious metals in order to maintain a favorable balance in the home country. cf. *mercantilism.*
(2) followers of the monetary theories of the Bullion Report (England 1810). cf. *"currency school" principle.*

bull market: an advancing stock market. [20]

bull pool: now prohibited by law, a

form of manipulation that consisted of a formally organized fund contributed by financial interests that sought to cause prices to rise. A pool manager was chosen and an agreement entered upon that stipulated the division of profits or losses and that none of the members should make individual transactions in the particular security being manipulated.

bull position: the existing position of market optimists or bulls.

bulls: speculators who anticipate that prices will rise.

bump

(1) *general:* to dismiss a worker.

(2) *labor relations:* slang, to reassign work from an employee of lower seniority to another of higher seniority to retain the older worker and fire the younger one.

bunched securities: repeated sales of the same stock at similar or identical prices as shown repeatedly on the ticker tape of an exchange.

bunco: a swindle.

bunco game: one of a variety of methods of swindling.

Bundesbank: established in 1875, the central bank of West Germany, located in Frankfurt.

bundle: slang, a large amount of money.

bundle of rights: the legal rights that go with property ownership: the rights to sell, lease, build, mortgage, improve, and so on.

B-unit: a large trading unit whose value varies from day to day. It is composed of equal proportions of different currencies: American dollar, German mark, French franc, Swiss franc, and British pound. [105]

buoyant: advancing stock; securities that continue to climb in value.

burden: cost of manufacture or production not directly identifiable with specific products; factory overhead or service cost; indirect costs; and apportionable costs. [43]

burden of proof: the duty of proving a position taken in a court of law. Failure in the performance of that duty calls for judgment against the person on whom the duty rests. Thus, the burden of proof that the paper written is not the valid will of the testator is upon the person who contests the will. [37]

Bureau of Customs: an agency of the U.S. Treasury Department established in its present form in 1927, responsible for the collection of customs tariffs, vessel licensing and regulation, and other functions. It maintains offices in all ports of entry.

Bureau of Employment Security: a part of the U.S. Department of Labor; it is responsible for the U.S. Employment Service, providing a nationwide job placement service, training programs, and developing resolutions of manpower problems; and the Unemployment Insurance Service, providing assistance to state agencies in unemployment insurance programs and making available to the states information on job opportunities.

Bureau of Labor Standards: formerly the Division of Labor Standards; as a part of the U.S. Department of Labor, it is concerned with developing and establishing better working standards, primarily in the field of labor legislation.

Bureau of Labor Statistics (BLS): a research agency of the U.S. Department of Labor; it compiles statistics on hours of work, average hourly earnings, employment and unemployment, consumer prices, and many other variables.

Bureau of the Budget: originally part of the U.S. Treasury Department, this federal agency was responsible for the presentation of the federal budget. Now under the Executive Office of the President, the bureau is called the Office of Management and Budget. see *Office of Management and Budget.*

Bureau of the Census: a federal unit in the U.S. Department of Commerce, responsible for conducting various censuses of population, housing, business, and so on. It assists other government groups in collecting pertinent data.

burn: slang, cheating a business partner out of his profits.

business

(1) *general:* the buying and selling of goods and services.

(2) *finance:* the activity of an individual, partnership, or organization involving production, commerce, and/or service.

(3) *personnel:* one's occupation or employment.

business agent: an elected or appointed representative of one or more local unions, with responsibility for negotiating contracts, administering existing contracts, and adjusting grievances. The agent is usually a full-time unionist, as contrasted with the shop steward or committeeman. The business agent may also have organizing duties.

business credit: the privilege of deferring payment for purchases, extended to customers by the vendors of items and services.

business cycle: any interval embrac-ing alternating periods of economic prosperity and depression. see *compensatory fiscal policy, contraction, expansion, inflation, recession, recovery, reflation.*

business data processing: use of automatic data processing for a wide variety of commercial operations.

business day: any day on which the offices of the consumer's financial institution involved in an electronic fund transfer are open to the public for carrying on substantially all of its business functions. [105]

business ethics: socially accepted rules of behavior that place pressure on business executives to maintain a high sense of values and to be honest and fair in their dealings with the public.

business index (indices): a time series that presents economic data (i.e., the Federal Reserve Board's Index of Industrial Production).

business insurance trust: a trust of life insurance policy contracts created in connection with a business enterprise. The term is applied both to a trust created for the liquidation of business interests and to a trust created for credit purposes or otherwise for the benefit of a business enterprise. [32]

business life insurance: life insurance purchased by a business enterprise on the life of a member of the firm. It is often bought by partnerships to protect the surviving partners against loss caused by the death of a partner, or by a corporation to reimburse it for loss caused by the death of a key employee. [58]

business manager

(1) *general:* the individual responsible for overseeing a firm, department,

or other unit, to ensure smooth operations.

(2) *labor relations:* a business agent. see *business agent.*

business paper: see *commercial paper.*

business risk: that part of a firm's risk that is caused by the inherent risk of the firm's investment (asset) operations. It is not concerned with how the firm finances its assets.

business solvency: a situation where a company has more assets than liabilities.

business transaction: the act of business involving purchasing or selling or other exchanges in value.

business transfer payments: transfers from business to persons which are charges against business products but for which no services are rendered currently. Major items of this type are corporate gifts to nonprofit institutions and allowance for consumer bad debts.

business trust: an unincorporated business organization in which title to the property is given to trustees to hold, manage, or sell. This structure is sometimes employed when a parcel of land is divided, improved, or sold. Has been referred to as a *Massachusetts trust* or *common law trust.*

bust: a severe decrease in business activity leading to high unemployment, low incomes, and low profits.

busted convertible: a convertible whose convertibility is valueless because the underlying equity is low in price.

butterfly spread: the simultaneous purchase or sale of three futures contracts in the same or different markets. For example, buying 10 soybean fu-

tures contracts in January, and other 10 for an April delivery, and at the same moment selling (going short) 20 soybean contracts for May of the same year. Borrowing power and profits may result. In addition, any profits are held until after the tax year ends. see also *spread, straddle.*

buttonwood tree: on May 17, 1792, 24 men (the original founders of the New York Stock Exchange) declared themselves "brokers for the purchase and sale of public stocks." A buttonwood tree (sycamore) once stood at that location.

buy

(1) *general:* the quality of a purchase (e.g., a good buy).

(2) *finance:* to acquire ownership of something in exchange for a monetary consideration.

"Buy American" statutes: regulations, some dating back four decades, establishing standards for government procurement worldwide. Provisionally written into multilateral trade agreements, they typically add 6 to 12 percent to the bids of foreign suppliers in order to give domestic companies an advantage.

buy and put aside (away): a financial maxim that urges buying stocks, putting them away, and forgetting about them, with an expected result of increased profit.

buy back: buying an identical amount of the same stock that had been sold short in order to satisfy the agreement within the seller's contract and complete the sale. synonymous with *short covering;* see *bond buy-backs, short sale.*

buy down: a builder pays the bank a lump sum of money in advance to reduce the monthly interest charges on the mortgage. see *balloon, roll over.*

buyer credit: paying an exporter promptly by the overseas importer, who obtains the needed funds by means of a loan from a bank; the payment is usually made directly by a bank to an exporter.

buyers' market: a market characterized by low or falling prices, occurring when supply is greater than demand. The buyers tend to set the prices and terms of sale.

buyer's monopoly: a characteristic of the market of many sellers and one purchaser.

buyers' option: the legal right a buyer has to purchase a security, commodity, or other thing within the terms of the option contract.

buyers over: a situation of more buyers than sellers. cf. *overbought.*

buyer's right to route: the purchaser's privilege to determine the route of the shipment when the seller does not pay the freight charges. If the seller proceeds to alter the buyer's wishes, the seller is liable for any loss incurred.

buyers' strike: where purchasers of a product cease their purchases.

buyer's surplus: the difference between what buyers pay and what they would pay if they had to.

buy-in: when a seller of securities fails to make delivery of them within the period stipulated. The purchaser can then buy them elsewhere if he or she had given prior written notice to the seller, and may charge the seller all costs and differences involved. cf. *sell-out.*

buying basis: the difference between the cost of a cash commodity and a future sold to hedge it.

buying forward: purchase of an item in large quantities in anticipation of future demand. [105]

buying hedge: a hedge that is initiated by taking a long position in the futures market equal to the amount of the cash commodity that is eventually needed. see also *hedge.*

buying in: when a seller does not hand over his securities at the expected time, the purchaser obtains shares wherever he or she can find them, and the seller becomes responsible for all added expenses.

buying long: buying stocks, bonds, or commodities outright with the expectation of holding them for a rise in price and then selling. cf. *selling short.*

buying on a shoestring: acquiring stocks or commodities with the minimum margin.

buying on balance: occurs when a stockbroker's orders to buy exceed his or her cumulative orders to sell.

buying on margin: purchasing securities without paying the full price immediately. Margin regulations are closely controlled by the SEC. see *margin, marginal trading, margin call.*

buying on scale: a procedure for purchasing securities where the broker is told to purchase a given number of shares at given intervals of a price decline. Since the buyer does not know how low the price can drop, by buying on scale as the price declines, his average cost per share also declines. synonymous with *scale buying.*

buying order: instructions given to a broker or agent to purchase or sell securities or commodities.

buying outright: paying with cash only; buying an item with 100 percent cash. In securities, the opposite of margin.

buying power: money available for spending and consumption. A combination of liquid assets plus available credit.

buying rate: the publicized quotation for buying such things as foreign exchange, commodities, and bills of exchange which a bank or other buyer employs to inform the trader of his desire to buy.

buying signals: a progression of prices on a stock chart that exceeds the normal range. It is used as an indication that self-stabilizing forces will soon respond to cause a reversal in trend. [105]

buying the intermarket spread: an investment strategy involving taking a hedge position in two securities simultaneously. If the speculator believes that banks are going to come under increased pressure, buying a future contract for Treasury bills and, at the same time, selling short a futures contract for bank CDs. see *intermarket spread*. cf. *selling the intermarket spread*.

buying to minimum inventory: the policy of adding to inventory of a specific good only when the inventory has fallen to a stated minimum.

buy on bid: a strategy whereby an individual can purchase a listed stock from an odd-lot trader who is selling at the bid price instead of waiting to execute an odd-lot sale following the next round-lot sale, which may be an indefinite time.

buy on close (or opening): to buy at the end (or beginning) of the session at a price within the closing or (opening range). [2]

buy on the offer: a strategy of purchasing an odd lot, thus avoiding the delay that might be involved with a market order. Instead of waiting for the next round-lot sale to establish the price of the odd-lot transaction, a buy on the offer order is executed at the lowest quoted asking price plus the odd-lot differential.

buy order: order to a broker, investment representative, bank, or manufacturer, to purchase a specified quantity of security or item.

buy out: to purchase all the assets, stock, and so on, of an ongoing organization; to purchase the interest in a firm that is owned by another.

buy-sell agreement: an agreement wherein owners of a business arrange to transfer their respective ownership interests upon the death of one, or upon some other event, to provide continued control of the business or other desired end. [37]

buy ticket: a form prepared in multiple copies, used by the investment department to instruct the order department to purchase a security. [37]

BV: see *book value*.

BW: see *bid wanted*.

by-bidder: a person who makes fictitious bids at an auction, on behalf of the owner or seller of the items, to obtain a higher price or to encourage further bidding.

by-laws: rules accepted by board members of a firm or other organization for governance. Such rules cannot be in opposition to laws imposed by government.

by-product: the residue arising at various stages in production of a principal commodity (e.g., by-products of the meat-packing industry are glue, bone, hair, etc.).

by-product method of cost accounting: a system of allocating costs between a principal product or products and a by-product or by-products. The main feature of the system is the initial costing of the by-product at the point where it first appears separately on some arbitrary basis (usually zero cost) and charging to the main product or products all other costs up to this point. Net proceeds of by-products are usually considered to be reductions of the cost of the main product.

by tale: see *tale*.

byte: a sequence of adjacent binary digits operated on as a unit and usually shorter than a computer word.

C
- (1) see *cash.*
- (2) see *cent.*
- (3) the currency component of money. [81]

C$: Canadian dollar.

CA
- (1) see *capital account.*
- (2) see *capital appreciation.*
- (3) see *capital assets.*
- (4) see *cash account.*
- (5) see *chartered accountant.*
- (6) see *current account.*
- (7) see *current assets.*
- (8) see *custodian account.*

cabbage: slang, paper money, banknotes, or other funds.

cabinet crowd: the section of the bond trading unit of the New York Stock exchanges that handles trading in active bonds. synonymous with *book crowd* and *inactive crowd.*

cable: slang, the dollar/sterling spot exchange rate.

cable rate: the charge for a cable transfer, contrasted with the check (demand draft) rate, and the rate for 30-, 60-, and 90-day bills of exchange. The cable rate is at all times higher than the check rate. see *check rate.*

cable transfer: see *transfer.*

CAD: see *cash against documents.*

cadastre: the official inventory of the real property in a community, the cadastre is used for determining taxes and its appraised value.

caeteris paribus: latin for "other things being equal." The usual assumption in economic theory under which only a few phenomena are permitted to vary at one time; to facilitate tracing the effects of the variations.

CAF: see *C&F.*

Cafeteria plan: an approach to employee benefits whereby participants choose from a menu offering day care and legal, medical, and dental coverage. see *zebra plan.*

calculating machine: a machine designed to make mathematical calculations in addition to straightforward addition and subtraction.

calculator: a device that performs arithmetic operations based on data and instructions placed manually or on punched cards.

calendar: in securities, the dates of forthcoming new issues.

calendar spreading: the simultaneous purchase and sale of options within the same class having different expiration dates.

calendar year experience: experience developed on premium and loss transactions occurring during the 12 calendar months beginning January 1, irrespective of the effective dates of the policies on which these transactions took place.

call
(1) *banking:* to demand payment of a loan secured by collateral because of failure by a borrower to comply with the terms of the loan.
(2) *computers:* the branching or transferring of control to a specified closed subroutine.
(3) *finance:* to demand payment of an installment of the price of bonds or stocks that have been subscribed.
(4) *investments:* see *calls.*

callable
(1) *banking:* that which must be paid on request, as a loan.
(2) *finance:* a bond issue or preferred stock, all or part of which may be redeemed by the issuing corporation under definite conditions, before maturity.

callable bond: see *bond, callable.*

callable capital: that portion of a company's capital not paid up and on which the firm's directors can call for payments to be made.

callable preferred stock: preferred stock which can be called in for payment at a price stated on the certificate by the corporation at its option.

call-back: the act of reading back posting media to the postings, or checks making up a list to the listing of the items. One person reads the amounts to another person, who is checking the "run" for accuracy. Call-backs are often made when a balance or settlement is not accomplished, the call back being one form of proving the accuracy of a run of items. [10]

call date: the date on which a bond may be redeemed before maturity at the option of the issuer. [52]

called bond: see *bond, called.*

called preferred stock: preferred stock, containing call provisions, which is redeemed by a corporation. [37]

call feature: a provision on a senior security (debt or preferred stock) that allows the firm to buy back the security at a prespecified price prior to maturity.

call loan: a loan payable on request. cf. *day loan.*

call money: currency lent by banks, usually to stock exchange brokers, for which payment can be demanded at any time.

call money market: an activity of brokers and dealers having call funds secured by stock exchange collateral and government securities to meet their money needs to cover customers' margin accounts and their own securities inventory.

call of more: the right to call again for the same amount of goods previously bought. Used primarily in the purchase of options.

call option: giving the option buyer the right to buy 100 shares of stock at a stated price at any time before a deadline, at which point the option expires.

call premium
(1) the premium payable by the issuer if he or she redeems a callable bond before maturity. It will be fixed in

the indenture and normally decreases as maturity approaches.

(2) the premium payable by an issuer when he or she redeems, if appropriate, preferred stock at an amount in excess of par or stated value. [43]

call price: the price at which a callable bond is redeemable; used in connection with preferred stocks and debt securities having a fixed claim. It is the price that an issurer must pay to voluntarily retire such securities. Often the call price exceeds the par or liquidating price in order to compensate the holder of the called security for his or her loss of income and investment position resulting from the call. [30]

call protection: convertibles issued in recent years offering protection of two to three years. After that, the company can force conversion of the bonds into stock. It usually does so when the convertible trades 25 to 30 percent above its call price. While the protection is in place, though, the convertible's price has unlimited potential and will continue to trade at a premium over the conversion value. If a bond is called, the investors runs the risk of losing some accrued interest.

call provision: the call provision describes the terms under which a bond may be redeemed by the issuer in whole or in part prior to maturity. [52]

call purchase: the buying of commodities when the seller has some option of pricing at a later date within a given range of the existing price. cf. *call sale.*

call report: agencies such as the Comptroller of the Currency and Federal Reserve Banks require periodic status reports from banks under their jurisdiction. The precise date is not given in advance so as to minimize manipulation of the information.

calls: an option contract that entitles the holder to buy a number of shares of the underlying security at a stated price on or before a fixed expiration date. [5] see *puts and calls.*

call sale: an agreement for the sale of a commodity where the price is set by the purchaser in the future. The setting of the price is at the "call" of the purchaser and is within a few points above or below the price of a stated future on the day of fixing the price of the contract. Opposite of *call purchase.*

cambism: engaging in the sale of foreign monies.

cambist

(1) *finance:* an individual who buys and sells foreign currencies.

(2) *international:* a handbook in which foreign country funds are converted into currency tables of the country for which the handbook is issued.

cambistry: the study of exchange of foreign currencies, with emphasis on identifying the least expensive procedure for remitting to a foreign nation.

Cambridge equation: see *cash balance equation (exchange form).*

cameralism: synonymous with *kameralism.*

Can.: see *cancellation.*

Canadian Bank Act: see *Bank Act, Canada.*

Canc.: see *cancellation.*

cancel: to mark or perforate; make void. [61]

canceled checks: checks that have been paid and charged to the depositor's account; then stamped or perforated with the date of the payment and the drawee bank's name or clearinghouse number. These checks are retained in the files of the bank until a statement of the depositor's account is sent to him or her. [31]

canceling machine: a machine used for canceling checks; passbooks; and other records in a bank. [10]

cancellation: the annulment or rendering void of any bank instrument upon payment; the termination of a policy or bond before its expiration, by either the bank or other party. Almost invariably, the contract states the type of notice necessary before cancellation becomes effective.

cancellation, pro rata: cancellation with a return of premium proportionate to the unexpired period for which premiums were paid. [12]

cancellation, short-rate: cancellation upon request of an insured, with a return of less than the proportionate amount. [12]

cancellation clause: a provision giving one or both parties the right to cancel the agreement in the event of a specified occurrence.

cancellation evidence: a terminated policy, or any legal notice of cancellation.

"cannibalism": in banking; occurs when customers transfer funds from passbook and other low-yielding accounts into accounts that carry interest rates at close to money market levels.

canons of taxation: the principles advanced by Adam Smith that taxes (a) should be in proporation to revenue received, (b) should be certain and not arbitary, (c) should be levied at a time convenient for taxpayers, and (d) should cost as little as possible to collect.

canvass: to call on prospective customers in person or by telephone to sell

banking services to determine interest or gather information.

Cap.
(1) see *capital.*
(2) see *capitalization.*

capacity
(1) *banking:* the largest amount of insurance a bank will accept on one risk.
(2) *finance:* one of the three elements of credit.
(3) *law:* competency or legal authority. cf. *non compos mentis.*

capacity costs: synonymous with *fixed cost.*

capias ad respondendum: a judicial writ commencing actions at law (e.g., the order directing the sheriff to place the defendant in custody).

capital
(1) *general:* the amount invested in a venture. see *equity, fixed capital.*
(2) *banking:* describes a long-term debt plus owners' equity.
(3) *finance:* the net assets of a firm, partnership, and so on, including the original investment, plus all gains and profits.

capital account: an account maintained in the name of the owner or owners of a business and indicating his or their equity in that business—usually at the close of the last accounting period.

capital adequacy rules: federal regulations that require large banks to maintain capital equal to a certain percentage of their assets, which consist principally of loans.

capital and surplus: found in a condensed statement of a bank's condition showing the bank's financial status. The two accounts, capital and surplus, are brought together because the surplus account of a bank corresponds to capital surplus, and pays no dividends.

capital appreciation: an increase or other appreciation in a capital asset's value.

capital asset pricing model (CAPM): a model used to estimate the required rate of return (discount rate) for an asset. It is based on the notion that the required rate of return equals the risk-free interest rate plus a beta-related risk premium.

capital assets: a collective term that includes all fixed assets, consisting of furniture and fixtures, land, buildings, machinery, and so on: as differentiated from property consumed; that is, property that yields income or reduces expenses. cf. *capital expenditure, capital investment.*

capital budget: a budget that itemizes expenditures to be used for building and for purchasing capital goods, and which identifies the source of the funds required to meet the expenditures.

capital charges: sums required to satisfy interest upon, and amortization of, monies invested in an enterprise. [62]

capital consumption: that portion of a firm's investment used in part or in its entirety in the process of production.

capital cost: the cost of improvements extending the useful life of property and/or adding to its value.

capital distribution: see *liquidating dividend.*

capital expenditure: see *expenditure.*

capital expenditures budget: the estimate of cash expenditures for new equipment purchases or for other fixed assets during a future fiscal period.

capital flight: a large transfer of money from one nation to another as a hedge against poor economic or political conditions.

capital formation: the development or expansion of capital goods as a result of savings.

capital gain (or loss)
(1) *general:* the gain or loss from the sale of a capital asset above or below the cost or appraised value.
(2) *finance:* the difference (gain or loss) between the market or book value at purchase or other acquisition and that realized from the sale or disposition of a capital asset. see *long-term capital gain (loss).*

capital gains distribution: a distribution to investment company shareholders from net long-term capital gains realized by a *regulated investment company* on the sale of portfolio securities. [30]

capital gains tax: a tax that is placed on the profit from selling a capital asset, often stock.

capital goods: items ordinarily treated as long-term investment (capitalized) because of substantial value and life (e.g., industrial machinery).

capital growth: an increase in market value of securities; a long-term objective pursued by many investment companies. [23]

capital improvement program: see *long-term budget.*

capital intensive: characterized by the need to use additional capital to increase productivity or profits.

capital investment: a collective term representing the amount invested in capital or fixed assets or in long-term securities, as contrasted with funds invested in current assets or short-term securities. Generally speaking, capital investments include all funds invested in assets that during the normal course of business are not expected to be returned during the coming fiscal period.

capitalism: an economic system based on freedoms of ownership, production, exchange, acquisition, work, movement, and open competition. see *laissez-faire.*

capital issues: stocks and bonds that are more or less permanent and fixed, as contrasted with short-term notes and accounts payable.

capitalist

(1) *general:* an individual investor in a business.

(2) *finance:* in Marxist terms, an individual who owns or shares in the ownership of the means of production and employs others. cf. *people's capitalism, private enterprise.*

capitalization

(1) *general:* the sum of all monies invested in a firm by the owner or owners; total liabilities.

(2) *banking:* the method of appraising property by deducting the estimated normal expenses from the amount of income the property is expected to yield. The resulting net profit does not necessarily represent the actual property value.

(3) *finance:* the total value of all securities in a firm.

capitalization of income: estimating the existing investment value of property by lowering anticipated future income to its present worth.

capitalization rate

(1) the relationship of income to capital investment or value, expressed as a percentage.

(2) the (percentage) rate at which an anticipated future income stream is discounted to present worth (i.e., market value). [6]

capitalization rate(s), basis for split: justification of the use of split rates is confined to two basic assumptions, as follows. (a) Investment in land and investment in building represent different degrees of risk and, therefore, require the application of a different rate in the capitalization of the income attributed to each: (i) land value is presumed to be stable and to earn a constant return to perpetuity; (ii) terminable lives of buildings require a higher rate to ensure return of capital investment within their estimated economic life, in addition to a return on the investment or capital value. (b) Income attributable to land and return to building are predictable, separable, and identifiable. [6]

capitalization rate(s), methods of selection of: a band of investment, sometimes designated synthetic, in which the current mortgage rate and rate for equity capital are combined in the same proportion as each (mortgage and equity) bears to the total value estimate. The accuracy of this method depends upon the correctness of the appraiser's estimate of the availability of mortgage money at the rate and long-value ratio set forth, and the degree to which the rate of return on equity capital has been verified by reference to comparable sales. [6]

capitalization rate(s), net

(1) the rate of interest expected to be earned on an investment.

(2) the rate of interest at which anticipated future net income is discounted, exclusive of provision for recapture of capital investment. [6]

capitalization rate(s), over all: net (capitalization) rate plus provision for recapture of total investment (i.e., land and improvements). This is the rate used in the property residual technique and is applied to net income before depreciation. [6]

capitalization rate(s), safe: the net rate of return on a virtually riskless and completely liquid investment, generally accepted as the savings bank interest rate or interest being paid on long-term government bonds, in a stable market; usually known as the *safe rate.* [6]

capitalization rate(s), source of: the market is the only source of capitalization rates which provides provable support for those rates. [6]

capitalization rate(s), split: in the capitalization process denoting an application of different rates to portions of total net income presumed to be earned by fractional parts of an improved property—for example, one rate applied to claimed earnings of land and another applied to net income said to be earned by the building. [6]

capitalization ratios: the percent that each of the following or its components is of total capitalization: bonds, other long-term debt, preferred stock, common stock and retained income, capital surplus, and premium on capital stock. [3]

capitalize
(1) *general:* to classify a cost as a long-term investment item instead of a charge to current operations.
(2) *banking:* to divide income by an interest rate to obtain principal.
(3) *finance:* to convert into cash that which can be used in production; to issue shares to represent an investment.

capitalized cost: the original cost of an asset plus the net charges incurred to prepare or complete it for its stated use.

capitalized surplus: the transfer of a corporation's paid in or earned surplus to capital stock by issuing a stock dividend; by increasing the par or stated value of the capital stock, or by simple resolution of the board of directors. [105]

capitalized value: the asset value (principal) of a given number of income dollars determined on the basis of an assumed rate of return. For example, the capitalized value of a $500 perpetual income at a rate of 5 percent is $10,000 (obtained by dividing $500 by 0.05). [67]

capitalized-value standard: the amount obtained by dividing the annual earnings by a stipulated interest rate. Used to determine the value of a business. synonymous with *earning-capacity standard.*

capital levy: any tax placed on capital. This tax is usually quite small, from $1/4$ or $1/2$ of 1 percent per year.

capital liability: a fixed liability (e.g., a corporate bond) that is created to acquire fixed assets or for purposes of funding.

capital loan: a loan that cannot be repaid without disposing of capital assets, in contrast to a loan, for example, to purchase merchandise, the sale of which will provide funds to repay the loan. [50]

capital loss: see *long-term capital loss.*

capital market: a place or system in which the requirements for capital of a business can be satisfied.

capital movements: the shifts in indebtedness and in gold stocks serving as balancing items when determining the international payments of a nation.

capital net worth: the total assets of a business less the liabilities.

capital outlay: expenditures for the acquisition of or addition to fixed assets; included are amounts for replacements and major alterations but not for repair. cf. *operating expense.*

capital paid in: the amount paid in for Federal Reserve Bank stock owned by member banks. [40]

capital program: see *long-term budget.*

capital rating: a rating given by a mercantile organization when appraising the net worth of a firm.

capital rationing: a situation where the firm's investment budget is not large enough to permit accepting all economically desirable projects.

capital readjustments: any fundamental, voluntary changes in the capital structure of a firm, involving the modification of the debt.

capital rent: the price paid for the use of improvements permanently affixed to land.

capital requirement: the total monetary investment needed to create and operate any business.

capital resources: resources of a fixed or permanent character, such as land and buildings, which cannot ordinarily be used to meet expenditures. [49]

capital risk: a risk created when a bank has to pay out funds to a counterpart in the deal without knowing whether the counterpart is able to meet its side of the bargain. cf. *delivery risk.*

capital stock: the specified amount of stock a corporation may sell as authorized by the state granting the corporate charter. If the stock has a stated value

per share, such value is known as par value. see *common stock.*

capital stock discount and expense: a balance sheet account. The excess of par value over the price paid in by the shareholder is capital stock discount. Expenses incurred in connection with the issuance and sale of capital stock which are not properly chargeable to "organization," and which have not been charged to "surplus" are included in capital stock discount and expense. [3]

capital stock subscribed: the temporary capital account containing a record of capital stock subscribed for but as yet not issued because the subscriptions have not been fully paid.

capital stock tax: a tax on the stock of a corporation usualy computed as a percentage of par value or assigned value. A special form of capital stock tax was the declared value capital stock tax, which was combined with an excess profits tax.

capital structure: the distribution of a corporation's capital among its several component parts, such as stock, bonds, and surplus. [39]

capital sum: the original amount of an estate, fund, mortgage, bond, or other financial dealing, together with accrued sums not yet recognized as income.

capital surplus: the excess of assets over liabilities plus the value given to issued capital stock, less amounts in paid-in or earned surplus.

capital turnover: the rate at which an organization's assets are converted into cash. synonymous with *investment turnover.*

CAPM: see *capital asset pricing model.*

captive: a mine or plant; the product of

which is used entirely by a parent company instead of being sold to the public. A large user of coal, cement, paper, or oil which is not in the business of marketing these products but it is a large user of them, may own and operate captive mines, wells, or mills.

captive insurance company: an insurance firm owned by one or more companies which are not insurance firms and which undertakes some or all of its owners' insurance business.

captive warehouse: synonymous with *warehouse; private.*

carat: the unit of weight for gems equal to approximately 3.2 grains; a twenty-fourth part of pure gold.

carbon plan: a variation of the single posting plan wherein a carbonized ledger is created as a carbon copy of the original statement. [10]

card, column: lines of a punched card that are used for punching holes, with each column representing a specific symbol in data processing.

card, computer: usually, the keypunched card used in automatic data processing.

card, hopper: the portion of a card-processing machine that holds the cards to be processed and makes them available to a card-feed mechanism.

card, punch: a card that has been or will be punched with holes to represent letters, digits, or characters.

card-activated nite drop: a separate machine device used for deposits (primarily commercial) after normal banking hours. This device can be attached to the electronics controlling an ATM at the same location. The plastic card can be coded to allow a special transaction which can activate the de-

vice, thus allowing a deposit and providing a receipt for the customer. [105]

card base: the total number of plastic cards outstanding by an issuing institution. This can be expressed as a percentage of the total personal deposit account base. [105]

card carrier: see *card mailer.*

cardholder: any person to whom a credit card is issued for personal, family, household, agricultural, business, or commercial purposes. [105]

cardholder account: record kept by the bank on each account for which a card has been issued. [105]

cardholder accounting: the position of debits, credits, adjustments, and payments to cardholder accounts for the purpose of accounting and reporting to the cardholder. [105]

cardholder agreement: written understanding stating the terms and conditions of card usage and payment by the cardholder. [105]

cardholder bank: the bank that has issued a bank card to an individual. The term is frequently used in conjunction with the intercharge arrangements to identify the card or issuing bank. [105]

cardholder base: the total number of cardholder accounts belonging to a specific bank. [105]

cardholder history file: record containing historical data on each cardholder account; minimum information: current balance, credit limit, high credit, and delinquency experience. [105]

cardholder master file: a record of all cardholder accounts. [105]

cardholder profile: describing the demographics of a bank's cardholder base or a survey panel of that base. [105]

cardholder statement: the billing summary produced and mailed at specific intervals, usually monthly. [105]

card imprint: printing appearing on a sales draft, credit voucher, or cash advance draft. A mechanical device (imprinter) is used to produce the imprint. It includes the embossed characters of the credit card and the merchant or bank name and identification numbers. [105]

card issuer

(1) the financial institution that authorizes the issuance of a card for which the institution; or its agent, carries the liability for the use of the card. The issuer retains full authority over the use of the card by the person to whom the card is issued.

(2) any bank or organization that issues, or causes to be issued, bank cards to those who apply for them. [105]

card mailer: a carrier used in mailing to the cardholder a card which may contain specific instructions for the cardholder regarding the card use.

card network: the geographic area in which the cards issued by a particular institution have some matter of acceptability. [105]

card pick-up: an order to have outside agencies, merchants, or bank personnel pick up a credit card that is being misused. [105]

card reissue: process of preparing and distributing bank cards to cardholders whose cards have expired or will expire in the near future. [105]

card reproducer: a device that reproduces a punch card by punching another identical card.

card security number (CSN): a hidden or difficult-to-reproduce number on or in the plastic of a card for fraud deterrence purposes. [105]

care of securities: the action of an investor following the purchase and payment for a security.

Carey Street: British term for *bankruptcy*.

CARICOM: founded in 1973; headquartered in Guyana, the Caribbean Community and Common Market.

carnet: a document of international customs permitting temporary duty-free import of specific items into certain nations. see *admission temporaire*.

carriage paid: see *freight paid to*.

carrier: the bank's insurance department that writes and fulfills the conditions of the insurance policy.

carrier's lien: the carrier's right to hold the shipper's property as security until the shipping obligation is paid. cf. *general lien*.

carry

(1) *general:* to enter or post.

(2) *banking:* the interest cost of financing the holding of securities.

(3) *banking:* to provide the difference between a partial down payment and the total price of a product or service.

(4) *computer:* a condition occurring during the operation of addition when the total of two digits in the same column equals or exceeds the numbering system (e.g., when 2 is exceeded in a binary system).

(5) *finance:* the act of a broker in providing money to customers who trade by margin accounts; to hold stocks; to be *long* of stock.

carryback: in federal income taxes, the amount of a taxpayer's business loss, subject to adjustments, deductible from the net income of three preceding years. cf. *carryover.*

carry forward

(1) *general:* to transfer the balance of an account from one balance sheet to another.

(2) *federal income taxes:* to declare an item of expense as minimal until a later time period when revenue is received.

carry income (loss): the difference between the interest yield of a dealer's portfolio and the cost of funds which support that portfolio. [90]

carrying broker: any broker or commission house maintaining a client's account.

carrying charge

(1) *general:* the continuing cost of owning or holding any property or items.

(2) *banking:* the amount of charges added to the price of a service to compensate for deferred payment.

(3) *finance:* the fee charged by investment brokers for handling margin accounts.

carrying market: a market in which more distant positions are quoted at a premium over the nearby positions, and where this premium is high enough to compensate for the carrying charges. [11]

carrying-over day: any postponed day of delivery. Used on the London Stock Exchange. see *backwardation.*

carrying value: the value of a fixed asset remaining after its accumulated depreciation reserve has been deducted from its original depreciable cost. [49]

carryover: in federal income taxes, the amount of a taxpayer's loss that was not absorbed as a carryback; may be

deducted as taxable income of succeeding years. see *carryback.*

carryover clause: a clause to protect a broker for a specified time, usually beyond the expiration date of the property listing.

carryover funds: monies authorized in a particular budgetary period which an administrative agency can encumber and then spend in a succeeding budgetary period.

cars: slang, used by commodity traders as a synonym for the term "contracts."

carte a memoire: a credit card developed in France which has an integrated circuit that enables a user to record more than 100 transactions on the card, updating the balance each time without the need to communicate with a central computer. see *"smart" credit cards.*

cartel: a group of separate business organizations that have agreed to institute approaches to alter competition by influencing prices, production, or marketing. Rarely as effective as a monopoly. see *monopoly, oligopoly;* cf. *consortium.*

Carter bonds: see *bond, Carter.*

carve-out: a means of financing by transfering income from future production or selling such advance earnings to another party for expanding credit.

case note: slang, a $1 bill.

case of need: when an exporter draws a bill on a foreign importer, he or she gives instructions "Refer to XYZ Co. in case of need." XYZ Co. is usually an agent or subsidiary, with power to act, or merely serves as a source of advice. Should something go wrong, the bank collecting the bill proceeds to contact the agent.

Cash.: see *cashier.*

cash: an all-embracing term associated with any business transaction involving the handling of currency and coins.

cash account: a cash basis account, where all purchases are completely paid for. cf. *margin account.*

cash advance: cash loan obtained by a cardholder through presentation of his or her credit card at a bank office, or by mail request. [105]

cash advance balance: that portion of the total balance representing any unpaid portion of cash advance loans previously issued. [105]

cash advance draft: a document executed by a cardholder that shows a cash advance obtained through using a bank card. [105]

cash advance reimbursement fee: a fee paid or received as compensation for granting a cash advance to a cardholder. [105]

cash against documents (CAD): when the purchaser must make payment for items before the receipt of the shipping papers that will give him or her control of the items once they are surrendered to him or her.

cash assets: assets described on a financial statement represented by actual cash on hand, and the total of bank deposits.

cash audit: an examination of cash transactions during a given time period to determine whether all received cash has been documented.

cash balance: all cash on hand.

cash balance equation (exchange form): in monetary theory, the cash balance equation is $P = M/KT$, where P is the average price level of T, M the quantity of money, T the total business transactions, and K the fraction of receipts held in idle cash and hence $1/V$ in the Fisher equation. synonymous with *Cambridge equation.*

cash basis: the system of accounting under which revenues are accounted for only when received in cash, and expenditures are accounted for only when paid. [49]

cash before delivery (CBD): payment is required prior to delivery of goods.

cash board: in a commodity exchange, the area of blackboard used for the recording of sales of cash commodity contracts. see *spot commodity.*

cashbook: a book of original entry where the cash receipts journal and the cash payments journal are put together, forming one book.

cash break-even point: assuming a plant organized for a given ideal volume of output, if units of output are put on the x axis and total dollars on the y axis, the cash break-event point is the intersection of the total cash revenue curve with the cash outlay curve (excluding interest and dividends).

cash budget: a schedule of expected cash receipts and disbursements.

cash bus: a cabinet on wheels where tellers store cash in the teller's cage or wicket during the day. This cabinet has sufficient room for the cash till and also storage under lock and key for packaged specie money that may be required for making change in large orders. The teller wheels the cash bus into the vault after balancing the cash at the end of the day. [10]

cash buying: the purchase of securities or commodities outright for immediate delivery of the item.

cash card: a card given by a retailer or store owner to a customer guaranteeing a discount for a cash payment. It is a substitute for credit cards; some merchants give cash-paying customers up to 8 percent discount.

cash commodity: a specific lot of a commodity bought through a cash transaction for immediate delivery, though delivery may be deferred.

cash credit: the British custom of allowing check overdrafts to a specified amount.

cash credit discount: in installment cash credit, the discount is the charge for the credit service which is deducted from the total amount of the loan before the borrower receives the balance in cash. [55]

cash delivery: same-day delivery of traded securities.

cash discount: a deduction from the selling price permitted by the seller for merchandise sold on credit, represented in terms of a percentage; made to encourage the prompt payment of the invoice covering the goods or services purchased.

cash dispenser: a machine capable of giving out cash representing a withdrawal from a deposit account or an extension of credit. synonymous with *ATM, cashomat.* see also *unattended banking terminal.*

cash dividend: declared dividends payable in cash, usually by check.

cash earnings: the profits or net income of an organization. These earnings include all depreciation and amortization accruals.

cashed check: check accepted by a bank in exchange for cash. Usually such an item can be identified by a teller's stamp or cash-out symbol. [31]

cash flow: the reported net income of a corporation, plus amounts charged off for depreciation, depletion, amortization, and extraordinary charges to reserves, which are bookkeeping deductions and not actually paid out in cash. Knowledge of these factors results in a better understanding of a firm's ability to pay dividends. cf. *net cash flow.*

cash flow statement: a statement of the income and payments of a company. [105]

cash forecasting: the projection of the cash needs of a company during an upcoming acounting period. This is done to determine the borrowing requirements during a specific future period. [105]

cash grain: grain for immediate delivery. synonymous with *spot grain.*

cashier: a bank's officer or representative responsible for the custody of the bank's assets, and whose signature is required on official documents.

cashier's account: the ledger account of a bank that is primarily used to record cashier's checks.

cashier's check: a bank's own check signed by a cashier, becoming a direct obligation of the bank. Upon issue to a customer, it becomes a loan and a debit in the cashier's account. It differs from a certified check in that it is drawn against the funds of the bank itself, not against the funds found in a specific depositor's account. cf. *certified check, register(ed) check.* synonymous with *official check, treasurer's check.*

cash-ins: redemptions of investment company securities.

cash in the chips: slang, to conclude a business transaction; to sell one's share of a company.

cash in vault: coin and currency actually held by the banks on their own premises. [40]

cash items: items listed in a firm's statement that are the equivalent of cash, such as bank deposits, government bonds, and marketable securities.

cash letter: a transit check with listing tapes, transmitting items from one bank to another for collection. Frequently, the items contained in the cash letter are grouped into several batches with a listing tape attached to each batch. The totals are recapped on the transmittal form letter. Generally, these are associated with mail deposits received from other banks. [31]

cash letter of credit: a letter addressed by a bank to its correspondent bank to make available to the party named in the letter, funds up to a specified amount within certain time limitations. The sum named in the letter is deposited with the bank before the letter is issued, hence the designation *cash letter of credit*. [10]

cash loan: see *policy loan*.

cash management: payment and collection services to corporate customers to speed collection of receivables, control payments, and efficiently manage cash. [105]

cash management account (CMA): a bank-type development of Merrill Lynch in partnership with Bank One of Ohio, based in Columbus, where affluent clients are offered a Visa credit card and checking to draw against their investment balances. The account was initially offered in 206 of Merrill Lynch's 382 offices in the United States.

Cash Management Bill: U.S. Treasury bills introduced in 1975 to raise funds quickly for a short period; ranging from 9 to 20 days to maturity, with notice of their offering given up to 10 days ahead. All payment must be made in federal funds.

cash market: as contrasted with the *futures market*; synonymous with *spot market*.

cash method of accounting: a system used especially in computing income tax, in which income is not credited until it is actually or constructively received and expenses are not charged until they have been paid; to be distinguished from the accrual method, in which income is credited when the legal right to the income occurs and expenses are charged when the legal liability becomes enforceable. [105]

cash method of handling purchases: the technique whereby purchases are recorded only when they are paid, by recording the invoice in the cash payments journal.

cashomat: see *cash dispenser*.

cash on delivery (COD): describes any purchase made with the expectation that the item(s) will be paid for on delivery. cf. *franco delivery*.

cash on hand: cash drawer money, vault cash, and demand deposits in commercial banks or regional Federal Home Loan Banks. [59]

cash over: a general ledger account to which tellers' cash overages are credited. see *cash over and short*. [10]

cash over and short: the difference between the cash on hand and the balance of the cash account or cashbook. When the cash on hand is over the balance of the cash account or cashbook, the cash is over; when less than that of the balance, the cash is short.

cash paid receipt: receipt given to a

customer when making a bank card payment in cash. It contains the community office number, date of payment, and teller's initials. [105]

cash payment: a payment made by cash at a community office. [105]

cash payments journal: a special journal in which all cash payments, and only cash payments, are entered.

cash position: the percentage of cash to the total net assets; the net amount after the deduction of current liabilities.

cash price: the current price of the cash commodity of a designated quality available for immediate delivery.

cash receipts journal: a special journal in which all cash receipts, and only cash receipts, are entered.

cash refund annuity: a life annuity providing that a lump-sum payment will be made to a beneficiary in an amount equal to the excess, if any, of the amount paid by the annuitant toward the annuity over the sum of the annuity payments received by the annuitant to the date of death. [52]

cash register: a machine used to provide an immediate record of every cash transaction by having a convenient place for sorting and keeping the funds used in daily transactions.

cash register totals: daily totals for all transactions; including cash sales, charge sales, receipts on account, and so on.

cash release ticket: a slip either handwritten or machine printed by which a teller charges himself for the amount of cash on a deposit. [10]

cash report: a statement, prepared on a daily basis, showing the cash position of the organization for each day.

cash reserve
(1) *banking:* requirements for banks to maintain a sufficient portion of deposits as required by federal law.
(2) *finance:* funds readily available to be converted into cash in an emergency. see entries under *liquid.*

cash sale
(1) *general:* the surrender of cash at the time of sale.
(2) *finance:* a transaction on the floor of an exchange that calls for delivery of the securities the same day. In "regular way" trades, the seller is to deliver on the fifth business day.

cash short: a general ledger account to which tellers' cash shortages are charged. [10]

cash statement: a classified summary of cash receipts and disbursements.

cash substitution ticket: see *cash release ticket.*

cash surrender value: the sum total of money paid by a bank upon cancellation of its life insurance policy. see *surrender value.*

cash ticket: a slip or ticket used as a substitute for cash included in a deposit. The teller verifies and retains the cash, recording the amount on the cash ticket. [31]

cash till: a tray built with compartment bins to help tellers sort and have ready for easy access the various denominations of currency. [10]

cash trade: any transaction in securities and commodities paid in full with cash for immediate delivery of goods. see *for cash.*

cash value: describes the amount available to the owner of a life insurance policy when the policy is surrendered to the insurer.

cash with fiscal agent: deposits with fiscal agents, such as commercial banks, for the payment of matured bonds and interest. [49]

casting: slang, any coin.

cast up: to add up a total, as "to cast up an account." synonymous with *footing.*

casual forecasting: predictions on the future activity of bank products or services which can be made if enough data have been collected to determine the "cause" of success or failure. [105]

casualty loss: property loss resulting from a sudden, unexpected, or unusual cause, such as fire, storm, shipwreck, or theft.

cathode ray tube (CRT): a visual display device that translates the data from a computer memory and visually presents the information in human language form. The CRT enables batches or blocks of information in memory to be instantly accessed, read, and displayed on a screen. In an on-line or real-time data-processing system, the device permits instant or impromptu display of any desired information.

cats and dogs
(1) *general:* items that do not have satisfactory sales turnover and accumulate inventory.
(2) *finance:* highly speculative stocks.

causa mortis: see *gift causa mortis.*

cause of action: created by intrusion on a person's legal right by a breach of contract or of a legal duty toward one's person or property.

caveat
(1) *finance:* a notice to cease payment.
(2) *law:* "let him beware" (Latin); a warning. A notice filed by an interested party with a proper legal authority directing others to cease or refrain from an act until the person filing can be heard from fully.

caveat emptor: "let the buyer beware" (Latin). When merchandise is sold without a warranty by the vendor, the purchaser takes the risk of loss as to defects. see *without recourse;* cf. *caveat subscriptor.*

caveator: one who files or sends a *caveat.*

caveat subscriptor (venditor): "let the seller beware" (Latin). Unless the seller states no responsibility, he or she is liable to the purchaser for any alterations from the written contract. cf. *caveat emptor.*

CB
(1) see *bond, callable.*
(2) see *bond, coupon.*

CBCT: see *Customer-Bank Communication Terminal.*

CBCT ruling: an interpretive ruling by the Comptroller of the Currency (May 19, 1975) stating that CBCTs do not constitute branches and permitting national banks, without regard to state branching law, to establish these facilities on a proprietary basis within 50 miles of a branch and outside that 50-mile radius only with an offer to share with other institutions. [105]

CBD: see *cash before delivery.*

CBOE: see *Chicago Board Options Exchange.*

CC
(1) see *cancellation clause.*
(2) see *cancelled checks.*
(3) see *cash commodity.*
(4) see *cashier's check.*
(5) see *cold canvassing.*

CCA: see *Credit Control Act of 1969.*

CCC: see *Commodity Credit Corporation.*

CCCS: see *Consumer Credit Counseling Services.*

CCS: see *Central Certificate Service.*

C&D: see *cats and dogs.*

CD

(1)   see *cash discount.*

(2)   see *certificate of deposit.*

(3)   see *cum dividend.*

CE

(1)   see *capital expenditure.*

(2)   see *cash earnings.*

(3)   see *caveat emptor.*

(4)   see *commodity exchange.*

CEA

(1)   see *Commodity Exchange Authority.*

(2)   see *Council of Economic Advisers.*

cease and desist order

(1)   *labor relations:* directions to management or the union, issued usually by the National Labor Relations Board, to halt an unfair labor practice. see *Taft-Hartley Act.*

(2)   *law:* a court or governmental agency demand that a person or firm cease an activity.

CEC: see *Commodities Exchange Center.*

cede: a company reinsuring liability with another company "cedes" business to that company (i.e., it yields or grants business by agreement).

CEDEL: Centrale de Livraison de Valeurs Mobilières; a computerized system for delivery and settlement for Eurobonds and related securities based in Luxembourg, with membership exceeding 850 institutions.

cedi: monetary unit of Ghana.

ceding company: the original insurance company that has accepted the risk cedes part of that risk to a reinsurer.

cédule: a European concept; the warehouse receipt used in transfers or assignments. see *warehouse receipt.*

CEF: see *closed-end fund.*

CEIC: see *closed-end investment company.*

ceiling price: usually during wartime, a maximum price established by government regulation on goods and services. cf. *floor.*

Celler Antimerger Act: an extension of the Clayton Antitrust Act, this 1950 addition prohibits a corporation from acquiring the stock or assets of another corporation if the effect would be a substantial lessening of competition or a tendency to monopoly.

cent: the coin of lowest worth in the United States, equal to one-hundredth of a dollar ($0.01).

center: an affiliate's location(s) for the operation of its bank card program or a center location providing identical processing services (e.g., authorization, interchange) for more than one affiliate. [105]

Center for Financial Studies, Inc.:   organized in 1977, this Connecticut nonprofit corporation directs the operation of the Center for Financial Studies on the campus of Fairfield University. The center is a joint undertaking by the university and the savings bank industry. Funds to construct the center were raised through a subscription by National Association of Mutual Savings Banks member savings banks. Upon completion of the center in late 1979, most of NAMSB's education programs were transferred there. [8]

Central American Clearing House: created in 1961 to establish a multilateral mechanism for clearing international payments between the Central American central banks.

Central American Common Market: created in 1960 and headquartered in Guatemala; purports to encourage economic integration between its members: Costa Rica, Guatemala, Nicaragua, and El Salvador.

central bank

(1) *banking:* a banker's bank. see *banker's bank.*

(2) *government:* a bank holding the main body of bank reserves of a nation and the prime reservoir of credit (e.g., Bank of England, Bank of France).

Central Certificate Service (CCS): a privately run depository through which members effect security deliveries between each other via computerized bookkeeping entries, thereby reducing the physical movement of stock certificates.

Centrale de Livraison de Valeurs Mobilières: see *CEDEL.*

central file: records of a company having data on the firm's customers placed in a form to allow an evaluation of the profitability and services provided to the customer.

Central Industry Fund, Inc.: this nonprofit corporation was organized in 1961 to provide technical and capital assistance to new and existing savings banks. Over the years, it has assisted institutions with special problems regarding location, management succession, and overall operation. [8]

central information file (CIF): in most banks, a ledger record of the bank services used by its customers, indicating in which office or offices the business is handled. [10]

central liability: the grouping together on one record of all liabilities of a borrower, such as loans both direct and indirect, consumer credit, letters of credit, guarantees, and other accommodations. The purpose of this record is to prevent overextensions of credit to the borrower, show what is currently due from him, and provide a history of his borrowing. [10]

central processing unit (CPU): a unit of a computer that incorporates the circuits controlling the interpretation and execution of instructions.

central proof: a system for effecting economy of operation by centralizing all proof and distributing functions in a single department of a bank. see *proof department.* [31]

central rate: a rate established under a temporary regime (based on an International Monetary Fund executive board decision of December 18, 1974) by a country which temporarily does not maintain rates based on a par value in accordance with the relevant fund rules but does maintain transactions in its territories. Central rates are in certain respects treated as par values, and the concept was introduced primarily to allow fund members who, prior to August 15, 1971, had an effective par value to base their exchange rates on a stable rate subject to specified margin requirements during the period when the par value of the U.S. dollar was not effective. The temporary regime provides for the possibility of margins of $2\frac{1}{4}$ percent either side of the central rate. After the change in the par value of the U.S. dollar on May 8, 1974, a number of countries have replaced their central rates with new par values. [42]

Central Reserve Cities: established

by the National Bank Act, New York City and Chicago are central reserve cities. see *reserve city bank.*

central reserve city bank: a member bank in New York City or Chicago that held legal reserves of state banks. Presently, this specialized treatment has largely disappeared.

century: slang, a $100 bill.

CEO: see *chief executive officer.*

Cert.: see *certificate.*

certain: French term for *indirect quotation.*

certificate

(1) *finance:* the piece of paper that is evidence of ownership of stock in a corporation. Watermarked paper is finely engraved with delicate etchings to discourage forgery. see *savings certificates.*

(2) *government:* a form of paper money, issued against silver or gold deposited in the U.S. Treasury.

(3) *law:* any written or printed document of truth that can be used as proof of a fact.

certificate account: a savings account containing a fixed amount of funds deposited for a fixed term. The customer is charged a penalty for premature withdrawal, but is paid interest at a rate higher than that on passbook accounts if the deposit remains untouched for the full term. see also *savings certificate.* [59]

certificate check: see *certified check.*

certificated securities: the quantity of a specific commodity held in warehouses that have been approved by a commodity exchange, and which is certified as deliverable on future contracts.

certificate financial statement: a financial statement of a corporation that

is accompanied by the report of a public accountant. [105]

certificate of accounts: the statements released by a certified public accountant stating the accountant's evaluation of a company's books of account that have been audited and/or from which he or she has prepared statements.

certificate of analysis: to assure the importer that goods conform to ordered specifications, a document requiring an overseas seller to accompany the bill of exchange drawn against a shipment as outlined in the letter of credit. see also *certificate of inspection.*

certificate of beneficial interest: a statement of a share of a firm's business when such ownership has been deposited with a trustee. The certificate holder receives the income from and holds an interest in the firm's assets, but relinquishes management control. Used when a business is operated as a trust.

certificate of claim: a contingent promise of the Federal Housing Administration to reimburse an insured mortgagee for certain costs incurred during foreclosure of an insured mortgage provided the proceeds from the sale of the property acquired are sufficient to cover those costs. [44]

certificate of convenience and necessity: a special permit (which supplements the franchise), commonly issued by a state commission, which authorizes a utility to engage in business, construct facilities, or perform some other service. [3]

certificate of deposit (CD): a negotiable, nonnegotiable, or transferable receipt payable to the depositor for funds deposited with a bank, usually interest bearing. see also *certificate of deposit (demand), certificate of deposit (time), variable interest plus.*

certificate of deposit (demand): a negotiable or transferable receipt issued for funds deposited with a bank and payable on demand to the holder. These receipts do not bear interest and are used principally by contractors and others as a guarantee of performance of a contract or as evidence of good faith when submitting a bid. They may also be used as collateral.

certificate of deposit (time): a negotiable or transferable receipt for funds deposited with a bank, payable to the holder at some specified date (not less than 30 days after issuance) and bearing interest.

certificate of incorporation: the franchise or charter issued by a state to the original petitioners of an approved corporation. Such franchise or charter constitutes the authority granted by the state for the organization to transact business as a corporation.

certificate of indebtedness
(1) a short-term note issued by a governmental agency, describing the current debt.
(2) an unsecured promissory note, the holder having a general creditor's recourse against general assets.

certificate of inspection: a document released by a trade association or agency authorized to inspect an importer's goods to assure the purchaser that the items correspond to those identified in the letter of credit. see also *certificate of analysis.*

certificate of insurance: evidence that an insurance policy has been issued, showing the amount and type of insurance provided. It may be used as

evidence of reinsurance between companies, and it is the document containing specific details of property covered by master or open policies. see *commercial set.*

certificate of lender and loan applicant: bank's certification to FmHA that it would not make a loan to an applicant without the FmHA loan guarantee. [105]

certificate of manufacture: in foreign trade, a statement signed by an exporter that goods ordered by the importer have been finished and set aside for shipment. This document is used with a letter of credit for the benefit of the exporter.

certificate of no defense: when a mortgage is sold, the certificate signed by the borrower that identifies the mortgage indebtedness.

certificate of occupancy: a permit issued by a building department verifying that the work meets the local zoning ordinances and the structure ready for occupancy.

certificate of origin: a certificate declaring that goods purchased from a foreign country have indeed been produced in that country and not another.

certificate of ownership: see *proprietorship certificate.*

certificate of participation: a certificate by an investment company issued in place of shares to show a proportionate interest. Also used to show interests in a loan or mortgage where there are many lenders.

certificate of registry: a statement by the registration authority of a nation that a named ship is registered under the flag, who the owners are, the tonnage, and so on.

certificate of release: a certificate

signed by the lender indicating that a mortgage has been fully paid and all debts satisfied.

certificate of title: a title company certification that the seller possesses sound, marketable, and/or insurance title to the property. If a title company issues this certificate and a defect is identified at a later time, the title company will indemnify the holder. see *title insurance.*

certificates: U.S. paper money circulated in the form of a receipt for silver or gold coins. The U.S. silver certificates are the best known. The redemption privilege was revoked by Congress on June 14, 1968. [27]

certificates of debt: certificates indicating that a loan or some other form of debts remains to be paid.

certification

(1) *banking:* an assurance by a bank that the drawer of a check has sufficient funds on deposit to cover payment on the check and that monies have been set aside to meet the incoming obligation. *Certification* is usually stamped across the face of the check. see also *cross check.*

(2) *labor relations:* determination by the National Labor Relations Board or an appropriate state agency that a particular union is the majority choice, hence the exclusive bargaining agent, of all employees in a particular bargaining unit.

certification department: that part of a bank where certification tellers process checks and record which checks are certified.

certification of disaster loss: statement to FmHA of crop production or physical losses due to natural disaster. This is used only for the emergency disaster and emergency livestock loan programs. [105]

certification of origin: a document issued to certify the country of origin of goods. [105]

certification teller: a teller whose duty is to certify or accept checks of depositors. In large banks this may be his or her only duty, but in smaller banks it is usually combined with others. [10]

certified check: the check of a depositor drawn on a bank; the face of the check bears the word "accepted" or "certified," with the date and signature of a bank official or authorized clerk. The check then becomes an obligation of the bank, and regulations require that the amount of the check be immediately charged against the depositor's account. cf. *cashier's check.*

certified mail: a service that provides a receipt to the sender and a record of delivery at the office of address. It is handled in the ordinary mail without insurance coverage. This service is not available to foreign countries. [24]

certified public accountant (CPA): an accountant who has been certified by the state as having met that state's requirements of age, education, experience, and technical qualifications. Not all who practice accounting are certified.

certiorari, writ of: a directive from an appellate court to a lower court declaring that the record of a case pending in the lower court is to be forwarded to the upper court for review.

cesser clause: a statement in a charter agreement that a charterer's obligation terminates when the freight is loaded. The owner of the carrier can, however, have a lien on the freight for appropriate charges.

cession number: a number assigned by an underwriting office to identify reinsurance premium transactions. [54]

cestui: a beneficiary of a trust.

cestui que trust: French adaption of a Latin phrase designating the person for whose benefit a trust has been established. synonymous with *beneficiary.*

ceteris paribus: the assumption that the values of all variables and parameters other than those being analyzed are constant.

C&F: cost and freight to named overseas port of import. Under this term, the seller quotes a price including the cost of transportation to the named point of destination. [61]

CF: see *cash flow.*

CFR: see *Code of Federal Regulations.*

CFTC: see *Commodity Futures Trading Commission.*

CG
(1) see *capital gain (or loss).*
(2) see *capital goods.*

CGT: see *capital gains tax.*

CH: see *clearinghouse.*

chain banking: a form of multiple-office banking under which a minimum of three independently incorporated banks are controlled by one or more individuals. cf. *branch banking.*

chain discount: a series of discounts taken on a base lessened successively by the amount of the preceding discount. For example, a chain discount of 40, 10, and 2 on 100 equals 47.08 percent discount.

chain of command: the organizational design for the flow of communications outlining directing toward authority, peers, and subordinates.

chain of title: the succession of conveyances from some accepted starting point from which the present holder of real property derives his title. [62]

chain store: one of a number of retail stores, all owned and managed by one firm.

chain-store tax: a progressive tax levied by many states on chain stores when the number of these stores exceeds a certain maximum. The tax is frequently levied in the form of a fee exacted to obtain a license. see *chain store.*

chairman of the board: the highest ranking executive of a corporation. In some cases the firm's president is also the chairman of the board.

chamber of commerce: an organization of business executives created to advance the interests of its members.

chancellor of the exchequer: the person in the United Kingdom in charge of the receipts and payments of the government. A function similar to the Secretary of the Treasury in the United States.

Chandler Act: passed by Congress in 1938, this act revised the federal law on financial reorganization of corporations, including bankruptcy.

change: money returned following a purchase, when a larger sum of money was given than was required (e.g., on a sale purchase of $0.98, a $1.00 handout returns $0.02 in change).

change in amount consumed: increase or decrease in the amount of consumption expenditures resulting from a change in personal income.

change in business inventories: represents the value of the increase or decrease in the physical stock of goods held by the business sector valued in current period prices. These inventories are in three stages of production: raw materials, semifinished goods, and finished goods ready for sale or shipment. An inventory increase is regarded as investment because it represents production not matched by current consumption; an inventory decrease is regarded as *negative investment* because it reflects consumption in excess of current production. [73]

CHAPS: Clearing House Automated Payments System (London).

Chapter 11: see *Bankruptcy Reform Act of 1978.*

character: a letter, digit, or other symbol that is used as part of the organization, control, or representation of data in a computer.

character and object classification of expenditures: a classification that focuses on the nature of spending apart from the functions served. It distinguishes among purchases of goods and services for current operation and capital outlay, assistance and subsidies, interest on debt, and insurance benefits and repayments.

charge
(1) *general:* a cost or expense allotted to a specific account.
(2) *banking:* to purchase for credit without making an immediate payment; usually to be paid following billing.
(3) *finance:* a demanded price.
(4) *law:* a judge's instruction to a jury.

charge account: line of credit that may be used repeatedly up to a certain specified limit. synonymous with *open-end credit, revolving credit.* [78]

charge account banking: permits consumers to arrange a line of credit with a bank or lending institution; us-

able to make purchases in many participating establishments. The plan may provide simply a 30-day charge account or installment payment service. [28]

charge authorization phone system: equipment permitting direct contact from a sales department to the credit office for the purpose of authorizing charges. Equipment is often selective so that calls may be directed to the individual in charge of a particular alphabetical group. [41]

charge back: a transaction that the cardholder bank returns either to its own merchant or to the merchant bank because the transaction fails to meet certain established criteria. [105]

charge-back rules: the rules governing the right of a card-issuing bank to charge back to the signing merchant bank sales made that do not conform to agreed-on standards. [105]

charge customer: a customer to whom merchandise is sold on account.

charged-off paper: see *write-off.*

charge notice: see *debit memo.*

charge off: to treat as a loss; to designate as an expense an amount originally recorded as an asset. cf. *write-off.*

charge-out: designates the release of debits or credits to other departments for further handling. Before such items are released, their package totals are recorded on a charge-out sheet. Later, the totals are included in the final proof. [31]

chargeplate: describes a device bearing the name of the credit customer and other descriptive data.

charges and miscellaneous revenue: nontax revenue derived chiefly from fees, assessments, and other reimbursements for current services and from rents and sales of commodities or services furnished incident to the performance of particular general government functions.

charge send: authorized credit purchase of merchandise taken by a customer.

charge ticket: that written memorandum which a bookkeeper uses as a guide in posting a debit item to an account. synonymous with *debit ticket*. [31]

charge wire: see *reverse money transfer*.

charitable bequest: a gift of personal property to a legal charity by will. [37]

charitable devise: a gift of real property to a legal charity by will. [37]

charitable lead (or up-front) trust: a trust for a fixed term of year wherein a charity is the income beneficiary and the remainder goes to a noncharitabe beneficiary. [105]

charitable remainder: an arrangement wherein the remainder interest goes to a legal charity upon the termination or failure of a prior interest. [37]

charitable remainder annuity trust: a trust that provides a sum certain, not less than 5 percent of initial fair market value of all property placed in trust, to be distributed at least annually to a noncharitable beneficiary, with remainder to a qualified charity. [105]

charitable remainder trust: an arrangement wherein the remainder interest goes to a legal charity upon the termination or failure of a prior interest. [105]

charitable remainder unitrust: a trust that provides a fixed percentage, not less than 5 percent of net fair market value of property, valued annually, to be distributed at least annually to a noncharitable beneficiary, with remainder to a qualified charity. [105]

charitable trust: a trust created for the benefit of a community ordinarily without a definite beneficiary—for example, a trust for educational purposes. synonymous with *public trust*. [32]

charter: the contract between a private corporation and the state, identifying the articles of association granted to the corporation by authority of the legislative act. Powers and privileges granted are included.

charter agreement: the contract between the owner of transportation and the party using the transportation. This may be an outright lease or simply an agreement by the owner to furnish transportation.

chartered accountant (CA): in the United Kingdom, Canada, and Australia, a certified accountant.

chartered banks: banks that operate under a government and state charter as opposed to private banks. [27]

Chartered Life Underwriter (CLU): the professional designation awarded by the American College of Life Underwriters to those who have completed the prescribed series of examinations and have satisfied the organization's experience requirement.

Chartered Property & Casualty Underwriter (CPCU): the professional designation awarded by the American Institute for Property and Liability Underwriters to those who have completed the prescribed series of examinations and have satisfied the organization's experience requirement.

charterer: an individual or organization, usually a state agency, who grants a business the right to incorporate and transact business.

charterparty: an agreement whereby owners of a vessel place it at the disposal of a merchant, the charterer, for the conveyance of a cargo of items. Sometimes the charterparty serves as security for a banker's loan to a shipowner. see also *charterparty assignment.*

charterparty assignment: a contract whereby a shipowner and the charterer (the earnings payable) is assigned to a bank as security for its loan to the shipowner, usually to help finance a ship's construction. see *charterparty.*

chartist: an individual who interprets stock market activity and predicts future movement, usually over a short period, from a graphic depiction of price and volume on charts. cf. *Dow theory.* synonymous with *technician.*

chartist's liability: an estimated risk involved in purchasing a security or selling it short following an analysis of a chart pattern.

chart of accounts: a list of account titles giving the order of arrangement and classification of accounts found in the general ledger.

charts: records of price changes in a security or market average placed on graph paper with the relevant volume of transactions.

chattel: derived from "cattle." All property that is not real property. A structure on real property is a chattel real; movable properties (e.g., automobiles) are chattels personal. see *replevin;* cf. *chose(s) in action, goods and services;* synonymous with *personal property.*

chattel, personal: any item of movable property besides real estate. [62]

chattel, real: an interest in land, such as a leasehold, which is less than a freehold estate. see *tenancy at sufferance, tenancy at will, tenancy for years.* [32]

chattel mortgage: an instrument prepared by a debtor (the mortgagor) transferring a chattel's interest to a creditor (mortgagee) for the purposes of providing security for a debt. If the debt is not paid, the mortgagee can sell the chattel and use the monies received to satisfy the debt outstanding.

chattel mortgage agreement: a legal agreement with a purchase of merchandise on an installment basis. Provides that the buyer accepts title to goods on delivery but gives the seller a mortgage on such merchandise that may be foreclosed under certain conditions and by prescribed legal procedure. [41]

chattel mortgage method: a method of obtaining a security interest in a dealer's inventory using a separate mortgage for each transaction. [105]

chattel personal: an article of personal property; to be distinguished from an interest in real property. [105]

chattel real: a nonfreehold interest in real property. The principal types are leases regardless of their length and estates at will.

cheap money: money that is available at relatively low rates of interest.

check

(1) *general:* a process for determining accuracy.

(2) *banking:* the Federal Reserve Board defines a check as follows: "a draft or order upon a bank or banking house purporting to be drawn upon a deposit of funds, for the payment of a certain sum on money to a certain person therein named, or to his order, or to

bearer, and payable instantly on demand."

(3) *computers:* the process of testing machine validity or the correctness of the results yielded by a program. cf. *debug.*

checkable: that which can be withdrawn against a checking account, such as checkable bank deposits.

check authorization/verification: an inquiry process undertaken to reduce the risk of accepting a fraudulent check or a check written for an amount that exceeds the account balance. Check authorization systems may be provided and maintained by the party accepting the check, by a financial institution, or by a third party engaged in such a business. These systems may be designed to access bank records directly or may rely on secondary data sources. In some systems, check approval is accompanied by a guarantee of payment.

checkbook: a book containing blank checks furnished by banks to depositors to permit them to withdraw funds from their checking accounts. A customer may keep a complete record of his or her deposits, withdrawals, and balance, by means of stubs or a register book. [31]

checkbook money: synonymous with *deposit currency.*

check bouncer: slang, an individual who writes checks against nonexistent bank accounts or against accounts with insufficient funds to cover the check.

check bouncing protection: a service provided to customers where a line of credit is associated with their checking accounts. Checks written on insufficient checking account deposits are paid, for a fee, by drawing automatically on this credit line. [105]

check clearing: the movement of checks from the banks where they are deposited back to those on which they are written, and funds movement in the opposite direction. This process results in credits to the accounts of the banks of deposit and corresponding debits to the accounts of the paying bank. The Federal Reserve operates a nationwide check-clearing system, though many checks are cleared by private sector arrangements. [1]

check credit: a bank service whereby a customer is granted a certain amount of credit, draws checks against this credit at times, and repays the bank periodically.

check credit plan: a type of installment loan plan normally used in conjunction with a customer's regular checking account in a commercial bank, including a revolving line of credit combined with personal checking privileges; the line of credit may be drawn upon as needed by the individual and repaid in monthly installments. [105]

check currency: demand deposits generated by a bank loan that is subject to withdrawal by check as opposed to coin or paper money.

check desk: that section of a bookkeeping department through which all incoming and outgoing debit and credit items pass. It assembles and controls all final proof figures for the bookkeeping department. The term is also applied to a proof department for incoming and outgoing items. [10]

check digit: a suffix digit that a computer, by a programmed mathematical formula, can use to test the validity of the account number. [105]

check files: the files in which all paid and canceled checks are stored until they are ready to be returned to the depositors with their statements. Check files may simply be drawers in a bookkeeper's desk, or in large banks a section of the bookkeeping department charged with the responsibility of filing checks and providing them with the statements before mailing. [10]

check filing: the process of placing canceled checks in storage to facilitate the periodic mailing of customers' statements. [31]

check guarantee: a term that identifies a service provided through a plastic card that guarantees payment up to the defined limit, when the merchant follows proper steps in accepting the check. [105]

check guarantee services: a bank service that guarantees payment of a check to merchants and banks. [105]

checking account: a demand account subject to withdrawal by check of funds on deposit.

checkless banking: describes a banking system in which checks are not required for monetary exchange; funds are transferred electronically. [105]

checkless society: describes the predicted absence or need for checks as a medium for transferring funds. The realization of this futuristic concept will come about with the universal usage of bank credit cards, widespread adoption of common machine languages, the ability of financial and commercial concerns of all types and sizes to communicate on-line and in real-time processing, and a complete program for automatic transfer of funds within a bank or between cooperating banks. The depositor's universal bank credit card will authorize debits to his or her account for purchases and services which he or she is presently paying for with a check. Settlements between all banks, to accommodate payments of their customers, are also made automatically. [10]

checklist: an adding machine list of a depositor's checks that are to be charged to his checking account. The number of checks used to make a list varies with the individual bank. The number of checks attached to a list is usually indicated on the list to be used for account analysis. The object of a list is to cut down on the number of items posted to a depositor's account, since only the total of the list appears on the depositor's statement. [10]

check number: the sequential numbers located in the top righthand corner of customer checks. Check numbers are used for the customer's record-keeping purposes. [105]

checkoff: the withholding of wages by an employer for direct payments to a union of dues and assessments. The Taft-Hartley Act states the union members must give written permission for these sums to be deducted. The checkoff cannot exist for longer than one year or until the termination of the union contract, whichever date comes first. A checkoff can also be used to deduct assessments for nonunion members.

check on us: checks drawn on a bank and presented to it for deposit or payment. [50]

checkout: when a block does not prove and the difference is not located by verifying the addition of the deposit tickets and comparing the check amounts with the listings, it is necessary to resort to a checkout. This consists of matching each item shown on the deposit tickets with a similar amount appearing on the block listing tapes, which will establish that the depositor has done one of the following: included a check without listing it, listed a check but failed to include it, or listed a check incorrectly. [31]

check processing: the internal receiving, recording, and perhaps the redistribution of checks written by customers of the institution or deposited by such customers and drawn on another institution. This includes the traditional posting, or recording, of the check in the individual customer's account, the microfilming, and the balancing of all such items received. [105]

check-protecting   equipment: machines that prevent a change in the check amount or in the name of the payee.

check rate: the basic rate for foreign exchange trades, used to calculate all other rates. synonymous with *demand rate.*

check register: the form of the cash payments journal used with a voucher system.

check requisition: a written request made to the accounting department of a firm for the preparation of a check. [59]

check-routing symbol: a device to facilitate the handling and routing of transit items through banks that remit at par all over the United States. The check-routing symbol is the denominator of a fraction, the numerator being the ABA transit number. The entire fraction is located in the upper right-hand corner of a check. The check-routing symbol is composed of three or four digits. The first digit in a denominator of three figures or the first two digits in a denominator of four figures identify the Federal Reserve District (1–12) in which the drawee bank is located. The next to the last digit designates the Federal Reserve Bank head office or branch through which the item should be cleared and also any special clearing arrangement. (The head office is indicated by the number 1. Branches, if any, arranged alphabetically, are indicated by numbers 2 to 5. Numbers 6 to 9 are used to designate special collection arrangements.) The last digit shows whether the item is acceptable for immediate or deferred credit. [10]

check safekeeping: see *free check storage account.*

check serial number: the magnetic characters imprinted in the auxiliary On-Us field. These figures correspond to the number on each check used by the maker as identification. see *account reconciliation plan.* [31]

check services: a service that provides the customer with a method of paying specialized bills with a bank card. [105]

check stub: that portion of a check form kept permanently in a checkbook as a record of the check that is attached to it.

check the market

(1)   in over-the-counter markets, asking for price quotations from several firms to determine the best quotes and the depth of the market.

(2)   determing if the market for an issue has changed since the last time it was quoted and/or sold.

check trading: selling bank checks to a customer, who is expected to repay the amount of the check plus interest in installments.

check truncation: the conversion of information on a check into electronic impulses after a check enters the processing system. It is called truncation because the physical processing of the check is cut short. see *truncation*. [105]

check vertification: used to identify the capability of verifying demand deposit account balances via a terminal. This may be used as a prelude to a point-of-sale system. [105]

check verification guarantee: systems providing retail merchants with varying degree of insurance against bad check losses by (a) verifying the authenticity of the check and/or its presenter, or (b) guaranteeing payments of the check by the bank. [33]

checkwriter: the device used to imprint the amount of a check on its face, in order to make alteration difficult. [105]

cheque: *check* in French or British English.

chermatistic: the pursuit of profit and wealth, in general.

cherry pie: slang, money easily obtained or from activities other than one's regular occupation.

Chg.: see *charge.*

Chicago Board of Trade: the world's largest grain exchange where spot or futures contracts are completed in a host of agricultural products.

Chicago Board Options Exchange (CBOE): an exchange set up by the Chicago Board of Trade and using the facilities provided by the Board for open-market trading of certain stock options. Prior to the 1973 opening of the CBOE, options had been handled on an individually negotiated basis. [105]

Chicago Mercantile Exchange: organized in 1919 as a national market place of trading in cash and futures contracts for commodity items, including butter, eggs, potatoes, pork bellies, hogs, cattle, sorghums, turkeys, and lumber.

Chicago School Theory: an economic approach stating that the basic equation controlling the macro-economic path of a state's economy is a function of the interaction between money supply and the speed of its turnover.

chicken feed: slang, small amount of money; small change.

chief clerk: usually a junior officer or a senior clerk whose duties consist of handling various transactions of an important nature, such as notary work, protests, wire transfers, and technical negotiable instruments. In branch banking, the chief clerk is a junior officer who is charged with the supervision of personnel and the general operations of the branch. [10]

chief executive officer (CEO): the person accountable to the board of directors for the activities and profits of the firm.

Chinese Wall: a policy barrier between the trust department and the rest of the bank designed to stop the flow of information to prevent use by the trust department of any material inside information, which may come into the possession of other bank departments, in making investment decisions. [105]

CHIPS: see *Clearing House Interbank Payment Systems.*

chisel: slang, borrowing money with the expectation of not paying.

chose: anything that is personal property. [37]

chose(s) in action: a right to, but not

possession of, funds or property; the actual taking possession may result from some other event. The right may be enforced by a court ruling and may cover debts, mortgages, negotiable instruments, insurance policies, and warrants. see *chose.*

chose(s) in possession: tangible personal property in actual possession (e.g., an automobile), as contrasted with a *chose in action.* see *chose;* cf. *corporeal property, goods and services.*

Chq.: see *cheque.*

Christmas Club account: a savings account whereby a customer deposits a specified sum each week in order to accumulate a lump sum for Christmas expenditures. [31]

chumming: artificially inflating the market's volume to attract other orders in some issues which stock exchanges compete in.

churning: the repetitive buying and selling of securities when such activity has a minimal effect on the market but generates additional commissions to a stockbroker.

CI
(1) see *capital intensive.*
(2) see *cash items.*
(3) see *compounded interest.*

CID: see *civil investigative demands.*

CIF
(1) see *central information file.*
(2) see *Corporate Income Fund.*
(3) see *cost, insurance, and freight.*

Cincinnati Stock Exchange: created 1887; most of its traded stocks are *unlisted,* including securities listed and traded on other stock exchanges.

Cincotta-Conklin Bill of 1976: a New York state law permitting state savings banks and savings and loan associa-

tions to offer checking accounts like commercial banks, but at no cost.

CIO: see *Congress of Industrial Organizations.*

cipher-proof: a method of balancing whereby certain figures are automatically subtracted from a control total. If the balance results in zero, it is proved that all figures were added and listed correctly. Sometimes referred to as zero balance. [32]

circle: a practice when a customer indicates an interest in buying and an underwriter agrees to provide a given quantity of a new issue subject to pricing.

circuity of action: when a bill of exchange is returned to the person who has already signed it, he or she may renegotiate it, but this person has no claim against individuals signing the bill between the time he or she initially signed it and its return to him or her.

circular: any prospectus; a publication providing information on a security and distributed widely.

circular bond: see *bond, circular.*

circular letter of credit: a document, frequently issued by a bank, that is not addressed to any particular agency or bank. The issuing bank accepts drafts on it when they are within the terms of the letter.

circulating capital: synonymous with *working capital.*

circulating capital good: any capital good item when in use that is consumed by a single use (e.g., gasoline used to make a car engine function).

circulating medium: money; any form of exchange that is accepted without endorsement.

circulation
(1) *banking:* the total value of the

issued bank notes of a bank that are in use, as distinguished from those being held in the bank's reserve.

(2) *finance:* the total of all currency in use at a given period. see *velocity of circulation.*

circulation statement: published monthly by the U.S. Treasury Department showing amounts of currency outstanding and in circulation, currency by denominations and coin, and the comparative sums of money in use.

circumfiduciation: the shifting of certificates of deposit money to other investments.

circumstantial evidence: if from specific facts and circumstances, according to the experience of mankind, an ordinary, intelligent person may infer that other connected facts and circumstances must necessarily exist, the latter facts and circumstances are considered to be proved by circumstantial evidence.

City: *The City* is London's financial center. synonymous with *The Square Mile.*

city bond: see *bond, municipal.*

city collection department: a department in a bank which handles the collection of items payable within a city, and receives and collects these items by messenger. As a general rule, those items which cannot be collected through the local clearinghouse owing to their being drawn on nonmembers, or drafts with documents attached which require special handling, pass through this department. [10]

city items: negotiable items, notes, and checks that are drawn upon individuals or institutions located in the same local or city in which they were deposited.

civil action: a court proceeding or suit by one person against another for protection of a private right or the prevention of a wrong. It includes actions ex contractu, ex delicto, and all equity suits.

civil bond: see *bond, civil.*

civil corporation: an artificial being, created by law for the purpose of engaging in the business purposes stated in its charter that has been granted by the state.

civil investigative demands (CIDs): created in legislation signed by President Ford on September 30, 1976, to give the Antitrust Division of the Justice Department added investigative authority. In civil antitrust investigations, these instruments are analogous to subpoenas issued in criminal investigations. CIDs may be issued to a company, its executives, or a third party, such as a competitor, to obtain documents or to require oral testimony.

civil law: law based on statutes, as distinguished from common law. A law that examines relationships between people, as opposed to criminal law.

civil loans: loans contracted by a federal, state, or municipal agency.

Civil Rights Act of 1964, Title VII: creating the federal Fair Employment Practices Law, covering all industries affecting interstate commerce. It bars discrimination by employers, unions, and employment agencies based on race, color, sex, religion, or national origin. Employers and unions may not discriminate in regard to apprenticeship, training, or retraining programs. Employers, unions, and employment agencies may not retaliate against any person opposing, making a charge, testifying, or taking part in probes or proceedings regarding any practice deemed to be unlawful under the act; or publishing or printing notices or advertisements indicating discrimination. Employment agencies are forbidden to discriminate by failing or refusing to refer applicants on the basis of race, color, religion, sex, or national origin. The law is administered by the Equal Employment Opportunity Commission, which has five members. see also *Civil Rights Act of 1968, Fair Employment Practices Committee.*

Civil Rights Act of 1968: guarantees to all citizens equal treatment in matters pertaining to housing and real estate. Prohibits discrimination because of race, color, religion, national origin, or sex against individuals trying to obtain financing for a home or property. see also *Civil Rights Act of 1964, Title VII.*

Ck.: see *check.*

CL

(1) see *call loan.*
(2) see *capital loss.*
(3) see *cash letter.*
(4) see *common law.*
(5) see *current liabilities.*

claim

(1) *banking:* a demand by an individual or a corporation to recover, under a policy of insurance, for loss that is covered by that policy.
(2) *law:* a demand for payment, reimbursement, or compensation for damages or injury as identified in a contract or under law.

claim against estate: a demand made upon the estate to do or to forebear some act as a matter of duty. A common example would be the claim submitted by a creditor for a debt owed him or her by the decedent at the time of his or her death. [37]

claim agent: the person authorized by an insuring underwriter to pay a loss(es).

claimant: the person asserting a right or presenting a claim for any loss suffered.

claim audit: a survey of a policy record to determine the payment due an insured under a claim. [12]

claim letter: a letter requesting payment or compensation for injury, damage, or misrepresentation in a business transaction.

claim ratio: see *loss ratio.*

claims reported by U.S. banks (long-term): long-term claims reported by U.S. banks represent commercial bank loans to foreigners. These loans may go to private business, individuals, or foreign governments. A large part of these comprise loans for foreign corporations, including loans to finance ship mortgages, U.S. exports, plant expansion, and to refinance debts outstanding. A loan is considered long-term if its repayment schedule is for more than one year. The flow in the opposite direction appears in long-term liabilities reported by U.S. banks. [73]

claims reported by U.S. banks (short-term): short-term claims include loans extended to foreigners with a maturity of less than one year. Loans to foreign banks for the purpose of financing general trade transactions on foreign accounts and short-term bank claims in foreign currencies that represent correspondent balances held in the bank's own account abroad are included. Nonbank claims such as outstanding collections held in the bank's custody or short-term investments in foreign money market assets are also included. [73]

claims reported by U.S. residents other than banks (long-term): those claims reported by private business firms resulting from their export transactions. These claims assume various forms. A common example is "supplier's credit." This is the long-term financing extended to a foreigner by a U.S. corporation in order that it may sell its product abroad. Long-term loans made to foreigners by insurance companies are also included. [73]

claims reported by U.S. residents other than banks (short-term): includes those claims reported by U.S. brokerage houses. These claims may be in the form of a cash account held by the broker. Also included are other short-term financial assets held abroad such as the unused proceeds of loan flotations by U.S. corporations in foreign capital markets. [73]

class
(1) *general:* to place in ranks or divisions.
(2) *banking:* a category of employees in the schedule of group insurance, denoting the amounts of coverage for which the members of the class are eligible. see also *Class A stock, classification.*

class action: a legal action in which one or more persons move against an organization on behalf of themselves as well as an aggrieved group or "class" of citizens deemed to be affected by the same condition.

Class A stock: as distinguished from Class B stock, common, a stock that usually has an advantage over other stock in terms of voting rights, dividend or asset preferences, or other special dividend provisions.

Class B stock: see *Class A stock.*

classical management: the first schools of management thought, including scientific management, functionalism, and bureaucracy.

classification: the underwriting or rating group into which a particular risk must be placed. Pertains to type of business, location, and other factors; not to be confused with *class,* but see *class rate.*

classification rating: the class to which a commodity is assigned for purposes of applying class rates in transportation.

classified: a securities issue of more than one class, usually presented in series from "A" on.

classified bond: see *bond, classified.*

classified loan: a loan made by a bank to a customer and subsequently criticized by examiners as being substandard.

classified property tax: the descriptions of properties by owners for the purpose of setting assessment with respect to market value and tax rates.

classified risk: in life insurance, the scaling of premiums to compensate for substandard health or other risks.

classified stock: equity security divided into groups such as Class A and Class B, the difference defined within the charter and by-laws of a corporation. Usually, these differences affect the right of voting. see *Class A stocks.*

classified taxation: a tax structure in which real property is categorized by function, with differing tax rates applied to each class. In such situations, some classes are excluded from paying any tax.

class of options: options contracts of the same type (call or put) covering the same underlying security. [5]

class I railroads: railroad companies having gross annual operating revenues in excess of $1 million.

class price: the price established for a group of buyers of the same commodity, with other prices established for different groups of buyers of that commodity. In effect, price discrimination based on the ignorance of buyers.

class rate: a type of insurance rate applicable to risks that are so similar in character that it is unnecessary to go to the expense of differentiating among them as to varying factors of hazards.

class system: a term occasionally applied to the stagger system of electing directors. Only a portion of the board has to stand for election in any one year. Each director's term runs for more than one year, so only one class of directors, or one portion of the full board, must win stockholder support at any one annual meeting.

claused bill of exchange: a bill of exchange bearing on its face a clause specifying the underlying transaction or the rate of exchange to be used.

claused bill of lading: see *clean bill of lading.*

Clayton Antitrust Act of 1914: hailed by the union movement as labor's Magna Carta. It was in part designed to remove labor from the purview of the Sherman Antitrust Act and to limit the use of injunctions against labor by the courts. The law has not been successful in the latter respect, however, because of the interpretations of the courts. cf. *Robinson-Patman Act of 1936, Sherman Antitrust Act of 1890.* see also *Celler Antimerger Act.*

clean
(1) see *clean bill of exchange.*
(2) see *clean bill of lading.*
(3) in Great Britain, a price quoted excluding accrued interest cf. *dirty.*

clean bill of exchange: a bill of exchange having no other documents, such as a bill of lading affixed to it.

clean bill of lading: a bill of lading receipted by the carrier for goods received in appropriate condition (no damages or missing items); does not bear the notation "Shippers Load and Count." cf. *over, short, and damaged.*

clean bond: see *bond, clean.*

clean credit: any letter of credit from a bank against which the foreign seller can draw a bill without documentary support. This credit is available only to firms having the best credit reputation.

clean draft: a sight or time draft which has no other documents attached to it. This is to be distinguished from *documentary draft.* [10]

clean float: see *floating currency.*

clean letter of credit: a letter of credit that does not demand such documents as bills of lading as a condition of acceptance by a bank. Such letters are issued only to prime risks.

clean payment: payment not encumbered by documents. [105]

clean up: slang, to take all available profits in a market; to make a substantial and rapid profit.

clean-up fund: provided as one of the basic services of life insurance. A reserve to cover costs of last illness, burial, legal and administrative expenses, miscellaneous outstanding debts, and so on. synonymous with *final expenses fund.*

clear

(1) *general:* to make a profit or gain.

(2) *banking:* having passed through or having been collected by a clearinghouse. see also *clearing and settlement.*

(3) *computers:* to replace information in a storage device by zero.

(4) *finance:* free from encumbrance.

clearance

(1) *general:* an act of clearing.

(2) *banking:* the adjustment of debits and credits in a clearinghouse.

(3) *finance:* a certificate of authority by a customs official permitting a ship to leave after having met customs requirements.

clearance fees: the change incurred in a commodity exchange following the clearing of a trade.

cleared: the time when an individual who has contracted for a stock pays for it and receives delivery. Many brokerage firms make a specialty of clearing transactions, charging other firms for this service.

clearing

(1) *general:* freeing a machine or device from obstruction or other barriers that minimize efficiency; erasing unnecessary information or data.

(2) *investments:* the physical transfer of cash and securities between the purchasers and sellers.

clearing account: an account designed to facilitate the distribution of certain items which usually affect more than one class of accounts, such as those for the production and distribution of power, the production and handling of materials and supplies, and for shop operations. [18]

clearing agreement

(1) an agreement between two or more nations to buy and sell goods and service among themselves according to a specified rate of exchange.

(2) any local, national, or international plan for the periodic mutual exchange by banks of charges against them by others in the plan and the settlement of adverse balances.

clearing and settlement: the process whereby checks or other records of financial or point-of-sale transactions are moved (physically or electronically) from the point at which they were originated to the organization (bank, thrift institution, or other agency) that keeps the accounts for, and expects to collect from and account to, the responsible payor. The settlement process completes the internal financial transactions among the (possibly) many parties involved in the clearing operation.

clearing bank: bank that has been designated by an interchange agreement to be the settlement bank for bank card transactions. [105]

clearing checks: the return of checks to the bank on which they were drawn for payment.

clearing contracts: the substitution of principals to transactions to aid in the settlement of accounts. see *futures.*

clearing credit: the total amount of checks presented by a clearinghouse bank drawn on the other participating banks. [105]

clearing debit: the total amount of checks presented to a clearinghouse bank by the other participating banks. [105]

clearing draft: a draft drawn on a clearing member in settlement of paper or electronic data entered into interchange by another clearing member. [105]

clearinghouse: an association of banks in a city, created to facilitate the clearing of checks, drafts, notes, or other items among the members. It also formulates policies and rules for the mutual welfare of all members. see *Stock Clearing Corporation.*

clearinghouse agent: a bank that is a clearinghouse member and which accepts checks of another bank, not a member, for settlement through the clearinghouse. synonymous with *redemption agent.*

clearinghouse association: a voluntary association of banks within the same city that has been established to facilitate the daily exchange of checks, drafts, and notes among its members and to settle balances caused by these exchanges.

clearinghouse balance: the sum of the debit and credit totals or balances at the end of the banking day.

clearinghouse certificate: prior to the formation of the Federal Reserve System, debit balances resulting from clearinghouse exchanges were settled in gold. In times of financial stress, member banks pooled their securities with the clearinghouse, to be used for the settlement of balances in lieu of gold. Clearinghouse certificates were issued against this pool of securities by the manager of the clearinghouse association to settle the exchange balances of debtor banks whose own resources were inadequate. The New York Clearing House Association resorted to the use of clearinghouse certificates 10 times in its history, the first

being at the outbreak of the Civil War in 1861. [10]

clearinghouse exchanges: synonymous with *exchanges.*

clearinghouse funds

(1)　monies within the banking system that are transferable from bank to bank through the Federal Reserve System. Federal funds are available on a daily basis, whereas clearinghouse funds require three days to clear.

(2)　funds used to settle transactions on which there is a one-day float. [105]

Clearing House Interbank Payment Systems (CHIPS): an automated clearing facility operated by the New York Clearing House Association which processes international funds transfers among its members. CHIPS is a system that moves dollars between 100 New York financial institutions—mostly major U.S. banks, branches of foreign banks, and Edge Act subsidiaries of out-of-state banks. see *Edge Act.*

clearinghouse statement: released by large clearinghouse association, a weekly report showing the surplus, capital, undivided profits, average net demand deposits, and average time deposits of its member banks.

clearing member: a member of a clearinghouse who is also an exchange member. Since not all exchange members are members of a clearinghouse, they clear their transactions with a clearing member.

clearing member bank: a bank, though not a member of the Federal Reserve System, permitted to collect its out-of-town checks via the Federal Reserve check-collecting system. By maintaining a balance with the Federal Reserve Bank in their district a bank may be allowed to become a clearing member.

clearing price: synonymous with *settlement price.*

clearings: the incoming cash letters of items which must be proved, sorted, returned if necessary, and for which settlement must be made. [31]

clearing the market: in securities and commodities, the satisfying of all buyers or sellers by moving the price.

clear title: synonymous with *good title, just title,* and *marketable title.*

Clifford trust: a ten-year trust to reduce income taxes by diverting the income from property placed in trust from the grantor to a beneficiary, usually a member of the grantor's family in a lower income tax bracket. At the end of the trust period of ten years or more, the trust property reverts to the grantor. synonymous with *ten-year trust.*

climax: the termination of rather long-lasting rising or declining price movement, often accompanied by significant securities trading volume. synonymous with *blowing off.* see *selling climax.*

clique: a gentlemen's agreement by a number of persons to manipulate securities by matched orders and short or wash sales. An illegal practice based on the concerted action of individuals rather than any structured organization.

CLOB: see *composite limit order book.*

CLOC: see *clean letter of credit.*

clock stamp: a mechanical or electric time recording device for imprinting upon an inserted document the time of arrival, and frequently the date upon which the item was received or transmitted. Such devices are frequently used in safe deposit and security deposit vaults. [10]

close

(1) *general:* to transfer the balances of revenue and expense accounts at the end of an accounting period (e.g., close the books). see *accounting cycle.*

(2) *banking:* to sign legal papers indicating that the property has formally changed ownership.

(3) *finance:* to conclude a sale or agreement.

(4) *investments:* the short period before the end of the trading session when all trades are officially declared to have been confirmed "at or on the close."

closed account: an account with equal debits and credits.

closed corporation: a corporation whose shares are held by only a few people, usually in positions of management.

closed-end credit: this type of credit (usually installment) involves an agreement with a customer specifying the total amount involved, the number of payments, and the due date of each payment. [105]

closed-end fund: an investment firm whose shares are traded on a securities exchange or the over-the-counter market.

closed-end investment company: a management investment company that has raised its capital by means of a public offering, over a limited period of time, of a fixed amount of common stock (and which may also have raised capital by the issuance of senior securities). The stock of a closed-end investment company is bought and sold on securities exchanges or over-the-counter markets, as are the securities of business corporations. [23]

closed-end mutual fund: unlike ordinary mutual funds, which sell unlimited shares that can always be redeemed at their net asset value, closed-end funds have only a set number of shares outstanding. The shares are traded on the major exchanges and the price rises and falls with demand.

closed indent: an importer's purchase order to an exporter which must be filled with goods from a specified manufacturer or firm. cf. *open indent*.

closed mortgage: a mortgage that cannot be paid off until maturity occurs.

closed out: a situation where the margin purchaser or short seller is unable to "cover" or make up the new amount of margin resulting from the price fluctuation of his securities. He is now closed out or sold out by his broker.

closed shop

(1) *computers:* pertaining to the operation of a computer facility in which most productive problem programming is performed by a group of specialists rather than by the problem originators.

(2) *labor relations:* an agreement in which only employees who were union members in good standing before being hired could continue to work. The closed shop was outlawed by the Taft-Hartley Act.

closed stock: the sale of complete sets only or the sale without assurance that replacements will be available.

closed trade: a transaction concluded by selling a security that has been paid for previously, or the converting of a short sale (i.e., purchasing a security that had earlier been sold short).

closely held: the ownership of a company's common stock by a single individual, family, or a few holders that is not placed on the market for significant trading.

close money: term applied when changes in prices between successive stock transactions are fractional, or when the last bid and asked quotations are hardly different.

close out: to liquidate; to make a final disposition.

close prices: a market condition whereby prices fluctuate only minor amounts and the spread between bid and asked prices is small. see *spread*.

close (closing) the books: the date set by a corporation's board of directors for the declaring of dividends resulting in the temporary closing of their stock transfer books.

closing account: an account in which various ledgers accounts are merged for summary and ultimate transfer to a final statement.

closing agreement: any final or definitive agreement. Used particularly to refer to final settlement of income tax liability and to real estate deals.

closing a mortgage loan: the consummation of a loan transaction in which all appropriate papers are signed and delivered to the lender, the making of the mortgage becomes a completed transaction, and the proceeds of the mortgage loan are disbursed by the lender to the borrower or upon the borrower's order. [44]

closing charges: the expenses or costs incurred in the sale, transfer, or pledging of property, such as recording fees and title examination fees, which must be provided for and distributed between the parties upon the consummation of the transaction. [44]

closing costs: the expenses incurred by sellers and buyers in the transfer of real estate ownership (e.g., attorney's fee, title insurance, survey charge, recording deed and mortgage). see *Real Estate Settlement Procedures Act.*

closing entries: journal entries made at the end of an accounting period to close (bring to zero balance) all revenue, expense, and other temporary accounts.

closing of transfer book: in corporations, setting a date after which changes of stock ownership for purposes of dividends and notices of meetings will not be accepted for a period to avoid confusion at dividend and meeting times.

closing price: the price of securities quoted at the end of the stock exchange day.

closing purchase: a transaction in which a writer liquidates his position by purchasing an option having the same terms as an option previously written (sold). [5]

closing range: commodities, unlike securities, are frequently traded at differing prices at the opening or close of the market. Purchasing or selling transaction at the opening can be filled at any point in such a price range for a particular commodity.

closing sale: a transaction in which an investor who had previously purchased an option demonstrates intent to liquidate his or her position as a holder by selling in a closing sale transaction an option having the same terms as the option previously purchased.

closing statement: an accounting of funds in a real estate sale.

closing the books

(1) the entries of a bookkeeper at the end of a period that permits balancing and preparation of financial statements.

(2) action by a transfer agent that records the stock transfer so that a list of stockholders eligible to receive a dividend is prepared. Stocks sell ex-dividend the day following the closing of the books. see *ex-dividend.*

closing the ledger: recording the closing entries in the general journal, posting them to the ledger, and ruling and balancing the ledger accounts.

closing (or passing) title: the formal exchange of money and documents when real estate is transferred from one owner to another. see *objection to title, paper title, presumptive title, quiet title suit, title defect.*

cloud on title: any claim or existing shortcoming that interferes with the title to real property. see *abeyance, curing title;* cf. *marketable title, perfect title.*

CLU: see *Chartered Life Underwriter.*

"club"

(1) a grouping of nations involved in a financial arrangement, often an LDC debt rescheduling. cf. *Paris Club.*

(2) a Euromarket term for a loan syndication technique, where various responsibilities are carried out by the lead bank and comanagers. Fees are reduced using this approach. [91]

club account: the popularity of the Christmas Club account has led banks to open other types of club accounts on the same basis. It is a convenient method of saving small amounts regularly for a definite purpose. Popular names for the newer club accounts are "budget savings," "vacation club," "travel club," and "all purpose club." Many depositors are using these club accounts to accumulate savings for annual premiums on life insurance, taxes, and vacations. [10]

CM
(1) see *call money.*
(2) see *call of more.*
(3) see *cheap money.*

CMA: see *Cash Management Account.*

Cmdty.: see *commodity.*

CMEA: see *Council for Mutual Economic Assistance.*

Cmm.: see *commission.*

Cn.: see *consolidated.*

Cncld.: see *cancel.*

Cnl.
(1) see *cancel.*
(2) see *cancellation.*

C note: slang, a $100 bill.

Co.: see *company.*

CO
(1) see *call option.*
(2) see *coinsurance.*
(3) see *covered option.*

coassignee: a person or company to whom some property right has been assigned jointly with another person or company.

COBOL: common business-oriented language. A general-purpose (machine) language designed for commercial data utilizing a standard form. It is a language that can present any business program to any suitable computer and also act as a means of communicating these procedures among people.

COC: see *Comptroller of the Currency.*

COD: see *cash on delivery.*

code of accounts: a chart of accounts classified by digits referring to account types. [105]

Code of Federal Regulations (CFR): a codification of regulations made by various federal agencies and indexed as such. [105]

codicil: a written instrument that is made subsequent to the will to which it applies. The codicil modifies certain desires and bequests of the testator.

COE: see *current operation expenditures.*

coefficient of cross-elasticity: the arithmetic relationship between a percentage change in the price of an item and the actual percentage change in the sales of a substitute or competitive item.

coefficient of relative effectiveness: term employed in the Soviet Union: the expected payoff or percent rate of return on capital investment. Similar to the concept of marginal efficiency of investment.

coemption: purchasing the entire supply of any commodity, usually for purposes of gaining a monopoly.

coexecutor: a trustee or person who acts jointly with another executor. see *executor.*

coffee and cake: slang, earning just enough income to pay for the necessities of life; a small salary.

cofinancing: financing a nation in parallel by institutions such as the International Monetary Fund, the World Bank, and commercial banks. May include situations where commercial lendings are made with cross-default clauses relating to IMF or World Bank loans. Default on the latter is taken as default on the commercial loans. [92]

cognovit: a plea used to avoid a trial, by a defendant who admits the right of the plaintiff. It is a written acknowledgment, by a defendant, of his or her liability in a civil suit to avoid the expense of contending.

cognovit note: a form of note (legal evidence of indebtedness) which is both a promissory note and chattel mortgage. The borrower, within the wording of the instrument, waives his or her right of action to the chattel property in case of his or her default in any payments agreed to in the transaction. [10]

COI
(1) see *certificate of incorporation.*
(2) see *certificate of indebtedness.*

coin: a piece of stamped metal authorized by a government for use as currency; specie.

coinage: the process of manufacturing metal money. Called gratuitous if no charge is made. cf. *brassage, seigniorage.*

coin-counting machine: a machine used in banks to count accurately and swiftly large volumes of specie, or coins. The machine has a hopper into which are fed all denominations of coins. The machine is regulated to sort out coins from the smallest size (dime) to the largest (half dollar). The coins are automatically counted as they are sorted, one denomination at a time, and are then packaged in coin wrappers. [10]

coining rate: the mint ratio.

coin pack: a technique of roll-wrapping a cylindrical stack of disks such as coins.

coinsurance
(1) *general:* insurance held jointly with others.
(2) *banking:* a provision in a policy that requires the insured to carry additional insurance equal to a certain specified percentage of the value of the property. The inclusion of this provision, whether mandatory or optional, usually gives to the insured rates lower than would otherwise apply.

coinsurer: one who shares the loss sustained under an insurance policy or policies. Usually applied to an owner of property who fails to carry enough insurance to comply with the coinsurance provision and therefore inevitably suffers part of the loss himself.

COLA: see *cost of living adjustment.*

cold call: contacting a potential investment customer without prior notice in order to make a sale or arrange for an appointment.

cold canvassing: determining potential investment customers without assistance from others or from references (e.g., selecting every tenth name in the telephone directory within a given location and having a salesman, or other person, call on these persons).

cold in hand: slang, a person without funds.

Coll.
(1) see *collateral.*
(2) see *collection.*

collapse
(1) *general:* a sudden drop in business activity or business prices.
(2) *finance:* failure or ruin of a specific firm.

collapsible company: a firm established to manufacture, construct, produce property, or to buy inventory, stock in trade, or property held primarily for sale to customers, unrealized receivables or fees, or assets held three years.

collar pricing: rather than fix the exact stock price at the time of a merger agreement, companies agree on a range—the collar—within which the final price will fall. The actual price is based on an average of the buying company's stock price during the 10 to 20 days before the deal is actually closed. The purpose is to avoid the tendency of the buyer's stock to a dive on the merger news as traders and investors unload their shares through fears of dilution.

Collat.: see *collateral.*

collate: to combine items from two or more ordered sets into one set having a specified order.

collateral: security (e.g., one's home, automobile, jewelry) left with a creditor to assure the performance of the obligator. When the obligator has performed, the creditor must return the collateral. see *hypothecate.*

collateral bond: see *bond, collateral.*

collateral heir: a person not in the direct line of the decedent from whom he inherits real property, as, for example, a nephew of the decedent who receives a share of his uncle's estate. see *direct heir, heirs.* [37]

collateralized loan: a loan granted a customer upon the pledge of liquid assets or illiquid assets. Should the borrower be unable to repay, the lender sells the collateral.

collateral loan: a loan obtained by the pledge of title to personal property. see *hypothecated account.*

collateral mortgage: a document used in connection with a loan which effects a lien on real estate, where the purpose of the loan is not for the purchase of the property offered as security. [105]

collateral mortgage bonds: collateral trust bonds that have been secured by a deposit of mortgage bonds.

collateral note: a promissory note secured by the pledge of specific property. [50]

collateral pledge: the agreement under which a third party pledges a savings account or other property as additional security for the lender's mortgage-secured advance of funds by check and extending credit. [59]

collateral security: property security, as distinguished from personal security.

collateral surety: commercial paper, such as stocks or bonds, that has have been placed with a lender as security for the payment of a loan.

collateral trust bond: see *bond, collateral trust.*

collateral trust notes: bonds secured by the deposit of other stocks or bonds. These notes are usually issued by investment trusts, railroads, and holding companies.

collateral value: the estimate of value of the thing put up as security for a loan made by a lender. With securities and commodities, the lender is usually restricted in his or her valuation by rules of an appropriate agency, such as the exchange or Federal Reserve Board.

collected funds: cash or checks deposited in the bank which have been presented for payment and for which payment has actually been received. [105]

collectible: that which can be converted into cash. synonymous with *liquid.*

collecting bank: a bank that collects payment on the bill sent by a remitting bank. [85]

collection

(1) *general:* presentation for payment of an obligation and the payment thereof.

(2) *banking:* the getting of money for presentation of a draft or check for payment at the bank on which it was drawn, or presentation of any item for deposit at the place at which it is payable. see *float, value date.*

collection activity: process of contacting delinquent cardholders either by mail or by phone in an effort to obtain payment. [105]

collection agent: a person or bank that handles checks, drafts, coupons, and related items for another person or bank with the purpose of trying to collect such instruments.

collection analyst: a person in the collection division of the credit office, responsible for determining status and subsequent collection procedure of customers' past-due accounts. [41]

collection basis of reporting: a method of reporting the receipts of takes by the Internal Revenue Service at the time of receipt of returns by collecting officers in the field (as compared with Treasury statements of receipts on the basis of reports of deposits made in Treasury accounts). The collection basis provides detail of collections by type of tax. [70]

collection charge: a bank's charge made for the collection of checks, coupons, drafts, notes, and acceptances that have been drawn on the bank, corporations, or persons out of the location of the sending bank. see also *exchange charge.*

collection clerk: a bank representative involved in the collection of checks, drafts, and other items drawn on out-of-town points.

collection correspondent: a person in the collection division of a credit office, responsible for handling collection matters by mail. [41]

collection cycle: the activity taking place between the extension of credit and the receipt of payment.

collection department: the department that handles checks, drafts, coupons, and other items received from a depositor with instructions to credit his or her account after final payment has been received. In large cities, the collection department is usually divided into four sections (i.e., city collection, country collection, coupon collection, and foreign collection). [10]

collection expense: all expenses incurred in the collection of notes, drafts, or accounts.

collection fee: the percentage paid an agent for his or her services in collecting premiums. [12]

collection item: items (drafts, notes, acceptances, etc.) received for collection and credited to a depositor's account after final payment. Collection items are usually subject to special instructions regarding delivery of documents when attached, protest, and so on, and in most banks are subject to a special fee for handling called a collection charge. synonymous with *collection.* [31]

collection ledger: a ledger that is part of the bookkeeping records of a bank transit unit showing the holding charges to other banks for checks and items while in transit or in the process of being collected. synonymous with *float ledger.*

collection letter: a letter of transmittal containing special handling instructions which accompanies items to be handled for collection and credit after payment. [31]

collection manager: supervisor of the collection division of the credit office. Usually (although not always) responsible to the credit manager. Handles all collection matters. [41]

collection on delivery (COD): the request that the cost of goods and other charges be collected at the time the items are delivered.

collection percentage: the amount collected during a given period, usually one month, expressed as a percentage against the total amount owed by all customers at the beginning of a period. [41]

collection period
(1) the period of time that it takes such items as checks and notes to clear.
(2) the collection period of accounts receivable used by credit men as one measurement of their efficiency. [4]

collection ratio: the ratio of receivables (accounts, interest, and notes) to net sales, indicating the efficiency of an enterprise in the collection of its customers' accounts.

collection reminder: reminder to customer that payment or payments are past due. Can be printed, typed, or in the form of a statement or sticker insert. [41]

collection service: a system of methods and procedures used to obtain payment of past-due consumer accounts receivable.

collection teller: a teller whose regular duty is the handling of collections. [10]

collective bargaining: negotiations between an employer or group of employers and a labor union for a contract covering employees in a bargaining unit. First established as a legal right by the National Industrial Recovery Act of 1933, and reconstituted by the Wagner Act and other subsequent legislation. The process is regulated by the National Labor Relations Board. Executive Order 10988 extended limited collective bargaining rights to federal employees.

collective investment fund: a pooled investment trust under which the funds of pension and profit-sharing plans that are approved by the Internal Revenue Service are commingled for investment. [37]

collective ownership: possession of an item in common, with no particular part or proportion assigned to anyone.

collective reserve unit (CRU): an international currency or unit of money for use along with currencies in the reserves of banks around the world.

collector of the customs: a U.S. Treasury Department official responsible for the collection of import duties at a port of entry.

collect shipment: a shipment for which freight charges and advances are made by the delivering carrier from the consignee.

Coll. L.: see *collection letter.*

Coll. Tr.: see *bond, collateral trust.*

collusion
(1) *general:* a secret agreement to defraud.
(2) *labor relations:* a conspiracy between an employer and the certified representative of his or her employees to defraud the employees represented while providing the semblance of a genuine bargaining relationship.

collusive bidding: bidding by suppliers who have arranged among themselves to submit to potential buyers bids that are similar or even identical.

colon: monetary unit of Costa Rica and El Salvador.

colorable title: a claim to ownership supported by some facts or circumstances tending to support the claim.

color blind: slang, an individual not opposed to cheating or stealing; a person who is unable to tell the difference between other people's money and his or her own.

color of title: an appearance of title founded upon a written instrument which, if valid, conveys title.

Co. Ltd.: a closed corporation.

columnar journal: a journal having special columns for the classification of transactions.

Com.: see *commerce.*

comaker: an individual who signs the note of another person as support for the credit of the primary maker. see *unsecured loan;* synonymous with *co-signer.*

comanager: in a Euroloan, the lender ranking next to the lead manager.

combination: the bringing together of several companies in a united effort to eliminate or control competition and/or effect economies.

combination bond: see *bond, combination.*

combination in restraint of trade: an agreement between people or firms to restrict competition in the sale, production, or distribution of a good or service.

combination orders: two orders, with the cancellation of one contingent upon the execution of the other.

combination packages: some form of term insurance with a tax-deferred annuity. Taxes are paid on the savings when the money is withdrawn. If the insurance portion is not expensive and the sales costs are not high, the combi-nation is comparable to and sometimes better than a cash-value policy.

combination rate: the rate charged for carrying freight between two points not on the same railroad, which is the sum of all the local rates between the point of origin, the junction points of the two or more railroads, and the point of destination. A combination rate is used when no joint rate exists.

combined cash journal and daily financial statement: bookkeeping forms for use in accounting systems that omit the use of a ledger.

combined financial statement: as distinguished from consolidated statements; used to present the financial position and the results of operations of a group of companies under common control or common management. Intercompany transactions are eliminated in the same manner as in consolidated statements. [43]

come across: slang, to pay money owed.

COMECON: see *Council for Mutual Economic Assistance.*

Comex: see *Commodity Exchange, Inc.*

comfort letter: a common condition of an underwriting agreement in connection with the offering for sale of securities registered with the SEC whereby an independent auditor issues a letter to the underwriter reporting on the limited procedures followed with respect to unaudited financial statements or other financial data. [43]

Com'l. Ppr.: see *commercial paper.*

Comm.: see *commission.*

commerce: trade between states and nations.

commerce clause: the clause in the U.S. Constitution which reserves to the federal Congress the regulation of commerce between the states and with foreign nations. Much federal legislation concerning business rests on this clause in Article I, Section 8.

commercial account: in general, a checking account; a bank account established for the purpose of enabling the depositor (usually a business person) to draw checks against the balance maintained. see *checking account.*

commercial agency: an organization that offers facilities in the field of credit and collections. synonymous with *mercantile agency.*

commercial and industrial loans: loans for business purposes except those secured by real estate. [40]

commercial auction: an agent business unit that effects the sale of goods through an auctioneer, who, under specified rules, solicits bids or offers from buyers and has power to accept the highest bids of responsible bidders and, thereby, consummates the sale. [48]

commercial bank: an organization chartered either by the Comptroller of the Currency and known as a national bank or chartered by the state in which it will conduct the business of banking. A commercial bank generally specializes in demand deposits and commercial loans. see also other entries under *bank.*

commercial bar: a brick, or bar of precious metal, usually gold or silver, used in the arts and industry area, as distinguished from one created for monetary use, (i.e., a jeweler's bar, which is usually smaller than the bar used for monetary purposes).

commercial bills: bills of exchange resulting from a commercial business transaction as contrasted with non-commercial bills (i.e., banker's bills).

commercial blanket bond: see *bond, commercial blanket.*

commercial borrower: one who borrows for some purpose having to do with business or commerce. [28]

commercial borrowing

(1) loans made to retailers and wholesalers, as differentiated from those loans made to manufacturers.

(2) loans made to private individuals (i.e. personal loans, car loans), as differentiated from loans made to companies.

commercial code: the Uniform Commercial Code, describing commercial law. It excludes laws dealing with real property.

commercial credit: credit extended by firms with which an organization does business.

commercial credit company: a firm engaged in certain forms of financing, especially the purchasing of accounts receivable, the extension of credit to retail dealers, and the discounting of installment accounts. synonymous with *discount house,* and *sales finance company.*

commercial credit document: a general expression for the paper or document, such as a bill of lading and/or warehouse receipt, accompanying an extension of commercial credit.

commercial discounts: discounts given to encourage prompt payment of a commercial account.

commercial draft: an order for the payment of money drawn by a seller of goods on the buyer's account at a bank. Once the draft is accepted and payment made to the seller, the buyer may obtain his or her goods. [59]

Commercial Exchange of Philadelphia: first opened in 1854 as the Corn Exchange Association of Philadelphia, changing in 1868 to its present name. This exchange deals in grains, feeds, and flour commodities.

commercial forgery policy: a contract of insurance protecting a person accepting checks in payment for services or goods.

commercial invoice: a statement showing the record of the transaction between a buyer and seller that has been prepared by the seller.

commercial lending: loans to businesses to meet short- or long-term needs. [105]

commercial letter of credit: an instrument by which a bank lends its credit to a customer to enable him to finance the purchase of goods. Addressed to the seller, it authorizes him to draw drafts on the bank under the terms stated in the letter. [50]

commercial loan: commercial loans are principally loans made to businesses for the financing of inventory purchases and the movement of goods, as distinguished from personal loans or consumer credit loans. Commercial loans are short-term loans or acceptances (time drafts accepted). see also *loan. [10]*

commercial mortgage: a loan secured by real estate, and for which the real estate is used or zoned for business purposes or multiunit dwellings, or is part of a real estate investment portfolio. [105]

commercial overhead: those expenses of a business other than materials, direct labor, manufacturing expense, and income taxes. The principal categories are selling, administration, financial, and staff functions.

commercial paper

(1) *general:* any notes, drafts, checks, or deposit certificates used in a business.

(2) *banking:* in 1978 the Bankers Trust Company sold several issues of clients' commercial paper—short-term IOU's issued by corporations. The securities industry has tried unsuccessfully to get the Federal Reserve Board to prohibit that sale on grounds that it violated the Glass-Steagall Act, which separates commercial from investment banking. see *Glass-Steagall Act of 1933.*

(3) *finance:* unsecured short-term (under 270 days) promissory notes issued by corporations of unquestioned credit standing and sold to corporate and individual investors.

commercial-paper house: principals and dealers who purchase commercial paper at one rate and attempt to sell it at another.

commercial paper names: established borrowers who are frequently in the commercial paper market.

commercial property: property to be used for business purposes, as contrasted with residential, agricultural, or industrial functions.

commercial report: see *credit report.*

commercial set: the four major documents covering a shipment, namely, the invoice, the bill of lading, the certificate of insurance, and the bill of exchange.

commercial stocks: U.S. Department of Agriculture stocks of grain at major grain centers.

commercial teller: an employee

whose prime function is paying and receiving funds for bank customers.

commercial treaty: an arrangement between two or more nations setting forth conditions under which the nationals of one nation, party to the agreement, can conduct business in the other contracting nation or nations.

commercial year: a business year; unlike the calendar year, it consists of 12 months of 30 days each, totaling 360 days.

commingled accounts: when several bank trust department accounts are managed as one account to take advantage of economies available to large investments, the accounts are referred to collectively as a commingled account. Banks may not sell shares to the public that would increase the size of these accounts and make them, in effect, open-ended investment companies or mutual funds. A recent Supreme Court decision, however, allows bank holding companies to advise, sponsor, and organize closed-end investment companies, which sell only a certain number of shares that are then traded in the open market like common stocks. Commingled accounts are testing the validity of the Glass-Steagall Act. see *Glass-Steagall Act of 1933.*

commingled fund: a common fund in which the funds of several accounts are mixed. [37]

commingled investment fund: a bank-operated trust fund in which accounts of individual customers are commingled and lose their identity. Each customer, in effect, owns a share of the entire fund. Such a fund differs only in detail from a mutual fund. [74]

commission
(1) *general:* the amount paid to an agent, which may be an individual, a broker, or a financial institution, for consummating a transaction involving sale or purchase of assets or services. cf. *override.*
(2) *banking:* agents and brokers are usually compensated by being allowed to retain a certain percentage of the premiums they produce, known as a commission.

commission broker: an agent who executes the public's orders for the purchase or sale of securities or commodities. see *dealer.* [20]

Commission des Opérations de Bourse: the French government agency responsible for supervising its stock exchange.

commissioner of banking: a state's banking department manager who regulates the state chartered banks in his state. In some states, known as *superintendent of banking.*

commissioners' values: the values of securities as determined by the National Association of Insurance Commissioners to be used by insurers for valuation purposes when preparing financial statements. [12]

commission house: a broker who purchases and sells only for customers and does not trade his or her own account.

commission merchant: an agent, transacting business in his own name, who usually exercises physical control over the goods consigned to him and negotiates their sale. The commission merchant usually enjoys broader powers as to prices, methods, and terms of sale than does the broker, although he must obey instruction issued by his principal. He generally arranges delivery, extends necessary credit, collects, deducts his fees, and remits the balance to his principal.

Most definitions state that the commission merchant has possession of the goods he handles. In its strict meaning, the word "possession" connotes to some extent the idea of ownership; in its legal meaning it involves a degree of control, somewhat of a misnomer when applied to an agent; the fact is disregarded in this definition since this usage is commonly accepted in the trade. [13]

commission trade: securities or commodities transactions where the brokerage firm receives a commission, as contrasted with tradings, usually over-the-counter, in which it serves as a principal and buys and sells for its own account and does not charge any commission.

commitment: an advance agreement to perform in the future such as by an association to provide funds for a mortgage loan. [59]

commitment and disclosure statement: a written acknowledgment by a lender, required under the Truth-in-Lending Act, in which the lender stipulates under what conditions funds will be lent to the applicant. [105]

commitment fee: a fee charged when a bank has granted an overdraft or term loan which is not being fully used. [93]

commitment fee (loan): any fee paid by a potential borrower to a lender for the lender's promise to lend money at a specified rate and within a given time in the future. [105]

committee deed: see *deed, committee.*

committee for incompetent: an individual or a trust institution appointed by a court to care for the property or the person (or both) of an incompetent; similar to a guardian, conservator, or curator. [32]

Committee on Uniform Securities Identification Procedures: see *CUSIP.*

committees: on stock exchanges, bodies that aid in the operation of the exchange performing responsibility for admissions, conduct, and so on.

commodities: a basic product, usually but not always agricultural or mineral, which is traded on a commodity exchange. [105]

Commodities Exchange Center (CEC): a facility for the four major New York commodity exchanges, opened in July 1977. Each exchange retains its own autonomy, clears transactions through separate clearing units, and shares in a single computer quotation system. CEC combines the Commodity Exchange, the New York Coffee and Sugar Exchange, the New York Mercantile Exchange, and the New York Cotton Exchange. See also *New York Coffee and Sugar Exchange, New York Mercantile Exchange.*

commodities futures contract: a contract to purchase or sell a specific amount of a given commodity at a specified future date. [105]

commodity: an item of commerce of trade. cf. *spot market.*

commodity agreement: an agreement between two or more countries covering the production and distribution of commodities, existing quantities of which exceed normal world demands. This agreement usually identifies provisions for control of production, exports, prices; and the means of expanding existing markets. synonymous with *international commodity agreement.*

commodity collateral loan: any loan made with a commodity, such as cotton, coffee, or sugar, as collateral.

Commodity Credit Corporation (CCC): an instrument of the federal government, created by the Agricultural Adjustment Act in 1933 to provide financial services to carry forward public price support activities with respect to certain agricultural commodities.

commodity dollar: synonymous with *commodity theory of money.*

commodity exchange: an organization usually owned by the member-traders, which provides facilities for bringing together buyers and sellers of specified commodities, or their agents, for promoting trades, either spot or futures or both, in these commodities. see *Commodity Exchange, Inc.* [48]

Commodity Exchange Act: federal legislation of 1936 establishing the Commodity Exchange Commission to regulate trading in the contract markets and other power to prevent fraud and manipulation in commodities and set limitations in trading for the purpose of preventing excessive speculation.

Commodity Exchange Authority: a unit of the U.S. Department of Agriculture, responsible for enforcing the Commodity Exchange Act of 1936.

Commodity Exchange Commission: the U.S. secretary of commerce, secretary of agriculture, and attorney general are designated by the Commodity Exchange Act of 1936 as the Commodity Exchange Commission.

Commodity Exchange, Inc. (Comex): formed in 1933 by the merger of the New York Hide Exchange, the National Metal Exchange, the National Raw Silk Exchange, and the New York Rubber Exchange. Presently, silver, copper, and mercury are the commodities futures traded. In 1980, Comex absorbed the Amex Commodities Exchange, an offshoot of the American Stock Exchange.

Commodity Futures Trading Commission (CFTC): a federal agency established in April 1975, responsible for coordinating the commodities industry in the United States, with primary concern for detecting and prosecuting violators of the Commodity Exchange Act. see also *Tax Reform Act of 1976.*

commodity income statement: an income statement prepared for each of the major traded commodities.

commodity loan: a loan made to a grain producer by the Commodity Credit Corporation.

commodity market: the market or public demand for the purchase and sale of commodity futures. [105]

commodity paper: notes, drafts, or other documents with warehouse receipts or bills of lading for commodities. Should default occur, the lender can sell the commodities up to the value of the loan and the expense of collection.

commodity price: a price for a commodity is quoted on a cash (spot) basis, or on a future basis, the difference to be accounted for by the charges involved in carrying the commodity for the period of the delivery of the future.

commodity rate: the rate of interest charged by banks on notes, drafts, bills of exchange, and other related documents issued on stable commodities.

commodity reserve theory: a monetary theory under which money would be convertible into one commodity at a specified rate or the commodity convertible into money at the same rate at the option of the holder of either the money or the commodity. One variation of the theory substitutes a bundle of staple commodities for one commodity alone.

commodity standard: a suggested monetary system that proposes to substitute a commodity or commodities for the precious metal or other base of a currency.

commodity surplus: the supply of a specific commodity that exceeds the market demands for a specific time period.

commodity tax straddle: a commodity investment in which a taxpayer has real capital gain that he wants to offset with a capital loss in order to defer his current-year tax liability. see also *straddle.*

commodity theory of money: the claim that the value of money is determined by the value of the commodity of which is is composed or which it represents. synonymous with *commodity dollar.*

commodity trading: the process of buying or selling contracts for future delivery of a commodity. [105]

commodity warehouse: see *warehouse, commodity.*

common business-oriented language: see *COBOL.*

common capital stock (common stock): represents the funds invested by the residual owners whose claims to income and assets are subordinated to all other claims. [3]

common carrier: a person or firm regulated by a public authority and operating under a franchise, which engages in the transportation of items or individuals in return for a fee, such service being made available at the same rates for all.

common disaster clause: a clause added to a life insurance policy to instruct the bank in paying the proceeds of policies when the insured and the named beneficiary die in the same disaster.

common expense: an expense arising from two or more forms of operation, the portion resulting from each form of operation not being distinguishable. For expenses common to freight and passenger service, prescribed rules are in effect with regard to their apportionment. [18]

common language for consumer credit: a standardized system of terminology and abbreviations for reporting the payment habits of credit users, developed by the Associated Credit Bureaus, Inc. [105]

common law: law that is based on precedent.

common law trust: see *business trust.*

common-law voting: one vote for each stockholder in a corporation, regardless of number of shares held. cf. *cumulative voting, ordinary voting.*

common machine language (MICR): the common machine language for mechanized check handling is a specially designed group of 10 Arabic numbers and four special symbols printed in magnetic ink in designated field locations along the bottom edge of a check. The Bank Management Commission of the American Bankers Association, in their 1959 publication number 147, stated the original intention of the MICR program as follows: "The concept of the Common Machine

Language, of course, is for the amount to be encoded by the first bank receiving the item for collection. This would permit all further handling in intermediate and paying banks to be primarily mechanical, resulting in tremendous economies in the banking system." This quotation assumes that eventually all banks will at least have their transit number routing symbol encoded on their checks, regardless of whether they intend to use equipment that will read the magnetic ink characters or not. see *magnetic ink character recognition.* [31]

Common Market: see *European Economic Community.*

common property: land generally, or a tract of land, considered as the property of the public in which all persons enjoy equal rights; a legal term signifying an incorporeal hereditament consisting of a right of one person in the land of another, as common of estovers, of pasture, of piscary, property not owned by individuals or government, but by groups, tribes, or in formal villages. [62]

common size statement: the device used in comparing statements, especially a statement from a small-sized concern with a statement of a concern many times larger in a similar line of business. To avoid misinterpretation and confusion frequently encountered while dealing with large amounts, the device operates as follows: the total value of each individual item (asset) is divided by the total of all like items (total assets), thus reducing each figure to a percentage of the whole. [10]

common stock: securities that represent an ownership interest in a corporation. If the company has also issued preferred stock, both common and preferred have ownership rights. The preferred normally is limited to a fixed dividend but has prior claim on dividends and in the event of liquidation, assets. Claims of both common and preferred stockholders are junior to claims of bondholders or other creditors of the company. Common stockholders assume the greater risk but generally exercise a greater degree of control and may gain the greater reward in the form of dividends and capital appreciation. Often used interchangeably with *capital stock.* see *leverage;* see also *voting right (stock).*

common stock dividends: dividends declared on common stock during the year whether or not they were paid during the year. Unless otherwise qualified, it is the amount of such dividends charged to retained income (earned surplus) and includes those payable in cash or stock. [3]

common stock equivalent: a security which, because of its terms or the circumstances under which it was issued, is considered in computing earnings per share to be in substance equivalent to common stock, (e.g., a convertible security). [43]

common stock fund: an investment firm having a portfolio consisting primarily of common stocks. Such a company can reserve the right to take defensive positions in cash, bonds, and other senior securities whenever existing conditions appear to warrant such action.

common stock index: a compilation showing the average current market value of common stock compared with their average market value at an earlier, base period.

common stock ratio: the stated value of common stock plus surplus reserves and surplus divided by the total value of bonds, preferred stock, common stock, surplus reserves, and surplus.

common trust fund: a fund maintained by a bank or a trust company exclusively for the collective investment and reinvestment of money contributed to the fund by the bank or trust company in its capacity as trustee, executor, administrator, or guardian and in conformity with the rules and regulations of the Board of Governors of the Federal Reserve System pertaining to the collective investment of trust funds by national banks, as well as with the statutes and regulations (if any) of the several states. [37]

communication system

(1) *general:* the means by which instructions and information pass from one bank to another. These include telex, cable, and mail in communications.

(2) *EFTS:* a service that moves messages among subscribers, including funds transfer transactions, that are subject to settlement by other means. [105]

community bank trust department: a trust department holding less than $100 million in trust assets. A community bank holds less than $100 million in deposits. [25]

community property: property that is owned jointly by a husband and wife by fact of their marriage. The state laws vary, but in states where community property applies, a husband and wife are considered to share equally in all of each other's property that is acquired during the marriage and in any income

received or increase in value occurring during the marriage.

community property law: law regarding property owned jointly by a man and wife. Insurance policies are often considered community property. [12]

Community Reinvestment Act (CRA) Statement: a description available for public inspection at each bank office indicating, on a map, the communities served by that office and the types of credit the bank is prepared to extend within the communities served. [78]

community trust: a trust ordinarily composed of gifts made by many people to a trustee for educational, charitable, or other benevolent purposes in a community. The property of the trust is trusteed, and distribution of the funds is under the control of a selected group of citizens who act as a distribution committee. There may be one trustee or, as is more often the case, several trustees (usually trust institutions of the community), each serving under identical declarations of trust in the administration of the property committee to its care and management. Some community trusts are known as *foundations.* [37]

commutation rights: in insurance, the right of the beneficiary at his or her option to receive in one sum the cash value of the remaining payments under an option selected by the insured of a life insurance policy.

commuter tax: any income tax levied by a town or city on people who work there but live elsewhere.

Comp.: see *compound.*

company: an association of people for reasons of carrying on some business activity.

company check: a check drawn by a

corporation, partnership, or other business entity on its account with a bank.

company store: a retail store owned and operated by a firm for the use of its workers and conducted as an adjunct to its traditional business.

company union: an employee organization, usually of a single company, that is dominated or strongly influenced by management. The National Labor Relations Act of 1935 declared employer domination to be an unfair labor practice.

company warehouse: synonymous with *warehouse, private.*

comparative advantage: a country or area has such an advantage in the manufacture of a particular item when its social cost of production for that item is less than the social cost experienced by other countries or areas for the same item.

comparative balance sheet: a balance sheet showing information for more than one fiscal period.

comparative profit and loss statement: a profit and loss statement showing information for more than one fiscal period.

comparative reports: financial reports giving the figures for more than one fiscal period.

comparative statement: the income, expense, profit and loss, balance sheet, or other financial statement of the same concern for two or more consecutive years that are analyzed to determine the increase or decrease in their component items, frequently for credit purposes. [10]

comparisons: the exchange of information between a broker and his bank or between two brokers to verify that each party's records of collateral held against loan are valid and in agreement. If there is disagreement, the parties can rapidly track down any difference.

comparison shopping:
(1) *general:* evaluation of a lender's annual percentage rate (APR), which tells the borrower the relative cost of credit, against the APRs quoted by other lenders. see *annual percentage rate.* [78]
(2) *banking:* an investor who compares certificates of deposits or other rates at several banks.

compensated dollar: a monetary unit where the gold content is periodically changed to retain the purchasing power level with some commodity index.

compensating balance: the lowest percentage of a line of credit that the customer of a bank is expected to maintain at all times.

compensating depreciation: a depreciation system dealing with the problem of fluctuating prices for the items being depreciated.

compensating payment: the sum of money just offsetting a given change in price or market condition.

compensating tariff: an increase in the tariff on a finished item (e.g., woolens) to compensate for an increase in the tariff on a raw material (e.g., wool) used in that commodity. If the tariff were raised on wool to protect farmers, then to maintain the same relative position of manufactures, an increase in the tariff on woolens is required.

compensation
(1) *general:* payment for any services or items.
(2) *law:* the settlement of any debt

by the debtor's establishment of a counterclaim against his ir her creditor.

compensation financing: see *compensatory official financing.*

compensation trading: when an exporter agrees to accept part-payment in items from the purchaser's nation in lieu of cash.

compensatory balance: the balance a borrower from a bank is required by the bank to keep in his or her account.

compensatory duty

(1) customs duty levied on important imported manufactured items to offset the increased costs of a domestic producer of similar items when such costs are attributable to a tariff on the raw materials used by such domestic manufacturer.

(2) a duty on an import commodity designed to offset an excise tax placed on the same commodity when manufactured in the importing nation. synonymous with *countervailing excise duty.*

compensatory finance: a general theory of government spending that the government budget should be unbalanced by a deficit during depression periods and unbalanced by a surplus during prosperity periods in an effort to secure stable economic conditions. cf. *fiscal policy.*

compensatory fiscal policy: an approach to reverse the direction of the business cycle when it is believed that it is becoming inflationary or deflationary. cf. *archmonetarist.* synonymous with *countercyclical (policy).*

compensatory official financing: a transaction carried out by an official agency to provide (or absorb) foreign exchange to (or from) an individual carrying on another transaction.

compensatory principle of money: the claim that the ratio between the mint and market values of two metals in a bimetallic monetary system will be maintained through normal operation of the forces of supply and demand.

compensatory principles of bimetallism: the principles applying when the currency of a nation is redeemable for fixed amounts of either gold or silver at the option of the currency holder. The principles is that the ratio between gold and silver established by the government will prevail in the free market by withdrawals from the mint or deliveries to the mint, according to the market price of one metal relative to the other is higher or lower, respectively, than that prevailing in the market for that metal.

competition:

(1) *general:* any rivalry.

(2) *finance:* the situation of a large number of manufacturers serving a large number of consumers, when no manufacturer can demand or offer a quantity sufficiently large to affect the market price. see *monopoly, oligopoly;* see also *invisible hand;* cf. *cutthroat competition, imperfect competition, nonprice competition.*

competitive bid: the awarding of a new stock issue to the highest bidder. In most cases, this nonnegotiated bid is made by investment banking groups.

competitive price: a price determined in the market by the bargaining of a number of buyers and sellers, each acting separately and without sufficient power to manipulate the market.

competitive profile: a resource containing a list of the bank's major competitors, growth comparisons of deposits and loan volume, product mixes, and service comparisons. [105]

competitive trader: a member of the exchange who trades in stocks for an account in which he or she has an interest. synonymous with *registered representative (trader)*. [20]

compile

(1) *general:* to collect, as with data.

(2) *computers:* to prepare a machine language program by means of a compiler. see *compiler.*

compiler

(1) *general:* a machine that compiles.

(2) *computers:* a routine that yields a specific program for a particular problem. The compiler converts computer instructions into a code that can be acted on by the computer.

complaint: the initial paper filed in court by the plaintiff in a lawsuit. It is referred to as a pleading—a statement of facts on which the plaintiff rests his or her cause of action.

complete audit: an audit in which an examination is made of the system of internal control and of the details of all the books of account, including subsidiary records and supporting documents, as to legality, mathematical accuracy, complete accountability, and application of accepted accounting principles. One of the main features of a complete audit is that the auditor is not expected to make any qualifications in his report except such as are imposed by lack of information, that is physical inability to get the fact. [49]

completed contract accounting: an accounting method that allows some companies with long-term contracts to deduct many expenses immediately but defer almost indefinitely reporting any revenue and profits to the Internal Revenue Service. The Treasury De-partment calls such deferrals an "interest-free loan" to the firms. This technique allows companys to report losses to the IRS while reporting profits to stockholders.

completed transaction: a sale property that has closed. In this transaction all legal and financial aspects are identified, and title to the property has transferred from seller to buyer.

completes: used in a floor report showing that an order to purchase or sell a block of stock has been carried out.

complete special audit: a complete audit of some particular phase of a governmental unit's activities, such as sinking fund transactions or a complete audit for all of a governmental unit's transactions for a shorter or longer period of time than the usual audit period. [49]

complete trust: a trust in which the trustee is not required to distribute income currently, or distribute amounts other than income, or make a charitable contribution. [37]

completion bond: see *bond, completion.*

complex trust: see *simple trust.*

compliance director: a member of a securities house who seeks to find fraud or unauthorized or unethical behavior, in the buying and selling of securities.

compliance examinations: specially designed examinations given by the three federal bank regulatory agencies. These examinations include procedures and standards, adopted by those agencies which will, for the first time, subject banks to a comprehensive review of their compliance with federal and state consumer credit statutes and regulations. [105]

compliance inspection report: a report given to a lender by a designated compliance inspector, indicating whether or not construction or repairs have complied to conditions established by a prior inspection. [105]

component operating firms: corporations that function as a unit of a holding company system. They are operating units of one parent company, which may merely hold stock in, and control the movement of, the existing operation companies or may, itself be an operating corporation.

composite: an insurance policy subscribed to by more than one firm on the same form.

composite check: a listing of payments to be made from an account, sent by the owner of the account to his or her depository institution with instructions to effect the payments and debit the account for the total amount. The payments are transmitted by the depository institution to the creditors for subsequent deposit by them in their respective accounts.

composite commodity standard: a monetary system concept where the value of the monetary unit is defined in terms of a selected number of commodities (composite commodity unit) instead of in terms of one or more precious metals.

composite demand: the sum of demands for an item or service beginning with any number of needs, all of which can be fulfilled by that particular item or service.

composite inventory: data accumulation on bank customers, including the most pertinent information that can be obtained about them.

composite limit order book (CLOB): a central electronic repository and display that automates all orders to buy and sell securities. It could eliminate the need for any exchanges by having buying and selling done directly by brokerage offices through a central computer system.

composite rate depreciation: a single depreciation rate to be applied against the total of depreciable assets or a group of such assets; based on an average of the rates applicable to individual items with some weighting of the relative importance of the several items.

composites: any data set that combines information from various sources to yield summary statistics concerning the securities industry. [105]

composite supply: an indefinite number and variety of items, each of which is able to satsify a particular need.

composite tape: a stock ticker printout that reports transactions occurring in national, regional, and over-the-counter exchange markets. [105]

composition: agreement between a borrower in financial difficulty and a lender, allowing the borrower to eliminate debt by paying only a portion of the total amount owed the lender. [78]

composition settlement: a creditor's acceptance of an amount smaller than that which he or she is legally entitled to from a debtor. By doing this the creditor waives any right to the full amount.

compound: to add interest to principal at time intervals for the purpose of establishing a new basis for subsequent interest computations.

compound abritrage: arbitrage achieved by using four or more markets. cf. *arbitrage.*

compound duty: a customs duty consisting of a specific duty to which is added an ad valorem duty. see also *customs duty.*

compounded: indicating the frequency with which interest is computed and added to the principal to arrive at a new actual balance.

compounded interest: interest created by the periodic addition of simple interest to principal, the new base thus established being the principal for the computation of additional interest.

compound-interest method of depreciation: taking the initial cost of a capital asset, deducting the expected salvage value at the time it is expected to be discarded and spreading the difference in equal installments per unit of time over the estimated life of the asset but then reducing the depreciation charge for each period by the amount of interest that such a charge would earn from the period of the charge to the time of discard.

compound tariff: consists either of (1) an ad valorem duty plus a specific duty or (2) a provision that ad valorem or specific duty will apply, whichever is higher.

comprehensive income: the change in equity (net assets) due to transactions and other events and circumstances from nonowner sources during a period. Comprehensive income does not include changes resulting from investments in the enterprise by owners and distributions from the enterprise to owners. [80]

compromise

(1) *general:* any agreement between two or more persons, usually in opposition, to settle their differences on areas of controversy without resort to legal action.

(2) *labor relations:* a settlement of a union-management dispute by an adjustment of differences by both sides, rather than resorting to outside involvement by a mediator or arbitrator.

Compt.: see *comptroller.*

comptroller: an executive officer whose job embraces the audit functions of the business.

Comptroller of the Currency (COC): a federal office created in 1863 to oversee the chartering and regulation of national banks.

comptroller's call: the Comptroller of the Currency may "call" upon all national banks to submit a complete financial report of their activities at any given date. Reports must, according to law, be submitted at his call at least three times a year. These "called reports" must also be published in all local newspapers in the town nearest to the bank. [10]

compulsory retirement: separation from employment at an age specified by union contract or company policy.

computer: a device capable of accepting information, applying a variety of actions on such data, and supplying the results of these processes. It usually consists of input and output, arithmetic, storage, communications, and control units. see *analogue computer, digital computer, first-generation computer, general-purpose computer, second-generation computer, third-generation computer.*

computer balancing: a section of the General Accounting Department responsible for balancing a register to NCR tapes. [105]

computer code: a machine code for a specific computer; any system of combinations of binary digits. synonymous with *machine code.*

computer science: the range of theoretical and applied disciplines connected with the development and application of computers.

concealment

(1) *general:* the willful withholding of any material fact(s) that would, if known, make the risk undesirable or would necessitate payment of a higher premium.

(2) *law:* the suppression of truth to the injury or prejudice of another. cf. *discovery practice.*

concentration account: a deposit account to which funds from other accounts held in the same name are periodically transferred. [105]

concentration ratio: in a specific industry, the breakdown of total business that is handled by a specified number of the largest organizations.

concern

(1) a business establishment, company, or firm.

(2) to be interested or anxious. [61]

concession

(1) *general:* any deviation from regular terms or previous conditions.

(2) *finance:* a reduction or rebate; an allowance from the initial price or rate.

concessionaire: the holder of a concession granted by a company, government, or other authorized body.

conciliation: in collective bargaining, the process whereby the parties seek to reconcile their differences. The discussion generated is advisory and par-

ticipation is not compulsory, but under the Taft-Hartley Act a union must notify the appropriate federal agency of an impending strike. Most conciliation work is conducted by the Federal Mediation and Conciliation Service. cf. *mediation.*

concurrent authority: exists when two or more brokers are given an open listing for property.

concurrent insurance: two or more insurance policies that provide the same coverage for the same property and the same interests.

Cond.: see *condition.*

condemnation

(1) *government:* the declaration by government that a structure is unsafe for use and is a menace to the safety of people.

(2) *law:* the taking of private property for public use. Under a condemnation proceeding, the property is taken with or without the consent of the owner, but upon the payment of just compensation. see *compensation, confiscation*; c.f. *eminent domain.* see also *excess condemnation.*

condensed balance sheet: a balance sheet where the details have been removed to give an easy, though accurate, reading of the assets, liabilities, and capital of the corporation. see *balance sheet.*

condensed statement: a financial statement grouping minor details together so that the statement can be more easily studied by the general public.

condition: a contractual clause, implied or expressed, that has the effect of investing or divesting with rights and duties the members of the contract.

conditional bond: see *bond, surety.*

conditional commitment for guarantee: FmHA's notice to a bank that the loan for which the bank is requesting a guarantee is approved for guarantee, subject to the conditions set forth in the commitment. [105]

conditional endorsement: an endorsement describing and imposing conditions upon a transferee. The instrument can still be negotiated within the terms of the condition, but the person who has made the conditional endorsement has the right to the proceeds of the instrument if the conditions are not fulfilled.

conditional gift: a gift of property by will which is subject to some condition specified in the will or in the trust instrument; opposed to an *absolute gift.* [32]

conditional indorsement: see *conditional endorsement.*

conditional sales: sales under a payment contract where title remains with the seller until final payment is made, but the property is transferred to the buyer at once. [28]

conditional sales contract: document used in installment sales credit arrangements, which withhold ownership title from the buyer until the loan has been paid in full. [78]

condition concurrent: a provision in a contract that two events must occur simultaneously, such as delivery of goods and their payment. A tender of performance by either party and rejection by the other creates liability on the part of the one rejecting.

condition of weekly reporting member banks: the Federal Reserve System release showing the changes in the reporting banks each week. These financial data, in part, show the changes in banks which represent more than half the banking resources of the United States.

condition precedent: a contract clause stating that immediate duties and rights will vest only upon the occurrence of an event. It is not a promise; therefore, its breach is not grounds for action against damages. However, it is the basis for a defense.

condition subsequent: a contract clause for the occurrence of an event that divests rights and duties (e.g., a fire insurance policy clause excusing the insurer from paying the policy if fire occurs and combustible materials were found within 5 feet of the area.)

condominium: individual ownership of a portion of a building that has other units similarly owned. Owners hold a deed and title. Owners pay taxes independently of other owners and can sell, lease, or otherwise dispose of the portion that the individual owns. Common areas, including halls, elevators, and so on, are jointly owned by the other tenants. see *lease-purchase agreement;* cf. *cooperative building.*

condominium conversion: changing rental units into condominiums, where the buyer gets title to a specified unit plus a proportionate interest in common areas. See *condominium.*

confession of a judgment: an admission by a party to whom an act or liability is imputed. [76]

confidence men: professional swindlers; people who cheat and defraud.

confidential risk report: a report established through investigations, of the physical condition of an insurer or his property, made prior to the issuance of a policy.

confirmation
(1) *investments:* a written order or

agreement to verify or confirm one previously given verbally, face to face, or by telephone. Executions of orders to buy or sell securities as substantiated in writing by brokers to their customers. see *dealer.*

(2) *law:* an assurance of title by the conveyance of an estate or right from one to another, by which a voidable estate is made sure or valid, or at times increased.

confirmed letter of credit: a foreign bank wishing to issue a letter of credit to a local concern may request a local bank in the city in which the beneficiary is located to confirm this credit to the beneficiary. The purpose of this confirmation is to lend the prestige and responsibility of the local bank to the transaction because the status of the foreign bank may be unknown to the beneficiary. The confirming bank assumes responsibility for the payment of all drafts drawn under the credit and usually charges a fee for doing so. [10]

confirming house: a firm that acts as intermediary between an overseas customer requiring goods and the home market seller. [105]

confiscation: the seizure of private property, without compensation, usually by a governmental agency. cf. *eminent domain, expropriation, nationalization.*

conformed copy: a copy of an original document with the signature, seal, and other such features being typed or otherwise noted. [37]

conforming mortgage loan: a mortgage loan that conforms to regularity limits such as loan-to-value ratio, term, and other characteristics. [59]

confusion of goods: the intermingling of the goods of two different owners, where the goods are difficult to separate once intermingled.

congeneric: meaning "of the same kind," this term has been used to designate one-bank holding companies that have diversified into areas beyond the traditional bounds of banking, but within the financial field. This term distinguishes them from the conglomerates, which are corporations that include business enterprises of all descriptions. [74]

conglomerate: the result of the merging of organizations producing differing items and services, to secure a large economic base, acquire sounder management, and gain greater potential profit. see *merger;* cf. *consortium.*

conglomerate merger: merger between companies in unrelated business lines.

Congress of Industrial Organizations (CIO): originally organized in 1935 as a committee (Committee for Industrial Organization) within the American Federation of Labor to spur unionization of mass production industries. Unions organized by the committee were expelled from the AFL in 1937, and the committee reorganized itself to form the Congress of Industrial Organizations in 1938.

connected load: in public utilities, the combined rating of all devices for receiving power on the customers' premises.

Cons.: see *consolidate, consolidated.*

consanguinity: blood relationship; to be distinguished from *affinity.* [37]

consent decree: in a case settlement, the instrument whereby the defendant agrees to cease certain actions that caused the action to be entered.

consent to pledge: a legal document

signed by a party who owns a particular asset, which gives permisssion for another party to pledge that asset as security for a loan. [105]

consent trust: a trust in which the consent of the settlor or some designated person is required before specified action by the trustee. [37]

consequential damage: the impairment of value which does not arise as an immediate result of an act, but as an incidental result of it. The impairment of value to private property caused by the acts of public bodies or caused by the acts of neighboring property owners. The term "consequential damage" applies only in the event no part of land is actually taken. The damage resulting from the taking of a fraction of the whole, that is, over and above the loss reflected in the value of the land actually taken, is commonly known as *severance damage*. [62]

conservator: a court-appointed official responsible for the protection of the interests on an estate.

Consid.: see *consideration*.

consideration
(1) *banking:* synonymous with *premium*.
(2) *law:* a requirement of valid contracts according to which all parties must provide something of value. cf. *forbearance, nudum pactum, quid pro quo*.

consignee: the ultimate recipient of goods; a shipping term.

consignment: the act of entrusting goods to a dealer for sale but retaining ownership of them until sold. The dealer pays only when and if the goods are sold.

consignment ledger: a subsididary ledger containing individual accounts with consignors.

consignment note: an instrument given when goods are dispatched, providing details of the items, the sender, and the individual to whom they are sent. The latter signs it upon arrival, providing proof of delivery.

consignment sale: a sales transaction completed by a consignee whereby items are sold for a consignor.

consignment shipment: a shipment of goods that is available to the importer for sale, at which time payment is made to the exporter. [105]

consignment terms: export trading on the basis that items exported on consignment remain the property of the exporter and are sold for the exporter by his or her agent.

consignor: the originator of a shipment.

consol(s):
(1) a bond that will never reach maturity; a bond in perpetuity.
(2) the name given to British government bonds.

console: the part of a computer used for communication between the operator or maintenance engineer and the central processing unit.

consolidate: to bring together various financial obligations under one agreement, contract, or note.

consolidated: the results obtained when the accounts of a parent company and its subsidiary companies are combined to reflect the financial position and results of operations of the group as if operated as a single entity. Such a consolidation involves intercompany eliminations and minority interest adjustments. [3]

consolidated accounting standards: the combined financial statements of a parent company and its subsidiaries. The consolidated accounting statements show assets, liabilities, and net worth for the total organization. [105]

consolidated balance sheet: a balance sheet showing the financial condition of a corporation and its subsidiaries. [20]

consolidated income statement: the combined statement of profit and loss for a group of firms controlled or owned by the same interests, thus eliminating duplications and intercompany profits and losses.

consolidated limit order book (CLOB): see *composite limit order book.*

consolidated mortgage: when two or more firms, each holding a mortgage on property, combine, and then the consolidated organization takes out a mortgage, the latter mortgage is referred to as a consolidated mortgage.

consolidated sinking fund: one sinking fund that is established to serve two or more bond issues. [49]

consolidated statement: see *combined financial statement.*

consolidated statement of financial position: a summary of a firm's financial position at a specific time.

consolidated statement of income: a financial summary of the activities of a firm at a specific time, noting the operations of all subsidiaries in which the company has a controlling interest.

consolidated tape: under the consolidated tape plan, the New York Stock Exchange and Amex ticket systems became the "consolidated tape" Network A and Network B, respectively, on June 16, 1975. Network A reports transactions in NYSE-listed securities that take place on the NYSE or any of the participating regional stock exchanges and other markets. Each transaction is identified according to its originating market. Similarly, transactions in Amex-listed securities, and certain other securities listed on regional stock exchanges, are reported and identified on Network B. [20]

consolidation: a combination of two or more organizations into one, to form a new entity.

consolidation loan: combines several debts into one loan, usually to reduce the annual percentage rate or the dollar amount of payments made each month, by extending them over a longer period of time. [78]

consolidation of bills: the borrowing of a lump sum of money for the payment of past-due bills; the money borrowed is then repaid in installments. [41]

consortium: a grouping of corporations to fulfill a combined objective or project that usually requires interbusiness cooperation and sharing of resources. cf. *cartel, conglomerate.*

conspicuous consumption: a term originated by Veblen to describe the phenomenon of consumers buying goods to show their position or status rather than for the other usefulness of the goods.

constant-cost industry: an industry in which average total unit cost remains the same as production volume increases or decreases.

constant costs: a statistical term indicating that prices, displayed in a time series, have been corrected to show a price level that existed at a certain date called the base period. see *base period.*

constant-dollar estimates: an estimate that removes the effects of price changes from statistical series reported in dollar terms.

constant-dollar plan: an investment plan under which funds are divided into two parts: a stock fund to purchase diversified common stock and a cash fund to be kept in liquid form. The plan calls for keeping the dollar (market) amount of the stock fund constant by selling on a rise and transferring to the cash fund, and vice versa in a price fall.

constant dollars: the actual prices of a previous year or the average of actual prices of a previous period of years.

constant factor: the periodic amount of principal and interest that is required to retire a loan.

constant payment: a fixed or invariable payment, a continually recurring payment. [62]

constant ratio: a method of comparing mortgage amortization (principal and interest) on an annual basis to the original amount of the mortgage. Expressed as a percentage. synonymous with *mortgage constant.*

constant yield rate: an installment finance method where a rate is computed on the total note as in the true discount rate for a contract of 12 monthly payments only.

construction bond: see *bond, construction.*

construction loan: funds extended on the security of real property for the purpose of constructing or improving a building. [39]

constructive receipt doctrine: income, although not actually reduced to a taxpayer's possession, which is credited to his or her account, set apart for him or her, or otherwise made available so that he or she may draw upon it at any time; used in determining what is included in the gross income of a taxpayer using cash method accounting. [105]

constructive side of the market: a long purchase of a stock with the anticipation that its market price will jump; a bullish position.

constructive trust: a trust imposed by a court of equity as a means of doing justice, without regard to the intention of the parties, in a situation in which a person who holds title to property is under a duty to convey it to another person; to be distinguished from an express trust and a resulting trust. [37]

consular invoice: an invoice covering a shipment of goods certified (usually in triplicate by the consul of the country for which the merchandise is destined. This invoice is used by customs officials of the country of entry to verify the value, quantity, and nature of the merchandise imported. [10]

consult account: a trust in which the trustee is required by the instrument to consult a designated party before taking action; to be distinguished from consent trust. [37]

consultant

(1) *general:* a specialist in any field of activity (e.g., psychological consultant, Wall Street consultant, engineering consultant), hired by an organization for the purpose of recommending solutions to a problem.

(2) *finance:* one with whom the fiduciary must confer in the administration of a fiduciary account. [37]

consumer: any person who uses goods and services.

consumer credit: credit extended by a

bank to a borrower for the specific purpose of financing the purchase of a household appliance, alteration, or improvement, a piece of equipment, or other personal needs. This form of credit is generally extended to individuals rather than to business executives.

consumer credit company (finance company): a company that specializes in lending small amounts of money to individuals [105]

Consumer Credit Counseling Services (CCCS): a unit of the Federal Home Loan Bank System. CCCS specializes in working with people who are overextended with debts and need to make arrangements with local creditors.

Consumer Credit Protection Act of 1968: see *Truth in Lending Act of 1968.*

consumer debentures: investment notes sold directly to the public by a financial institution. These notes are much like the certificates of deposit sold by banks and savings and loans. Unlike banks selling notes, these notes can be sold anywhere, at any interest rate determined to be found competitive by the institution.

consumer finance companies: companies licensed by a state for the special purpose of providing consumers with a reliable service for installment cash loans. [55]

consumer good: item bought and used by the final consumer for personal or household purposes.

consumer lease: a contract in the form of a bailment or lease for the use of personal property by a natural person primarily for personal, family, or household purposes. [105]

consumer loan: loans to individuals or families, the proceeds to be used for consumer, as contrasted with business or investment, purposes. [28]

consumer plant and equipment: the still unused service and uses that are built into the possession of a people as individuals and families, a form of personal and family wealth. [28]

Consumer Price Index (CPI): a measurement of the cost of living determined by the Bureau of Labor Statistics. see *cost of living index.*

Consumer Protection Act: see *Truth in Lending Act of 1968.*

consumer sale disclosure statement: a form presented by a dealer giving essential details on financing charges relative to a purchase on an installment plan. This is required under the Consumer Credit Protection (Truth-in-Lending) Act.

consumers' cooperatives: associations of ultimate consumers organized to buy items and services primarily for use by or resale to the membership.

consummation: a defined term under Regulation Z, meaning the actual time that a contractual relationship is created between borrower and lender, irrespective of the time of performance of a particular transaction. Depending upon the state law of contracts governing a particular association, consummation may occur at the time a loan is closed, at the time a lender accepts (as distinct from receives) a borrower's loan application, or at the time a firm commitment is given to make a loan. see *Regulation Z.* [59]

consumption: the final using of goods or services in the satisfaction of human wants.

consumption loan: a loan whose proceeds are used for personal purposes.

consumption tax: a tax on consumption. May be at the wholesale, manufacturing, or retail point.

Cont.: see *contract.*

contango

(1) *finance:* the cost factors when calculating from one given period to a future point.

(2) *investments:* a basic pricing system in futures trading. A form of premium or carrying charge; for example, instead of paying for the cost of warehousing silver bullion, paying insurance finance charges and other expenses (silver users prefer to pay more for a futures contract covering later delivery).

contemporaneous reserve accounting (CRA): a one-day lag allowing member banks of the Federal Reserve to calculate their required reserves and reserves held as vault cash for a week before making the final adjustments to their reserve balances on Wednesdays. This system is "contemporaneous" because, except for the one-day lag, assets and liabilities used in calculating reserves and required reserves are those of the same week. see *lagged reserve accounting.*

contest of a will: an attempt by legal process to prevent the probate of a will or the distribution of property according to the will. [37]

continental rate: the rate charged in Europe for foreign exchange and on bills of exchange.

contingency fund: assets set aside for use in unpredicted situations. see *contingent reserve;* cf. *sinking fund.*

contingency reserve: see *contingent reserve.*

contingent annuity: an annuity presently established and funded but with payments to commence upon the hap-

pening of an uncertain event, such as the death of a named person other than the annuitant.

contingent asset: an asset that may become actual or unqualified as situations presently unfulfilled are satisfied.

contingent beneficiary: see *beneficiary, contingent.*

contingent commission: a commission, the amount of which is dependent on the profitableness (or some other characteristic) of the business written by an agent or reinsurer. [53]

contingent duty: synonymous with *contervailing duty.*

contingent executor: an executor named in a will whose capacity as executor is dependent upon the action or nonaction of the principal executor. [37]

contingent fees: renumeration based or conditioned upon future occurrence or conclusions, or results of services to be performed. [62]

contingent fund: assets or other resources placed aside for unexpected expenditures, or for anticipated expenditures of an uncertain amount.

contingent interest: the right to property that depends for "vesting" or realization on the coming of some future uncertain occurrence.

contingent life tenant: a person whose life interest in an estate is dependent upon certain events occurring. [105]

contingent liability: the liability imposed on an individual, corporation, or partnership because of accidents caused by persons (other than employees) for whose acts the first party may be held responsible under the law. see *guaranteed debt, switch (contingent) order.*

contingent obligation: an obligation dependent upon other events; for example, in the case of income bonds, the payment of interest is contingent upon the earning by the corporation of an amount sufficient to pay the interest.

contingent order: a request to purchase or sell a security at a specific price which in contingent upon the earlier execution of another order; for example, "Purchase 50 ABC at ___ , if you can sell 50 XYZ at ___ ."

contingent payment order: a payment order that is executed only upon the receipt of a stipulated covering payment. [105]

contingent remainder: a future interest in property that is dependent upon the fulfillment of a stated condition before the termination of a prior estate; to be distinguished from vested remainder. see *remainder.* [37]

contingent reserve: the setting aside of a certain amount of profits to meet unanticipated needs of the business or some unexpected loss, the amount of which cannot be definitely ascertained at the time of budgeting.

contingent trustee: a trustee whose appointment is dependent upon the failure to act of the original or a successor trustee. [37]

continued bond: see *bond, continued.*

continuing account: a running or open book account where settlements are made regularly (e.g., 30 to 60 days).

continuing agreement: that portion of the broker's loan arrangement with a bank purporting to simplify the borrowing since the broker need not seek a loan application and sign a note each time he borrows. Following the signing of this agreement, the broker can borrow within the terms of the agreement on a continuous basis.

continuing guaranty: a form given to a bank by a person to guarantee repayment of a loan to another party. This guaranty promises payment by the guarantor in the event of default by the borrower, and is so worded that it may apply to a current loan, or to one made at a later date. The guaranty may or may not pledge collateral as security for the loan. [10]

continuity of coverage: a clause attached or contained in a fidelity bond which takes the place of another bond and agrees to pay the losses that would be recoverable under the first bond except that the discovery period has expired. This would be in a case where losses have been caused by a dishonest employee and have not been discovered, though they have occurred at various times stretching over a period of time, that time being a period under which several bonds have been insured. A chain of several bonds may be involved, each one superseding a prior obligation. Those losses will be covered if the chain of bonds is unbroken and each has included continuity of coverage clause. [56]

continuous audit: an audit where the detailed work is carried out continuously or at short, regular periods throughout the fiscal year, usually at the shortest intervals (weekly, monthly) when subsidiary records are closed and made available for audit in controllable form.

continuous budget: a budget that perpetually adds a month in the future as the month just ended is dropped.

continuous market: a securities or commodities market that is broad, enabling normal amounts to be sold with ease and little price variation.

contocurrent account: used in West Germany and parts of Switzerland to identify what is called in the United States a checking account.

contra: means that an account has an offsetting credit or debit entry. [59]

contrabalance: a balance in an account which is the opposite of the normal balance of that account (e.g., an accounts receivable account with a credit balance; such a balance is correctly shown as a liability). Asset valuation accounts, such as bad debt reserve, are contrabalances to the asset.

contraband: illegal or prohibited goods. see *smuggling.*

contract: an agreement between two or more persons, as established by law, and by which rights are acquired by one or more parties to specific acts or forbearance from acts on the part of others.

contract, breach of: see *breach of contract.*

contract account: general term describing a long-term credit arrangement for purchase of specific items described in the contract. Usually includes a service or carrying charge. see *chattel mortgage agreement, conditional sales contract, contract clause.* [41]

contract bond: see *bond, contract.*

contract broker: on the stock market, a member of the exchange trading for other members. Prior to 1919, the fee for this service was a flat $2 per 100 shares. Hence the contract broker is called a *two-dollar broker.* see *two-dollar brokers.*

contract clause: a clause in the Constitution of the United States (Article 1, Section 10) declaring that no state may pass laws diminishing the obligation of a contract. Although corporate franchises are accepted as contracts and protected by this clause, it cannot act as a bar to the regulatory and police powers of the state.

contract for deed: a written agreement between the seller and buyer of a piece of property, whereby the buyer receives title to the property only after making a determined number of monthly payments; also called an *installment contract* or *land contract.* [59]

contract grades: those grades or types of a commodity which may be delivered on the futures contract. Differentials based on federal standards have been established by the various commodity exchanges which provide premiums for superior grades or discounts for lower grades. [2]

contraction: a decline of economic activity in the business cycle. The opposite of expansion.

contract market: one of the 18 commodity exchanges, permitted under the Commodity Exchange Act to deal in futures contracts in the commodities.

contract month: the delivery month for a grain contract. Also, the month when grain is deliverable against future contracts.

contract of guarantee (line of credit): FmHA issues this to the lender testifying to its agreement to guarantee the bank's loan. [105]

contract of sale: a written document whereby an owner agrees to convey title to a property when the purchaser has completed paying for the property under the terms of the contract. [59]

contractor: a person who contracts to perform work or to supply materials under specified conditions. [44]

contract payable: sums due on contracts. [49]

contract purchasing: a form of purchasing defined in a contract for orders and deliveries, covering a time period, usually one year.

contract sale: a sale of real estate in which the seller retains title to the property until the buyer has made the required number of monthly payments. [59]

contracts in foreign currency: agreements to buy and sell an amount of one currency for another at an agreed rate of exchange. [105]

contractual liability

(1) liability assumed by contract.

(2) an additional coverage, for a specific exposure for which the basic liability policy does not provide. It may be obtained for an additional premium.

contractual plan: by common usage, an accumulation plan with a stated paying-in period and provision for regular investments at monthly or quarterly dates. Sustantially synonymous with *prepaid charge plan*. [30]

contrarian: popularized by David Dreman to describe the small investor who makes money in the stock market at a rate that exceeds the popular averages. By purchasing unpopular stocks, the buyer looks for investment-grade stocks that are out of favor in terms of their current price-earnings ratios. Obviously, the higher the price-earnings ratio on a stock—that is, the bigger the multiple of earnings that the market is

paying for it—the less likely it is to outperform both the market itself and stocks currently less in favor.

contrary market: market movement in an unexpected direction.

contributed capital: the payments in cash or property made to a corporation by its stockholders, in exchange for capital stock, in response to an assessment on the capital stock, or as a gift; paid-in capital; often, though not necessarily, equal to capital stock and paid-in surplus. [43]

contribution

(1) *general:* something given, such as time or money.

(2) *banking:* the bank's payment of, or obligation to pay, all or part of a loss.

(3) *law:* the sharing of a common loss or benefit, paid or to be paid by each of the parties involved.

contribution margin: the excess of total revenue over total variable cost.

contribution profit: sales revenue less the variable cost of producing the revenue.

control: a system under which all transactions or balances of a given type are included in a single total, so that the accuracy of their recording may be proved. [50]

control account: an account in the general ledger used to carry the total of several subsidiary accounts. Whenever any subsidiary account is affected, the same will be reflected in the control account total. Control accounts are also used as "total" accounts, controlling the accounts within a "book" or "ledger" in the bookkeeping department and the savings department. [10]

control card: a card which indicates the total dollar amount on deposit and the total number of accounts in a single ledger. Control cards are debited and credited according to each day's transactions and are used as a basis of proof when trial balances are taken. In addition to the control card for each ledger or section, there is a master control card for each unit, or for the bank as a whole. [39]

controlled account: where the principal authorizes the broker, with a power of attorney, to exercise his or her own discretion in the purchasing and selling of securities or commodities.

controlled commodities: commodities that are subject to the regulations of the Commodity Exchange Authority.

controlled company (corporation): a firm whose policies are controlled by another with ownership of 51 percent or more of its voting shares. see *Tax Reform Act of 1969;* cf. *working control.*

controlled economy: an economy that is regulated and greatly influenced by government. see *statism*; cf. *laissez-faire.*

controlled inflation: an economic situation that causes monetary and fiscal experts to urge creation or inflationary conditions, usually by increasing the supply of money in order to pull the economy out of a recession or deflation period into prosperity.

controlled market: see *free and open market.*

controller: see *comptroller.*

controlling account: an account, usually kept in the general ledger, which receives the aggregate of the debit and of the credit postings to a number of identical, similar, or related accounts called subsidiary accounts so that its balance equals the aggregate of the balance in these accounts. [49]

controlling interest: any ownership of a business in excess of 50 percent. However, a small percentage of shareholders may control the firm if the remainder of the stock is distributed among many owners and is not active in voting. see *working control;* cf. *minority interest.*

controlling records: a class of financial records within a bank composed of the controlling books or accounts of the bank. see *controlling account.*

controls: approaches by regulatory agencies to keep the economy in a healthy position. In most cases, governmental agencies act, by creating rules, to monitor the condition of the nation's economy.

control stock: securities belonging to those who have controlling interest in a company.

Conv.: see *convertible.*

convenience goods: products that the public wishes to purchase with a minimum of effort or time (toothpaste, cigarettes, sodas, paper, etc.).

convenient payment account: installment payment arrangement for purchase of either soft or hard goods. Usually carries a service or carrying charge. Specific payments required on specified dates. synonymous with *deferred payment account.* [41]

conventional billing: a system of rendering to a customer an itemized, descriptive statement of all purchases, cash payments, merchandise returned, and allowances made during a specific period, usually one calendar month. Original sales checks and other billing media are retained by the store. [41]

conventional fixed-rate mortgage: a mortgage with a fixed term, fixed rate, and fixed monthly payments which is fully paid off within 30 years or less. It is a mortgage without government insurance or guarantee. see also *conventional loan*. [66]

conventional loan: a mortgage loan, usually granted by a bank or loan association. The loan is based on real estate as security rather than being guaranteed by an agency of the government. This loan has a fixed interest rate and fixed payments for the life of the loan. see also *conventional fixed-rate mortgage.*

conventional tariff system: a system of tariff duties in which rates are largely or wholly set by bilateral or multilateral commercial agreements with other nations and subject to change. cf. *autonomous tariff system.*

conversion

(1) *general:* the process of changing from one system or one type of equipment to another.

(2) *banking:* a provision whereby a more permanent form of insurance may be elected without a medical examination if the request is made within the specified time and an additional premium is paid.

(3) *computers:* the process of changing from one method of data processing to another or from one data-processing system to another (e.g., using COBOL instead of FORTRAN).

(4) *law:* the unauthorized taking of another's goods or property.

conversion charge: the specified cost of converting from one class or series of an open-end fund to another issued by the same company or group of companies having the same sponsor. It is usually lower than the regular sales charge. [30]

conversion costs: a combination of direct labor and factor overhead in the manufacturing process.

conversion parity: the common stock price where the conversion value of a bond is equal to the existing market price of the convertible bond. see *conversion price.*

conversion point: the price (adjusted for accrued dividends) at which stock into which a bond is convertible will just equal the current market price of the bond plus accrued interest on the bond.

conversion premium: the percentage that the price of the convertible trades above its conversion value. One of the axioms of convertible bond trading is that the lower the premium, the more closely it will trade in step with the common. The higher the premium, the more likely the issue will trade on its merits as a bond.

conversion price: the price for which a convertible bond, debenture, or preferred stock of a firm can be exchanged by an owner for common stock or another security of the same organization.

conversion privilege: see *exchange privilege.*

conversion rate: an exchange rate from foreign to U.S. currency. [105]

conversion ratio: the number of shares of common stock received when a convertible bond or convertible preferred stock is exchanged with the same firm. The price is frequently given at the issue date of the bond or preferred stock, and may not be the same as the market price when the conversion takes place.

conversion value: value created by changing from one state, character, form, or use to another. [62]

convertibility: ease of exchanging one currency for that of another nation or for gold. see *soft currency.*

convertible: slang, any corporate stock that can be converted to a stock of another corporation.

convertible bond: see *bond, convertible.*

convertible currencies: includes the U.S. Treasury and Federal Reserve holdings of foreign currencies that are counted as part of official U.S. reserve assets. [11]

convertible debentures: like bonds, these carry a fixed interest rate and have a set maturity date. They may be traded in for a given amount of stock at any time at the option of the investor. The issuer, however, also has the right to call them in, to be redeemed either in cash or for common stock.

convertible hedge: an investment strategy of selling common stock short at the same time a long position is created in convertible bonds of the same firm. This form of hedging occurs when a decline is anticipated.

convertible money: money that can be exchanged at par for the standard or legal money.

convertible preferred stock: a security that can be exchanged at the owner's option for a fixed quantity of common shares of the same corporation.

convertibles: interest-paying debentures and dividend-paying preferred shares that can be exchanged for the common stock of the issuing company on a preset basis. The conversion privilege becomes valuable only if the mar-

ket value of the debenture or preferred stock is below that of the total value of the common shares into which it can be converted.

convertible security: usually a bond or preferred stock that may be converted into common stock at the option of the owner.

convertible wraparound mortgage: see *CWM.*

conveyance: a written statement called a deed, whereby ownership of property is passed from one person or organization to another.

conveyancing: the act of transferring title to real property.

cooking the books: slang; corporate accounting irregularities.

cooling-off period: the term for the period, usually 20 days, that must elapse before the filing of a registration for a new security and public sale, as declared by the SEC.

cooperative: anything owned jointly to the same end.

cooperative apartment: dwelling units in a multidwelling complex in which each owner has an interest in the entire complex and a lease on his or her own apartment, although he or she does not own the apartment as in the case of a condominium. [105]

cooperative bank: a term given in some states to an institution that operates as a savings and loan association. see *savings and loan association.* [39]

cooperative building: tenants residing in the building are stockholders in a corporation that owns the real estate. All are part owners of the corporation. Stockholders sign a proprietary lease with an operating organization, and in place of rent pay a proportionate fixed rate to cover operating costs, maintenance, and so on. cf. *condominium.*

cooperative central bank: a state-chartered mutual institution in Massachusetts to which all state savings associations (called cooperative banks) in Massachusetts must belong; it insures the savings accounts held by members and serves as a central credit facility. [59]

cooriginator: in bonding, where the clients of more than one surety company join for a specific contract. Such surety is known as cooriginator for its client's share. [54]

co-ownership: synonymous with *multiple ownership.*

copartnership (partnership): a company of partners, as distinguished from a proprietorship or a corporation. [76]

Copeland Act of 1934: so-called *Antikickback Law,* making it illegal for an employer or his or her agent to extract a payment as a condition of continued employment. The law prohibits employers or their agents from using force, threats, or other means to secure the return of any part of a worker's wages as a condition of retaining his or her job. Violators are fined.

copper a tip: slang, a person who reacts negatively to a tipster's advice.

Cor.: see *corpus.*

cordoba: monetary unit of Nicaragua.

core inflation: the underlying rate at which prices would rise even in the absence of any excessive demand pressure or any sharp increases in prices, or strikes in key businesses.

corner the market: to purchase a security on a scale large enough to give the purchaser control over the price.

Corp.: see *corporation.*

corporate agent: trust companies act as agents for corporations, governments, and municipalities for various transactions. In each case, a fee is charged for the particular service rendered. [10]

Corporate Bankruptcy Act: see *National Bankruptcy Act. of 1898.*

corporate bond: see *bond, corporate.*

corporate bond equivalent: the semiannual equivalent rate of return for a security whose interest payments are not on a semiannual basis.

corporate-bond unit trusts: similar to GNMA trust units, but without monthly return of principal. Yield is close to a point less. see *Government National Mortgage Association.*

corporate depositary: a trust institution serving as the depositary of funds or other property. see also *depositary, depository.* [37]

corporate fiduciary: a trust institution functioning in a fiduciary capacity, such as an administrator, trustee, executor, or guardian.

Corporate Income Fund (CIF): a short-term series investment vehicle. It is a unit trust that is similar to a money market fund with a fixed portfolio of high-grade investment paper.

corporate indenture: an agreement made by a bank to act as an intermediary between a corporation making a public bond offering and the purchasers of the bonds. The bank agrees to act as a trustee by protecting the interest of the lenders (bondholders). [105]

corporate profits after taxes: the earnings of U.S. corporations organized for profit after liability for federal and state taxes has been deducted. [73]

corporate profits before taxes: the

net earnings of corporations organized for profit measured before payment of federal and state profit taxes. They are, however, net of indirect business taxes. They are reported without deduction for depletion charges and exclusive of capital gains and losses and intercorporate dividends. [73]

corporate profits tax liability: federal and state taxes levied on corporate earnings of a given year; a measurement of taxes for the year in which they are incurred, not necessarily for the year in which they are paid.

corporate records: the records of a corporation required by incorporation laws. A listing of all shareholders, their addresses, quantity of stock, date of purchase, and price paid for shares is obligatory.

corporate resolution: a document given to a bank by a corporation defining the authority vested in each of its officers who may sign and otherwise conduct the business of the corporation with the bank. Corporate resolutions usually are given with or without borrowing powers. These powers are granted by the board of directors of the firm. [10]

corporate shell: a firm having no fixed assets except for its name, cash, and perhaps a stock exchange listing. Some shells are illegal or carry on illegal activities.

corporate stock
(1) equity shares of a corporation classified as common, preferred, or classified.
(2) sometimes, bonds of a municipality.

corporate surety: insurance provided by a surety company as compared to surety provided by a person. The writ-

ing of bonds by a corporation as obligor.

corporate surplus: as of the date of the balance sheet, the equity in the assets not offset by the capitalization, current or deferred liabilities, or unadjusted credits. It includes appropriations for additions to property, for retirement of funded debt, reserves for sinking and other funds, and other appropriations not specifically invested. [18]

corporate tax equivalent: the rate of return needed on a par bond to produce the same after-tax yield to maturity as a given bond.

corporate trust: a trust created by a corporation, typical of which is a trust to secure a bond issue. [37]

corporate trustee: a trust institution serving as a trustee. [37]

corporation
(1) *general:* an organization having purposefulness, declared social benefit, derived powers, legal entity, permanence, and limited liability.
(2) *law:* individuals created by law as a legal entity, vested with powers and ability to contract, own, control, convey property, and discharge business within the boundaries of the powers granted. cf. *firm.*

corporation account: a checking or savings account owned by a corporation and established in accordance with a resolution adopted by its board of directors.

corporation bond: see *bond, corporate.*

corporation charter: a document issued by the state or federal government giving a group of persons the right to act as a legal person in the conduct of an enterprise and specifying at least some of the conditions of operation.

corporation de facto: despite a minor failure to comply with the regulations for incorporation, a legal entity that thereafter has exercised corporate powers.

corporation de jure: a corporation formed by fulfilling the requirements of the law permitting the formation of the corporation.

corporation finance: the function within a firm responsible for providing funds needed by the organization. This includes raising initial capital, working capital, emergency funds, expansion capital, and so on.

corporation income tax: a progressive tax levied on earnings of corporations and Massachusetts trusts by either a state or the federal government.

corporation securities: securities of a business corporation, as distinguished from municipal or government securities.

corporation sole: a one-man corporation, the authority, duties, and powers of which are attached to and go with the office and not the natural person who for the time being holds the office. [37]

corporation tax: a federal or state tax levied on the profits of a corporation. [105]

corporators: the group which in certain states elects the trustees of a mutual savings bank. The number of corporators is not limited, and the group is self-perpetuating. [39]

corporeal: pertaining to a right or group of rights of a visible and tangible nature. [62]

corporeal heraditament: tangible property that can be inherited.

corporeal property: real or personal property having form or structure (e.g., house, furniture, land, fixtures). cf. *chose(s) in possession.*

corpus: a term used in trust companies and trust accounting to describe all the property in a trust, also referred to as the "body" of the trust. A corpus may consist of real estate, stocks, bonds, and other personal property, cash in the form of bank accounts, and any items that the donor may wish to have included. [10]

correction: any price reaction within the market leading to an adjustment by as much as one-third to two-thirds of the previous gain.

correction voucher: a form used by tellers to facilitate the correction of any errors made in the recording of transactions on electronic data-processing equipment. [59]

correlation: a relationship or dependence. Reflecting the principle that two things or variables are so related that change in one is accompanied by a corresponding or parallel change in the other.

correspondency system: the origination and administration of mortgage loans for investors by independent loan correspondents. [22]

correspondent: a securities firm, bank, or other financial organization that regularly performs services for another in a place or market to which the other does not have direct access. Securities firms may have correspondents in foreign countries or on exchanges of which they are not members. Correspondents are frequently linked by private wires. Member organizations of the New York Stock Exchange with offices in New York City may also act as correspondents for out-of-town member organizations that do not maintain New York City offices. [20]

correspondent bank: a bank that is the depository for another bank. The correspondent bank accepts all deposits in the form of cash letters and collects items for its bank depositor.

corset: a strategy whereby the more money that banks accumulate for lending over six months, the bigger the deposits with a central bank will have to be.

cosigner: synonymous with *comaker.*

cost: the value given up by an entity in order to receive goods or services. Cost is the value given up to get an item in the volume needed, shipped to the desired location. All expenses are costs, but not all costs are expenses.

cost accounting: a branch of accounting dealing with the classification, recording, allocation, summarization, and reporting of current and prospective costs. It provides the means by which management can control manufacturing costs.

cost and freight: see *C&F.*

cost and insurance: a shipping term indicating that the price includes the cost of goods and insurance. Freight charges are not included. [105]

cost approach to value: a method of estimating the value of real property by deducting depreciation from the cost of replacement and adding the value of the land to the remainder. see *appraisal.*

cost basis: the orginal price or cost of an asset usually based on the purchase price or, in the case of assets

received from an estate, on the appraised value of the assets at the death of the donor or some anniversary or other fixed date. [37]

cost-benefit analysis: a branch of operations research that aids in evaluating the implications of alternative courses of action. This method is primarily concerned with the selection of equipment, products, and so on, before they become available.

cost bond: see *bond, cost.*

cost center: in accounting, the establishment of areas to reflect the scope of responsibility of a supervisor (such as a department or process) and the accumulation of costs under the control of these areas.

cost curve: a graphical presentation with dollars of cost on the vertical axis and quantity of product on the horizontal axis, the curve connecting the costs of varying quantities of product.

cost effectiveness: see *cost-benefit analysis.*

cost factors: the various expenses that must be met by a supplier of consumer credit, and which therefore influence the charges he or she will make for credit services. [55]

costing: synonymous with *cost accounting.*

cost, insurance, and freight (CIF): a quoted price that includes the handling charges, insurance, and freight costs up to delivery, usually up to a port of entry. cf. *cost and freight* (see under *C&F.*).

cost ledger: a subsidiary record wherein each project, job, production center, process, operation, product, or service is given a separate account where all items entering into its cost are posted in the required detail. Such accounts should be so arranged and kept that the results shown in them may be reconciled with and verified by a control account or in the general books. [49]

cost of capital: the rate of return that a firm must pay to acquire investment funds.

cost of funds: interest (dividends) paid or accrued on savings, Federal Home Loan Bank advances, and other borrowed money during a period as a percent of average savings and borrowings.

cost of goods sold: the purchase price of goods sold during a specified period, including transportation costs.

cost of insurance: the cost or value of net insurance protection in a given year. [12]

cost of living

(1) *general:* the average cost to an individual of providing the basics of life. see *price control.*

(2) *finance:* the average of the retail prices of all goods and services required for a reasonable living standard. see *Consumer Price Index.*

cost of living adjustment (COLA): an increase or decrease of wages based on the increase or decrease in the purchasing power of money. Inflation and deflation are primary causes for a cost of living adjustment. see *escalator clause.*

Cost of Living Council: established in 1971, a committee of government appointees responsible for administering a 90-day freeze on wages and prices.

cost of living index: popular term for the Consumer Price Index issued monthly by the U.S. Department of Labor, Bureau of Labor Statistics. A measurement of changes in prices of goods and services purchased by moderate-income families. Wages of workers whose union contracts contain an escalator clause fluctuate with the cost of living index.

cost of merchandise sold: in accounting, the total cost of the units of merchandise sold during a fiscal period. It is determined by subtracting the cost of ending merchandise inventory from the costs of the beginning merchandise inventory plus inventory purchased (or manufactured) during the fiscal period involved.

cost of money

(1) *bank card:* the expense, expressed as an annual percentage, which is charged by the bank to a credit card operation for the use of funds.

(2) *lending:* a calculated figure that considers the respective costs of the several sources of bank funds to establish a cost that must be covered by a bank's rate structure on loans. [105]

cost of occupancy: the periodic expenditure of money necessary to occupy a property, exclusive of the expenses directly attributable to the conduct of a business. [6]

cost of reproduction: the cost of replacing a building as of any given date (usually current). [59]

cost of sales: the composite value of the product at the time it is offered for sale. This is composed of the manufacturing cost plus a proportionate percentage of selling and administrative expenses and profit. [38]

cost or market, whichever is lower: a conservative basis of inventory valuation. [105]

cost-plus contracts: an agreement whereby a buyer pays a seller or producer the costs of the product in addition to a percentage of the costs for the seller's profit.

cost plus fixed fee (CPFF): a contract used for some types of construction, development programs, and research programs whereby costs are not estimable beforehand. The compensation is the sum of all expenses incurred plus a specific fee. [105]

cost-plus pricing: the practice of setting a selling price by adding a profit factor to costs. [105]

cost-push inflation: an inflationary cycle that results from increasing supply and labor costs. They lead to increased prices for goods. As the cost of living rises, workers demand wage increases, and the cycle repeats. [105]

cost records: all ledgers, supporting records, schedules, reports, invoices, vouchers, and other records and documents reflecting the cost of projects, jobs, production centers, processes, operations, products, or services, or the cost of any of the component parts thereof. [49]

costs and expenses: costs of conducting business that are paid from revenues received by the firm.

cost schedule: a tabular arrangement showing the cost of each quantity of production.

cost-share: to share the cost(s) of, such as to *cost-share* a business.

cost standard: the cost of a specific activity, process, or product, that has been specified and is referred to for control and reporting. Deviations in actual costs from the established standards usually must be explained. [105]

cost theory of capitalization: where a firm's capitalization is determined by the out-of-pocket investments in fixed assets, the regular working capital needed to run the firm, advertising, and other related costs.

cost unit: a term used in cost accounting to designate the unit of product or service whose cost is computed. These units are selected for the purpose of comparing the actual cost with a standard cost or with actual costs of units produced under different circumstances or at different places and times. [49]

cost-volume profit analysis: a method used for measuring the functional relationships between the major aspects of profits and for identifying the profit structure of an organization.

cosurety: one of a group of surety companies executing a bond. The obligation is joint and several, but common practice provides a stated limit of liability for each surety.

cotrustee: a person, trust organization, or bank permitted to provide trust functions, acting with another as a trustee.

Cotton Futures Act: the United States Cotton Futures Act was legislated in 1915 to standardize transactions in cotton futures. In 1936, the Commodity Exchange Act was amended to cover other commodities, including cotton.

Council for Mutual Economic Assistance (CMEA) (COMECON): founded in 1949 to aid the development of member states (Bulgaria, Cuba, Czechoslovakia, German Democratic Republic, Hungary, Mongolia, Poland, and Romania) through joint utilization and coordination of activities.

Council of Economic Advisors (CEA): in accordance with the Employment Act of 1946, a group of economists charged with advising the president on a variety of matters, including the preparation of the budget message to Congress. see also *Joint Economic Committee.*

Council on Wage and Price Stability (COWPS): a federal agency responsible for the monitoring of wage and price increases in the private sector; reviews government policies contributing to inflation and reports findings to Congress and the president. Dismantled by the President in 1981.

counter cash: that part of the actual cash of a bank kept by the tellers in their cages. [31]

counter check: a form of check provided by a bank for the convenience of the depositor. A counter check may be cashed only by the drawer personally. [50]

counterclaim: a defendant's claim that the defendant is entitled to recover from the plaintiff.

countercyclical (policy): leveling the ups and downs of the business cycle with budget deficits during depression and surpluses during prosperity. synonymous with *compensatory fiscal policy.*

counter deposits: a deposit presented at the teller's window by a customer. Other forms include deposits by mail, clearings, collections, or internal sources. [31]

countererror: in accounting, an error (over or short) that is offset by an error of equal amount, thus creating a balance which is correct without disclosing that two or more of the transactions apparently proved are actually in error. [31]

counterfeit: imitation or fraudulent money.

counterfeit card
(1) device or instrument that has been printed, embossed, or encoded like a bank card, but which is not a card because it is not authorized by an issuer.
(2) a card that has been validly issued by an issuer and which has been changed without the authorization of the issuer. [105]

counterfeit currency coverage: a bond that protects an insured against loss through the receipt in good faith of counterfeited or altered currency or coin.

counterfeit paper: paper arising from the use of a counterfeit card showing the purchase of goods and/or services from a merchant or a cash advance. [105]

counter item: any item accepted or originated at the bank teller window as contrasted with those received by mail, clearings, or from internal departments. [10]

countermand: to cancel an order that has not yet been carried out.

counteroffer: if the one to whom an offer is extended proposes terms different from those set forth in the original offer and thus rejects the original offer, he or she is in effect making a counteroffer. An effort to accept an offer conditionally is a *counteroffer.*

counterpart monies: local currency equivalents of dollar assistance given to nations by the United States following World War II that are in turn used to purchase U.S. goods or services. cf. *tied loan.*

counterpurchasing: placing an order with a manufacturer in one country with the expectation that merchandise of equal value and/or quantity will be sold in the opposite direction to the other nation.

countersignature

(1) *banking:* the signature of a licensed agent or representative on a policy, which is necessary to validate the contract.

(2) *law:* a signature added to a document to authenticate it. cf. *attestation.*

counterspeculation: action by the government in a controlled economy designed to counteract the power of buyers or sellers to influence price (and thus speculate) by estimating the price that would prevail in the absence of restrictions by sellers or buyers and then guaranteeing that estimated price. The guaranteed price is achieved by government purchases or sales.

countertrade: methods used to sell products to countries that do not have the cash to pay for them, that is, when a company agrees to buy or market abroad products of another nation valued at up to the entire cost of the selling firm.

countervailing credit: see *back-to-back.*

countervailing duty: a customs duty levied by an importing nation as a protective surtax to offset an export bounty paid by the exporting nation. synonymous with *contingent duty.*

countervailing excise duty: synonymous with *compensatory duty.*

countervailing tariff: an extra tariff imposed by one nation to offset the export bounty granted by another nation.

country bank: a national or state bank that is not located in a Federal Reserve city. Country banks' legal reserve requirements are usually less than for large city banks.

country check: a transit check; an item drawn on an out-of-town bank; a check drawn upon a bank out of a central reserve or reserve city.

country club billing: a billing system in which the account statement is accompanied by copies of original invoices. [36]

country code: a three-digit code to identify uniquely the country to which the transaction data generated by the card should be routed. [105]

country collections: all items that are being sent outside the city in which the sending bank is located. A banker will speak of "city collection," which are items drawn on banks and business houses upon whom drafts are to be collected within the city of the bank's location; and "country collections," which are sent out of the city to the bank's correspondents for collection and payment. [10]

country item: see *country collections.*

country price: the price farmers receive when they sell their commodity in an area removed from the central market. It is frequently quoted as so many points or cents "on" or "off" a certain futures price.

coupon: the portion of a bond that is redeemable at a given date for interest payments. cf. *talon.*

coupon account: type of credit extension whereby books of coupons having a stated value are sold on an installment payment basis. Coupons are used in issuing stores as cash. Payment for the coupon book is stretched over a period of time. Coupon accounts are generally used for credit customers of limited responsibility, and whose buying must be closely controlled. [41]

coupon bond: see *bond, coupon.*

coupon book: a set of payment cards or computer cards that the borrower returns to the association one at a time with regular loan repayments, or with deposits for savings accounts such as a club account. [59]

coupon collection: being negotiable, coupons are collectable like any other negotiable instrument. The owner of the bond from which the coupon was clipped signs a "certificate of ownership" and attaches the coupon to this certificate. It is then either cashed by the bank, or deposited by the depositor as a credit to his or her account. Coupons are collected by banks under special transit letters which require considerably more description than is required for check collections. [10]

coupon collection teller: the person in a coupon collection department who processes coupons presented for payment.

coupon envelope: a special envelope provided by a bank for the deposit of interest payments on loans. [105]

coupon ledger: the ledger used by a bank or trust company to record the receipt of monies in order to pay coupons, disbursements for their redemption when presented for payment, and the numbers of coupons paid.

coupon-paying department: found within a bank or trust company, a department chosen as paying agent by corporations and others to pay matured coupons and bonds.

coupon payment form: a form sent to a credit bureau after an inquiry has been made by telephone. The proper coupon is attached to it. [76]

coupon payments account: to show the total coupon checks outstanding, a bank or trust company will create a general ledger account to identify coupon redemption payments.

coupon rate: the interest rate specified on interest coupons attached to a bond. synonymous with *nominal interest rate*. [49]

coupon shell: used in certain localities to describe the envelope in which maturing coupons are enclosed for collection. [10]

coupon system: see *Associated Credit Bureaus of America, Inc.*

coupon teller: a bank teller responsible for controlling the redemption of matured coupons that have been presented for payment.

coupon transmittal form: a form used to request a credit report by mail. The proper coupon is attached to it. [76]

coupon yield: interest on a bond on an annual basis divided by its face value, stated in percentage. This is not usually equal to the current yield or yield to maturity. [105]

court account: accounts that require court accountings and approval in their normal conduct. Probate, guardianship, conservatorship, and testamentary trust accounts are the most common. [37]

courtage: a European term for brokerage fee.

courtier: French term for *broker.*

court bond: see *bond, court.*

courtesy box: collection box equipped with mail chute for motorists. [24]

court trust: a trust coming under the immediate supervision of the court such as a trust by order of court or, in some states, a trust under will. [37]

covenant: a contract pertaining to an undertaking, a promise, or an agreement to do or forbear from doing that which has legal validity and is legally enforceable.

covenant of equal coverage: synonymous with *negative pledge clause.*

"cover": shorts are said to "cover" when they buy back the contracts they had previously sold, thereby liquidating their position. [2]

coverage

(1) *general:* synonymous with *insurance* or *protection.*

(2) *finance:* the ratio of assets to cover specific liabilities.

covered arbitrage: arbitrage between financial instruments dominated in differing currencies, using forward cover to eliminate exchange risk.

covered margin: the interest rate margin between two instruments denominated in differing currencies, after taking account of the cost of forward cover.

covered option: an option in which the seller (or writer) owns the underlying security, as opposed to the uncovered (or naked) condition, under which the option is written against cash or other margin.

covered writing: the most common, and perhaps easiest to understand, strategy is writing calls against a long position in the underlying stock. By receiving a premium, the writer intends to realize additional return on the underlying common stock in his portfolio or gain some element of protection (limited to the amount of the premium less transaction costs) from a decline in the value of that underlying stock. The covered writer is long the underlying stock or a convertible security such as warrants, convertible bonds, convertible preferreds, or a listed option of the same class. He is willing to forsake possible appreciation in his underlying

issues in return for payment of the premium. [15]

covering

(1) *finance:* the act of meeting one's obligation.

(2) *investments:* buying a stock previously sold short. [20]

cover payment: an arrangement by which a correspondent bank is reimbursed for payment made in accordance with instructions of the sending bank. [105]

coverture: the legal status of a married person. [105]

COWPS: see *Council on Wage and Price Stability.*

CP

(1) see *closing price.*

(2) see *closing purchase.*

(3) see *collar pricing.*

(4) see *commercial paper.*

(5) see *condition precedent.*

CPA: see *certified public accountant.*

CPCU: see *Chartered Property & Casualty Underwriter.*

CPFF: see *cost plus fixed fee.*

CPI: see *Consumer Price Index.*

CPM: see *critical path method.*

CPN: see *commercial paper note.*

CPS

(1) see *convertible preferred stock.*

(2) see *cumulative preferred (stock).*

CPU: see *central processing unit.*

CQ respondent bank: banks that have exchanged authorized signature lists, and/or engage in an exchange of services, and/or have an account or accounts with each other. [105]

Cr.

(1) see *credit.*

(2) see *creditor.*

CR: see *cash reserve.*

CRA: see *contemporaneous reserve accounting.*

crash: a sudden and disastrous drop in business activity, prices, security values, and so on, as occurred in October of 1929.

crawling peg: foreign exchange rates that permit the par value of a country's currency to change automatically by small increments, upward or downward, if in actual daily trading on the foreign exchange markets the price in terms of other monies persists on the floor or ceiling of the established range for a given period.

cream: slang, insurance policyholders having the lowest premiums, in part because they are the best risks.

creampuff sale: an expression suggesting that real property is easily sold.

creative financing: any of various home mortgage arrangements to make buying more affordable.

creator: a trustor or settlor; a person who creates a trust by will or a voluntary trust.

Cred.
(1) see *credit.*
(2) see *creditor.*

Crediscope: a more objective system of reporting trade data from creditor's ledgers. It was introduced in 1977. [76]

credit
(1) *general:* an entry recorded on the right side of a ledger. cf. *debit.*
(2) *banking:* funds remaining in a bank account. see also *bank credit.*
(3) *finance:* sales or purchases that are accompanied by a promise to pay later.

credit acceptance: notification to a customer that his or her credit application has been accepted and an account is now available for his or her use. [41]

credit adjustment: a correction issued and posted to a cardholder account which reduces the balance of the account. [105]

credit agency: firms that provide credit and collection information.

credit analyst: an expert who determines by examining a person's present and past activities whether the person has earned credit. [41]

credit application: a form filled out by a borrower wanting credit, or an interview, which seeks information about an applicant regarding residence, employment, income, and existing debt. [78]

credit approval department: that aspect or department of a bank card operation which is responsible for the processing of new cardholder applications to determine if the applications are approved or declined. May include the responsibility for limit control. [105]

credit association: a group of local retail credit granters forming a dues-paying association. In most cases the local association with 10 or more members is a unit of the National Retail Credit Association. Usually known as the Retail Credit Association. [41]

credit authorization/verification: an inquiry process undertaken to reduce the risk of credit fraud or of extending credit in excess of an imposed credit limit.

credit authorizor: see *authorizor.*

credit balance: see *balance of account.*

credit bank: synonymous with *commercial bank.*

credit barometrics: financial ratios applied to balance sheets and profit and loss statements that aid in credit analysis.

credit bill: a bill of exchange where the

debtor has arranged in advance for credit with the drawee.

credit bureau: an agency holding central files of data on consumers in a given trade area. These bureaus collect personal data, data on paying habits of individuals, and so on, and make impartial reports for credit granters.

credit card: a card issued by an organization entitling the bearer to credit at its establishments (e.g., Exxon's credit card used at gas stations). There are single-purpose cards issued by a specific firm, multipurpose cards (e.g., American Express, Carte Blanche), and bank cards (e.g., MasterCard and Visa).

credit card center: the physical facility where credit card operations are conducted. [105]

Credit Card Issuance Act: federal regulation, which became effective in October 1970, that regulates the issuance of credit cards and the extent of a cardholder's liability in case a card is used without permission. [105]

credit clearing: see *credit interchange.*

credit company
(1) a commercial credit organization.
(2) a firm that operates as a factor and takes paper subject to recourse rather than without recourse.

credit contract: a written statement showing how, when, and how much you will pay for goods and services.

credit control: any policy purporting to expand or contract credit, such a policy being applied by governments, banks, a central banking organization, or other agencies.

Credit Control Act of 1969: federal legislation giving the Federal Reserve System standby authority to control the price and allocation of credit if authorized by the president, one that has never been invoked. Expected to expire June 30, 1982.

credit criteria: the standards applied to cardholder applications or to previous account records in order to determine approval or rejection of the application for the issuance of a credit card, the establishment of a line of credit, or the increase of a line of credit. [105]

credit currency: currency that does not have full convertibility into standard money. synonymous with *fiduciary money (or standard).*

credit decline: notification to a customer that his or her credit application has not been accepted.

credit department
(1) *general:* in a nonbank the department of a company that establishes lines of credit for various customers and authorizes the extension of credit. In addition, most mercantile credit departments also have responsibility for the collection of the accounts.
(2) *banking:* a department in a bank where credit information is obtained, assembled, and retained for reference purposes. Credit applications for loans are presented to this department by a loan officer. The credit department gathers all available information on the customer, and prepares it for the confidential use of the loan officer. Based on the findings of the credit departments, which will make an analysis of the credit information, the loan officer is in a position to make a decision as to whether the loan application should be rejected. The credit department also obtains information

and answers credit inquiries for its bank correspondents, who may have a business transaction pending that will involve credit knowledge on a local business. [10]

credit entry: an entry placed on the right-hand side of an account.

credit facilities: a business system set up to offer credit services to those who possess personal or business credit. [28]

credit file: an assembly of facts and opinions which indicates the financial resources of an individual (or an enterprise), his or her character, and his or her record of performance, especially toward financial obligations. [44]

credit folder: synonymous with *credit file*.

credit footing of an account: the columnar total written at the foot of the credit money column in an account.

credit for tax on prior transfers: federal estate tax credit allowed for federal estate tax already paid on the transfer of property to the present decedent from a transferor who died within 10 years before, or within two years after, the present decedent's death. [105]

credit grantor: a misused term indicating that credit is supplied to consumers by business. The true concept is that business supplies only the facilities through which those who possess credit can use it. [28]

credit history: a continuing record of a borrower's debt commitments and how well these have been honored. [78]

credit information: information on a person, company, or subject made available to a credit analyst.

credit instrument: a written guarantee to pay, which serves the purpose of money in consummating commercial exchanges, although actual money or bank notes are not used.

credit insurance: where the insurance company reimburses a wholesaler, producer, jobber, or service organization for losses caused by the nonpayment of accounts receivable or the debtor's insolvency.

credit interchange: the sharing among suppliers of data shown by the ledger about accounts.

credit interchange bureau: an organization that serves as a clearinghouse for its members credit requests.

credit interviewer: an individual who secures from a credit applicant needed data for establishing worthy credit.

credit investigation: an inquiry made by a lender to verify data given in a credit application or to investigate other aspects the creditor believes to be relevant to credit worthiness. see *acid test ratio.*

creditism: a Carter administration term marking the shift to control of credit in the war against inflation.

credit letter: another title for a cash letter. see *cash letter.* [10]

credit life insurance: synonymous with *mortgage life insurance.*

credit limit: amount, established with or without agreement of the customer, to which credit purchases may be authorized. [41]

credit line: see *line of credit.*

credit losses: the money lost by a finance company or other credit-granting institution when a debt is not paid. This loss may be increased by the cost of collection activities before the debt is finally written off as uncollectable. [55]

credit manager: individual responsible for the credit function of a credit card plan, including the approval of new applications and the establishment and/or increase of credit lines. [105]

credit mechanism: see *credit facilities.*

credit memo

(1) a posting medium authorizing the credit to a specified account of a certain named amount that bears the complete description of the transaction, the date, and the signature of the party responsible for the authorization of the credit.

(2) a detailed memorandum forwarded from one party or firm to another, granting credit for returned merchandise, some omission, overpayment, or other cause. [10]

credit mixte: a combination of conventional government export financing and concessionary loans that are made interest free or at very low rates.

credit money: fiduciary money that is not completely backed by a precious metal.

creditor: one who is due money from another. synonymous with *lender.* see *guaranty.*

creditor country: a nation which on a net basis is owed more by another nation than it owes it, thereby establishing a favorable balance of trade.

creditors: those to whom one owes an obligation (usually financial).[28]

creditor's bill: a proceeding commenced by one or more unpaid creditors petitioning a court of equity to appoint a receiver to manage the affairs of a debtor who is not meeting his or her obligations.

creditors' committee: a group of persons who seek to arrange some settlement on behalf of each person or firm having claims on a business in financial difficulty; the common procedure is for all claims to be assigned to this body for settlement. [76]

creditor's notice: in probate the notice published stating the decedent's death and the name of the executor or administrator to whom claims should be presented for payment. [37]

creditor's position: that portion of the market price of a property which is represented by or can be obtained through a first mortgage. [62]

credit party: the party to be credited or paid by the receiving bank. [105]

credit proxy: the sum of member bank deposits plus nondeposit items. Often referred to as adjusted credit proxy.

credit rating

(1) *banking:* the amount, type, and form of credit, if any, which a bank estimates can be extended to an applicant for credit.

(2) *finance:* an estimate of the credit and responsibility assigned to mercantile and other establishments by credit investigating organizations.

credit rating book: the list of established credit users in a region together with a code letter showing general credit rating.

credit record: a complete and permanent record of your credit performance. [41]

credit report: a confidential report made by an independent individual or organization that has investigated the financial standing, reputation, and record of an applicant for insurance.

credit reporting agencies: organizations structured to supply to business and industry the information they need to reach credit, sales, financial, and general management decisions.

credit risk: the risk assumed for the

possible nonpayment of credit extended.

credit sales department: recommended by the National Retail Credit Association to designate the place where credit and collection functions are carried on. [41]

credit scoring system: a statistical measure used to rate credit applicants on the basis of various factors relevant to credit worthiness. [78]

credit service charge: the charge made for the use of credit facilities. [28]

credit side: the right-hand side of an account.

credit slip: document showing the return of merchandise by a cardholder to a merchant, or other refund made by the merchant to the cardholder. A copy of this document is used by the bank to credit the cardholder's account. synonymous with *credit voucher* and *refund slip.*

credit standing: one's present credit worthiness as determined by his or her past credit performance. [28]

credit system: a creditor may use a demonstrably and statistically sound, empirically derived credit system obtained from another person, or may obtain credit experience from which such a system may be developed. [105]

credit terms: specification of the terms for the payment of a credit obligation.

credit ticket: a bank bookkeeping memorandum or posting medium on which the transaction leading to a credit entry in a ledger account is described in detail. [31]

credit transaction: every aspect of an applicant's dealings with a creditor regarding an application for, or an existing extension of, credit. [105]

credit transfer: a voucher giving bookkeeper authority to credit an account according to instructions on the voucher. cf. *debit transfer.*

credit transfer system: a computer system which will make available collected funds already in a customer's account to an account maintained by the retailer. [105]

credit union: a cooperative financial organization established within and listed to a specific group of people. see *Federal Credit Union, share draft.*

credit voucher: synonymous with *credit slip.*

credit worthy (credit worthiness): receiving a favorable credit rating; an individual or business is thereby entitled to use the credit facilities of the organization(s) who requested the information. see *open credit.*

creeping inflation: a gradual but continuing increase in the general price level by as little as 2.5 percent a year. cf. *flation.*

"cremation": the act of destroying by fire certain records of the bank. The legal counsel of the bank advises the bank which records and documents may be destroyed, as a result of having outrun the statute of limitations according to the laws of the state in which the bank is operating. The term also applies to the destruction by fire of certain bonds and coupons that have been redeemed by a bank acting as fiscal agent for the issuing corporation or govermental agency. The cremation of paid securities is by agreement between the bank and the issuing agency. [10]

Crime of 1873: in 1873 the coinage laws were revised and the standard silver dollar was omitted (i.e., silver was demonetized). This was done because very little silver had come to the mint after 1834 since the market value of silver was higher than the price paid by the Treasury. The law was later called the "Crime of '73."

crime of receiving: receiving, possessing, concealing, storing, bartering, selling, or disposing of any property, money, or other thing of value with the knowledge that it has been stolen. [59]

critical path method (CPM): in planning and scheduling, a complex series of operations, the sequence of events that are most critical as to timing; the longest path of activities in a system. CPM is based on the network analogue principle and was first used in 1957 by E.I. Du Pont de Nemours and Co., to improve the planning, scheduling, and coordination of its new-plant construction effort. cf. *program evaluation and review technique (PERT)*

crop year: a commodity term referring to the period from the harvest of a crop to the next year, varying with different crops.

cross bill: see *redraft.*

cross-border lending: lending of funds by a U.S. bank to less-developed countries.

cross check: the placing of two diagonal lines across the front of a check and the addition of a term or series of words to determine the negotiability of the check such as to one's banker if his name is inserted between the lines. Rarely used in the United States, but found in parts of Europe and Latin America.

cross-currency exposure: when a firm's debt servicing requirements in a currency are not covered by its revenue-generating capabilities in that currency.

cross-default clause: a loan agreement clause stating that default on any other loans to the borrower will be regarded as default on this one.

crossed sales: synonymous with *crossed trades.*

crossed trades: forbidden by both the securities and commodities exchanges, a manipulative technique where a broker or several brokers offset an order to purchase with an offer to sell and fail to execute the orders on the exchange. The transaction, is therefore, not recorded and can suggest that one of the parties to the cross failed to obtain the price that would have been obtained on the exchange. synonymous with *crossed sales.*

cross-elasticity: describes the impact on the demand for one product of price changes of a related product. For example, when the price of butter goes up, the price of margarine, a substitute, usually rises as well. see *coefficient of cross-elasticity, elastic demand.*

crossfoot: to add figures horizontally across columns. [43]

cross-freight: the situation in which goods are shipped from one part of the country to another for processing and then back to the original point for sale, or where; for example, some peaches are shipped from New York City to Boston for sale and others from Boston to New York City for sale.

crossing: a practice by a broker who performs the act of seller and purchaser of the same stock. When a broker has such an order, he or she is required by the exchange to put the stock up for sale at a price that is higher than his or her bid price to fulfill the minimum variation permitted in the security, prior to concluding the transaction.

cross order: in the stock market, an order to a broker to buy and sell the same security. If the buy order and sell order are from two different persons, the broker must execute them through the exchange, and may not directly pair them. If the orders are from the same person or collusive where by two persons, it is a wash sale. see *wash sale.*

cross purchase: where a broker, without recourse to the market, fulfills an order to buy and an order to sell the same stock. The practice is forbidden by the New York Stock Exchange.

crossrate: the determination of the rate of exchange of two foreign currencies by using the rate of exchange of each currency in a third nation's currency.

cross remainders: dispositive provisions of a will or trust agreement wherein there is provision that surviving life beneficiaries shall be entitled to receive or share in the income of the deceased beneficiary. [105]

cross-selling: employee efforts to sell financial services other than the service that he or she is performing. [105]

crowd
(1) *general:* the aggregate of key persons involved in any activity; those who control the day-to-day decisions of the firm.
(2) *investments:* brokers who transact business in securities on the trading floor of an exchange.

crowding out: a term used by former Secretary of the Treasury William Simon to describe the negative impact of large government deficits on economic growth.

CRT: see *cathode ray tube.*

CRU: see *collective reserve unit.*

Crude Oil Windfall Profit Tax Act of 1980: see *windfall profits tax.*

crunch: an economic squeeze; a crisis created by some financial pressure.

crush margin: the gross profit that a processor makes from selling oil and meal, minus the cost of buying the soybeans.

crush spread: a futures spreading position in which a trader attempts to profit from what he or she believes to be discrepancies in the price relationship between soybeans and its two derivative products.

cruzeiro: monetary unit of Brazil.

CS
(1) see *capital stock.*
(2) see *closing sale.*
(3) see *common stock.*
(4) see *condition subsequent.*

CSN: see *card security number.*

C-speck: slang, a $100 bill.

Csv.: see *cash surrender value.*

CT
(1) see *cable transfer.*
(2) see *cash trade.*

CTB: see *bond, collateral trust.*

Ctfs.: see *certificate.*

Cts.: see *cent.*

CU: see *credit union.*

Culpeper Switch: a computerized Federal Reserve facility located in Culpeper, Virginia, which serves as a central relay point for messages transmitted electronically between Federal Reserve districts on the Fedwire. Messages moving billions of dollars of funds and securities daily are processed by Culpeper in electronically coded form. They originate in commercial banks, are sent to Reserve Banks, and then are transmitted to Culpeper, where they are switched to other Reserve Banks and, in turn, to other commercial banks. [1]

Cum.: see *cumulative.*

cum coupon: international bond market term for dealings in a bond where the purchaser acquires the right to receive the next due interest payment. cf. *cum-dividend, ex-coupon.*

cum dividend: as distinguished from the *ex-dividend,* the dividend included. The purchaser of a stock cum dividend has the right to receive the declared dividend.

cum right: the stockholder's right to acquire shares of a new issue of stock in a company in direct proportion to existing holdings. see also *rights.*

cumulative: an arrangement whereby a dividend or interest which, if not paid when due or received when due, is added to that which is to be paid in the future. [37]

cumulative dividend: a dividend on cumulative preferred stock payable, under the terms of issue, at intervals and before any distribution is made to holders of common stock.

cumulative preferred (stock): a stock whose holders are entitled, if one or more dividends are omitted, to be paid on the omitted dividends before dividends are paid on the company's common stock.

cumulative voting: each share of stock may cast as many votes for one director of the firm as there are directors who seek elected office.

curable depreciation: depreciated property that is still considered to be economically useful.

curator: an individual or a trust institution appointed by a court to care for the property of a minor or an incompetent person. In some states a curator is es-

sentially the same as a temporary administrator or a temporary guardian. [37]

Curb broker: an old name for a member of the Curb Exchange. see *Curb Exchange.*

Curb Exchange: the name used before 1953 for the American Stock Exchange in New York City. See *American Stock Exchange.*

curing title: the removal of a claim from a title, to make it marketable.

Curr.: see *currency.*

currency: paper money and coin issued by a government or central bank, which circulates as a legal medium of exchange. [7]

currency availability clause: a Euromarket clause providing that banks can switch their lending to a different currency should the original currency be no longer available.

currency band: a carefully defined area within which a nation's money fluctuates on both sides of its official parity. Set at 2.25 percent each side of the parity at the 1971 Washington Smithsonian Agreement.

currency bloc: nations that use a common currency base; for example, the British sterling bloc exists for Great Britain and many of her present and former colonies.

currency bond: see *bond, currency.*

currency cocktail: a unit of account based on a number of currencies.

currency code: code identifying the currency of the transaction amount (the three-letter ISO code is recommended). [105]

currency convertibility: the ability to exchange for gold, as well as for other currencies.

currency exchange (swap): a long-term exchange of currency between two firms in different nations.

currency parities: as agreed upon by members of the International Monetary Fund, funds of all of the world's major nations are set in relation to the U.S. dollar.

currency pouch: a zipper pouch in which a cashier places and locks the money from the cash drawer at time of closing the cash drawer. [55]

"currency school" principle: a principle developed in England in the nineteenth century, maintaining that under a purely metallic currency any loss of gold to foreign countries or the reverse would result automatically in a corresponding decrease or increase in currency in circulation and thus immediately influence the price level. Under a mixed currency of gold and convertible paper, the same effect would not occur automatically, but would be brought about only by regulation of the quantity of paper money to conform to the quantity of gold. This principle was essentially embodied in Peel's Bank Charter Act of 1844. cf. *"banking school" principle.*

currency shipment: the responsibility of the Federal Reserve Bank and other large city banks to supply other banks with an appropriate quantity and quality of coins, paper money, and orders for the transfer of money.

currency transferability: the ability of a currency to be easily exchanged for another currency by any and all of its owners.

current: in budgeting and accounting, designates the operations of the present fiscal period as opposed to past or future periods. [49]

current account: a running account between two companies, reflecting the movement of cash, merchandise, and so on.

current account balance: the difference between the nation's total exports of goods, services, and transfers and its total imports of them. It excludes transactions in financial assets and liabilities. [1]

current and accrued assets: generally consists of items realizable or to be consumed within one year from the date of the balance sheet. Includes cash, working funds, and certain deposits, temporary cash investments, receivables, materials and supplies including fuel, and prepayments. [3]

current and accrued liabilities: generally consists of obligations incurred, accrued, or declared, including short-term borrowing, all of which are either due and payable, payable on demand or, in any event, contemplated to be paid within one year. [3]

current and collectable: money that flows or passes from hand to hand as a medium of exchange. [61]

current (floating) assets: the assets of a company that are reasonably expected to be realized in cash, or sold, or consumed during the normal operating cycle of the business.

current assets to current debt: obtained by dividing the total of current assets by total current debt. Current assets are the sum of cash, notes, and accounts receivable (less reserves for bad debts), advances on merchandise, merchandise inventories, and listed federal, state, and municipal securities not in excess of market value. Current debt is the total of all liabilities falling due within one year. [4]

current budget
(1) the budget prepared for the succeeding fiscal year, or in the case of some state governments, the budget prepared for the succeeding biennium.
(2) the budget in force during the current fiscal year or biennium. [49]

current capital: circulating capital or gross working capital.

current cost: what it would cost today to replace an asset or to require equivalent productive capacity.

current debt: the sum of all liabilities due within the year from the statement date, including current payment on mortgages, funded debts, and serial notes. Liability reserves are included, but reserves for depreciation are excluded.

current debt to inventory: dividing the current debt by inventory; yields yet another indication of the extent to which a business relies on funds from the disposal of unsold inventories to meet its debts. [4]

current debt to tangible net worth: obtained by dividing current debt by tangible net worth. Ordinarily, a business is in trouble when the relationship between current debt and tangible net worth exceeds 80 percent. [4]

current delivery: delivery during the present period such as this month for commodities. [2]

current dollars: the actual prices of goods and services each year.

current exit value: what a company could sell an asset for (or remove a liability) in today's market.

current expensing: President Reagan's idea for reviving American capital spending and improving productivity allowing a business to deduct from its taxable income the cost of all capital assets, except land and buildings, in the year in which the goods are acquired.

current income: wages, salary, profit, or other income of the immediate period of time, this month, this year. [28]

current liabilities: money owed and payable by a company, usually within one year. [20]

current operation expenditures: expenditures for salaries and wages, supplies, material, and contractual services, other than capital outlays.

current prices: security prices prevailing in the market as a specified time period.

current ratio: the relationship between total current assets and total current liabilities. It is calculated by dividing current assets by current liabilities.

current resources: resources to which recourse can be had to meet current obligations and expenditures. Examples are current assets, estimated revenues of a particular period not yet realized, transfers from other funds authorized but not received, and, in case of certain funds, bonds authorized and unissued. [49]

current return: the present income from any investment.

current value accounting: an accounting approach that requires the measurement of individual assets (e.g., factories, machines, and supplies) in current prices rather than in terms of the actual dollar costs at which they were acquired in earlier years.

current yield: an expression as a portion of the annual income to the investment; for example, if annual income is $10 and investment is $100, the current yield is 10 percent. see *return*.

curtail schedule: a list of the amounts

by which the principal of an obligation is to be reduced by partial payments and of the dates when these payments are to become due. [44]

curtesy: a husband's life interest in the property of his deceased spouse. cf. *dower.*

cushion bond: see *bond, cushion.*

cushion checking (credit): a check overdraft plan that is also an instant loan. When a check is issued in excess of the customer's account balance or a request is made to transfer from the customer's cash reserve to his or her checking account, a loan is made for up to 36 months plus a modest interest charge.

CUSIP: the American Bankers Association's Committee on Uniform Securities Identification Procedures that established alphabetical and numerical descriptions of securities traded on the exchanges and in over-the-counter markets.

custodian: a banking institution that holds in custody and safekeeping the securities and other assets of an investment company. [23]

custodian account: any financial account (i.e., bank, securities) created for a minor, as provided by state law.

custodianship: the relationship between a trust firm or bank where the bank controls the customer's property subject to the owner's instructions. To be differentiated from the safe depository function where the bank does not control the customers property but merely provided a place for safe keeping.

custody: the banking service that provides safekeeping for a customer's property under written agreement, and additionally calls for the bank to collect and pay out income, and to buy, sell, receive, and deliver securities when ordered by the principal to do so. [105]

customer-bank communication terminal (CBCT): the name given to remote (i.e., not on bank premises) electronic devices through which customers may withdraw, deposit, or transfer funds from or to their checking or savings accounts. cf. *automated teller machine.*

customer draft: see *sight draft.*

customer ownership: the legal ownership of securities by customers of a corporation.

customer risk: see *credit risk.*

customer's agreement and consent: the form required by a member firm of the New York Stock Exchange of any client holding a margin account. The client's signature indicates agreement to follow the rules of the exchange, the SEC, and the Federal Reserve Board.

customer's broker(man): see *registered representative (trader).*

customer's costs: in public utilities, the costs of maintaining meters, billing, collecting, and keeping customers' accounts.

customer's free credit balance: the funds in a client's brokerage account, other than from a short sale, which is at the dispersal of the client.

customer's ledger: a ledger that shows accounts receivable of each customer.

customers' liability: an account in a bank's general ledger as an offset to existing letters of credit that have not been paid but remain guaranteed. see *letter of credit.*

customers' man: synonymous with *registered representative (trader).*

customers' net debit balances: credit

of New York Stock Exchange member firms made available to help finance customers' purchases of stocks, bonds, and commodities. [20]

customer's representative: employees of security firms who are regularly employed in the solicitation of business or the handling of customers' accounts, or who advise customers about the purchase or sale of securities.

customer's room: the area within a broker's office available for customers. The space usually contains a quotation board, a ticker, and other information available from investment services.

customhouse: the place for the payment of import duties in the United States and for the payment of import and export duties in other nations.

customhouse bond: see *bond, customhouse.*

customs: taxes imposed by a government on the import or export of items. cf. *duty, tariff.*

customs broker: a licensed person who handles the preparation of paper and carries out the steps in securing clearance of goods through customs.

customs duty: a tax levied and collected by custom officials in discharging the tariff regulations on imports.

customs invoice: a document that contains a declaration by the seller, the shipper, or the agent of either as to the value of the goods covered. [105]

customs union: an agreement by two or more trading countries to dissolve trade restrictions such as tariffs and quotas among themselves, and to develop a common external policy or trade (e.g., trade agreement).

cut: an expression used in banks to denote the taking of a total of a pack of checks sorted and going to one destination. The term is most frequently used in banks equipped with proof machines. Since these machines can list a large number of checks on a tape, it has been found more convenient to "cut a tape" by taking totals at intervals of between 100 and 200 items per total. The term also is applied to canceling checks. [10]

cutback rate: in transportation, that part of a rate incurred in connection with transit shipments at the transit point.

cut notes: paper money issues that have been officially bisected or quartered and each portion given its own value, normally indicated by overstamping. This has usually been an emergency measure due to a shortage of coins. [27]

cutoff: to effect better control over huge volumes of checks passing through the proof department in large banks, these banks have periodic "settlements" or "cutoffs" of work. Each cutoff is balanced and items are immediately released from the proof department after each settlement. This not only affords better control, but permits transit items to be mailed in several deliveries each business day. [10]

cutoff date: a specific day chosen for stopping the flow of cash, goods, or other items for closing or audit reasons. Usually this occurs if an inventory is scheduled when sales or purchases are to take place.

cut-rate: slang, inexpensive; an item offered at less than the usual price.

cut slip: a slip of paper upon which is imprinted or written the total of a particular "cut." The cut slips are retained and used to "settle" a proof machine when the settlement is made. [10]

cutthroat competition: intensive competition that may lead to the bankruptcy of a major competitor, allowing the survivor to raise prices considerably. see *rate war.*

cutting a loss

(1) *general:* ceasing development, production, or sales of a failing item.

(2) *investments:* terminating an unprofitable market position and accepting the loss involved before it grows larger.

cutting a melon: slang, making an extra distribution of money or stock to shareholders, usually when preceded by an unusually profitable transaction (e.g., the sale of a subsidiary).

Cv.: see *convertible.*

Cvt.: see *convertible.*

CWM: convertible wraparound mortgage; a mortgage making it possible for builders to offer below-market, fixed-rate, fully amortized loans to home buyers during periods of high interest rates without requiring forfeiture of the builder's profit through interest rate buy-downs or subsidies.

Cy.: see *currency.*

CY: see *current yield.*

cycle: the grouping of cardholder accounts to provide for a distribution of work load and easier account identification.[105]

cycle billing: the matching of alphabetical breakdowns to specific days to assist in customer billing. Each breakdown is a cycle and occurs on the same day every month.

cycle mailing: the practice adopted by a number of banks of dividing the depositors' accounts into groups termed "mailing cycles," and the mailing of the statements at stipulated intervals during the month. Proponents of this practice claim that it decreases the cost and confusion experienced when all statements for all depositors are mailed at the same time (usually at the end of the month.) [10]

cycle period: a specific period of time during which both debit and credit transactions are accumulated for billing. [105]

cycle posting: the practice of dividing accounts to be posted into groups termed "cycles" and posting these accounts at stipulated intervals during the month. [10]

cyclical fluctuations: periodic variations in a time series frequently indicative of a business cycle.

cyclical inflation: periodic variations in a period when there is a sudden increase in the general price level. cf. *secular inflation.*

cyclical stocks: securities that go up and down in value with the trend of business, rising faster in periods of rapidly improving business conditions and sliding very noticeably when business conditions deteriorate.

cyclical theory: see *cyclical stocks.*

cyclical unemployment: unemployment connected with fluctuations in business activity reflected by business cycles.

D
(1) see *delivery*.
(2) see *discount*.
(3) see *dollar*.
(4) checkable deposits of depository institutions. [81]

DA
(1) see *depletion allowance*.
(2) see *discretionary account*.
(3) see *dollar (cost) averaging*.
(4) see *dormant account*.

D/A: see *documents against acceptance.*

DAC: see *Development Assistance Committee.*

dace: slang, 2 cents.

D/A drafts: documents on acceptance. Time drafts (trade acceptances) payable at some time in the future. [105]

daily balancing: procedure by which all monetary transactions received within a given 24-hour period are balanced. [105]

daily interest account: a savings account that pays interest daily from the date of deposit to the date of withdrawal. [59]

daily reports: skeleton copies of insurance policies prepared for the agent and the bank, consisting of the declarations page and fill-in endorsements.

daily reserve calculation: a daily calculation to determine the "reserves" necessary to meet the "lawful reserve" requirements. see *lawful reserve.* [10]

daily statement: a daily transcript of the balances shown on the accounts in the bank's general ledger. [31]

daily transaction tape: in fully automated demand deposit accounting, the magnetic tape record of each day's debits and credits to all accounts, usually in account number sequence. [105]

Daily Treasury Statement: a listing of transactions that clear through the U.S. Treasurer's account. For each business day it reflects cash deposits, cash withdrawals, and the status of the Treasurer's account.

daisy chains: oil sale overcharges through transactions designed primarily to increase the price of crude oil.

dalasi: monetary unit of Gambia.

damage liability: automobile insurance that pays for damage to another car or to property not belonging to the insured. [105]

damages

(1) *banking:* loss sustained to a person or his or her property.

(2) *banking:* loss in value to remaining property when a portion of one's property is expropriated.

(3) *law:* money awarded by the court to the plaintiff to be paid by the defendant, as compensation for the plaintiff's loss.

data

(1) *general:* a representation of facts, concepts, or instructions in a formalized manner, suitable for communication.

(2) *computers:* any representation such as characters or analog quantities to which meaning is, or might be, assigned.

(3) the plural "data" is often incorrectly construed as singular. "Data" is the plural of "datum."

data bank: a comprehensive collection of information on a principal subject and related areas.

data base: a collection of information specific to an operation, business, or enterprise.

data capture: the act of collecting data into a form that can be directly processed by a computer system. Some electronic funds transfer systems are designed to capture transaction data at the precise time and place the transaction is consummated.

datamation: the flow of information by way of a computer. Formed from the words "data" and "automation."

data processing

(1) *computers:* the execution of a systematic sequence of operations performed on data.

(2) *computers:* any procedure used for receiving data and yielding a specific result.

(3) synonymous with *information processing.*

data reduction: the process of transforming large masses of data into useful, condensed, or simplified intelligence.

Data Universal Numbering System: a numbering system designed and maintained by Dun & Bradstreet for universal numerical identification of commercial business establishments. [105]

date: the point in time, fixed by the year, month, and day, when an occurrence takes place. see also *effective date.*

date of acceptance: the date when a time draft is accepted, or honored.

date of acquisition: the effective date of purchase of an asset. [105]

date of draft: the date when a draft is drawn.

date of maturity: the date on which a debt must be paid. Usually applied to those debts evidenced by a written agreement, such as a note, bond, and so on.

date of payment of dividends: the date when declared dividends are to be paid.

date of the note: the date of issue.

date of trade: the day when an order to buy or sell is executed.

dating: a technique of extending credit beyond the time it was originally given. Often used as an inducement to dealers to place orders far in advance of the coming season.

datum: the singular form of *data.*

day book: a record book in which all financial transactions are noted without regard to debit or credit. Later the journal entries are made from the day book. Sales checks, petty cash slips, and other devices have largely replaced the day book.

daylight exposure: the total open position allowed to a bank's foreign exchange department during a business day.

daylight overdraft: occurs when a bank overdraws its reserve account during the day even if the account is replenished by the end of the day; a practice frowned upon by the Federal Reserve Board.

daylight overdrafts: loans that banks make to customers during the business day with the expectation they will be repaid by 5 P.M.

daylight trading: making a purchase followed by a sale of a security on the same day, to avoid a holding position in the shares traded overnight or longer.

day loan: a one-day loan, granted for the purchase of stock, for the broker's convenience. Upon delivery, securities are pledged as collateral to secure a regular call loan.

day order: an order to buy or sell that, if not executed, expires at the end of the trading day on which it was entered. [20]

day points: used in connection with transit work and the general ledger in a bank. The term is applied to the number of days required to send transit letters to distant points geographically by the best means of transportation. Because of the adequacy of transportation today, banks average their availability for collection of transit items into one day, two days, and three days.

When transit letters are sent out, the bank knows the number of days it will take to collect the items. On the day that collection should be accomplished, the totals of all transit letters scheduled for credit that day are transferred from a deferred account to the available asset account "due from banks." see also *due from banks*. [10]

days of grace: the reasonable length of time allowed, without suffering a loss or penalty, for postponed payment or for the presentment for payment of certain financial documents. see *grace period*.

day-to-day loans: synonymous with *call loan*.

day-to-day money: synonymous with *call money*.

day trading: in anticipation of a rapid price change, the purchasing of a stock and selling it again, or selling it short, on the same day.

day trust: see *passive trust*.

D&B: see *Dun and Bradstreet*.

Db.: see *debenture*.

DC: see *daisy chains*.

DD
(1) see *declaration date*.
(2) see *deferred delivery*.
(3) see *delayed delivery*.
(4) see *demand draft*.
(5) see *due date*.

ddd policy: a package policy providing blanket fidelity, forgery, and broadform burglary coverage by specific insuring agreements.

DDP: see *direct deposit of payroll*.

dead asset: an asset that is not productive of income under usual operations. A standby machine tool or a high-cost facility that is not used except in emergencies is a dead asset during the time it is not in use.

deadbeat

(1) *general:* a person who tries to evade paying for things.

(2) *finance:* a person who pays his or her entire charge every billing period, thus avoiding revolving credit charges.

dead broke: slang, penniless.

dead hand: used to indicate the continuing hold of a settlor or a testator, who has been dead for many years, upon living individuals or organizations that are confronted with conditions which the settlor or the testator could not have foreseen. [37]

deadheading: transportation for which no fee is paid. In railroading it would include the shifting of a train crew from one point to another, or the transportation of the holder of a pass.

dead market

(1) *general:* a dull selling day, marked by low volume, lack of consumer interest, or other factors creating poor sales.

(2) *investments:* a market marked by minor price changes and low volume.

dead pledge: an expression for a mortgage that is paid on time.

dead president: slang, a U.S. banknote; any piece of paper money.

dead rent: the fixed annual sum paid for a quarry or mine, in addition to royalty payments that vary in amount according to the yield.

deadweight tonnage (DWT): the weight that a vessel can carry when loaded to its load-line level. cf. *gross registered tonnage.*

deal: slang, a large transaction involving a change in ownership.

dealer: an individual or firm in the securities business acting as a principal rather than as an agent. Typically, a dealer buys for his or her own account and sells to a customer from the dealer's inventory. The dealer's profit or loss is the difference between the price he pays and the price he receives for the same security. The dealer's confirmation must disclose to the customer that he has acted as principal. The same individual or firm may function, at different times, as broker and dealer. [20]

dealer activities: a bank operating as a securities dealer by underwriting, trading, or selling securities. [105]

dealer financing: a dealer of commodities, such as household appliances, may make arrangements with a bank for the bank to finance the purchase of these appliances upon their sale by the dealer. The customers who purchase these items then become borrowers of the bank under "consumer credit" or "time sales" loans. The bank usually has the dealer endorse the notes of his customers as additional security for the loans, and has the dealer maintain reserves on each note with the bank as other security. These reserves are termed *dealer holdbacks* or *dealer reserves.* [10]

dealer holdbacks: see *dealer financing.*

dealer loan: see *dealer financing.*

dealer market: market for government securities trading, located primarily in New York City. [105]

dealer paper: the conditional sales contract that is purchased from a merchant who assigns his rights to the finance company. [55]

dealer rebate: some portion of interest received by a bank on a dealer-financed loan, which is paid to the dealer for arranging the loan through the bank. [105]

dealer reserves: see *dealer financing.*

dear: costly; expensive; priced unusually high.

dear money

(1) **banking:** the presence of high interest rates. see *hard money (currency).*

(2) **finance:** a situation created when loans are difficult to obtain because of the supply and demand for credit.

"death sentence": a clause in the Public Utility Holding Company Act of 1935 requiring that all such companies register with the Securities and Exchange Commission and that no more than three levels of corporations are permitted (a parent company, its subsidiary, and a sub-subsidiary). All holding companies exceeding these three levels must be dissolved (the death sentence).

Deb.: see *debenture.*

debase: to reduce the quality, purity, or content, or otherwise alter the accepted intrinsic value of the coinage of a realm.

debenture

(1) **general:** used to describe indebtedness, usually in long-term obligations, which is unsecured.

(2) **finance:** a corporate obligation that is sold as an investment.

(3) **law:** a voucher or certificate acknowledging that a debt is owed by the signor.

debenture bond: see *bond, debenture.*

debenture certificate

(1) a document authorizing payment of money granted as a bounty to an exporter of some domestic items.

(2) a customhouse document authorizing a rebate on duties paid on imported items to be exported.

debenture stock: stock issued under a contract to pay a specified return at specified intervals. In this sense, it may be considered a special type of preferred stock. It is to be distinguished from a debenture, which represents a bond in form as compared with a share of stock. [18]

debit

(1) **general:** any amount in dollars and cents that, when posted, will increase the balance of an asset or expense account and decrease the balance of a liability account. All asset and expense accounts normally have debit balances, and all liability, capital, and income accounts normally have credit balances. cf. *credit.*

(2) **banking:** a weekly premium life insurance agent's list of all the premiums he or she is required to collect.

(3) **investments:** that portion of the purchase price of stock, bonds, or commodities covered by credit extended by a broker to margin customers.

debit adjustment: a correction posted to a cardholder's account which is added to the balance owing. [105]

debit balance: in a customer's margin account that portion of purchase price of stock, bonds, or commodities covered by credit extended by the broker to the margin customer. see *balance of account.* [20]

debit card: a cash machine automator and a check guarantee. A recent innovation permitting bank customers to withdraw cash at any hour from any affiliated automated teller machine in the country, and to make cashless purchases from funds on deposit without incurring revolving finance charges for credit.

debit column: the left-hand side of an account or journal column.

debit entry: an entry placed on the left-hand side of an account.

debit footing of an account: the columnar total written at the foot of the debit money column in an account.

debit in error: a paperless debit entry that has been posted to a customer's account and which he or she maintains was not properly authorized by him or her. The rules of automated clearing-houses provide that receiving banks must allow customers a specified time frame during which they may unilaterally revoke debits in error. Regulation E also spells out the corrective time requirements when this occurs. [105]

debit memo

(1) a posting medium authorizing the debit to a specified account for a certain named amount which bears the complete description of the transaction, the date, and the signature of the party responsible for the authorization of the charge.

(2) a detailed memorandum forwarded from one party or firm to another charging for some omitted charge, disallowed or improper payment, or other causes. [10]

debit party: the source of funds for a payment on the receiving bank's books. [105]

debit ticket: a bank bookkeeping memorandum or posting medium on which the transaction leading to a debit entry in a ledger account is described in detail. [50]

debit transfer: a voucher giving a bookkeeper authority to charge on ac-

count according to the instructions on the voucher. Opposite of *credit transfer*. [41]

debt: money, services, or materials owed to another person as the result of a previous agreement. see also *effective debt, funded debt, gross debt, total debt.*

debt capital: funds borrowed to finance the operations of a business.

debt ceiling: a level controlled by Congress: the maximum limit on the federal debt. At times Congress has raised the debt ceiling.

debt collector: anyone, other than a creditor or his attorney, who regularly collects debts for others. [78]

debt discount: the difference between the proceeds of a loan and the face value of the note or bond, where the former is smaller. [105]

debtee: a creditor.

debt-equity swap: a transaction in which a company trades newly issued stock, or equity, for outstanding deep-discount bonds or debt.

debt financing: the long-term borrowing of money by a business, usually in exchange for debt securities or a note, for the purpose of obtaining working capital or other funds necessary to operational needs or for the purpose of retiring current or other indebtedness. [35]

debt instrument: a written promise to repay a debt; includes bills, notes, and bonds. [105]

debt limit: a maximum amount of money that a state or local government can borrow; usually set by legislation of the state involved.

debt monetization: the process by which the national debt is used to increase currency in circulation. Essentially, this is carried out by the purchase of government bonds by the Federal Reserve System, thus releasing Federal Reserve notes into circulation. These purchases may be effected through member banks.

debtor: one who owes money to another.

debtor bank: a bank which, following check distribution in a clearinghouse, has fewer claims against other banks than the other banks have against it.

debtor nation: a country whose citizens, companies, and government owe more to foreign creditors than foreign debtors owe them.

debtor's position: that portion of the market price of property which is in excess of a prime first mortgage, or mortgagable interest; the equity holder's position. [62]

debt ratio: total debt divided by total assets.

debt retirement: the slow reduction of a firm's debt through either a sinking fund or serial bonds. Debt reduction purports to improve the quality and the market price of a bond issue.

debt securities: fixed obligations that evidence a debt, usually repayable on a specified future date or dates and which carry a specific rate or rates of interest payable periodically. They may be non-interest bearing also. [35]

debt service: interest payments and capital reduction on government, industrial, or other long-term bonds. see *debt service fund.*

debt service fund: a fund established to finance an account for the payment of interest and principal on all general obligation debt, serial and term, other than that payable exclusively from special assessments and revenue debt

issued for and services by a governmental enterprise. Formerly called a *sinking fund.* [49]

debt service fund requirements: the amounts of revenue provided for a debt service fund so that all principal and interest payments can be made on schedule. [49]

debt-service ratio: payments made by a country to foreign debt as a percentage of the country's export earnings. [105]

debt service requirement: the amount of money required to pay the interest on outstanding debt, serial maturities of principal for serial bonds, and required contributions to a debt service fund for term bonds. [49]

debts written-off: see *credit losses.*

debt-to-net worth ratio: all liabilities divided by net value.

debug

(1) *computers:* to detect, locate, and remove mistakes from a routine or malfunction of a computer. see *post-mortem.*

(2) *computers:* to test a program on a computer to determine whether it works properly.

(3) synonymous with *troubleshoot.*

decal: emblem placed on merchant windows and doors to identify affiliation with a credit card plan. [105]

deceased account: a bank deposit account in the name of a deceased person. Upon notification of death, the bank segregates the decedent's account and withholds release of funds until a court of law authorizes payment to the legal heirs. see *frozen account.*

decedent: a deceased person.

decedent estate account: a savings account held in the name of a deceased person. [59]

deceit: conduct in business: one person, through fraudulent representations, misleads another person who has the right to rely on such representations as the truth, or is unable to detect the fraud. see *estoppel.*

deceleration principle: an economic statement asserting that this year's increases in prices and wages should be, generally, at least a half percentage point below average increases from the previous year.

decertification: an order by the National Labor Relations Board ending the representation rights of a union, pursuant to a vote of the workers, in an NLRB election. This is done following a petition which asserts that the union no longer represents the majority of the employees. see *Taft-Hartley Act.*

decision: a court's final judgment.

deck: a collection of computer cards.

declaration

(1) *general:* the full disclosure of items, property, or income, as with a customs declaration.

(2) *banking:* a statement by an applicant for insurance, usually relative to underwriting information. Sometimes, this is copied into the policy. cf. *evidence of insurability.*

(3) *law:* the first pleading in an action.

declaration date: the date on which payment of a dividend is authorized by a corporation's board of directors.

declaration of condominium ownership: a complex legal document with appropriate addenda which provides for qualifying a multiunit property for condominium development and sale in accordance with a local state's condominium act (law). [59]

declaration of dividend: the board of

director's action in which a decision is made to pay the stockholders of the corporation a portion of the earnings or surplus of the company.

declaration of trust: a written agreement that property to which one person holds title actually belongs to another person, for whose benefit the title is maintained. see *fiduciary, trust.*

declaratory judgment: a court's determination on a question of law, stating the parties' rights without ordering any action.

declare a dividend (to): the declaration or vote by a firm's board to pay shareholders a dividend from earned surplus.

declination: the rejection by a life insurance company of an application for life insurance, usually for reasons of health or occupation of the applicant. [58]

decline: a downward slump, trend. A lowering of the price for a commodity or a security. [61]

declining balance: a balance which decreases in the amount owned with each payment; the service charge is often computed on the declining balance. [41]

declining balance depreciation: a depreciation method that charges larger amounts of depreciation expense in earlier years and lesser amounts later.

declining-marginal-efficiency-of-capital theory: proposed by British economist John Maynard Keynes that when, at a given rate of consumption, more productive plans and equipment are created, the rate of return on new and existing capital equipment falls. synonymous with *falling-rate-of-profit theory.*

decreasing-cost industry: an industry

whose average total unit cost decreases as production volume increases over the usual range of production.

decreasing costs: costs that decline as output per unit increases.

decreasing returns: see *diminishing returns*.

decreasing term insurance: often used to cover the outstanding balance of a home mortgage, has a fixed annual cost. Initially, it offers large coverage for a small premium, but since its benefits decline over time, it should not be used as a primary insurance policy.

decree: the judge's conclusion in a suit in equity (e.g., an order that an agreement be put into effect immediately).

deduck: slang, an amount that is deducted from taxable income.

deductible: an amount that can be subtracted or taken away from a principal sum or amount. [105]

deductible clause: an insurance policy provision making the insured liable for the initial, often small portion of any loss sustained by the insured, thereby lowering the cost of the insurance.

deductible coverage: in insurance, a provision that only the loss in excess of a minimum figure is covered.

deduction: taking away, as from a sum or amount. Discount, rebate, method of reasoning. [61]

deductions from gross income: amounts allowed by the Internal Revenue Service, as deductions in arriving at gross income (e.g., rents, taxes, interest). see *Internal Revenue Service, itemized deductions, Tax Reform Act of 1976*.

deed: a formal, written agreement of transfer, by which title to an estate or other real property is transmitted from one person to another. see *deed, general warranty; deed, quitclaim*.

deed, administrator's: the legal instrument given by a person who is legally vested with the right of administration of an estate, especially of an estate such as that of a minor, or incompetent such as a lunatic, or of a testator having no competent executor. [62]

deed, bond for: an executory contract for the sale of land, with title remaining with the grantor until the purchase price is paid; ordinarily binding on both parties. [6]

deed, committee: a deed employed when the property of a child or a person declared incompetent is conveyed. A court-approved committee is obtained before the transfer. see *deed, guardian*.

deed, executor's: a deed by a person named by the decedent in his will to manage and settle his estate. [6]

deed, general warranty: a deed stating that a grantor is giving the grantee good title, free of debt. The most secure of deeds, it guarantees that the grantor will defend the title against any claims. It is a deed in full covenant. see *perfect title*.

deed, guardian: a deed to convey the property of an infant or incompetent. see *deed, committee*.

deed, mortgaged: a deed by way of mortgage which has the effect of a mortgage on the property conveyed and imposes a lien on the granted estate. [6]

deed, quitclaim: a document by which one's legal right to, title to, interest in, or claim to a specific property, or an estate held by oneself, or others, is forever relinquished to another; usually contains no warranty or statement against the claims that others might have in the property.

deed, special warranty: a deed in which the grantor defends property title against demands made by grantees, heirs, and other claimants. No other liability is assumed by the grantor. Trustees often use this deed when transferring title, and following a court decision, to convey tax titles.

deed, trust: a deed that establishes a trust. Generally, it conveys legal title to property to a trustee and states his authority and the conditions binding upon him in dealing with the property held in trust. Frequently, trust deeds are used to secure lenders against loss. In this respect, they are similar to mortgages. [62]

deed, trustee: a deed by a party who holds property in trust. [6]

deed absolute: synonymous with *deed given to secure a debt.*

deed description: a recitation of the legal boundaries of a parcel of land as contained in a deed of conveyance. [6]

deed given to secure a debt: a form of mortgage in which title to the property is handed over to the lender by the borrower as security for the repayment of a debt. synonymous with *deed absolute.* [59]

deed in lieu of foreclosure: a mortgagor's way of presenting title to the mortgagee to prevent foreclosure of property.

deed of assignment: the written statement, identifying an assignee, often a trust company, to be responsible for the activities of an insolvent firm.

deed of release: a deed that releases property from the lien of a mortgage.

deed of surrender: an instrument by which property is identified as an estate for life or an estate for years to a person who will receive it in reversion.

deed of trust: a deed that is placed in trust with a third party to ensure payment of the indebtedness or to assure that other conditions of the transaction are met. Upon satisfaction of the debt, the third party transmits the deed to the purchaser, freeing the third party from future responsibilities.

deed restrictions: provisions inserted in a deed limiting the use of the property conveyed by the deed. [44]

deemed transferor: the parent of the transferee of property who is more closely related to the grantor of the trust than the other parent of such transferee. Where neither parent is related to the grantor, the deemed transferor is the parent who has a "closer affinity to the grantor." [105]

deepening of capital: the adoption of more roundabout (but more efficient) methods of production which increase the ratio of the amount of capital employed in producing a given amount of goods.

deep in money: call options give the holder the opportunity to buy 100 shares of a given stock at a predetermined price and within a limited period of time, usually months. A call is "deep in (the) money" when the exercise price of the call is well below the present market price of the underlying shares.

Def.: see *deficit.*

defaced coins: coins that have been mutilated in some manner. [10]

de facto: "in actual fact" (Latin). In reality; actually; existing, regardless of legal or moral consideration (e.g., de facto segregation; de facto discrimination in employment). cf. *de jure.*

de facto corporation: following an effort, in good faith, to form a corporation under a value statute and there is a failure in some particular, the firm is said to be de facto (in fact) when there has been an exercise of corporate power. Only the state, not a third party, can challenge the firm's existence as a de facto corporation. cf. *de jure corporation.*

defalcation: occurs when an individual in a trust or fiduciary position is unable, by his or her own fault, to account for funds left in his or her hands. Often interchangeable with embezzlement or misappropriation of funds. cf. *peculation.*

default: the failure to do that which is required by law, or to perform on an obligation previously committed. The term is commonly used when some legally constituted governing body fails to pay the principal or interest on its bond or fails to meet other financial obligations on maturity.

defaulted paper: any obligation whose principal or interest is in default. Such obligation, security, or investment should be distinguished on all financial statements where they normally appear by showing those in default separately from those not in default. [49]

defeasance: a clause that provides that performance of certain specified acts will render an instrument or contract void. [62]

defease: see *defeasance.*

defeasible: able to be annulled or made void.

defection: French term for *default.*

defendant: an individual sued in a court of law; the individual answering the complaint of a plaintiff.

defensive investment: an investment policy that places its major effort on reducing both the risk of (eventual) loss and the need for special knowledge, skill, and continuous attention. cf. *speculation.*

defensive portfolio: the aggregate of investments unlikely to fluctuate greatly in value either up or down (i.e., preferred stocks, high-grade bonds).

defensive stocks: stocks that shift little in price movements and are rarely of interest to speculators. Held by long-term investors seeking stability, these stocks frequently withstand selling pressure in a falling market. synonymous with *protective stocks.*

defer: to delay payment to a future time. [78]

deferment charge: an additional charge on a precomputed loan which results in extending all fully unpaid installments one or more months and thus deferring the formal final interest maturity date. (This is similar to collecting interest only on a simple interest account for one month.) [55]

deferment short: the amount by which a payment is insufficient to pay the deferment charges being assessed on an account. [55]

deferrals: cash collected before revenue is recognized as being earned, or in which cash is disbursed before an expense is recognized as being incurred.

deferred annuity: an annuity contract that provides for the postponement or start of an annuity until after a specified period or until the annuitant attains a specified age.

deferred asset: an asset that is not

readily convertible into cash, subject to current settlement. [19]

deferred availability cash items: checks received for collection for which credit has not yet been given. The Reserve Banks credit the banks sending in the checks according to a time schedule based on the normal time required to collect payment on the checks. [40]

deferred bond: see *bond, deferred.*

deferred charges: expenditures that are written off over a time period.

deferred compensation: the postponement of distribution of a portion of current earnings until a later date, usually at retirement. The object of deferred compensation is to reduce current income taxes by postponing receipt of taxable income until a time when the receiver will likely be in a lower income tax bracket.

deferred consignment expenses: expenses recorded by a consignor that apply to consigned items sold in a future fiscal period.

deferred credit: a credit that has been delayed in posting for a reason. A deferred credit may be a deposit that came into a bank after business hours and is therefore entered on the books the next business day.

deferred debits: accounts carried on the asset side of the balance sheet in which are recorded items being amortized as charges against income over a period of years (such as debit discount and expense) and items held in suspense pending final transfer or disposition (such as extraordinary property losses, clearing accounts (net), retirement or other work in progress, etc.). [3]

deferred delivery: purchase of a cash commodity for delivery at some specified future date. synonymous with *forward delivery.*

deferred dividend: a stock dividend (preferred or common) that will not be paid until some action occurs.

deferred expense: an asset that has been created through the payment of cash by an entity before the time it will obtain benefits from that payment. Basically synonymous with *prepaid expense.*

deferred gross profit on installment sales: gross profit on installment sales realized in a future fiscal period.

deferred income (deferred credits): any income, such as premiums received on bonds that are sold, or rent received in advance, that does not apply to the year for which it was received. Consequently, the crediting of the income is deferred until such time as it is earned. Until then it is listed on a balance sheet as a current liability.

deferred interest
(1) the delay in paying interest. see *bond, deferred.*
(2) the postponement in crediting out-of-town checks deposited by people holding interest-bearing balances for interest purposes until the required days pass to collect them.

deferred liabilities: liabilities the settlement of which is deferred. [18]

deferred maintenance: the expenditure necessary to restore a fixed asset to "like new" condition. This differs from ordinary maintenance or repairs, which, in most cases, merely restore the asset to working order. An example would be the complete rebuilding of a lathe by replacing all bearings (whether worn or not), regrinding the lead screw threads, repainting the castings, replating the fittings, and so on. [38]

deferred payment account: synonymous with *convenient payment account.*

deferred payments

(1) *banking:* mortgage allowances for postponement of interest payments. A type of installment plan.

(2) *finance:* delayed payments postponed until a future time; usually against some future period.

deferred posting: the posting of items in the bookkeeping department on a delayed basis. All items received during one day's business are intersorted and posted on the next business day, as of the date received. [31]

deferred revenue: a liability that has been created through the receipt of cash by an entity before its performance of a service or sale of goods.

deferred serial bond: see *bond, deferred serial.*

deferred special assessments: special assessments that have been levied but are not yet due. [49]

deferred stock: stocks whose dividends are not to be paid until the expiration of a stated date, or until a specified event has taken place.

deferred tax: a tax liability accrued on income that is reported but not subject to income tax until a later time period.

deferring: in accounting, relieving the expense and/or income accounts of those portions of expenditures and receipts which are not yet actual expense or income, and diverting them to future accounting periods. cf. *accruing.*

deficiency

(1) *general:* the amount by which anything falls short of some require-

ment or expectation. The term should not be used without qualification. [49]

(2) *government:* the amount by which taxes are in excess of the taxes stated on a taxpayer's tax return, plus further earlier assessments and less earlier rebates.

deficiency contribution: that portion of the periodic payment by an employee or employer under a retirement plan which is allocated to paying or amortizing the unfunded accrued liability or actuarial reserve deficiency, or meeting the requirements for previous service. [52]

deficiency guarantee: a guarantee given to a lender, limited in amount to the deficiency suffered by the lender on realization of an asset in the event of the borrower's default.

deficiency judgment: a court order authorizing collection from a debtor of any part of a debt that remains unsatisfied after foreclosure and sale of collateral. [44]

deficiency supply bill: an appropriation for a purpose or project made following enactment of the annual budget or the regular appropriation bills.

deficit

(1) *general:* the excess of liabilities over assets; the excess of obligations and expenditures affecting a given budget period which is in excess of the budget established for the period.

(2) *finance:* indicating obligations or expenditures for items that are in excess of the amount allotted for those items in a financial budget.

deficit financing: exists when government expenditures exceed revenues and the difference is made up by borrowing. The objective is to expand business activity and yield an improvement in general economic conditions. The deficit is covered by release of government bonds. cf. *deficit spending.*

Deficit Reduction Act of 1984 (DEFRA): federal legislation of tax increases to raise some $50 billion through fiscal 1987. see also *Tax Reform Act of 1984.*

deficit spending: the spending of public funds raised by borrowing rather than by taxation. A fiscal activity often associated with the government that spends more than it collects from taxes and other revenues. Some fiscal policy experts point out that an increase in the deficit stimulates the economy, whereas a decrease in the deficit has the opposite effect. cf. *deficit financing.*

defined benefit pension plan: an Internal Revenue Service ruling making possible tax-deductible pension plan contributions as high as 100% of salary for professionals and business managers.

defined contribution plan: a pension plan that provides for an individual account for each participant and for benefits based on the amount contributed to the participant's account, including any income, expenses, gains, or losses. [105]

definitive: denoting a permanent stock certificate or bond issued to replace an existing document resulting from a change in the corporation involved, particularly a change impacting on the firm's financial structure.

definitive bond: see *bond, definitive.*

definitive certificate: see *definitive.*

deflation

(1) *general:* a decline in the general price level, resulting in an increase in the purchasing power of money.

(2) *finance:* the lessening of the amount of money in circulation.

deflationary gap: the amount by which demand falls short of full employment supply, thus lowering the real value of a nation's output.

deflator: a statistical device or divisor that removes the influence of some increase such as the changing value of currency.

DEFRA: see *Deficit Reduction Act of 1984.*

defraud: to deprive an individual, by deceit, of some right; to cheat; to withhold improperly that which belongs to another.

defray: to pay; to carry an expense; for example, a court settlement may include an amount of money to defray the legal costs of the winning party.

defunct company: a firm that has ceased to exist; a dissolved organization.

degree of combined leverage: a measure of the company's earnings-per-share variability created by the combined effects of operating leverage and financial leverage.

degree of financial leverage: a measure of the company's earnings-per-share variability created by fixed financing costs.

degree of operating leverage: a measure of the variability of the company's earnings before interest and taxes that is caused by fixed operating costs.

degressive taxation: a type of progressive taxation: the rates increase as the base amount taxed increases; and each addition to the tax rate is lower than the preceding one.

de jure: "by right" (Latin); rightful, legitimate, just; according to law or equity. A term describing a state of affairs or a condition existing based on right or law, as distinguished from one that exists de facto. cf. *de facto.*

de jure corporation: a firm that has followed the law dealing with establishing incorporation. A de jure corporation exists in both law and fact. cf. *de facto corporation.*

Delaware Banking Law of 1981: a comprehensive Delaware law aimed at out-of-state banks that would grant them a wide range of credit powers, unavailable in most states. These powers include the ability to charge interest rates not subject to any legal ceiling, to raise interest rates retroactively, to charge variable interest rates, to levy unlimited fees for credit card usage and to foreclose on a home in the event of default for credit card debts. The law also includes a provision that would lower taxes. It would allow, for example, New York banks that relocate in Delaware and earn more than $30 million a year to be taxed at a rate of 2.7 percent, compared with 8.7 percent for those Delaware banks earning under $20 million and a rate of 25.8 percent for banks that remain in New York.

delayed delivery: securities that were sold with the knowledge that delivery would not occur on the regular clearance date. see *clearing.*

delayed items: items representing transactions that occurred before the current accounting year. [18]

delayed opening: the situation created when buy and sell orders accumulate prior to the opening of a stock exchange.

del credere agency: when an agency, factor, or broker attempts to guarantee to his or her principal the payment of a buyer's debt, the agent (etc.) is functioning under a del credere agency.

delectus personae: "chosen or selected person" (Latin); for example, to designate a partner.

delinquency: failure to pay a debt when due.

delinquency percentage: the percentage of either dollar amount or number of accounts that are past due; calculated for dollar amount by dividing dollars delinquent by total dollars outstanding; calculated for number of accounts by dividing the number of accounts delinquent by the total number of active accounts. [105]

delinquency ratio: ratio of past due loans to total loans serviced. [105]

delinquent account: a cardholder account on which a payment or payments have not been made in accordance with the terms and conditions of the cardholder agreement. [105]

delinquent account receivable: a debt remaining unpaid after the due date. [43]

delinquent activity report: the periodic report displaying all of the activity on past due accounts. [105]

delinquent special assessments: special assessments remaining unpaid on and after the date on which a penalty for nonpayment is attached. [49]

delinquent tax: describing a tax that is unpaid after the date when the payment was expected.

delist: activity resulting in the removal or cancellation of rights, by the SEC, previously given to a listed security. This situation occurs usually when a security fails to meet some of the requirements for the listing privilege.

delivered at frontier: when the seller

is required to supply items that conform with the contract, at his or her own risk and expense, the seller must place the items at the disposal of the purchaser at the named place of delivery at the border at the specified time. The purchaser is responsible for complying with import formalities and for duty payment. cf. *delivered duty paid*. [95]

delivered duty paid: when the seller is required to supply items that conform with the contract, at his or her own risk and expense, the seller must place the items at the disposal of the purchaser, duty paid, and all required formalities having been complied with, at the named place of destination at the specified time. cf. *delivered at frontier*. [95]

delivery

(1) *general:* the transfer of the possession of an item from one person to another.

(2) *investments:* the transmission of the certificate representing shares bought on a securities exchange; delivery is usually made to the purchaser's broker on the fourth business day after the transaction. see *good delivery, settlement day*; see also *seller's seven sale.*

delivery date: formally, the first day of the month during which delivery is to be made under a futures contract. Since sales are made at the seller's option, however, the seller can make delivery on any day of the month, following proper notification to the buyer.

delivery month: a futures contract must stipulate one of the calendar months as the month of delivery. [2]

delivery notice: the notification of delivery of the actual commodity on the contract, issued by the seller of the futures to the buyer. The rules of the vari-

ous exchanges require that tender notices be issued on certain days, and in some cases, at certain hours. [2]

delivery points: those locations designated by futures exchanges at which the commodity covered by a futures contract may be delivered in fulfillment of the contract. [2]

delivery price: the price fixed by the clearinghouse at which deliveries on futures are invoiced and also the price at which the futures contract is settled when deliveries are made. [2]

delivery receipt: a document signed by the consignee acknowledging receipt of merchandise.

delivery risk: the risk that a counterpart will not be permitted to complete his or her side of the deal, although willing to do so. cf. *capital risk.*

Dem.

(1) see *demand.*

(2) see *demurrage.*

demand

(1) *general:* the willingness and capability to purchase goods or services.

(2) *finance:* a request to call for payment, or for the carrying out of an obligation. see *sight draft.*

(3) *law:* a claim, or the assertion of a legal right.

(4) see also *market demand.*

demand-and-supply curves: the graphic representation of the maximum purchasing and minimum selling prices given and accepted to traders in a particular commodity at a specific time and place, and the resulting market price.

demand bill: any sight bill of exchange.

demand costs: synonymous with *capacity costs, readiness-to-serve costs.*

demand deposit: a deposit on account

in a commercial bank on which checks can be drawn and funds taken out without any advance notification. Demand deposits are the greatest part of our money supply.

demand deposit (adjusted): the total of customers' deposits in reporting member banks subject to immediate withdrawal (checking accounts), excluding interbank deposits and deposits of the U.S. government, less checks in the process of collection. [40]

demand draft: a draft payable immediately upon sight or presentation to the drawee. synonymous with *sight draft.* see *draft.* [31]

demand loan: a loan that has no fixed maturity date but is payable on demand of the bank making the loan. Demand loans can be "called" by a bank at any time payment is desired.

demand mortgage: a mortgage that may be called for payment on demand. [44]

demand note: a note or mortgage that can be demanded at any time for payment by the holder. see also *scrip.*

demand price: the maximum price a purchaser is willing to pay for a stated quantity of a commodity or service.

demand-pull inflation: an increase in the price level created by an abundance of money pursuing too few commodities. The demand for items is greater than the capability to produce or supply them.

demand rate: synonymous with *check rate.*

demand schedule: a tabular arrangement showing the quantities of a product that buyers stand ready to purchase at different prices.

demand secured loan: a demand loan for which collateral is held as security

by the lender. The value of the collateral must be at least equal to that of the loan. [105]

demand sterling: used in London and other English banks; signt bills of exchange drawn in pounds.

demise charterparty: a charter by demise functions as a lease of the vessel itself, which for the time passes to the ownership of the charterer. see also *charterparty.*

demonization (demonetization)
(1) *banking:* the reduction in the number of government bonds and securities by a commercial bank, resulting in an increase in the value of deposit and paper currency, including federal reserve notes.
(2) *finance:* the withdrawal of specified currency from circulation.

demonetarize: see *demonization.* [2]

demonstration: the unexpected activity or sudden climb in value for any specific or group of stocks.

demonstrative gift: a gift, by will, or a specified sum of money to be paid from a designated fund or asset; as a gift of $1000 from a specified bank account. [37]

demonstrative legacy: see *legacy.*

demurrage: detention of a freight car or ship beyond time permitted for loading or unloading, with additional charges for detention.

demurrer: a method of procedure in a law suit: the defendant admits the validity of all the plaintiff's complaints but denies that the facts warrant a cause of action. cf. *cognovit, nonsuit.*

denial letter: FmHA's notice to a bank that it cannot guarantee a loan under the proposed conditions. [105]

denomination value: the face value of all currencies, coins, and securities.

de novo: slang, new banks.

Dep.

(1)   see *deposit.*

(2)   see *depositary.*

Department of Agriculture, U.S.: a federal agency established in 1889 to conduct farm educational and research programs, as well as to administer numerous federal agricultural aid programs and other projects to aid farmers and ranchers.

Department of Commerce, U.S.: a federal agency established in 1913 to promote domestic and foreign trade.

Department of Education, U.S.: this new federal agency, established in 1980, is a spinoff from the Department of Health, Education and Welfare. This agency is responsible for improving national programs in the field of education.

Department of Energy (DOE), U.S.: a federal agency established in 1977 to control oil price and allocations, to coordinate energy research and development efforts, to set rates for oil and oil-product appliances, and to energy conservation standards. see *Federal Energy Administration.*

Department of Health and Human Services, U.S.: following the creation of the Department of Education in 1980, this new cabinet unit replaced the Department of Health, Education and Welfare. This agency is responsible for improving national programs in health and social security.

Department of Health, Education and Welfare (HEW), U.S.: see *Department of Health and Human Services, U.S.*

Department of Housing and Urban Development (HUD), U.S.: a federal agency formed in 1965 responsible for national programs dealing with housing needs and urban renewal and development. see also *Government National Mortgage Association.*

Department of Justice, U.S.: a federal agency created in 1870 with supervisory powers over federal prosecuting agencies, representing the federal government to the courts. The department has jurisdiction over issues of antitrust and civil rights and supervises the government's activities relating to immigration.

Department of Labor, U.S.: a federal agency created in 1913 to advance workers' welfare, working conditions, and in general, employment opportunities.

Department of the Treasury, U.S.: a federal agency created in 1789 to impose and collect taxes and customs duties, to enforce revenue and fiscal laws, to disburse federal funds; to manage the public debt, and to coin and print money.

Department of Transportation (DOT), U.S.: a federal agency created in 1966 to promote a coordinated national transportation policy embracing all media except water transport. see *Federal Aviation Administration.*

department store banking: see *multiple banking.*

dependent: an individual who requires support from another, as distinguished from one who merely derives a benefit from the earnings of another. see *dependents.*

dependent covenants: two or more related agreements; the performance of one promise must take place before the performance of other promises (e.g., a buyer must pay for goods before the purchased items will be delivered).

dependents

(1) *banking:* an insured employee's spouse and unmarried children who meet certain eligibility requirements for coverage under a life plan.

(2) *taxation:* a relative or nonrelative receiving more than half of his or her support from a taxpayer; under Internal Revenue law an exemption is provided.

depletion

(1) an amount charged to current operating expenses over a period of time in order to write off the asset value of a wasting asset, such as a mine or an oil well. It is a noncash expense.

(2) the consumption or exhaustion of wasting property, such as royalties, patent rights, mines, oil and gas wells, quarries, timberlands, and other things that are consumed or worn out in the using. [105]

depletion accounting: natural resources, such as metals, oils, and gas, which conceivably can be reduced to zero over the years, present a special problem in capital management. Depletion is an accounting practice consisting of charges against earnings based on the amount of the asset taken out of the total reserves in the period for which accounting is made. A bookkeeping entry, depletion does not represent any cash outlay, nor are any funds earmarked for the purpose. [20]

depletion allowance: as permitted by the Internal Revenue Code, a deduction from taxable income derived from a wasting asset. The basis of the allowance is either a percentage of the gross income from specified property or a per-unit-of-product condition.

deployment: the distribution and placement of financial service terminals providing convenience to customers. This may occur in traditional market areas or new market areas. [105]

depo: short for *deposit*.

déport: French term for *discount*.

deposit: an amount of funds consisting of cash and/or checks, drafts, coupons, and other cash items that may be converted into cash upon collection. The deposit is given to a bank for the purpose of establishing and maintaining a credit balance.

deposit administration: a form of group annuity in which the contributions are held by the insurer, usually at a guaranteed rate of interest, until an employee's retirement, at which time an annuity is purchased. [105]

deposit analysis: a process by which account deposits are analyzed to determine that portion of the deposit which must be considered float and cannot be immediately credited to an account. [105]

depositary: an individual or institution identified as one to be entrusted with something of value for safekeeping (e.g., a bank or trust company).

depositary receipt: mechanism to allow for the trading of foreign stocks on U.S. stock exchanges when the overseas nation involved will not allow foreign ownership of the stock of domestic firms. The shares are therefore deposited with a bank in the country of corporation and an affiliated or correspondent bank in the United States issues depositary receipts for the securities. U.S. investors buy these receipts and can trade them on an appropriate American stock exchange in the same way as other stocks. The major purpose of the instrument is to officially identify ownership of the stock in the foreign country.

depositary trust company: a central securities certificate depositary in New York City through which clearing members of the Stock Clearing Corporation effect security deliveries between each other by computerized entries, thus minimizing the physical movement of certificates.

deposit banking: the activity of a commercial bank dealing with deposits, receiving checks on other banks, remitting on checks forwarded for the purpose of collection, and paying out deposits by check.

deposit book: a passbook of a customer of the bank showing the amounts of deposits made.

deposit ceiling rates of interest: maximum interest rates that can be paid on savings and time deposits at federally insured banks, savings and loan associations, and credit unions. Ceilings are established by the Federal Reserve Board, the Federal Deposit Insurance Corporation, the Federal Home Loan Bank Board, and the National Credit Union Administration. [1]

deposit correction slip: a form used to notify a depositor of an error made by the depositor. When the error is located, the bank makes out a deposit correction slip showing what the error was and the corrected new balance of the deposit. The depositor can then correct his or her records accordingly. [10]

deposit creation multiplier: the dollars of lending generated by an independent increase of one dollar in bank deposits.

deposit currency: checks and other credit items deposited with a bank as the equivalent of cash.

deposit date: the date on which paper is received by a bank from a merchant. [105]

deposit envelope: an envelope used by merchants to transport sales drafts and credit vouchers to banks for credit to their deposit accounts. [105]

deposit function: the business of receiving money on deposit for safekeeping and convenience. This function includes the receiving of demand deposits subject to check and the receiving of savings (time) deposits at interest. [31]

deposit funds: funds established to account for collection that either are held in suspense temporarily and later refunded or are paid into some other fund of the government or held by the government as banker or agent for others. cf. *escrow.*

deposit insurance: insurance to protect the depositor against bankruptcy of a bank or savings and loan institution (see, e.g., *Federal Deposit Insurance Corporation).*

deposit interest rate: limits set by the Federal Reserve System and Federal Deposit Insurance Corporation on interest rates that commercial banks can declare on time deposits. The bank is prohibited from paying any interest rates on demand deposits.

deposition: testimony not given in open court but instead taken by written or oral questionings, signed and witnessed, and ultimately used like testimony in court.

deposit liability: a bank's total liability

to customers shown by all demand deposits, time deposits, certificates of deposit and so on.

deposit line: the approximate average amount that a bank's customer usually maintains in a bank account.

deposit loan: loans that are made by the banker crediting the borrower's account with a "loan deposit" for the sum of the loan. This is different from giving the borrower currency when granting a loan.

depositor: an individual, partnership, business proprietorship, corporation, organization, or association is termed a depositor when funds have been placed in bank in the name of the person or entity.

depositor's life insurance: a form of life insurance granted a depositor, without cost, by certain financial institutions, which pays the depositor's beneficiary or estate the amount on deposit—but not in excess of a certain stipulated sum—at the time of death of the depositor. Such benefits are often limited to those depositors whose accounts were opened before they attained a stipulated age. [10]

depository: a bank in which funds or securities are deposited by others, usually under the terms of a specific depository agreement. Also, a bank in which government funds are deposited or in which other banks are permitted by law to maintain required reserves. [50]

depository agreement: see *mortgage certificate.*

depository bond: see *bond, depository.*

Depository Institutions Act of 1982: authorized the Federal deposit-insurance agencies to lend capital to thrift units that are running out of reserves. The Act broadened the powers of thrift units by allowing them to make commercial loans and to accept demand deposits, thereby opening up a new market for them. Short-term loans were also authorized.

Depository Institutions Deregulation and Monetary Control Act: legislation passed in the spring of 1980, the act committed the government to deregulating the banking system. It provided for elimination of interest-rate controls (known as Regulation Q) for banks and savings institutions within six years, and it authorized them to offer interest-bearing NOW accounts beginning in 1981 anywhere in the country. The act also wiped out all state usury laws on home mortgages above $25,000. It also modernized the mortgage instrument by repealing dollar limits, permitting second mortgages, and eliminating lending-territory restrictions. see *graduated-payment mortgage, pledged-account mortgage, variable-rate mortgage.*

Depository Institutions Deregulation Committee (DIDC): charged with deregulating the banks and savings industry. Created by Congress in the spring of 1980, it has a panel of five voting members: the Federal Reserve Board chairman, the Treasury secretary, and the chairmen of the Federal Home Loan Bank Board, the Federal Deposit Insurance Corporation, and the National Credit Union Administration.

In June 1981, it approved a plan to phase out interest rate ceilings on deposits at banks and savings and loan associations during the following four years.

On August 1, 1981, current ceilings on 2½ year certificates were removed. Also on that date, interest rate ceilings were eliminated for accounts maturing in four years or more at banks or thrift institutions.

On August 1, 1982, ceilings were eliminated for accounts maturing in three years or more. Interest on deposits maturing in two to three years were tied to the rate on two-year Treasury securities. Thrift institutions were allowed to pay as much as the Treasury rate, whereas commercial banks were held to 0.25 percentage point less.

On August 1, 1983, ceilings were eliminated on accounts maturing in two years or more, and the rates for deposits maturing in one to two years were tied to the one-year Treasury rate, without any differential between bank and savings and loan rates.

On August 1, 1984, ceilings were eliminated on accounts maturing in one or two years, and the rates for deposits maturing in less than a year were tied to the comparable Treasury rate without a differential between bank and savings and loan rates.

On August 1, 1985 ceilings were removed from accounts that matured in less than one year, except for passbook savings accounts. The committee did not decide what to do about the passbook accounts, although controls on them will end April 1, 1986, under a law passed by Congress in 1980.

depository receipt: short for American depository receipt. see *American depository receipt.*

depository transfer draft: a pre-printed, no-signature instrument used only to move funds from one account to another account in the same name at another bank. [105]

Depository Trust Company (DTC):   a central securities certificate depository through which members effect security deliveries between each other via computerized bookkeeping entries, thereby reducing the physical movement of stock certificates. [20]

deposit receipt: in banks where tellers' machines are now used, the machine issues a printed receipt for the deposit made. This receipt does away with the pen-and-ink entry made in the passbook used by checking account depositors. The bank furnishes a folder in which the depositor keeps his deposit receipts until he has received his bank statement. After verifying his statement for accuracy of entry of all deposits, he can destroy the receipts, since he has been properly credited by the bank as evidenced on his statement. [10]

deposits in federal reserve banks: deposit accounts held as follows: (a) *member banks*—deposits of member banks, which are largely legal required reserves; (b) *U.S. Treasurer*—general or checking accounts of the Treasury; (c) *foreign*—balances of foreign governments and central banks; and (d) *other*—other deposits, includes those of nonmember banks maintained for check-clearing purposes. [40]

deposit slip: an itemized memorandum of the cash and other funds which a customer (depository) presents to the receiving teller for credit to his or her account. [31]

deposit-taking company (DTC): a financial institution that can take deposits, make loans, discount bills, issue letters of credit, but cannot be called a bank. The concept originated in Hong Kong.

deposit ticket: a business form onto which a depositor itemizes all items that he or she wishes to deposit in a bank.

deposit warrant: a financial document prepared by a designated accounting or finance officer authorizing the treasurer of a governmental unit to accept for deposit sums of money collected by various departments and agencies of the governmental unit. [49]

depot: short for *deposit*.

depreciable: the state of any asset that is subject to depreciation. [105]

depreciable asset: property used in business or income production whose cost a taxpayer can recover as deductions from income over the useful life of the asset.

depreciable cost: the value of a fixed asset subject to depreciation. Sometimes this is the original cost, at other times, the original cost less an estimated salvage value.

depreciable plant: a utility plant. Usually a tangible plant in service which is subject to depreciation (wearing out, inadequacy, obsolescence, and other causes). [3]

depreciate
(1) in accounting, the process of reducing the book value of a fixed asset at periodic intervals to charge a portion of the assets' cost as an expense of the period in which it provides a service.
(2) to decrease in service capacity or usefulness. [105]

depreciated cost: cost less accumulated depreciation and less other valuation accounts, having the effect of reducing the original outlay to a recoverable cost; the book value of a fixed asset.

depreciated currency: resulting from the lowering in the exchange value of currency, funds not accepted at face or par value.

depreciation
(1) *general:* normally, charges against earnings to write off the cost, less salvage value, of an asset over its estimated useful life. It is a bookkeeping entry and does not represent any cash outlay, nor are any funds earmarked for the purpose. see *book depreciation, declining balance depreciation.* [20]
(2) *banking:* a decline in the value of property.

depreciation book: accrued depreciation shown on books of account. [6]

depreciation charges: charges made by private business and not-for-profit institutions against receipts, to account for the decrease in value of capital assets as a result of wear, accidental damage, and obsolescence, plus an estimate of corresponding depreciation in owner-occupied dwellings.

depreciation fund: funds or securities set aside for replacing depreciating fixed assets. [105]

depreciation method: the arithmetic procedure followed for reducing the book value of an asset over the years of its useful life. [105]

depreciation of money: the fall in the value of the monetary unit measured in terms of goods and services which the unit will buy compared with a base point in time. Sometimes restricted to change of the metal content of the monetary unit.

depreciation reserve: an account recording periodic charges to income to reflect the portion of the cost of a long-lived asset recovered. If the amount is kept in cash or a specific asset, it is referred to as a fund. When an asset is disposed of, the account is credited with all the depreciation charges previously made for that asset.

depressed market: a situation created when prices of goods or services are unusually low.

depression: an economic condition: business activity is down over a long period, prices drop, purchasing power is greatly reduced, and unemployment is high.

Depression of the 1930s: the Great Depression, a severe economic crisis that afflicted the United States and also affected worldwide business, is thought to have begun with the collapse of the stock market in October 1929 and finally ended in the early 1940s, when defense spending for World War II strengthened the general economy.

Deregulation Act: see *Depository Institutions Deregulation and Monetary Control Act.*

dereliction: the intentional abandonment of property. "Derelict property" is any property forsaken or discarded in a way indicating that the owner has no further use or need of it.

derivative deposit: a deposit that is created when a person borrows money from a bank (e.g., deposit currency). A customer is lent a sum, not in money but by credit to his or her account, against which he or she may draw checks as required.

derivative suit: in corporation law, a suit by a stockholder on behalf of the corporation, in which the stockholder alleges that the officers of the corpora-tion have failed to act to protect the interests of the corporation and therefore the particular stockholder is suing on behalf of the corporation.

derived demand: the demand for an item that grows out of the wish to fulfill the demand for another item (e.g., when a demand for community tennis courts is filled, it leads to increased sales of supplies for the courts and tennis equipment).

derogatory information: data received by a credit card issuer indicating that an applicant or cardholder has not paid his or her accounts with other creditors according to the required terms. [105]

descendant: one who is descended in a direct line from another, however remotely (child, grandchild, great-grandchild). [37]

descent: the passing of property, or title to the property, by inheritance, as contrasted with request or purchase.

description: items are sometimes described on the deposit ticket, by the teller or another clerk, as to the city or bank of payment. This provides a source reference record and assists in the calculation of uncollected funds. [31]

descriptive billing: a billing system in which an account statement is not accompanied by copies of original invoices. Instead, the statement contains sufficient detail to permit the customer to identify the nature, date, and amount of each transaction processed during the statement period. cf. *country club billing.*

descriptive labeling: the labeling of consumer goods by quality, size, and so on, to aid in judging the price, but without reference to recognized standards or grades.

descriptive statement: a bank account statement that contains one or more described entries for which no separate item is enclosed. Bill check, preauthorized payments, and direct payroll deposits necessitate some form of descriptive statement unless a substitute enclosure document is produced by the bank. [105]

desk, the: the trading desk at the New York Federal Reserve Bank, through which open market purchases and sales of government securities are made. The desk maintains direct telephone communication with major government securities dealers. A "foreign desk" at the New York Reserve Bank conducts transactions in the foreign exchange market. see also *foreign exchange desk.* [1]

de son tort: "of his own wrongdoing" (French). An expression found in such phrases as executor de son tort and guardian de son tort. [32]

desterilizing gold: the issuance by the Treasury of gold certificates to the Federal Reserve System covering gold previously bought by the Treasury but against which the Treasury had not yet issued gold certificates. cf. *sterilizing gold.*

destination clauses: marketing contracts to permit an oil monopoly to stipulate which countries should receive oil, preventing the oil from being diverted to the spot market. see *spot market.*

destructive competition: competition that forces prices to so low a level that poor service or commodities results and needed revenue is not realized by

competitors properly to maintain their properties.

detailed audit: an audit in which an examination is made of the system of internal control and of the details of all transactions and books of account, including subsidiary records and supporting documents, as to legality, mathematical accuracy, complete accountability, and application of accepted accounting principles for governmental units. [49]

details of charges: stipulates that a party in a transaction should pay the charges. [105]

details of payment: see *originator to beneficiary information.*

deterioration: a reduction of the quality and/or substance of a fixed asset, usually resulting from normal wear and tear from being used. The effect is to lower the value of the asset.

determination date: the latest day of the month on which savings may be deposited and still earn interest from the first day of the month; set by an association's board of directors, but usually the tenth day. [59]

detinue: a common law action to recover property.

Detroit Stock Exchange: established in Michigan in 1907, the majority of its transactions are in unlisted securities.

deutsche mark: West Germany's currency, replacing the old Reichsmark in 1948.

devaluation: an action taken by the government to reduce the value of the domestic currency in terms of gold or foreign monies.

development

(1) *general:* a gradual unfolding by virtue of which something comes to be.

(2) *finance:* a venture on a large scale.

Development Assistance Committee (DAC): a committee of the Organization for Economic Cooperation and Development whose function is to encourage the flow of funds from member nations to the developing countries.

development expense: the cost of developing products, processes, or other commercial activities to make them functional.

Development Finance Companies (DFCs): the financing of development finance companies by the World Bank commenced in 1950 with a loan of $2 million to the Development Bank of Ethiopia. By the end of fiscal 1975, bank lending to such intermediaries had reached almost $3 billion to 68 DFCs (including three regional DFCs serving the East Africa Community, Africa, and Latin America, respectively) in 44 countries and the three regions. see also *International Bank for Reconstruction and Development.* [16]

Development Loan Fund (DLF): created under the 1957 Mutual Security Act, the fund purports to administer long-range development loans. Loans, credit, and guaranties are authorized to assist private lending for economic development.

deviation

(1) *banking:* a rate or policy form differing from that published by a rating bureau.

(2) *statistics:* a measure of dispersion, calculated to be the difference between the particular number or item and the average, which is usually the arithmetic mean, or set of numbers or items.

devise: a gift, often real property, found in a last will and testament.

devisee: any person receiving title to real property in accordance with the terms of a will. see *devisor, lucrative title.*

devisen: German term for *foreign exchange.*

devises: French term for *foreign exchange.*

devisor: the donor of a gift of real property by will. see *devisee.*

devolution: the passing of real estate title by hereditary succession.

DFCs: see *Development Finance Companies.*

diagonal expansion: expanding a business by developing new products that can be produced by using equipment already employed in manufacturing its product or which contain much the same raw materials as the established product. The evolution of by-products frequently is the cause of diagonal expansion.

diary: a record kept of maturity dates for notes, bonds, and other instruments. see *tickler.*

dicta: rules or arguments given in the written statement of a judge that have no bearing on issues involved and are not critical for their determination (singular, "dictum").

DIDC: see *Depository Institutions Deregulation Committee.*

dies non: Latin, a day on which no business can be transacted.

differences account: see *over and short account.*

differential duty: a difference in the duty on the same commodity based on the origin of the commodity or some similar face. synonymous with *discriminating duty* and *preferential duty.*

differentials: the premiums paid for the grades higher than the standard growth (basic grades) and the discounts allowed for the grades lower than the basic grades. These differentials are fixed by the contract terms. [11]

diffusion theory of taxation: the theory that all taxes are spread over the whole population by price changes rather than coming to rest on the person who pays the tax.

digested securities: securities owned by investors who are not expected to sell them soon. cf. *stag.*

digit: a component of an item of data; a character position in a computer that may assume one of several values; one of the symbols 0, 1, . . ., 9 (e.g., the number 557 contains three digits but is composed of two types of characters, 5 and 7).

digital computer: a computer in which discrete representation of data is mainly used; performs arithmetic and logic processes on these data. The numbers express all quantities and variables of a problem. cf. *analogue computer.*

digitizing machine: a bank machine that reproduces the signature of a customer (which is stored on a card previously signed by the customer) at the top of each check. Thus, when a customer actually countersigns a check for a cash advance, the two signatures can be corroborated.

Dillon Round: the 1960–1962 international trade negotiations conducted under the auspices of GATT and followed in 1964 by the Kennedy Round and in 1973 by the Tokyo Round. see *Kennedy Round* and *Tokyo Round.*

dilution: the effect of a drop in earnings per share or book value per share, caused by the potential conversion of securities or by the potential exercise of warrants or options.

dime: a 10-cent coin, valued at 10 percent of a U.S. dollar.

diminishing balance accrual: accrual method for recognizing earned income by applying the Rule of 78 to the unearned interest balance on account. [105]

diminishing returns: a condition that exists when, in successively applying equal amounts of one or two factors of production (e.g., land and capital) to the remaining factor(s), an additional application produces a smaller increase in production than the preceding application. cf. *indifference schedule.*

dinar: monetary unit of Abu Dhabi, Aden, Algeria, Bahrain, Iraq, Jordan, Kuwait, Libya, South Yemen (Aden), Tunisia, and Yugoslavia.

dip: referring to prices, a mild setback or reaction.

Dir.: see *director.*

direct access: synonymous with *random access.*

direct cost: the cost of any good or service that contributes to the production of an item or service (e.g., labor, material); indirect costs (e.g., machinery upkeep, power, taxes) are not directly associated with the production. see *running costs*; cf. *indirect costs.*

direct debit: a method of collection used for certain claims, generally those which are repeated over a period of time, under which the debtor gives his or her bank a standing authorization to debit his or her account on sight of the direct debit issued by a creditor. [105]

direct debt: the debt that a unit has incurred in its own name or assumed.

direct deposit merchants: merchants who deposit directly through the U.S. mail. Incoming processing in accounting is responsible for servicing the merchants. [105]

direct deposit of payroll (DDP): a payroll system in which employee earnings are deposited directly to the employee's account at a depository institution.

direct earnings: earnings stated by a firm not showing any equity in the surplus earnings above dividend payments of units or affiliated companies. cf. *equity earnings.*

direct expenditures: payments to employees, suppliers, contractors, beneficiaries, and other recipients.

direct expense: synonymous with *direct cost.*

direct financing: raising capital without resorting to underwriting (e.g., by selling capital stock).

direct heir: a person in the direct line of ascent or descent of the descendent; as, father, mother, son, or daughter. see also *collateral heir, heirs.* [37]

direct inquiry: generally speaking, an inquiry about a person's credit standing made by one firm to another. As distinct from an inquiry to a credit bureau. [41]

direct investments: investments in foreign corporations where the investors have a controlling interest in the overseas firm.

direct labor: the cost of wages paid to workers.

direct lease financing: a form of term debt financing for fixed assets. Leases are similar to loans from a credit viewpoint because of considerations of cash flow, credit history, management, and projections of future operations. [105]

direct liability: a debtor's obligation arising from money, goods, or services received by him or her from another.

direct loan: a loan made directly to a customer for which the customer applied in person or by mail; opposed to a "sales contract," where credit is advanced to a customer through the purchase of a conditional sales contract from a merchant. [55]

direct materials: the cost of materials which become an integral part of a specific manufactured product or which are consumed in the performance of a specific service.

direct obligation: a drawer's obligation as the instrument maker, as contrasted with the indirect obligation of an endorser of the instrument.

director: a person elected by shareholders to establish company policies. The directors appoint the president, vice-presidents, and all other operating officers. Directors decide, among many other matters, if and when dividends are to be paid. [20]

directorate: a corporation's board of directors.

direct overhead: factory, selling, or other expenses related directly to a specific product and resulting in a direct cost.

direct payroll deposit: an electronic system which permits a corporation to pay its employee without formally preparing checks. The data processor serving the corporation generates paperless credit entries representing deposits and delivers such entries to its bank on or before each payday. The bank, through processing, extracts those paperless entries which are for its own customers and credits the employee's personal account. In turn, it sends the remainder of the entries to the local automated clearinghouse and, in so doing, becomes the originating bank for these entries. The ACH processes the entries, makes settlement between the originating and receiving banks on payday, and transmits the entries to the appropriate receiving banks. The receiving bank posts the entries on or before payday and consequently reflects such items on the customer's periodic statements. [105]

direct placement: the negotiation by a borrower, such as an industrial or utility company, directly with the lender, such as a life insurance company or group of companies, for an entire issue of securities. No underwriter is involved and that transaction is exempt from SEC filing.

direct quotation: quotation of fixed units of foreign currency in variable amounts of domestic currency. cf. *indirect quotation.*

direct reduction loan: a loan repayable in consecutive equal monthly payments of interest and principal sufficient to retire the debt within a definite period. "Direct" actually means that after the monthly interest payment has been taken out of the payment, the balance of the loan payment is applied directly to the reduction of the principal of the loan. [51]

direct reduction mortgage (DRM): a direct reduction mortgage is liquidated over the life of the mortgage in equal monthly payments. Each monthly payment consists of an amount to cover interest, reduction in principal, taxes,

and insurance. The interest is computed on an outstanding principal balance monthly. As the principal balance is reduced, the amount of interest becomes less, thereby providing a larger portion of the monthly payment to be applied to the reduction of principal. As taxes and insurance are paid by the mortgagee (lending association), these disbursements are added to the principal balance. This procedure follows throughout the life of the mortgage. [10]

direct sendings: items that are drawn on a particular bank, and sent directly to that drawee bank by another bank, are known as direct sendings. This is to be distinguished from a transit letter, which may be sent to a "correspondent bank" and which contains items on many drawee banks within a certain area. [10]

direct tax: the burden of a tax that cannot be easily shifted or passed on to another individual by the person on whom it is levied. cf. *indirect tax.*

direct verification: a method of bank audit whereby the auditor of a bank sends a request for the verification of the balances of deposits or loans as of a stated date to the depositors or borrowers. Verifications are returned directly to the auditor, confirming the correctness of balances or listing discrepancies. [10]

dirham: monetary unit of Morocco.

dirty

(1) a foreign exchange float where the value of the currency is controlled by the authorities rather than the market.

(2) a bill of lading that is qualified as to the condition of the items to which it relates.

(3)   in Great Britain, a stock which is cum-divided and close to the date for payment of interest. cf. *clean bill of exchange* and *clean bill of lading.*

Dis.:   see *discount.*

disagio: the charge made for exchanging depreciated foreign monies. cf. *agio.*

disaster clause: a Eurocredit loan agreement clause containing provisions for repayment of the loan if the Euromarket should disappear. cf. *break.* [87]

Disb.:   see *disbursement.*

disburse: to pay out money; to expend. [61]

disbursement: an actual payment of funds toward the full or partial settlement of an obligation.

disbursement schedule: a list or tabular statement of the amounts to be disbursed on specific dates in accordance with agreements entered into in a mortgage loan transaction. [44]

disbursement voucher: an order for making payments.

DISC: see *Domestic International Sales Corporation.*

discharge

(1)   *general:* to fire. synonymous with *dismiss.*

(2)   *law:* the release of one party from meeting his or her obligation under a contract because parties other to the contract have failed to meet their obligation(s).

discharge of bankruptcy: an order that terminates bankruptcy proceedings, usually relieving the debtor of all legal responsibility for certain specified obligations. [76]

discharge of contract: the fulfillment of a contract's obligations.

discharge of lien: the recorded release of a lien when debt has been repaid. [78]

disclaimer: a document, or a clause in a document, that renounces or repudiates the liability of an otherwise responsible party in the event of (a) noncompliance by such other party to certain conditions described in the instrument, (b) named external conditions, or (c) losses incurred because of a discrepancy in the goods delivered and the weight or count made by the shipper.

disclosure: all publicly owned corporations are required by the SEC to immediately inform the public of all information, positive or negative, that may influence any investment decision. see *full disclosure, insider.* see also *discovery practice.*

discontinuous market: as differentiated from continuously listed securities, the unlisted stocks and bonds forming a separate market.

discount

(1)   *finance:* the amount of money deducted from the face value of a note.

(2)   *foreign exchange:* the relationship of one currency to another. For example, Canadian currency may be at a discount to U.S. currency.

(3)   *investments:* the amount by which a preferred stock or bond sells below its par value. [20]

(4)   *investments:* "to take into account," as "the price of the stock has discounted the expected dividend cut."

discount broker: a broker who buys and sells stock. Since such brokers do not usually provide customers with other services, notably research, they tend to have lower fees than those of major brokerage firms.

discount charge: a finance charge deducted in advance. [78]

discount check: as determined by the New York Fed, the difference between the purchase price and the face value of a bill purchased from a Federal Reserve Bank.

discount clerk: a bank's representative working in the discount unit. Duties traditionally include the calculations of notes, acceptances and the maintenance of records of bills discounted.

discount corporation: any banking institution involved in the buying and discounting of trade and bankers' acceptance, commercial papers, bills of exchange, and so on. synonymous with *discount house.*

discounted value: the present value of future payments due or receivable, computed on the basis of a given rate of interest. [12]

discount from asset value: the percentage expression of the price of a share divided by its asset value.

discount house: synonymous with *commercial credit company, discount corporation,* and *sales finance company.*

discounting: occurs when an institution lends money to a business with a customer's debt obligation to the firm as security on the loan.

discounting a note receivable: selling a note receivable to a bank or to someone else.

discounting the news: when a stock's price or the level of a major market indicator climbs or falls in expectation of a good or bad occurrence, then barely moves when the actual development takes place and is announced, the stock is said to have "discounted the news."

discount loan: a loan on which the interest and/or charges are deducted from the "face amount" of the loan at the time it is made. [55]

discount market: differing from the bank's discounts for its own clients, the open market for commercial papers and acceptances. This market deals with banks of the Federal Reserve System, other banks, discount and commercial-paper houses, dealers of notes, and so on.

discount on purchases: a cash discount taken by a buyer.

discount on sales: a cash discount granted by a seller.

discount on securities: the amount or percentage by which a security (a bond or a share of stock) is bought or sold for less than its face or par value; opposed to premium on securities. [37]

discount rate: the Federal Reserve Bank's interest rate charged to member banks for loans. In most cases, higher interest rates lead to the lowering of security prices. see *easy money, prime interest (rate), tight money.*

discount register: a bank's book of original entry, in which a daily record is kept of all loan department transactions, such as loans made, payments received, and interest collected. [105]

discounts and advances: outstanding loans of the Federal Reserve Banks, primarily to member banks. [40]

discount store: a cut-rate store created to undersell its competitors.

discount tables: see *tables, discount.*

discount window: in 1980 a law was passed giving the Federal Reserve Board smoother control over the economy, requiring all banks and savings and loan associations to keep reserves behind checking-type deposits. One of the provisions of the law gives about 15,000 other banks and savings and loan associations the right to borrow from the Federal Reserve through its so-called discount window. It is felt by some analysts that this approach would hamper the Fed's ability to regulate the growth of reserves, the base for deposit and money creation.

discount yield: the ratio of the annualized discount to the par value. [107]

discovery practice: the disclosure by one party of facts or statements needed by the party seeking the discovery in connection with a pending cause or action. cf. *concealment.*

discretionary account: an account in which the customer gives the broker or someone else the authority, which may be complete or within specific limits, as to the purchase and sales of securities or commodities, including selection, timing, amount, and price to be paid or received. see *discretionary order.* [20]

discretionary fund: discretionary income enlarged by the amount of new credit extensions, which also may be deemed spendable as a result of consumer decision relatively free of prior commitment or pressure of need. [48]

discretionary income: what remains of disposable income, after essential living costs are paid. see *disposable income.* [78]

discretionary order: the customer specifies the stock or the commodity to be bought or sold, and the amount. His agent is free to act as to time and price. see *discretionary account.* [20]

discretionary policy: monetary policy, purporting to compensate for a business cycle, that leads to a decision by a person or government.

discretionary pool: a group of people authorized by others to act on their behalf in buying or selling securities or commodities.

discretionary spending power: designating money available to consume after necessities have been purchased. cf. *disposable income.*

discretionary trust
(1) a trust that entitles the beneficiary to use only so much of the income or principal as the trustee in its uncontrolled discretion shall see fit to give him or her to apply for his or her use.
(2) an investment company that is not limited in its policy to any one class, or type, of stock or security but may invest in any or all of a broad range of securities. [37]

discriminating duty: synonymous with *differential duty.*

discriminating taxation
(1) regressive taxes that impose a relatively greater burden on people of lower income than on people of higher income.
(2) taxation created to favor certain industries, often for the purpose of protecting domestic interests.
(3) any allowance or exemption in a tax system appearing to have little justification in equity or public policy and seen as favoring the beneficiary unjustly at the expense of other taxpayers.

Disct.: see *discount.*

diseconomies of scale: occur when costs increase as a business grows in size. For all firms, there is a point at which as the company becomes larger, costs also increase. see *law of increasing costs;* see also *internal economies of scale.*

dishoarding
(1) taking an item from storage and

placing it in use (i.e., removing currency from a safe deposit box and investing it).

(2) the act of reducing a stock of goods that was intended, when accumulated, to exceed normal future needs.

dishonored: describes a negotiable instrument offered for acceptance of payment that is turned down or cannot be obtained. see *notice of dishonor.*

disinflation: the result of a strategy to reduce the general price level by increasing the purchasing power of money.

disintermediation: the taking of money out of interest-bearing time accounts (e.g., savings and commercial bank accounts) for reinvestment at higher rates for bonds and so on.

disinvestment: the reduction of capital goods.

disk: a circular metal plate with magnetic material on both sides, continuously rotated for reading in a computer network.

disk pack: a set of magnetic disks designed to be placed in a computer central processing unit for reading and writing.

dismiss

(1) *general:* to release an employee.

(2) *law:* to dispose of a case without a trial. see *nolo contendere.*

dispatch earning: a saving in shipping costs arising from rapid unloading at the point of destination.

disposable income: personal income minus income taxes and other taxes paid by an individual, the balance being available for consumption or savings. see also *discretionary spending power.*

dispositive provisions: the provisions of a will or trust agreement relating to the disposition and distribution of the property in the estate or trust; to be distinguished from administrative provisions that relate to the handling of the property while it is in the hands of the executor or trustee. [37]

dispossess: to put an individual out of his or her property by force.

dissaving: a lowering of net worth, caused by spending more than one's current income.

disseisin: the forcible explusion of an owner from his or her land; the loss of property possession by claiming ownership. see *ejectment.*

dissent: the act of disagreeing. Thus, a widow's refusal to take the share provided for her in her husband's will and assertion of her rights under the law is known as her dissent from the will. see *dower.* [32]

dissolution (corporate): termination at the expiration of a corporation's charter, by order of the attorney general of the state, by consolidation, or by action of the stockholders.

dissolution (partnership): termination by the wishes of the partners at a specified time, or by operation of law because of incapacity, death, or bankruptcy of any partner.

Dist.

(1) see *discount.*

(2) see *exchange distribution.*

distant delivery: delivery during one of the more distant months and at least two months away.

distrain: to seize another's property as security for an obligation.

distress for rent: the taking of a tenant's personal property in payment of rent on real estate. see *general lien, landlord's warrant.*

distress selling: selling because of necessity; what happens when securities owned on margin are sold because lowered prices have hurt equities.

distributable net income (DNI): all income generated by a trust, less all deductible expenses paid by a trust, whether charged against principal or income. [105]

distributes: a person to whom something is distributed; frequently applied to the recipient of personal property under intestacy; to be distinguished from "heir"—a person who inherits real property. [32]

distributing syndicate: investment bankers, brokerage houses, and so on, who form a joint venture to sell an issue of securities. see *distribution.*

distribution

(1) *general:* the dividing up of something among several people or entities; the process of allocating income and expenses to the appropriate subsidiary accounts.

(2) *finance:* the division of aggregate income of a community among its members.

(3) *investments:* the selling, over a time period, of a large block of stock without unduly depressing the market price. cf. *secondary distribution.*

(4) *law:* the apportionment by a court of the personal property of a deceased person among those entitled to receive the property according to the applicable statute of distribution.

distribution cost analysis: when marketing an item in a particular location, the breaking down of all direct and indirect costs.

distribution in kind: the distribution of the assets of an estate in their original form and not the cash value of the property. Stocks and bonds are generally distributed among those entitled to receive them instead of being converted into cash for the purpose of effecting distribution. [37]

distribution of certificate account maturities: legislation of 1978; Federal Home Loan Bank System members may not accept certificate deposits that would cause the aggregate amount of certificates maturing in any consecutive three-month period to exceed 30 percent of an association's savings ($100,000 certificates excepted). [51]

distribution of risk: the spreading of investments over a number of stocks.

distribution shipment: a truckload of small goods that are transported at a truckload rate to a specified destination.

distributive share: the share of a person in the distribution of an estate. [37]

distributor: synonymous with *wholesaler.*

Div.: see *dividend.*

Divd.: see *dividend.*

divergence indicator: an indicator purporting to measure which member currency of the European Monetary System diverges from its central parity against the European Currency Unit. [96]

diversification

(1) spreading investments among different companies in different fields. Another type of diversification is offered by the securities of many individual companies whose activities cover a wide range.

(2) the purchase of varying assets in order to minimize the risk associated with a portfolio.

diversified holding company: a corporation that controls several unrelated companies. Holding companies do not participate in management of operations of their subsidiaries. [105]

diversified investment company: an investment company that practices diversification. The Investment Company Act of 1940 requires such a company to have at least 75 percent of its assets represented by cash, government securities, securities of other investment companies, and other securities limited in respect of any one issuer to an amount not greater than 5 percent of the value of the total assets of such investment company and not more than 10 percent of the outstanding voting securities of such an issuer. [23]

diversion privilege: the privilege of shipping in carload lots to a diversion point where inspection, grading, and reshipping may be done. The through rate plus a small charge is applicable.

diversity factor: in public utilities, the ratio of the noncoincident maximum demands for service of all customers in a group to the maximum demand of that group.

divest: to remove a vested right.

divestiture: the process of disposing of all or part of a business. see *spinoff.*

dividend: a portion of the net profits that has been officially declared by the board of directors for distribution to stockholders. A dividend is paid at a fixed amount for each share of stock held by the stockholder. cf. *Irish dividend.*

dividend appropriations: amount declared payable out of retained income (earned surplus) as dividends on actually outstanding preferred or common stock, or the amount credited to a reserve for such dividends. [3]

dividend check: a negotiable instrument in the form of a check drawn on a depository bank of the corporation issuing the dividend. It is signed by the secretary of the corporation.

dividend claim: a request made by the purchaser of stock upon the registered holder for the amount of a dividend where the transaction took place prior to the ex-dividend date, but the transfer could not be effected prior to the record date. [37]

dividend forecast chart: a chart prepared by a brokerage firm, indicating dividend yields for corporations that it considers for its customers.

dividend on: the sale of a stock with an understanding that the purchaser will receive the next dividend.

dividend order: a form which, when properly filled out, instructs a corporation to forward dividend checks to a specified address. [37]

dividend payer: a security or firm paying dividends, as contrasted with those firms and their securities which, because of poor performance or the process of plowing back their earnings, do not pay dividends.

dividend-paying agent: the agent of a corporation charged with the duty of paying dividends on the stock of the corporation out of funds supplied by the corporation. [37]

dividend payout: the fraction of earnings paid out as common dividends.

dividend payout ratio: the ratio of dividends per share of common stock to earnings per share of common stock.

dividend-price ratio: the ratio of the current dividend rate to the market price of a stock.

dividend rate: the indicated annual rate of payment to a shareholder based on a company's latest quarterly dividend and recurring extra or special year-end dividends.

dividend reinvestment plans: a service in which the bank, as agent, automatically reinvests the customer's dividends in a security. [25]

dividend requirements: the amount of annual earnings required to pay preferred dividends in full. [30]

dividends per share: the dollar amount of dividends paid to stockholders for each share owned of a corporation's common stock.

dividend warrant: any order to release a corporation's dividend to its rightful shareholder.

dividend yield: a stock's dividend per share divided by its market price per share.

divisional bond: see *bond, divisional.*

division of labor
(1) *general:* breaking a job down into the smallest number of operations without jeopardizing performance.
(2) *banking:* breaking a bank's job down into the smallest number of operations without jeopardizing performance.

Dix: slang, a $10 bill.

D&J: December and June (semiannual interest payments or dividends).

DJA: see *Dow Jones averages.*

dk: see *don't know.*

DL: see *demand loan.*

DLF: see *Development Loan Fund.*

Dlr: see *dealer.*

DM: see *deutsche mark.*

DMJS: December, March, June, September (quarterly interest payments or dividends).

DNI: see *distributable net income.*

DNR: see *do not reduce.*

DO: see *day order.*

DOA: see *Department of Agriculture, U.S.*

dobra: monetary unit of San Tóme and Principe.

DOC: see *Department of Commerce, U.S.*

dock: slang, penalizing an employee part of his or her pay for lateness, absence, or related matters.

doctrine of asset shiftability: banks need not seek supplementary liquidity in its loan portfolio, as this liquidity is available through the shifting of nonloan assets (secondary reserves) to the open market. [105]

document
(1) a form, voucher, or written evidence of a transaction.
(2) to instruct, as by citation of references.
(3) to substantiate, as by listing of authorities. [105]

documentary bill: see *documentary draft.*

documentary commercial bills: bills of exchange resulting from commercial transactions that are backed by bills of lading and other related instruments.

documentary credit: when a bank, in behalf of its customer makes payment to (or to the order of) a third party (a beneficiary) or is to pay/accept/negotiate bills of exchange drawn by the beneficiary; or authorizes such payments to be made, or such drafts to be paid/accepted/negotiated by another bank.

documentary draft: a draft accompanied by a shipping document, bill of lading, insurance certificate, and so on, these documents having intrinsic value. Instructions for disposition of the document usually accompany the draft. [31]

documentary stamp: a revenue stamp issued for the payment of a tax on documents, as deeds, checks, or wills. [62]

document of title: a piece of paper signed by the seller or carrier showing that the person named (buyer) has the right of ownership to the thing described in the document (e.g., a deed to land).

documents

(1) *general:* anything printed or written that is relied on to record or prove something.

(2) *computers:* written evidence of transactions showing a representation of stored information (e.g., printed paper, punch cards).

documents against acceptance: referring to domestic or foreign bills of exchange, notice that supporting statements will not be given to the drawee until acceptance of the bill.

documents against payment: referring to domestic or foreign bills of exchange, notice that supporting statements will not be given to the drawee until payment of the bill.

DOE: see *Department of Energy, U.S.*

DOG: see *days of grace.*

dog: slang, a promissory note.

DOJ: see *Department of Justice, U.S.*

Dol.: see *dollar.*

DOL: see *Department of Labor, U.S.*

dollar

(1) *general:* monetary unit of the United States. Also the currency for Guam, the Marshall Islands, Puerto Rico, the Ryukyu Islands, Solomon Islands, and the Virgin Islands (U.S.).

(2) *finance:* monetary unit of other nations, including Antigua, Australia,

Bahamas, Barbados, British Honduras, Brunei, Canada, Dominica, Ethiopia, Grenada, Guiana, Guyana, Hong Kong, Jamaica, Kiribati, Liberia, Montserrat, Nauru, Nevis, New Guinea, New Zealand, Singapore, Somoa (British), St. Kitts, St. Lucia, St. Vincent, Taiwan, Trinidad and Tobago, Tuvalu, and Zimbabwe.

dollar acceptance: an acceptance or any bill of exchange drawn in a foreign nation or in the United States that is payable in dollars.

dollar bill of exchange: see *dollar (cost) averaging.*

dollar bond: see *bond, dollar.*

dollar control: guiding inventory by the amount of funds rather than by the number of physical items.

dollar (cost) averaging: a system of buying securities at regular intervals with a fixed dollar amount. The investor buys by the dollars' worth rather than by the number of shares. If each investment is of the same number of dollars, payments buy more shares when the price is low and fewer when it rises.

dollar credit: a letter of credit permitting drafts to be drawn in dollars.

dollar deficit: see *dollar drain (gap).*

dollar diplomacy: the United States' attempt to influence another nation via the power of the American dollar.

dollar drain (gap): the amount by which imports from the United States into a foreign country exceed the nation's exports to the United States.

dollar exchange: banker's acceptances and bills of exchange drawn overseas that are paid in the United States or around the world in dollars, or conversely drawn in the United States and paid overseas in dollars.

dollar-month computation: a method

of computing earnings on savings accounts based on the premise that every dollar held in a savings account for one full year will earn the number of cents equivalent to the earnings rate. [59].

dollar premium: used in Great Britain for the added premium or cost that investors are required to pay to purchase dollars for investment outside the country.

dollar shortage: a nation's lack of sufficient money to buy from the United States, caused by a steady favorable balance of payments for the United States.

dollar stabilization

(1) acts by monetary authorities (i.e., the Federal Reserve Board, International Monetary Fund) to reduce the fluctuation of the international exchange value of the dollar.

(2) an idea of economist Irving Fischer that would result in a compensated dollar tied to commodities rather than gold.

dollar stocks: an English term describing American stocks.

domestic acceptance: any acceptance where the drawee and drawer are situated in the United States and consequently paid in this country.

domestic bill: any of several documents (i.e., sight or time drafts) drawn and payable within the same state.

domestic bill of exchange: synonymous with *inland bill of exchange.*

domestic corporation: a corporation carrying out business in the same state where it was established or incorporated.

domestic exchange: any check, draft, or acceptance drawn in one location and paid in another within the United States. synonymous with *inland exchange;* cf. *foreign exchange.*

Domestic International Sales Corporation (DISC): federal legislation of 1971 to help exporters meet foreign competition. Abolished January 1, 1985. see *Foreign Sales Corporations.*

domicile: a dwelling; a place of permanent residence. cf. *legal residence.*

domicile of corporation: the corporation's location for legal purposes; its legal residence.

domiciliary administration: the settlement of the portion of a decedent's estate which is located in the state of his domicile; to be distinguished from "ancillary administration," which relates to property elsewhere than in the state of the decedent's domicile. [37]

domiciliary trustee: the trustee of that portion of a decedent's or settlor's property which is located in the state of his domicile; to be distinguished from "ancillary trustee," who administers property elsewhere than in the state of the decedent's or settlor's domicile. [37]

dominion: in transferring property from one to another, the separation by the transferor from all power over the property and passing such power to the transferee.

donated stock: to raise working capital, a corporation may receive back from a shareholder any or all of the paid issues. Often done when the stock is offered as a payment for services rendered. Donated stock is nonassessable.

donated surplus: surplus arising from contributions without consideration, by stockholders and others, of cash, property, or the company's own capital stock. Donated surplus is a form of paid-in surplus. [43]

donative interest: an interest in property that is subject to gift. [37]

donee: one who receives a gift.

dong: monetary unit of Viet Nam.

donor: one who makes a gift.

donor (trust): a living person who creates a "voluntary trust." [10]

do not reduce: found in a securities limit order to buy or sell, the price given in the order is not to be lowered by the amount of cash dividend on the ex-dividend date. Does not apply to stock dividends or rights.

don't know (dk): an attempted confirmation or comparison of a stock transaction by one firm, with another firm denying knowledge of its existence. The comparison is marked "don't know" and returned. The member firm must inform the executing broker of this fact, and the floor broker is to investigate the situation immediately.

doomage power: the power of the government to base a tax assessment on any available data where the taxpayer fails or refuses to furnish a return.

dormant account: an account that has had little or no activity for a period of time.

dormant partner: a partner not known to the public at large who is entitled to participate in the profits and subject to the losses.

DOT

(1) see *date of trade.*
(2) see *Department of the Treasury, U.S.*
(3) see *Department of Transportation, U.S.*

double: an option either to purchase or sell a security or commodity at a special price.

double auction market: on the stock market, the process of constant varying of prices by those bidding (buyers) and asking (sellers) in order to make a market. A sales occurs when the highest bidder meets the price of the lowest asker.

double barreled: applied to tax-exempt bonds which are backed by a pledge of two or more sources of payment. For example, many special-assessment or special-tax bonds are additionally backed by the full faith, credit, and taxing power of the issuer.

double bottom: that portion of a charted time series showing two lows.

double bottom (top): the price action of a security or market average where it has declined two times to the same approximate level, indicating the existence of a support level and a possibility that the downward trend has ended.

double budget: segregating capital expenditures from recurring expense items so that an annual income statement will not be distorted during those years of heavy capital investment.

double charge: a single purchase in which the cardholder was charged twice. [105]

double counting (entry): in bookkeeping, since every transaction is entered two times, counting the same quantity twice when evolving a total; procedure used in determining the gross national product.

double-declining-balance method of depreciation: spreading the initial cost of a capital asset over time by deducting in each period double the percentage recognized by the straight-line method and applying that double percentage to the undepreciated balance existing at the start of each period. No salvage value is used in the calculation.

double eagle: a U.S. $20 gold piece.

double endorsement: a negotiable instrument or other document containing two endorsements, indicating that recourse can be made to the two companies or persons that endorsed the instrument.

double entry: the method of recording transactions that requires that any increase in one account reflect an increase or decrease in another account. The total debits of each entry must equal the total credits. see *journalize.*

double exemption: a municipal term applied to bonds that are exempt from both state and federal income taxation. [105]

double financing: fraudulent action on the part of a dealer who submits a credit application and receives a loan for the same customer from two different banks. [105]

double indemnity: a provision in a life policy, subject to specified conditions and exclusions, whereby double the face amount of the policy is payable if the death of the insured is the result of an accident.

double insurance: purchased to insure against the same risk twice. Usually, it is impossible to obtain more than the loss suffered. If a risk is insured against twice, one firm will claim contribution from the other. see *excess coverage clause, noncurrency.*

double liability: the liability of the stockholders of banks before banking legislation of the 1930s brought about the elimination of this feature for all national banks and most state banks.

Under the double liability provision, the stockholders of a bank, in the event of its liquidation, were held legally responsible for an amount equal to the par value of their stock in addition to the amount of their original investment. [39]

double option: synonymous with *spread* and *straddle.*

double posting: the posting of a debit amount or a credit amount to two accounts.

double sawbuck: a $20 bill.

double standard: see *bimetallism.*

double taxation: short for "double taxation of dividends." The federal government taxes corporate profits once as corporate income; the remaining profits distributed as dividends to stockholders are taxed again as income to the recipient stockholders. [20]

doubtful assets: assets that rarely bring full value upon liquidation.

doubtful loan: see *nonaccrual asset.*

dough: slang, money or cash.

Douglas amendment: amendment to the Bank Holding Company Act of 1956 that prohibits bank holding companies from acquiring out-of-state banks unless laws of the host state specifically permit such entry. see *Bank Holding Company Act of 1956.*

dower: a right for life by a married woman in a portion of the land owned by her husband, which becomes vested upon his death. In some states, a wife owns one-third of her deceased husband's real estate. see *tenant in dower;* cf. *curtesy.*

Dow Jones averages: the averages of closing prices of 30 representative industrial stocks, 15 public utility stocks, 20 transportation stocks, and an average of the 65 computed at the end of a trading day on the New York Stock Exchange. cf. *NYSE Common Stock Index, Standard & Poor's 500 Stock Average.*

down and out: slang, penniless.

down gap: an open space formed on a security chart when the lowest price of any market day is above the highest price of the next day.

down payment

(1) *banking:* money deposited as evidence of good faith for purchasing property upon contract signing.

(2) *finance:* a partial payment, made at the time of purchase, to permit the buyer to take the merchandise.

downside momentum: see *momentum.*

downside risk: the probability that the price of an investment will fall. [105]

downstairs merger: a merger of a parent corporation into a subsidiary.

downstream: describing movement of a business activity from a higher to a lower level (e.g., a loan from a parent company to one of its subsidiaries).

downstream borrowing: the borrowing of money by a corporation through the use of the credit standing of its subsidiaries.

down tick: a securities transaction at a price that is lower than the last different price. synonymous with *minus tick.* see *up tick.*

downturn: following a growth period, the downward movement of a business cycle or activity.

Dow theory: a theory of market analysis based on the performance of the Dow Jones industrial and transportation stock price averages. The market is said to be in a basic upward trend if one of these averages advances above a previous important high, accompanied or followed by a similar advance in the other. When both averages dip below previous important lows, this is regarded as confirmation of a basic downward trend. The theory does not attempt to predict how long either trend will continue, although it is widely misinterpreted as a method of forecasting future action. see *Dow Jones averages.* [20]

D/P: see *documents against payment.*

DPS: see *dividends per share.*

DR

(1) see *daily reports.*

(2) see *discount rate.*

drachma: monetary unit of Greece.

draft: an order in writing signed by one party (the drawer) requesting a second party (the drawee) to make payment in lawful money at a determinable future time to a third party (the payee).

draft envelope: a wrapper used by merchants to transmit sales drafts and credit slips to the bank for credit to their deposit accounts. [105]

draft number: the sequential number printed on formsets. [105]

drawback: any refund of taxes or duties already paid on account of imported items that have been reexported. A primary purpose of the drawback is to provide a type of government subsidy enabling the domestic manufacturer to compete more effectively with an overseas competitor.

draw-down: drawing funds made available under a Eurocredit.

draw-down request: an instruction to reduce the balance of the sender's account with the receiver by a payment to the sender's account at another financial institution. [105]

drawee: any party expected to pay the sum listed on a check, draft, or bill of exchange.

drawee bank: the bank upon which a check is drawn. [7]

drawer: any party who draws a check, draft, or bill of exchange for the payment of funds.

drawing account: money available to owners or salespeople to be used for expenses which will be deducted from future earnings. [61]

drawn bond: see *bond, drawn.*

drawn securities: any securities called for redemption.

drayage: charges made for moving freight on carts or vehicles in a terminal location or city.

Drayton Company Ltd.: founded in 1971 to reinsure programs underwritten by U.S. insurance companies, it is geared to the special insurance needs of the savings bank industry and is wholly owned by savings banks and The Central Industry Fund, Inc. The company's primary aim is to assure that savings banks will continue to enjoy the benefit of a stable and equitable insurance market. see *Central Industry Fund, Inc.* [8]

dried up: to come to a halt; the disappearance of either buying or selling order on the stock market.

drive
(1) a concerted upward or downward movement in the price of a security.
(2) the attempt to manipulate the price of securities or commodities by sellers to force prices downward. If proven, such action is illegal.

drive-in banking: because of traffic congestion and lack of parking space, many banks now have tellers' windows facing the outside of the building, or separate outside booths, for the convenience of depositors. The bank customer drives up to a teller's window.

DRM: see *direct reduction mortgage.*

drop: slang, a decline in the price of a stock or commodity.

drop shipper: a middleman who secures orders from buyers and sends the orders to manufacturers or other suppliers who ship directly to the buyers, and is usually responsible for collection of the purchase price.

dry run
(1) another name used by banks for the machine pay plan of journalizing the posting media before posting to the statement. see also *machine pay.* [10]
(2) also used to mean a *test period.*

dry trust: see *passive trust.*

D/S: days after sight; referring to the tenor of a bill of exchange.

DS: see *debenture stock.*

DT: see *Dow theory.*

DTC
(1) see *Depository Trust Company.*
(2) see *deposit-taking company.*

dual banking: some banks are chartered by the state in which they operate and others by the federal government. This allows for dual banking, where each independent component cooperates with the other to offer its clientele complete banking services.

dual billing and posting: posting a customer's purchases to ledger, as independent from the preparation of a bill for the customer.

dual control: a method of maintaining security whereby two individuals must be present during transactions involving risk. Dual control can be accomplished through the use of two keys or two combinations for entry into secured areas. [105]

dual currency account: an account kept by a bank with a bank in a foreign country in the foreign currency. [105]

dual dating: a practice of embossing two dates on the face of credit cards, the first date being the effective date and the second being the expiration date. [105]

dual exchange market: exists when the authorities operate two exchange markets, prescribing the use of one market for exchange transactions relating to specified types of underlying transactions and the use of the other permitted dealing in foreign exchange.

duality: effective in 1977, the ability of a single bank to be a card-issuing member of more than one credit card.

dual listing: securities listed on more than one stock exchange.

dual mutual funds: funds that divide their portfolios between capital growth investments and income investments.

dual plan: see *single-posting system.*

dual posting: see *double counting (entry).*

dual-purpose fund: see *split investment company.*

dual savings plan: a plan whereby two separate operations are required to post a savings deposit or a withdrawal to an account.

dual system of banking: banks may choose to operate under either a federal or state charter. Regulations and requirements vary, depending on whether a bank is regulated by a state or the federal government. Regulations also vary among states. [33]

Du. Dat.: see *due date.*

due (annuity): annuity payments to commence immediately. [12]

due bill: the acknowledgment of a debt that a debtor will render a service or merchandise.

due-bill-check: a due bill in the form of a check payable on the date of payment of a cash dividend, which prior to such date is considered a due bill for the amount of the dividend.

due care: the standard of conduct displayed by an ordinary, reasonable, prudent individual. see also *prudent man rule.*

due date: the date on which an instrument of debt becomes payable; the maturity date.

due diligence session: bringing together a firm's officials whose securities are to be issued with an underwriting syndicate in compliance with the Securities Act, to be questioned pertaining to a prospectus, registration of the security, and other relevant financial matters.

due from: specifies an obligation owed to you. [105]

due from account: title given to bank asset accounts that represents its funds on deposit with a corresponding bank. [105]

due from balance: British term for *nostro account.*

due from banks: title of an asset account in the general ledger. Subsidiary accounts under this title include each account of funds that a bank has on deposit with other banks. Legal reserve funds and funds placed on deposit with correspondent banks are among these accounts. [31]

due from banks, collections: any contingent asset account within the bank's financial ledger showing the aggregate balances that are due from other banks.

due from Federal Reserve Bank: any

asset account listed in a financial ledger of a member or clearing member bank showing the balance due from a Federal Reserve Bank. The figure shows the approximate cash reserve, as required by law, that is held with the Federal Reserve Bank.

due from Foreign Exchange Department: an asset account in the bank's financial statement showing the total funds within a foreign department for purposes of investment in foreign exchange activities.

due-on-sale: a clause in a conventional home mortgage stating that the balance of the existing mortgage must be paid to the lending bank when the home is sold by the owner.

due process of law: all actions of a court taken to ensure the rights of private individuals before the law; all legal steps to protect these rights. A court order to compel compliance with its wishes (e.g., a summons, issued to compel attendance in court).

due to: specifies an obligation owed by you. [105]

due to balance: British term for *vostro account*.

due to banks: the title of a liability account in the general ledger. Includes subsidiary accounts of funds that one bank has on deposit with another bank. [31]

due to fiscal agent: amounts due to fiscal agents, such as commercial banks, for servicing a unit's maturing interest and principal payments on indebtedness. [49]

dull: an inactive trading period; when prices of stocks move very little.

dummy: a person, such as a director elected to a board, who acts only for another person. The dummy has no

material ownership in the firm and allows the individual who has sponsored his or her election to control his or her vote on the issues before the directors.

dummy directors: synonymous with *dummy incorporators*.

dummy incorporators: usually, a minimum of three people who, when creating a new corporation, act temporarily as the incorporators and directors, then resign and transfer their interest to the true owners. synonymous with *dummy directors*.

dummy stockholder: one who holds in his or her name stock that belongs to another party, whose identity is thus concealed.

dump

(1) *computers:* to copy the contents of all or part of a storage, usually from an internal storage into an external storage. see also *memory, post-mortem;* cf. *search.*

(2) *investments:* to offer large blocks of stock for purposes of disposal, with little concern for price or the effect on the market. see *profit taking.*

dumped: see *trigger-price system.*

dumping

(1) *finance:* selling items to other countries below cost for purposes of eliminating surplus or to hurt foreign competition.

(2) *finance:* in the United States, selling imported items at prices less than the cost of manufacture. see *boomerang;* cf. *Antidumping Act of 1974.*

dun: to press for payment of a debt; to demand repeatedly what one is owed.

Dun and Bradstreet (D&B): the oldest and largest mercantile agency in the United States, offering credit data and ratings on business concerns.

Dun's Market Identifiers: a published system identifying firms with an absolute identification number and providing regular updated economic information on each company (e.g., address code, number of workers, and corporate affiliation).

duopoly: an industry containing two businesses selling the identical items. In a duopoly, both firms exercise control.

duopsony: exists when only two buyers are seeking a similar item. cf. *monopsony, oligopsony.*

duplicate bills: any bills in a set.

duplicate deposit ticket: a copy, usually in carbon, of an original deposit ticket. [10]

duplicate documents: documents in a set.

durability
(1) *general:* the lasting quality of an item.
(2) *finance:* money that can be used over an extended period or can be replaced at minimal cost.

durable merchandise: goods that have a relatively lengthy life (television sets, radio, etc.)

duress (personal): a threat of bodily harm, criminal prosecution, or imprisonment. An individual under duress at the time of entering into or discharging a legal obligation is unable to exercise freely his or her will with respect to the transaction. see *extortion.*

duress (property): forced seizure, or withholding of goods by an individual who is not entitled to possess them, and the demands made by such a person as a condition for the release of the goods.

dutch auction: an auction sale where the price on items is continuously lowered until a bidder responds favorably and buys.

duties: see *duty.*

duty
(1) *general:* an actual tax collected.
(2) *finance:* a tax imposed on the importation, exportation, or consumption of goods.
(3) *law:* a legal requirement established by law or voluntarily imposed by the creation of a binding promise. A legal right accompanies every legal duty.

duty card: synonymous with *tickler.*

duty drawback: a tariff concession allowing a rebate of all or part of the duty on goods imported for processing before being reexported.

duty free: describing items that are not affected by any customs duty. see *fee list.*

DWT: see *deadweight tonnage.*

dynamics: the consideration of the effect of the time dimension on economic situations.

dynamiter: a securities broker who attempts to sell fraudulent or unregistered stocks and bonds over the telephone. cf. *boiler room tactic.*

EA: see *Edge Act.*

each way: trading on both the buying and selling sides of a transaction; the broker earns a commission of 3 percent each way (i.e., 3 percent for selling and another 3 percent for executing the purchase order).

eagle: a U.S. $10 gold coin, first coined in 1795. The Treasury demanded the surrender of all gold coins in 1933.

EAM: see *electrical accounting machine.*

early vesting: see *vesting.*

earmarked: goods held aside for later use or development.

earmarked gold: a treasury or stabilization fund; quantities of gold found in the fiduciary reserves of one nation's central bank for another nation's central bank.

earned income: income derived from goods and services rendered as well as pension and annuity income. see *Tax Reform Act of 1976;* cf. *unearned income.*

earned premium: that part of an insurance premium which pays for the pro-tection the insurance company has already given on a policy. [56]

earned surplus: a firm's net profits available after the payment of dividends to shareholders.

earnest money: money given by a contracting party to another at the time of the signing of a contract to "bind the bargain"; this sum is forfeited by the doner if he or she fails to carry out the contract.

earning assets: loans and investments that together are the assets responsible for most of the bank's earnings. [67]

earning-capacity standard: synonymous with *capitalized-value standard.*

earning power: an employee's potential capacity on his or her job to earn wages over a period of time—usually the normal span of years during which the worker is productive.

earnings: the total remuneration received by a worker for a given period as compensation for services rendered, for work performed, as a commission, as overtime, and so on. cf.

payroll deductions, wage. synonymous with net income.

earnings assets: the loans and investments that, together, represent the source of most bank revenue. [105]

earnings credit: an offset to service charges on checking accounts, calculated on the basis of the average balance held in the account during the specified period. [105]

earnings per share: the portion of a corporation's net income that relates to each share of a corporation's common stock that has been issued and is outstanding.

earnings price (EP) ratio: earnings per share of common stock outstanding divided by the closing stock market price (or the midpoint between the closing bid and asked price if there are no sales) on a day as close as possible after the publication of the earnings. [3]

earnings report: a statement issued by a company showing its earnings or losses over a given period. The earnings report lists the income earned, the expenses, and the net result.

earnings statement: an analysis or presentation of the earnings of an enterprise in statement form. An income statement form is an earnings statement. [105]

easement right: see *access right.*

ease off: a slow decline in prices. [2]

easy money: money that can be obtained at low interest rates and with relative ease as the result of sufficient supply of a bank's excess reserves.

EBIT: earnings before interest and taxes.

EC: see *ex-coupon.*

ECOA: see *Equal Credit Opportunity Act.*

econometric model: a set of related equations used to analyze economic data through mathematical and statistical techniques. Such models are devised in order to depict the essential quantitative impact of alternative assumptions or government policies, and for testing various propositions about the way the economy works. [73]

economic: describes any action having to do with the evolution of goods and services that are purported to satisfy a human condition.

economic costs: payments to the owners of the requirements for manufacturing to convince them to supply their resources in a specified activity.

economic efficiency: synonymous with *Pareto optimality.*

economic growth rate: the percentage rate at which total annual output grows; an increase in real per capital income.

economic indicators: a classification of economic information, to be used in business cycle analysis and forecasting.

economic order quantity (EOQ): the optimum amount of inventory that will minimize total inventory costs.

economic profit: the residual profit after explicit and implicit costs have been paid. synonymous with *pure profit.*

Economic Recovery Tax Act of 1981 (ERTA): federal legislation, signed by President Reagan in August, 1981; includes the following provisions.

Tax rate cuts: (1981) credit of $1\frac{1}{4}$ percent against individual tax bills and 5 percent withholding rate reduction on October 1; (July 1982) tax rate reduction of 10 percent, followed by another in July 1983. By 1984, the top rate on $50,000 in earned income dropped from 49 percent to 38 percent; (1985)

cost-of-living wage and salary increased offset by widening tax brackets, raising "zero bracket" at low end, boosting personal exemptions.

Unearned income and capital gains: (June 9, 1981) the maximum tax on capital gains realized a drop from 28 percent (gain after 60 percent exclusion taxed at 70 percent) to 20 percent (gain after 60 percent exclusion taxed at 50 percent). Minimum holding period for long-term capital gain remains 12 months. (1982) Top rate on dividends, interest, rents, and royalties dropped from 70 to 50 percent, equal to maximum tax on salary income.

Marriage tax offset: (1982) if both spouses work, a 5 percent deduction from the salary of the lower-paid partner, up to $1500; (1983) a 10 percent deduction, up to $3000.

Pension deductions: (1982) tax deductions for contributions to Individual Retirement Accounts raised to $2000 and the 15 percent limitation canceled. The IRA provision is extended to employees already covered by pensions. Voluntary thrift plans as well as separate IRA accounts qualify.

Interest deductions: (1981–1982) exempt interest income up to $1000 ($2000 joint return) on special "All-Savers" savings certificates was offered for one year only. A deduction of $750 ($1500 joint return) of public utility stock dividends was allowed if paid into a reinvestment plan; (1985) exclusion of 15 percent of savings interest, less interest paid on consumer (but not on mortgage) loans.

Estate and gift tax reductions: (1982–1986) progressive exclusion from taxation of the first $250,000 of estate up to the first $600,000 of es-

tate; (1982) unlimited deduction for estate and gift transfers to a spouse; (1982) annual gifts excluded from taxation raised from $3000 to $10,000.

Stock option treatment: (1981) no tax at exercise on $100,000 per year in stock. Capital gains treatment on gain over option price at sale.

Depreciation and investment tax credits: (1981) accelerated depreciation rules and expanded tax credits for certain classes of real estate investment should shelter more income for investors. see also *All-Savers certificates, Individual Retirements Accounts, Keogh plan, Tax Reform Act of 1984.*

economic rent: the estimated income a propety should bring in the existing rental market. The economic rent can be either above or below the amount actually received. cf. *rack rent.*

economics

(1) *general:* the branch of the social sciences concerned with the production, distribution, and consumption of goods and services.

(2) *general:* a description of events dealing with consumption, distribution, exchange, and production of goods and services. see also *labor economics.*

economic sanction: a form of economic pressure (e.g., boycott, embargo) used to compel another country or group of countries to comply with international agreement.

economic value: the value given to an item as a function of its usefulness and its scarcity.

economies of scale: the result of production functions showing an equal percentage increase in all inputs leads output to increase by a large percentage. see *natural monopoly.*

ECR
(1) see *electronic cash register.*
(2) see *embossed character reader.*

ECU: the *European currency unit.*

ED: see *extra dividend.*

Edge Act: recreated a dual banking system for foreign banks by establishing a new class of Federal charters for them. It also gives the Federal Reserve Board the right to impose reserve requirements on foreign banks. The 1978 International Banking Act restated the broad purpose of the Edge Act statute, in which Congress requires the Fed to revise any of its regulations that unnecessarily disadvantage American banks in the conduct of business. The act also allowed U.S. banks to open offices across state lines to assist in foreign trade financing. see *International Banking Act of 1978.*

edge corporation: a foreign banking organization structured in compliance with the Federal Reserve Act.

EDP: see *electronic data processing.* see also *ADP.*

EDR: see *European Depository Receipt.*

educational tariff: tariff duties that protect a new home industry until that industry is capable of competing effectively with imported goods.

education loan: an advance of funds, insured under a program of the U.S. Department of Education, made to a student for the financing of his or her college or vocational training.

EE: see *equity earnings.*

EEC: see *European Economic Community.*

EEOC: Equal Employment Opportunity

Commission. see *Civil Rights Act of 1964, Title VII.*

effective: a declaration by the SEC of final authorization to begin distribution of a new issue of stock or bonds.

effective annual yield: the return on an investment, expressed in terms of the equivalent simple interest rate. [105]

effective date
(1) ***banking:*** the date on which an insurance binder or policy goes into effect and from which time protection is provided.
(2) ***law:*** the date on which an agreement or contract goes into effect; the starting date.

effective debt: the total debt of a firm, including the major value of annual leases or other payments that are equivalent to interest charges.

effective demand
(1) the actual purchases being made, as distinguished from those that could be made by persons with the ability to buy but no such desire or with desire but no funds.
(2) the quantity demanded at the normal price.

effective exchange rate: any spot exchange rate actually paid or received by the public, including any taxes or subsidies on the exchange transaction as well as any applicable banking commissions. The articles of agreement envisage that all effective exchange rates shall be situated within permitted margins around par value. [42]

effective gross revenue: total income less allowance for vacancies, contingencies, and sometimes collection losses, but before deductions for operating expenses. [62]

effective interest rate (or yield): the

rate or earning on a bond investment based on the actual price paid for the bond, the coupon rate, the maturity date, and the length of time between interest dates; in contrast to *nominal interest rate*. [49]

effective par: with preferred stocks, the par value that would ordinarily correspond to a given dividend rate.

effective yield: the rate of return realized by an investor who purchases a security and then sells it.

efficient market hypothesis: stock market theory that says competition for stock market profits is so keen that observed stocks prices are good estimates of the "true" value of the stocks.

EFT: Electronic Funds Transfer.

EFTA: see *European Free Trade Association*.

EFTS: see *electronic funds transfer system*.

EI
(1) see *earned income*.
(2) see *exact interest*.
(3) see *ex-interest*.

EIB: see *Export-Import Bank*.

eighth stocks: stocks on which the odd-lot differential, when added to a purchase order or subtracted from a sell order, of one-eighth of a point is applied to the following round-lot sale. Eighth stocks sell below 60, while quarter stocks sell above 60.

ejectment: the legal action brought to retain possession of property and to receive damage monies from the person who illegally retained it. see *right of possession, seisin;* cf. *landlord's warrant*.

ekuwele: monetary unit of Equatorial Guinea.

EL: see *even lots*.

elastic currency: see *elasticity*.

elastic demand: demand that changes in relatively large volume as prices increase or decrease. When a small change in price results in a greater change in the quantity people buy, the demand for the item is said to be elastic. The demand for jewelry, furs, and second homes is considered to be elastic. see *cross-elasticity*.

elasticity
(1) *general:* the impact on the demand for an item created by changes in price, production, or other factors affecting demand. see *coefficient of cross-elasticity*.
(2) *banking:* the ability of a bank to meet credit and currency demands during times of expansion and to reduce the availability of credit and currency during periods of over expansion. see *Federal Reserve Notes*.

elasticity of demand: see *elastic demand*.

elasticity of expectations: the ratio of the relative rise in expected future prices of commodity X to the relative rise in price in the preceding period (sometimes compared with a preceding price, not its rise).

elasticity of substitution: the rate at which one factor of production will be substituted for another in response to a change in their relative prices. Similarly as to the consumer, the rate at which one commodity will be substituted for another in response to a change in their relative prices.

elastic money: currency or money supply that increases or decreases with the economy's needs. Elasticity is affected by decisions of monetary authorities or by making currency related to bank loans by the rediscount device.

elastic supply: supply that changes in

relatively large volume with a minor change in price.

election: the choice of an alternative right or course. Thus the right of a widow to take the share of her deceased husband's estate to which she is entitled under the law, despite a contrary provision in the will, is known as the widow's election. [32]

electrical accounting machine (EAM): conventional punch-card equipment, including sorters, tabulators, and collectors.

electronic banking: banking transactions conducted via computerized systems, effecting efficiency and lower costs.

electronic cash register (ECR): a cash register in which electronic circuitry replaces electromechanical parts.

electronic data processing (EDP): data processing largely performed by electronic devices.

electronic funds transfer (EFT): see *electronic funds transfer system(s) (EFTS).*

Electronic Fund Transfer Act: passed by Congress in 1978, but the effective date of most of its provisions was delayed until May 10, 1980, to allow time for the federal bank regulatory agencies to develop a comprehensive set of implementing regulations. Essentially a consumer protection measure, the art requires financial institutions to disclose to new customers the terms and conditions of EFT services, including the consumer's liability for unauthorized transfers; and to describe the type and availability of EFT services offered, and the service charges. The law covers the consumer's right to receive documentation

of transfers and to have errors corrected promptly; preauthorized transfer procedures; and the institution's liability if it fails to make or stop transfers. see *Regulation E.* [14]

electronic funds transfer system(s) (EFTS): a loose description of computerized systems that process financial transactions or process information about financial transactions, or effect an exchange of value between two parties. see *Bank Wire System, Fedwire, Hinky Dinky, paperless item processing system, pre-authorized payment, prestige card, service counter terminal.*

electronic handshake: see *Intermarket Trading System.*

electronic terminal: an electronic device, other than a telephone, operated by a consumer to initiate an electronic fund transfer; includes, but is not limited to, point-of-sale terminals, automated teller machines, and cash-dispensing machines. [105]

eleemosynary: describes the classification of quasi-public corporations and organizations engaged in charitable work. cf. *not-for-profit corporation.*

eligible acceptance: see *eligible paper.*

eligible bill: see *eligible paper.*

eligible borrower: a borrower who meets the eligibility standards set by FmHA for participation in its guaranteed loan programs. [105]

eligible commercial paper: a negotiable instrument, having met certain requirements, that is eligible for rediscounting at a special rate by member banks of the Federal Reserve System.

eligible investment: any income-producing investment that is considered to be a sound repository for the funds of savings banks and similar institutions.

eligible lender: FmHA will consider guaranteeing loans made by any federal or state chartered bank, Federal Land Bank, Production Credit Association, and other lending institutions approved by FmHA. [105]

eligible paper: instruments, securities, bills, and so on, accepted by a financial institution (i.e., a Federal Reserve Bank) for the purpose of rediscounting.

eligible stock: a stock in which banks, charitable organizations, trustees, and so on, may invest funds committed to their care.

Elkins Act: federal law of 1903 supplementing the Interstate Commerce Act of 1887, prohibiting rebates and tightening penalty provision of the law.

embargo
(1) *finance:* a condition resulting in the failure to accept freight at a specified location because of some crisis at the point of destination; the prohibition of handling certain goods.
(2) *government:* an official order prohibiting the entry or departure of commercial ships at its ports, especially as a wartime measure. see *blockade, sanction.*

embezzlement: the fraudulent appropriation "to one's own use" of the money or property entrusted to an individual's care. see also *defalcation.*

emboss: a process of printing identifying data on a bank card in the form of raised impressions. [105]

embossed character reader (ECR): a device that reads embossed characters on a bank card. [105]

embossing: the mechanical raising of data from an otherwise flat surface of a bank card for subsequent automatic or manual reading. [105]

Emergency Banking Relief Act of 1933: federal legislation returning to the president World War I power relating to transactions in credit, currency, silver and gold, and foreign currencies, and the fixing of a $10,000 fine and 10 years of imprisonment for violators. Also authorized the president to fix regulations on Federal Reserve member banks.

emergency dispute: a strike or the threat of a strike that would affect the national welfare and/or safety. Under the Taft-Hartley Act, the president is authorized to determine whether a dispute imperils the nation's well-being, and if it does, to take appropriate action, which is usually to create a fact-finding board.

Emergency Home Finance Act: federal legislation of 1970; created the Federal Home Loan Mortgage Corporation, under the Federal Home Loan Bank System, to provide a secondary market for conventional loans as well as Federal Housing Administration and Veterans Administration mortgages; extended from 20 to 30 years the period allowed for associations to accumulate Federal Savings and Loan Insurance Corporation-required reserves. [51]

eminent domain: the inherent right of certain legally constituted governing bodies to take title to and possession of real property, for the public good, with just compensation to the owner. cf. *confiscation.*

emolument: compensation for personal services in the form of wages, commissions, awards, or other personal benefits.

emphyteutic lease: a perpetual lease whereby the owner of an uncultivated parcel has granted it to another in perpetuity or for a lengthy period on condition the leasee will improve the land.

empirical credit system: a credit scoring system, based on creditors; experience with borrowers, allotting certain points to attributes describing the applicant. [78]

employ: to hire or engage the services of an individual or his or her equipment.

employable: describes people in the population who are able to work and fall within certain age limits. cf. *hardcore unemployed.*

employee: a general term referring to all those who work for a wage or salary and perform services for an employer.

employee benefit trust: a trust that holds the assets of a pension, profit-sharing, stock bonus, or thrift plan, operated for the benefit of a corporation's employees or a labor union's members. [25]

Employee Retirement Income Security Act of 1974 (ERISA): on Labor Day, 1974, President Ford signed into law the Employee Retirement Income Security Act. The purpose of ERISA is to protect the interests of workers who participate in private pension and welfare plans and their beneficiaries. ERISA reaches 1.5 million plans and approximately 40 million workers and affects assets now held in private pension and welare plans totaling more than $200 billion.

Title I, administered by the Department of Labor, deals with protection of employee benefit rights. Title II is composed of amendments to the Internal Revenue Code. Title III deals with the division of responsibilities among the Department of Labor, the Internal Revenue Service, and the Pension Benefit Guaranty Corporation. Title IV deals with plan termination insurance and establishes the Pension Benefit Guaranty Corporation.

ERISA is designed to guarantee that workers are not required to satisfy unreasonable age and service requirements before becoming eligible for pension plan participation, that persons who work for a specified minimum period under a pension plan are assured of at least some pension at retirement age; that the money will be there to pay pension benefits when they are due; that plans and plan funds are administered and managed prudently; that employees know their rights and their obligations under the plans; that spouses of pensioners are given adequate protection; that the benefits of workers in certain defined benefit pension plans are protected in the event of a plan termination; and that the federal taxing power is protected by ensuring the equitable operation and soundness of pension plans.

The law also allows an employee not covered by a pension plan other than Social Security to put aside, on a tax-defered basis, a certain amount of money for retirement. see *Individual Retirement Account;* see also *Keogh plan.*

employee stock ownership plans (ESOPs): programs created to give the worker a feeling of participation in the management and direction of a company. Thus workers are encouraged to purchase stock of the company. see *compensation, retirement, self-employed.*

employee stock repurchase agreement: a plan under which stock in a corporation is sold to employees with an agreement providing for repurchase by the corporation.

employees trust: a trust established by an employer (usually a corporation) for the benefit of employees. [37]

employer rights: see *management prerogatives.*

Employment Act of 1946: a law designed to seek the federal government's promotion of full employment. Provision is also made for continuing study of economic trends and the submission of the President's Economic Report by the Council of Economic Advisers. The act also directs the president to present an annual economic report to Congress with legislative recommendations. see *reconversion.*

emporium: the major market of an area or products.

EMS: see *European Monetary System.*

EMTS: electronic money transfer system.

EMU: see *European Monetary Union.*

encipher: synonymous with *encode.*

enclosure sale: a sale in which property placed as security for a debt is sold to pay the debt.

encode
(1) to place magnetic ink characters of the E 13B type font specified by the ABA on the face of a document during the processing of items through an encoding machine.
(2) to apply a code, frequently one consisting of binary numbers, to represent individual characters or groups of characters in a message.
(3) to substitute letters, numbers, or characters for other numbers, letters, or characters, usually with the intent of hiding the meaning of the message from everyone except those who know the enciphering scheme. synonymous with *encipher.* [21, 31]

encoder
(1) a device capable of translating from one method of expression to another.
(2) the encoding process usually refers to inscribing or imprinting MICR characters on checks, deposits, or other bank documents. [105]

encoding: synonymous with *imprinting.*

encoding strip: on bank checks, the area in which magnetic ink will be deposited to represent characters; the clear band. [105]

encroachment
(1) *general:* the gradual expansion of a low-value district into a higher economic residential section.
(2) *law:* the infringement of another's property without the owner's consent.

encumbered: property to which one has title, but against which a claim has been made or granted to another.

encumbrance (incumbrance)
(1) *general:* that which holds back or weighs down.
(2) *banking:* a claim or interest in land or other property that although its value depreciates, does not prevent transfer or sale.
(3) *finance:* the amount expected to be paid for items ordered before they are received.

encumbrance account: in governmental accounting, a budgetary device to ensure that appropriations will not be overexpended. As expenditures are authorized, an encumbrance account is established to reduce available appropriations. When actual expenditure is determined, the entry is reversed and the appropriation is reduced by the amount expended.

End.: see *endorsement.*

endiguer: French term for to *hedge.*

end loan: a mortgage for a house buyer when the house is complete.

end money: a special fund created in the event that the costs of a project exceed original estimates.

endogeneous: those variables or facts explained within the framework of an economic model. [57]

endogenous theory of business cycle: any theory of the business cycle tracing the cause or causes of the cycle to economic movements or adjustments inherent in the very nature of the modern economy.

endorse: the act of placing one's name on an instrument, usually on the back, either by signing or by rubber stamping, so as legally to pass title of the instrument to another party. May also refer to the endorsing of a note by a second party guaranteeing payment in the event of default by the maker. Also spelled "indorse." [31]

endorsed bond: see *bond, endorsed.*

endorsee: the person to whom a negotiable item payable or endorsed to order is negotiated by endorsement and delivery. Also spelled "indorsee."

endorsement

(1) *general:* a show of support, a verification.

(2) *finance:* a signature written on the back of an instrument constitutes an endorsement. An endorsement is required on a negotiable instrument in order to transfer and pass title to another party, who becomes a "holder in due course." The endorser, in signing the endorsement, guarantees that he or she is the lawful owner of the instrument, knows of no infirmity in the instrument, accepted it in good faith for the value received, and is a holder in due course and has the legal capacity to transfer title to another party in the normal course of business.

(3) *insurance:* when circumstances require that a policy be changed (e.g., change of name, addition of property, or change in coverage), such changes are made by attaching to the policy an endorsement—a form bearing the language necessary to record the change. cf. *scratch endorsement.*

(4) also spelled *indorsement.*

endorsement date: the date appearing on the interchange advice and endorsed on paper by the clearing member first entering the paper into interchange. The date must be the same date as that on which the paper is mailed to the card issuer's clearing member. [105]

endorser: one who endorses; the person who transfers his or her title to an instrument to another by endorsement. Also spelled *indorser.*

endorsing: signing a check, note, or other financial instrument purporting to transfer it to another person.

endosser: French term for to *endorse.*

endowment

(1) *general:* a gift to an institution, usually for a specific purpose. In most cases, the gift permits the giver to declare a deduction on his taxes.

(2) *insurance:* a life term contract providing for the payment of the face amount of the policy at a specified age, at the end of a specified period, or upon the death of the insured.

endowment, pure: an insurance plan, that provides for payment of the face amount to the insured only upon survival to the end of a fixed period. Does not allow for payment of benefits to a beneficiary on prior death of the insured. [12]

endowment insurance: life insurance on which premiums are paid for at a given period, during which the insured is covered. If the person survives beyond the end of the premium period, he or she collects the face value.

endowment term: period of time from date of issue to maturity of an endowment contract. [12]

end sentinel: end-of-text character which signals the end of the message or of the information encoded on the magnetic strip on the bank card. [105]

Energy Research and Development Administration (ERDA): federal agency, in the Department of Energy, responsible for government activities in energy research and development, including demonstration of commercial feasibility and practical application of fossil, nuclear, solar, and geothermal energy, and programs of energy conservation.

Energy Tax Act of 1978: federal legislation dealing with excise taxes imposed on gas guzzlers; changes in motor fuels excise taxes; the repeal of excise taxes on buses; benefits of van pooling among employers and employees; additional investment credits to encourage business energy conservation; a push for geothermal exploitation and development; elimination of the excise tax on rerefined lubricating oil; and tax credits for energy saving in the home. Housing credits apply to qualified energy-saving devices installed in a personal residence after April 19, 1977. An individual received 1978 credits for 1977 expenditures if the work was done after April 19, 1978. See *Revenue Act of 1978.*

enfeoff: to give a gift of ownership to property.

enforced liquidation: the condition created by the failure of a security owner to maintain sufficient equity in a margin account.

English disease: synonymous with *stagflation.*

engross: to purchase a sufficient quantity of a commodity to secure a monopoly for purposes of reselling at a higher price.

enjoin
(1) *general:* to command or direct.
(2) *labor relations:* a court action to prevent a union from engaging in an illegal stoppage or strike action. An employer or corporation may also be enjoined during a labor dispute. see *injunction.*
(3) *law:* to stop, to forbid.

entail: to limit or curtail the succession to property by ordinary rules of inheritance. cf. *primogeniture.*

enterprise: any business venture requiring risk.

enterprise debt: debt that is to be retired primarily from the earnings of publicly owned and operated enterprises. see also *bond, revenue.* [49]

enterpriser: any person or group of persons who assume the risks of a business enterprise. synonymous with *entrepreneur.*

entirety (estate by): the property of husband and wife passed on to the survivor on the death of one. The estate is called "entirety" because the law looks on the husband and wife as one.

entity: see *corporation.*

Entree: a debit card produced by Visa (formerly BankAmericard).

entrepôt trade: reexporting imports from a warehouse. When the items are not sold from bonded warehouses, and duty has been paid, the reexporter may be entitled to a refund of the duty.

entrepreneur: one who assumes the financial risk of the initiation, operation, and management of a given business or undertaking. see *threshold companies.* synonymous with *enterpriser.*

entry

(1) *general:* a recording of data in an account or account book.

(2) *computers:* an input received from a terminal device attached to a computer.

Environmental Protection Agency (EPA): federal agency founded in 1970. It develops and enforces standards for clean air and water, establishes standards to control pollution from pesticides, toxic substances, and noise, and approves state pollution abatement plans.

EOM: end of month. In figuring discounts, EOM means that computation is made from the end of the month rather than the date of shipment or invoice date.

EOM dating: a policy of commencing credit terms as of the month's end. For example, 7/20 EOM means that a 7 percent cash discount is taken if the invoice is paid by the 20th of the month following the invoice date. Invoices dated after the 25th of the month are considered to be dated in the following month.

EOQ: see *economic order quantity.*

EP

(1) see *earning power.*

(2) see *effective par.*

EPR: see *earnings-price ratio.*

EPS

(1) see *earnings per share.*

(2) electronic payment system.

EPT: see *excess profits tax.*

Epunts: a European financing technique whereby the unit of account is a payment guarantee, the value of which is expressed in terms of gold, as are free-world currencies. The unit is not a gold obligation itself but has a value based on gold. Each unit represents slightly less than nine-tenths of a gram of gold, the same as the basis of the value of the American dollar. The holder of a matured bond that is expressed in Epunts can request payment in any one of 17 currencies, irrespective of the kind of currency the holder used when he or she made the purchase. The name Epunts comes from the European Payments Union, formed in 1947 to facilitate currency exchange, to which 17 nations belonged. The union no longer exists.

Equ.: see *equity.*

equal coverage: a corporation indenture protective clause providing that in the case of an additional issue of bonds, the subject bonds shall be entitled to the same security as that of the earlier issue.

Equal Credit Opportunity Act (ECOA): federal legislation prohibiting creditors from discriminating against credit applicants on the basis of sex or marital status. After March 1977, discrimination in credit on the basis of race, color, religion, national origin, age, and receipt of public assistance was prohibited. Compliance with the law comes under the jurisdiction of the Federal Trade Commission.

equal dignity: a reference to mortgages or other legal obligations so that all have equal ranking to prevent one from taking precedence over another. see *parity clause;* cf. *first lien, overlying mortgage, second lien, subordinated interest, tacking, underlying mortgage.*

Equal Employment Opportunity Commission (EEOC): see *Civil Rights Act of 1964, Title VII.*

equalization fund: see *Exchange Stabilization Fund.*

equalizing dividend: a dividend paid to correct irregularities caused by changes in established regular dividend dates. [105]

Equal Pay Act of 1963: a federal law requiring that men and women performing equal work be paid equal wages, and applying to employers and workers covered by the Fair Labor Standards Act. The act prohibits lowering pay for men to equalize rates.

equal pay for equal work: the concept, frequently written into contract language, that like work shall command like pay, regardless of sex, race, or other individual characteristics of the employees.

equation price: a price attained by the adjusting action of competition in any market at any time, or in a unit of time, such that the demand and supply become equal at that price.

equilibrium interest rate: the interest rate that keeps the price level constant. This rate coincides with the rate that keeps money incomes constant only in a stationary economy.

equilibrium price
(1) *general:* the price that maximizes a firm's profitability.
(2) *finance:* the price of goods determined in the market by the intersection of a supply and demand curve.

equilibrium quantity
(1) *general:* the quantity that maximizes a firm's profitability.
(2) *finance:* the quantity of goods determined in the market by the intersection of a supply and demand curve.

equimarginal principle: the quantity of money, goods, or services that a person believes he or she should receive for some other item or service.

equipment leasing: the renting of expensive equipment to save a substantial and immediate cash outlay. In most cases the leasing agreement includes a maintenance arrangement with the lessor on the leased items.

equipment obligations: equipment bonds, equipment notes, or car-trust notes secured only by lien on specific equipment. [18]

equipment trust
(1) a corporate trust established for the purpose of financing the purchase of equipment.
(2) a device or trust used to help firms obtain equipment by either the Philadelphia-Lease Plan or the New York Conditional Sales Plan. see *equipment trust certificate.* [37]

equipment trust bond: see *bond, equipment trust.*

equipment trust certificate: a type of security, generally issued by a railroad, to pay for new equipment (e.g., locomotives). Title to the equipment is held by a trustee until the notes are paid off. An equipment trust certificate is usually secured by a first claim on the equipment. [20]

equitable asset: an asset held by the executor of an estate but subject to debts only by a decree of an equity court for satisfaction of certain obligations.

equitable charge: a charge on property imposed by and enforceable in a court of equity, as distinguished from a charge enforceable in a court of law. A conveyance of real property, absolute on its face but intended only as security for a loan, may constitute an equitable charge on the property. [105]

equitable conversion: permitting real property to be converted into personal property. Real property owned by a partnership is, for the purpose of the partnership, personal property, because to determine a partner's interest, the real property must be reduced to cash.

equitable mortgage: a written statement making certain property security for a debt.

equitable ownership: the estate or interest of a person who has a beneficial right in property, the legal ownership of which is in another person. For example, a beneficiary of a trust has an equitable estate or interest in the trust property. cf. *legal partnership.* [37]

equitable right of redemption: a defaulted borrower's right to redeem his property, by full payment of the mortgage debt, up to the date of the mortgage foreclosure sale. [59]

equitable title: the right that exists in equity to secure total ownership to property when its title is in someone else's name.

equities: used synonymously with *common stocks* or *capital stocks* to designate securities that are owned capital rather than owed capital. The stockholders' equity in a company may be stated inclusive or exclusive of preferred stock. [67]

equity
(1) *general:* the value placed on the distribution of income.
(2) *banking:* the difference between liens against property and the current market value.
(3) *investments:* the ownership interest of common and preferred stockholders in a company. [20]
(4) *investments:* the excess of value of securities over the debit balance in a margin account. see *margin call.*
(5) *law:* the law of trusts, divorce, injunctions, and other rules of performance are enforced in courts of equity to determine fairness, right, and justice.

equity capital: stockholders' or owners' investments made in an organization.

equity conversion: synonymous with *reverse-annuity mortgage.*

equity earnings: a portion of surplus earnings of a subsidiary company, over dividend payments, that are unreported by the parent company. synonymous with *indirect earnings, undisclosed earnings, unreported earnings.*

equity financing: the selling of capital stock by a corporation.

equity funding: any combination of mutual fund shares and insurance. In such a plan, the buyer purchases his mutual fund shares and then the shares are pledged as collateral for the loan that is used to defray the cost of the premium on an insurance policy. see *investment company.*

equity income: net operating income less loan interest.

equity mortgage: home mortgage contract in which the lender reduces the interest rate by a certain percentage in return for the same percentage of profit when the borrower sells a home.

equity of redemption: see *equitable right of redemption.*

equity receivership: rarely found nonstatutory proceeding against insolvent debtor.

equity securities: any stock issue, common or preferred.

equity stake mortgage: low interest rates on a mortgage, one-third less on the average, in return for one-third of the profits when the property is sold.

equity trading: increasing the earnings of a business by borrowing funds at a rate of interest less than the rate of profit that can be earned by such borrowed monies when applied to the normal activities of the firm.

equity transaction: a transaction resulting in an increase or decrease of net worth or involving the transfer between accounts making up the net worth.

equity turnover: the ratio that measures the relationship between sales and the common stockholders' equity. It is used to compute the rate of return on common equity.

equivalent bond yield: a measurement of the rate of return on a security sold on a discount basis that assumes actual days to maturity and a 365-day year.

ER
(1)	see *earnings report.*
(2)	see *ex-rights.*
(3)	excess reserves of depository institutions.

ERDA: see *Energy Research and Development Administration.*

ERISA: see *Employee Retirement Income Security Act of 1974.*

erratic fluctuations: short-term changes that are difficult to measure and predict because they tend to be unexpected.

error account: a suspense account serving as a place to record errors, such as till overages or shortages.

error resolution: Regulation E outlines the requirement for error resolution and the liability and consequences for the bank and its customer. [105]

errors and omissions: insurance coverage for liability arising out of errors or omissions in the performance of professional services other than in the medical profession; applicable to such services as engineering, banking, accounting, insurance, and real estate.

ERTA: see *Economic Recovery Tax Act of 1981.*

ES
(1)	see *earned surplus.*
(2)	see *exempt securities.*

escalator clause
(1)	*general:* provides for an adjustment of wages in accordance with such factors as cost of living, productivity, or material costs. Escalator clauses are designed to keep real wages reasonably stable during the term of a contract.
(2)	*banking:* provides for increased payments in the event of unforeseen occurrences (e.g., increased fuel or maintenance costs).
(3)	*finance:* permitting adjustments of price or profit in a purchase contract, under specified conditions.

escape law
(1)	*general:* in a maintenance-of-membership agreement, a provision setting a period during which union members may withdraw from membership without effect on their employment.

(2) **law:** a contractual provision outlining the circumstances under which either party may be relieved of any obligation previously incurred or agreed to.

escheat: the reversion of property to the government when a person dies without leaving a will and has no heirs, or when the property is abandoned.

escheat law: pertaining to the reversion of land to the state by the failure of persons having legal title to hold the same.

escrow: a written agreement or instrument setting up for allocation funds or securities deposited by the giver or grantor to a third party (the escrow agent), for the eventual benefit of the second party (the grantee). The escrow agent holds the deposit until certain conditions have been met. The grantor can get the deposit back only if the grantee fails to comply with the terms of the contract, nor can the grantee receive the deposit until the conditions have been met. see also *billed escrow;* cf. *deposit funds.*

escrow agent: see *mortgage department.*

escrow agreement: an arrangement whereby two parties agree to place a sum of money in the hands of a third party for conditional delivery under specified circumstances.

escrow analysis: the periodic examination of escrow accounts by the mortgagee to verify that current monthly deposits are sufficient to provide the necessary funds to pay taxes, insurance, and other bills when they are due. [105]

escrow bond: see *bond, escrow.*

escrow closing: a type of loan closing in which an escrow agent accepts the loan funds and mortgage from the lender, the down payment from the buyer, and the deed from the seller. [59]

escrow funds: as applied to mortgage loans, represents reserves established for the repayment of taxes and insurance when due. Reserves are collected monthly by the mortgagee as part of the regular payment. [31]

escrow officer: an officer of a financial institution designated as the escrow agent or the custodian of the funds, securities, deeds, and so on, deposited until their release by agreement upon the completion of the agreed-upon act. [10]

escudo: monetary unit of Azores, Cape Verde Islands, Guinea-Bissau, Madeira, Mozambique, Portugal, Portuguese East Africa, and Timor.

ESD: see *ex-stock dividend.*

ESOPs: see *employee stock ownership plans.*

Est.: see *estate.*

estate

(1) **general:** any right, title, or other interest in real or personal property.

(2) **law:** all assets owned by an individual at the time of his or her death. The estate includes all funds, personal effects, interests in business enterprises, titles to property (real estate and chattels), and evidence of ownership, such as stocks, bonds, and mortgages owned, and notes receivable.

estate account: an account in the name of the estate of a decedent, administered by the executor or administrator of the estate. [39]

estate at will: of indefinite duration; the estate allows the lessee possession as long as both lessor and lessee mutually agree to it.

estate duty: a British term for the tax

on property of a deceased individual. synonymous with *inheritance tax* in the United States.

estate in common: see *tenancy in common.*

estate in fee simple: the absolute right to ownership in real estate. [105]

estate in reversion: the remaining portion of an estate that the grantor retains after certain interests in it have been transferred to another.

estate in severalty: an estate held by one person only. No other party has any part of it.

estate in tail: see *entail.*

estate plan: a definite plan for the administration and disposition of one's property during one's lifetime and at one's death; usually set forth in a will and one or more trust agreements. [37]

estate tax: a state or federal excise tax placed on an estate, to be paid before property is transferred to heirs. This is different from an inheritance tax, which is levied against the receivers of the estate. see *Tax Reform Act of 1976.* cf. *succession tax.*

estate tax bond: see *bond, estate tax.*

estimated balance sheet: the estimate of assets, liabilities, and proprietorship at the end of a future fiscal period.

estimated cost: the expected cost of a product to be manufactured. It includes standard costs projected to future operations.

estimated gross national product: an estimation of the GNP based on the combined estimates of its four main components: consumer spending; spending by business firms; spending by local, state, and federal governments; and net foreign spending. [105]

estimated profit and loss statement: the estimate of income, expenses, and net profit for a future fiscal period.

estimated revenues: the account title used in governmental accounting to set up the budgeted revenues for a period. The estimated revenues are compared against the actual revenues at the end of the period.

estimated tax: for corporations, the projected tax liability, minus tax credits permitted by law, above $100,000.

estoppel: a legal stoppage; when an individual who knows the truth but does not reveal it makes another believe something to be truthful, and that person acts to his detriment based on belief of the facts given to him, the giver of the untruthful information must reveal the full details of the situation. see *deceit.*

estoppel certificate: an instrument indicating the unpaid principal balance of a mortgage plus the amount and rate of interest thereon.

ET: see *estate tax.*

ETA: see *Energy Tax Act of 1978.*

et al.: (abbreviation of *et alii,* Latin) "and others" (who are specified elsewhere in the document.)

étalon de change-or: French term for *gold exchange standard.*

étalon-or: French term for *gold standard.*

EURCO: see *European Composite Unit.*

Eurobill of Exchange: a bill of exchange drawn and accepted in the usual fashion but expressed in foreign currency and accepted as being payable outside the country whose currency is being used.

Eurobond: a bond released by a U.S. or other non-European company for sale in Europe. In this market, corporations and governments issue medium-term securities, typically 10 to 15 years in length. see *Eurocredit sector.*

Euro-Canadian dollars: Canadian dollars dealt in the Euromarkets.

Eurocard: a European credit card developed by the West German banking system that is accepted in most western European countries.

Eurocheque: a credit card for purchasing goods in several western European countries.

Eurocommercial paper: commercial paper issued in a Eurocurrency. see *Eurocurrency.*

Eurocredit: any lending made using Eurocurrency. see *Eurocurrency.* [87]

Eurocredit sector: a sector of the Euromarket, where banks function as long-term lenders by constantly rolling over short- and medium-term loans at rates that fluctuate with the cost of funds. see *Eurobond.*

Eurocurrency: monies of various nations deposited in European banks that are used in the European financial market. synonymous with *Euromoney.*

Eurodollar collaterized certificates of deposits (CDs): certificates of deposit of at least $100,000 to foreign investors issued by federally chartered and Federal Savings and Loan Insurance Corporation-insured institutions.

Eurodollar deposits: bank deposits, generally bearing interest and made for a specific time period, that are denominated in dollars but are in banks outside the United States. [106]

Eurodollars: short-term, high quality source of funds to banks; deposits in foreign branches or banks denominated in dollars.

Euroequity: equity share denominated in a currency differing from that of the nation in which it is traded.

Eurofrancs: Swiss, Belgian, or French francs traded on the Eurocurrency markets.

Euroguilders: Dutch guilders traded in the Eurocurrency markets.

Euromarket (Euromart):
(1) see *Eurobond.*
(2) see *Eurocredit sector.*
(3) see *European Economic Community.*

Euromarks: Deutschmarks traded in the Eurocurrency market.

Euromart: see *European Economic Community.*

Euromoney: synonymous with *Eurocurrency.*

European Coal and Steel Community (ECSC): known as the *Schuman Plan,* it was proposed in 1950 by Jean Monnet, a leader in European confederation; its major functions are the pooling of resources and the placement of duty restrictions on coal, iron, and steel in trade among the nations of France, West Germany, Italy, Belgium, The Netherlands, and Luxembourg. see *European Economic Community.*

European Common Market: see *European Economic Community.*

European Composite Unit (EURCO): a nonofficial, private unit of account based on member currencies of the European Community; includes a quantity of each of the European Communities' currencies, in a proportion that reflects the importance of the country.

European currency band: see *snake system.*

European Currency Unit (ECU): money made up of nine European currencies: the Deutschemark, French franc, British pound, Italian lira, Belgian franc, Dutch guilder, Danish krone, Luxembourg franc, and Irish punt—plus 20 percent gold. synonymous with *European Monetary Unit.*

European Depository Receipt (EDR): patterned after the American depository receipt to facilitate investments by Americans in securities of foreign nations. The EDR was first issued in London in 1963, to facilitate international trading in Japanese securities. It is a negotiable receipt covering certain specified securities which have been deposited in a bank in the country of origin of the securities. Their use in trading eliminates the necessity of shipping the actual stock certificates, thus making transfer of ownership easier, faster, and less costly. [97]

European Economic Community (EEC): an agreement made in 1957 among France, Italy, West Germany, Belgium, The Netherlands, and Luxembourg (the original "Inner Six" nations) for the purposes of establishing common import duties and the abolishing of tariff barriers between borders. Denmark, Ireland, and England joined the EEC in 1973, and in 1975 many countries of Africa and the Caribbean became members. Greece became a member in 1981. Spain and Portugal were admitted in 1985. synonymous with *Common Market, Euromarket (Euromart).*

European Free Trade Association (EFTA): in 1959 Austria, Denmark, Norway, Portugal, Sweden, Switzerland, and the United Kingdom (the original "Outer Seven") established common regulations for tariffs and trade. Subsequently, Iceland became a member and Finland an associate member. see *European Economic Community.*

European Investment Bank: created by the Rome Treaty as a finance institution of the European Economic Community, this bank assists in financing projects within the Common Market.

European Monetary System (EMS): intended to move Europe toward closer economic integration and to avoid the disruptions in trade that can result from fluctuating currency values. France, West Germany, Belgium, Luxembourg, The Netherlands, Ireland, and Denmark all plan to prevent their currencies from rising or falling in value against each other any more than 2.5 percent. Italy will keep its lira from fluctuating against the other currencies by more than 6 percent. see *European Monetary Union.*

European Monetary Union (EMU): created on January 1, 1979, the union is Europe's response to U.S. monetary profligacy. Under EMU, currencies of member nations would rise together, rather than fluctuating separately. Founding members were Germany and France, but the expectation is that all nine Common Market members will join, with invitations going out to non-Common Market countries as well. see *European Monetary System.*

European Monetary Unit: synonymous with *European Currency Unit.*

Eurosterling: a sterling deposit acquired by a bank outside the United Kingdom.

Euroyen: Japanese yen traded in the Euromarkets.

evening up: a profit to offset a loss.

even lots: lots or number of stock shares sold in units of 100 or multiples thereof. see also *board lot.*

even-par swap: the sale of one block of bonds and the simultaneous purchase of the same nominal principal amount of another block of bonds, without concern for the net cash difference.

even up: a securities term describing an evenly divided balance of security buyers and sellers. Prior to the opening of the exchange, it refers to the opening prices of the day which show minimal changes from the closing prices of the previous days trading.

evergreen credit: a revolving credit free of a maturity date, but giving the bank the opportunity, once each year, to convert into a term loan.

every-normal granary: a device designed to stabilize the price of agricultural commodities through the purchase by the government of excess production for storage and the sale by the government from that storage in years of low production.

eviction: the depriving by due process of law land or property in keeping with the judgment of a court. see *disseisin, ejectment.*

Evid.: see *evidence.*

evidence: the testimony of witnesses and information presented to a court.

evidence of insurability: any statement or proof of a person's physical condition and/or other factual information affecting his acceptability for insurance. cf. *declaration.*

EW: see *ex-warrants.*

Ex.: see *exchange.*

exact interest: interest compounded on a 365-days-per-year basis. see *compounded interest, ordinary interest, simple interest.*

ex-all: indicates that the seller has sold a security but reserved for himself the right to all pending advantages. These would include rights, warrants, and dividends in money or kind which may be granted to the security.

Examination Objectives: a subsection in the Comptroller's Handbook describing, for each banking activity, the goal of primary importance to the examiner. Certain objectives determine the scope of specific areas of examination interest. Other objectives ensure compliance with laws, rules, and regulations. [105]

examination of title: the review of the chain of title on a piece of real estate as revealed by an abstract of title from the public records pertaining to the property. [105]

Examination Procedures: a subsection in the Comptroller's Handbook for each banking activity which includes the procedures that an examiner is required to perform. These procedures are supervisory in nature and help the examiner to accomplish the target objectives for each subject area. [105]

examine for bank endorsement: an act performed generally in a bank's proof department or bookkeeping department whereby clerks examine the backs of all checks to see that the bank which forwarded the items has properly endorsed them. The bank endorsement is very important because banks use it to trace the path of an item through the banks through which it has passed. The whole system of returning items for infirmity through the channels from which they came relies to a great extent upon clear, legible bank endorsements. [10]

examine for endorsements: an act performed to determine whether an item has been properly endorsed so as to complete its negotiability. Tellers, or clerks who receive the items from tellers, check endorsements so that the depositor of any item can be readily determined. It is the responsibility of bookkeepers to see that items are properly endorsed before they are paid by the bank. Many cases involving the negotiability of an instrument have arisen because of improper, incomplete, or faulty endorsements on the instrument. [10]

examine for missorts: bookkeepers are required to examine checks before posting them to determine that they are drawn on accounts in their particular ledger, or that they are actually drawn on the drawee bank. There are two types of missorts: checks sorted to the wrong ledger, or checks drawn on another bank where a depositor may maintain another account but is using a similar style of check. [10]

ex-ante saving: a form of planned saving which may be more or less than ex-ante investment (planned investment). cf. *ex-post saving.*

exception: in title-insuring practice, an item that may not be covered by title insurance because it limits in some way the owner's right to his or her property; exceptions may include easements, liens, and deed restrictions. [59]

exception item: item that cannot be paid by drawee bank for one reason or another, such as stop payment or insufficient funds. [105]

exception report: see *exceptions.*

exceptions: transactions, either monetary or nonmonetary, which fail to meet the parameters of the system: usually displayed periodically on a listing called an *exception report.* [105]

excess bank reserves: the deposits that a member bank has with the Federal Reserve Bank over and above the amount required to be on deposit there.

excess condemnation: in condemnation proceedings, taking more land or property than is truly required for the government project in question.

excess coverage clause: a statement that in the event of a loss, a specific insurance will be considered in excess of any other insurance held against the identical risk. see *double insurance.*

excess demand curve: reflects the quantity demanded less the quantity offered at each price.

excess equity: a situation where the cash value of an account is in excess of the amount required for margin in the buying of securities.

excess insurance: a policy or bond covering the insured against certain hazards, applying only to loss of damage in excess of a stated amount. The risk of initial loss or damage (excluded from the excess policy or bond) may be carried by the insured himself or may be insured by another policy or bond, providing what is known as primary insurance.

excess(ive) interest: the difference between the minimum rate of interest contractually guaranteed on dividends, or proceeds left with a firm and the interest actually credited.

excessive purchases: the number assigned by management representing the number of purchases posted to an account in a day, above which the account is listed on a printout for manual attention. When this figure is exceeded, a code indicating an excessive purchase condition may be displayed by the authorization system when the account file is accessed. [105]

excess loan: an illegal bank loan made to one customer that is in excess of the maximum stated by law. Directors of banks approving such loans have been held by court decisions to be personally liable for the bank's losses.

excess of loss reinsurance: reinsurance that indemnifies the ceding company for the excess of a stipulated sum or primary retention in the event of loss.

excess profits tax: a tax added to the normal tax placed on a business. It is usually levied on profits above what the law declares as normal during periods of wartime.

excess reserves: designates the amount of funds held in reserve in excess of the legal minimum requirements, whether the funds are on deposit in a Federal Reserve Bank, in a bank approved as a depository, or in the cash reserve carried in its own vaults.

Exch.: see *exchange.*

exchange

(1) *general:* an organization or place for carrying out business or settling accounts.

(2) *finance:* the volume of monies available for use.

(3) *investments:* any exchange for trading in securities or commodities. see *clearinghouse, foreign exchange, stock exchanges.*

exchange acquisition: a method of filling an order to purchase a block of stock on the floor of an exchange. Under certain circumstances, a member broker can facilitate the purchase of a block by soliciting sell orders. All

orders to sell the security are lumped together and crossed with the buy order in the regular auction market. The buyer's price may be on a net basis or on a commission basis. [20]

exchange against actuals: synonymous with *exchange of spot.*

exchange bureau: a consumer reporting agency cooperatively maintained and operated by banks engaged in installment credit activities. [105]

exchange charge: has a variety of meanings. Sometimes it refers to a remittance charge, which is a charge that some banks deduct in paying checks drawn upon themselves when they are presented through the mails from out-of-town points for the service of remitting the proceeds to these distant points. The term may also refer to a charge for drafts on other cities or to a charge which banks make for collecting out-of-town items. Generally called *collection charges.* [50]

exchange controls: governmental restraints limiting the right to exchange the nation's currency into the currency of another country.

exchange current: the current rate of exchange.

exchange depreciation: the decline of a foreign currency or currencies which a currency experiences. This is usually created by a reduction in the base, such as gold, of the currency but can also be caused by other factors, such as monetary funds, stabilization, or government action.

exchange distribution: a method of selling large blocks of stock on the floor of an exchange. Under certain circumstances a member-broker can facilitate the sale of a block of stock by soliciting and inducing other member-brokers to solicit orders to buy. Individual buy orders are lumped together with the sell order in the regular auction market. A special commission is usually paid by the seller; ordinarily the buyer pays no commission. [20]

Exchange Equalization Fund: the stabilization fund of the United Kingdom, originally created to help the British Treasury meet the problems that arose from the suspension of gold in 1931.

exchange for futures: transferring to a seller the cash commodity of a long futures position by the purchaser of a cash commodity. Any difference between the spot and futures contract is settled with cash.

exchange for physical: synonymous with *exchange of spot.*

exchange jobber: a banker who buys foreign exchange in large amounts for resale at a margin to smaller banks or individuals.

exchange of securities: resulting from a merger or consolidation, a technique where the securities of one corporation are exchanged for those of a second firm on a mutually agreeable basis.

exchange of spot (or cash commodity) for futures: the simultaneous exchange of a specified quantity of a cash commodity for the equivalent quantity in futures, usually due to both parties' carrying opposite hedges in the same delivery month. Also known as *exchange for physical* or *exchange against actuals.* In grain the exchange is made outside the "pit." [2]

exchange privilege: enables a mutual fund shareholder to transfer his investment from one fund to another within the same fund group if his needs or objectives change, generally with a small transaction charge. [23]

exchange rate: refers to the price of one currency in relation to that of another.

exchanges: all checks, drafts, notes and other instruments that are presented to a clearinghouse for collection. synonymous with *clearinghouse exchanges.*

Exchange Stabilization Fund: a department of the U.S. Treasury established in 1934 with the "profits" derived from the reduction in the gold content of the dollar for the purpose of stabilizing the foreign exchanges.

exchange value: the value of any good considered as the quantity of other things that will be given in exchange for it.

exchequer: that account of the Chancellor of the Exchequer of the United Kingdom used to handle the revenues and payments of the kingdom. This account is maintained in the Bank of England and parallels the U.S. Treasury Department's account in the 12 Federal Reserve Banks.

Excise, Estate and Gift Tax Adjustment Act of 1970: federal legislation; extended excise tax rates on automobiles and telephone service until January 1972. Sped up collections on estate and gift taxes.

excise taxes: taxes levied by the federal and state governments on the manufacture, sale, or consumption of commodities, or taxes levied on the right, privilege, or permission to engage in a certain business, trade, occupation, or sport.

Excise Tax Reduction Act of 1954: federal legislation; dismantled Korean War excise tax structure. All excise tax rates in excess of 10 percent were reduced to 10 percent, except for the 20 percent cabaret tax. see *Excise Tax Reduction Act of 1965.*

Excise Tax Reduction Act of 1965: federal legislation; repealed excise taxes on several items and provided for systematic reductions in the rates on transportation equipment and communication services. see *Excise Tax Reduction Act of 1954.*

exclusion

(1) *general:* any restriction or limitation.

(2) *banking:* a provision of an insurance policy or bond referring to hazards, circumstances, or property not covered by the policy.

(3) *taxes:* an amount excluded from taxable income.

exclusive allowance: the portion of an annuity payment that can be excluded from taxable income each year. This amount is determined by dividing the annuitant's investment in the contract by his life expectancy. In a tax-deferred-annuity (TDA) program, the amount of annual contribution that may be excluded from taxable income by a participant is specified by law.

exclusive listing: an arrangement whereby a broker becomes the sole agent of the owner of a property, assuming the sole right to sell or rent the property within a specified time period.

ex-coupon: without the coupon. A stock is sold ex-coupon when the coupon for the existing interest payment has been removed.

Exctr.: see *executor.*

exculpatory clause: a clause that relieves the landlord of liability for personal injury to tenants as well as for property damages. The clause does not necessarily protect the landlord against liability to a third party.

Ex. D.: see *ex-dividend.*

Ex. Div.: see *ex-dividend.*

ex-dividend (ex div; XD): identifying the period during which the quoted price of a security excludes the payment of any declared dividend to the buyer, and the dividend reverts to the seller.

ex-dividend date: the day on and after which the right to receive a current dividend is not transferred automatically from seller to buyer. [37]

execute

(1) *computers:* to carry out an instruction or perform a routine.

(2) *law:* to complete or make valid, as by signing, sealing and delivering.

execute an order: the fulfillment of a buy or sell order where every execution is accompanied by a confirmation from the broker to the customer.

executed: signed, sealed, and delivered, as of contracts or other written agreements.

execution: the actual filling of a customer's order.

execution date: see *posting date.*

executive compensation: the total monies paid to an executive, including the regular salary, plus additional payments (e.g., bonuses or director's fees). It does not include warrants or options to purchase stock. see *compensation.*

executor: a party (person, bank, etc.) identified in a will to administer the estate upon the death of the maker of the will (the testator) and to dispose of it according to the wishes of the testator.

executor de bonis non: the individual or corporation named in the will to take over and complete the settlement of an estate in those cases in which the original executor, for one reason or another, has failed or been unable to do so. Unless the testator himself names such a successor executor, the court appoints an administrator de bonis non. [37]

executor de son tort: one who, without legal authority, assumes control of a decedent's property as if he were executor and thereby makes himself responsible for what comes into his possession. [37]

executor of an estate: the person appointed by a testator to execute his or her will or to see its provisions carried into effect after his or her decease. [76]

executor's deed: see *deed, executor's.*

executory: until all parts of a contract are performed, the contract is said to be executory as to the part not performed.

executrix: a woman identified in a will to administer the estate upon the death of the maker of the will (the testator) and to dispose of it according to the wishes of the testator.

exemplary damages: monies or fines imposed by a court (a) in punishment of the defendant, (b) to make an example of the wrongdoers, and (c) to deter others from doing the same thing.

exemplified copy: a copy of a record or document witnessed or sealed certified to as required by law for a particular transaction. [37]

exempt: free from burden or liability.

exempt employees

(1) *general:* employees who are not subject to the rulings of seniority.

(2) *labor relations:* employees not subject to wage and overtime provisions of the Fair Labor Standards Act.

Such employees may or may not be covered by a union contract. see *Fair Labor Standards Act of 1938.*

exemption

(1) *income taxes:* a token deduction from gross income allowed for the taxpayer and others in his family where at least half of their support can be shown. Additional deductions are given for people over 65 years of age and for blindness. see *Tax Reform Act of 1976.*

(2) *law:* a person free from a duty required by some law (e.g., one relieved from jury duty because of prejudice of the subject).

exempt securities: stocks that do not require the regular margin when bought on credit.

exercise notice: a notice issued by a clearinghouse that was formed to ensure stock deliveries, obligating a customer to send the securities covered by an option against payment of the exercise price. see *exercise price.*

exercise price: the fixed price for which a stock can be purchased in a call contract or sold in a put contract. see *puts and calls.* synonymous with *striking price.*

exercise ratio: number of shares of common stock that may be exchanged for each warrant owned.

ex gratia payment: a payment made by an insurance company, but one for which it is not liable under the terms of the insurance policy.

exhaust price: the price at which a broker is forced to sell a security that was margined and subsequently dropped in price.

exhibit

(1) *general:* a display or public show.

(2) *law:* anything presented in a court to assist in proving a set of allegations.

Eximbank (Ex-Im Bank): see *Export-Import Bank of the United States.*

Ex. Int.: see *ex-interest.*

ex-interest: having no interest. synonymous with *flat.*

existing mortgage: a mortgage that is encumbering a property. After the property has been sold, the mortgage may or may not remain.

exogenous: those variables or facts not explained within an economic model but imposed upon the model by outside forces. [57]

exoneration: the act of relieving one of what otherwise would be or might be a liability or a duty.

exonumia: a numismatic term applicable to all nongovernment monetary issues. [27]

Exor.: see *executor.*

exotic: a currency in which a large international market does not exist.

Exp.
(1) see *expense.*
(2) see *exports.*

expansion
(1) *general:* extending or broadening the operation or area of a business.
(2) *finance:* a business cycle fluctuation characterized by an increase in industrial activity.

ex parte: upon, from, or in the interest of one side only. Ordinarily implies a hearing or examination in the presence of, or on papers filed by, one party and in the absence of, and often without notice to, the other. [18]

expected exit value: the nondiscounted amount of cash a company expects to realize from holding a partic-ular asset. cf. *present value of expected cash flow.*

expected return: the profit that is anticipated from a business venture.

expected yield: the ratio of expected return over the investment total, usually expressed as a percentage on an annual basis.

expendable fund: a fund whose assets may be applied by administrative action for general or specific purposes.

expenditure: an actual payment, or the creation of an obligation to make a future payment, for some benefit, item, or service received. If the expenditure is for the purpose of acquiring or improving a relatively permanent asset, it is termed a *capital expenditure.* If the amount involved is charged to some operating account, it is a *revenue expenditure.*

expense: the cost of resources used to create revenue. Expense is the amount shown on the income statement as a deduction from revenue. Expense should not be confused with cost. All expenses are costs, but not all costs are expenses.

expense account
(1) *general:* an account carried in the general ledger in which all operating expenses are recorded. Expenses are deducted from gross profits, or the total of all income accounts, to compute the net profit of the business for the period.
(2) *finance:* money advanced to an employee, usually an executive, for travel, daily costs, and other items that are accepted by the organization as justified; monies paid by an employee that are reimbursed by the employer after the expenditures have been accepted.

expense account cards: a type of card issued to a cardholder which is used exclusively for that cardholder's business expenses. [105]

expense constant: a flat amount included in some premiums, which covers the minimum expense of an insurance transaction.

expense fund: a fund, required by law, held by a mutual savings bank or directors of a nonstock bank to ensure the financial stability of the bank at the time of its dealings with the public.

expense loading: used in rate making to denote the amount which is added to the pure premium in order to provide for the expenses of the insurance company. see *pure premium.* [56]

expense ratio: the percentage of the premium used to pay all operating costs.

experience
(1) *general:* events during one's lifetime; usually pertaining to acquired knowledge or skill.
(2) *banking:* the premium and loss record of an insured or of a class of coverage.

experience rating
(1) *general:* the basis for an adjustment, according to the employer's unemployment or accident record, of the rate the employer pays for unemployment insurance or workmen's compensation insurance.
(2) *banking:* a type of individual risk rating that, based on insured experience on the risk, measures the extent to which a particular risk deviates from the average of its class and reflects this deviation in the rate for the risk. see *basic rating,* cf. *judgment rates.*

expiration
(1) *general:* termination, cessation.
(2) *banking:* the date on which a policy will cease to be in effect, unless previously canceled.
(3) *investments:* the last day on which the option may be exercised. [5]

expire: to arrive at the termination period of an agreement, contract, or other instrument.

expired account: an account on which the originally agreed period for payment has elapsed, but an unpaid balance remains due. [55]

expired card: a bank card that has passed its expiration date. [105]

ex-pit transaction: the buying of cash commodities at a specified basis outside the authorized exchange.

explicit interest: the amount of money or goods paid on a loan.

export: to ship an item away from a country for sale to another country.

export bounty: a subsidy paid by the government of the country from which goods are exported.

export credit: a commercial letter of credit issued for the purpose of financing a shipment of goods to a foreign country. [50]

Export-Import Bank of the United States (Eximbank) (Ex-Im Bank): this independent federal banking corporation, established in 1934, facilitates and aids in financing exports and imports and the exchange of commodities between the United States and foreign nations; it offers direct credit to borrowers outside the United States as well as export guarantees, export credit insurance, and discount loans.

export license: a document issued by a government permitting a stated amount of a specified commodity to be exported. A license is usually required for such items as gold, arms, munitions, and drugs.

export quotas: fixed amounts of goods that may be exported. Export quotas are determined by the government and may be used for the sake of national defense, to support price control schemes, and so on.

export rate: a transportation rate applicable only to domestic shipment of goods en route to a foreign country.

exports: items produced in one country and sold to another.

export tax: a duty on items exported from a country. The U.S. Constitution prohibits the use of an export tax.

Export Trade Act: see *Webb-Pomerene Act of 1918.*

ex-post facto law: "after the fact" (Latin). A law applying retroactively: forbidden by Article 1 of the U.S. Constitution. That is, a law that would serve to convict an individual for an activity that had not been declared illegal when the person is accused of having performed it.

ex-post saving: realized saving. If hoards are considered as constant, ex-post saving must equal ex post investment. cf. *ex-ante saving.*

exposure: when a bank has lent funds (or engaged in foreign exchange dealing with) or invested in a company or country.

Express Company money orders: money orders, similar to postal and bank money orders.

express trust: a trust stated orally or in writing, with the terms of the trust definitely prescribed; to be distinguished from a *resulting trust* and a *constructive trust.* [37]

express warranty: a statement of conduct by a seller to a buyer that a specific condition exists in the character of goods.

expropriation: the act of taking private property for public purpose, or the modification of the right to private property by a sovereignty or any entity vested with the proper legal authority; for example, property under eminent domain is expropriated. cf. *confiscation.*

ex-quay: where the seller places the items at the disposal of a buyer at the agreed quay at the agreed time. [95]

Ex. R.: see *ex-rights.*

ex-rights: without the rights. Corporations raising additional money may do so by offering their stockholders the right to subscribe to new or additional stock, usually at a discount from the prevailing market price. The buyer of a stock selling ex-rights is not entitled to the rights. see *ex-dividend, rights.* [20]

ex-ship: where the seller places the items at the disposal of a buyer at the agreed time, on board the ship at the usual unloading point in the named port. The buyer pays import duty. [95]

ex-stock dividend: without any stock dividend; for example, when the stock dividend is held as the property of the seller. cf. *ex-dividend.*

ex-store: selling term for commodities in warehouse. [11]

Extd.: see *extended.*

extend(ed)

(1) *general:* to multiply the unit price by the quantity of units to ascertain the total cost on an invoice.

(2) *banking:* to allow a period of time for the payment of a debt beyond the date originally set.

(3) *law:* describes a contractual ob-

ligation that has been prolonged beyond the originally stated date of maturity or termination.

extended bond: see *bond, extended.*

extended fund facility: where the International Monetary Fund lend funds over a three-year period rather than the usual one-year period.

extended term insurance: permanent plans of life insurance providing term coverage for the face amount of policy, in lieu of cash settlement, when premiums are discontinued for a fixed period.

extension

(1) *banking:* moving the maturity date to a later time, resulting in prolongation of the terms of a loan. see *lockup.*

(2) *finance:* the granting of borrowing rights, or the permission to buy without immediate payment.

(3) *law:* a postponement by agreement of the parties of the time set for any legal procedure.

extension agreement: a written authorization by creditors involved in bankruptcy proceedings to postpone the due date of their bills, with the hope that the debtor will be able to improve his or her financial condition and honor the debts at a later time. [105]

extension fee: a charge made on an installment loan for postponing the due date of a payment. [105]

extension of credit: the granting of credit in any form. [105]

extension of mortgage: an agreement which prolongs the terms of a mortgage.

external audit: an examination intended to serve as a basis for an expression of opinion regarding the fairness, consistency, and conformity with accepted accounting principles of statements prepared by a corporation or other entity for publication. [43]

external bill: a bill of exchange drawn in one country but payable in another country. cf. *foreign bill.*

external bond: see *bond, external.*

external debt: the debt held by person outside a country.

externalities: external benefits or costs of activities for which no compensation is offered. synonymous with *spillovers.*

external public debt: that part of the public debt owed to nonresident foreign creditors, made payable in the currency of the nation of the creditors, as to both interest and principal.

external security audit: a security audit conducted by an organization or individuals independent of the one being audited. [105]

extinguish: to wipe out, settle, or conclude, as with a debt or obligation.

extinguishment fund: a sinking fund.

extortion: the taking of something of value from someone by force; fear of exposure and threat of force are also instruments of extortion, which is sometimes aimed at inducing the victim to pay the extortioner more than is due him or her in a legitimate connection. cf. *duress (personal).*

extra: short form of "extra dividend." A dividend in the form of stock or cash in addition to a company's regular or usual dividend. Not to be confused with *ex-dividend.*

extractive industry: a business that takes products directly from nature, especially from land or water (e.g., lumber, coal, or oil).

extra dating: adding days beyond the regular date for invoice payment. Extensions are usually for 3- or 60-day periods.

extra dividend: see *extra.*

extra expense insurance: designed for the business firm (e.g., a bank) that must continue to operate following a loss, usually at great additional expense. It is not to be confused with business interruption insurance because it does not protect against interruption of business.

extraordinary gain or loss: income or loss to an entity caused by an unusual and infrequent event, unrelated to the ordinary activities of the entity.

extraordinary income: a listing of income of a business that does not result from ordinary operations, as found in the firm's financial statements. [105]

extraordinary items: income statement captions (extraordinary income and extraordinary deductions) which segregate material gains and losses, less applicable income taxes, arising out of current-year transactions that are of a character significantly different from the typical or customary activities of the company. Included would be such items as the sale or abandonment of a plant or a significant segment of the company's investments or business, major changes in accounting procedures, and condemnations. [3]

extraordinary property losses: an amortizable (deferred debit) account, which includes the depreciated value of property abandoned or damaged by circumstances that could not have been reasonably anticipated and which is not covered by insurance. [3]

extrapolation: the estimate of an unknown value beyond the range of a series of identifiable values (e.g., projecting the world's population in A.D. 2500).

ex-warrants: without warrants. When a security is sold ex-warrants, the warrants are retained (exercised) by the seller. see *ex-rights.*

ex-works: where the seller places the items at the buyer's disposal at the agreed time, at the agreed place, but the purchaser is responsible for all export and import duties, shipping, and so on. [95]

F: used on a ticker tape after a foreign stock symbol to show that the stock has been sold by a foreign owner.

F&A: February and August (semiannual interest payments or dividends).

FA

(1) see *face amount.*

(2) see *facilitating agency.*

(3) see *fixed assets.*

(4) see *floating assets.*

(5) see *frozen asset.*

FAA: see *Federal Aviation Administration.*

FAC: Federal Advisory Council. A group of 12 advisors representing the 12 Federal Reserve districts, which meets several times a year to confer with the Board of Governors of the Federal Reserve System.

face amount: the principal sum involved in a contract. The actual amount payable by the company may be decreased by loans or increased by additional benefits payable under specified conditions or stated in a rider.

face of a note: the amount stated on a note. synonymous with *principal.*

face of policy: the first or front page of the insurance policy. It usually includes the name of the insurance company and the insuring clauses. [56]

face value: the principal value of an instrument. It is on the face value that interest is computed on interest-bearing obligations such as notes and bonds. The legal entity issuing a note, bond, or other obligation contracts to repay the face value of the obligation at maturity. synonymous with *par value.*

facilitating agency: any organization aiding an individual or firm in taking title to goods (i.e., a stock exchange).

facsimile signature: a mechanically imprinted signature placed on an instrument, check, bond, security, and the like. Although such signed checks are accepted as equal to hand-signed ones, banks usually have certain stipulations that must be met prior to honoring them.

factor

(1) *general:* an individual who carries on business transactions for another. see also *factors.*

(2) *finance:* an agent for the sale of goods or services, authorized to sell

279

and receive payment for the times or services.

(3) finance: a financial organization whose primary business is purchasing the accounts receivable of other companies, at a discount, and taking the risk and responsibilities of making collection.

factorage: the commission collected by a factor.

factor cost: a product's market price where all costs are deducted that are not factors of production such as transfer payments and depreciation.

factoring

(1) banking: a method commonly employed by an installment loan department of a bank for computing the amount of interest to be refunded or credited because a 12-month loan is being liquidated before maturity. It is also a method for accruing earned discount.

(2) finance: selling accounts before their due date, usually at a discount.

factors

(1) general: ingredients needed for the production of any good or service. The primary factors are land, labor, capital, and enterprise.

(2) finance: limited agents who buy accounts receivables from small firms at a discount. Funds are advanced upon the delivery of duplicate invoices as evidence of sale and delivery of the goods. Factors frequently perform all accounting functions in connection with the accounts receivable, in which case purchasers are notified to remit directly to the factor. see also *factor.*

factor, 78th: a method commonly employed by the installment loan and other departments of a bank for com-

puting the amount of interest to be refunded or recredited when a 12-month loan is liquidated prior to maturity. Also, a method used for accruing earned discount. [10]

factor's lien: a factor's right to retain the merchandise consigned to him or her for reimbursal for all advances previously made to the consignor. cf. *particular lien.*

factory overhead: manufacturing costs, excluding direct material and direct labor.

factory overhead incurred: manufacturing costs accumulated during a given accounting period.

facultative: describes a specific transaction, one risk at a time, with the ceding and acceptance being optional on the part of the ceding company and the reinsurer. That is, the reinsuring company may exercise its "faculty" to accept or reject the risk offered.

fail(s)

(1) general: a business venture that does not prove financially viable.

(2) investments: a broker's inability to deliver stocks he or she owes another broker within the required five business days. One broker's failure to deliver results in another broker's failure to receive.

failure: the inability to fulfill normal business obligations; becoming insolvent or bankrupt.

FAIR Certificate: *f*ree from tax *a*ffordable, *i*nsured *r*ewarding; the 1981 Savings and Loan Association strategy with Congress to allow a savings certificate that would be free from federal income tax, offered in affordable denominations, insured by a federal agency, and pay a significant net turn. see *All-Savers certificates.*

Fair Credit Billing Act: an amendment to the federal Truth in Lending Law that protects charge account customers against billing errors by permitting credit card customers to use the same legal defenses against banks or other "third party" credit card companies that they previously could use against merchants.

Fair Credit Reporting Act of 1971: federal legislation giving the user of credit, the buyer of insurance, or the job applicant the right to learn the contents of his or her file at any credit bureau. see also *Freedom of Information Act of 1966.*

Fair Debt Collection Practices Act: an amendment to the Consumer Practices Act, signed by President Carter, its basic objective is to eliminate abusive and bitterly unfair debt collection practices, such as threats of financial ruin, loss of job or reputation, and late evening telephone calls. The law became effective in March 1978.

Fair Employment Practices Committee: a committee set up by Executive Order 8802 in 1941 to "investigate complaints of discrimination." Fair employment practices were made part of federal law by the Civil Rights Act of 1964. see *Civil Rights Act of 1964, Title VII.*

Fair Labor Standards Act of 1938: a federal statute setting minimum hourly wages, providing for payment of time and one-half for work beyond 40 hours a week, and regulating employment of those under 18 years of age. Known as the Wage and Hour Law, it is administered by the U.S. Department of Labor. The act has been amended to include standards for computing working time and increases of the minimum wage, rules for computing overtime pay, and requirements for equal pay for equal work without regard to sex. There are more than 40 exemptions applying to professionals, executives, and salespersons. Similar statutes have been passed by state legislatures.

fair market value: a value arrived at by bargaining between informed buyers and sellers.

fairness: the ability of financial statements to convey unambiguous, adequate information concerning a particular firm's activities. [105]

fair price: the price that results in a fair return on funds invested or which has an appropriate markup on goods or services sold to claim a reasonable profit.

fair rate of return: the profit that a public utility can earn to pay interest and dividends and expand facilities, as determined by federal and state law. see *rate regulation.*

fair return: income on invested capital allowing a firm to raise additional capital for normal growth.

fair trade acts: laws passed by various states in which retailers are obliged to maintain specified prices on select goods. In recent years fair trade pricing has been withdrawn by a great number of retailers and manufacturers.

fair value: under the Investment Company Act, value determined in good faith by the board of directors for those securities and assets for which there is no market quotation readily available. [30]

fairy godfather: slang, a potential business supporter.

fall: the failure of a seller to deliver securities to the purchaser or to a specific place of delivery as contracted. [105]

falling-rate-of-profit theory: synonymous with *declining-marginal-efficiency-of-capital theory*.

fall out of bed: a crash in stock prices; a sharp drop in the market.

false pretense: any untrue statements or representations made with the intention of obtaining property or money. [56]

family allowance plan: a scheme providing every family, rich or poor, with a certain amount of money based exclusively on the number and age of its children. Family units above specified levels would return all or a portion of the money with their income taxes; those below specified income levels would retain the funds.

family income rider: a special policy provision added to a basic term life insurance policy, stating that a specified monthly income is to be paid to the beneficiary for the remainder of the income period if the insured dies before the expiration of the term.

Fannie Mae: see *Federal National Mortgage Association*.

Farm Bankruptcy Act of 1933: federal legislation that allowed farmers added time to pay off their debts. The provisions of the act expired in 1949.

Farm Credit Administration: the U.S. agency responsible for the cooperative farm credit system, providing long- and short-term aid to farmers.

farmer-owned reserve (FOR): established in 1977 to promote grain price stability. In principle, for FOR stabilizes prices by releasing stored grain to the market when prices are high and removing grain when prices are low. see also *payment-in-kind program*. [99]

Farmers Home Administration (FmHA): an agency of the federal government that makes, participates in, and insures loans for rural housing and other purposes. [59]

farm out: to subcontract.

farm price: the price received by farmers for their products as reported each month by the U.S. Department of Agriculture.

Farm Relief Act of 1933: see *Agricultural Adjustment Act of 1933*.

farm stock: the grain stock held by farmers.

farm subsidies: monies given or loaned, under stringent regulation, by the U.S. Department of Agriculture to producers of certain farm products when the market price drops below the percentage of agricultural parity or if a portion of acreages is used for pasturage or for purposes of conservation. see *price support*; cf. *Brannan plan*.

farm surplus: farm products purchased by the U.S. government for purposes of keeping agricultural prices stable. These surpluses remain in warehouses until disposed of (e.g., as overseas sales or as food distributed to needy people).

FAS: see *free alongside ship*.

FASB8: Statement of Financial Accounting Standards No. 8; governs corporations' financial accounting and reporting for foreign currency transactions, and sets standards for foreign currency financial statements incorporated in the financial statements of a firm by consolidation, combination, or the equity method of accounting. [101]

Fas-Cash: a copyrighted system designed to expedite the handling of cash by the teller. Currency is precounted and strapped by the teller before banking hours. The currency is strapped in packages of from $2 through $9, and from $10 through $100. This permits the teller to select rapidly nearly any combination of precounted packages of currency, and he or she is required only to get the correct change from an automatic cashier. For example, a customer wants to cash a check for $38.75. The teller selects a $30 and an $8 package of currency and selects $0.75 from the automatic cashier. This is a very fast method of handling customers at the teller's window. [10]

fas price: the amount charged an importer, including such expenses as insurance, warehousing, trucking, and lighterage up to the loading tackle of a ship. Full risk of ownership remains with the seller up to the loading on a vessel.

fate (inquiry): an inquiry on the position of a bill of exchange to determine if it has been accepted, paid, and so on. short for *please advise fate.*

fat snake: slang, a monetary union to create a European fixed system. see *European Monetary System, European Monetary Union.*

favorable trade balance: when a nation's total value of exports is in excess of its total value of imports.

FB: see *bond, fidelity.*

FBA: see *Farm Bankruptcy Act of 1933.*

FC
(1) see *fixed capital.*
(2) see *fixed charges.*
(3) see *floating capital.*
(4) see *futures contract.*

FCA: see *Farm Credit Administration.*

FCBA: see *Fair Credit Billing Act.*

FCC: see *Federal Communications Commission.*

FCI: see *Federal Crime Insurance.*

FCPA: see *Foreign Corrupt Practices Act of 1977.*

FCRA: see *Fair Credit Reporting Act of 1971.*

Fcs.: see *franc.*

FCU: see *Federal Credit Union.*

Fd.
(1) see *fund.*
(2) see *funding.*

FDCPA: see *Fair Debt Collection Practices Act.*

Fdg.: see *funding.*

FDIC: see *Federal Deposit Insurance Corporation.*

FE
(1) see *foreign exchange.*
(2) see *futures exchange.*

FEA: see *Federal Energy Administration.*

feature
(1) **general:** the components of an item or service that yield a benefit.
(2) **investments:** the more active stocks in the general list.

FECOM: European Monetary Cooperation Fund.

Fed: slang, the Federal Reserve System.

Federal Advisory Council: a committee of the Federal Reserve System that advises the Board of Governors on major developments and activities.

Federal agency issues: interest-bearing obligations evidencing debt of the U.S. government agencies or departments. [105]

Federal Aviation Administration (FAA): in the U.S. Department of Transportation, the agency chartered "to provide for the regulation and promotion of civil aviation in such manner as to best foster its development and safety, and to provide for the safe and efficient use of the airspace by both civil and military aircraft." The FAA was established in 1959.

federal bonds: see *bond, federal.*

federal budget expenditures: in the unified budget concept, expenditures of all federal agencies and trust funds. Expenditures are distinguished from net lending, and total budget outlays are the sum of expenditures and net lending. Expenditures of public enterprise funds and trust revolving funds are shown net of the receipts of such funds.

federal budget receipts: in the unified budget concept, receipts, net of refunds, of all federal agencies and trust funds. Interfund and intragovernmental transactions are excluded. Proceeds of borrowing or receipts of public enterprise and revolving funds are not included.

Federal Communications Commission (FCC): established in 1934 to regulate interstate and foreign commerce in communications by both wire and radio activity. Jurisdiction now includes radio, television, wire, cable, microwave, and satellite. The FCC consults with other government agencies on matters involving radio communications and with state regulatory commissions on telegraph and telephone matters; it also reviews applications for construction permits and relevant licenses.

Federal Contract Compliance Office (OFCC): a unit of the U.S. Department of Labor, created in 1962; responsible for drawing up uniform sets of rules to guide the government agencies that enforce affirmative action programs. Prohibits discrimination by race or sex by employers holding federal contracts.

Federal Corrupt Practices Act: see *Hatch Act.*

Federal Credit Union: a cooperative association organized under the Federal Credit Union Act for the purpose of accepting savings from people, making loans to them at low interest rates, and rendering other financial services to members.

Federal Crime Insurance: insurance against burglary, larceny, and robbery losses offered by the federal government in which the Federal Insurance Administration has determined that such insurance is not readily available from commercial companies. This Department of Housing and Urban Development program began in 1971.

federal debt limit: a limit imposed by law on the aggregate face amount of outstanding obligations issued, or guaranteed as to principal and interest, by the United States; guaranteed obligations held by the secretary of the Treasury are exempted.

federal deficit: a public or federal debt; the difference that exists between revenue and government expenditures.

Federal Deposit Insurance Corporation (FDIC): a government corporation that insures the deposits of all banks that are entitled to the benefits of insurance under the Federal Reserve Act. The FDIC was created through the Banking Act of 1933 and was affected by amendments of 1935. All national banks and all state banks that are members of the Federal Reserve System are required by law to be members of the FDIC. Mutual savings bank are also encouraged to join.

Federal Deposit Insurance Corporation Assessment: the annual premium, equal to $1/12$ of 1 percent of deposits, which FDIC member banks pay for insurance coverage. [105]

federal discount rate: the interest rate charged on federal funds. The interest is charged on a discount basis and is a key factor in determining the prime rate charged for commercial loans. [105]

Federal Energy Administration (FEA): a federal agency launched in 1973 to develop and implement federal energy policy, including the allocation of resources. Absorbed in 1977 into the U.S. Department of Energy.

Federal Equal Credit Opportunity Act of 1977: legislation prohibiting discrimination when responding to credit requests on the basis of race, color, religion, national origin, sex, marital status, or age; because all or part of a person's income derives from any public assistance program; or because a person in good faith has exercised any right under the Truth in Lending Law. Gives married persons the right to have credit information included in the name of both the wife and the husband if both use or are responsible for the account. The right was created, in part, to ensure that credit histories will be available to women who are later divorced or widowed.

federal expenditures: federal purchases of goods and services, transfer payments, grants-in-aid to state and local governments, net interest paid, and subsidies, less current surplus of government enterprises.

Federal Farm Loan Act: established in 1916, this legislation was passed to provide long-term credit for farmers, to provide capital for agricultural development, to create standard forms of investment based upon farm loans, to furnish a market for U.S. bonds, to cre-

ate government depositaries and financial agents for the United States, and for other purposes.

Federal Financial Institutions Examination Council: see *Financial Institutions Regulatory and Interest Rate Control Act.*

federal funds: funds available at a Federal Reserve Bank, including excess reserves of member banks and checks drawn in payment for purchases by the Federal Reserve Bank of government securities.

federal funds payment/transfer: payment effected by check or wire transfer against a bank's account with a Federal Reserve Bank. [105]

federal funds purchased: short-term borrowing of reserves from another bank. [105]

federal funds rate: the interest rate charged on loans by banks that have excess reserve funds (above the level required by the Federal Reserve) to those banks with deficient reserves. The Fed funds rate is closely watched as an early warning indication of major changes in the national economy. see *legal reserve.* [33]

federal funds sold: temporary transfer of reserves to another bank. [105]

federal government securities: all obligations of the U.S. government. see *Treasury bill, Treasury note.*

Federal Home Bank: one of 11 regional banks established in 1932 to encourage local thrift and home financing during the Depression. The banks are owned jointly by various savings and loan associations. The Federal Home Loan Bank Board serves as a management body.

Federal Home Loan Bank System: a system established in 1932 to serve as a mortgage credit reserve system for home mortgage lending institutions. Members may obtain advances on home mortgage collateral and may borrow from home loan banks under certain conditions. [44]

Federal Home Loan Mortgage Corporation (FHLMC) (Freddie Mac): established in 1970, responsible for aiding the secondary residential mortgages sponsored by the Veterans Administration and Federal Housing Administration in addition to nongovernment protected residential mortgages.

Federal Housing Administration (FHA): the government agency that carries out the provisions of the National Housing Act, approved in June 1934. The FHA promotes the ownership of homes and also the renovation and remodeling of residences through government guaranteed loans to home owners.

Federal Housing Administration mortgage: a mortgage made in conformity with requirements of the National Housing Act and insured by the Federal Housing Administration. [22]

Federal Housing FHA Insured Loans: insured mortgages from private lending institutions to stimulate homeownership and rental opportunities to American families. Applicants who wish to participate in a single-family mortgage insurance program must apply to a HUD-approved mortgage lender, who then applies to HUD. Interest rates are set by the FHA on these loans. [66]

Federal Insurance Contributions Act (FICA): federal legislation that defines Social Security taxes and benefits. FICA deductions are made on paychecks to support this program. see *payroll tax.*

federal insurance reserve: a general loss reserve required to be established by a federal association under the rules and regulations of the Federal Savings and Loan Insurance Corporation. [59]

Federal Intermediate Credit Banks (FICB): regional banks created by Congress to provide intermediate credit for ranchers and farmers by rediscounting the agricultural paper of financial institutions.

federal internal revenue collections: total federal taxes collected through the Internal Revenue Service. These monies make up 99 percent of all federal taxes (customs and a few miscellaneous taxes are excluded). see *federal tax collections.*

Federal Labor Relations Authority: created on January 1, 1979, one of the major agencies to replace the Civil Service Commission, it is responsible for overseeing labor-management relations.

Federal Land Bank (FLB): supervised by the Farm Credit Association, one of 12 banks that offers long-term credit to farmers. Strictly speaking, the Land Banks are a competitor to thrifts. However, regulations limit their participation in housing loans to 15 percent of their total investments. Also, their money is limited to farmers and ranchers.

Federal Loan Bank: one of 12 district banks, originally established in 1916, to make available long-term mortgage loans, at equitable terms, to farmers to enable them to own their own farms. The Federal Loan Bank System is the largest holder of farm mortgages in the world.

Federal Maritime Commission: an agency created in 1936 to regulate foreign and domestic ocean commerce, mainly by overseeing agreements reached by a variety of rate-making conferences of ship carries.

Federal Mediation and Conciliation Service (FMCS): an independent agency created in 1947 as the successor to the U.S. Conciliation Service. Its functions include providing mediators for labor-management disputes in which interstate commerce is involved.

Federal National Mortgage Association (FNMA): an independent agency, originally chartered in 1938 and reconstituted in 1954. Its major function is to purchase mortgages from banks, trust companies, mortgage companies, savings and loan associations, and insurance companies to help these institutions with their distribution of funds for home mortgages. Nicknamed *Fannie Mae*.

Federal Open Market Committee (FOMC): the Federal Reserve System's most important policy-making group, with responsibility for creating policy for the system's purchase and sale of government and other securities in the open market.

Federal Power Commission (FPC): an agency established in 1930 to regulate interstate operations of private utilities in matters of their issuance of securities, rates, and location of sites. In 1977 the FPC was made part of the Department of Energy.

Federal Reserve Act: legislation signed by President Wilson on December 23, 1913, establishing the Federal Reserve System to manage the nation's money sypply.

Federal Reserve agent: chairman of the board of a Federal Reserve District Bank (a Class "C" director) who is responsible for maintaining the collateral for all Federal Reserve notes held within his bank.

Federal Reserve Bank: one of 12 banks created by and operating under the Federal Reserve System. Each Federal Reserve Bank has nine directors. The banks and districts are listed under *banker's bank.*

Federal Reserve Bank account: as mandated by Federal Reserve regulations, the account kept by all member banks and clearing member banks with a Federal Reserve Bank in its district. It shows the cash balance due from a Reserve Bank to guarantee that the member bank has sufficient legal reserves on hand.

Federal Reserve Bank collections account: shows the sum of monies for out-of-town checks distributed for collection by a Federal Reserve check collection system that are not presently available in reserve but being collected.

Federal Reserve bank float: Federal Reserve Bank credit on uncollected deposits.

Federal Reserve bank note: U.S. paper money released prior to 1935 by Federal Reserve Banks and secured by U.S. bonds and Treasury notes authorized to be used for that purpose. These notes have been retired from circulation.

Federal Reserve Board: the seven-member governing body of the Federal Reserve System; the governors are appointed by the President, subject to Senate confirmation, for 14-year terms. Created in 1913 to regulate all national banks and state-chartered banks that are members of the Federal Reserve System, the board possesses jurisdiction over bank holding companies and also sets national money and credit policy.

Federal Reserve branch banks: see *banker's bank.*

Federal Reserve Bulletin: a monthly journal issued by the Board of Governors of the Federal Reserve System dealing with issues in banking and finance.

Federal Reserve Chart Book: a monthly and semiannual publication of the Board of Governors of the Federal Reserve System, presenting charts of interest to the financial community.

Federal Reserve check collection system: the system, established in 1916, by which the Fed accepts out-of-town checks from the banks at which they were deposited or cashed, routes the checks to drawees, and credits the sending bank. It handles over 60 million checks each business day.

Federal Reserve cities: see *banker's bank.*

Federal Reserve credit: the sum of the Federal Reserve credit as measured by the supply that its banks have given to member bank reserves. It is composed primarily of earning assets of the Federal Reserve Banks.

Federal Reserve currency: paper money issued by the Federal Reserve Banks that circulates as a legal medium of exchange and is legal tender. [105]

Federal Reserve notes: when certain areas require large volumes of currency, or in seasons of the year when the public demand for currency is very heavy, Federal Reserve Banks have the power under the Federal Reserve Act to issue notes. When the need for currency relaxes, Federal Reserve Banks retire these notes. Federal Reserve notes are issued to member banks through their respective Federal Reserve Banks in denominations of $1, $5, $10, $20, $50, $100, $500, $1000, $5000, and $10,000. Federal Reserve notes answer the need for an elastic currency with full legal tender status.

Federal Reserve notes of other banks: the total amount of Federal Reserve notes held by Reserve Banks other than the Reserve Bank that issued them. [40]

Federal Reserve Open Market Committee: a committee of the Federal Reserve System that has complete charge of open market operations, through which the Fed influences the growth of the nation's money supply. It includes the members of the Board of Governors of the Federal Reserve System and five representatives of the 12 Federal Reserve Banks. [33]

Federal Reserve requirements: the amount of money that member banks of the Federal Reserve system must hold in cash or on deposit with a Federal Reserve Bank, in order to back up their outstanding loans. The requirement is expressed as a percentage of outstanding loan volume. [105]

Federal Reserve routing symbol: see *American Bankers Association.*

Federal Reserve System: the title given to the central banking system of the United States as established by the Federal Reserve Act of 1913. The system regulates money supply, determines the legal reserve of member banks; oversees the mint, effects transfers of funds, promotes and facilitates the clearance and collection of checks, examines member banks, and discharges other functions. The Federal Reserve System consists of 12 Federal Reserve Banks, their 24 branches, and the national and state banks that are members of the system. All national banks are stockholding members of the Federal Reserve Bank of their district. Membership for state banks or trust companies is optional. see *Federal Reserve Board.* see also *banker's bank.* [31]

Federal Reserve Wire Network: see *Fedwire.*

Federals: items drawn on banks in a large city in which a Federal Reserve Bank is located, although the banks do not belong to the city's clearinghouse association.

Federal Savings and Loan Association: one of the associations established by the Home Owners' Loan Act of 1933, and amended in the Home Owners' Loan Act of 1934, which brought existing and newly formed mutual savings banks and building and loan associations under a federal charter. see *Federal Savings and Loan Insurance Corporation.*

Federal Savings and Loan Insurance Corporation (FSLIC): an organization created in 1934 for the purpose of insuring the shares and accounts of all federal savings and loan associations and of such state-chartered savings and loan associations as apply for insurance and meet the requirements of the corporation. [39]

Federal Savings Association: a savings association chartered and regulated by the Federal Home Loan Bank Board. [59]

federal tax collections: all internal revenue collections, plus customs collections and railroad unemployment insurance taxes collected by the Railroad Retirement Board, before refunds.

Federal Tort Claims Act of 1946: permits the United States to be sued for property or personal damages under circumstances such that if the federal government were an individual, it would be liable. Before passage of this act, the government could be sued only with its permission.

Federal Trade Commission (FTC): established in 1914; the enabling legislation also declared unfair methods of competition illegal. Amended by the Wheeler-Lea Act of 1930; enforces antitrust laws; seeks voluntary compliance or civil remedies. see *Equal Credit Opportunity Act.*

federal trust funds: see *trust funds, federal.*

Federal Wage-Hour Act: see *Fair Labor Standards Act of 1938.*

fed funds: see *federal funds.*

Fed Funds Bill: see *Cash Management Bill.*

fed funds rate: the rate of interest payable on federal funds; considered the key short-term interest rate because it indicates the intentions of the government. [90]

Fed intervention hour: the period when the Fed typically enters the market to conduct its various open market operations, usually shortly before noon Eastern time.

Fed open-market operations: the Fed increases the supply of bank reserves by buying U.S. government securities, and reduces reserves by selling them. Temporary reserve injections are made through repurchase agreements

(RPs), while temporary draining is accomplished through matched sale-purchase agreements (reverse RPs). Traders and analysts analyze these operations to determine whether the Fed is making reserves more or less plentiful, resulting in lower or higher interest rates.

Fedwire: a communications network linking Federal Reserve Banks, branches, and member banks; used both to transfer funds and to transmit information. cf. *Bank Wire System.*

fee
(1) *banking:* an inheritable estate in land. cf. *fee simple estate, freehold.*
(2) *finance:* a remuneration for services.

fee checking account: a type of checking account on which a fixed fee is charged for each check written or item deposited. This distinguishes it from the regular checking account plan, which sometimes requires a minimum balance and the service charge is computed on a measured activity analysis of the account. The fixed fee may be charged before any checks are written, in which case the book of blank checks is sold to the depositor. The fixed fee may be charged at the time the checks or deposits are posted to the account, in which case the bookkeeper posts the service charge immediately after posting the check or deposit to the account. [10]

fees and royalties from direct investments: reported by companies with direct investments abroad. They represent income received by U.S. parent companies from their foreign affiliates for patent royalties, licensing fees, rentals, management services, other home office charges, and research and development. [73]

fee simple estate: an absolute fee; an estate of inheritance without limitation. This form of estate is not qualified by any other interest and upon the owner's death passes unconditionally to the heirs.

fee tail: an estate limited to a person and the heirs of his or her body; fee tail male if male heirs, fee tail female if female heirs. In most states, estates in fee tail have been abolished, generally by converting them into fee simple estates. [105]

FEIA: see *Foreign Earned Income Act of 1978.*

felony: any major crime (e.g., murder, arson, rape) punishable by a greater penalty than for a misdemeanor or minor offense. In many states of the United States, felony is defined by statute as crimes punishable by imprisonment or death. see also *misdemeanor, tort.*

feoffment
(1) *general:* the granting of a fee.
(2) *banking:* the granting of land by the act of taking possession. see *enfeoff.*

FEPC: see *Civil Rights Act of 1964, Title VII.*

feverish market: a condition of a stock or commodity market where prices change rapidly and no direction is easily identified.

FF.&C.: see *full faith and credit.*

FFLA: see *Federal Farm Loan Act.*

FHA: see *Federal Housing Administration.*

FHB: see *Federal Home Bank.*

FHLBS: see *Federal Home Loan Bank System.*

FHLMC: see *Federal Home Loan Mortgage Corporation.*

FI: see *foreign investment.*

fiat money: money circulated by government decree and having no precious metal backing. see *gold exchange standard;* cf. *full-bodied money, real money.*

fiat standard: see *managed money.*

FICA: see *Federal Insurance Contributions Act.*

FICB: see *Federal Intermediate Credit Banks.*

fictitious paper (spooks): fraudulent action on the part of a dealer whereby forged contracts in the names of mythical persons are sold to a bank. [105]

fictitious registration: a document issued by a country or state official to identify the exact ownership of a business, where the name of the business does not do so. [105]

Fid.: see *fiduciary.*

fidelity bond: see *bond, fidelity.*

fidelity insurance: coverage against loss from embezzlement or theft by employees.

fiduciary: an individual, corporation, or association, such as a bank, to whom certain property is given to hold in trust, according to an applicable trust agreement. The property is to be utilized or invested for the benefit of the property owner to the best ability of the fiduciary. Administrators and executors of estates, and trustees of organizations, are common examples of fiduciaries. Investments of trust funds, are usually restricted by law.

fiduciary accounting

(1) *general:* maintaining property accounts in the hands of a trustee, executor, or administrator.

(2) *banking:* estate accounting.

fiduciary bond: see *bond, fiduciary.*

fiduciary loan: an unsecured loan.

fiduciary money (or standard): currency not secured completely by any precious metal. synonymous with *credit money.*

fiduciary return: an income tax return prepared by a fiduciary on behalf of a trust or estate. [37]

fiduciary service: a service performed by an individual or corporation acting in a trust capacity. A banking institution authorized to do a trust business may perform fiduciary services, for example, by acting as executor or administrator of estates, guardian of minors, and trustee under wills. [50]

fiduciary standard

(1) a monetary system in which the monetary unit is defined in terms of paper money.

(2) a monetary system based on a precious metal and the coinage thereof, where the face value of the coins is very little more than a substance on which to stamp an arbitrary value.

field warehousing: an approach for receiving collateral pledged in business loans. The warehouseman usually leases part of the borrower's facility and appoints a custodian to care for the items.

field warehousing loan: a loan made on inventories held in field warehouses established on the premises of the borrower.

fieri facias: "that you cause it to be made" (Latin). A court order directing the sheriff to impose a tax on goods or personal property of the defendant, to satisfy the judgment of a plaintiff.

FIFO (first in, first out)

(1) *general:* relates to inventory

FIGURE   292

valuations, and the balance sheet figures for inventory should be qualified accordingly. This simply means that the cost shown for the first shipment of a particular item is used for valuations. This could inflate or deflate profits.

(2) *finance:* a method of computing dividends or interest and the effect withdrawals have on earnings for the period. The FIFO method is considered to be using the oldest money on deposit for withdrawals during the interest period. It was originally designed to discourage withdrawals by exacting the maximum penalty.

(3) see *LIFO.*

figure: slang, meaning "00" and denoting an exchange-rate level.

file

(1) *general:* any collection of informational items similar to one another in purpose.

(2) *law:* to place a legal document on public record.

filing: giving public notice of a lender's assignment of collateral. The information is recorded with the appropriate governmental authority by presenting applicable documentation. [105]

filing fee: a charge made for the recording or official notation of documents required for evidencing a security interest or lien. [105]

fill

(1) *general:* to complete an order for goods or services.

(2) *investments:* to satisfy the demand for a security at a specific time by selling an amount equivalent to the quantity of shares bid for at the highest quoted price. see *hit the bid.*

fill order: an order that must be filled immediately (or cancelled).

fin.: see *finance.*

final expenses funds: synonymous with *clean-up fund.*

final sales: the total of net sales to consumers, governments, and foreigners. Final sales exclude sales made to producers except sales of durable plant and machinery.

final underwriting account: a complete and final list of participating underwriters drawn from written responses to underwriting invitations extended by a syndicate managers and listed alphabetically within each bracket.

finance

(1) *general:* to raise money by sale of stock, bonds, or notes.

(2) *finance:* describes the theory and practice of monetary credit, banking, and comprehensive promotion methods. This theory covers investment, speculation, credits, and securities.

(3) *government:* to raise money by taxation or bond issue, and to administer revenue and expenditures in a governmental organization. More recently, this activity has become known as *public finance.*

finance and control: planning, directing, and measuring the result of a firm's monetary activities.

finance bill: any draft drawn by one bank on a foreign bank against securities retained by the overseas institution.

finance capitalism: the period in the United States from about 1865 to 1929 when industrial empires came into the possession of few bankers and investors.

finance charge: the cost of a loan in dollars and cents as required by the

Truth in Lending Act. see *Truth in Lending Act of 1968.* [78]

finance company: any institution other than a bank that makes loans to businesses or individuals. see *sales finance company.*

finance lease: a lease transaction for a lessor's service is a financial one where the lessee assumes responsibilities, such as maintenance, taxes, insurance, and so on, related to the possession of the equipment. Finance leases are usually full-payout agreements.

finance unit: a nondelivery postal branch or station for financial services and acceptance of mail. [39]

financial accounting: recording and interpreting revenues, expenses, assets, and liabilities of a company. [105]

Financial Accounting Standards Board (FASB): an independent accounting organization formed in 1973, responsible for creating "generally accepted accounting principles." FASB is a self-regulatory organization whose impact is on accounting firms and practitioners.

Financial Accounting Standards No. 8: see *FASB8.*

financial break-even point: assuming a plant organized for a given output, if units of output are put on one axis and total dollars on the other axis, the financial break-even point is the intersection of the total cash revenue curve and the total cash outlay curve, including interest and dividends.

Financial Center Development Act of 1981: legislation of the State of Delaware, the act has provisions designed to alter the state's banking and tax codes in order to convince out-of-state banks to establish subsidiaries in Dela-

ware. The tax provision, replacing a flat 8.7 percent franchise tax on banks, calls for a regressive income tax on banks starting at 8.7 percent and declining to 2.7 percent for all income over $30 million. The bill also includes an elimination of interest rate ceilings on all consumer transactions; permission for banks to charge customers additional expenses, such as cash withdrawal fees and transaction fees, on top of interest costs; permission for a lender to foreclose on a borrower's home in the event of default, and an allowance for a retroactive raise in interest rates on credit card transactions.

financial counseling: expert advice given to a family with respect to money and credit management. [55]

financial expense: the interest expense on long-term debts.

financial flexibility: the ability of an enterprise to take effective actions to alter the amount and timing of future cash flows so that it can respond to unexpected needs and opportunities. [80]

financial guaranty: a bond the insurer guarantees that it will pay a fixed or determinable sum of money.

financial institution: an institution that uses its funds chiefly to purchase financial assets (deposits, loans, bonds) as opposed to tangible property. Financial institutions can be classified according to the nature of the principal claims they issue: nondeposit intermediaries include, among others, life and property/casualty insurance companies and pension funds, whose claims are the policies they sell, or the promise to provide income after retirement; depositary intermediaries obtain funds mainly by accepting deposits from the public.

financial insolvency: a situation created when a company is unable to pay its debts as they mature even though its assets may exceed the liabilities.

Financial Institutions Regulatory and Interest Rate Control Act: federal legislation of 1978; modified authority to invest in state housing corporation obligations; increased Federal Savings and Loan Insurance Corporation insurance limits for IRA and Keogh accounts from $40,000 to $100,000; permitted FSLIC to issue cease-and-desist orders against associations, directors, officers, employees, and agents; authorized cease-and-desist orders against associations, holding companies, their subsidiaries, and service corporations; expanded criteria for removal of a director interlocks among depository institutions; created interagency Federal Bank Examination Council to encourage uniformity in financial institutions supervision; authorized Federal Home Loan Mortgage Corporation purchase of secured home improvement loan packages; amended Consumer Credit Protection Act establishing rights and responsibilities for electronic funds transfer; established procedural safeguards for dissemination of financial institution records to federal agencies; extended Regulation Q authority for rate control and rate differential until December 15, 1980. [51]

financial instrument: any written instrument having monetary value or evidencing a monetary transaction. [105]

financial intermediaries: organizations operating in money markets that permit buyers and sellers, borrowers, and lenders, to meet easily. see *financier.*

financial investment: purchasing sound stocks or bonds as contrasted to real investment in a capital asset such as real estate or plant equipment.

financial lease: long-term, noncancelable lease.

financial leverage: the ability of fixed-charge financing to magnify the effects of profits (losses) on earnings per share.

financial management
(1) the function of making sure that funds are available in adequate amounts when needed.
(2) the function of raising and providing funds for capital purchases as well as for operating expenses. [105]

financial markets: the money and capital markets of the economy. The money markets buy and sell short-term credit instruments. The capital markets buy and sell long-term credit and equity instruments.

financial paper: accommodation paper, that is, a short-term loan not supported by a specific commercial transaction or transfer of goods. cf. *commercial paper, commodity paper.*

financial plan: the pattern of stocks and bonds issued at the time the corporation is organized, or after failure when it is reorganized.

financial position: the status of a company, combining the assets and liabilities as listed on a balance sheet.

financial ratios: the relationship that exist between various items appearing in balance sheets and income accounts and occasionally other items. These ratios are used to measure and evaluate the economic condition and operating effectiveness of a firm.

financial reports: reports of union financial affairs required to be filed with the U.S. Secretary of Labor by the Taft-Hartley Act. [5].

financial risk: in investments, used in contradistinction to interest rate risk and purchasing power risk to refer to the risk of default in performing the obligations of a security.

financial service terminal: an electronic device used in conducting activity for an EFT system. Such a device may be an ATM, POS terminal, or similar devices. The terminal accepts, through automatic or manual input, specific electronic instructions which it transmits to the authorizing data processor for proper response to the customer at the terminal. [105]

financial solvency: a normal business condition: current assets are above current liabilities. cf. *insolvency.*

financial statement: any statement made by an individual, a proprietorship, a partnership, a corporation, an organization, or an association, regarding the financial status of the "legal entity."

financial structure: mix of the firm's total financing sources, both long and short term.

Financial Times (of London): considered by professionals as one of the best English-language newspapers for business and financial news.

financial uncertainty: the probability of financial changes occurring in the company issuing a specific security. [105]

financier: an individual who earns a living by supplying money for other people's businesses and in turn receives a cash profit or retains a percentage of the business. see *financial intermediaries.*

financing: involves the purchase of or advance of funds against paper arising from installment sales by a dealer. [105]

financing statement: the statement, filed by a creditor, giving a record of a security interest or lien on the debtor's assets. [105]

finder's fee
(1) *general:* payment given to an individual for bringing together a buyer and seller.
(2) *banking:* payment to someone for acquiring a potential buyer with a property. A fee is usually paid when the seller and the buyer conclude an arrangement.

fine
(1) a penalty charged a violator by a government, court, or other authority for breaking a law or rule.
(2) a relatively low interest rate or margin, as when a loan is made at the finest rate.
(3) the purity of precious metals.

fine metal: the degree of purity of precious metals.

fineness: the degree of purity when speaking of gold or silver coin. United States coin was formerly nine-tenths fine or pure and one-tenth alloy.

fine tuning: the manipulation of discretionary monetary and fiscal policy to offset changes in the level of economic activity.

fireworks: slang, the rapid climb in price for a security or group of securities.

firm
(1) *general:* the acceptance of an obligation to perform, deliver, or accept, as "a firm bid," "a firm offer."

(2) *finance:* any business, corporation, proprietorship, or partnership.

(3) *law:* an unincorporated business or a partnership. Unlike a corporation, a firm is not recognized as a separate person apart from those managing it (i.e., it is not an entity).

firm bid (or offer): in over-the-counter markets a number of bids are nominal or informational and can vary with the order size. To guarantee that the bid or offer quoted is for a given size transaction, the inquirer requests a firm quotation that is binding upon acceptance, as distinguished from the informational quotation.

firm commitment

(1) for loans, a lender's agreement to make a loan to a specific borrower on a specific property within a given time period. In the secondary market, a buyer's agreement to purchase loans under specified terms.

(2) FHA or MIC agreement to insure a loan on a specific property with a designated borrower. [105]

firming of interest rate: a period during which interest rates are rising and the supply of money tends to become less plentiful. [67]

firming of the market: a period when security prices tend to stabilize around a certain level after a downward movement. [67]

firm order: a definite order than cannot be canceled. It may be written or verbal.

firm price: an obligation to the maker of a state price that must be met if accepted within a specified time period.

first board: the delivery dates for futures as determined by the administration of an exchange.

first deed of trust: a deed of trust that is recorded first and is the first lien.

first-generation computer: a computer utilizing vacuum tube components. This equipment was predominantly made from 1953 to 1960.

first in, first out: see *FIFO.*

first lien: a first mortgage. cf. *equal dignity.*

first mortgage: the mortgage on property that takes precedence over all other mortgages. A first lien. see also *prior lien, underlying mortgage.*

first notice day: first day on which transferable notices can be issued for delivery in a specified delivery month. [11]

first preferred stock: dividend stocks that are preferred over common stock of the corporation. It ranks ahead of the second preferred issue.

firsts: the top grade of any item.

first teller: the paying teller in a bank.

first-use notice: the announcement sent to a cardholder when a debit transaction is posted to an account for the first time. The purpose of this notice is to thank the cardholder for using his or her account and to act as a security measure if the bank card was never received by the cardholder of record. [105]

fiscal: relating to financial matters.

fiscal agency services: services performed by the Federal Reserve Banks for the U.S. government. These include maintaining accounts for the Treasury Department, paying checks drawn on the Treasury, and selling and redeeming Savings Bonds and other government securities. [1]

fiscal agent: a bank or trust company acting under a corporate trust agreement with a corporation. The bank or trust company may be appointed in the capacity of general treasurer of the corporation, or may be appointed to perform special functions as fiscal agent. The principal duties of a fiscal agent include the disbursement of funds for payment of dividends, redemption of bonds and coupons at maturity, and the payment of rents. [10]

fiscal charges: expenses or charges that are normal for a given type of business and must be incurred in order to engage in a given type of business.

fiscal dividend: the increase in federal revenues resulting from an increase in gross national product at any given level of tax rates.

fiscal drag: the tendency of a high-employment economy to be restrained from its full growth potential because it is incurring budgetary surpluses.

fiscalists: believers who insist that fiscal policy is the primary means for altering the level of economic activity by the government.

fiscal monopoly: monopolization by a government of the manufacture and sale of certain commodities in general use for the purpose of getting revenue for the Treasury.

fiscal period: A 12-month accounting period for which business activities are reported.

fiscal policy: a planned course of action on budgetary issues.

fiscal year (FY)

(1) *general:* a corporation's accounting year. It can be any 12 consecutive months (e.g., February 1 of one year through January 31 of the next). Most companies operate on a calendar year basis.

(2) *government:* the fiscal year of the U.S. government begins October 1.

Before 1976 the government's FY began on July 1.

Fisher equation: in monetary theory, the Fisher equation is $PT = MV$, where P is the general price level, T the total volume of transactions, V the transactions velocity of money, and M the quantity of money.

"five and five" power: a noncumulative general power of the donee to appoint in each calendar year the greater of $5,000 or 5 percent of the value of the trust at the end of the year. [105]

five-case note: slang, a $5 bill.

five Cs of credit: a method of evaluating credit-worthiness, including character, capacity, capital, collateral, and conditions. [105]

five percenter: persons who, for a fee of 5 percent or higher, use their alleged connections with public officials to secure federal government contracts for business clientele.

five percent redemption fund: the amount of funds retained by all Federal Reserve Banks held on deposit with the U.S. Treasury.

five-spot: slang, a $5 bill.

fix: setting the cost of an item or service. cf. *price fixing.*

fixation: the setting of a price in the future, as used in commodity call purchase and call sale trades.

fixed annuity: an annuity contract providing payments that remain constant throughout the annuity period. These payments do not vary with investment experience.

fixed assets: permanent assets required for the normal conduct of a business, which normally are not converted into cash during the period after they were declared fixed (e.g., furniture, land, buildings). see *illiquid.*

fixed-balance bonus account: a savings account that pays earnings above the passbook rate if the balance in the account exceeds a specified minimum for a specified term. [59]

fixed budget: a corporation's budget, set for a specific time period in advance that is not subject to change during the budgetary period.

fixed capital: capital invested, usually by stock-and bondholders; as distinguished from current assets, which are partly supplied by banks.

fixed charges: business expenses that are not related to the level of operations.

fixed cost (or expense): a cost or expense, for a fixed period and a range of activity, that does not change in total but becomes progressively smaller per unit as the volume increases. synonymous with *period cost*; see also *capacity costs*; cf. *direct cost*.

fixed credit line: synonymous with *irrevocable credit.*

fixed debt: the permanent debt extending over a length of time, such as that represented by bonds.

fixed exchange rate: a concept within the European Monetary System, where all members except Britain maintain fixed exchange rates between their currencies, promoting monetary stability in Europe and throughout the world. see also *European Monetary System.*

fixed income: income that does not fluctuate with the general price level. People on fixed income have the most difficulty when prices are rising (e.g., retired pensioners in a period of inflation).

fixed-income market: any debt-bearing instrument, among them U.S. Government bonds, tax-exempt bonds, corporate bonds, financial futures, and money market funds.

fixed income security: a preferred stock or debt security with a given percentage or dollar income return.

fixed insurance annuities: variable premiums pay either a lump sum or a guaranteed minimum monthly income at retirement. Yield varies. First-year guarantee for each annual contribution is usually competitive with bank certificates of deposit. Reinvested funds in account tend to earn somewhat less.

fixed investment: measures additions to and replacements of private capital brought about through purchase of durable equipment and structures for business and residential purposes. Fixed investment expenditures are reflected in GNP in two ways. First, capital investment increases GNP by the value of the asset in the period in which the investment is made. Second, the effects of previous years' fixed investments show in the products produced with the help of the capital. These products are of all types: consumer goods, additional capital goods, exports, and government purchases. [73]

fixed investment trust: an investment company created as a nondiscretionary trust and is limited to an agreed-upon list of securities.

fixed liabilities: all liabilities that will not mature within the ensuing fiscal period (e.g. mortgages due 20 years hence, bonds outstanding).

fixed obligation: an obligation that is fixed at the time the agreement is made and continues to run during the life of the agreement (e.g., interest on bonds except income or adjustment bonds).

fixed price: the lowest sale price of a new issue, below which a purchase cannot be made. This price is usually set by the underwriter of the security.

fixed-price contract: the agreement whereby a buyer pays a seller or producer a stipulated amount.

fixed rate: see *fixed exchange rate.*

fixed-rate mortgage: a home mortgage with a fixed interest rate, usually long term; there are equal monthly payments of principal and interest until the debt is paid in full.

fixed register asset: a record (book, card, or sheet) that contains the details of the cost price and the depreciation of the fixed assets. [73]

fixed test asset: the ratio of fixed assets to fixed liabilities.

fixed-to-tangible-net-worth asset: fixed assets represent depreciated book values of buildings, leasehold improvements, machinery, furniture, fixtures, tools, and other physical equipment, plus land, if any, and valued at cost or appraised market value. The ratio is obtained by dividing fixed assets by tangible net worth. Ordinarily, the relationship between fixed assets and tangible net worth should not exceed 100 percent for a manufacturer, and 75 percent for a wholesaler or retailer. Beyond these limits, so disproportionate an amount of capital is frozen into machinery or "brick and mortar" that the necessary margin of operating funds for carrying receivables, inventories, and day-to-day cash outlays, as well as maturing obligations, becomes too narrow. This not only exposes the business to the hazards of unexpected developments, such as a sudden change in the business climate, but creates possible drains on income in

the form of heavy carrying and maintenance charges should a serious portion of fixed assets lie idle for any length of time. [61]

fixed trust: an organization created by a trust indenture between investors and a trustee for the purpose of the joint investment of trade. [105]

fixing the price

(1) *finance:* establishing a price on something arbitrarily rather than through the free enterprise system.

(2) *investments:* computing the price at which a commodity will be billed for rapid delivery. see *spot market.*

fixture

(1) *general:* any equipment or furnishing (e.g., lamps, shelves) added to rented space for purposes of aiding in business acitivity.

(2) *law:* any chattle or personal property that is attached to real property in a permanent fashion.

flagging an account: temporarily suspending activity on an account until brought up to date or for other relevant reason. see *rubricated account.*

flag of convenience: the national flag flown by a ship that is registered in a country other than that of its owners (e.g., to escape taxes and high domestic wages).

flash estimate: the Commerce Department's earliest estimate of the gross national product.

flash prices: a technique used whenever an exchange ticker tape runs late. The latest prices of two groups of 50 stocks are printed at 5-minute intervals.

flat

(1) *finance:* with no interest.

(2) *investments:* describes the price

at which a bond is traded, including consideration for all unpaid accruals of interest. Bonds that are in default of interest or principal are traded flat. Income bonds, which pay interest only to the extent earned, are usually traded flat. cf. *loaned flat.*

flatbed imprinter: a device that leaves an image of embossed characters from a credit card on all copies of a sales draft form set as a result of a manual horizontal movement of the imprinter head. [105]

flat broke: slang, penniless.

flat cancellation: the cancellation of a policy as of what would have been its effective date, before the company has assumed liability. This requires the return in full of any paid premiums. cf. *pro rate cancellation.*

flat income bond: see *bond, flat income.*

flation: neither inflation or deflation; a period of economic stability. cf. *creeping inflation.*

flat lease: synonymous with *straight lease.*

flat rate: in public utilities, a flat rate requires each customer to pay a fixed sum per period without regard to use.

flat (rate) yield: see *interest yield.*

FLB

(1) see *Federal Land Bank.*

(2) see *Federal Loan Bank.*

fleece: slang, to take money or property from an unknowing person (the "sheep") by unfair activity. synonymous with *swindle.*

fleet policies: marine insurance policies covering all or many of the ships operating under one ownership/management.

Fletcher-Rayburn Act: see *SEC.*

flexible account: see *charge account.*

flexible budget: a budget, usually referring to overhead costs, that is established for a range rather than for a single level of activity. Direct materials and labor are sometimes included in the flexible budget.

flexible exchange rates: where exchange rates of varying world currencies freely change in reaction to supply and demand conditions, free from governmental maneuvers to hold a fixed rate where one currency is exchanged for another.

flexible loan insurance plan: a new type of mortgage, this device calls for using a portion of the borrower's down payment to set up a savings account. The account is then pledged over to the lender and gradually drawn upon to supplement the low monthly payments made by the borrower during the initial years of the loan. Popularly referred to as *flip.* An example of a *pledged-account mortgage.*

flexible mortgage: there are two types. see *renegotiable-rate mortgage* and *variable-rate mortgage.*

flexible-payment mortgage: an interest-only type of loan for the first five years. Two major restrictions apply: each monthly payment must cover at least the interest due, and after five years, payments must be fully amortizing. A rarely used mortgage because it offers the home buyer only a slight reduction in monthly payments during the early years. see also *graduated-payment mortgage, pledged-account mortgage, reverse-annuity mortgage, rollover mortgage, variable-rate mortgage.*

flexible reimbursement plan: where an employer creates a pool, usually several hundred dollars, for each employee to draw on for health needs. In case of illness, the employee may draw money from his or her pool to pay the first charges on medical bills, called the deductible, before the company-paid health insurance assumes the burden. If any of the money is not used, it becomes the employee's. synonymous with *health expense account.*

flexible-spending accounts: see *cafeteria plan, zebra plan.*

flexible tariff: a tariff permitting administrative officials to use discretion in altering tariff rates to deal with emergency conditions disturbing competitive conditions between nations, particularly where the conditions give rise to dumping.

flier: a speculative purchase of investment, usually made by an individual who does not usually speculate or actively trade in the market.

flight of capital: the movement of capital, which has usually been converted into a liquid asset, from one place to another to avoid loss or to increase gain. see also *flight of the dollar.*

flight of the dollar: purchasing foreign securities with dollar exchange, to escape the adverse impact of inflation, deflation, or other economic condition.

flip: acronym for *flexible loan insurance plan.*

flip mortgage: a graduate-payment scheme offered in some states.

flipping: the practice of refinancing a consumer's retail installment contract in the form of a cash loan so that an interest rate higher than the 19.2 percent ceiling can be charged.

float

(1) *banking:* the amount of funds in the process of collection represented by checks in the possession of one bank but drawn on other banks, either local or out of town. see *uncollected funds.*

(2) *investments:* the portion of a new security that has not yet been bought by the public. cf. *undigested securities.*

floatation (flotation)

(1) *finance:* the process of financing a business activity.

(2) *investments:* launching an issue of securities. see *float.*

floater: see *floating-rate CD* or *floating-rate note.*

floating assets: synonymous with *current assets.*

floating capital: funds that are not a permanent investment, (i.e., invested in items manufactured). synonymous with *working capital.*

floating charge: a business loan that is secured on assets rather than on a particular item. The lender has priority of repayment from the fund of assets that exist when a receiving order is made against the firm.

floating currency: one whose value in terms of foreign currency is not kept stable (on the basis of the par value or a fixed relationship to some other currency) but instead is allowed, without a multiplicity of exchange rates, to be determined (entirely or to some degree) by market forces. Even where a currency is floating, the authorities may influence its movements by official intervention; if such intervention is absent or minor, the expression *clean float* is sometimes used. [42]

floating debt: any short-term obligation; usually, the portion of the public debt held in Treasury bills or other short-term obligations.

floating exchange rate: fluctuation in

the rate of exchange of a nation's currency when its value is no longer fixed in terms of gold or another national currency.

floating policies: marine insurance policies issued for a lump sum insured sufficient to cover all voyages expected by the insured over a period.

floating-rate bond: see *bond, floating-rate.*

floating-rate CD (FRCD): a certificate of deposit whose coupon is variable and normally linked to the interbank money market rate. [105]

floating-rate note (FRN): used by banks to raise dollars for their Euromarket operations, a mixture of the rollover credit market with the Eurosecurities market. [102]

floating rates: the automatic determination of appropriate exchange rates by market forces, not a nation's reserve holdings. Nations that do not follow these rates are pressured into line; otherwise, they would see the value of their currency driven to unacceptably low levels or driven up to the point where no other nation would be able to purchase their goods.

floating securities
(1) securities purchased for speculation and resale, retained in the name of a broker.
(2) stock of a corporation ready for sale on the open market.
(3) new issues of securities that have not been completely purchased.

floating supply: in municipal bond terminology, the overall amount of securities believed to be available for immediate purchase, in the hands of dealers and speculators who wish to sell as distinct from investors who may

be willing to sell only for a special reason. [67]

float ledger: synonymous with *collection ledger.*

float one: slang, to cash a check or take a loan.

floor
(1) *government:* the minimum level determined by regulation, law or contract for wages, prices, and so on.
(2) *investments:* the huge trading area where stocks and bonds are bought and sold on an exchange. see also *pit.*

floor broker: a member of a stock exchange who executes orders on the floor of the exchange to buy or sell listed securities.

floor limit: the largest amount for which a merchant may accept noncash payment (check or credit card) without obtaining an authorization. A zero floor limit calls for authorization for every transaction, and this is becoming more feasible as the time and cost of obtaining authorization decline.

floor partner: a member of a stock exchange and a brokerage firm partner who transacts his or her firm's business on the floor of that exchange.

floor-plan insurance: insurance of a dealer's floored inventory to protect a bank's equity in the inventory. [105]

floor planning: any method such as a trust receipt by which the borrower keeps possession of goods that are pledged as security for a loan.

floor report: confirmation of an executed order on an exchange trading floor, such as price, number of shares, and the name of the security.

floor trader: any member of the stock exchange who trades on the floor for his own account. An exchange member who executes his own trades by being personally present in the pit or place provided for futures trading. [20]

flotation: see *floatation.*

flowchart

(1) **general:** a graphical representation of the definition, analysis, or solution of a problem, in which symbols are used to represent operations, data, flow, equipment, and other variables.

(2) **operations research:** a system analysis tool that displays a picture of a procedure. May be general or detailed. see *methods study.*

flower bond: see *bond, flower.*

flow-through method: an accounting method under which decreases or increases in state or federal income taxes resulting from the use of liberalized depreciation and the investment tax credit for income tax purposes are carried down to net income in the year in which they are realized. [3]

FLRA: see *Federal Labor Relations Authority.*

FLSA: see *Fair Labor Standards Act of 1938.*

fluctuation: the ups and downs of prices (see, e.g., *erratic fluctuations*). see *hedging, yo-yo stocks.*

fluctuation harnessing: applied to the investment formula known as dollar cost averaging because a constant dollar amount is invested at regular intervals, regardless of price.

fluid capital: see *floating capital, working capital.*

fluid savings: savings that have neither been spent nor invested.

flurries: unexpected, short-lived price fluctuations in the trading of securities, usually brought on by news.

fly-by-night activity: figuratively, an unsound operation; literally, one that is expected to move under cover of darkness to avoid payment to creditors.

FMAN: February, May, August, November (quarterly interest payments or dividends).

FMC: see *Federal Maritime Commission.*

FMCS: see *Federal Mediation and Conciliation Service.*

FmHA: see *Farmers Home Administration.*

FmHA guaranteed loan: a loan made by a bank and guaranteed by FmHA against loss due to default by the borrower. [105]

FmHA insured loan: a loan made directly by FmHA to a borrower. FmHA also services this type of loan. [105]

FMV: see *fair market value.*

FNMA: see *Federal National Mortgage Association.*

FOB: freight (free) on board: a term identifying the point from which a store is to pay transportation on incoming shipments. When the shipping point is FOB, the store must pay all charges from the vendor's shipping point. When the shipping point is FOB store, the vendor must pay all charges up to the store's receiving dock. cf. *free alongside ship.*

FOIA: see *Freedom of Information Act.*

fold: slang, to go into bankruptcy.

folding money: slang, paper banknotes.

FOMC: see *Federal Open Market Committee.*

FOR: see *farmer-owned reserve.*

for a turn: a commitment in a stock made with the expectation of gaining a quick, though small profit.

forbearance: surrendering the right to enforce a valid claim in return for a promise. This consideration binds a promise.

forbearance agreement: a verbal or written agreement providing that the association will delay exercising its rights (in the case of a mortgage loan, foreclosure) as long as the borrower performs certain agreed-upon actions. [59]

for cash

(1) *general:* items or services sold for 100 percent of funds.

(2) *investments:* a transaction demanding that sold stocks be delivered to the purchaser on the same day.

force account: a method employed in the construction and/or maintenance of fixed assets whereby a governmental unit's own personnel are used instead of an outside contractor. [49]

forced billing: a means used to secure payments for freight delivery when no bill can be found.

forced loan: any draft drawn against uncollected funds that is honored by a bank with the expectation that the uncollected monies will clear, becoming a forced loan should the uncollected funds not clear for reasons of insufficient balance, forgery of the draft, and the like.

forced sale: the sale or loss of property when one does not wish to dispose of it, as in bankruptcy. synonymous with *judicial sale.* see *involuntary alienation.*

forced saving: occurs when consumers are prevented from spending a portion of their income on consumption.

for deposit only: a restriction to an endorsement, limiting the negotiability of a check. [105]

forecasting: projecting events of the future utilizing current data.

foreclose (foreclosure): a legal process whereby a mortgagor of a property is deprived of his or her interest therein, usually by means of a court-administered sale of the property. see *deed in lieu of foreclosure, referee's foreclosure deed;* cf. *mother hubbard clause;* see also *equity of redemption, shortcut foreclosure.*

foreign agency: an agency of a domestically domiciled company located outside the country. The primary consideration is that the legal relationship is one of agency as contrasted to branch or subsidiary operation.

foreign bank: any bank other than the subject bank. Items of other banks included with the bank's are considered to be on a "foreign bank." The term may also refer to a banking concern outside the continental limits of the United States. [31]

foreign bill: a bill drawn in one state and payable in another state or nation. cf. *external bill.*

foreign bill of exchange

(1) the system by which the balances arising out of transactions between countries are settled.

(2) the currency used in making the settlement. [50]

(3) a draft, directing that payment be made in a foreign currency.

foreign card: bank card issued by another bank. synonymous with *out-of-area card* or *out-of-plan card.*

foreign check: a check drawn on a bank other than that to which it is presented for payment. [105]

foreign collections: bills of exchange that have either originated overseas and are import or incoming collections or those which are export or outgoing collections in that they are payable in another country.

foreign company: a company in any other state than the one in which it is incorporated or chartered.

foreign corporation
(1) a private corporation chartered in a foreign nation and conducting business within the United States.
(2) a private corporation within the United States doing business in one state but chartered in a different state.

foreign correspondent: a bank in another nation serving as agent for a U.S. bank maintaining sufficient balances.

Foreign Corrupt Practices Act of 1977: federal legislation designed to avoid improper corporate payments abroad. Under the act, corporate violators can be fined up to $1 million and others are liable for fines up to $10,000—not payable by the company—and five years in prison.

foreign crowd: the name given for New York Stock Exchange traders of foreign bonds.

foreign currency: the currency of any foreign country which is the authorized medium of circulation and the basis for record keeping in that country. Foreign currency is traded in by banks either by the actual handling of currency or checks, or by establishing balances in foreign currency with banks in those countries. [10]

foreign currency account: an account maintained in a foreign bank in the currency of the country in which the bank is located. Foreign currency accounts are also maintained by banks in the United States for depositors. When such accounts are kept, they usually represent that portion of the carrying bank's foreign currency account that is in excess of its contractual requirements. [10]

foreign department: a division of a company that carries out the needed functions for the company to engage in foreign operations of a business nature, such as exports, imports, and foreign exchange.

foreign deposits: those funds held in accounts in financial institutions outside the United States payable in the currency of the country in which the depository is located. [105]

foreign direct investments: the flow of foreign capital into U.S. business enterprise in which foreign residents have significant control. [73]

foreign draft: a draft drawn by a bank on a foreign correspondent bank. [105]

foreign drawings and remittances service: a service through which foreign exchange banks make their due from accounts available to their correspondents for use in arranging foreign exchange transfers. [105]

Foreign Earned Income Act of 1978: extends pre-1976 tax rules for U.S. citizens working abroad to tax years commencing with 1978. Thereafter, a whole new set of deductions reflect excess living costs abroad.

foreign exchange (F/X): instruments used for international payments (i.e., currency, checks, drafts, and bills of exchange).

foreign exchange broker: a person, company, or bank that engages in buying and selling foreign exchange, such as foreign currency or bills.

foreign exchange desk: the foreign exchange trading desk at the New York Federal Reserve Bank. The desk undertakes operations in the exchange markets for the account of the Federal

Open Market Committee, as agent for the U.S. Treasury and as agent for foreign central banks. see also *desk, the.* [1]

foreign exchange markets: those in which the monies of different countries are exchanged. Foreign exchange holdings—sometimes referred to as foreign exchange—are holdings of current or liquid claims denominated in the currency of another country. [73]

foreign exchange position: see *FX position.*

foreign exchange rate: the price of one currency in terms of another.

foreign exchange risk: the risk of suffering losses because of adverse movement in exchange rates.

foreign exchange trading: the buying and selling of foreign currencies in relation to either U.S. dollars or other foreign currencies. [105]

foreign exchange transactions: the purchase or sale of one currency with another. Foreign exchanges rates refer to the number of units of one currency needed to purchase one unit of another, or the value of one currency in terms of another. [1]

foreign income: income earned by Americans from work performed in another country. Under the Tax Reform Act of 1976, the amount of annual income that can be excluded from taxable income by Americans working abroad was reduced from $20,000 (in some cases from $25,000) to $15,000. Foreign employees of U.S. charitable organizations are able to exclude $20,000 each year.

foreign inquiry: an inquiry made to a credit bureau for information on a per-

son or firm from an other-than-normal service area of the bureau. [41]

foreign investment: the purchase of assets from abroad.

Foreign Investors Tax Act: federal legislation of 1966 establishing a tax ceiling (30 percent) for overseas investors in U.S. securities, the purpose of which is to stimulate foreign investment in the United States and aid in lowering the deficit in the U.S. international account.

foreign items
(1) transit items payable at an "out-of-town" bank.
(2) bills of exchange, checks, and drafts that are payable at a bank outside the jurisdiction of the U.S. government. [10]

foreign money: see *foreign currency.*

foreign sales corporations (FSCs): federal legislation of 1984. With such a corporation, a parent U.S. company pays up to 15 percent less tax on its exports.

foreign trade: trade between persons who are residents of different nations.

foreign trade financing: any of the payment methods used to settle transactions between individuals in different countries. [105]

foreign trade multiplier: the concept that fluctuations in exports and/or imports may lead to significant variations in national income.

foreign trade zone: a free port or area where foreign items can be imported without being required to pay duties on the condition that it is not used domestically and is shipped to another nation.

foreign transaction: an interchange item or an international transaction either originating or routed to a point outside the United States or Canada. [105]

forex: short, for *foreign exchange.*

forfeit: a thing lost to its owner by way of penalty for some default or offense.

forfeiture: the automatic loss of cash, property, or rights, as punishment for failure to comply with legal provisions and as compensation for the resulting losses or damages.

Forg.:   see *forgery.*

forged check: one on which the drawer's signature has been forged. [50]

forgery: false writing or alteration of an instrument to injure another person or with fraudulent intent to deceive (e.g., signing, without permission, another person's name on a check to obtain money from the bank).

forgery bond: see *bond, forgery.*

forint: monetary unit of Hungary.

form: the insurance policy itself and any endorsements or riders that may be included. [56]

formula clause: the provision of a will or trust agreement stating a formula whereby the executor or trustee can determine the federal estate-tax value of property; usually employed in connection with the marital deduction under the Revenue Act of 1954. [37]

formula investing: an investment technique. One formula calls for the shifting of funds from common shares to preferred shares or bonds as the market, on average, rises above a certain predetermined point—and the return of funds to common share investments as the market average declines. see *dollar (cost) averaging.* [20]

Fort Knox: a U.S. Army reservation in Kentucky where the U.S. government stores its gold bullion and the majority of the nation's gold, most of which is held as security for the gold certificate account of the Federal Reserve Banks.

FORTRAN: acronym for the formula translation system. A language primarily used to express computer programs by arithmetic formulas.

forward buying: the buying of an actual or spot commodity where delivery is for the future rather than as a current delivery.

forward commitment: an investor's agreement to make or purchase a mortgage loan on a specified future date. [22]

forward contract: a contract between a customer and a bank whereby each agree to deliver at a specified future date a certain amount in one currency in exchange for a certain amount in another currency at an agreed rate of exchange.

forward cover: an arrangement of a forward foreign exchange contract to protect a foreign currency buyer or seller from unexpected exchange rate fluctuations.

forward deal: an operation consisting of purchasing or selling foreign currencies with settlement to be made at a future date. [105]

forward delivery: synonymous with *deferred delivery.*

forward exchange: a foreign bill of exchange purchased or sold at a stated price that is payable at a given date.

forward exchange rate: an exchange rate (price) agreed upon today that will be utilized on a specified date in the future.

forward exchange transaction: a purchase or sale of foreign currency for future delivery. Standard periods for forward contracts are one, three, and six months. [42]

forward-forward: a deal for a future date in an instrument maturing on a further forward date; the instrument is usually a certificate of deposit and the object may be to extend the term of the deal.

forwarding: carrying information from one page to another in an account or journal.

forwarding agent: an individual or firm whose function it is to collect goods and to ship or deliver them as instructed.

forward margin: the margin between today's price of a currency and the price at a future date.

forward market: the claim to sell or purchase securities, foreign currencies, and so on, at a fixed price at a given future date. This market is one that deals in futures.

forward movement: the rising tendency in the price of a security or commodity or an average.

forward prices: a proposal for minimizing price uncertainty and encouraging greater stability in farming by utilizing the price system as an adjustment mechanism.

forward rate: see *forward exchange rate.*

forward sales: sales for shipment or delivery in the future that are not on a standardized futures contract by a trader in cash or spot goods.

forward selling: the sale of an actual or spot commodity where delivery is for a future or forward date, as distinct from a current delivery.

FOT: see *free on truck.*

foul bill of lading: a bill of lading identi-

fying shortage or damage that existed at the time of shipment.

foundations: see *community trust.*

founders' shares: see *founder's stock.*

founder's stock: stock given to the developers or founders of a new corporation for services rendered by them.

fourth market: the buying and selling of unlisted securities directly between investors.

FP: see *fixed price.*

FPC: see *Federal Power Commission.*

FPS: see *first preferred stock.*

Fr.: see *franc.*

FRA: see *Federal Reserve Act.*

fraction: generally applied to holdings of less than one share, resulting from rights and stock dividends. Because they are not entitled to dividends, they are usually disposed of by sale or rounded out, by the purchase of additional fractions, to full shares. [37]

fractional currency: any currency that is smaller than a standard money unit (e.g., any coin worth less than $1).

fractional lot: less than a round lot. see *fraction.*

fractional money: coins of smaller value, such as the half-dollar, quarter, dime, and nickel in the United States.

fractional reserve: under the U.S. commercial banking system, a bank is required by law to maintain only a portion of any deposit as reserves. The difference is then permitted to be lent to borrowers.

franc: monetary unit of Belgium, Benin, Burundi, Cameroons, Central African Empire, Chad, Comoros, Congo (Brazzaville), Dahomey, Djibouti, France, French Somaliland, Gabon, Guadeloupe, Ivory Coast, Liechtenstein, Luxembourg, Madagascar, Malagasy,

Mali, Martinique, Monaco, New Caledonia, New Hebrides Islands, Niger, Oceania, Réunion Island, Rwanda, Senegal, Switzerland, Tahiti, Togo, and Upper Volta.

franchise

(1) *general:* a privilege given to a dealer for the distribution of a manufacturer's product.

(2) *government:* a privilege given by a government to utilize public property or to create a monopoly.

(3) *law:* a certificate of incorporation.

franchise clause: provides that payment shall not be made unless the loss or damage equals or exceeds a specified amount, known as the *franchise.*

franchise plan: bank card plan for which right-of-use has been granted by one bank or association to another for a fee. [105]

franchise tax: the tax levied on a corporation to conduct business under its corporate name.

franco delivery: the full delivery of items to a consignee, with all charges paid, as with a prepaid delivery.

franken: monetary unit of Liechtenstein.

fraud: intentional misrepresentation of the truth in order to deceive another person. Aspects of fraud include the false representation of fact, intentionally made (see *scienter*), with the intent that the deceived person act thereon; knowledge that the statement would deceive; and knowledge that the person deceived acted leading to his injury. see also *bad faith, deceit, lapping, voidable contract.*

fraud account: an account on which the credit card has been used by an individual other than the cardholder of record and without the knowledge or consent of the cardholder of record. Usually the result of a lost, stolen, or never-received credit card. [105]

fraud bond: see *bond, fraud.*

fraud loss: losses (charge-offs) stemming from the fraudulent use of a bank card. [105]

fraudulent conveyance: conveyance of property entered into by a debtor with the objective of defrauding creditors.

Frazier-Lemke-Long Act: see *Farm Bankruptcy Act of 1933.*

FRB: see *Federal Reserve Bank.*

FRCD: see *floating-rate CD.*

FRCS: Federal Reserve Communications System.

Freddie Mac: see *Federal Home Loan Mortgage Corporation.*

free alongside ship (FAS): when an exporter delivers merchandise "free alongside ship," he pays all charges involved up to the moment of delivery. cf. *FOB, free overside.*

free and clear: the absence of any liens or other legal encumbrances on property.

free and open market: a market in which supply and demand are freely expressed in terms of price. Contrasts with a controlled market, in which supply, demand, and price may all be regulated. [20]

free astray: freight that is miscarried or delivered at the wrong location, then is billed and forwarded to the correct location without additional charge.

free balance: the minimum balance that a commercial bank allows a checking account customer to maintain without being charged a service fee. The free balance varies by commercial bank.

free banking: the concept that any group of incorporators of a bank that can fulfill the standards should be given a charter. Since 1933 this concept has been changed where the need for the service must be shown.

free bond: see *bond, free.*

free checking account: a service offered by banks where demand deposit customers do not pay a fee for the privilege of writing checks. [105]

free check storage account: an example of what the banking industry calls check safekeeping, or truncation. It is a process that cuts off the normal cycle of check flow—from check to payee to bank and back to the check-writer—before it is completed.

free coinage: the obligation of the U.S. government to accept for coinage unlimited quantities of a specified metal or metals under the law. cf. *gratuitous coinage.*

free crowd: see *active crowd.*

Freedom of Information Act (FOIA) of 1966: federal legislation, amended in 1974 and 1976, establishing the principle that the public has the right, with certain exceptions, to information collected and kept by federal government agencies. Its aim is to make government records and decision making more accessible to public scrutiny by preventing agencies from arbitrarily withholding information. see also *Fair Credit Reporting Act of 1971.*

freedom shares: U.S. savings notes sold from 1967 through the mid-1970s.

free enterprise: the condition under which a firm or individual is able to function competitively without excessive government restrictions.

free gold: the amount of gold in the Treasury in excess of gold needed to meet gold certificates and other indebtedness due in gold.

free goods: items that are so abundant that it is not profitable to attempt to charge for them (e.g., sunlight).

freehold: the holding of a piece of land, an office, and so on, for life, or with the right to pass it on through inheritance.

free item: an item received by the processing bank which is not listed on the cash letter or deposit where it is enclosed. [105]

free list: a statement prepared by a customs department of items that are not liable to the payment of duties.

freely convertible currency: a currency that may be used by citizens and foreigners without restriction. [105]

free market: describes the unrestricted movement of items in and out from the market, unhampered by the existence of tariffs or other trade barriers.

free (freight) on board: see *FOB.*

free on board airport (FOBA): where a seller agrees to place goods in the hands of an air carrier or his or her agent at the named airport of departure. [95]

free on rail (FOR): the cost of the goods plus carriage to a specified rail terminal plus the cost of loading onto the rail trucks. synonymous with *free on truck.* [95]

free on truck (FOT): synonymous with *free on rail.* [95]

free overside: in export price quotations: the seller pays all costs and accepts full responsibility for the goods until they have been safely unloaded at the place of importation in a foreign country; thereafter, the buyer will pay all costs such as customs duty.

free period: that extent of time for which no finance charges will be levied provided that payment in full is made. Usually, the time period between the billing date and 25 days from that date. [105]

free-period cost of funds: charge expressed as a percentage for funds used to finance outstandings from the time a merchant account is credited for sales deposited until finance charges thereon are billed to a cardholder. [105]

free port: a port where no duties are paid on either imports or exports.

free reserves: a Federal Reserve Bank term describing the margin by which excess reserves exceed the bank's borrowings.

free riding

(1) *investments:* prohibited by law, the buying and rapid sale of securities, where no personal funds are given for the original purchase.

(2) *investments:* the withholdings by brokerage firms of new stocks that are expected to climb higher than the initial public offering. Prohibited by the SEC.

free silver: see *free coinage.*

free supply: in the commodities industry where total stocks less what is owned or controlled by the government.

free surplus: that portion of retained earnings available for common stock dividends, that is, after deducting any amounts appropriated or legally restricted by reason of such items as preferred stock dividends in arrears, the repurchase of treasury stock, or loan agreements calling for a minimum cash balance or a minimum liability ratio. Dividends payable in common stock are a general exception to most restrictions on dividends arising from loan agreements. [43]

free trade: trade among countries in the absence of policy restrictions that may interfere with its flow.

free trade zone: where imports are distributed with little or no customs duties and regulations.

free working capital: synonymous with *working capital* and *net current monetary assets.*

freeze

(1) *general:* to fix prices at present levels. as with a price freeze. A freeze rarely takes place except during national crises or wartime.

(2) *government:* governmental seizure or impounding of property, goods, and so on. This action demands an executive order or the passage of a law, usually during emergencies.

(3) see also entries under *frozen.*

freight: all merchandise, goods, products, or commodities shipped by rail, air, road, or water, other than baggage, express mail, or regular mail.

freight absorption: when a seller does not charge a customer with freight out, the seller is said to have absorbed the freight.

freight allowed: an agreement whereby a business pays the transportation charges on incoming goods but is permitted to charge back all or part of that cost to the vendor.

freight forwarder: the intermediary between a consignor or consignee of a shipment and the transport carriers, customs officials, and other third parties with whom the consignor would normally deal.

freight inward: freight paid on shipments received.

freight outward: freight paid by a seller on outgoing customer shipments.

freight paid to: where a seller must forward the goods at his or her own expense to the agreed destination and is responsible for all risks of the goods until they are delivered to the first carrier. [95]

freight release: when items are shipped with freight payable at their destination, a remittance for the amount of freight due is made to the vessel owner, who either endorses a freight release on the bill of lading or retains the bill and issues a freight release as a separate document.

Friedmanite: one who upholds the monetary theories of Milton Friedman, who advocates direct control of money supply by governments in lieu of tax manipulations, government projects, and so on. cf. *neo-Keynesian.*

friendly counter: a newer trend in bank lobby design. The friendly counter is an open counter where depositors and customers of a bank may transact business with the teller. The counter has no grille work other than a gate that the teller may open for the depositor to pass large packages over the counter. The friendly counter has a ledge constructed over the counter. Forms, working supplies, and so on, are under this ledge, and are beyond the reach of persons who might try to perpetrate illegal acts in the bank. [10]

fringe benefits: nonwage benefits (paid vacations pensions, health and welfare provisions, life insurance, etc.) whose cost is borne in whole or in part by the employer.

FRN: see *floating-rate note.*

front-end fees: fees payable at the beginning of a loan.

front-end finance: finance for the ini-

tial part of a contract or project; usually used in export finance referring to that part of a loan not covered by export credit insurance.

front-end loading: fees and other charges which are levied more heavily to begin with and then taper off.

frozen

(1) *general:* not easily available.

(2) *finance:* when the conversion of something of value into money is impossible, the thing is said to be frozen. cf. *liquid.*

frozen account

(1) an account on which payments have been suspended until a court order or legal process again makes the account available for withdrawal. The account of a deceased person is frozen pending the distribution by a court order grant to the new lawful owners of the account. see *deceased account, sequestered account*; cf. *blocked accounts.*

(2) where a dispute has arisen regarding the true ownership of an account, it is frozen to preserve the existing assets until legal action can determine the lawful owners of the asset.

frozen asset: any asset that cannot be used by its owner because of pending or ongoing legal action. The owner cannot use the asset; nor can he or she dispose of it until the process of the law has been completed and a decision passed down from the courts.

frozen credit: a loan, normally called and matured, but because of economic factors is recognized by a creditor that such a step would precipitate bankruptcy and thereby preclude any substantial payment. Consequently, such credits can be carried or extended with the hope of liquidation when the debtor has recovered. synonymous with *frozen loan*.

frozen loan: synonymous with *frozen credit*.

frozen out: action of one party to a transaction preventing or forcing a withdrawal from that transaction by a second party. The second party in this situation is *frozen out*.

FRS: see *Federal Reserve System*.

FS
  (1) see *financial statement*.
  (2) see *futures spread*.

FSC: see *foreign sales corporations*.

FSLA: see *Federal Savings and Loan Association*.

FSLIC: see *Federal Savings and Loan Insurance Corporation*.

FTC: see *Federal Trade Commission*.

FTCA: see *Federal Tort Claims Act of 1946*.

fudge factor: to offset errors made by economists, an adjustment of model findings to fit known facts. This factor is introduced whenever its forecasts appear to be suspiciously out of line with the real world.

full-bodied money: gold; currency that is worth its face value as a commodity. cf. *fiat money*.

full-cost pricing: the practice that includes all appropriate manufacturing costs in determining inventory.

full coverage: any form of insurance coverage that provides for payments of losses in full, subject to the limit of the policy, without application of a deductible. cf. *ordinary life*.

full disclosure: as described by the Securities Exchange Act of 1934; every company that has securities listed on an exchange must register with the SEC and file annual and other reports

disclosing financial and other data for the information of the investing public. Management must also disclose basic financial information used in stockholder's meetings.

full faith and credit: a pledge of the general taxing power for the payment of obligations.

full faith and credit debt: a municipality's debt that is a direct obligation of the municipality.

full liability: liability not shared with others.

full-line forcing: the practice of requiring a buyer, as a condition of the sale to him or her of one or more popular or highly desired items in a vendor's line of merchandise, to purchase less popular or less desired items in the line.

full lot: usually, 100 shares of stock traded on the New York Stock Exchange. synonymous with *round lot* or *board lot*. cf. *odd-lot orders*.

full-paid stock: see *capital stock*.

full payment: the amount of money owed on a single account that, if paid, will reduce the account to a zero balance. [105]

full-payout lease: see *finance lease*.

full recourse: type of dealer financing whereby a dealer sells or assigns to a bank installment sales paper a dealer originates with an unconditional guaranty; should the purchaser become delinquent, the dealer accepts full responsibility for the paper. [105]

full-service bank: a commercial bank that is capable of meeting the total financial needs of the banking public. Because the charters of some financial institutions limit their activities, this term draws attention to the advantages enjoyed by customers of a commercial bank. cf. *Hinky Dinky, multiple banking, one-stop banking.*

full stock: an equity stock with a par value of $100. see also *capital stock.*

fully funded: a method of financing a pension or annuity plan whereby its entire cost is fully provided on an accrual basis. [52]

fully invested: a portfolio having no assets in the form of cash or cash equivalent.

fully modified pass-through: see *pass-through certificates.*

fully paid stocks: legal issues where the corporation has received at least the equivalent of its par value in goods, services, or currency.

fully registered: generally applied to bonds that are registered as to principal and income. In this form, a bond is not negotiable and interest is remitted by the disbursing agent to the registered owners. [37]

fully vested: describes an employee covered by a pension plan who has rights to all the benefits bought with the employer's contributions to the plan, even when the worker is not employed by that employer at retirement.

functional cost analysis program: a study based on data submitted by individual banks to the Federal Reserve System to compare various totals and cost ratios. [105]

functional costing: classifying costs by allocating them to the various functions performed (warehousing, delivery, billing, etc.).

functional discount: a deduction taken to effect differing prices to different customers (e.g., retailers get 40 percent off the list price, wholesalers 40 to 50 percent off).

functional finance: the analysis of financial matters for purposes other than the usual problems of balancing budgets (e.g., for the effects on national income).

functional income distributions: wages, rents, interests, and profits paid to manufacturers in return for supplying their labor, land, capital, and management talents.

functional obsolescence: created by structural defects that reduce a property's value and/or market ability.

fund

(1) *general:* an asset of any organization set aside for a particular purpose. Not to be confused with general fund. see *sinking fund.*

(2) *finance:* cash, securities, or other assets placed in the hands of a trustee or administrator to be expanded as defined by a formal agreement.

fund accounts: all accounts necessary to set forth the financial operations and financial condition of a fund. [49]

fundamental disequilibrium: an International Monetary Fund expression indicating a substantial and persisting variation between the par exchange rate of a national currency and its purchasing-power parity with the currencies of other countries.

fundamental research: an analysis of industries and companies based on such factors as sales, assets, earnings, products or services, markets, and management. As applied to the economy, fundamental research includes consideration of gross national product, interest rates, unemployment, inventories, and savings, see also *technical research.* [20]

fundamentalist: a financial analyst who employs mathematical data for evolving opinions and recommendations regarding the status and future of markets.

fundamental product: offering to the market that is immediately recognized as what is being sold, such as a savings account. [105]

fundamentals: a Wall Street school of thought that purports to predict stock market behavior by examining the vital statistics of a stock, the firm's management, earnings, and so on.

fund balance: the excess of the assets of a fund over its liabilities and reserves except in the case of funds subject to budgetary accounting where, prior to the end of a fiscal period, it represents the excess of the fund's assets and estimated revenues for the period over its liabilities, reserves, and appropriations for the period. [49]

fund balance receipts: receipts that increase the fund balance of a fund but which are not property included in current revenues. Examples are taxes and accounts receivable previously written off as uncollectible. [49]

fund balance sheet: a balance sheet for a single fund. see *fund*. [49]

funded debt

(1) *general:* exists when the method of paying off the debt and its interest is determined for specific periods.

(2) *finance:* usually, interest-bearing bonds of debentures of a company; may include long-term bank loans but does not include short loans or preferred or common stock. [20]

funded debts to net working capital: funded debts are all long-term obligations, as represented by mortgages, bonds, debentures, term loans, serial notes, and other types of liabilities maturing more than one year from the statement date. This ratio is obtained by dividing funded debt by net working capital. Analysts tend to compare funded debts with net working capital in determining whether or not long-term debts are in proper proportion. Ordinarily, this relationship should not exceed 100 percent. [4]

funded debt unmatured: unmatured debt (other than equipment obligations), maturing more than one year from date of issue. [18]

funded deficit: a deficit eliminated through the sale of bonds issued for that purpose. see also *bond funding*. [49]

funded insurance trust: see *unfunded insurance trust*.

funded reserve: a reserve invested in earmarked interest-bearing securities.

fund group: a group of funds which are similar in purpose and character. For example, several special revenue funds constitute a fund group. [49]

funding: the gathering together of outstanding debts of a business, leading to a reissuing of new bonds or obligations for the purpose of paying off debts.

funding bond: see *bond, funding*.

funds: a sum of money or stock convertible to money, assets. [61]

funds, corporate: a general funds mix of industrial and utility issues of varying maturities. Typically, about half the securities mature in more than 20 years. High-yield funds have less than 20-year maturity periods.

funds, government: the U.S. government has a large selection of load and no-load funds of high quality.

funds, municipal: most big fund sponsors have muncipal bond funds, some general funds with securities of good grade, and some "high-yield" filled with speculative issues.

funds management: the continual arrangement and rearrangement of a bank's balance sheet in an attempt to maximize profits, subject to having sufficient liquidity and making safe investments. [105]

fund surplus: see *fund balance.*

fungible: describes goods or securities, any unit is the equal of any other like unit (e.g., wheat, corn).

funny money: convertible preferred stocks, convertible bonds, options, and warrants that appear to have characteristics of common stock equity but which did not reduce reported earnings per share before 1969.

future depreciation
(1) that loss from present value which will occur in the future.
(2) sometimes used to indicate the future annual charge necessary to recapture the present building value over its economic life or the annual amount necessary to amortize total investment. [6]

future estate
(1) *general:* an estate developed for the purpose of possession, to be taken at an identified later date or upon occurrence of a future event.
(2) *law:* a *nonpossessory estate.*

future exchange contract: a contract for the purchase or sale of foreign exchange to be delivered at a future date and at a rate determined in the present.

future income: earnings or other income which seems to be reasonably certain for some time to come. [41]

futures
(1) *finance:* foreign currencies bought or sold based on a rate that is quoted as of some future date.
(2) *investments:* contracts for the sale and delivery of commodites at some future time, made with the expectation that no commodity will be received immediately. see *gray market, hedging, Tax Reform Act of 1976.*

futures call: the sale of commodities where delivery is made upon the request of the seller on any trading date for a specified month.

futures commission broker: a firm or party engaged in soliciting or accepting and handling orders for the purchase or sale of any commodity for future delivery on or subject to the rules of any contract market and who, in or in connection with such solicitations or acceptance of orders, accepts any money, securities, or property (or extends credit in lieu thereof) to margin any trades or contracts that result therefrom. They must be licensed under the Commodity Exchange Act when handling business in commodities covered thereby. [2]

futures commission merchant: see *futures commission broker.*

futures contract: the right to buy or sell a commodity at a specified price on a specified future date. The price is established when the contract is made in open auction on a futures exchange.

futures exchange: an organization created for the trading of commodity futures.

futures market: any commodity exchange trading in futures.

futures spread: the simultaneous purchase and sale of contracts in either the same or different commodities. In the case where one commodity is involved, the contracts must be in different delivery months. The aim of a futures spread is to take advantage of the difference, or spread, in the prices of two future contracts that have some direct economic relation to each other. A trader buys one contract, and sells the other short—sells it without owning it—in the hope that one part will move more than the other. see *spread, straddle.*

future sum: the money that a borrower agrees to repay for an obligation. It is the interest or discount, plus service or other charges, added to the total amount borrowed.

future worth: the equivalent value at a future date on time value of money.

FV: see *face value.*

F/X: see *foreign exchange.*

FX (foreign exchange) position: a bank's net holdings of any commitments in foreign exchange in any particular currency at any given point in time. [105]

FY: see *fiscal year.*

G: gold.

GA

  (1) see *general account.*

  (2) see *general average.*

  (3) see *gross asset.*

GAAP: generally accepted accounting principles. see *Financial Accounting Standards Board.*

gain: any benefit, profit, or advantage, as opposed to a loss.

gain on disposal: the sale of a noncurrent asset for more than book value.

galloping inflation: the rapid and unlimited rise of prices; swiftly increasing inflation that, if not controlled and minimized, could lead to a major crisis in the economy. synonymous with *hyperinflation, runaway inflation.*

gambling: in securities, the random buying and selling of these items without intelligently investigating prospects.

GAO: see *General Accounting Office.*

gap analysis: a technique to measure interest rate sensitivity. [107]

gap management: the identification of those assets and liabilities that are interest sensitive. [105]

garage: the transfer of liabilities or assets to a center which has little connection with the underlying transaction, usually to shift profits into a low-tax area.

garage, the: slang, the annex to the New York Stock Exchange trading floor where Post 30, for inactive stocks, and six of the other 18 trading posts are lodged.

garbage: unwanted and meaningless information in computer memory or on tape. see *GIGO.*

Garnet St. Germain Depository Institutions Act of 1982: instructs the Depository Institutions Deregulation Committee to authorize money market deposit accounts (MMDAs), requiring that the account be "directly equivalent to and competitive with money market mutual funds." In addition, it specified that the account have no minimum maturity and that it allowed up to three preauthorized or automatic transfers and three transfers to third parties (checks) per month. [98]

garnishee: a debtor of a defendant who possesses money or property that a third party (a plaintiff) wishes to acquire to satisfy a debt due him or her by the defendant; an individual upon whom a garnishment is served.

garnishment: a writ from a court directing an employer to withhold all or part of the money due an employee in wages and to pay such funds to the court or to the plaintiff in the action (the person to whom the employee is indebted) until a given debt is liquidated. cf. *offset.*

gateway: a place at which freight is interchanged or interlined between carriers or where a carrier joins two operating authorities for the provision of through service.

gather in the stops: to sell a security in sufficient supply to lower the price to a level where numerous stop orders are known to be entered. synonymous with *uncover the stops.* see *snowballing.*

GATT: see *General Agreement on Tariffs and Trade.*

GAW: see *guaranteed annual wage.*

GB: see *bond, guaranteed.*

GD
   (1) see *good delivery.*
   (2) see *gross debt.*

GDP: see *gross domestic product.*

GE: see *gross earnings.*

gearing: in Great Britain, the relationship between equity capital and fixed interest capital. synonymous with *leverage* in United States.

geets: slang, money, purchasing power.

gelt: slang, money.

general account: an account appearing in the bank's general ledger; all ac-

counts other than those of depositors and depositories.

General Accounting Office: an independent nonpolitical agency established in 1921 that audits and reviews federal financial transactions and examines the expenditures of appropriations by federal units. The GAO is directly responsible to Congress.

General Agreement on Tariffs and Trade (GATT): a 1947 arrangement among 23 nations to make numerous mutual tariff concessions. Additional countries have joined GATT. see *Kennedy round.*

general asset currency: see *asset currency.*

general audit: an audit that embraces all financial transactions and records and which is made regularly at the close of an accounting period. [49]

general average: a contribution by all the parties in a sea adventure to make good a loss sustained by one of their number because of sacrifices voluntarily made of part of the ship or cargo to save the remaining part and the lives of those on board from an impending peril.

general banking law: the banking law of an individual state under which the banks organized in that state are authorized to do business. [50]

general bonded debt: the outstanding bonded indebtedness of a governmental unit with the exception of utility and special assessment bonds.

general control expenditures: expenditures (for personnel administration and other general administration) of the legislative and judicial branches of the government, the office of the chief executive, auxiliary agencies, and staff services.

general deposit: funds of banking deposits that are combined in the bank, as differentiated from special deposits that are kept separately and for which the bank serves as a bailee.

general depository: any Federal Reserve member bank authorized to handle deposits of the Treasury.

general equilibrium analysis: an economic inquiry in which the interaction of all markets is considered.

general examination: a detailed examination of all national banks undertaken every two years by the Comptroller of the Currency. [105]

general expenditures: total expenditures less utility, sales of alcoholic beverages, and insurance trust expenditures when used in reference to state or local governments separately. When combined for state-local totals, these items become direct general expenditures to avoid duplicating intergovernmental payments. cf. *general revenue.*

general fixed assets: those fixed assets of a governmental unit which are not accounted for in an enterprise, trust, or intragovernmental service fund. [49]

general fund: money that can be utilized (i.e., money that has not already been authorized for a particular project).

general gift: a gift, by will, of personal property which is not a particular thing as distinguished from all others of the same kind. [32]

general indorsement: synonymous with *blank endorsement.*

generalists: stocks trading at more than $100 a share. The name is derived from the General Electric Com-

pany. Its stock used to trade above the century mark.

generalized scheme of preferences (GSP): a system of tariff reductions and quota increases purporting to aid less developed nations.

general journal: an accounting record into which journal entries are made.

general ledger: the most important bank record. Every transaction that takes place in the bank during the business day is reflected through various departmental subsidiary records to the general ledger. see also *suspense account.*

general legacy: see *legacy.*

general lien: a lien against an individual but not against his real property. It gives the right to seize personal property until a debt has been paid. The asset involved does not have to be that which created the debt. see *distress for rent, vendor's lien;* cf. *particular lien.*

general loan and collateral agreement: synonymous with *broker's loan.*

general long-term debt: a long-term debt legally payable from general revenues and backed by the full faith and credit of a governmental unit. see *long-term debt.* [49]

general management trust: a trust that is not limited to any particular stock in which to invest.

general mortage: a mortgage covering all properties of a debtor and not restricted to one parcel.

general mortgage bond: see *bond, general mortgage.*

general obligation bond: see *bond, general obligation.*

general obligations (GO): long-term borrowings that are backed by the full faith, credit, and taxing powers of the issuing locality rather than income generated by a specific project.

general partner: a partner who, along with others, is liable for the partnership debts.

general power of appointment: the power of the donee (the one who is given the power) to pass on an interest in property to whomsoever he or she pleases, including himself or herself or his or her estate. see *power of appointment.* [37]

general property tax: a tax on the assessed value of property, computed as a percentage of the total value.

general-purpose computer: a computer designed to handle a wide variety of problems (e.g., sorting, or a file processing activity).

general reserves: funds set aside for the sole purpose of covering possible losses. Includes the Federal Insurance Reserve, reserve for contingencies, and any reserve "locked up" for losses. [59]

general revenue: total revenue less utility, sales of alcoholic beverages, and insurance trust revenue when used in reference to state or local governments separately. When combined for state-local totals, it refers only to taxes and charges and miscellaneous revenue, to avoid duplicating intergovernmental revenue. cf. *general expenditures.*

general revenue sharing: funds distributed to states and local general-purpose governments by the federal government under the State and Local Fiscal Assistance Act of 1972. [70]

general sales tax: a tax on most items, collected at the time of purchase. In many states purchases of food and medicine are excluded from this law. see also *sales tax.*

general tariff: see *single-schedule tariff.*

general warranty deed: see *deed, general warranty.*

generation skipping tax: see *unified credit.*

generic identification: the association of a group of cardholders as a single unit, that is, cardholders of several banks belonging to the same association, such as Visa or MasterCharge cardholders.

generic product: the essential benefit the buyer expects to receive from the fundamental product. When a customer opens a checking account, he or she is not buying paper checks, but is buying a bill-paying convenience. [105]

Gen. Led.: see *general ledger.*

Gen. Mtge.: see *general mortgage.*

gen-saki: a Japanese short-term money market; a market for conditional bond sales. A market where securities firms sell or buy bonds, usually for two or three months, while simultaneously including an agreement to repurchase them.

gentlemen's agreement: an unsigned, unsecured contract based on the faith of the involved parties that each will perform.

genuine and valid: a term indicating the acceptability of a check that is completed properly and drawn against sufficient funds. [105]

GES: see *gold exchange standard.*

gestor: one who acts for another, in law. [61]

GICs
(1) see *guaranteed income contracts.*

(2) see *guaranteed investment contracts.*

Giffin effect: the situation noted by Sir R. Giffin that a rise in the price of all goods will, in the case of the poor whose incomes do not increase, cause an increase in the quantity of staple items of food consumed despite the increase in their price in order to make the income cover the needs.

gift: the value of a donated asset acquired without cost to the recipient or regard to its donor. The use of the gift may or may not be restricted. [49]

gift causa mortis: a gift made in the anticipation of death to avoid inheritance taxes. cf. *gift inter vivos.*

gift certificate: a certificate having an identified cash value, to be used in purchasing goods or services from the issuing store or business.

gift inter vivos: a gift of property given during the donor's life to another living person. cf. *gift causa mortis.*

gift tax: a graduated, progressive tax imposed by some state governments and the federal government. This tax is paid by the donor, or individual making the gift, not the donee, the recipient of the gift.

GIGO: garbage in, garbage out; the acronym for the concept that results produced from unreliable or useless data are equally unreliable or useless.

gilt-edged: the highest-quality securities.

gilt-edged bond: see *bond, gilt-edged.*

gilt-edge security: a security where the risk factor is at a minimum (i.e., a U.S. government bond).

Ginnie Mae: see *Government National Mortgage Association (GNMA).*

Ginnie Mae trusts: closed-end unit investment trusts made up of Ginnie Mae certificates. The cost is $1000 per unit with a sales charge of around 4 percent. The monthly payments cover earned interest and amortization—the same as having direct participation in Ginnie Mae certificates, which are available only in the larger denominations. see *Government National Mortgage Association.*

Ginnie Mae II: started in July 1983, similar to the original Ginnie Mae with other advantages. Lets originators join together to issue jumbo pools, which combine mortgages from different issuers into a single package, as well as continue to be sole issuers. There is only one central paying agent, the Chemical Bank, leading to greater efficiency in payments and transfers. Holders of Ginnie Mae II are paid on the twenty-fifth day of the month, in contrast to the fifteenth day of the month for the original Ginnie Mae; thereby the 10-day delay lowers the yield on the securities by about five points. see also *Ginnie Mae trusts.*

GIRO: developed in the banking system of Germany, the payment system in which a bank depositor instructs his or her bank to transfer funds from his account directly to creditor accounts and to advise the creditors of the transfer.

give an indication: expressing an interest in a new security issue by entering a firm buy order for a stated amount.

give an order: directing a broker to purchase or sell a security in a certain amount which may include specifications of a price or time limit.

give-out order: in securities and commodities, an order to a broker given out by him or her to a specialist for execution.

give-up: occurs when a member of a stock exchange on the floor acts for a second member by executing an order for him with a third member. see *two-dollar brokers.*

give-up order: securities not accepted for direct sale by a participating underwriter.

GL: see *go long.*

glamour stock

(1) *general:* any popular security.

(2) *investments:* a successful security that attracts a substantial following and whose price rises on a continuous basis.

Glass-Steagall Act of 1933: a legislative saefguard designed to prevent commercial banks from engaging in investment banking activities; also authorized deposit insurance. In recent years, attempts have been made to change this act. After a long period of contentment with the restrictions, the banking industry, especially the American Bankers Association, has begun to test the limitations on several fronts, including commercial paper, commingled accounts, money market funds, municipal revenue bonds. see *bond, municipal revenue; commercial paper; commingled accounts; money market funds.*

glut: to oversupply (e.g., a glut of oil on the market).

GNMA: see *Government National Mortgage Association.*

GNMA certificate unit trusts: backed by government-guaranteed mortgages. Maturities of 12 years or less. Big brokerage houses sweep monthly checks for interest and returned principal from mortgage amortization into a market-rate money fund. Requires periodic reinvestment decision.

GNMA mortgage-backed securities: securities guaranteed by GNMA and issued primarily by mortgage bankers (but also by others approved by GNMA). The GNMA security is pass-through in nature, and the holder is protected by the "full faith and credit of the U.S. government." It is collateralized by FHA or VA mortgages. [105]

gnomes: financial and banking people involved in foreign exchange speculation. The term was coined by Great Britain's Labour ministers during the 1964 sterling crisis.

GNP: see *gross national product.*

GO

(1) see *general obligations.*

(2) see *government obligations.*

go-down: in the Far East, a commercial storage warehouse.

go-go fund: an investment purporting to acquire sizable earnings in a short time period, resulting in risky, speculative market activity.

going ahead: when a broker decides to make a trade for his or her own account, fair practice requires that he or she fill all his or her customer's orders first. A dishonest broker will "go ahead" (i.e., transact his or her own business first).

going business: any business that over a period of years has been profitable, properly managed, and financially responsible, and holds prospects for continued prosperity.

going public: describes a situation when a firm's shares become available on a major exchange, as distinguished from being held by a few shareholders.

going short: selling a stock or commodity short.

going value (going-concern value): the value that an enterprise has as a unit, as opposed to the total value of each of its parts taken separately.

gold bas: see *bullion*.

gold bond: see *bond, gold*.

gold brick: slang, worthless, and often fraudulent, securities that initially appear sound and worthy.

gold bullion standard: a monetary standard according to which (a) the national unit of currency is defined in terms of a stated gold weight, (b) gold is retained by the government in bars rather than coin, (c) there is no circulation of gold within the economy, and (d) gold is made available for purposes of industry and for international transactions of banks and treasuries.

gold certificate account: gold certificates on hand and due from the Treasury. The certificates, on hand and due from the Treasury, are backed 100 percent by gold owned by the U.S. government. They count as legal reserve, the minimum the Reserve Banks are required to maintain being 25 percent of their combined Federal Reserve note and deposit liabilities. (40)

gold clause: contract term defining a money debt in terms of a U.S. dollar of a specified weight and quality of gold.

gold clearance fund: today, known as the *Interdistrict Settlement Fund*.

gold cover
(1) the gold reserve of a state or international organization which is a reserve against its currency or similar obligations. see *Gold-Cover Repeal Act*.
(2) a legal requirement, now defunct, for U.S. Federal Reserve notes that a specific percentage of the value of an issue of paper currency must be backed by an actual gold reserve.

Gold-Cover Repeal Act: federal legislation of 1968 which repealed the requirement that the U.S. paper currency (Federal Reserve notes) be backed by a gold reserve of 25 percent of the value of currency outstanding, thereby freeing more than $10 billion in gold reserves for international exchange activities. see also *gold cover*.

gold currency system: a monetary system where currency and gold can be freely converted one into the other at established rates.

golden parachutes: employment contracts for top management, usually long term, providing for continued compensation in the event control of a company changes hands.

golden passbook: see *time deposit (open account)*.

gold exchange standard: an international monetary agreement according to which money consists of fiat national currencies that can be converted into gold at established price ratios.

gold exporting point: the rate of exchange at which the importer of goods can at the same cost buy gold and export it in payment of his or her imports.

gold fixing: in London, Paris, and Zurich, at 10:30 A.M. and again at 3:30 P.M., gold specialists or bank officials specializing in gold bullion activity determine the price for the metal.

gold hoarding: with the hope of guaranteeing the value of their money, people who convert their funds into gold bullion and hold on to it over an extended time period.

gold importing point: the rate of exchange at which the exporter can at the same cost arrange to have gold sent to him or her in payment for his or her goods.

gold market: a foreign exchange market dealing in gold. [105]

gold points: the range within which the foreign exchange rates of gold standard countries will differ. Gold points are equal to the par rate of exchange plus and minus the cost of transporting gold. The cost of insurance is included.

Gold Pool: seven representatives of central banks of the United States, the United Kingdom, Belgium, Italy, Switzerland, the Netherlands, and the Federal Republic of Germany, who, operating through the Bank for International Settlements of Basle, seek to maintain equilibrium in the price of gold by purchasing and selling on the markets within certain minimum and maximum levels.

gold price: see *two-tier gold price.*

gold production: as listed by the *Federal Reserve Bulletin,* appearing monthly, the estimated gold production in countries of the free world.

Gold Reserve Act: federal legislation of 1934 authorizing the devaluation of the dollar in terms of gold by from 50 to 60 percent at the discretion of the president and ordered the acquisition by the Treasury of all gold held by the Federal Reserve Banks in return for gold certificates. Coinage of gold was abolished, as was the redemption of money in gold.

gold reserves: gold, retained by a nation's monetary agency, forming the backing of currency that the nation has issued.

gold settlement fund: the fund of gold certificates deposited by the 12 Federal Reserve Banks with the Interdistrict Fund of the Federal Reserve System and used for clearance of debits and credits of each Reserve Bank against the other 11 banks in order to save transportation of money between the banks.

gold standard: applied to a monetary agreement according to which all national currencies are backed 100 percent by gold and the gold is utilized for payments of foreign activity. cf. *limping standard.*

gold stock: value of gold owned by the government. [40]

gold tranche position in International Monetary Fund: represents the amount that the United States can draw in foreign currencies virtually automatically from the International Monetary Fund if such borrowings are needed to finance a balance-of-payments deficit. The gold tranche itself is determined by the U.S. quota paid in gold minus the holdings of dollars by the fund in excess of the dollar portion of the U.S. quota. Transactions of the fund in a member country's currency are transactions in monetary reserves. When the fund sells dollars to other countries to enable them to finance their international payments, the net position of the United States in the fund is improved. An improvement in the net position in the gold tranche is similar to an increase in the reserve assets of the United States. On the other hand, when the United States buys other currencies from the fund, or when other countries use dollars to meet obligations to the fund, the net position of the United States in the fund is reduced. [73]

go long: purchasing stock for investment or as speculation. see *short sale.*

good: any item of merchandise, commodity, and so on, having value. [105]

good deal: slang, a desirable business opportunity.

good delivery: certain basic qualifications must be met before a security sold on an exchange may be delivered; the security must be in proper form to comply with the contract of sale and to transfer title to the purchaser. [20]

good faith: trust. [28]

good faith bargaining: applied to the requirement that both parties to a labor dispute meet and confer at reasonable times, with minds open to persuasion with a view to reaching agreement on new contractual terms. A requirement to reach agreement on any proposal is not implied.

good-faith check: the check that must be included with a bid on a bond sale. The bidding notice ordinarily provides that if the bonds are awarded to a syndicate that does not pick them up as agreed, the good-faith check will be held as liquidated damages. The good-faith checks of unsuccessful bidders are returned. [105]

good-fors: usually applied to emergency low-denomination notes, which state on the face that they are "good for" a specified amount. [27]

good money: if two kinds of money of equal nominal value are in circulation, the general public may prefer one over the other because of metal content and will tend to hoard the "good money" and spend the "bad money," driving the good money out of circulation. see *Gresham's Law.*

goods and services

(1) *general:* the result of industrial work, equaling the gross national product for one year.

(2) *law:* any movable personal property, excluding livestock and excluding intangible property such as leases. cf. *chattel, chose.*

goods on approval: obtained when a potential buyer requests and receives from a seller the right to examine items for a stated time period before deciding whether to purchase the goods.

good-this-month order (GTM): a customer's request to a broker for the purchase or sale of stocks or commodities, the order being good this month only. see *day order, open order.*

good-this-week order (GTW): a customer's request to a broker for the purchase or sale of stocks or commodities, the order being good this week only. see *day order, open order.*

good through: a request to purchase or sell stock at a stated price limit for a stated time period, unless it is executed, canceled, or altered as to price. May appear as GTW (good through week), GTM (good through month), and so on.

good ticket: slang, financially successful.

good-'til-canceled order (GTC): an order to buy or sell that remains in effect until it is either executed or canceled. cf. *orders good until a specified time, resting order.* [20]

good title: synonymous with *just title, marketable title.*

"good to the last drop": an exchange system whereby all clearinghouse members are required to make good in the event that one of their number does not or cannot comply with transferring the debits and credits that have resulted from the day's trading. see also *"marks to the market."*

goodwill: the intangible possession

that enables a business to continue to earn a profit in excess of the normal or basic rate of profit earned by other businesses of similar type.

go private: the process by which a corporation buys up its own stock which was in public hands. [105]

go public: to raise money for a corporation by offering stock for public sale. see *new issue, registration.*

go (going) short: selling a security short, that is, selling a security not owned, or owned but not delivered. cf. *go long.*

Gosplan: the state planning commission of the Soviet Union responsible for general economic planning.

gouge: slang, to acquire an excessive profit, by either overcharging or defrauding.

gourde: monetary unit of Haiti.

governing committee: a governing body of a recognized stock exchange.

governmental accounting: the composite activity of analyzing, recording, summarizing, reporting, and interpreting the financial transactions of governmental units and agencies. [49]

government bond: see *bond, government.*

government check: checks drawn on the Treasurer of the United States and collected through the Federal Reserve Banks. [105]

government depository: a bank that has been chosen to receive deposits of a government or its agency. Usually used to differentiate a bank designated as a depository for the U.S. government.

government deposits: funds of the U.S. government and its agencies which are required to be placed in de-

positories designated by the secretary of the Treasury.

government expenditures: gross expenditure amounts without deduction of any related receipts.

government monopoly: a monopoly owned and controlled by either a local, state, or federal government (e.g., U.S. Postal Service, water supply systems).

Government National Mortgage Association (GNMA): an agency of the Department of Housing and Urban Development. Its primary function is in the area of government-approved special housing programs, by offering permanent financing for low-rent housing. Nickname, Ginnie Mae. see *Ginnie Mae trusts.*

government obligations (GO): instruments of the U.S. government public debt that are fully backed by the government, as contrasted with U.S. government securities—that is, Treasury bills, notes, bonds, and savings bonds.

government revenue: all money received other than from issue of debt, liquidation of investments, and agency and private trust transactions. Includes tax collections, charges and miscellaneous revenue, intergovernmental revenue, utility, sales of alcoholic beverages, and insurance trust revenue for all funds and agencies of a government. Revenue is net of refunds and other correcting acts.

"governments": as used in the United States, all types of securities issued by the federal government (U.S. Treasury obligations), including, in its broad concept, securities issued by agencies of the federal government. [67]

government saving: tax receipts less government expenditures.

government securities: securities issued by U.S. government agencies for example, Federal Land Bank bonds and Federal Home Loan Bank notes. These securities are not guaranteed by the federal government.

government securities dealers: firms, including a few large banks with their own dealer units as well as non-bank dealers, that finance significant inventories of U.S. government stocks via borrowing from banks and corporations.

GP
(1) see *going public.*
(2) see *gold points.*
(3) see *grace period.*
(4) see *gross profit.*

GPAM: see *graduated-payment adjustable mortgage.*

GPMs: see *graduated-payment mortgage.*

GR
(1) see *gross receipts.*
(2) see *gross revenue.*

grace period
(1) *general:* most contracts provide that the policy will remain in force if premiums are paid at any time within a period (the "grace period") varying from 28 to 31 days following the premium-due date.
(2) *banking:* the period when a mortgage payment becomes past due, before it goes into default.

grade creep: slang; in personnel compensation systems, the tendency to upgrade the rating and pay for a specific job. Under this concept, a highly inflationary trend is encouraged.

graded tax: a form of local taxation; an attempt to place an increasingly heavy burden on land values and at the same time a lessening burden for land improvements. The primary objective is to dissuade owners from keeping their land unimproved—specifically, by building on the property.

grades (grading): the classification into well-defined grades of major commodities. The standardization in quality difference of staple commodities for purposes of identification during trading periods.

graduated-payment adjustable mortgage (GPAM): a GPM with an adjustable rate; the borrower and lender share interest rate risk. see *graduated-payment mortgages, price-level-adjusted mortgage.*

graduated payment adjustable mortgage loan: a mortgage instrument that combines features of the graduated payment mortgage and the adjustable mortgage loan was authorized by the Federal Home Loan Bank Board in July 1981. Lenders are now able to offer mortgage loans where the interest rate may change to reflect changes in the market place and where the monthly payments for the first 10 years may be set at a lower amount than required to fully amortize the loan.

graduated-payment mortgage (GPM): first insured by the Federal Housing Administration in 1977, where payments are much lower at first than for traditional level-payment mortgages. Prices then rise gradually and level off after a few years. The idea is to put home ownership within reach of young people who might otherwise be forced by spiraling housing prices and high interest rates to remain renters. see also *flexible-payment mortgage, pledged-account mortgage, price-level-adjusted mortgage, reverse-annuity mortgage, rollover mortgage, variable-rate mortgage.*

graduated securities: stocks that have moved from one exchange to another (e.g., from the American Stock Exchange to the New York Stock Exchange).

graduated tax: a progressive tax; the rate of tax per unit of the tax base increases as the number of units increases.

graft: a financial or other gain achieved through the abuse of a person's position or influence.

grain bill: a bill of exchange drawn against grain shipments.

grain exchanges: commodity exchanges that trade in spot and futures of grain.

grain pit: part of a trading area of a commodity or grain exchange where pit traders or commodity brokers transact business. The pit is really a series of concentric rings, with each ring indicating a different contract period.

grand: slang, $1000.

grandfather clause: any condition that ties existing rights or privileges to previous or remote conditions or acts. More popularly used when a new regulation goes into effect, to exempt people already engaged in the activity being regulated.

grandfathered activities: nonbank activities, some of which would normally be impermissible for bank holding companies, but which were acquired or engaged in before a particular date. Such activities may be continued under the "grandfather" clause of the Bank Holding Company Act—some until 1981 and some indefinitely. [1]

grant: a clause in a deed reflecting the transfer of title to real property.

grantee: an individual to whom a grant is made; the person named in a deed to receive title to property.

granter: a person who offers credit.

grantor: an individual who makes a grant; a person who executes a deed giving up title to property.

grants-in-aid: payments made by one government unit to another for specified purposes. They represent federal support for a state or locally administered program, or state support for a local program. cf. *revenue sharing.*

gratuitous coinage: a government policy of producing coins from metal without cost to the owner of the metal.

gratuity: a gift or donation.

gravelled: a London Stock Exchange term, synonymous with *bottom out.*

graveyard market: a securities market where those who are in cannot get out and those who are out cannot get in.

gravy: money that is in excess of what is anticipated; money easily earned.

gravy train: slang, a chance to receive excessive funds for little or no work.

gray knight: an opportunistic second bidder in a company takeover, not sought out by the target, who attempts to take advantage of the problems between the target and the initial bidder. cf. *white knight.*

gray market: sources of supply from which scarce items are bought for quick delivery at a premium well above the usual market price. Individuals engaged in this legal activity speculate on future demands. cf. *black market.*

green: slang, paper money.

greenbacks

(1) inconvertible notes used during the Civil War that were legal tender for all public and private debts except interest on the national debt or import duties.

(2) presently, used to refer to any of the paper money issues of the Federal Reserve Banks or the U.S. Treasury.

greenlining: a response of community citizens who withdraw their accounts from lending institutions that they believe practice redlining. see *redlining.*

green power: the power of money.

Gresham's law: describes the fact that bad money tends to drive out good money. Refers to the way in which people protect themselves from loss by spending money of questionable value and holding onto money of known better value. cf. *quantity theory. see good money.*

grift: slang, money made dishonestly, especially by swindling.

gross
(1) *general:* 12 dozen.
(2) *finance:* the total amount before any deductions have been made.

gross asset: all property in possession of a company. Gross assets are the total of the ledger and nonledger assets. [42]

gross bonded debt: the total amount of direct debt of a governmental unit represented by outstanding bonds before deduction of sinking fund assets. see *direct debt.* [49]

gross book value: the dollar amount at which an asset is carried on a firm's books, without making a deduction for accumulated depreciation or any other contra accounts. [105]

gross charge: the ratio between the interest charge on a discount interest loan and the discounted amount disbursed to the borrower. [59]

gross debt: all long-term credit obligations incurred and outstanding, whether backed by a government's full faith and credit or nonguaranteed, and all interest-bearing short-term credit obligations.

gross deposits: all deposits, without any exclusions or deductions. This would include all forms of demand and time deposits (i.e. those due banks and government deposits).

gross domestic product (GDP): the total value of a nation's output, income, or expenditure produced within a nation's physical borders.

gross earnings: the total income of a business, usually segregated as to type in financial income statements.

grossed-up net redemption yield: British term for net redemption yield on a security, divided by the proportion of marginal income retained by the investor following tax.

gross estate: all of a person's property before debts, taxes, and other expenses or liabilities have been deducted; to be distinguished from *net estate,* which is what is left after these items have been taken into account. [37]

gross income: revenues before any expenses have been deducted.

gross income multiplier: a figure by which effective gross income is multiplied to obtain an amount that indicates the capital value of property. [44]

gross interest: the full price paid for something, including the cost of the capital and the cost of the administration of the transaction.

gross lease: a lease of property under which the lessor agrees to meet all charges which would normally be incurred by the owner of that property. [62]

gross line: the amount of insurance a company has on a risk, including the amount it has reinsured. "Net lines" plus reinsurance equals the "gross line."

gross margin
(1) the amount, determined by subtracting the cost of goods sold from net sales, which covers operating and financial expenses and provides net income. synonymous with *gross profit*.
(2) the dollar difference between the net sales and the net cost of goods sold during a stated time frame. Gross margin percentage is calculated by dividing net sales into this figure.

gross national debt: the total indebtedness of the federal government, including debts owed by one agency to another.

gross national disproduct: the total of all social costs or reductions in benefits to the community that result from producing the gross national product (e.g., the pollution of rivers is part of the gross national disproduct).

gross national expenditure: the full amount spent by the four sectors of the economy (household, government, business, and foreign) on the nation's output of goods and services. It is equal to the gross national product.

gross national income: synonymous with *gross national product*.

gross national product (GNP): the total retail market value of all items and services produced in a country during a specified period, usually one year. Distribution is presented in terms of consumer and government purchases, gross private national and foreign investments, and exports.

gross national product deflator: a price index or combination of indexes which reveals changes in the price level over a number of years according to constant values and for a larger eco-nomic segment than is usually embraced by other price indexes.

gross national product gap: the difference between potential and actual GNP as calculated by the Council of Economic Advisors. [108]

gross operating income: an accounting term that includes income received from the ordinary operation of the business before deducting expenses of operation. [59]

gross private domestic investment: purchases of newly produced capital goods plus the value of the change in the volume of inventories held by business. Purchases include all new private dwellings, whether leased to tenants or owner occupied.

gross profit: operating revenue less the cost of goods sold. see *gross margin*. [77]

gross profit ratio: the ratio to sales of the difference between sales and the cost of merchandise sold.

gross rate: see *flat rate*.

gross receipts: total receipts prior to deducting expenses.

gross registered tonnage: the tonnage of a vessel as registered; calculated not on weight but by cubic capacity (100 cubic feet = 1 registered ton). cf. *deadweight tonnage*.

gross revenue: total revenues received from selling goods or performing services. A revenue before any deductions have been made for returns, allowances, or discounts. Often called *gross sales*.

gross sales: total sales, over a specified period, before customer returns and allowances have been deducted.

gross savings: the sum of capital consumption (depreciation), and personal and corporate savings.

gross spread: a banking term used to determine underwriting fees. see *underwriter.*

gross variance: the total difference between actual and standard attainment under a standard cost system. Gross variance is generally broken down into volume and efficiency components. [38]

gross volume: total dollar amount of all merchant sales and cash advances. [105]

gross yield: the return obtained from an investment before the deduction of costs and losses involved in procuring and managing the investment. see *net yield.* [44]

gross yield to redemption: British term for interest yield on a security plus the annual capital gain should the security be held to redemption.

ground floor: slang, a low price security with expectations of considerable increase in value.

ground lease: a contract for the rental of land on a long-term basis. [105]

ground rent
(1) a price paid each year, or for a term of years, for the right to occupy a parcel of real property.
(2) rent paid for vacant land. If the property is improved, ground rent is that portion attributable to the land only. [105]

group annuity: a pension plan providing annuities at retirement to a group of persons under a master contract. It is usually issued to an employer for a group of employees. [105]

group banking: a form of banking enterprise whereby a group of existing banks form a holding company. The holding company supervises and coordinates the operations of all banks in the group. A majority of the capital stock of each bank in the group is owned by the holding company.

group enrollment card: a document signed by an individual eligible for group insurance as notice of his or her wish to participate in the group plan. In a contributory case, this card also provides an employer with authorization to deduct contributions from an employee's pay.

group insurance: any insurance plan under which a number of employees and their dependents are covered by a single policy, issued to the employer or often to an association with which the employees are affiliated, with individual certificates given to each insured person. see *noncontributory.*

group life insurance: life insurance, usually without medical examination, on a group of people under a master policy. It is typically issued to an employer for the benefit of employees. The individual members of the group hold certificates as evidence of their insurance. [58]

Group of Ten: composed of the prosperous countries of the world who fix and regulate their policies in international monetary activities. Members are Belgium, Canada, France, Great Britain, Italy, Japan, the Netherlands, Portugal, Spain, Sweden, the United States, and West Germany. Switzerland is an unofficial member.

group sale: a sale of securities shared pro rata by each of the selling syndicate members, as contrasted to a designated sale, where only certain members participate.

growing equity mortgage: a home mortgage with a fixed interest rate, but monthly payment may vary according to an agreed schedule or index. synonymous with *rapid-payoff mortgage*.

growth fund: a mutual fund whose holdings are made up primarily of growth stocks. The more speculative of these are often referred to as go-go stocks.

growth in earnings per share: annual percentage growth in primary earnings per share for the restated five-year period ending December 31, based on the least-squares method.

growth recession: coined by Solomon Fabricant, a period in which the economy slows dramatically but keeps sputtering forward. While the economy grows, the decline in the rate of expansion is seen as almost as traumatic as an outright contraction.

growth stock: stock of a corporation whose existing and projected earnings are sufficiently positive to indicate an appreciable and constant increase in the stock's market value over an extended time period, the rate of increase being larger than those of most corporate stocks.

GS
(1) see *glamour stock*.
(2) see *government securities*.
(3) see *gross sales*.
(4) see *gross spread*.
(5) see *growth stock*.

GSA: see *Glass-Steagal Act of 1933*.

GSL: see *guaranteed student loans*.

GSP: see *generalized scheme of preferences*.

GT: see *gift tax*.

GTC: see *good-'til-canceled order*.

Gtd.: guaranteed.

GTM: see *good-this-month order*.

GTW: see *good-this-week order*.

Guar.: see *guarantee*.

guarani: monetary unit of Paraguay.

guarantee: a written statement assuring that something is of stated quantity, quality, content, or benefit, or that it will perform as advertised for a stated period. In some cases, all or part of the purchaser's money will be refunded if the item fails to meet the terms of a guarantee. see *guaranty*.

guaranteed account: an account, the prompt and full payment of which is guaranteed by a responsible agency or person. Usually, guaranteed accounts are those for minors whose legal credit responsibility is deemed insufficient for granting unsupported credit or individuals whose payment record or other factors make necessary the guarantee of a more responsible person. [41]

guaranteed annual wage (GAW): a plan whereby an employer agrees to provide his employees a special minimum of employment or income for a year. Unions argue that GAW plans add to income and employment stability. Management argues that GAW does not take into account the fluctuations in demand for goods, and is thus a poor business practice. cf. *Halsey premium plan*.

guaranteed bond: see *bond, guaranteed*.

guaranteed debt: obligations of certain semipublic and public corporations that are guaranteed by the federal government as contingent liabilities.

guaranteed deposits: see *Federal Deposit Insurance Corporation*.

guaranteed division: a dividend on the capital stock of a firm, which has been guaranteed to be paid at specific intervals. [105]

guaranteed income contracts (GICs): agreements that promise a rate of return no matter how well or poorly an insurance company's investment portfolio performs.

guaranteed insurability: an option that permits the policyholder to buy additional amounts of life insurance at stated times with evidence of insurability.

guaranteed interest
(1) rate of interest return specified in the policy as the rate at which reserves will be accumulated.
(2) rate of interest paid on funds deposited with the company, either for advance premium deposits or in accordance with the settlements options. [12]

guaranteed investment contracts (GICs): public bonds which typically promise a fixed rate of return for relatively short periods—3 to 10 years.

guaranteed letter of credit: travelers' letters of credit or commercial letters of credit; the party requesting the credit issuance does not pay the bank in cash for the equivalent amount of the credit upon its issuance. The bank substitutes its own credit for people or firms, to encourage more domestic and foreign trade.

guaranteed mortgage: a mortgage with a guarantee of payment of principal or interest or both. The Federal Housing Administration and the Veterans Administration offer the majority of these mortgages today.

guaranteed stock: usually, preferred stock on which dividends are guaranteed by another company; under much the same circumstances as a bond is guaranteed. [20]

guaranteed student loans (GSL): loans primarily made by banks, savings and loan associations, and credit unions, and some colleges. The federal government pays the full 9 percent interest on loans for college students while they are enrolled.

guarantee of signature: a certificate affixed to the assignment of a stock certificate or registered bond or to other documents by a bank or stock exchange house, vouching for the genuineness of the signature of the registered holder. [37]

guarantees: federal credit aid in which the federal government pledges its financial liability for loans made by private or state or local government institutions.

guarantees against price decline: guarantees given by a manufacturer to distributors that if his or her price to them declines within a given period after purchase, he or she will reimburse them for the amount of the decline on remaining stock. [9]

guarantor: one who makes a guaranty; an individual who by contract is prepared to answer for the debt, default, and miscarriage of another. see *guaranty.*

guaranty: a contract, agreement, or undertaking involving three parties. The first party (the guarantor) agrees to see that the performance of a second party (the guarantee) is fulfilled according to the terms of the contract, agreement, or undertaking. The third party is the creditor, or the party, to benefit by the performance.

guaranty fund: a fund which a mutual savings bank in certain states must create through subscriptions or out of earnings to meet possible losses resulting from decline in value of investments or from other unforeseen contingencies. In other states, such a fund is known as the *surplus fund*. [39]

guaranty savings bank: a savings bank with features of both a mutual savings bank and a stock savings bank.

guaranty stock: basic stock that is not withdrawable and which protects the interest of all other investors against losses. [59]

guardian: an individual chosen by a court to oversee the property rights and person of minors, persons adjudged to be insane, and other incompetents.

guardian account: an account in the name of a guardian who acts on behalf of and administers the funds for the benefit of the ward. [39]

guardian ad litem: a particular guardian chosen for the single purpose of carrying on litigation and preserving a ward's interests but who has no control or power over the ward's property.

guardian deed: see *deed, guardian.*

guardian de son tort: a person, though not a regularly appointed guardian, who takes possession of an infant's or an incompetent person's property and manages it as if he or she were guardian, thereby becoming accountable to the court.

guardianship account: an account in the name of a guardian who acts on behalf of and administers the funds for the benefit of the ward.

GUC: see *good-'til-canceled order.*

guerrilla financing: loans devised on their own outside conventional channels. A strategy to protect an individual seller who lends money privately to the individual buyers who might get saddled with a risky, illiquid asset when cash comes in gradually as the buyer pays off the note.

guerrillas: municipal bond syndicates that attempt to outbid independent bidders on new bond issues. synonymous with *barracudas.*

guilder: monetary unit of the Netherlands, Netherlands Antilles, and Surinam.

guillotine clause: slang, a clause that permits the lender to call a loan if the mortgage conditions are not met.

gulf riyal: monetary unit of Dubai and Qatar.

gunslinger: Wall Street slang for *speculator.*

gutter market: the outdoor securities market that existed in 1914 during World War I when the exchange was closed. Trading was conducted on New Street near the New York Stock Exchange building.

gyp 'ems: slang, for graduated-payment mortgages. see *graduated-payment mortgages.*

HA: see *house account.*

habeas corpus: a writ ordering an official having custody of a person alleged to be unlawfully detained to return the individual before a court to determine whether the imprisonment was legal.

habendum clause: a deed of mortgage clause that defines the extent of the property being transferred. It reads: "To have and to hold the premises herein granted unto the party of the second party (i.e., the grantee), his heirs and the assigns forever."

hacking the pie: slang, what occurs at the end-of-the-year meeting of partners when they divide up a firm's profits.

haggling: see *higgling.*

haircut finance: a borrowing made against securities as collateral.

half-buck: slang, a half-dollar (50 cents).

half-life: the time that elapses until half the principal amount of a block of bonds has been redeemed.

half-stock: common or preferred stock having a par value of $50.

hallmark: an impression made on gold and silverware introduced in the beginning of the fourteenth century in England to identify the quality of the metal used.

Halsey premium plan: incentive wage plan which provided for a guaranteed wage in addition to an extra bonus for performance in excess of the norm.

hammering the market: the persistent selling of securities by speculators operating on the short side who believe that prices are inflated and that liquidation is imminent. When the market is primarily affected by the bears, these individuals are said to be *hammering the market.*

handbill: paper currency.

handling charge: see *interchange fee.*

hand signals: a system used by brokers during the early days of the American Stock Exchange to communicate executions and quotations to their clerks.

hang-out loan: a loan lasting longer than its lease.

hard: see *hard currency.*

hard cash: metallic currency, as distinguished from paper money.

hard currency: currency whose value is expected to remain stable or increase in terms of other currencies; alternatively, a freely convertible currency may be referred to as *hard*.

harden: following a drop in the price for securities, a surge in buying leading to a price increase.

hard loan: a foreign loan that must be paid in hard money.

hard money (currency)

(1) *finance:* currency of a nation having stability in the country and abroad.

(2) *finance:* coins, in contrast with paper currency, or soft money.

(3) *finance:* describes a situation in which interest rates are high and loans are difficult to arrange. synonymous with *dear money*.

hard sell: slang, attempting to sell goods or services in an aggressive, often unpleasant fashion.

hard spot: a security or group of securities holding strong in a generally weak market.

hard stuff: slang, money.

hardware

(1) *general:* mechanical equipment used for conducting an activity.

(2) *computers:* the electric, electronic, and mechanical equipment used for processing data, consisting of racks, tubes, transistors, wires, and so on. cf. *software*.

Harter Act: legislation protecting a ship's owner against claims for damage resulting from the behavior of the vessel's crew, provided that the ship left port in a seaworthy condition, properly manned and equipped.

Hart-Scott-Rodino Act: federal legislation of 1976, requiring companies to notify the Federal Trade Commission and the Justice Department of their plans to buy more than $15 million or 15 percent of a company. see also *Herfindahl index*.

Hatch Act: the Federal Corrupt Practices Act; Section 313 of this law was amended by Section 304 of the Taft-Hartley Act to make it unlawful for (a) banks and corporations authorized by Congress to make a contribution or expenditure in connection with election to any political office or activity; and (b) any corporation or labor organization to make a contribution or expenditure in connection with any election or political activity.

Hawley-Smoot Act: legislation of 1930 that raised tariffs, spurring foreign retaliation and a decline in world trade.

hazard insurance: a form of insurance coverage for real estate that includes protection against loss from fire, certain natural causes, vandalism, and malicious mischief. see also *homeowner's insurance.* [59]

HC: see *holding company*.

head tax: a tax imposed on immigrant aliens on their entry to the United States.

head teller: a teller in a bank who sometimes has the title of assistant cashier. The head teller is usually custodian of the reserve cash in the bank's vault. It is his or her responsibility to see that an "economical" quantity of cash is on hand at all times to meet the normal demands of the banks customers. It is his responsibility to assemble the cash figures for all tellers at the end of the business day, and prepare the cash report for the general ledger. He is also responsible for the work of all tellers in the bank, and he must recount cash for a teller who comes up with a difference at the end of the day. He must fully report any overage or shortages that may appear, and assist where possible to locate the difference. [10]

health expense account: synonymous with *flexible reimbursement plan*.

heart attack market: the market's reaction following President Eisenhower's heart attack in 1955 when the Dow Jones Industrial Average dropped 31.89 points, 6.5 percent.

heavy market: a declining securities and commodities market created when the supply of bids for buying shares exceeds the demand for them, resulting in a price drop.

hedge: to offset. Also, a security that has offsetting qualities. Thus one attempts to "hedge" against inflation by the purchase of securities whose values should respond to inflationary developments. Securities having these qualities are "inflation hedges." see *arbitrage, puts and calls, short sale.* [30]

hedge clause: a disclaimer that disavows legal responsibility for the accuracy of information from outside sources.

hedge fund: a partnership of people who pool their resources for purposes of investment. cf. *investment company.*

hedger: an individual who is unwilling to risk a serious loss in his or her cash position and takes a counterbalancing position in order to avoid or lessen loss.

hedging: a type of economic insurance used by dealers in commodities and securities, manufacturers, and other producers to prevent loss due to price fluctuations. Hedging consists of counterbalancing a present sale or purchase by a purchase or sale of a similar commodity or of a different commodity, usually for delivery at some future date. The desired result is that the profit or loss on a current sale or purchase be offset by the loss or profit on the future purchase or sale.

hedging clause: a protective statement of warning for securities customers that customarily reads: "The information furnished herein has been obtained from sources believed to be reliable, but its accuracy is not guaranteed."

heirs: people who receive(d) the title to property upon the death of an ancestor or other testator.

heirs-at-law: the persons who inherit the real property of a person who dies without a valid will disposing of his or her property. [105]

held over: see *holdovers.*

held to maturity: see *Moody's Bond Yield.*

hell-or-high-water contract: see *take-or-pay contract.*

Hepburn Act: the 1906 act of Congress permitting the Interstate Commerce Commission to announce rate changes and make them effective within 30 days until suspended by a court. The act also expanded the jurisdiction of the Commission to cover pipelines and sleeping cars.

hereditament: property that can be inherited.

Herfindahl index: a mathematical standard for determining when an industry is so concentrated that mergers will be anticompetitive. see also *Hart-Scott-Rodino Act.*

hesiflation: a concept suggested by former Secretary of the Treasury Henry H. Fowler for a reduced growth pattern in the economy combined with strong inflationary pressures. cf. *stagflation.*

HHFA: see *Housing and Home Finance Agency.*

HI: see *hot issue.*

hiccup: slang, a short-lived drop in the stock market.

Hicksian IS-LM framework: see *IS-LM model.*

hidden amenities: desirable aspects of property that are provided but not always given attention on first inspection.

hidden assets: assets of a firm that are not easily identifiable by examining the balance sheet.

hidden clause: in a contract, any obscure provision that stipulates requirements that may be against the buyer's interests.

hidden inflation: inflation not revealed by economic indicators, usually resulting in a lowering of quality.

hidden reserve: by undervaluing assets or overvaluing liabilities, a hidden reserve is created; that is, the surplus amount thus created is not apparent from an examination of a financial statement.

hidden tax: a tax included in the price of goods and services that is not easily identifiable by the payer of the tax.

higgling
(1) when the buyer offers a low price and the seller asks a high price, and through bargaining, a third price is arrived at to satisfy both parties.
(2) sometimes referred to as *haggling*.

high balance: account upon which the outstanding balance exceeds the authorized credit limit. see *high credit, over-limit account.* [105]

high credit: highest amount of credit extended to a particular customer at one time. [41]

highest credit: the greatest amount owed by the consumer within the last year or on the last installment contract. [76]

high finance
(1) *general:* utilizing another's funds in a speculative fashion, which may result in a loss to the funds' owner.
(2) *finance:* borrowing to the maximum of one's credit.
(3) *finance:* extremely complicated transactions.

high flyers: high-priced speculative securities that move up or down several points in a trading day.

high grade: describes an item of superior quality (e.g., high-grade stock).

high posting: see *postlist.*

high-powered money: see *monetary base.*

high-premium convertible debenture: a bond with a long-term equity kicker packaged to offer some protection against inflation. Designed primarily for the bond buyer, it carries a higher return than conventional convertible debentures.

high-ratio loan: mortgage loans in excess of 80 percent of the sales price or value, whichever is less. [105]

high-volume accounts: an account whose activity is so unusually large as to warrant special handling. [31]

highway trust fund: a trust fund through which is financed the expanded program of federal highway aid. Appropriations based on certain highway user tax collections are made to the fund, and from it, federal payments to states for highways are made.

hi-lo index: the moving average of individual stocks that attain new highs and new lows each day, indicating a weakening or improving market in general. At the same time, an established indicator (e.g., Dow Jones Industrials might show no action or even opposite movement in blue-chip issues).

H. in D.C.: see *holder in due course.*

Hinky Dinky: the name of a Nebraska supermarket chain whose employees operate in-store terminals provided by First Federal Savings and Loan of Lincoln, Nebraska, to permit First Federal customers to make deposits and withdrawals in the store. This service is significant because (a) it enables off-premises access to accounts maintained at a depository institution, and (b) the accounts bear interest. see *service counter terminals.*

hire purchase: used in Great Britain for purchases made on time payments or on the installment plan.

hi-risk: displayed on a merchant inquiry screen if a fraud transaction occurred at the outlet during the current month. [105]

historical cost: the principle requiring that all information on financial statements be presented in terms of the item's original cost to the entity. The dollar is assumed to be stable from one time period to another.

historical rate: assets such as inventories, property, plant, and equipment are translated into dollars at the rate in effect when the assets were acquired.

hit the bid: selling at the highest bid price quoted for a stock.

hoarding: to collect for the sake of accumulating; a planned effort by persons to accumulate items beyond normal need (e.g., purchasing dozens of cartons of cigarettes in anticipation of a price hike).

HOI: see *house of issue.*

hokeys: see *Home Owners' Loan Corporation Bonds.*

HOLC: Home Owners Loan Corporation. A federal corporation organized in 1933 for the purpose of making loans to owners of small homes who were either delinquent in their payments and in danger of losing their homes or on the verge of becoming delinquent.

hold: used to indicate that a certain amount of a customer's balance is held intact by the bookkeeper until an item has been collected, or until a specific check or debit comes through for posting. [31]

holder: the bearer possessing an instrument.

holder in due course: a person who has taken an instrument under the following conditions; (a) that it is complete and regular upon its face; (b) that he or she become a holder of it before it was overdue, and without notice that it had been previously dishonored, if such was the fact; (c) that the holder took it in good faith and for value; and (d) that at the time it was negotiated to him or her, the holder had no notice of any infirmity in the instrument or defect in the title of the person negotiating it. see *endorsement.*

Holder in Due Course Rule: a Federal Trade Commission rule, effective May 14, 1976, which requires sellers to assure that consumers retain the right to assert claims and defenses against whoever holds the debt instrument used to purchase goods or service. [105]

holder of record: dividends are declared payable to stockholders owning shares on a specific date. Such stockholders are said to be "holders of record."

hold harmless: a clause agreeing to assume the liabilities or losses involved.

holding company: a corporation that owns the securities of another, in most cases with voting control. synonymous with *parent company* and *proprietary company.* see *group banking, holding company (multiple-bank), holding company (one-bank).*

holding company (multiple-bank): a bank holding company, however defined, that owns or controls two or more banks. [74]

holding company (one-bank): at present, there is no legal definition of a one-bank holding company. A very broad definition would be any company that owns or controls a single bank. [74]

holding company affiliate: a legal term fully defined in the Banking Act of 1933. Generally, it pertains to any organization that owns or controls any one bank either through stock ownership or through any means that allows it to elect a majority of the bank's directors. [74]

holding the line: monetary or fiscal policies used to prevent or discourage prices from climbing above a current level. Measures include freezing prices, increasing bank reserves, increasing the discount rate, and restricting consumer loans.

holding the market: to minimize the decline in the price of a security, a sufficient quantity of the stock is purchased to support the interest in a particular share.

holdovers: used, usually in large banks, to describe a portion of work that has to be processed by a twilight shift or a night force. The 40-hour workweek makes it frequently necessary for the bank to employ three shifts. Since the business day starts officially at midnight, work that has not been processed by the twilight force is "held over" to the night force, which starts processing the remaining work. The work, for control purposes, is credited to the twilight force, and recharged as "hold-overs" to the night force. [10]

hollow note: a $100 bill.

holographic will: a will entirely in the handwriting of the testator. [105]

home banking: a concept in banking, pioneered in 1980 by Banc One Corporation in Columbus, Ohio. By connecting a device to TV sets and telephones, customers will be able to call up information about bills and bank accounts on their TV screens and pay bills with a push of a button. Since this approach does not allow deposits and cash withdrawals, it isn't considered a branch bank.

home conversion: borrowing against your home.

home debit: a self-check; any draft or check drawn upon a bank and subsequently brought to the same institution for deposit or payment.

home financing: the providing of funds, secured by a mortgage, for the purchase or construction of a residential structure containing one, two, three, or four dwelling units. [59]

home improvement loan: an advance of funds, usually not secured by a mortgage and usually short-term, made to a property owner for the upgrading of his property, such as maintenance and repair, additions and alterations, or replacement of equipment or structural elements. [59]

Home Loan Bank Act (System): see *Federal Home Loan Bank System.*

Home Loan Bank Board: an agency that roughly parallels for the Federal Home Loan Bank System the duties of the Board of Governors of the Federal Reserve Bank System.

Home Mortgage Disclosure Act: a federal law requiring certain financial institutions to disclose information about their home mortgage activities to the public and to government officials. [105]

homeowner's insurance: a broad form of insurance coverage for real estate that combines hazard insurance with personal liability protection and other items. [59]

Home Owners' Loan Act of 1933: federal legislation establishing the Home Owners' Loan Corporation with $200 million from the Reconstruction Finance Corporation; the corporation was authorized to release up to $2 billion in bonds to exchange for mortgages. see *Federal Savings and Loan Association.*

Home Owners' Loan Corporation Bonds: authorized by the Home Owners Loan Act of 1934, $2 billion of bonds could be sold or exchanged for mortgages by the Home Owners Loan Corporation. Nicknamed "hokeys." The Corporation is now defunct and all bonds have been recalled.

homeowner's policy: an insurance policy that covers personal liability as well as home damages caused by fire, wind, or hail. [105]

homestead association: the name used by some savings associations in the state of Louisiana. [59]

homestead estate: a type of estate ownership in land, permissible in a number of states, that protects the possession and enjoyment of the owner against the claims of creditors and from execution and sale for his or her general debts, provided that he or she has a family. [59]

homogenization: the blurring of the traditional distinctions among a nation's financial institutions, where banks, thrift institutions, and credit unions have moved onto each other's turf but increasingly are facing stiff competition from nonregulated, nonfinancial institutions.

Hon'd: see *honored.*

honeycombed with stops: a securities market containing entries of many stop orders.

honor: to pay or to accept a draft complying with the terms of credit.

honor bond: see *bond, honor.*

honored: when attributed to a draft or a note, the paper was either accepted or paid.

Hopkinson rate: in public utilities, a rate made up of two parts. The demand charge is a specific charge for fixed capacity costs. The energy chart is based on the variable output costs.

HOR: see *holder of record.*

horizontal audit: a method of testing the practical operation of internal controls by observing the accounting procedures. This is done by a public accountant. [105]

horizontal intergration: the expansion of a business by acquiring other firms or divisions engaged in the same stage of production of the same product. [105]

horizontal merger: a combination formed when two or more businesses producing the same goods or service merge.

horizontal price fixing: an agreement on prices among competitors at similar levels of distribution.

hot card: used to describe a card being used on an account on which excessive purchasing is taking place. Usually a lost or stolen card or otherwise indicative of unauthorized purchasing. [105]

hot card list: a list of delinquent accounts or stolen plastic cards. see *restricted card list*. [105]

hot issue: a stock in great demand, often when sold for the first time. A typical symptom is a rapid price rise with the original purchaser making a quick profit.

hot money: money that is received through means that are either illegal or of questionable legality.

"hots": in Great Britain, Treasury bills on the day they are issued, with their full term to run.

hot stuff: an indication for good selling propaganda within literature pertaining to a stock issue, whether truthful or not.

house account
(1) *general:* any account belonging to a client that has not been nor ever may be assigned to a firm's representative.
(2) *investments:* an account created by a brokerage company for its own use.

house bill: any bill of exchange drawn by a central office against a branch or affiliate.

house cleaning: slang, the reorganization of a firm, by rearranging positions and often releasing employees.

household saving: household disposable income less the existing household consumption.

house of issue: an investment banking firm engaged in underwriting and distribution of security issues.

house organ: a publication (newspaper, magazine) issued periodically by a company to its employees to keep them informed about the company, its personnel, and pertinent activities.

housepaper: a commercial bill of exchange drawn and accepted by firms in the same group, as a subsidiary, and accepted by its parent firm.

Housing Act of 1949: established national housing goals of "a decent home and suitable living environment for every American family"; provided grants to municipalities for public housing and slum clearance; set up a program of financial assistance for rural areas. [51]

Housing Act of 1961: authorized new programs for federal involvement in housing, including subsidized rental housing for low- and moderate-income families, and Federal Housing Administration insurance of liberal term loans for repair and modernization in declining urban areas; expanded funds for Federal National Mortgage Association special assistance functions. [51]

Housing and Community Development Act of 1977: raised ceilings on single-family loan amounts for association lending, federal agency purchases, Federal Housing Administration insurance and security for Federal Home Loan Bank advances;

raised ceilings on conventional and FHA home improvement loans. [51]

Housing and Home Finance Agency: a single agency created in 1977, responsible for major housing programs and activities of the federal government.

HR 10: see *Keogh Plan (HR 10).*

HSA: see *Hawley-Smoot Act.*

HUD: see *Department of Housing and Urban Development, U.S.*

hull: in marine insurance, the basic body of a vessel, as distinct from its cargo or equipment.

human resource accounting: the reporting and emphasis of the relevance of skilled and loyal employees in a firm's earning picture.

hung up: a situation of an investor whose money is tied up in securities that have dropped in value below the original purchase price, the selling of which will lead to a major loss.

hurdle rate: required rate of return, or minimum acceptable rate of return imposed on a proposed investment.

hush money: slang, money given to assure the silence of the receiver; a bribe.

hybrid basis accounting: a system of accounting that combines cash basis and accrual basis accounting. [59]

hybrid computer: a computer for data processing using both analog and digital representations of data.

hyperinflation: synonymous with *galloping inflation.*

hypothecary value: the value as-

signed by a lender to the collateral pledged to secure a loan.

hypothecate: to promise and place property to secure a loan. The identified property is said to be hypothecated.

hypothecated account: an account that is pledged or assigned as collateral for a loan. Savings accounts and trust accounts are usually selected for purposes of hypothecation.

hypothecated asset: things pledged without transferring possession or title.

hypothecated stock
(1) stock pledged as collateral for a loan.
(2) pawned stock.

hypothecation
(1) *banking:* an agreement or contract that permits a bank or a creditor to utilize the collateral pledge to secure a loan, in case the loan is unpaid at maturity. see *respondentia.*
(2) *investments:* the pledging of securities as collateral, for example, to secure the debit balance in a margin account. [20]

hysteresis: the nonreversibility of an economic function; for example, if in expansion, the cost curve goes down, then after the expansion an effort to contract to the original position will not proceed along the same cost curve. This is due to the fact that not all economies (or diseconomies) inherent in the expansion are lost in the contraction.

I

I

(1) see *interest*.

(2) the nominal market interest rate. [81]

IA

(1) see *inactive account*.

(2) see *intangible asset*.

IAA: see *Investment Advisers Act*.

IADB: *Inter-American Development Bank*.

IBA

(1) see *Independent Bankers Association of America*.

(2) see *International Banking Act of 1978*.

(3) see *Investment Bankers Association*.

IBANCO: a nonstock membership corporation responsible for administering and promoting the blue, white, and gold card program throughout the world. [105]

IBEC: see *International Bank for Economic Cooperation*.

IBFs: see *international banking facilities*.

IBRD: see *International Bank for Reconstruction and Development*.

ICA

(1) see *Interstate Commerce Act of 1887*.

(2) see *Investment Company Act of 1940*.

ICC

(1) see *International Chamber of Commerce*.

(2) see *Interstate Commerce Commission*.

ICE: see *International Commercial Exchange*.

ICS: see *issued capital stock*.

ID

(1) see *immediate delivery*.

(2) see *income debenture*.

(3) see *interim dividend*.

(4) see *interlocking directorate*.

(5) the discount rate. [81]

idemsonans: describes a legal document in which absolute accuracy in the spelling of names is not demanded. (e.g., "Eliot" or "Elliott" would be acceptable as designation of a person named Elliott).

identification: the procedure by which a bank teller or other employee assures himself as far as possible (through documents, contact with another bank, and other means) that the person with whom he is dealing is the person he or she claims to be. [39]

identifying number: a number provided by the Internal Revenue Service for tax purposes. In the case of an individual, it is his or her Social Security number. [105]

idle money

(1) *banking:* inactive bank deposits. see *unclaimed balances.*

(2) *finance:* uninvested available funds.

idle time

(1) *general:* time when an employee is unable to work because of machine malfunction or other factors not within the control of the worker. Usually the worker receives compensation during idle time.

(2) *computers:* the part of available time during which the computer is not in use.

IDP (integrated data processing)

(1) *computers:* a collection of data-processing techniques built around a common language, in which duplication of clerical operations is minimized. see also *ADP.*

(2) *systems:* data processing carried out, organized, and directed according to a systems approach.

IEEPA: see *International Emergency Economic Powers Act of 1977.*

IET: see *interest equalization tax.*

IF: see *insufficient funds.*

IFC: see *International Finance Corporation.*

IFE: see *Institute of Financial Education.*

if issued: see *when issued.*

ignorantia juris neminem excusat: "ignorance of the law is not excuse"

(Latin). The principle according to which you can be cited for parking illegally even if you say you didn't see the "No Parking" sign.

II: see *institutional investor.*

IID: see *investment in default.*

illegal: describes behavior contrary to the basic principles of law. An illegal act is forbidden by law, whereas an unlawful act, though not forbidden by law, is not given the protection of the law.

illegal operation: the process resulting when a computer either cannot perform the instruction part or will perform it with incorrect and irrelevant results. This shortcoming is often caused by built-in computer limitations.

illiquid

(1) *finance:* not easily convertible into cash; the opposite of liquid. Illiquid assets can be converted into cash, but usually at a major loss in value. Fixed assets are illiquid assets.

(2) *law:* not established by any documentary evidence.

illusory: appearing false. If that which seems to be a promise is found not to be a promise, it is said to be illusory.

IMF: see *International Monetary Fund.*

IMM: see *international money management.*

immediate and deferred credit: items sent to a Federal Reserve Bank are generally divided into separate cash letters which contain items for immediate credit and items for deferred credit. [31]

immediate annuity: an annuity commencing one month, one quarter, half a year, or one year after the effective date of payment.

immediate beneficiary: a beneficiary of a trust who is entitled to receive immediate benefits from the trust property, whether or not limited to income; opposed to ultimate beneficiary. synonymous with *primary beneficiary*. [37]

immediate credit: when a depositor draws on cash and home debit items in the form of withdrawal or check, while checks drawn on other banks are subject to "deferred availability" until they are collected, by the bank in which they have been deposited.

immediate delivery: an arrangement whereby an investor selects mortgages, generally from a mortgage banker's off-the-shelf inventory, for delivery, acceptance, and payment within a limited period, usually 30 days. [22]

immediate order: an order that must be executed at a state price as soon as it reaches the exchange floor, or be canceled. synonymous with *fill order* and *kill order*.

Immediate Payment Zones: an area served by one of approximately 40 check-clearing facilities at Federal Reserve Banks, their branches, and various separate regional centers. Immediate payment zones were established as the result of a Federal Reserve Board (FRB) policy statement (June 1971) that directed the expansion of regional check-clearing facilities for overnight clearing of most commercial bank checks. One objective of the FRB is to expand the zones as much as possible in order to minimize the shipping and processing of checks at the local level, where most remain throughout their lifetimes. A long-range goal is to effect immediate payment from bank to bank throughout the country via FedWire. [105]

immigrant remittances: funds of im-

migrants that are sent out of the country.

immovable: describes real property that cannot be moved (e.g., land, trees, structures).

immunity: that which confers the ability to escape from the legal duties or penalties imposed on others (see, e.g., indemnity).

immunization fund: a technique to protect pension-fund bond investments from sharply rising interest rates. To eliminate the risk of losing principal, the fund invests in government securities. The bank's actuaries fix the proportions of longer-term, medium-term and short-term securities by formulas that take into account differences in yields and the timeliness of cash flows from the securities.

Imp.
  (1) see *import*.
  (2) see *improvement*.

impact loan: a medium-term loan, usually five years, to a Japanese firm by a foreign bank in foreign currency.

impaired capital: when the capital of a firm is indeed less than the capital stated.

impaired credit: the reduction of credit given to a corporation resulting from the bank's decision that its credit worthiness has weakened. see *credit, line of credit*.

impaired risk: a risk that is substandard or under average.

impair investment: a money or near-money expenditure which does not result in capital formation, being either for consumption or a transfer and acquisition of existing capital.

impairment
  (1) *general:* the total, where liabilities exceed assets by reason of losses.

(2) *finance:* the amount by which stated capital is reduced by dividends and other distributions, and by losses.

imperfect competition: circumstances under which prices are usually altered by one or more persons. This occurs because of unusual conditions in the market or advantages secured by some buyers or sellers.

impersonal account: a ledger account bearing a title which is not a personal name.

implicit costs: costs originating within the business that are the responsibility of the owner (e.g., time, money).

implicit interest: synonymous with *imputed interest.*

implicit price deflator for gross national product: a measure of the average change in market prices of goods and services represented in the national income and product accounts, compared to average levels in a base period.

implied contract: a contract agreement that can be assumed by the nature of the actions of two parties but which does not entail an express agreement. [105]

implied easement: infringement on property that has been left unchallenged over a period of time. The infringement is apparent from continued and lengthy use.

implied trust: a trust created by operation of law or by judicial construction, to be distinguished from an express trust, which is created by express language, oral or in writing. [37]

import: to receive goods and services from abroad; an imported item.

import credit: a commercial letter of credit issued for the purpose of financing the importation of goods. [50]

import duty: any tax on items imported.

import letter of credit: see *import credit.*

import license: permission received from a government to import stated quantities of enumerated items.

import quota: a protective ruling establishing limits on the quantity of a particular product that can be imported.

imports of goods and services: represent the sum of all payments for merchandise imports, military expenditures, transportation and travel costs, other private and U.S. government services, and income and service payments to foreign parent companies by their affiliates operating in the United States. By far the largest component of this category is merchandise imports, which includes all goods bought or otherwise transferred from a foreign country to the United States. [73]

imposition: a demand or tax (e.g., bridge tolls, tariffs) on items or property made by a taxing authority.

impost: a tax, usually an import duty.

impound: to seize or hold; to place in protective custody by order of a court (e.g., impounded property, impounded records).

imprest (petty cash) fund: a fund of a designated amount out of which payments for expenses of small amounts are made; a system commonly employed in business.

imprinter: device supplied to each merchant who affiliates with a bank card plan to produce an image of the embossed characters of the bank card on all copies of sales drafts and credit slips. [105]

imprinter fee: the amount charged by the bank to a merchant for use of a bank-owned imprinter. [105]

imprinting: to place on the face of a document the magnetic ink characters specified by the American Bankers Association. synonymous with *encoding*. [31]

improvement: a change made in an asset to improve its condition with the expectation that it will also increase its value.

improvement lien: see *special assessment*.

improvement mortgage bond: see *bond, improvement mortgage*.

imputed: describes a value estimated when no cash payment is made, in order to establish that value.

imputed cost: a cost that is not specified but instead is implied to exist by the policies of the organization (e.g., interest that would have been earned on cash spent to purchase inventories).

imputed income: income received in some form other than money, usually stated in terms of goods or services. Imputed income includes wages paid in kind, rental value of owner-occupied homes, food and fuel produced and consumed on farms, and interest payments by financial intermediaries, which do not explicitly enter the national accounts. [105]

imputed interest: an estimate of value, charge, or interest due for using capital even though a cash payment has not been made. synonymous with *implicit interest*.

In.: see *income*.

inactive account: an account that has

little or no movement. The balance may be stationary, neither deposits nor withdrawals having been posted to the account for a period of time. cf. *idle money*. synonymous with *dormant account*.

inactive asset: that part of total assets that are not in continuous productive use in any business. An emergency generator not in use for an extended time period would be an inactive asset.

inactive bad debt account: an account charged off and judged to be uncollectible. [55]

inactive corporation: one which neither operates property nor administers its financial affairs. If it maintains an oganization, it does so only for the purpose of complying with legal requirements and maintaining title to property or franchises. [18]

inactive crowd: synonymous with *cabinet crowd*.

inactive market: a market condition characterized by a lower volume of activity than its usual.

inactive post: a trading post on the floor of the New York Stock Exchange where inactive securities are traded in units of 10 shares instead of the usual 100-share lots. Better known in the business as Post 30. see *round lot*. [20]

inactive stock (bond): an issue traded on an exchange or in the over-the-counter market in which there is a relatively low volume of transactions. Volume may be a few hundred shares a week or even less. see *cabinet crowd*.

inactive trust: a trust in which the trustee has no duty except to hold title to the property. [37]

inadvertent error: a mechanical, electronic, or clerical error that is not intentional. [78]

inalienable: not able to be sold or transferred. synonymous with *non assignable.*

in-and-out: the purchase and sale of the same security within a short period—day, a week, even a month. An in-and-out trader is generally more interested in day-to-day price fluctuations than dividends or long-term growth. [20]

INAS: see *Interbank National Authorization System.*

in balance: see *trial balance.*

Inc.

   (1) see *income.*

   (2) see *incorporate.*

incentive: a motivational force that stimulates people to greater activity or increased efficiency.

incentive bonus: cash payments, usually made at the end of the year, based on some measurement of individual performance and not equal in percentage or amount for individuals in the group being rewarded. [105]

incentive fee: synonymous with *performance fee.*

incentive pay: a wage system based on the productivity of a worker above a specified level. It may take the form of a piece rate, rate for performance above a fixed standard, or rate arrived at by some other method agreed upon.

incentive stock options: like traditional qualified options, there is no tax when you exercise the options. A person must hold the stock for at least one year from the date of exercise, and two years from the date the option was granted. When the stock is sold, the differences between the option price

and the sale price is taxed as a capital gain rather than as ordinary income.

incentive taxation: the use of taxation not only for purposes of public revenue but to encourage economic development along any given line.

incestuous share dealing: the buying and selling of one another's company securities for purposes of creating a tax or other financial advantage.

inchoate: newly begun or incomplete.

inchoate interest: a future interest in real estate.

incidence of taxation: see *tax incidence.*

incidents of ownership: the rights of the insured or his or her estate to the economic benefits of an insurance policy which makes the proceeds of the policy subject to estate tax. [105]

in-clearing items: items received by a bank as a result of a clearinghouse exchange are commonly called incoming clearings, or shortened to "in-clearings." [31]

income: money or its equivalent, earned or accrued, arising from the sale of goods or services. see *gross income, net income, profit, revenue.*

income account: an account in the general ledger of a bank. Expenses are listed under the assets, and the total expenses are usually deducted from the income accounts total to show the net profit to date as a portion of the undivided profits accounts.

income and expense statement: a summary of the incomes and costs of operation over a specified time period. synonymous with *profit and loss statement.*

income and profit: income and profit involve net or partially net concepts and refer to amounts resulting from the deduction from revenues, or from operating revenues, of cost of goods sold, other expenses, and losses, or some of them. The terms are often used interchangeably and are generally preceded by an appropriate qualifying adjective or term such as "gross," "operating," "net . . . before income taxes," and "net." [77]

income approach to value: a procedure for property appraisal in which the value on the net amount of income produced by the property is used. This value is determined by subtracting the total income of the property from expenses to determine net profit.

income available for fixed charges: total income less miscellaneous deductions, which consist of expenses of miscellaneous operations, taxes on miscellaneous operating property, miscellaneous rents and tax accruals, loss on separately operated properties, maintenance of investment organizations, income transferred to other companies, and miscellaneous income charges. [8]

income averaging: see *averaging*.

income basis: the ratio of the dollars of interest or dividend to the price paid for the security rather than to the face or par value.

income beneficiary: a person who, by the terms of a will or a trust instrument, is entitled to receive income from property for a specified number of years or for life. [37]

income bond: see *bond, income*.

income capital certificates: Federal Home Loan Bank Board Certificates that are agreements to pay back a corporation's loan, plus interest, when and if associations in financial difficulty get into a better position. Payments are installments, and are always less than the association's net income. Income capital certificates were initiated in September 1981.

income coverage
(1) *direct:* the extent to which net income from portfolio investments (after deduction of any prior interest or preferred dividend requirements) covers the requirements of a specific senior obligation, whether bank loans, debentures or preferred stock; in computing the coverage for bank loans or debentures, interest actually paid is added back to net income. The coverage figure may be expressed in dollars, as a percentage, or as a ratio.
(2) *overall:* the amount by which net income from portfolio investments plus interest actually paid covers total interest charges, if any, senior preferred dividends, if any, and the dividend requirement of the subject issue. [30]

income debenture: a corporate bond paying interest only when earned. By means of a subordinate venture, the interest it bears is senior to stock dividends.

income deductions: includes interest on long-term debt, amortization of debt discount, expanse and premium-net, taxes assumed on interest, interest on debt to associated companies, other interest charges, interest charged to construction (credit), miscellaneous amortization and income deductions (any nonrecurring income deductions of a material amount should be noted). [3]

income distribution: the way in which personal income is dispensed throughout the various socioeconomic levels in a nation.

income dividends: payments to mutual fund shareholders of dividends, interest, and short-term capital gains earned on the fund's portfolio securities after deduction of operating expenses. [23]

income effect: the change in the quantity of an item demanded because a person's purchasing power has been altered.

income fund: an investment company whose primary objective is generous current income. May be a balanced fund, common stock fund, bond fund, or a preferred stock fund. [30]

income in kind: goods or services received by an individual directly as income rather than through money payments. cf. *real income*.

income in respect of a decedent (IRD): income items and deductible obligations that would have been receivable or payable by the decedent had he or she lived and that are received or paid by his or her estate or successor to the property have the same tax consequences to the estate or successors when received or paid and retain the same character they would have had in the hands of the decedent. [105]

income interchange: sales drafts received by a cardholder bank. [105]

income portfolio: an aggregate of securities held primarily because they generate a steady income.

income property: property, usually commercial, industrial, or residential, owned or purchased for a financial return expected.

income return: monies earned from an investment over the period of one year. see *yield*.

income statement

(1) *general:* the profit and loss statement of a given concern for a particular period of time.

(2) *banking:* a copy of the income cash ledger for a particular trust account.

income stock: a stock, the earnings on which are mainly in the form of dividend income, as opposed to capital gains. It is considered a conservative, dependable investment, suitable to supplement other income. Well-established corporations with a consistent record of paying dividends are usually considered income stock. [105]

income tax: a tax on annual earnings and profits of a person, corporation, or other organization. Traditionally, there are federal, state, and city taxes, although not all states and not all cities tax income.

income velocity of money: the average number of times each year that a dollar is spent on purchasing the economy's annual flow of final goods and/or services—its gross national product.

income yield: in Great Britain, the return during the next 12 months in interest payments on a security.

incoming clearings: see *in-clearing items*.

incoming exchanges: those checks presented by member banks to a clearinghouse for clearing purposes. see *clearinghouse*.

incoming mail: checks and drafts received through the mail for deposit from other banks and depositors. [31]

incompetent: one who is incapable of managing his or her affairs because of mental deficiency or undeveloped mentality. Children and idiots are incompetents in the eyes of the law. [62]

incontestable: a clause stating that after a certain period, the insurance policy may not be disputed except for nonpayment of the premiums.

inconvertible money: irredeemable funds; circulating money that cannot be converted into the standard. United States money has been inconvertible since 1933 because it is not redeemable in gold. see *fiat money.* synonymous with *irredeemable money.*

incorporate: to form into a corporation; become a corporation. [62]

incorporated trustee: any trust company or bank under its charter and by law that can serve as a fiduciary.

incorporation: the procedure in obtaining a state charter to form a corporation.

incorporation by reference: a reference in one document to the contents of another document in such a manner as to give legal effect to the material to which reference is made. [32]

incorporeal: of no material substance; existing with no physical properties (e.g., rights, privileges).

incorporeal property: intangible, personal property (i.e., without body); includes property rights, mortgages, and leases. see *choses in action.*

increasing cost: the situation in which average total unit costs of a business increase as the volume of business increases. True over large ranges of output for farming, mining, fishing, and lumbering, the so-called extractive industries. cf. *constant costs, decreasing costs.*

increasing-cost industry: an industry that experiences increases in resource prices or in manufacturing costs as it expands when new firms enter it.

incremental: describes the additional investment required for a project or additional cash flows resulting from a project.

incumbrance: see *encumbrance.*

incur: to sustain or become liable for, usually in reference to a cost, expense, loss, or debt. [105]

incurably depreciated: describes damaged property that is beyond rehabilitation or property that is uneconomical to repair.

incurred losses: loss transactions occurring within a fixed period, usually a year. For example, calendar-year incurred losses are customarily computed in accordance with the following formula: losses paid during the period, plus outstanding losses at the end of the period, less outstanding losses at the beginning of the period.

indebtedness: a debt is owed; any form of liability.

indefeasible: incapable of being annulled or rendered void; as, an indefeasible title to property. [37]

indemnify: to compensate for actual loss sustained. Many insurance policies and all bonds promise to "indemnify" the insureds. Under such a contract, there can be no recovery until the insured has actually suffered a loss, at which time he or she is entitled to be compensated for the damage that has occurred (i.e., to be restored to the same financial position enjoyed before the loss).

indemnity

(1) *general:* payment for damage; a guarantee against losses.

(2) *finance:* a bond protecting the insured against losses from others failing to fulfill their obligations. see *bond, indemnity.*

(3) *investments:* an option to buy

or sell a specific quantity of a stock at a state price within a given time period.

(4) **law:** an act of legislation, granting exemption from prosecution to certain people.

indemnity bond: see *bond, indemnity.*

indent: the request from a purchaser to an importer to import specific items at a stated price. The importer has a given time period in which to accept or refuse the offer.

indent.: see *indenture.*

indent house: a firm specializing in importing goods pursuant to specific orders from domestic buyers. The advantage of the firm lies in its contacts and experience, particularly in procuring the lowest possible price.

indenture

(1) **finance:** a written agreement under which debentures are issued, setting forth maturity date, interest rate, and other terms. [20]

(2) **law:** an agreement binding one person to work with or without pay for another for a stated period (e.g., apprenticeship). An obsolete agreement.

(3) see *trust indenture.*

indenture bond: see *bond, indenture.*

independent audit: an audit performed by an independent auditor. see also *audit report, independent auditor.*

independent auditor: an auditor who is independent of the governmental unit or agency whose accounts are being audited.

independent bank: a bank that operates in one locality. The directors and officers are generally local to the community.

Independent Bankers Association of America: created in 1930, an association to promote the interest of independent banking in the United States

as a vibrant, contributing force within the economy.

independent broker: members on the floor of the New York Stock Exchange who execute orders for other brokers having more business at that time than they can handle themselves, or for firms who do not have their exchange member on the floor. Formerly known as the two-dollar brokers—from the time when these independent brokers received $2 per 100 shares for executing such orders. Their fees are paid by the commission brokers. see *commission broker.* [20]

independent executor: an executor of a will, who, after filing has inventory, does not make further accounting to the probate court; recognized by statute in only a few states. [37]

indeterminate appropriation: an appropriation that is not limited either to any definite period of time or to any definite amount, or to both time and amount. [49]

index

(1) **general:** an ordered reference list of the contents of a file or document, together with keys or reference notations for identification of location of those contents.

(2) **government:** a statistical yardstick expressed in terms of percentages of a base year or years. For example, the Federal Reserve Board's index of industrial production is based on 1967 as 100. In April 1973 the index stood at 121.7 which meant that industrial production during that month was about 22 percent higher than in the base period.

indexation: formally adjusting wages and other kinds of incomes such as rents, pensions, or interest payments to changes in inflation.

indexed bond: see *bond, indexed*.

index fund: a mutal fund whose investment objective is to match the composite investment performance of a large group of publicly traded common stocks, generally those represented by the Standard & Poor's 500-Composite-Stock Index. [23]

index futures: where contracts are promises to buy or sell a standardized amount of a stock index by a specified date. Futures are regulated by the Commodity Futures Trading Commission, and the contracts are available only from brokers licensed by the CFTC. cf. *index options*.

indexing: an increasingly popular form of investing: investments are weighted in line with one of the major stock indices (e.g., Standard & Poor's 500-Composite-Stock Index.).

index linking: relating wages, prices, interest rates, or loan values to an index, usually of prices.

index number: a mathematical device or number which is used to express the price level, volume of trade, and so on, of a given period, in comparison with that of a base period the value for which is given as 100. Useful in comparing relative changes in various phenomena from month to month or year to year.

Index of National Enervation and Related Trends (INERT): a U.S. Department of Commerce measure of the rate of increase of the figure for the gross national product.

index options: top options represent the right, but not the obligation, to buy or sell a specific value of an index at a set price by a specific date. Options are regulated by the SEC and are available through stockbrokers. cf. *index futures*.

indicated interest: synonymous with *open interest*.

indicated market: the price when a trader believes a security might be bought or sold when there is not a firm bid or offer upon which to base a more definite opinion.

indicated yield: used to describe the current return or yield to maturity of stocks and bonds.

indicators: any quantity (average, composite, or index) that is correlated to the performance of the stock market or to general economic conditions. Indicators are observed in an attempt to predict market conditions. [105]

indifference schedule: a table illustrating all combinations of two commodities that are equally satisfactory or yield the same total utility to a recipient at a specified time.

indirect business tax and nontax liability: all tax liabilities incurred by business, except for corporate income and social insurance taxes, plus general government nontax revenues from business. Nontax liabilities consist mainly of certain charges for government products and services, fines and penalties, donations, and special assessments by state and local governments.

indirect compensation: incentive bonuses or cash profit sharing earned and received in cash in the same year. Indirect compensation includes all cash payments received in addition to base salary or guaranteed year-end bonuses. [105]

indirect control: control of an individual, a corporation, or other legal person, as exercised through an intermediary. [18]

indirect costs: costs not usually identifiable with or incurred as the result of the manufacture of goods or services, but applicable to a productive activity generally. Included are costs from manufacturing operations (wages, maintenance, overhead, etc.). see *running costs.*

indirect earnings: synonymous with *equity earnings.*

indirect exchange: a strategy employed in arbitrage of foreign exchange in purchasing foreign exchange in one market and quickly selling it in another market at a rate that produces a profit over the purchase price plus the expenses of the transaction.

indirect expense: expenses such as rent, taxes, and insurance which cannot be specifically charged to the department or cost center that benefit from them. They are generally accumulated for a period and the total then distributed on some equitable basis. [38]

indirect exporting: exporting through a middleman, such as an export merchant.

indirect foreign exchange standard: see *gold exchange standard.*

indirect labor costs: wages of nonproduction employees, such as maintenance crews, inspectors, timekeepers, tool crib attendants, and sweepers.

indirect liability: a party who endorses the note of a maker for a bank or guarantees a note as guarantor for a maker is said to have indirect liability on the note.

indirect loan: purchase by banks of loan contracts between retail merchants and customers. [105]

indirect origination: the purchase of a ready-made loan from a source other than a regular lender (such as a subdivision contractor, or a mobile home or home improvement dealer), usually as part of an on-going business relationship between the association and the seller. see also *loan origination.* [59]

indirect quotation: quotation of fixed units of domestic currency in variable units of foreign currency. cf. *direct quotation.*

indirect standard: the monetary system that does not directly convert its currency into a standard metal such as gold or silver but allows, as a right of ownership, the exchange of the domestic currency into the currency of a nation that is on a metal standard. The ratio of exchange is credited and held with only occasional changes.

indirect tax: a tax, the burden of which can be easily passed on to someone else by the individual who is required by law to pay the tax to the government. Most excise taxes are indirect taxes. cf. *direct tax.*

individual account: an account in the name of one individual, as contrasted with an account or a corporation, a partnership, or an account in two or more names. [50]

individual banker: a private banker; an unincorporated bank, found in only a few states.

individual policy pension trust: a type of pension plan, frequently used for small groups, administered by trustees who are authorized to purchase individual level premium policies or annuity contracts for each member of the plan. The policies usually provide both life insurance and retirement benefits. [58]

individual proprietorship: synonymous with *proprietorship*.

Individual Retirement Accounts (IRA): originally, individual pension accounts available to anyone not covered at work by a qualified pension plan. Effective January 1, 1982, all wage earners, including those already in company pension plans are able to make tax-deductible contributions to IRAs. An individual can now put away an extra $2000 a year, or a total of $2250 if there is a nonworking spouse, and let the earnings accumulate tax-free until age 59¹/₂. see *Employer Retirement Income Security Act of 1974*; see also *Economic Recovery Tax Act of 1981, Keogh plan*.

Indm.: see *indemnity*.

indorsee: see *endorsee*.

indorsement: see *endorsement*.

indorser: see *endorser*.

induced investment: new capital formation caused by an upturn in consumer buying.

industrial bank: a financial institution originally organized to extend loans to employees. The bank derives its funds through a form of worker savings. Most industrial banks have now been merged into commercial banks. cf. *labor banks*.

industrial collateral: a category of stock exchange collateral where brokers who borrow in the call money market present to the lending institution either industrial or regular collateral. This collateral is represented by the firm's traded stocks.

industrial credit: debt incurred by industrial or business firms to meet payrolls, buy raw materials, build new plants. [55]

industrial insurance: life insurance on an individual in an amount under $1000, with premiums payable weekly to an agent who calls at the insured's home to collect. see *debit*. synonomous with *weekly premium insurance*.

industrialist: an individual who owns, controls, or plays a critical role in the operation of an industrial organization.

industrial life insurance: see *industrial insurance*.

industrial loan commitments: amount of loans to industrial borrowers which have been approved but for which the funds have not yet been advanced to them. [40]

industrial loans: loans outstanding to industrial borrowers under an amendment to the Federal Reserve Act which authorized the Federal Reserve Banks to make loans to certain business firms unable to get credit from other financial institutions on reasonable terms. This authority was terminated in August 1959. [40]

industrial production: a measure issued by the Federal Reserve mid-month for the previous month, of the physical output of factories and mines.

industrial psychology: the branch of applied psychology concerned with the behavior and motivation of individual workers. Activities include testing, selection, training, and other aspects of individual and/or group interactions on the job.

industrial relations: any activity, event, or interaction between employer and employee. It commences with the job interview and lasts throughout the working lifetime of an employee. The most popular usage of the term limits it to union-management relations.

industrial revenue bond: see *bond, industrial revenue.*

industrials: corporate securities of firms involved in the production and/or sale of services or commodities.

industry

(1) *general:* trade, business, production, or manufacture.

(2) *government:* as determined by the Standard Industrial Classification (SIC) system of the U.S. Bureau of the Census, any commercial activity identified by this listing.

industry funds: mutual funds whose investment is restricted to high-yield, senior securities. The goal of an industry fund is to obtain high levels of income and preserve capital. [105]

inelastic demand (inelasticity): exists when a price increase leads to a higher total sales, revenue, or a price decrease leads to a lower sales revenue. A perfectly inelastic demand occurs when the demand for an item does not change with changes in price.

inelastic supply: a condition in which the quantity of an item produced does not alter, or changes minimally, with a price change.

ineligible bills: in Great Britain, bills not eligible for rediscount at the Bank of England.

inequities: rates or conditions substantially out of line with those paid or existing for comparable work in a plant, locality, or industry.

INERT: see *Index of National Enervation and Related Trends.*

INET: see *Interbank Network Electronic Transfer.*

infant industry argument: a dispute in support of import restrictions, claiming that specific new domestic firms have not reached their ultimate level of technical superiority and consequently required temporary protection from products from abroad.

infirmity: in the creation or transfer of title, any known act or visible omission in detail, that would invalidate the instrument.

inflation: an increase in the price level creating a decrease in the purchasing power of the monetary unit. cf. *deflation, flation, hesiflation, hyperinflation, overheating, prime interest (rate), simultaneous inflation and unemployment, speculation, stagflation.*

inflation, runaway: see *galloping inflation.*

inflation accounting: the bookkeeping practice that shows the impact of inflation on corporate assets and profits.

inflationary gap: the amount by which government and private spending exceeds the amount needed to maintain a stable price level and full employment.

inflationary spiral: in a time of rising prices, employees demand higher wages, which in turn increases costs, leading sellers and producers then to demand still higher prices. see *stabilization policy, wage stabilization*; cf. *Pigou effect concept.*

inflation hedges: see *hedge.*

inflationitis: slang for "the dollar-ain't-worth-a-hill-o'-beans blues."

inflump: see *simultaneous inflation and unemployment.*

informatics: see *information science.*

information

(1) *general:* the meaning that a human assigns to data by means of the conventions used in their representation.

(2) *computers:* the collection of

data, numbers, characters, and so on, which is processed or produced by a computer.

information processing: synonymous with *data processing.*

information retrieval

(1) *general:* the methods and procedures for recovering specific information from stored data.

(2) *general:* a technique for cataloguing data all related to one field so that such data can be called for at any time with speed.

(3) *computers:* a branch of computer science relating to the methods for storing and searching quantities of information.

information science: the study of how data are processed and transmitted through digit processing equipment. synonymous with *informatics.*

infrastructure: the basic structure of a nation's economy, including transportation, communications, and other public services, on which the economic activity relies.

infringement

(1) *general:* encroaching on someone else's property (i.e., trespassing). cf. *intrusion.*

(2) *law:* the production of an item that yields the same results by the same action as a patented item. A patent infringement.

(3) *law:* the reproduction of a registered trademark and its use on merchandise to mislead the public into believing that the items bearing the reproduced trademark are the product of the true owner of the trademark. A trademark infringement.

in gear: the parallel rise of two or more indicaters of an economic condition or activity; for example, when the Dow Jones Industrial Average and the Transportation Averages both rise, they are *in gear.*

ingot: a bar of metal cast from a mold.

ingress: the ability to enter property or land.

inher.: inheritance.

inherit: to acquire the property of a person who dies intestate. see also *devolution.*

inheritance: the act of inheriting; any possession coming as a gift; any characteristic passed on by heredity. see *Tax Reform Act of 1976.*

inheritance taxes: taxes levied by the states on property received by inheritance or by succession; a tax on inherited property. cf. *estate tax, succession tax.*

inheritance tax return: the return that the executor or administrator is required to make to the state on the basis of which the inheritance tax due the state is calculated and paid; to be distinguished from the federal estate tax return. [37]

inheritance tax waiver: a release, signed by the appropriate state taxing official, relinquishing any claim of the state to the assets of an estate, or a portion thereof, under consideration. [59]

initial issue: credit cards sent out at the inception of a credit card plan. [105]

initial margin: the amount a buyer is requested to deposit with a broker before commencing trading. cf. *maintenance margin.* see also *margin, margin call.*

initiation fee: in the securities business, the initial membership levy for a newly elected member to an exchange. Thereafter, most exchanges have annual dues.

Inj.: see *injunction.*

injunction: a court order advising the party that if it does commit the enjoined-against act, there will be a penalty. A temporary restraining order is issued for a limited time. A permanent injunction is issued after a full hearing. In 1932 the Norris-LaGuardia (Anti-Injunction) Act forbade the federal courts to issue injunctions unless certain conditions were fulfilled first. see also *blanket injunction.*

injunction pendente lite: a court remedy before the hearing of the merits of a suit, for the express purpose of preventing the doing of any act whereby the conditions in the conflict might be substantially altered. see also *lis pendens.*

in kind: value in goods and services as distinguished from value in money.

inland bill of exchange: a bill drawn and payable in the same state. [39]

inland exchange: synonymous with *domestic exchange.*

in lieu tax: a substitute for property taxes in the case of public utilities. Usually, a tax based on gross earnings.

innocent purchaser: an individual who in good faith does not expect any hidden property defects to appear when he or she has gained title to real property.

innovation theory of the cycle: emphasizes the role of innovations (all forms of cost reduction or new products) in stimulating investment and hence incomes. As the innovation becomes widely adopted, this effect on incomes disappears due to the fact that the profit margin narrows and further new investment declines. Since innovations are not developed uniformly through time but come in groups, incomes rise and fall.

in personam: a legal judgment binding the defendant to a personal liability. cf. *in rem.*

in-plant banking: a banking service whereby facilities for banking transactions are provided to employees on the company's premises. [105]

in proof: see *prove.*

input/output (I/O): a general term for equipment used to communicate with a computer.

inquiry balance: the amount of funds that will be displayed to the holder of a bank services card requesting a balance inquiry. [105]

in rem: a legal judgment that binds, affects, or determines the status of property. cf. *in personam.*

Ins.: see *insurance.*

inscribed: government bonds such as savings bonds whose records are held by the Federal Reserve Banks rather than the U.S. Treasury.

in shape for sale: describing the condition in which a security will make a good delivery. [37]

inside director: a director of a corporation who maintains a significant stock interest and may be employed by the corporation.

inside information: see *tips.*

insider: an individual who, because of his or her employment position, has special information dealing with the financial status of a firm before that information is released to the public or to stockholders. see *smart money.*

insider reports: monthly reports required by the SEC that must be filed by officers, directors, and stockholders owning more than 10 percent of a corporation whose securities are listed on any national securities exchange.

in sight: a commodities term describing the quantity of goods that are to be delivered to a particular location.

insolvency: the inability to pay one's debts as they mature. Even though the total assets of a business might exceed its total liabilities by a wide margin, the business is said to be insolvent if the assets are such that they cannot be readily converted into cash to meet the current obligations of the business as they mature.

insolvent: an individual who has ceased to pay his or her debts or is unable to pay such debts as demanded by creditors. see *bankrupt, bankruptcy.*

inspection report: information gathered by a mercantile source and compiled in report form to be used to supplement underwriting material in the selection of risks. The primary purpose of the report is to verify information given on the application. [12]

Inst.
(1) see *installment (instalment).*
(2) see *instant.*
(3) see *instrument.*

installment (instalment): a partial payment on the purchase price for any item, sold with the agreement that the remaining monies will be paid on a specified due date.

installment account: see *charge account.*

installment bond: see *bond, serial.*

installment buying: acquiring goods or services with no down payment or a small down payment; to be followed by payments at regular intervals.

installment cash credit: money loans directly to an individual and repaid through periodic payments over a specified length of time. [55]

installment contract: synonymous with *contract for deed.*

installment credit: a form of consumer credit involving regular payments; permitting the seller to reacquire the item bought if the buyer fails to meet the payment schedule.

installment financing: that form of financing which involves the repayment or amortization of an obligation by payments of fixed amounts at regular intervals. [55]

installment interest: the interest on a loan payable in equal amounts at regular intervals over a period of time.

installment loan: synonymous with *personal loan.*

installment payments: periodic payments made to discharge an indebtedness. synonymous with *amortization payments.*

installment refund annuity: see *annuity, installment refund.*

Installment Sale Revision Act of 1980: this legislation liberalized the rules for postponing tax on property that is sold on the deferred-payment basis.

installment sales (homes): homeowners wanting to sell their homes who act as lenders can reap a tax benefit by allowing purchasers to pay in installments. The Internal Revenue Service allows sellers to spread their gain over a number of years instead of reporting it all in the year of sale, and thus to defer most of the capital gains tax on the profit.

installment sales credit: a one-shot loan used to buy "big ticket" items, such as cars or appliances. A down payment is usually required and a contract is signed for the balance due, plus interest and service charges. The debt is repaid in equal installments over a specified period of time. Generally involves three parties: the buyer, the seller, and the lender. [78]

instant (inst.): a business term designating the present month (e.g., on the 10th inst.) cf. *proximo.*

Institute of Financial Education: a national educational organization, affiliated with the United States League of Savings Association, dedicated to increasing the professional skills of savings association personnel through classroom courses, home study, executive training programs, seminars, workshops, clinics, and other methods. Formerly called the *American Savings and Loan Institute.* [59]

institution: an organization (e.g., bank, insurance company, investment company pension fund) holding substantial investment assets, often for others.

institutional house: a brokerage firm that serves financial institutions and profit-sharing plans rather than individual investors. [105]

institutional investor: a company having substantial funds invested in securities (e.g., a bank, labor union, college).

institutional lender: a financial institution that invests in mortgages either directly or through the purchase of mortgages or mortgage-backed securities in the secondary mortgage market. [105]

institutional market: the market for short terms and commercial paper. This market is used by corporations and financial institutions needing cash or having cash to invest in large quantities for short periods of time. [105]

institutional pot: the percentage, usually 20 percent, of an offering of a security that has been set aside by managers for large institutional orders.

Instl.: see *installment (instalment).*

instrument: any written document that gives formal expression to a legal agreement or act.

instrumentalities: agencies of the federal government whose obligations are not the direct obligation of the federal government.

instrumentality: a subordinate agency.

insufficient funds: used when a depositor's balance is inadequate for the bank to pay a check that has been presented. A service charge is often placed on the customer when the balance is not sufficient to pay the check.

insular bond: see *bond, insular.*

insurable interest (life version): the monetary interest of the beneficiary of a life insurance contract in the continued life of the person insured. Insurable interest exists only to the extent that the beneficiary will suffer financial loss as the result of the death of an insured.

insurable interest (property and liability version): any interest in or relation to property of such nature that the occurrence of an event insured against would cause financial loss to the insured.

insurance

(1) *general:* a method whereby those concerned about some form of hazard contribute to a common fund, usually an insurance company, out of which losses sustained by the contributors are paid. see also *self-insurance.*

(2) *law:* a contractual relationship that exists when one party (the insurer), for a consideration (the premium), agrees to reimburse another party (the insured) for loss to a specified subject (the risk) caused by designated contingencies (hazards or perils), or to pay on behalf of the insured all reasonable sums for which he or she may be liable to a third party (the claimant).

insurance binder: a written evidence of temporary hazard or title coverage that runs for a limited time and must be replaced by a permanent policy. [105]

insurance company: an organization chartered under state or provincial laws to act as an insurer. In the United States, insurance companies are usually classified as fire and marine, life, casualty, and surety companies and may write only the kinds of insurance for which they are specifically authorized by their charters.

insurance coverage: the total amount of insurance that is carried.

insurance policy: broadly, the entire written contract of insurance. More specifically, it is the basic written or printed document, as well as the coverage forms and endorsement added to it.

insurance premium: see *premium.*

insurance trust: an instrument composed wholly or partially of life insurance policy contracts.

insurance trust expenditures: cash payments to beneficiaries of contributory social insurance programs (employee retirement funds, unemployment compensation, sickness insurance, etc.). Excludes cost of administration, intergovernmental expenditures for social insurance, and noncontributory payments to former employees.

insurance trust revenue: revenue from contributions required of employers and employees for financial social insurance programs operated by state and local governments, plus earnings on assets held for such systems.

insurance underwriting: see *underwriting.*

insured: the person(s) protected under an insurance contract.

insured account: a savings account, up to but not exceeding the prescribed maximum amount, that is held in an association whose accounts are insured by the Federal Savings and Loan Insurance Corporation or a bank belonging to the Federal Deposit Insurance Corporation.

insured association: an association whose savings accounts are insured by the Federal Savings and Loan Insurance Corporation. [59]

insured bank: a bank that is a member of the Federal Deposit Insurance Corporation.

insured closing letter: a document given to the lender by a title insurance company which insures the lender against the failure of the title company's agent to perform his or her duties according to the lender's instructions [105]

insured deposits: deposits in banks, which are guaranteed by the FDIC against loss due to bank failure. [105]

insured life: the person on whose life the policy is issued. [58]

insured loan: a loan insured by FHA or a private mortgage insurance company. [105]

insured member: an individual, a partnership, an association, a corporation, a trustee under a trust or a custodian of public funds, holding an account at an insured association. [59]

insurer: the party to the insurance contract who promises to indemnify losses or provide service.

intangible asset: an asset that has no substance or physical body; it is incorporeal. The most widely known types of intangible asset are goodwill and patented rights. These assets are purchased, sometimes for very substantial outlays of capital. Their value to the purchaser lies in the use he or she can make of them, although they cannot be seen. see *chose(s) in action.*

intangible (personal) property: rights to personal property as distinguished from the property itself (e.g., stocks, bonds, notes, and contracts).

intangible tax: a state tax levied on all deposits in a bank (stocks, bonds, notes, etc.), excluding certain exempted items. The tax is against the individual accounts.

intangible value: the value of a company's intangible assets. [105]

integrated company: a firm that has united its multiple units or items for the purpose of widening its market territory to achieve efficiency, and improve costs.

integrated data processing: see *IDP.*

inter alia: among other things.

Inter-American Development Bank: established in 1959 to encourage economic development of 21 member nations in Latin America. Twenty representatives from Latin American countries and the United States initiated this effort. see also *Alliance for Progress.*

Interbank: the New York-based origi-nator of Master Card. Interbank is a nonprofit institution originally formed by a group of banks to combat Bank of America's credit card system.

interbank bid rate: the rate at which the clearing member purchased or made a bona fide offer to purchase U.S. dollars for immediate delivery from another financial institution in exchange for transaction currency. [105]

interbank borrowing: usually done when banks find themselves temporarily low on liquidity and approach banks that have an excess of liquidity in order to borrow funds.

interbank demand deposits: deposits held for other commercial or savings banks; the breakdown shows the amounts for domestic (United States) and foreign banks. [40]

interbank loan: a credit extended from one bank to another. [105]

Interbank National Authorization System (INAS): the national authorization network used to approve Master Card credit transactions. [36]

Interbank Network Electronic Transfer (INET): a national electronic data transfer system operated by ICS (Interbank Card Association). [105]

interbranch: a term associated with any action or function that takes place between or among the various branches of a bank. As an example, an interbranch memorandum would be sent to all branches within a banking organization to inform them of some action, function, or decision to be instituted. All branches would receive the same message, so that all would be coordinated and put the action into effect at the same time in the same manner. [10]

interchange

(1) a concept for a national network of EFT participants that allows customers the use of EFT services outside their normal market area. For credit cards, the practice has long been done in the processing of foreign cardholder activity through local merchants (e.g., a California customer buys a hat in New Orleans). The draft settles through interchange without the actual transmission of the paper.

(2) the exchange of debit and credit transaction data between merchant banks and cardholder banks based on an agreement between the participants. [105]

interchangeable bond: see *bond, interchangeable.*

interchange authorization: an amount at or below which an authorizing member may authorize transactions on behalf of an issuer and over which authorization must be obtained from such issuer. [105]

interchange fee: charge levied and collected by either the merchant bank or card-issuing bank for the processing of interchange transactions. [105]

interchange register: a listing of all transactions between a merchant bank and a cardholder bank. [105]

intercommodity spread: a position between two related commodities; for example, a long wheat and a short corn position is an intercommodity spread. see *interdelivery spread, intermarket spread.*

intercompany market: a market for borrowing and lending of funds between nonbanking firms, without any involvement of banks.

intercorporate stockholding: an unlawful condition where a corporation holds stock in other corporations and this interferes with competition (e.g., restraint of trade).

interdelivery (or intramarket) spread: the most common type of spread consisting of buying one month and selling another month in the same commodity. An example of such a spread would be long December corn/short September corn. see also *intercommodity spread, intermarket spread.*

Interdistrict Settlement Fund: a U.S. Treasury gold certificate fund held for the account of and subject to the control of the Federal Reserve System to minimize the time and expense of settlement of the inter-Federal Reserve Bank transactions.

interest: the price paid for the borrowed use of a commodity, usually money. see *money rates;* cf. *pure interest.*

interest accrued: interest earned but not yet due or payable.

interest and penalties receivable on taxes: the uncollected portion of interest and penalties receivable on taxes. [49]

interest bearing: a debt instrument (i.e., note bond or mortgage) upon which interest is computed. This is distinguished from equities, upon which dividends are declared.

interest bearing note: a note in which the maker agrees to pay the face of the note with interest.

interest charges: the carrying charges on a client's margin account that compensates a broker for his or her responsibility and the cost of finding funds needed to maintain it. This rate is usually somewhat higher than a broker's rate at the bank.

interest coverage: applies to the frequency with which interest charges are earned; found by dividing the sum of the fixed charges into the earnings available for such charges, either before or after deducting income taxes.

interest earned but not collected: represents interest on loans which has not been collected in advance, but is due and payable at specified times. Interest on demand loans usually comes into this class, collection being made each month, each quarter, or longer period of time, based upon bills being sent to the borrower for interest due. This is an asset (resources) account in the general ledger. synonymous with *interest receivable*. [10]

interest equalization tax (IET): a form of foreign-exchange control established by the U.S. government in the early 1960s whereby any U.S. resident has to pay a special tax on any purchase of overseas securities.

interest expense: the expense incurred for interest on a debt.

interest-free loan: see *completed contract accounting*.

interest on long-term debt: interest on outstanding bonds (mortgage and debenture), receivers' certificates, and miscellaneous long-term debt, notes, and so on, issued or assumed by the utility and which are due one year or more from date of issuance. [3]

interest only account: an account which in the last two calendar months has made one or more payments of which nothing was applied to principal (ledger card balance). Loans made during the last two calendar months are excluded. [55]

interest-only mortgage: where mortgage payments are smaller for a set period, with the principal paid off when the property is sold.

interest on the unpaid balance: interest charged at an agreed rate, calculated on the balance remaining on the obligation. [105]

interest payable: a liability representing accrued interest owed by a business.

interest penalty: a fee or additional charge made when the terms of a financial contract are altered. [105]

interest period: a rollover credit made available to a borrower on the understanding that he or she may select to borrow for periods varying typically between one month and one year.

interest rate: a percentage expressing the relationship between the interest for one year and the principal.

interest rate arbitrage: the movement of funds from one money market center to another through the foreign exchange market in order to obtain higher rates of interest. [105]

interest rate peg: monetary policy followed from 1942 to 1951 where the Federal Reserve System adjusted the amount of money in order to maintain a constant interest rate on Treasury securities. see *Monetary Accord of 1951*.

interest rate risk: in investments, used in contradistinction to financial risk and purchasing power risk to refer to the risk that the interest rate may change, thus affecting the market value of a security even though its obligations continue to be met.

interest rate swap: the exchange of two financial assets (liabilities) which have the same present value but which generate different streams of receipts (payments). see also *swap contract*. [107]

interest rate uncertainty: the market price of the security may change as interest rate levels change. [105]

interest receivable: synonymous with *interest earned but not collected.*

interest receivable on investments: the amount of interest receivable on investments, exclusive of interest purchased. Interest purchased should be shown in a separate account. [49]

interest receivable on special assessments: the amount of interest receivable on unpaid installments of special assessments. [49]

interest-sensitive assets: items on which the interest received or paid can be changed in the near future. [105]

interest short: a term describing the amount by which a payment is insufficient to pay the accrued interest on an account. [55]

interest table: a broad term given to any mechanical indexing device, or chart, permitting independent calculation of simple or compound interest, the discount or present value, and the like, on varied amounts for certain or varied times. [10]

interest waived: refers to the amount of interest due on an account which is relinquished due to certain circumstances and arrangements made for repayment of an account. [55]

interest warrant: a firm's request for payment of interest due on its notes, debts, and so on. see *warrant.*

interest yield: the uniform rate of interest on investments computed on the basis of the price at which the investment was purchased, giving effect to the periodic amortization of any premiums paid or to the periodic accrual of discounts received. [52]

interest yield equivalent: the mea-surement of the rate of return on a security sold on a discount basis, which assumes actual days to maturity and a 360-day year.

interfund accounts: accounts in which transactions between funds are reflected. see *interfund transfers.* [49]

interfund loans: loans made by one fund to another. [49]

interfund transfers: amounts transferred from one fund to another. [49]

intergovernmental expenditures: payment to other governments as fiscal aid or as reimbursements for the performance of services for the paying government. synonymous with *revenue sharing.* cf. *direct expenditures.*

intergovernmental revenue: revenue received from other governments as fiscal aid, shared taxes, and reimbursements for services performed. synonymous with *shared revenue.*

interim bond: see *bond, interim.*

interim borrowing: the sale of short-term paper in anticipation of bond issuance. see also *bond anticipation notes.* [49]

interim certificate: see *bond, interim certificate.*

interim closing: any closing of the books of account that occurs at some time other than at the end of a fiscal year and which does not involve the summarizing of the income and expense accounts. [105]

interim dividend: any dividend given to shareholders ahead of the full (regular) dividend.

interim loan: a short-term construction loan made to finance improvements on real property. [22]

interim receiver: a court-appointed individual asked to protect a debtor's property until an official receiver is appointed.

interim report: a report, made monthly, quarterly, or semiannually, to stockholders informing them of current developments and results. The interim report serves as a supplement to an annual report.

interim statement: a financial statement prepared before the end of the current fiscal year and covering only financial transactions during the current year to date. see *statement.* [49]

interim warrants: see *interim borrowing.*

interlocking directorate: the condition in which one or more members of the board of directors of one business also are members of the board of directors of other corporations.

interlocutory decree: issued before a final court decree; an intermediate decree that does not resolve the matter but settles some portion of it.

intermarket spread: involves purchasing a commodity deliverable on one exchange and selling the same commodity deliverable on another exchange (e.g., long Chicago December wheat/short Kansas City December wheat). see *intercommodity spread, interdelivery spread.*

Intermarket Trading System: a computerized system connecting the six exchanges in the nation (American Stock Exchange, Boston Stock Exchange, Midwest Stock Exchange, New York Stock Exchange, Philadelphia Stock Exchange, and Pacific Stock Exchange) which transmits commitments to buy or sell to each simultaneously. Price information is displayed on a video screen at each exchange where traders then accept or reject the prospective transaction on the basis of the price. sometimes referred to as *electronic handshake.*

intermediary bank(s): bank(s) excluding ordering bank and beneficiary's bank that participate in a funds transfer. [105]

intermediary bank advice charges: information specifying who to charge for advising the intermediary bank and how to apply these charges. [105]

intermediary bank advice identifier: information used in contracting the intermediary bank in order to send an advice (e.g., phone number, cable address). [105]

intermediary bank advice instructions: additional information which pertains to notification of the intermediary bank (e.g., bank's name, hours of availability). [105]

intermediary bank advice method: a code that specifies the method to be used to notify the intermediary bank that the account has been credited or that funds are available (e.g., phone, letter, wire). [105]

intermediary bank identifier: a code that uniquely identifies the intermediary bank. [105]

intermediary bank identifier type: a code that specifies the type of identifier used for the intermediary bank. [105]

intermediary bank method of payment: specifies how payment is to be made to the intermediary bank. [105]

intermediary bank name and address: identifies the intermediary bank by name and, optionally, the intermediary bank's postal address. [105]

intermediate bond: see *bond, intermediate.*

intermediate credit bank: one of the 12 Federal Intermediate Banks established in 1923 to provide banks and other financial institutions with a rediscounting facility for agricultural paper of an intermediate term.

intermediate-term credit: credit that is generally extended over a period of 3 to 10 years.

intermediate trend: movements within the framework of the primary or major trend. The price of a security can move in one direction 10 to 30 points and then back the opposite way. It is composed of many smaller movements in price.

intermediation: the investment process in which savers and investors place funds in financial institutions in the form of savings accounts and the financial institutions in turn use the funds to make loans and other investments. [59]

interminate bond: see *bond, intermediate*.

internal audit: a business audit carried out by the firm itself on a continuous basis. cf. *look back*.

internal bond: see *bond, internal*.

internal check: coordinated methods and measures adopted by an organization to check the accuracy and validity of data and to safeguard assets.

internal controls: methods and measures employed to promote efficiency, encourage acceptance of managerial procedures and policies, check the validity of management data, and protect assets.

internal debt: the debt of a nation.

internal economies of scale: factors that bring about increases or decreases to an organization's long-run average costs or scale of operations resulting from size adjustments with the company as a product unit. They occur primarily because of physical economies or diseconomies. see *diseconomies of scale*.

internal items: debit or credit memoranda prepared by or for an officer of the bank to adjust the balance in the general ledger and for a customer's account. Examples include corrections, loan proceeds, special customer charges, and certification entries. [31]

internal memory: the internal parts of a data-processing machine capable of retaining data.

internal national debt: that part of the national debt owed to persons within the country owing the debt.

internal rate of return (IRR): rate of return an investment is anticipated to earn.

internal revenue: in the United States, federal income from all taxation other than customs duties.

internal revenue bond: see *bond, internal revenue*.

Internal Revenue Code of 1954: federal legislation; provided for a complete revision of the Internal Revenue Code of 1939. Includes provisions for dividend credit and exclusion, retirement income credit, and accelerated depreciation. Changes in tax laws since 1954 have been enacted as amendments to this code.

Internal Revenue Service (IRS): the federal agency empowered by Congress to administer the rules and regulations of the Department of the Treasury, which includes the collection of federal income and other taxes. It is divided into 9 regions with 64 districts and is also responsible for the investigation and prevention of tax frauds.

internal security audit: a security audit conducted by personnel responsible to the management of the bank or department being audited. [105]

International Bank for Economic Co-operation (IBEC): established in 1964 and headquartered in Moscow; responsible for the organization and execution of payments between members of Comecon and non-Comecon nations.

International Bank for Reconstruction and Development (IBRD—The World Bank): proposed at Bretton Woods in July 1944, commencing operation in June 1946. After phasing out activities of reconstruction, primary efforts are made to provide loans for economic development. see *International Monetary Fund.* see also *Development Finance Companies.*

international banking: bank operations dealing with foreign exchange, making of foreign loans or serving as investment bankers for foreign nations, provinces, municipalities, and companies.

International Banking Act of 1978: federal legislation designed to remove many of the competitive advantages that foreign banks had over their domestic counterparts. The Federal Reserve Bank is now authorized to impose reserve requirements on foreign banks, for example, and for the first time there are restrictions on their ability to take deposits nationwide. Its basic purpose is to apply the McFadden Act of 1927, which forbids branching by American banks across state lines, to foreign banks. Until passage of this new act, foreigners have been free to open branches in any state which allowed them in. see *Edge Act.*

international banking facilities (IBFs): specially designated offices in the United States, identified by the Federal Reserve Board, permitting banks to take deposits from and make loans to nonresidents, including overseas subsidiaries of U.S. companies.

International Chamber of Commerce (ICC): created in Paris in 1919; provides an arbitration court for settling international business disputes and responsible for the "Uniform Customs and Practice for Documentary Credits."

international checks (cheques): traveler's checks acceptable and payable in other nations (i.e., the American Express Travelers checks).

International Commercial Exchange: established in 1970, following the passage of the Commodity Exchange Act, to create a currency futures trading market. An international commercial exchange clearing association was also formed. This institution replaced the New York Produce Exchange.

international commodity agreement: synonymous with *commodity agreement.*

International Development Association: an auxiliary credit agency of the World Bank to handle requests for soft loans to developing nations to be repaid over a longer time interval than traditional, and at times to be repaid in the borrowing state's own currency. see also *World Bank Group.*

International Emergency Economic Powers Act of 1977: this federal law grants the president authority "to deal with any unusual and extraordinary threat, which has its source in whole or substantial part outside the United States, to the national security, foreign policy, or economy of the United States, if the president declares a national emergency with respect to such a threat." President Carter, utilizing this law in November 1979 froze all official Iranian assets in the United States.

international exchange: see *foreign exchange*.

International Finance Corporation: established in 1956, this investing organization purports to aid in the expansion of private business in less developed industrial nations. see also *World Bank Group*.

international liquidity: the total for all internationally acceptable currencies in the monetary system of the world.

International Monetary Fund (IMF): to restore orderly exchange practices following World War II, the IMF was formed and became operational on March 1, 1947. Member nations can borrow foreign currencies from the fund under specified conditions. Membership in the fund is a prerequisite to membership in the International Bank for Reconstruction and Development. see *Bretton Woods Agreement of 1944, special drawing rights.*

international money management (IMM): strategies used by firms with multinational cash flows to maximize earnings from interest and exchange rate movements while reducing exposure to risk. [94]

international money order: a money order issued by a bank, express company, or post office which is payable overseas. see also *money order*.

International Organization for Standardization (ISO): the central body for the formation and dissemination of industry standards for all national bodies. ANSI is the U.S. member of ISO. [105]

international payments mechanism:

the organization of markets whereby the monies of different nations are exchanged. see *swap*.

international postal money order: a money order issued by a post office which is payable overseas.

international securities: securities traded in major securities markets of the world, with trading on a listed or unlisted basis.

international trade: foreign trade measured by merchandise exports and imports of a country for a stated period, often one year.

international unit: a statistical device used to put data from a number of nations on a uniform base so that the different economies can be compared.

interpleader: when an individual who has an obligation to pay for services or goods does not know which of two or more claimants should receive his or her obligation, he or she brings a suit requiring the claimants to litigate between themselves.

interpositioning: when brokerage houses create an arrangement to create business when acting in behalf of two principal companies in a stock transaction. Abuses of interpositioning are illegal under SEC regulations.

interproduct competition (direct): firms offering products from different product classes to the same market, such as a brokerage firm's securities competing with high-interest CDs for corporate dollars. [105]

interproduct competition (indirect): firms offering products from different product classes but competing for prospects with limited purchasing power. [105]

in terrorem clause: a provision of a will or trust agreement intended or, at any rate, calculated to frighten a possible beneficiary into doing or refraining from doing something at the peril of forfeiting his possible benefits—such as a provision that would disinherit any named or potential beneficiary who contested the will. [37]

interrupt

(1) *computers:* to stop a process in such a way that it can be resumed without destroying work already done.

(2) *operations research:* to stop a current control sequence.

(3) *systems:* a break in the normal flow of a system or routine, permitting the flow to be restarted from that point at a later time.

interstate branching bill: a concept that allows banks from other states to open branches with broad services in a different state, and vice-versa. In principle, interstate branch banking creates a free trade zone, but presently remains prohibited by the McFadden Act of 1927.

interstate carrier: a common carrier whose business extends beyond the boundaries of one state.

interstate commerce: commerce, including the transporting of goods and services across the boundaries of more than one state.

Interstate Commerce Act of 1887: see *Act to Regulate Commerce of 1887*.

Interstate Commerce Commission (ICC): a federal agency established to enforce the Interstate Commerce Act and other related acts affecting common carriers engaged in interstate commerce.

Interstate Land Sales Full Disclosure Act of 1968: federal legislation requiring all large land-sales promoters to furnish prospective buyers with a detailed and accurate report on the land and to spell out buyers' rights in the transaction.

intersympathy between stocks: the tendency for price action of securities within the same group to be similar.

intervention: a monetary agency's transaction to maneuver the exchange rate for its currency or the level of its foreign exchange reserves.

intervention currency: the foreign currency a country uses to ensure by means of official exchange transactions that the permitted exchange rate margins are observed. Intervention usually takes the form of purchases and sales of foreign currency by the central bank or exchange equalization fund in domestic dealings with commercial banks. [42]

interview: a conversation designed to yield information for purposes of research or assistance in guidance, counseling, or treatment. see *interview, structured; interview, unstructured*.

interview, exit: a conference with an employee before termination of his or her relationship with the organization to determine reasons for leaving, future plans, and general attitudes toward the job and company.

interview, structured: an interview in which the asking of definite questions closely controls the subjects discussed.

interview, unstructured: an interview in which the interviewer does not determine the format or subject to be discussed, thus leaving the interviewee in major control of the conversation.

interview bias: influence resulting from the presence of personal prejudice of the individual conducting the interview.

inter vivos: "between living persons" (Latin). In the term "trust inter vivos" or "inter vivos trust," the same as living trust. see also *gift inter vivos.* [32]

intestacy: the condition resulting from a person's dying without leaving a valid will. [32]

intestate: not having a valid will; when a person dies intestate, his or her estate is persented for settlement to administrators. see *escheat.*

intestate succession: the descent and distribution of property of a person who dies without a valid will. [37]

in the black: slang, describing a business that is functioning with a profit.

in the money: a situation in which the striking price is below the market price of the underlying stock for a call, or the striking price is above the market price of the underlying stock for a put. [5]

in the red: slang, describes a business that is functioning at a loss.

Intl.: *international.*

in toto: in the entire amount.

intrabranch: used to express an action or function that is ordered to take place within an individual branch or office, and does not affect the action of other branches or offices of an organization. An example would be a personnel problem such as tardiness or absenteeism that applies only to one office or branch of an organization. An intrabranch memorandum would be sent to all departments within the one office or branch involved. [10]

intracity: an action or function taking place within one city. As an example, intracity clearings between banks within one city. This is to be distinguished from intercity clearings or col-

lections, which means the exchange of items through transit between different cities. [10]

intracommodity spread: a position in the same commodity but different months on the same exchange.

intraday high and low: the highest and lowest price obtained by a security during a specific market session which defines the trading range for a day.

intragovernmental service fund: a fund established to finance and account for services and commodities furnished by a designated department or agency to other departments and agencies within a single governmental unit. Amounts expended by the fund are restored thereto either from operating earnings or by transfers from other funds, so that the original fund capital is kept intact. Formerly called a *working capital fund.* [49]

intramarket spread: see *interdelivery spread.*

intraproduct competition (direct): firms offering from the same product class to the same market, such as bank ABC, Visa card, and bank XYZ's Master Charge card. [105]

intrastate commerce: commerce conducted solely within a state's geographic borders.

intrastate securities: over-the-counter shares issued and distributed within only one state.

intrinsic value

(1) *general:* the market value of the material in a thing (e.g., the value of the metal in a gold tooth filling).

(2) *investments:* the excess of the market value of the underlying stock over the striking price of the option for a call, or the excess of the striking price

of the option over the market value of the underlying stock for a put. [5]

intrusion: forcefully taking possession of another's real property.

Inv.: see *invoice.*

inventory: the name given to an asset of a business. Inventories are of two general types: direct and indirect. (a) Direct inventory in an industrial concern consists of raw materials, work-in-process, and finished goods. Direct inventories represent various stages of fabrication; in commercial and retail businesses, they are inventories purchased for resale. (b) Indirect inventories, in general, are all supplies used to carry on the business and not purchased for resale. Indirect inventories are usually considered as deferred assets.

inventory financing: the attempt to find the necessary capital for a firm by borrowing funds with inventory used as collateral.

inventory float: the rate of use of a company's inventory. [105]

inventory of stores for resale: the value of goods held by a governmental enterprise for resale rather than use in its own operations. [49]

inventory of supplies: the cost value of supplies on hand. [49]

inventory to net working capital: merchandise inventory is divided by net working capital. This is an additional measure of inventory balance. Ordinarily, the relationship should not exceed 80 percent. [4]

inventory turnover: the number of times, on the average, that inventory is replaced during a period. It is calculated by dividing cost of goods sold by average inventory.

inventory valuation adjustment: cor-porate profits and income of unincorporated enterprises include inventory profit or loss in customary business accounting. Current output in the national income accounts, however, includes only the value of the change in volume in inventories.

inverse demand pattern: exists when price and volume vary at the same time and more is sold at a high price than at a lower one.

inverted market: a commodity futures market where distant-month contracts are selling lower than near-month contracts.

invested capital: the amount of capital contributed to a company by its owners.

investment: the use of money for the purpose of making more money, to gain income or increase capital, or both.

investment adviser: a person or firm that advises clients on investments and is required to register under the Investment Advisers Act of 1940 with the SEC.

Investment Advisers Act: federal legislation of 1940 to regulate investment advisers, in order to protect the public from misrepresentation and dishonest investment tactics, by identifying specific unlawful activities. All investment advisers are required to register with the SEC, the administrator of the Investment Advisers Act.

investment analysts: individuals whose profession is the study and comparison of securities. Investment analysts usually serve brokerage houses or investment institutions. [105]

investment banker: the middleman between the corporation issuing new securities and the public. The usual practice is for one or more investment bankers to buy outright from a corporation a new issue of stock or bonds. The group forms a syndicate to sell the securities to individuals and institutions. The investment banker is the underwriter of the issue.

Investment Bankers Association: a national fraternity of investment bankers engaged in investment banking activities. The IBA was founded in 1912.

investment banking: the financing of the capital requirements of an enterprise rather than the current "working capital" requirements of a business.

investment banking house: one that engages in the merchandising of corporate and government securities by purchasing them in large blocks and selling them to investors. It helps to finance the capital, or long-term, credit requirements of business organizations, whereas the commercial bank finances their short-term credit requirements. [50]

investment bill: a bill of exchange purchased at a discount with the intention of holding to maturity as an investment.

investment broker: one who negotiates only cash transactions and not those on margin.

investment certificate: a certificate issued by an association which shows the amount of money an individual has invested with it. Such certificates do not carry any stockholders' liability and have no voting rights. [51]

investment club: a voluntary grouping of people who pool their monies to build up an investment portfolio, which it is hoped, will give members a better return per individual than each would have expected separately.

investment company: a company or trust that uses its capital to invest in other companies. There are two principal types: the closed-end type and the open-end, or mutual fund. (a) Shares in closed-end investment companies are readily transferable in the open market and are bought and sold like other shares. Capitalization of these companies remains the same unless action is taken to change, which is seldom. (b) Open-end funds sell their own new shares to investors, stand ready to buy back their old shares, and are not listed. Open-end funds are so called because their capitalization is not fixed; more shares are issued as people want them. see *reinvestment privilege*; cf. *hedge fund, monthly investment plan, no-load funds, regulated investment company, split investment company.*

Investment Company Act of 1940: federal legislation requiring the registration and regulation of investment companies with the SEC.

investment cost theory of rate making: in utility and railroad rate making, investment cost is the cost of acquisition by the present owner of property devoted to public use. On this base the rate of return is computed.

investment counsel: one whose principal business consists of acting as investment adviser; a substantial part of the person's business consists of rendering investment services. [20]

investment credit: credit given to a firm for the purchase of property, equipment, or other identified fixed assets.

investment dollar: dollars in London that are available for the purchase of dollar securities. In times of great demand these dollars are quoted at a premium, and the amount of the premium changes daily. As there are only so many dollars available in the investment pool, the rate charged to secure them changes rapidly throughout the business day, whenever there is an unusual demand for American securities. synonymous with *security dollars*.

investment income: any income resulting from monies invested in securities or other property.

investment in default: investment in which there exists a default in the payment of principal or interest. [49]

investment in fixed assets: the book value of fixed assets. [49]

investment manager: those individuals or companies that perform the service of managing the investments of institutions or individuals. Investment managers charge a fee for performing this service. [105]

investment market

(1) a place where securities and other investments are sold.

(2) the state of trade in investments.

investment media: any area in which capital is invested (i.e., securities, certificates, insurance, commodities, and business ownership).

investment multiplier: the reciprocal of the marginal propensity to save. The ratio of the change in national income consequent upon a change in investment to that change in investment. When there is an increment of aggregate investment, other things unchanged, national income will change by an amount that is K times the investment. K is the investment multiplier. Hence, the greater the marginal propensity to consume, the greater the investment multiplier.

investment objective: the goal (e.g., long-term capital growth, liberal current income, etc.) which an investor (whether an individual, an investment company, or other institution) pursues. [23]

investment policy: the means employed in pursuit of an investment objective. [23]

investment portfolio: the list of securities owned by a bank, an individual, or a business enterprise.

investment powers: the power of a fiduciary regarding the investments in the account. [37]

investment property: real estate acquired for profit.

investment savings account: a savings account, usually represented by a certificate for each unit of savings placed in the account, on which earnings ordinarily are mailed to the account holder when payable rather than credited to the account. [59]

investment securities: investments purchased for a portfolio, as opposed to those purchased for resale to customers. Those eligible for investments by banks include U.S. Treasury and government agency bonds, notes, and bills, state and municipal bonds, and corporate bonds. [105]

investment tax credit: an incentive for making long-term investments that reduces a firm's federal tax obligation by a specified percentage of the new investment costs.

investment trust: any firm, company or trust that takes its capital and invests it in other companies. see *closed-end investment company, mutual fund*.

investment turnover: synonymous with *capital turnover*.

investment underwriting: see *underwriting*.

investor: an individual whose principal concerns in the purchase of a security are regular dividend income, safety of the original investment, and if possible, capital appreciation. see *long position*; cf. *speculator*.

investors funds: actually retail (repos) or repurchase agreements that are not funds at all. synonymous with *money funds*. see terms above.

Investors Service Bureau: a facility of the New York Stock Exchange which answers written inquiries from individual investors on all aspects of securities investing. Major areas of inquiries involve finding local brokerage firms that take small orders or accounts, explaining investing methods and listed securities, clarifying exchange operations, and providing instructions for tracing dubious securities. [20]

invisible exports: services, financial or personal, rendered by citizens of one nation to foreigners. These may consist of insurance, freight and passenger charges, interest on domestic bonds, dividends of domestic corporations, and so on.

invisible hand: a term first used by Adam Smith to describe the ability of the perfectly competitive market to bring about the greatest benefit for all, even when all merchants selfishly maximize their own profits.

invisible imports: services, financial or personal, rendered by foreigners to the natives of a given country. These may consist of freight and passenger charges, insurance and banking services, and so on.

invisible items of trade: items, such as freight and insurance charges, which, though not shown as exports or imports, are considered along with exports and imports in determining the balance of payments between two or more nations. cf. *visible items of trade*.

invisible trade balance: as contrasted with the import and export of goods, the trade balance created by the import and export of services, (i.e., consulting and advisory services).

invoice: an instrument prepared by a seller of goods or services and rendered to the buyer. The instrument usually lists all items making up the bill for the convenience of the buyer, and to prevent disagreements, the amount is stated on the instrument.

involuntary alienation: forced sale of real estate.

involuntary bankruptcy: see *bankruptcy*.

involuntary investor: an investor who has purchased securities at a high price and therefore cannot sell his shares without a substantial loss; he becomes an investor. see *locked in, trader*.

involuntary lien: a lien on property demanded without the consent of the owner. Construction of sewers and sidewalks near an owner's property and property tax increases are examples. synonymous with *lien in invitum*.

inward collection: in Great Britain, the collection of payment on a bill from a British firm.

I/O: see *input/output*.

IOU: an informal written agreement acknowledging a cash debt (i.e., I owe you).

IP: see *issue price*.

IRA: see *individual retirement accounts*.

IRD: see *income in respect of a decedent*.

Irish dividend: a trade term for an assessment imposed on a security instead of a dividend.

iron law of wages: the concept that wages tend to equal what the employee needs to maintain a subsistence level of living. synonymous with *subsistence theory of wages*.

iron man: slang, a silver dollar.

IRR: see *internal rate of return*.

irredeemable: lacking any provision to repay in money or in kind or to exchange for something of equal value.

irredeemable bonds: see *bond, irredeemable*.

irredeemable money: synonymous with *inconvertible money*.

irregular: a commodity or security market condition where some prices or averages advance while others decline, with no recognized movement of the overall market in any particular direction.

irregular savings account: a savings account containing a contractual variation as to time, notice, systematic buildup, additional earnings, earnings penalty, or similar provision. [59]

irreparable harm: injury or damage that is so constant and universal that no fair of reasonable redress can be achieved in court. Therefore, the plaintiff seeks resolution by injunction.

irrevocable beneficiary: where the stated beneficiary of a policy cannot be changed without the permission of the beneficiary or by his or her death.

irrevocable credit: a credit that cannot, before the date it expires, be cancelled, revoked, or withdrawn without the consent of the person in whose favor the credit is given. Used mostly in foreign travel and trade, but also used in domestic business. synonymous with *fixed credit line*.

irrevocable documentary credit: where a bank issuing credit gives an irrevocable undertaking to pay a seller provided that specific conditions are fulfilled.

irrevocable letter of credit: a contract by an issuer to accept drafts as conditioned by the contract and to charge them against his or her account. The letter is good for a given period of time.

irrevocable trust: a trust that cannot be set aside by its originator.

IRS: see *Internal Revenue Service*.

IS: see *income statement*.

ISB: see *Investors Service Bureau*.

ISF: see *Interdistrict Settlement Fund*.

IS-LM model: explains the notion of policy mix, where the *IS* curve (depicts equilibrium in goods and services market) is the locus of combinations of interest rate and real economic activity consistent with equilibrium in the goods and services market. The curve is downward sloping because lower interest rates induce higher levels of investment, which increase real income through the multiplier. The *LM* curve (depicts equilibrium in money market) is the locus of combinations of interest rate and real economic activity consistent with the equilibrium in the money market. [81]

ISO: see *International Organization for Standardization*.

issue: any of a company's securities, or the act of distributing such securities. [20]

issued capital stock: a portion of a firm's stock retained by stockholders or repurchased by the firm to be held as treasury stock. Such stock represents the difference between authorized and unissued capital stock.

issue price: the price for a new security sold to the public, determined by an underwriter or syndicate. see *syndicate, underwriter.*

issuer: with reference to investment company securities, the company itself. [30]

issuer identifier: that portion of the primary account number (PAN) which identifies the card issuer and/or primary processing endpoint, when combined with the major industry identifier. [105]

issue value: the value of a share of stock at which it is issued by a corporation.

Istituto Centrale per il Credito a Medio Termine: Italian government agency which pays interest rebates on or refinances export credits granted by Italian banks.

IT: see *income tax.*

itemized appropriation: a restriction of an appropriation to be made only for and in the amounts listed. A step-by-step listing of all pertinent funds set aside to pay a specific cost. cf *lump-sum appropriation.*

itemized deductions: a listing of allowed expenses which are subtracted in arriving at taxable income. see *Tax Reform Act of 1976.*

itemized statement: a recap of account activity for a designated period of time. [105]

item number: a sequential number assigned by the computer input program to identify the position within a batch of a specific item. [105]

items: as used in bank collections, a flexible term broad enough to include instruments payable in money generally. The term is often used in combinations such as cash items, noncash items, collection items, city items, and out-of-town items. [50]

ITO: International Trade Organization.

ITS: see *Intermarket Trading System.*

IVA: see *inventory valuation adjustment.*

J: see *judgment.*

JA: see *joint account.*

jack: slang, money.

jacket: a wrapper or enclosure for an official document. [49]

JAJO: January, April, July, October (quarterly interest payments or dividends).

jawbone: slang, establishing financial credit by presenting clear, objective information.

jawboning: slang, pressured urging by an influential individual to submit to specific rules and regulations. cf. *moral suasion.*

J&D: June and December (semiannual interest payments or dividends).

J-curve: describing the expected impact of a devaluation on a nation's trade balance.

JD: see *job description.*

jeeps: 9.5 percent GPMs. see *graduated-payment mortgages.*

jell: slang, to complete a business transaction or sale of goods.

jeopardy assessment: the power of the government to make an immediate assessment and seizure upon claim of income taxes where there is danger of either the taxpayer leaving the country or of assets disappearing.

jeopardy assessment bond: see *bond, jeopardy assessment.*

jeopardy clause: a Eurocurrency agreement clause stating that should certain events curtail a lender's activity or the operation of the Euromarkets, other designated actions (i.e., the substitution of another agreed rate of interest) will come into effect. [83]

JIT: see *Job Instruction Training.*

Jnt. Stk.: see *joint stock company.*

JO: see *joint ownership.*

job: in foreign exchange, a bank dealing on its own behalf with other banks.

job account: an account pertaining either to an operation that occurs regularly or to a specific piece of work, showing all charges for material and labor used and other expenses incurred, together with any allowances or other credits. [49]

job analysis: a systematic study of the specific tasks required for a particular job, set of conditions, rate of pay, and so on. Usually, a statement of the per-

380

sonal qualities needed to perform a given job.

jobber

(1) a merchant middleman who purchases from an importer or producer or some large wholesaler and sells to retailers.

(2) in Great Britain, an individual or firm dealing in stock as a principal rather than as a broker. Stockjobbers are not permitted to deal with the public since this function is reserved to stockbrokers.

job classification: evaluation of job content and required skills, for the purpose of setting up wage brackets for each classification.

job content: for a given classification, the duties, functions, and responsibilities.

job definition: the statement of task requirements; there is a job definition for each job in the company.

job depth: the amount of control an employee can exert to alter or influence his or her job and the surrounding environment.

job description: a statement, usually in writing, of the responsibilities, approaches, conditions, and other relevant factors built into a job.

job dilution: the approach of dividing the tasks of a job into levels of skill. The parts needing higher skill are to be performed by skilled employees and the remaining tasks are carried out by relatively unskilled employees who have a lower level of training.

job enlargement: a procedure for increasing the scope and responsibilities of a job to increase satisfaction to the employee. cf. *loose jobs (rate)*.

job evaluation: a systematic rating of job content on factors such as skill, re-

sponsibility, and experience. The evaluation is primarily used to minimize wage inequities.

Job Instruction Training (JIT, J.I.T.): a program of training workers within industry based on a specific outline of procedures, including rules for getting ready to instruct and rules on how to train.

job lot: a form of contract having a smaller unit of trading than is featured in the regular contract.

job method of cost accounting: a system of allocating costs among various products by maintaining a ticket for each "job" and cumulating thereon the various charges incurred at each step in production.

job placement: the assignment of a person to a job.

job range: the number of operations a job occupant performs to complete his or her work.

job rotation: a personnel practice that involves moving an employee from one work station to another to increase overall performance by promoting a greater understanding of the multiple tasks in the organization.

job satisfaction: given in terms of the positive or negative aspects of an employee's attitude toward his or her job or some part of it.

job security: usually described in a union contract, a means of protecting a worker's job. Often invoked when new methods or machines are introduced.

job specification (specs): a carefully written description of a specific job with duties and opportunities described. It identifies the requirements of the job and the desired qualifications needed for a worker to perform effectively. see also *job standardization*.

job standardization: the use of clearly defined techniques for work procedures and the requirements to be met to reduce individual variations to be found in a specific work task. cf. *job classification.*

Job Training Partnership Act: federal legislation of 1982 to replace CETA in an attempt to turning management of training programs for unemployed and other groups over to the private sector and less to local governments.

jogging: the procedure of recording on a storage device the occurrence of particular types of transactions or system activities. [105]

John Doe: a name given in legal proceedings to a party whose true name is unknown. [61]

joint account: an account owned by two or more people, subject to deposit or withdrawal by all signatures of all joint owners. In banks, any account owned by two or more parties is referred to as a joint account regardless of whether all parties or any one of the parties may sign checks.

joint adventure: two persons entering into a single business for their mutual benefit, as with partners.

joint and last survivor (annuity): payments made jointly to two or more annuitants, and continuing until death of the last survivor. [12]

joint and several account: when two or more persons desire to deposit in a jointly owned account, and the account is drawn against either by check or withdrawal order, the signature of any one of the owners will be honored.

joint and several guaranty: an indorsement in which the liability for an entire bond issue may be enforced against all obligors jointly or against any one of them separately. This is a form of guaranty frequently found when a railroad terminal is used by more than one railroad. [105]

joint and severally: a term frequently encountered in loan transactions when several persons sign a note for a loan. When the term "jointly and severally" is used, each person is legally obligated to become liable for the payment of the note; the group involved must also become liable.

joint and survivorship: a phrase usually applied to annuities under which during the lifetime of both husband and wife, they are joint beneficiaries of the annuity and, after the death of either, the survivor becomes the sole beneficiary. [105]

joint bond: see *bond, joint and several.*

joint combination rate: a joint rate in transportation which is obtained by combining two or more rates published in one tariff.

Joint Commission on the Coinage: created by the Coinage Act of 1965, to determine whether the nation requires new coinage and if so, what form it should take.

joint contract: two or more people who make a promise to another are joint obligors to the contract and to the other party identified.

joint control bond: see *bond, joint control.*

joint cost: a cost that is common to all the segments in question that can be assigned to the segments only by means of arbitrary allocation.

joint demand: demand created when two or more commodities are used together, if at all, and are therefore wanted at the same time.

joint deposit: see *joint account.*

Joint Economic Committee: created under the Employment Act of 1946, the Congressional counterpart to the president's Council of Economic Advisers, to gather appropriate data on economic matters, to make recommendations, and so on.

joint endorsement: an endorsement made by two or more payees or endorsees.

joint liability: a liability shared by two or more people. In the event of legal proceedings, persons jointly liable must be acted against as a group. [105]

joint life insurance: insurance on two or more persons, the benefits of which are payable on the first death to occur.

jointly and severally: see *joint and severally.*

joint mortgage: any mortgage that has been signed by two or more mortgagors, being the joint obligation of all signers.

joint note: a note with more than one maker. Should there be a default, the holder sues all the makers on a joint basis as distinguished from a "joint and several" action that is against one or all the makers.

joint ownership: the interest in property of two or more people.

joint production costs: the costs of two or more produced goods that are made by a single process and are not identifiable as individual products up to a certain stage of production, known as the split-off point.

joint-product method of cost accounting: a system of allocating costs between two or more products produced simultaneously by distributing costs on some index basis (e.g., selling price, space occupancy, direct labor, etc.).

joint rate: in railroading, a single, consolidated rate charged for carrying freight between two points not on the same railroad and arranged by agreement between the railroads involved carrying the items from consignment point to destination.

joint return: in U.S. income taxation, a return reporting the income of both the husband and the wife. This return renders each fully liable for the total tax due.

joint-stock banks: in England, the name for all commercial banks. This term does not apply to the Bank of England, private banks, and so on.

joint stock company: an association that is neither a partnership nor a corporation but has some of the characteristics of each.

joint supply: see *joint cost.*

joint tenancy: two or more people holding equal ownership of property. Upon the death of one of the parties, the decedent's interest automatically passes on to the surviving owner(s). see *undivided right.*

joint tenants by the entireties: an account held in two or more names from which either owner may withdraw funds but for which each owner is considered to own all the funds. [105]

joint tenants with right of survivorship: property (bank account, safe deposit box) held in two or more names, to which any single owner has access without notifying the others. Right of survivorship indicates that in the event of the death of one owner, the remaining tenant(s) immediately becomes owners of the property. [105]

joint venture: a commercial undertaking by two or more people, differing from a partnership by relating to the disposition of a single lot of goods or the termination of a specific project.

joint will: a single will of two or more individuals.

JOJA: July, October, January, April (quarterly interest payments or dividends).

Jour.: see *journal*.

journal: a record of original entry. This record may be written in pen and ink at the time a transaction is made, or may be created either in original printing or carbonized as the posting of the entry is made by machine. cf. *ledger*.

journal entry: the interpretation of a business transaction, display of the bookkeeping treatment accorded the transaction, and an explanatory description of the transaction. [105]

journalize: the process of recording a transaction in an entity's records using the double-entry system. Debits, credits, and any necessary explanations are recorded in the journal.

journal voucher: a voucher provided for the recording of certain transactions or information in place of or supplementary to the journals or registers. The journal voucher usually contains an entry or entries explanations, references to documentary evidence supporting the entry or entries, and the signature or initials of one or more properly authorized officials. [49]

Jr.: see *junior*.

JSC: see *joint stock company*.

JSDM: June, September, December, March (quarterly interest payments or dividends).

judgment: a debt or other obligation, as determined by the decision or decree of a court.

judgment account: an account on which legal action has been taken and judgment obtained. [55]

judgmental system: a nonstatistical measure of evaluating credit worthiness. [78]

judgmental system of evaluating applicants: as used in the Equal Credit Opportunity Act, any system for evaluating the creditworthiness of an applicant, other than a demonstrable and statistically sound, empirically derived credit system. That system allows for the use of any pertinent element of creditworthiness, including any information about the applicant that a creditor obtains and considers and that has a demonstrable relationship to a determination of creditworthiness. [105]

judgment bond: see *bond, judgment*.

judgment creditor: an individual who has proved a debt in court or has won an action for the recovery of a debt.

judgment currency clause: a clause found in a Eurocurrency credit agreement protecting lenders against any loss arising from the fact that the loan is made in one currency and judgment given by the courts in still another.

judgment debt: any debt contested in a suit at law and proved to be valid.

judgment debtor: an individual who has been ordered by the court to make a payment to another.

judgment in personam: a judgment against a person, directing a specific defendant to do or not to do something.

judgment in rem: a judgment against a thing, as contrasted with a judgment against an individual (e.g., bank account, personal property). see *judgment lien*.

judgment lien: a charge rendered in a state or federal court on a piece of land or personal property against one who owes a debt. When applied to personal property, it is generally termed an *attachment*. see *attachment*. [51]

judgment note: a note authorizing a creditor to enter a judgment against a debtor in case of nonpayment, without the need for court action.

judgment rates: rates established by the judgment of the underwriter utilizing his or her professional skills and experience, without the application of a formal set of rules or schedule.

judgments payable: amounts due to be paid by a governmental unit as the result of court decisions, including condemnation awards in payment for private property taken for public use. [49]

judicial accounting: an account of proceedings prepared for submission to a court having jurisdiction. [37]

judicial review
(1) *labor relations:* an action brought before a court to determine the legality of decisions issued by a labor relations board. The review is concerned only with whether the decision is in violation of a statute; the merits of the case are not at issue.
(2) *law:* a legal examination of a situation ordered, sanctioned, prescribed, or enforced by a judge or court (e.g., a judicial proceeding).

judicial sale: a sale of real or personal property ordered by a legal body or court. synonymous with *forced sale*.

judicial settlement: the settlement of an account in accordance with the order, judgment, or decree of a proper court, the effect of which in many states is determined by statute. [32]

juice man: slang, a loaner of money at exorbitant interest rates. synonymous with *loan shark*.

jumbo CDs: certificates of deposit in minimum denominations of $100,000.

jumbo certificates: bank certificates earning in excess of 10 percent interest.

junior: an exchange by holders of securities maturing within one to five years for issues with original maturities of five or more years. [71]

junior advance refunding: an operation where the securities eligible for exchange mature in from one to five years. [65]

junior bond: see *bond, junior*.

junior equity: common stock. The junior position refers to the fact that the claims of holders of common stock are subordinate to holders of preferred stock, in the event of the liquidation of a corporation. [105]

junior interest
(1) a legal right that is subordinate to another interest.
(2) a mortgage participation junior to another participation.

junior issue: an issue whose claim for dividends or interest, or for principal value, comes following that of another issue, called a senior issue.

junior lien: a lien against a property that has a senior lien made and recorded. The rights are enforceable only after previous liens have been satisfied.

junior mortgage: a second or third mortgage that is subordinated to a prior mortgage. cf. *equal dignity*.

junior refunding: an exchange by holders of securities maturing within one to five years for issues with original maturities of five or more years. [71]

junior securities: common stocks and other issues whose claims to assets and earnings are contingent upon the satisfaction of the claims of prior obligations. [30]

junk bond: see *bond, junk.*

jurisdiction

(1) ***government:*** authority given by the Constitution to the courts to try cases and determine causes. Different courts get differing cases, based on the nature of the offense, the amount of the claim involved, and other factors.

(2) ***labor relations:*** the area of work or group of employees for which a union claims the right to bargain collectively.

jurisdiction risk: a risk inherent in placing funds in a center where they will fall under the jurisdiction of a foreign legal authority, which may become hostile, or which may apply biased legal procedures; can arise in any international transaction.

just compensation: a government payment for property taken under eminent domain which reflects a fair market value for the taken property and includes compensation for incidental loss of value which may result with respect to the remaining holdings of the property owner.

jury of executive opinion: a forecasting approach utilizing the opinions of senior executives.

justified price: a fair market price that a buyer will give for property.

just title: a title that will be supported against all claims. Considered to be a proper title. synonymous with *clear title,* and *good title.*

JV: see *joint venture.*

Kaffirs: used by European investors when describing mining shares from South Africa.

kale seed: slang, money.

kameralism: a concept of mercantilism concerned with the production of wealth by the state and how the wealth is used; sometimes spelled *cameralism.*

KD

(1) see *knocked-down price.*

(2) Kuwaiti dinar.

keelage: the charges paid by a ship entering or remaining in certain ports.

keepwell: a letter of comfort where a provision is made by a parent of a borrowing subsidiary in which the parent specifies that its subsidiary will conform to certain requirements.

Kennedy Round: during President Kennedy's Administration, a 1964 series of world tariff negotiations to reduce tariffs. The sixth round of tariff reductions under the auspices of the General Agreement or Tariffs and Trade. cf. *Dillon Round.*

Keogh plan (HR 10): a form of tax-qualified retirement plan established by a nonincorporated business or self-employed individual. Investment contributions and appreciation are generally tax deferred until actually received in the form of benefits. Formerly defined under the Self-Employment Individuals Tax Retirement Act of 1962. Until January 1, 1982, in each taxable year, the contributed amount could not exceed $7500 or 15 percent of annual earned income, whichever was less. Under the Tax Reform Act of 1976, for individuals with less than $15,000 of adjusted gross income, the minimum contribution would remain at the lesser of $750 or 100 percent of self-employed income. Effective January 1, 1982, a self-employed person or an individual who has outside self-employment income can put as much as $15,000 every year in a Koegh plan, double the old limit. But the 15 percent of earnings restrictions stays in effect for Keoghs. see *Economic Recovery Tax Act of 1981, Individual Retirement Accounts.*

kerb dealing: dealing in commodity markets which occur once the official market has closed.

Kerr-Smith Tobacco Control Act of 1934: federal legislation, amended in 1935, provided for processing taxes in the tobacco industry to finance a quota system for growers, including penalties for marketing beyond individual quotas.

key account: a merchant who is of particular importance to a card plan in terms of either volume or prestige or both. [105]

key industry: an industry that because of a unique characteristic, holds major importance in the country's economy (e.g., steel, automobile).

key man insurance: protection of a business firm against the financial loss caused by the death or disability of a vital member of the firm; a means of protecting the business from the adverse results of the loss of an individual possessing special skills or experience. [105]

Keynesian economics: developed by the British economist John Maynard Keynes, a system showing that national income and employment are dependent upon real investments and consumer spending. see *liquidity preference, New Economics, paradox or thrift, savings and investment theory;* cf. *Friedmanite, quantity theory.*

keystone pricing: nominal pricing in which the marked price is intended as higher than the selling price to make the buyer feel that he or she is getting a bargain.

KI: see *key industry.*

kickback

(1) *government:* an illegal rebate given secretly by a seller for granting an order or contract, as with a payoff.

(2) *labor relations:* the racketeering practice of forcing employees, as a condition of employment, to return a part of the wages established by law or by union contract to the employer. Outlawed in federally financed employment. see *Antikickback Law.*

kick in: slang, to contribute money, to pay one's share.

killing: slang, describes an unusually profitable trade.

kill order: synonymous with *immediate order.*

kin: persons of the same blood or members of the same family. [37]

kind

(1) monetary unit of Papua.

(2) when used in "distribution in kind" the distribution of the property itself, not its cash value.

kindred: persons related by blood. [105]

kinked demand: a firm's demand curve which becomes continuous at the market price. This is associated with the phenomenon of an industry in which there are few firms but no price leader.

kip: monetary unit of Laos.

kite (kiting)

(1) *banking:* writing a check in an amount sufficient to overdraw the account, but making up this deficiency by depositing another check, likewise in excess of deposits, and issued on some other bank. This unorthodox procedure is considered to be evidence of fraudulent intent (e.g., mailing in the rent when your account has insufficient funds, but counting on receiving and depositing some money before the

landlord has a chance to present the check for collection. see *forgery*.

(2) *finance:* sometimes used for an accommodation bill.

kiting stocks: the manipulation of stock prices to unprecedented high levels.

knocked-down price: a lowered or reduced price; a seller's asking price that has been lowered for purposes of making the sale.

Kondratyev wave: a major contribution of the Russian economist Nikolai Dmitriyevich Kondratyev, whose thesis was that business activity in the major western nations assumes a rhythmic wave pattern over very long periods. Using price indexes and other eco-nomic gauges for such countries as the United States, Great Britian, and France, he contended that sort of "super" business cycle exists, extending over roughly over half a century.

koruna: monetary unit of Czechoslovakia.

KP: see *Keogh Plan.*

krona: monetary unit of Iceland and Sweden.

krone: monetary unit of Denmark and Norway.

KS: see *kiting stocks.*

kwacha: monetary unit of Malawi and Zambia.

kwanza: monetary unit of Angola.

kyat: monetary unit of Burma.

L

L: a new definition of money supply of the Federal Reserve Board: a broad measure of liquid assets, equaling M3 plus other liquid assets not included elsewhere, such as term Eurodollars held by U.S. residents other than banks; bankers' acceptances; commercial paper; Treasury bills and other liquid Treasury securities; and U.S. Savings Bonds. see also *M3*.

LA

(1) see *legal asset*.

(2) see *liquid assets*.

labor banks: banks whose stock is owned by labor unions and their membership. cf. *industrial bank*.

Labor Department, U.S.: see *Department of Labor, U.S.*

labor economics: a specialty in the field of economics concerned primarily with the relationship between the worker and his or her job. Areas covered include supply of labor, hours and wages, conditions of work, and other forces relating to the general economic welfare of the worker.

labor exchange bank: a scheme appearing in the nineteenth century with the aim of facilitating exchange of commodities in proportion to their labor content.

labor force: defined by the U.S. Bureau of the Census, people over 14 years of age who are gainfully employed, looking for work, or absent from work (e.g., because of illness or vacation).

labor grade: job or job groups in a rate structure, set usually through job classifications and evaluations, or by agreement with a union.

labor-hour method of depreciation: taking the initial cost of a capital asset, deducting the expected salvage value at the time it is discarded, and spreading the difference on the basis of labor hours of use in an accounting period as a percentage of the total labor hours of use expected to constitute the life of the asset.

labor intensive: describing the use of additional personnel to increase output or earnings. see also *labor pool*.

Labor-Management Relations Act of 1947: see *Taft-Hartley Act*.

labor mobility: the ease with which

workers change positions and jobs. Horizontal mobility pertains to the way workers move from job to job at a similar skill level. Vertical mobility pertains to the way workers change jobs by moving up and sometimes down the occupational ladder.

labor pool: the established source of trained people from which prospective workers are recruited. see also *labor intensive.*

labor relations: a general term to identify all matters arising out of the employer-employee relationship. see also *industrial relations.*

labor-saving equipment: any machine or mechanized equipment that reduces the need for labor by a reduction of workers or by curtailing the number of hours of potential employees. In the 1960s automation was considered to be a technological breakthrough that would result in displacement of workers. cf. *automation.*

labor theory of value: expounded by Karl Marx to describe the exploitation of workers in a capitalist system. He claimed that the exchange value of any good was measured by the amount of labor required for its manufacture. Since labor was not only the measure but also the source of all value, every product could be identified as relating directly to the human effort or the quantity of labor involved in production.

labor turnover: see *turnover.*

laches: neglect to do a thing at the proper time, such as undue delay in asserting a right or asking for a privilege. [105]

LAFTA: see *Latin American Free Trade Area.*

lag: the delay between two computer events.

lagged reserve accounting (LRA): a Federal Reserve ruling of September 1968, changing the timing of reserve accounting by extending the one-day lag to a two-week lag. Under this system, required reserves for each settlement week (seven days ending each Wednesday) are based on deposit liabilities held two weeks earlier. Average vault cash held two weeks earlier is counted as a part of reserves in the current week, and vault cash in the current week is counted as reserves two weeks in the future.

lagged values of variables: values of variables pertaining to previous time periods. For example, consumption expenditures today might be related to both today's income and yesterday's income. Yesterday's income is a lagged variable. [57]

lagging indicator: a numerical index which exhibits trends similar to those of the stock market, after the fluctuations have taken place in the stock market. Lagging indicators are followed by those seeking to verify specific trends. [105]

laissez-faire

(1) *general:* a term used to describe a leadership style of minimal involvement.

(2) *finance:* a policy of the classic capitalistic model, suggesting that government should not interfere with the economy. cf. *controlled economy, statism.*

lamb: an inexperienced speculator.

lame duck

(1) *general:* an individual going out of office shortly; thus thought to be ineffectual or helpless.

(2) *investments:* a speculator whose venture has failed.

(3) *investments:* a member of a stock exchange who is unable to meet his or her debts.

land banks: see *Federal Land Bank.*

land certificate: a legal document indicating proof of ownership of land or property. Contains a description of property and the owner's name and address.

land contract: installment contract drawn between buyer and seller for the sale of property. Occasionally used as a substitute for a mortgage, except that ownership of the property does not pass until payment of the last installment. [78]

land development loan: an advance of funds, secured by a mortgage, for the purpose of making, installing, or constructing those improvements necessary to produce construction-ready building sites from raw land. [59]

landesbanken: state savings banks of Germany.

land freeze: government limit on the sale or transfer of land.

landlord: the owner of leased property; the lessor.

landlord's warrant: to obtain overdue rental payments, the landlord secures a court-approved warrant that permits him or her to take possession of the lessee's personal property in the leased premises until the debt is paid. Should the debt remain, the landlord can sell the personal property at public auction. see *distress for rent*; cf. *ejectment, reentry.*

land patent: a governmental document providing proof of title to land. cf. *land warrant.*

land poor: usually, a person who owns land but because of taxes or other obligations is short of funds.

land revenue: any form of payment derived from ownership of land. It may take various forms (farm produce, forest rights, mineral deposits, ect.).

land tax: a tax levied on the ownership of real property. An assessed valuation determines the rate of the tax. see also *cadastre.* synonymous with *ad valorem taxes* or *property tax.*

land trust: title to land held by a trustee in the interest of the beneficiaries of a trust.

land trust certificate: an instrument granting participation in benefits of the ownership of real estate, while the title remains in a trustee.

land value tax: a governmental levy on the value of land only (i.e., not including structures or agricultural produce on it).

land warrant: a government document given as proof of ownership to anyone buying public land.

language

(1) *general:* a set of representations, conventions, and rules used to convey information.

(2) *computers:* a defined character set used to form words, symbols, and so on, and the rules for combining these into useful communications.

language translator: a general computer term for any assembler, compiler, or other routine that accepts statements in one language and produces equivalent statements in another language.

Lanham Act of 1947: federal legislation governing trademarks and other symbols for identifying goods sold in interstate commerce. As amended, it allows a manufacturer to protect his brand or trademark in the United States by having it recorded on a government register in the U.S. Patent Office, provides for the legal right to register any distinctive mark, and so on. see *trademark.*

lapping: theft from a customer that is covered by theft from another customer by placing false entries in account books. see *fraud.*

lapse

(1) ***banking:*** the failure of the insured to pay the cost of the premium when due, or within the days of grace allowed.

(2) ***banking:*** the discontinuance of a right by the passage of time, as when the grace period of a mortgage ends or the date of a lease has passed.

(3) ***law:*** the termination of a right through disuse or failure to meet standard obligations over a fixed time period.

lapsing schedule: a form on which are recorded the costs of fixed assets or the total yearly additions to a group of fixed assets, together with the details of the distribution of their costs over accounting periods succeeding their purchase.

larceny: the unlawful taking of the personal property of another without the individual's consent and with intent to deprive him or her of the ownership and use of it. This offense is defined by statute in nearly all states and provinces, but there are some differences in the definitions.

La Salle Street: the financial center of Chicago.

last in, first out: see *LIFO.*

last sale: the final price in the transacting of a security during the trading day or at the end of the day.

last trading day: the last day during which trading in a futures contract is permitted during the delivery month. All contracts which have not been offset by the end of trading on that day must therefore be settled by delivery or agreement.

last will: the will last executed by an individual; all former wills are revoked by the last one.

late charge: a special fee demanded in connection with any payment on a mortgage loan or other obligation that is not made when due. [44]

late payment: a payment made after the due date on which an additional charge may be imposed. [78]

late posting payment: payment received and credited after the billing date. [105]

late tape: when the ticker tape of an exchange cannot report transactions fast enough and it runs 5 or more minutes late.

latifundism: the holding of land in sizable estates.

Latin American Free Trade Area (LAFTA): headquartered in Uruguay; founded in 1960 with the goals of trade liberalization and a system of reciprocal credits between members for financing payments imbalances. Members include Argentina, Bolivia, Brazil, Chile, Colombia, Ecuador, Mexico, Paraguay, Peru, Uruguay, and Venezuela.

laundered money: funds sent through numerous depositories one after another, in an attempt to conceal the source of the money. [105]

lawful money: all forms of money that are endowed by federal law with legal tender status for the payment of all debts, both public and private.

lawful reserve: banking laws establish the lawful reserves that must be maintained by banks for the protection of depositors' accounts. These reserves were established by the Federal Reserve Act of 1933 and 1935 for national banks, and by the banking laws of the various states for state-chartered banks. The Federal Reserve Board is vested by law with power to change the lawful reserve for national banks in order to control the supply of credit throughout the United States. This board may increase the reserve requirements in order to curtail the extension of credit, or it may decrease the reserve requirements in order to permit the expansion of credit. The various state laws follow a similar pattern, being more strict in some respects and less strict in others. The lawful reserves are required to be available at all times in the form of cash, and under certain conditions, government securities, either in the vaults of the bank, or in lawful bank depositories authorized by government or state officials. [10]

law of increasing costs: that the average total unit cost in a production process increases as the volume of a firm increases. see *diseconomies of scale, marginal cost.*

laws of descent: laws governing the descent of real property from ancestor to heir; to be distinguished from laws, rules, or statutes of distribution governing the disposition of personal property. [32]

lawsuit: a claim in a court of law. [61]

lay corporation: any corporation formed for purely secular purposes, profit-making or otherwise, hence any corporation other than an ecclesiastical one.

lay days: agreed-upon days that a chartered vessel is permitted without penalty to remain in port for loading and unloading.

lay off: slang, spreading a large loan risk among others to prevent potential loss.

layoff loan: considered to be one within the legal limit of the country bank but taken by the city bank to aid a country bank that is highly loaned up.

LB: see *bond, legal.*

L/C
 (1) see *letter of credit.*
 (2) see *line of credit.*

LC
 (1) see *leverage contract.*
 (2) see *loan capital.*
 (3) see *loan crowd.*

LCL: see *less-than-carload lot.*

L. Cr.: see *letter of credit.*

L&D: see *loans and discounts.*

LDC: see *less developed country.*

leader: a person who at a given time and place, by his or her actions, modifies, directs, or controls the attitudes or behavior of others, often referred to as followers.

leaders
 (1) *general:* any item that shows strong selling power in a market situation.
 (2) *investments:* individual securities or groups of shares that set the pace of a climbing or declining market.

leadership: in a group or organization, the exercise of command and direction in a skillful and responsible fashion.

leadership training: provided by means of workshops, conferences, seminars, and other programs designed to upgrade skills and to offer information of use to those in leadership positions.

leading indicators: 12 indicators, issued by the Bureau of Economic Analysis, chosen for their record in predicting turns in the business cycle, released late in the month for the previous month.

leads and lags: changes in the pattern of international payments terms. Should a devaluation of a nation's currency be feared, its importers with overseas currency obligations will rush to pay to avoid their debts becoming greater following devaluation; they *lead* payments. Conversely, exporters will benefit by not rushing to convert export receipts in foreign currency; they *lag* payments.

lead underwriter: an insurance underwriter who is the first of a number of underwriters to accept a line on a risk.

leakage: any factor or pressure that prevents new capital formation from exerting its full effect on the national income.

lease: a form of contract transferring the use or occupancy of land, space, structures, or equipment, in consideration of a payment, usually in the form of rent. Leases can be for a short period or as long as life. In a lease, the lessor gives the use of the property to a lessee.

lease (regular or commercial): agreement to occupy and use space for a definite term at a fixed monthly rental. [24]

leaseback: a seller who remains in possession as a tenant after completing the sale and delivering the deed. cf. *sell and leaseback agreement.*

lease broker: an individual in the business of securing leases for speculation and resale in areas where land plays or exploration work is being carried out.

leased fee interest: an interest of the owner in a leased property.

leased life insurance: a leasing firm life insurance policy in which the business then leases the policy to its original owner in consideration of a fee presumably lower than the cost of the original coverage.

lease financing: a specialized area of finance dealing with renting property owned by the lender, financing the leases of a company engaged in rentals, and financing the purchase of an item to be leased out by the borrower. [105]

lease ground: a lease that provides for occupancy and use of a parcel of unimproved land often, though obviously not always, for the construction of a building. In the event the lessee is to assume all property charges, more descriptive terminology would be *net ground lease. [6]*

leasehold: an estate or interest a tenant holds for a number of years in the property he or she is leasing.

leasehold obligation: an obligation in a leasehold, to pay a specified rental for a specified number of years.

leasehold value: the market value of a lease may increase or decrease over what was originally paid.

lease-purchase agreement: an agreement providing that a portion of a tenant's rent can be applied to the price of purchase.

Led.: see *ledger.*

ledger: a record of final entry in bookkeeping. An account is established for every type of transaction, and a ledger account is posted with every transaction affecting this particular account. cf. *journal.*

ledger asset: those assets for which accounts are maintained in the general ledger. [42]

ledger balance: the record of the balance in a customer's account, according to the bank's records. The ledger balance may not reflect all deposits if the bank has not yet received actual payment for them. [105]

ledger control card: a monthly record to date of the total debits, credits, and balances of the customer accounts it represents. In demand deposit accounting, this card is the final record of its group to be updated. [31]

ledger journal: a record that functions as both journal and ledger. [105]

ledger proof card: a record prepared daily containing total debits and credits affecting a given group of accounts. In demand deposit accounting, this card follows the customer account cards. Its reconciliation with the daily updating totals is the control for its group. [31]

left-hand side: the rate at which a bank offers a foreign currency. [105]

legacy (bequest): a gift of personal property made in a will. There are four common types of legacy: (a) *specific legacy*—a gift of a particular piece of property, as an automobile, or an investment that has been specifically described; (b) *demonstrative legacy*—one payable in cash out of a particular designated fund; (c) *general legacy*—a gift of money in a certain sum; and, (d) *residual legacy*—includes all the remaining personal property after the payment of all obligations, charges against the estate, and all other legacies.

legal asset: any property, including securities, that can be used for payment of a debt.

legal bond: see *bond, legal.*

legal capital

(1) that portion of the paid-in capital of a corporation that comprises the par or stated value of the stock.

(2) that portion of a corporation's net assets restricted as to withdrawal under corporate law. [105]

legal charity: one that comes within the legal definition of a charity. [105]

legal common trust fund: a common trust fund invested wholly in property that is legal for the investment of trust funds in the state in which the common trust is being administered. The term is employed most often in or with respect to common trust funds in states that have a statutory or court-approved list of authorized investment for trustees where the terms of the trust do not provide otherwise. [37]

legal entity: any individual, proprietorship, partnership, corporation, association, or other organization that has, in the eyes of the law, the capacity to make a contract or an agreement and the abilities to assume an obligation and to discharge an indebtedness. A legal entity is a responsible being in the eyes of the law and can be sued for damages if the performance of a contract or agreement is not met.

legal interest: the maximum rate of interest permitted by state law; this rate is used in contracts in which no rate has been stated. cf. *usury.*

legal investments

(1) investments that savings banks, insurance companies, trustees, and other fiduciaries (individual or corporate) are permitted to make by the laws of the state in which they are domiciled, or under the jurisdiction of which they operate or serve. Those investments which meet the conditions imposed by law constitute the legal investment list.

(2) investments that governmental

units are permitted to make by law. see *legal list.* [49]

legal list: a list of investments selected by various states in which certain institutions and fiduciaries, such as insurance companies and banks, may invest. Legal lists are often restricted to high-quality securities meeting certain specifications. see *prudent man rule.* [20]

legal monopoly: a privately owned organization that is granted an exclusive right by the government to function in a specified market under strict control and pricing by the government (e.g., public utilities).

legal name: an individual's personal first and last name, used as identification when entering into certain transactions. The name must be currently in use for financial purposes and must be used without fraudulent intent. [105]

legal obligations: a debt or promise to perform, that can be enforced by legal means if necessary. [28]

legal opinion
(1) the opinion of an official authorized to render it, such as an attorney general or city attorney, as to legality.
(2) in the case of municipal bonds, the opinion, usually of a specialized bond attorney, as to the legality of a bond issue. A preliminary legal opinion is made in advance of the original sale of the bonds, a final opinion, after the bonds have been issued and sold. [49]

legal ownership: an estate of interest in property which is enforceable in a court of law; to be distinguished from *equitable ownership.* [37]

legal partnership: an estate or interest in property that is enforceable in a court of law. cf. *equitable ownership.* [105]

legal person: often applied to a corporation that is allowed to own property, to sue, to be sued, and to exercise many of the rights accorded to natural persons.

legal rate of interest: the maximum rate of interest that is permitted by the laws of the state having jurisdiction over the legality of a transaction. Interest in excess of this legal rate is termed usury. see *usury.* cf *usurious rate of interest.* [10]

legal reserve: part of a bank's cash assets that must be retained as protection for depositors; ruling from the Federal Deposit Insurance Act.

legal residence: where a person lives. The law does not require anyone to spend a majority of his or her time in a certain place for it to be categorized as a legal residence. However, federal law recognizes only one legal residence for an individual. cf. *domicile.*

legals: see *nonlegals.*

legal security: a stock or bond that can be bought by a fiduciary and retained for beneficiaries.

legal tender: any money that is recognized as being lawful for use by a debtor to pay a creditor, who must accept same in the discharge of a debt unless the contract between the parties specifically states that another type of money is to be used.

legal title: the claim of right to property that is recognized by law.

legatee: an individual to whom a legacy is given by will.

legend: the text on a bank note. [27]

lek: monetary unit of Albania.

lempira: monetary unit of Honduras.

lend: to give up something of personal value, for a definite or indefinite period of time, without relinquishing ownership. see *loan.*

lender: an individual or financial institution making a trade of placing an interest on money, as with a money lender, with the expectation that the money (or other item) will be returned with the interest. see *note.*

lender-dealer agreement: in mobile home lending, a document that spells out the exact conditions under which lender and dealer will do business, and the rights and responsibilities of each. [59]

lender of funds: see *promissory note.*

lender of last resort: the name given to a central bank that will lend to individual banks whenever they experience large withdrawals.

lender's agreement: the signed agreement between the bank and FmHA describing the bank loan servicing and other responsibilities. [105]

lender's loss payable clause: a provision in an insurance policy that establishes a lender's interest in real property for insurance purposes; once such endorsement has been added to the policy, any claim drafts are written to the mortgagor and mortgagee as joint payees. [59]

lending flat: when a security sold short is borrowed for purposes of delivery and the borrower does not have to pay a charge for the privilege of borrowing it. When a security is lent flat, no fee is charged the borrower.

lending institution: a finance company, bank, loan or other organization that lends money and makes money by advancing funds to others. see also *personal finance company.*

lending rate: the interest rate charged to borrowers by lenders.

lending securities: securities that can be borrowed by a broker representing a short seller.

leniency clause: in a promissory note, a clause spelling out the association's willingness to adjust loan payments temporarily if a borrower is experiencing several financial difficulties through no fault of his or her own. [59]

leone: monetary unit of Sierra Leone.

less developed country (LDC): a country showing (a) a poverty level of income, (b) a high rate of population increase, (c) a substantial portion of its workers employed in agriculture, (d) a low proportion of adult literacy, (e) high unemployment, and (f) a significant reliance on a few items for export. see also *underdeveloped country.*

lessee: a tenant.

lessor: a landlord.

less-than-carload lot (LCL): used by railroad to designate freight shipments of less than a carload each.

let: to lease, demise, or convey, thus a sign "to let."

letter of administration: evidence of appointment issued by a court to an individual or a trust instruction to settle the estate of a decedent who failed to name an executor. [37]

letter of advice: a note giving instructions.

letter of allotment: an allotment notice.

letter of attorney: a document showing a power of attorney.

letter of conservatorship: a certificate of authority issued by the court to an individual or corporate fiduciary to serve as conservator of the property of a person; corresponds with *letters of guardianship*. [37]

letter of credit: an instrument or document issued on behalf of a buyer by a bank on another bank or banks, or on itself. It gives a buyer the prestige and the financial backing of the issuing bank. The acceptance by the bank of drafts drawn under the letter of credit satisfies the seller and the seller's bank in the handling of the transaction. The buyer and the accepting bank also have an agreement as to payment for the drafts as they are presented. see also *circular letter of credit, confirmed letter of credit, irrevocable letter of credit, revolving letter of credit, straight letter of credit, traveler's letter of credit, unconfirmed letter of credit.*

letter of demand: see *payoff statement.*

letter of dispute: letter with a customer's signature explaining the nature of his or her dispute. [105]

letter of hypothecation: an instrument executed by the pledgor of items or the documents of title.

letter of indication: a bank's letter of identification given to a traveler who has bought a letter of credit.

letter of intention: a pledge to purchase a sufficient amount of open-end investment company shares within a limited time (usually 12 or 13 months) to qualify for the reduced selling charge that would apply to a comparable lump-sum purchase. [30]

letter of license: a letter by a creditor permitting a debtor to proceed as stated to avoid bankruptcy.

letter of lien: a document signed by a purchaser, stating that specific items are held by him or her in trust for the seller. As the buyer pays for the items, the agreement becomes null and void. synonymous with *letter of trust.*

letter of moral intent (LOMI): an undertaking by a firm falling short of a legal guarantee, usually given by a parent firm in respect of a subsidiary.

letter of trust: synonymous with *letter of lien.*

letters of administration: a certificate of authority to settle a particular estate issued to an administrator by the appointing court. cf. *letters testamentary*. [105]

letters of conservatorship: a certificate of authority issued by the court to an individual or corporate fiduciary to serve as conservator of the property of a person; corresponds with letters of guardianship. [105]

letters of guardianship: see *letters of conservatorship*.

letters patent: a government-issued instrument granting a right or conveying title to a private person or organization.

letters testamentary: a certificate of authority to settle a particular estate issued by the appointing court to the executer named in the will; to be distinguished from letters of administration. cf *letters of administration*. [37]

letter stock: an unregistered stock, usually issued by a new, small firm to avoid the expense of a formal underwriting. These securities are sold at a discount to mutual funds and investors specializing in speculative purchases.

lettuce: slang, money, especially paper money.

leu: monetary unit of Romania.

lev: monetary unit of Bulgaria.

level accrual: accrual method of recognizing earned income by dividing interest balance by the number of months to maturity. [105]

level-payment plan: an amortization plan that provides for equal monthly payments covering both principal and interest during the term of the mortgage. Part of each payment is applied to interest as earned, and the rest of the payment is credited to principal. [44]

level-premium life insurance: life insurance for which the premium remains the same from year to year. The premium is more than the actual cost of protection during the earlier years of the policy and less than the actual cost in the later years. The building of a reserve is a natural result of level premiums. The overpayments in the early years, together with the interest that is to be earned, serve to balance out the underpayments of the later years. [58]

leverage: the effect on the per share earnings of the common stock of a company when large sums must be paid for bond interest or preferred stock dividends, or both, before the common stock is entitled to share in earnings. Leverage may be advantageous for the common stock when earnings are good but may work against the common stock when earnings decline. [20]

leverage charge plan: an accumulation plan under which the selling charges are spread over the entire life of the program; that is, a sales charge obtains on each separate purchase, the amount varying with the size of the purchase. [30]

leverage contract: the right to buy or sell a commodity at a specified price on a specified future date without rigid variation margin requirements of recognized commodity exchanges. The customer puts up 25 percent of the value of the contract and pays a premium of 2 percent over the prevailing market price, commissions, and interest on the unpaid balance of the contract.

leveraged lease: a lease transaction in which the financing of equipment is divided into debt and equity portions and placed separately with different investors.

leverage factor: the ratio of working assets to price of the leverage security. [30]

leverage ratios: relationships among balance sheet values that measure the extent to which owners, rather than creditors, finance a business. [105]

leverage stock: junior security of a multiple-capital-structure company, generally a common stock, but the term may also be applied to a warrant, or to a preferred stock if the latter is preceded by funded debt or bank loans. [30]

levy
(1) *general:* a tax assessment.
(2) *finance:* a demand made on the members of a company for a contribution of added working capital or to make good on a loss.
(3) *government:* to assess, declare, and receive a sum of money against a person or property for public objectives.

levy (writ of)
(1) *general:* placing a lien on land or other property of a defendant.
(2) *law:* the instrument authorizing

the sheriff to take a defendant's property to satisfy a plaintiff's judgment.

Li.: see *liabilities.*

liabilities

(1) *banking:* the funds a bank owes. The largest liability for a bank is deposits. see *accrued liabilities, capital liability, contingent liability, current liabilities, deferred liabilities, fixed liabilities, long-term liabilities reported by U.S. banks.*

(2) *finance:* all the claims against a corporation. see *indirect business tax and nontax liability.*

liability: a debt or obligation stated in terms of money.

liability account: see *segregated account.*

liability for endorsement: a contingent liability arising from the endorsement of an obligation owing by another, and continuing until it is ascertained that the original debtor has met or failed to meet the obligation. In the case of the default of the original debtor, the contingent liability becomes a direct one of the endorser. [105]

liability hedge: a strategy for a bank to make its liabilities less sensitive to rate changes. When a bank takes in interest-sensitive deposits (e.g., six-month money market certificates, it can fix, or very nearly fix, the cost of reissuing or rolling over the certificates simply by short-selling securities for future delivery.

liability insurance: protection against the loss of property or earning power of a business or individual. Liability insurance is of various specific types: accident, health, property damage, collision, and so on. [105]

liability ledger: see *note notice.*

liability reserve: an amount set up to show a liability such as income taxes but in the form of a reserve to show that the amount is estimated.

LIBOR: see *London Inter-Bank Offered Rate.*

license: a right to engage in certain activities for which permission is needed.

license and permit bond: see *bond, license and permit.*

licensed lender: a consumer finance office authorized to conduct business in the state in which it is located.

licensee: a bank that has been granted the right to issue bank cards and operate a bank card plan by a licensing authority such as Visa U.S.A. or Interbank Card Association. [105]

license tax: a tax upon individuals or corporations for the right of engaging in some business enterprise.

liée: French for *swap.*

lien: a claim on property to secure payment of a debt or the fulfillment of a contractual obligation. The law may allow the holder of the lien to enforce it by taking possession of the property.

lien affidavit: an affidavit either stating that there are no liens against a particular property or documenting and describing any existing liens. see *recordation; cf. no lien affidavit.*

lienee: a person possessing a right of lien on the property of another person.

lien in invitum: a lien placed on property without the owner's approval. synonymous with *involuntary lien.*

lienor: the holder of a lien. see *voluntary conveyance or deed.*

lien placement fee: cost of recording with the secretary of state the security interest of a bank on the title of any new or used car. [78]

lien theory: a theory of real estate law which holds that a mortgage conveys to the mortgagee a claim to, or lien on, the mortgaged property. [59]

"life": synonymous with *LIFFE* (London International Financial Futures Exchange).

life annuity: see *annuity life.*

life beneficiary: a person who receives benefits from an estate, generally in the form of income, during his or her lifetime; sometimes called a life tenant if the estate consists of real property. [37]

life contingency: probability of living or dying. Tables relating to life contingency may be found in rate manuals. [12]

life cycle hypothesis: a theory of the saving decision stating that consumers save to be able to maintain a stable level of consumption in the future. see also entries under *marginal propensity.*

life estate: an estate in real or personal property that terminates when the owner dies. The future of the property (i.e., after the owner's death) is usually provided for when the estate for life is prepared.

life insurance: insurance providing for payment of a stipulated sum to a designated beneficiary upon the death of the insured. Various plans of life insurance are available to fit the differing needs of many classes of insureds—for example, endowment plans, which pay back the face amount of the policy to the insured if he or she survives the specified period of the policy, or annuity contracts, under which savings are accumulated and paid back in periodic payments of guaranteed lifetime income to the annuitant if he or she survives the specified period.

life insurance in force: the sum of the face amounts, plus dividend additions, of life insurance policies outstanding at a given time. Additional amounts payable under accidental death or other special provisions are not included. [58]

life insurance trust: a trust created by an individual for the benefit of his or her heirs, the major portion of which is in the form of life insurance.

life interest: the estate or interest that a person has in property for his or her own life or for another person's life, or for an indefinite period limited by a lifetime. [105]

life of delivery: the time period from the beginning of commodity trading in the delivery to the date of the last transaction.

life tenant: a beneficiary having possession of certain property for the duration of his or her life. An estate or interest in property held during the life of a specified person, called *life estate.*

LIFFE: London International Financial Futures Exchange. synonymous with *"life."*

LIFO (last in, first out)

(1) *general:* dealing with the valuation of inventories: the price shown on the last incoming shipment of a particular item is the one that will be used for current valuations and cost.

(2) *banking:* a method of determining the effect of withdrawals on savings account dividends or interest computations. With LIFO, withdrawals are made from money that was de-

posited last. The withdrawal penalty under this plan is loss of interest on the last money deposited. cf. *FIFO.*

lift check: a check that is not drawn on a bank but through the bank against the maker. Many corporations issue payroll checks in the form of lift checks. The bank through which the items are drawn accumulates a group of these items and delivers them to the maker upon receipt of a regular check in payment of the total. [31]

light gold: gold coins that have been reduced in weight, either by error of the mint or as the result of usage.

limit

(1) in commodities, the maximum allowed price fluctuation in any day before trading is suspended.

(2) the restriction on the number of futures contracts any one individual or firm may hold.

light piece: slang, a silver coin, usually a 25-cent piece.

lilangeni: monetary unit of Swaziland.

limit

(1) in commodities, the maximum allowed price fluctuation in any day before trading is suspended.

(2) the restriction on the number of futures contracts any one individual or firm may hold.

limitations of actions (statutes of): the law for each state identifying the definite time limit to the period within which a law suit can be brought under law. The terms within the statutes vary by state; however, the time within which a commercial case action should be brought is usually six years.

limit control: the component of a bank card operation which has the responsibility of monitoring cardholder balances relative to credit limits and of taking appropriate action when credit limits are exceeded. [105]

limited (Ltd.): see *limited company.*

limited audit: an audit in which the effectiveness of the system of internal control and the mathematical accuracy, legality, propriety, and completeness of all transactions are determined by examining only selected items. The assumption is that the transactions selected for examination are representative of the entire group from which selected, and, therefore, if no errors are found in them, the unchecked items in the group are also correct. see also *complete audit.* [49]

limited check: a check limited as to the amount. Such checks have inscribed on their face a legend that the item is void if for more than a certain amount. Limited checks are frequently used in payroll payments by check, with the maximum amount shown on the face. This is done to frustrate attempts to raise the amount of the check. The date by which a check must be presented for payment also constitutes a limitation. [10]

limited coinage system: the U.S. Mint's program under which the right of the individual to bring bullion for purposes of being coined is limited.

limited company: a British business corporation; "Ltd." indicates registration under the Companies Act and formally establishes the limited liability of stockholders.

limited depositary: a Federal Reserve System member bank which under stated restrictions can receive governmental deposits.

limited-dividend corporation: a corporation upon which a limitation is placed regarding the maximum amount of dividends on its capital stock. Following creation of the needed and desirable surplus and reserves, such a corporation's prices can be reduced to the point where earnings were sufficient to meet the maximum dividend requirements and to maintain reserves.

limited facility branch office: a branch office that operates subject to certain limitations, such as the services it may offer or the number of its personnel. [59]

limited guardianship: some states have created a limited guardianship which allows a partially disabled or incompetent person to delegate limited powers and authority to the limited guardian. [105]

limited legal tender: moneys that formerly were legal tender in payment of debts up to a specified amount (e.g., pennies were legal tender up to 25 cents). This was changed by law on June 5, 1933.

limited liability: the legal exemption of stockholders from financial liability for the debts of the firm beyond the amount they have individually invested. see *partnership;* cf. *nonassessable stock.*

limited life: a characteristic of a single proprietorship or partnership; in both cases the business ceases to exist on the death of either of the owners.

limited open-end mortgage: an indenture under which additional bonds may be issued, but which establishes certain limits, or measures, of maximum amounts that may be issued. [37]

limited order: an order in which the customer has set restrictions with re-

spect to price. see *composite limit order book, market order, no-limit order, percentage order, stop limit order.*

limited partner: a member of a partnership who is not personally liable for incurred debts of the partership. By law, at least one partner must be fully liable.

limited parntership: see *limited partner.*

limited payment life: a policy providing permanent protection, but premiums are payable only for a specified, limited number of years.

limited power of appointment: a power of the donee (the one who has the power) to pass on an interest in property that is limited in some way—as to or for whom or to the time within which he must exercise the power; also known as special power; the opposite of general power of appointment; all powers that are not general are special or limited powers. [37]

limited price order: an order to buy or sell a stated amount of a security at a specified price, or at a better price according to the directions within the order. cf. *limited order.*

limited-reduction plan: an amortization plan that provides for only a limited amount of principal reduction prior to the expiration date of the loan. [105]

limited resource agreement: an indirect lending arrangement where a dealer sells or discounts installment contracts to a bank and is liable in case of default for a limited time, a limited dollar amount, or both. [105]

limited tax bond: see *bond, limited tax.*

limit move: the greatest change in the

price of a futures contract allowed during any trading period, as determined by the contract market's regulations.

limit order: see *limited order.*

limit up, limit down: commodity exchange restrictions on the maximum upward or downward movement permitted in the price for a commodity during any trading session day.

limping standard: a modification of the gold monetary standard leading to the acceptance of certain silver coins as standard money to the extent that they are made unlimited legal tender and not required to be redeemed in gold.

Lincoln Incentive Management Plan: a combination profit-sharing and incentive plan, developed by J.F. Lincoln in 1934, leading to better worker performance and sizable extra payments for the employee.

line
(1) in Great Britain, a large quantity of stock or shares.
(2) in Great Britain, an acceptance of a risk by an insurance underwriter and, should there be more than one underwriter, each underwriter's proportion of the sum assured.

lineal descendant: a person in the direct line of descent, as child or grandchild; opposed to collateral heir. [37]

line and staff authority: a part of the organization identified by those having the right to decide and to order others to perform activities (line), and those having the right to plan, recommend, advise, or assist, but not empowered to order others to perform activities (staff).

linear programing: a mathematical technique used in operations re-search to optimize a business operation subject to given resources and restraints; bears no relation to computer programming. [45]

line authority: authority that is exerted downward (i.e., over subordinates) in an organization.

line chart: a chart constructed on graph paper showing the price range of a security on a particular day, week, or month. The closing price is noted and a separate chart of volume is usually recorded, helping chartists so predict future price movements.

line functions: functions that contribute directly to bank objectives (such activities as accepting and processing deposits, investing). [105]

line manager: a high-level officer having direct responsibility for carrying out a superior's requests and authorized to pass along his or her own orders to subordinates. see also *line organization, middle management.*

line of credit: an agreement between a bank and a customer: the bank agrees, over a future period, to lend the customer funds up to an agreed maximum amount. The bank has the option to withdraw from the agreement if the financial status of the borrower changes, or if the borrower fails to use the line of credit for its intended use as set forth in the agreement. The customer may borrow as much of the "line" as is required and pay interest on the borrowed portion only. A line of credit is widely used by large organizations to finance future commitments and for purchases of inventory. May be "advised"—that is, the customer is officially notified of the existence of the line—or "guidance"—that is for the bank's internal use only.

line of discount: the maximum credit that a bank will extend to a retailer on the basis of his or her accounts payable, which the merchant discounts with the bank.

line organization: the oldest and least complex company structure, where top officials have total and direct authority and subordinates report to only one supervisor.

linkage
(1) *computers:* coding that connects two separately coded routines.
(2) *finance:* the pressures an industry can exert on the rest of the economy.

liquid: capable of being readily converted to cash. Usually the assets of an entity are considered to be most liquid when they are in cash or marketable securities. synonymous with *collectible.*

liquid.: see *liquidation.*

liquid asset fund: see *money market fund.*

liquid assets: those assets that are easily converted into cash (e.g., government bonds). see also *flight of capital.*

liquidate
(1) *general:* to convert (assets) into cash.
(2) *banking:* to discharge or pay off an indebtedness.
(3) *finance:* to settle the accounts of, by apportioning assets and debts.

liquidated claim: a claim or debt in which the amount due is fixed by law or has been ascertained and agreed upon by the parties and no bona fide dispute regarding the amount exists between the parties. [105]

liquidated damages: the payment by all parties of an agreed sum of money as damages for breaching their contract. The courts can declare the amount to be a penalty and unenforceable if the amount is excessive.

liquidating dividend: the declared dividend in the closing of a firm, to distribute the assets of the organization to qualified stockholders.

liquidating market: a securities market where aggressive selling occurs at relatively low prices.

liquidating value: the anticipated value of a particular asset that will be realized in case of liquidation of a business. [10]

liquidation: the winding up of the affairs of a business by converting all assets into cash paying off all outside creditors in the order of their preference, and distributing the remainder, if any, to the owners in proportion, and in the order of preference, if any, of ownership.

liquidation cost per installment: the primary costs involved in the payment of each installment, including teller time, bookkeeping, and collection expenses. [105]

liquidation cost per loan: the cost involved in removing a loan from the active file, canceling, and returning a note. [105]

liquidator: a person who liquidates; a person legally in charge of liquidating a business.

liquid cushion: the protection provided by holdings of cash or of securities (such as short-term marketable government bonds) that are readily convertible into cash. [105]

liquidity
(1) *finance:* the solvency of a business, which has special reference

to the speed with which assets can be converted into cash without loss.

(2) *investments:* the ability of the market in a particular security to absorb a reasonable amount of buying or selling at reasonable price changes. [20]

liquidity preference: part of Keynesian theory; the preference of people to hold their assets in cash rather than in a less liquid form, as with an investment. see *Keynesian economics;* cf. *marginal propensity to invest.*

liquid ratio: the ratio of readily available current assets to current liabilities.

liquid saving: individuals' saving consisting of, or easily and quickly convertible into, cash. These consist of currency, bank deposits, shares in savings and loan associations, and securities. Included are holdings of persons, unincorporated businesses, trusts, and not-for-profit institutions. [70]

liquid securities: stocks, bonds, and so on, easily marketable and converted to cash. [28]

liquid trap: the liquidity preference theory of John Maynard Keynes. The concept that at some low interest rate, the speculative desire for cash becomes infinitely elastic. cf. *quantity theory.*

lir.: see *lira.*

lira: monetary unit of Italy, San Marino, Turkey, and Vatican City.

lis pendens: a pending suit. see also *injunction pendente lite, pendente lite.*

listed securities (stocks): any bonds or stocks that have been admitted for trading on a stock exchange and whose issues have complied in every way with the listing requirements of the exchange.

lister: a broker who sells property from a listing.

listing: a seller's preference to offer a property with one or more real estate brokers; the broker who successfully sells the property receives a commission.

listing agreement: a mutual agreement between a firm seeking to have its securities identified on that exchange and the sponsoring stock exchange. see *listed securities (stocks), listing requirements.*

listing requirements: securities listed on the New York Stock Exchange require that (a) the corporation have net tangible assets of $16 million; (b) the corporation issue a minimum of 1,000,000 publicly held shares, including at least 2000 round-lot shareholders; (c) the publicly held shares have a market value of at least $16 million; (d) the corporation have had $2.5 million of net income or more prior to federal taxes in the latest year and $2 million or more in each of the preceding two years; and (e) the corporation fulfill certain other requirements as to debt, capital, national interest, and so on.

list price: the price, often published, which makes no allowance for trade or other discounts, rebates, or commissions.

LIT: see *life insurance trust.*

litigant: a person engaged in a law suit.

litigation: the act of carrying on a lawsuit.

Little Board: the American Stock Exchange. cf. *Big Board.*

Little Steel: a description used in

World War II to identify all steel companies, excluding the U.S. Steel-Corporation (Big Steel).

lives in being: lives in existence at a given time. see *rule against perpetuities.* [37]

living trust: a voluntary trust created from the assets of a living person.

LL: see *limited liability.*

Lloyd's: an association of English insurance underwriters, the oldest of its kind in the world. The Corporation of Lloyd's also provides a daily newspaper *(Lloyd's List and Shipping Gazette),* a clasification of ships *(Lloyd's Register of Shipping),* and other publications.

L.M.E.: see *London Metal Exchange.*

LO

(1) see *limited order.*

(2) see *lowest offer.*

load: the portion of the offering price of shares of open-end investment companies that cover sales commissions and all other costs of distribution. The load is usually incurred only on purchase; there is seldom any charge when the shares are sold. cf. *no-load funds.*

load charge: the commission charged to a mutual fund shares purchaser covering sales, promotion, and distribution costs.

load funds: mutual funds sold by sales representatives. For the shares they sell, there is a sales charge or load. cf. *no-load funds.*

loading

(1) *general:* the amount added to net premiums to cover a company's operating expenses and contingencies; includes the cost of securing new business, collection expenses, and general management expenses.

Precisely: the excess of the gross premiums over net premiums.

(2) *finance:* money added to an installment agreement to cover selling and administrative overhead, interest, risk, and so on.

(3) *investments:* monies added to the prorated market price of underlying securities, representing fees and overhead.

loading charge: a premium, usually from 6 to 8 percent, charged by open-end investment funds on selling new securities, to cover selling costs.

load up: to buy a security or commodity to one's financial limit, for purposes of speculation.

loan: a business transaction between two legal entities whereby one party (the lender) agrees to "rent" funds to the second party (the borrower). The funds may be "rented" with or without a fee. This fee is called interest or discount. Loans may be demand or time loans, depending on the agreement as to maturity. Loans may also be short-term or long-term. cf. entries under *lend.*

loanable funds theory of interest: a concept that the interest rate is determined by the demand for, and supply of, loanable funds only, as distinguished from all money.

loan application: a form used by banks to record the formal request for a loan by a borrower. The form is specially designed by each bank to incorporate the necessary information that the bank desires having on record. The loan application may be a simple form or a more complex one, containing information relative to the assets, liabilities, income, insurance, and contingent obligations of the borrower, as well as the purpose for which the loan is intended. [10]

loan bill: a bill of exchange drawn for more than the customary time period, usually over 30 days' sight.

loan capital: part of a corporation's capital formed by long- and short-term creditors (i.e., banks, noteholders).

loan-closing payments: expenses incurred when a mortgage loan is set (mortgage costs, legal fees for preparing the papers, appraisal and recording fees, etc.).

loan committee: the group of persons responsible for approving applications for loans and thereby committing the institution to making those loans, subject to the applicants' acceptance of the loan terms. [59]

loan consent agreement: the agreement that a securities broker must receive authorizing him to lend securities carried for a customer's account. A loan consent agreement is required by the SEC.

loan contract: the written agreement between a borrower and lender of funds, in which terms and conditions of the loan are set forth. [105]

loan crowd: stock exchange members who will borrow or lend securities to investors who have sold short. These individuals usually meet at a designated place of the exchange. see *short sale.*

loan department: the department of the bank where all the paperwork as well as the actual loan transactions are handled. All notes and other negotiable instruments and all collateral securities are filed in this department, which is bailee or custodian of these instruments and securities. The "loans made register," the record of original entry for all loans, is created here. The note notice and maturity tickler are filed here for ready reference. The liability ledger containing the complete loan record of each borrower is made and kept in this department. This department is the principal source of revenue for the operations of the bank. [10]

loaned flat: sometimes securities are sold short, requiring the seller to borrow them if this becomes necessary to make delivery. When he or she is able to borrow without making an interest payment for the shares, the seller is dealing in a stock that is *loaned flat.* see *loan stock.*

loaned stock: stock loaned to a short seller of his broker to fulfill the terms of a short selling contract by delivering shares. The borrower pays the lender of the security the market value of the stock in money and the lender either pays interest on the money or receives a premium for lending it.

loan fee: any charge made to the borrower in connection with an association loan, and particularly a charge made in connection with a new mortgage loan; in the latter case, also called *a loan origination fee* or *premium of initial servicing fee.* [59]

loan fund: a fund whose principal and/or interest is loaned to individuals in accordance with the legal requirements and agreements setting up the fund. Such a fund is accounted for as a trust fund. see also *trust fund.* [49]

loan guaranty certificate: a certificate issued by the Veterans Administration advising a lending institution of the percentage of a particular loan that is guaranteed. [105]

loan guarantee fee: the fee FmHA

charges the bank for its guarantee. This fee is usually 1 percent of the total loan and is nonrefundable. [105]

loan information sheet: in secondary market transactions, a listing of loans being offered for sale, showing principal balance, term, loan-to-value ratio and other items. [59]

loan-in-process account: an accounting category representing funds remaining to be disbursed on mortgage loans that have been closed. [59]

loan interest: the amount of money paid for the use of capital or borrowed funds.

loan ledger: the liability ledger.

loan loss provision: a charge for anticipated loan losses, which appear on an income statement as an operating expense.

loan loss reserve: an account established based on a bank's loss experience to compensate for expected losses from the loans extended. [105]

loan market: places, such as banks, financial institutions, and trust companies, where loans are made.

loan maturity: date when a note becomes due and payable. [105]

loan modification provision: a clause in a mortgage permitting the borrower to defer one or more payments in the event of financial difficulties.

loan note guarantee: FmHA's signed commitment setting forth the terms of its guarantee to the bank. [105]

loan note guarantee report of loss: bank's report to FmHA of a loan default. [105]

loan officer: an officer of the bank who is designated with the responsibility of interviewing customers who may become borrowers. Certain officers have the power to grant loans. Large loans are approved by a loan committee consisting of appointed officers and directors of the bank. [31]

loan origination: all the steps taken by an association up to the time a loan is placed on its books, including solicitation of applications, application processing, and loan closing. see also *indirect origination.* [59]

loan origination fee: see *loan fee.*

loan participation agreement: in secondary market transactions, a contract under which the seller-servicer agrees to supply, and the buyer to purchase, interests in blocks of loans at a future date; the agreement sets forth the conditions for individual transactions, and the rights and responsibilities of both parties. [59]

loan passbook: a book in which loan payments, escrow account disbursements, and other loan account transactions are entered for the customer's records. [59]

loan policy: a title insurance policy prepared by a title insurance company to a holder of a mortgage.

loan price: the price at which growers can secure government loans under a price support system.

loan proceeds: the net amount of funds that banks disburse from the borrower's loan account.

loan processing: all the steps taken by banks from the time a loan application is received to the time it is approved, including application taking, credit investigation, evaluation of the loan terms, and other steps.

loan rate: the rate charged for borrowing money at a specific date for a stated period. cf. *legal interest.*

loan register: a loose-leaf or bound journal in which the details of loans are entered, usually in the order in which they are granted. [10]

loan relief: when the principal walks away via a cash or an exchange deal from an encumbrance that he or she had on a particular piece of property. [62]

loan repayments: repayments of outstanding loan principal to the association, whether in the form of regular installments or prepayments; excludes payments of interest, loan fees, and similar items of income. [59]

loans adjusted: the face value of customers' notes held (including bankers' acceptances and commercial paper purchased in the market) less interbank loans and reserves for losses on loans. [40]

loans and discounts: used by banks to designate all funds outstanding on loans. [31]

loans and investments adjusted: the total of loans adjusted, U.S. government securities, and other bank eligible securities. [40]

loans and notes payable: obligations outstanding in the form of loans and notes payable or other similar evidences (except interest coupons) of indebtedness payable on demand or within a time not exceeding one year from date of issue. [18]

loans and notes receivable: obligations in the form of demand or time loans and notes receivable, or other similar evidences (except interest coupons) of money receivable within a time not exceeding one year from date of issue. [18]

loans and other long-term assets: a part of total transaction in U.S. government assets, this account includes the flow of capital abroad resulting from all loans and credits with an original maturity of more than one year made by the federal government to foreign countries. Most of these credits finance U.S. exports of goods and services. [73]

loan schedule: a listing of due date, amount of payment, balance after payment, and other information relevant to a specific loan. [105]

loan servicing: all the steps taken to maintain a loan, from the time it is made until the last payment is received and the loan instruments are canceled. [59]

loan settlement statement: a document, prepared for and presented to the borrower at a loan closing, showing all disbursements to be made from the loan proceeds. [59]

loan shark: an unauthorized money-lender who charges excessive interest for instant cash, accepting poor credit risks, and so on. A racketeer who threatens punishment if the repayment is not on schedule. see also *usury.*

loans in process: loans on which the bank has made a definite commitment but has not disbursed the entire loan proceeds.

loans made register: see *note notice.*

loans receivable: amounts that have been loaned to persons or organizations, including notes taken as security for such loans. The account is usually found only in the trust and agency funds balance sheet. [49]

loan stock: securities that have been loaned to a broker or short seller to fulfill the terms of a short-selling contract by delivering shares.

loans to nonbank financial institutions: loans outstanding to nonbank financial institutions, subdivided as follows: sales finance, personal finance, factors, business credit companies; and others, including mortgage companies, mutual savings banks, savings and loan associations, insurance companies, and federal agencies. [40]

loan teller: an employee in the loan department who handles loan transactions. This teller is the custodian of cash in the loan teller's cash till (except in larger banks), and handles all direct transactions involving loans for the loan officer, upon the officer's recommendations and approval. The teller usually computes the interest based upon the rate set by the loan officer, accepts collateral over the counter, and performs all duties of a regular teller, but dealing specifically with the functions of the loan department. [10]

loan term: the time period granted for repayment of a loan. [59]

loan to facilitate: a mortgage loan in which the association provides the borrower with funds to purchase real estate that the association has acquired in salvage of mortgage loans. [59]

loan-to-value ratio: the ratio between the amount of a given mortgage loan and the appraised value of the security for that loan, expressed as a percentage of the appraised value. [105]

loan value
(1) *general:* the amount of money that can be borrowed on a life insurance policy.
(2) *banking:* the amount a lending organization will lend on property.

loan-value ratio: the ratio of a property's appraised value in proportion to the amount of the mortgage loan.

loan voucher: a document required by some state laws, itemizing, identifying, and detailing the distribution of funds covered by the face amount of the note, including such items as discount or loan charges, fees, insurance premiums, rebates, and checks issued. [55]

lobby: the main banking room of a bank where depositors and customers of the bank may transact business with the bank. The ordinary business is transacted through the teller, whereas loans, credit extensions, trust operations, and the more complex matters of finance are handled in privacy in offices away from the bank lobby. [10]

LOC: see *letter of credit.*

local clearings: *local items.*

local items: checks drawn on other banks in the same city as the bank currently holding them. synonymous with *local clearings.* [31]

local rate: in railroading, the rate charged for carrying freight between two points on the same railroad.

lock-away: a British term for a long-term security.

lock box: a specialized service by which a bank acts as an agent in directly receiving and collecting a customer's incoming payments.

locked in: an investor is said to be locked in when he or she does not sell a security because its profit would immediately become subject to the capital gains tax. see *Tax Reform Act of 1976.*

locked market: a market in which the trader is willing to bid for and after a particular security at a single price. [105]

lockup

(1) *banking:* a note or obligation that has been renewed, the time of repayment having been extended beyond the original due date.

(2) *investments:* securities that have been withdrawn from circulation and placed in a safe deposit box as a long-term investment.

loco: in the commodities market, meaning "at" (i.e., silver may be traded "loco London").

logo: a symbol used by a particular company or individual for identification purposes, often imprinted on letterheads and checks.

Lombard loan: a central bank loan supported by collateral such as stock and bonds. Term used primarily in England and parts of Europe.

Lombard rate: German for the rate of interest charged for a loan against the security of pledged paper.

Lombard Street: the financial area in London.

LOMI: see *letter of moral intent.*

London interbank offered rate (LI-BOR): a measure of what major international banks charge each other for large-volume loans of Eurodollars, or dollars on deposit outside the United States.

London Metal Exchange: members, approximately 110, deal in copper, lead, zinc, and tin.

London Stock Exchange: a major European stock exchange, formed in 1773.

long: signifies ownership of stocks. "I am long 100 U.S. Steel" means that the speaker owns 100 shares. Specifically, holding a sizable amount of a security or commodity in anticipation of a scarcity and price rise. see *carry.*

long account: synonymous with *long interest.*

long and short haul clause: the provision in the Interstate Commerce Act, as amended, which prohibits carriers from charging higher rates for a short haul than for a longer haul which includes the short haul.

long draft: a draft for more than the customary time period.

longer-term loan (term loans): funds loaned to business for more than one year, usually to acquire fixed assets. [105]

long-form mortgage clause: provides for the assumption of responsibility, for the satisfaction of the mortgage by the mortgagor when he or she takes title; the mortgagor does not simply acquire the property.

long green: slang, paper money.

long hedge: the buying of futures made as a hedge against the sale of a cash commodity.

long interest: the collective retention of a particular stock, or group of stock. symonymous with *long account.*

long market: an overbought market.

long of exchange: when a trader in foreign currency holds foreign bills in an amount exceeding the bills of his or her own that have been sold and remain outstanding, the trader is long of exchange.

long on the basis: one who has bought cash or spot goods and has hedged them with the sale of futures. He or she has therefore bought at a certain basis on or off futures and expects to sell at a better basis with the future for a profit. [2]

long position: describes a holder of

securities who expects an increase in the price of his or her shares or holds these securities for income.

long pull: the buying of a security with the expectation of a holding position over a period of time hoping for a rise in the value of the stock.

long-range planning: a systematic procedure for directing and controlling future activities of a firm for periods longer than a year. It predicts the future and establishes a strategy of action and expected results.

long run: the period of time in which all costs (including the fixed costs) of a particular firm are to be considered variable.

long sale: in the commodities market, hedging sales or sales created due to spot commitments. see *short sale.*

long side: a long interest.

long squeeze: a market situation in which longs are forced to liquidate their positions because of falling prices.

long stock: securities that have been bought in anticipation of increasing prices.

long-term budget: a budget prepared for a period longer than a fiscal year, or in the case of some state governments, a budget prepared for a period longer than a biennium. If the long-term budget is restricted to capital expenditures, it is called a capital program or a capital improvement program. [49]

long-term capital gain: realized when capital assets that have been held for longer than 12 months are sold at a profit. see *Tax Reform Act of 1976.*

long-term capital loss: realized when capital assets that have been held for

longer than 12 months are sold at a loss. see *Revenue Act of 1978, Tax Reform Act of 1976.*

long-term corporate bond: see *bond, long-term corporate.*

long-term debt: liabilities that become due more than one year after the signing of the agreement. Usually, these are formal legal agreements demanding periodic payments of interest until the maturity date, at which time the prncipal amount is repaid.

long-term financing: the issuance and sale of debt securities with a maturity of more than one year and preferred and common stock for the purpose of raising new capital, refunding outstanding securities, or for the divestment of investments in securities not permitted to be held under the Public Utility Holding Company Act of 1935. [3]

long-term investment

(1) security or other asset purchased for its income flows rather than for rapid capital gains.

(2) investment held for more than six months. [105]

long-term liabilities reported by U.S. banks: include long-term deposits—in excess of one year—by foreigners in U.S. banks, mainly by foreign officials or international agencies. Some of these liabilities consist of deposits used to finance U.S. imports, plant expansion, and other financial transactions which would involve U.S. banking services, such as a foreign government's line of credit to a U.S. bank. The flow in the opposite direction appears in claims reported by U.S. banks: long-term. [3]

long-term mortgage: a home mortgage running 40 or more years.

long-term receivables and investments: a group of assets, including money owed to the firm on a long-term installment basis, plus the firm's investments in affiliated and other firms.

long-term trend: the direction in which market prices appear likely to move over a future time period.

look back: the auditing of past records to locate errors that have come to the attention of a bank's auditing department. cf. *internal audit.*

lookback options: where an investor has the right to buy gold at its lowest price during the life of the "call" option, while those who bought "puts" may sell the metal at its highest price.

loophole certificate (CD): under present regulations, federally insured banks are permitted to pay the market interest rate—that pegged to the weekly auction of Treasury bills—only on deposits of $10,000 or more. With the loophole certificate of deposit, the saver is loaned, generally at an annual rate of 1 percent, the difference between his or her deposit sum and the $10,000. For example, if the depositor has only $5000, the bank issues a passbook loan for the other $5000. The loan is automatic and requires no collateral. It is only a paper transaction and the consumer never touches the money. It is credited to his account at the beginning and extracted six months later.

loose jobs (rate): exist when the earnings for a worker are not in line with pay for similar positions requiring similar skills. see *incentive pay, piece rate (wage).*

loot: slang, money, especially large sums of it.

Lorenz curve: a graphic device for plotting the degree of inequality in the distribution of income.

Loro Account: denoting the account of a third party, for example, a London bank paying $1 million to the Chase Manhattan Bank for the credit of the Loro Account of the Dresdner Bank, which is held by the Chase Manhattan Bank.

Los Angeles Stock Exchange: see *Pacific Coast Stock Exchange.*

loss

(1) *general:* any item that can be listed as an expense.

(2) *finance:* the excess of the cost or depreciated cost of an asset over its price of sale.

loss carryback: a tax provision allowing a business experience a loss to recalculate taxable income in prior years by offsetting the current loss against previous years' income. [105]

loss carry forward: business losses from previous years deducted from profits in the current and subsequent years, for purposes of reducing tax expenses.

loss carryover: see *loss carry forward.*

losses: the dollar figure that has been charged off to bad debt or fraud loss expense. [105]

loss leader: an article sold in the retail trade below cost so as to attract buyers for other items.

loss on bad debts: an expense resulting from failure to collect amounts due from charge customers.

loss on disposal: the result of a sale of noncurrent asset for less than the book value or unrecovered cost.

loss on fixed assets: the loss or expense resulting when the book value of a fixed asset is greater than the actual value at the time the asset is sold.

loss on sale of assets: an expense account for noting losses that result when assets are sold for less than the book value.

loss outstanding: a tabulation of losses that an insurance firm has in the form of claims but which it has not settled.

loss payable clause: provides for payment to a party (e.g., mortgagee or lienholder) in addition to the insured, for any losses to the insured property according to the extent of that party's interest in the property at the time of the loss.

loss ratio: a percentage arrived at by dividing the amount of the losses by the amount of the insured premium. Various loss ratios are computed (e.g., earned premium to incurred losses, written premium to paid losses).

loss reserve: a part of assets retained by a bank in available form to meet expected claims (i.e., insurance coverage on a mortgage).

lost card: a bank card that has been reported to the credit card issuer as lost or misplaced by the cardholder of record. [105]

lost in transit: an item lost between the center and either the clearinghouse or community office. [105]

lost opportunity: a professional money managers description for investments that are not earning the current available rate of interest.

lost policy release: a statement signed by the insured releasing the bank from all liability resulting from a lost or mislaid contract of insurance.

lot
(1) *general:* any group of goods or services making up a single transaction.
(2) *banking:* a parcel of land having measurable boundaries.
(3) *investments:* a quantity of shares, usually 100. cf. *block, odd-lot orders.*

low: the lowest price paid for a purchase of securities at a specific time period.

lowest offer: the lowest price that a person will accept in the sale of a stock at a specific time.

low grade: of inferior quality, applied to merchandise, stocks, and so on.

low interest: an account on which the rate has been reduced to 12 percent per annum simple interest or less. [55]

LP
(1) see *limited partner.*
(2) see *linear programming.*
(3) see *long position.*

LR
(1) see *listing requirements.*
(2) see *loan rate.*

LRA: see *lagged reserve accounting.*

LS
(1) see *letter stock.*
(2) see *listed securities (stocks).*

LSE: see *London Stock Exchange.*

Lshld.: see *leasehold.*

LT
(1) see *legal tender.*
(2) see *legal title.*

LTCG: see *long-term capital gain.*

LTCL: see *long-term capital loss.*

Ltd.: see *limited company.*

LTD: limited to any security or purpose.

lucrative title: a title that is obtained by a person who pays less than the true market value of the property; title to property obtained as a gift. see *devise, gift causa mortis, gift inter vivos.*

lump sum: full payment made in one sum, and at one time. [12]

lump-sum appropriation: usually a government appropriation having no specific instructions as to how the funds appropriated should be spent. cf. *itemized appropriation.*

lump-sum distribution: with respect to pension plans, the distribution of an individual's benefits in the form of one payment rather than in equal installments over a specified period of time or the individual's lifetime. The Internal Revenue Code imposes certain requirements in order for the distribution to qualify for special tax treatment. [105]

lump sum purchase: a group of assets obtained for an indicated figure, without breakdown by individual assets or classes of asset.

luxury tax: a tax imposed on items not considered essential for daily living. In most cases, goods so taxed are expensive.

M: the equilibrium nominal money stock. [81]

M1: see *M-1A*.

M-1A: recent money supply definition of the Federal Reserve Board (1980), replacing the old M1 definition; currency plus demand deposits at commercial banks. This is essentially the same as the old M1 with one exception: it excludes demand deposits held by foreign banks and official institutions. see also *L, M-1B, M2, M3, M4, M5*.

M-1B: recent money supply definition of the Federal Reserve Board (1980); equals M-1A plus other checkable deposits at all depositary institutions, including NOW accounts, automatic transfer service, credit union share drafts, and demand deposits at mutual savings banks. see also *L, M-1A, M2, M3, M4, M5*.

M2: recent money supply definition of the Federal Reserve Board (1980); equals M-1B plus savings and small-denomination time deposits at all depositary institutions, overnight repurchase agreements (RPs) at commercial banks, overnight Euro-dollars held by U.S. residents other than banks at Caribbean branches of member banks, and money-market mutual fund shares. see also *L, M-1A, M-1B, M3, M4, M5*.

M3: recent money supply definition of the Federal Reserve Board (1980); equals M2 plus large-denomination time deposits at all depositary institutions and term repurchase agreements at commercial banks and savings and loan associations. see also *L, M-1A, M-1B, M2, M4, M5*.

M4: (defunct) includes M2 plus large negotiable CDs at banks. [33]

M5: (defunct) includes M3 plus large negotiable CDs at banks, savings banks, credit unions, and savings and loans. [33]

MA

(1) see *margin account*.

(2) see *market averages*.

machine: any piece of equipment used to regulate force or motion; a combination of mechanical devices and powers to carry out a task. cf. *hardware*.

machine, scanning: a machine that facilitates the input of data by reading printed data and converting them into machine language.

machine accounting: a record-keeping system that uses electromechanical, but not electronic, machines for the posting of account records and ledgers. [59]

machine address: the direct, absolute, unindexed address expressed as such or resulting after indexing has been carried out. synonymous with *absolute address, specific address*.

machine code: an operation code that a machine is designed to recognize. synonymous with *computer code.*

machine instruction: an instruction that a machine can recognize and execute.

machine language: information or data expressed in a code that can be read by a computer or by peripheral equipment without further interpretation.

machine-oriented language: a programming language that is more like a machine language than a human language.

machine pay: a plan of checking account posting whereby all media, both checks and deposits, are posted to a journal only on the first "run" of the media. The old balances of all affected accounts are picked up, the media posted, and new balances extended as in any posting run. The affected accounts may or may not be offset, depending upon the using bank's preference. The machine pay journalizing mechanically shows up items to be returned for insufficient funds, or paid as overdrafts. The run also establishes totals for checks, deposits, and new balances of affected accounts. The subsequent run on the depositor's statements must then prove to the machine pay run for checks, deposits, and new balances, verifying that the items were posted correctly, checks as checks, deposits as deposits, and the right accounts selected. [10]

machine readable: describing material that can be sensed or read by a specific device.

macroeconomics: the study of statistics (e.g., total consumption, total employment) of the economy as a whole rather than as single economic units. synonymous with *aggregate economics.*

macro-hedge: a hedge designed to reduce the net portfolio risk of an organization. cf. *micro-hedge.* [107]

"made to the order of": see *order.*

magic mortgage: lending method enabling buyer to purchase a house with a very low down payment but requiring a yearly interest fee to the insurer of the loan. The term derives from MGIC, Mortgage Guarantee Insurance Corporation, which promoted the idea.

magic sixes: a group of stocks, often considered undervalued, that meet certain requirements, all of them having to do with the number 6. A magic six stock must trade at less than 60 percent of book value. It must also have a maximum price-earnings ratio of 6. Finally, the annual dividend, or yield, is equal to more than 6 percent.

magnetic disk: a storage device in which information is recorded on the magnetizable surface of a rotating disk. A magnetic disk storage system is an array of such devices, with associated reading and writing heads which are mounted on movable arms. [45]

magnetic ink character recognition (MICR): the recognition by a computer of characters printed with magnetic ink. cf. *optical character recognition.*

magnetic tape

(1) *computers:* a tape with a magnetic surface on which data can be stored by selective polarization of portions of the surface.

(2) *computers:* describes a storage system in which information is recorded on the magnetizable surface of a strip of synthetic or steel tape.

mail deposit: a deposit received by the bank through the mail rather than over the counter. The bank credits the customer's account and mails a receipt back to the customer. [31]

mailgram: a low-cost, written message transmitted electronically by Western Union and delivered by the U.S. Postal Service. [24]

mailing holder: see *card mailer.*

mail order (MO): a written direction received by mail from a cardholder wishing to have the purchase amount charged to his or her account. Special authorization procedures usually govern mail orders. [105]

mail teller: this name is used to designate the teller or division that handles deposits received by mail. [31]

mail transfer: see *transfer.*

main frame: the major part of the computer, the arithmetic or logic unit. synonymous with *central processing unit.*

main location: the head office location of a merchant. [105]

main storage: the general-purpose storage of a computer.

maint.: see *maintenance.*

maintenance

(1) *general:* the upkeep of any form of property (land, machinery, tools, etc.).

(2) *banking:* all expenditures made to preserve an asset's value.

(3) *computers:* the updating of object program master files, selection of programs, and control of production procedures.

(4) *computers:* any activity intended to eliminate faults or to keep hardware or programs in satisfactory working condition, including tests, measurements, replacements, adjustments, and repairs. see *debug.*

(5) *investments:* the sum of cash or securities deposited in a brokerage account to fulfill the broker's margin requirements.

(6) *law:* support or sustenance that a person is legally bound to give to another.

(7) *law:* interfering unlawfully in a suit between others by assisting either party (e.g., giving one party money).

maintenance bond: see *bond, maintenance.*

maintenance margin: the amount of money required by a clearinghouse to retain a futures position. It is less than the initial margin and allows the flexibility needed to permit minor price fluctuations.

maintenance of investment organization: the charges to income for the directly assignable organization and administration expenses that are incident to the carrier's investments in leased or nonoperating physical property, and in stocks, bonds, or other securities. [18]

maintenance reserve: an amount reserved to cover costs of maintenance. [62]

major industry identifier: the first digit of the Primary Account Number, signifying the major industry issuing the plastic card. [105]

majority-owned subsidiary: a subsidiary for which more than 50 percent of the outstanding voting capital stock is owned by the parent company or by another of the parent's majority-owned subsidiaries. [105]

majority stockholders: those who own more than 50 percent of the voting stock corporation, thus having controlling interest. see *working control.*

major trend: the direction stock prices move over a period of time regardless of temporary shifts contrary to trend. synonymous with *primary movement.*

make (making) a line: a stock's price pattern which fluctuates within a relatively narrow range for some time, indicating either accumulation or distribution of the security. Chartists follow these formations for clues on price direction.

make a market: to stand ready to buy or sell, adjusting bid and offer prices to balance purchases and sales. [67]

make good: to discharge an obligation or debt.

maker
(1) *general:* a manufacturer, processor, or producer of merchandise or products.
(2) *law:* an individual, firm, or other legal entity who signs a note, check, or other negotiable form as a responsible party.

make the cash: to decide whether the funds on hand, following receipts and payments, balance with the record of sales payments of obligations.

make-up day: in Great Britain, the day of the month on which figures are compiled for reporting to the Bank of England; usually the third Wednesday of each month.

making a market
(1) *general:* the promotion or stimulation of interest in any good or service.
(2) *investments:* the coming to terms between two brokers, one attempting to buy and the other to sell a particular security.

making a price: the price a seller gives indicating a willingness to accept at the request of the purchaser, or vice versa.

making-up price: the price of a delivered security.

mala fides: see *bad faith.*

malfeasance: a wrong doing; a criminal act (e.g., a public official taking graft). cf. *misfeasance.*

malicious: describes an improper act done purposefully without excuse.

maline: a state of mind that is noncaring of the law and other's rights.

Maloney Act: see *National Association of Securities Dealers.*

managed currency: a currency whose quantity is increased or decreased according to changes in the general price level or other objectives. The management is by the government of a country or its central bank. The management may be designed to influence the internal price level of a nation or the ratio of that price level to the price levels of other nations, or both, or to pursue other objectives.

managed money: a monetary system in which government tries to control the circulation of money to achieve a specific goal, such as the stabilization of prices.

management: the individual or group of individuals responsible for studying, analyzing, formulating decisions, and initiating appropriate actions for the benefit of an organization.

management accounting: a resource of management that supplies financial information at all levels to be used in the planning and administering of the business.

management audit: a system for examining, analyzing, and appraising a management's overall performance. Ten categories of the audit are economic function, corporate structure, health of earnings, service to stockholders, research and development, directorate analysis, fiscal policies, production efficiency, sales vigor, and evaluation of executive performance.

management by crisis: a leadership style that purports to clear away shortcomings and failures by waiting until things get so bad that people will accept drastic measures. It is usually destructive and fails to attain stated organizational goals.

management by exception: the practice, by an executive, of focusing attention primarily on significant deviations from expected results.

management by objectives: see *MBO.*

management company: a firm that manages and sells the shares of open-end investment companies and claims a fee or commission.

management development: leadership training for middle- or top-level personnel to upgrade their skills.

management fee: the charge made to an investment company for supervision of its portfolio. Frequently includes various other services and is usually a fixed percentage of average assets at market. [30]

management game: a dynamic training approach utilizing a model of the business world. In most cases, this problem-solving technique attempts to examine broad business issues in a classroom setting free of real-world consequences.

management information system (MIS): a specific data-processing system that is designed to furnish management and supervisory personnel with current information in real time. In the communication process, data are recorded and processed for operational purposes. The problems are isolated for referral to upper management for higher-level decision making, and information is fed back to top management to reflect the progress in achieving major objectives.

management science: the formulation of mathematical and statistical models applied to decision making and the practical application of these models through the use of digital computers.

management stock
(1) stock owned by the management of a corporation.
(2) stock having extra voting privileges, thus gaining control over a corporation.

manager: a bank involved in managing a Eurocredit or an issue of a security.

managing agency accounts: an agency account concerning which the agent has managerial duties and responsibilities appropriate to the kind of property and in conformity with the terms of the agency; to be distinguished from a safekeeping or custody account. [37]

managing agent: the service by which

an agent assumes an active role in administering another's property. [105]

managing underwriter: the syndicate organizer, also referred to as the syndicate manager or the principal underwriter. [26]

mandate: a court order to an authorized agency or officer to enforce a decree, judgment, or sentence to the court's satisfaction.

mandate of protest: see *notice of dishonor*.

mandatory: obligatory; as a power of a trustee which the trustee must exercise, mandatory power, the equivalent of a direction. [37]

mandatory sharing: required sharing among similar, or perhaps dissimilar financial institutions in a given market area or graphic locale. In this situation, all institutions affected provide identical services, accessibility, and transaction activity. [105]

MANF: May, August, November, February (quarterly interest payments or dividends).

manifest: a document listing the contents, value, origin, destination, carrier, and time that a cargo is shipped.

manipulation

(1) *general:* artful approach, often in an unfair or fraudulent fashion.

(2) *investments:* an illegal operation. Buying or selling a security for the purpose of creating a false or misleading appearance of active trading or for the purpose of raising or depressing the price to induce purchase or sale by others. see *rigged market, stock jobbing;* see also *SEC*. [20]

Mann-Elkins Act: an act of Congress in 1910 revising laws governing interstate commerce by including communication systems (now under Federal Communications Commission jurisdiction) and by broadening the powers of the Interstate Commerce Commission.

manual: a listing of information, instructions, prices, and so on, that is a handy reference book; a handbook.

manual accounting: a record-keeping system of hand-posting account transactions to the proper subsidiary ledgers, journals, and general records. [59]

manual of operation: the written instructions, usually prepared by, or with the approval of, the accounting, auditing, comptroller's, or methods department, covering the procedure to follow and the responsibilities of the party or parties in the handling of the transactions within and affecting the operations of a given business or financial institution. [10]

MAPS: acronym for multivariate analysis, participation, and structure. A management-development technique allowing members to define their task groups and choose the people most appropriate for working in them. see *Monetary and Payments System Planning Committee*.

Marg.: see *margin*.

marge à terme: French for *forward margin*.

margin

(1) *general:* the difference between the cost of sold items and the total net sales income. see *contribution margin, profit*.

(2) *finance:* the difference between the market value of collateral pledged to secure a loan and the face value of the loan itself. see also *remargining*.

(3) *investments:* the amount paid by the customer when he or she used a broker's credit to buy a security. Under

Federal Reserve regulations, the initial margin required in past decades has ranged from 50 to 100 percent of the purchase price. see *Regulation T.*

margin account: any brokerage account where listed stocks can be bought with the aid of credit given by the buyer's broker.

marginal activity: a commercial venture barely able to meet its expenses from its revenues.

marginal analysis: the analysis of economic information by examining the results of the value added when one variable is increased by a single unit of another variable. see *direct cost.*

marginal borrower: a borrower who will reject an opportunity to borrow if the interest charge is increased.

marginal buyer: a buyer who will refuse to buy at any given price if the price is increased.

marginal cost: the increase in the total cost of production that results from manufacturing one more unit output. see *law of increasing costs.*

marginal cost pricing: pricing each good so that the price covers all direct costs, plus the variable part of overhead.

marginal efficiency of capital
(1) the relation between the prospective yield of a capital asset and its supply price or replacement cost.
(2) the rate of discount that would make the present value of a series of annuities given by the returns expected from the capital asset during its life just equal to its supply price.

marginal land: land that will merely repay the cost of products grown on it and will not yield increased revenue.

marginal lender: a lender or investor who will refuse to lend or invest if the rate of interest is lowered.

marginal pair: the marginal seller and marginal buyers plus the first seller whose price is above the market price and the first buyer whose price is just below the market price.

marginal producer: a producer who is just able to meet his costs of production with little actual profit.

marginal productivity theory of interest: an interest theory explaining the interest rate as tending under competitive conditions to equal the marginal addition to output by the last unit of capital when the amount of available capital is assumed fixed.

marginal propensity to consume (MPC): reflected by the percentage of increases in income that is spent for consumption purposes.

marginal propensity to invest (MPI): reflected by the percentage of increases in sales that is spent on investment items. cf. *liquidity preference, oversaving, quantity theory.* synonymous with *accelerator.*

marginal propensity to save (MPS): reflected by the percentage of increases in income that individuals save. cf. *life cycle hypothesis, multiplier principle, oversaving, quantity theory.*

marginal revenue: the added revenue a business receives from the sale of one additional unit. In the short run, under conditions of competition, this is the same as the market price.

marginal risk: the risk that a customer goes bankrupt following entry into a forward contract when the bank must close its commitment in the market, thereby running the risk that the exchange rate has shifted unfavorably in the interim. The risk is confined to the marginal amount of such a movement. cf. *capital risk*.

marginal seller: a seller who refuses to sell if the price is lowered.

marginal tax rate: tax rate paid on any additional dollars of income.

marginal trading: the purchase of a security or commodity by one who borrows funds for part of the purchase price rather than paying for the entire transaction with his or her own money.

marginal utility: the additional usefulness of any added unit of a good or service. [105]

margin buying: using credit given by a broker to purchase securities.

margin call
(1) *banking:* if a borrower has securities pledged as collateral for a loan, and a declining market for the securities forces the value of the securities downward, the bank is responsible for seeing that the margin requirements are maintained. The bank will request more margin from the borrower, who will either have to pledge more collateral or partially pay the loan, to meet the established margin requirements. synonymous with *margin notice*.
(2) *investments:* a demand upon a customer to put up money or securities with a broker. The call is made when a purchase is made or when a customer's equity in a margin account declines below a minimum standard set by the exchange or firm. [20]

margined securities: stocks purchased on credit or held as collateral in a margin account. The securities cannot be withdrawn until the debit balance owing in the account has been fully paid.

margin notice: synonymous with *margin call*.

margin of profit: operating income divided by sales. Income taxes are usually excluded, and depreciation is usually included in the operating expenses.

margin of safety
(1) *general:* the balance of income left after payment of fixed charges.
(2) *finance:* the difference between the total price of a bond issue and the true value of the property for which it is issued.

margin requirement: the portion of a total purchase price of securities that must be put up in cash.

margins: the limits around the par value within which a spot exchange rate of a member nation's currency is allowed to move in actual exchange market dealings and public transactions.

marine protection and indemnity insurance: insurance against legal liability of the insured for loss, damage, or expense arising out of or incident to the ownership, operation, chartering, maintenance, use, repair, or construction of any vessel, craft, or instrumentality in use in ocean or inland waterways, including liability of the insured for personal injury or death, and for loss of or damage to the property of another person.

marital deduction: assured by provisions in federal tax laws to prevent double taxation of an estate at the time of the death of a spouse. It permits the deceased to leave up to one-half of his or her estate to the spouse, with this amount deductible from the taxable estate. see *Tax Reform Act of 1976*.

Mark.: see *market*.

markdown

(1) *general:* a reduction of an originally established selling price.

(2) *investments:* a revaluation of stocks based on a decline in their market quotations.

markdown cancellation: additions that do not raise the selling price above that at which the goods were offered for sale prior to a markdown.

market: people possessing the ability and desire to purchase, or prospects for a product or service; an estimated or realized demand for an item or service.

marketability: the rapidity and ease with which a given asset can be converted into cash. cf. *liquid.*

marketable: that which can be sold, e.g., property that can be sold to a purchaser within a reasonable period.

marketable securities: securities existing in a ready, active market.

marketable title: title to property that is free of defects and will be accepted by a lawyer without objection. cf. *cloud on title, perfect title.* synonymous with *clear title, good title.*

market acceptance: the banks, bankers, business firms, and corporations involved in transactions in bank acceptance. [105]

market analysis: an aspect of market research involving the measurement of the extent of a market and the determination of its characteristics. see *chartist, Dow theory.*

market area: that territory within which the purchase or sale of a commodity affects the price generally prevailing for that commodity.

market audit: a method for studying the marketing activities and structure of a bank or financial institution. It is designed primarily to identify areas in which improvements are necessary to boost profits. cf. *management audit.*

market averages: a major securities barometer showing the trend and conditions of the market; that is, the American Stock Exchange Index, the Dow Jones averages, the New York Stock Exchange Index, and Standard & Poor's 500-Corporate-Stock Index.

market cycle: in securities, a period of rising prices followed by a period of lower prices. These cycles roughly correspond to a business cycle of recovery, prosperity, recession, and depression.

market data approach to value: in appraising, the estimation of the market value of a property by comparing it with similar properties sold recently. [59]

market demand: the total amount of a bank service that is wanted at a specified price at a specific time.

market equilibrium: the balance that occurs when buyers and sellers decide to stop trading at the prevailing prices.

market factors: statistical series such as population, number of families, and income, which are used for setting sales potential for any selection of the market. [9]

market financing: that part of the general business function of providing and managing funds and credit which is directly related to the transactions involved in the flow of goods and services from producer to consumer or industrial user. [13]

market-if-touched order (MIT): an order to buy or sell at the market immediately if an execution takes place at a certain price stated in the order.

market index: data expressed as a percentage of a base in which a part of the market is stated as a percentage of the entire market.

marketing: activities that accelerate the movement of goods or services from the manufacturer to the consumer; that is, everything connected with advertising, distribution, merchandising, product planning, promotion, publicity, research and development, sales, transportation, and warehousing of goods or services.

marketing cooperative: an association of producers to market their products jointly (e.g., California Fruit Growers Exchange).

marketing profile: resource providing information to allow bank management to assess the future intelligently with respect to problems and opportunities, areas of potential and growth, and how the market is changing. [105]

marketing research: the process of gathering, recording, and analyzing information pertaining to the marketing of the services of banks and financial institutions. see *market research.*

market instinct: the ability to interpret accurately the significance of the price and volume shifts in securities.

market is off: the analysis of the state of the market which shows that prices have dropped from an earlier closing.

market leaders: securities of major corporations (e.g., Standard Oil of New Jersey, International Business Machines), because of their importance in their own industry, are considered primary indicators of the economic health of the economy in general and the security market in particular.

market letter: printed sheets mailed by brokerage houses and investment advisory services which attempt to interpret conditions in the market and make recommendations for investment opportunities.

market liquidity: the condition of a securities market reflecting the supply and demand forces, assisting an investor to purchase or sell stocks at prices relatively close to the previous sale.

market maker: a broker or bank that is prepared to make a two-way price to purchase or sell, for a security or a currency on a continous basis.

market off: an expression indicating that prices on the various stock exchanges were down for the day.

market order: an order to buy or sell stocks or bonds at the price prevailing when the order reaches the market. cf. *limited order, no-limit order, percentage order, stop order.*

market out clause: found in underwriting statements of securities; the underwriter reserves the privilege of terminating an agreement to sell securities at a stated price if unfavorable market conditions occur, rendering sale at this price unprofitable.

market oversight surveillance system: see *MOSS.*

marketplace: a general term identifying business and trade activities.

market potential: the expected sales of a commodity, a group of commodities, or a service for an entire industry in a market during a stated period. [13]

market price

(1) *finance:* the price established in the market where buyers and sellers meet to buy and sell similar products; a price determined by factors of supply and demand rather than by decisions made by management.

(2) *investments:* the last reported price at which the stock or bond sold.

market rate: the interest rate charged a firm in order to borrow funds.

market ratio: the power of one good to command another in exchange for itself in a free market. Often used with reference to the relative value of gold and silver.

market report

(1) any news about or condition of the securities market.

(2) a report from the trading floor of an exchange that a particular transaction has been executed at the stated price found in the report. The report can be either written or verbal.

market research: that part of marketing research dealing with the pattern of a market, measuring the extent and nature of the market, and identifying its characteristics. Market research precedes marketing research. see *marketing research.*

market risk: the possibility of a decline in the price of a specific security; the loss that the holder of an investment may have to assume at the time of sale. [105]

market securities

(1) as a verb, to offer securities for sale on a market.

(2) as an adjective, those securities traded in a public market as distinguished from those with a limited market.

market sentiment: the public or mass psychology that affects the buying or selling trend of securities. They may be positive, negative, or mixed.

market share: a bank's percentage of the industry's total sales.

market stabilization: attempts to stop the working of the full and free forces in a market by some agency, such as the underwriter of an issue or a sponsoring investment banker; usually prohibited by the SEC. One exception is made when an initial offering is registered with the SEC receiving authorization to "peg" or stabilize prices of an issue. Sometimes a secondary offering receives such permission.

market swing: movements of the average prices of a security or commodity market which are of a cyclical or secondary trend.

market uncertainty: the probability that investor's attitudes may shift, thus causing the market price of the investment to change. [105]

market value

(1) *finance:* the price that property will command on the open market. The price for which an owner is prepared to sell property and the amount a purchaser is willing to pay. see *reasonable value.*

(2) *investments:* the price of a security or commodity on the daily quotation, indicating the amount required for buying or selling.

market vs. quote: the market price of a security is the price at which the last order was executed; a quote designates the current bid and ask. [105]

markka: monetary unit of Finland.

mark signature: when a person is unable to write his own name, a mark or other indication (e.g., an "X") is affixed to a legal instrument.

"marks to the market": where all autonomous clearinghouses indicate the accounts of the exchange's members at the end of every day. They do this by transferring the debits and credits that have resulted from the day's trading. see also *"good to the last drop."*

mark the market: checking the last

sale prevailing for stocks retained in a margin account to determine if the account fulfills minimum margin requirements of the Federal Reserve Board, the Stock Exchange, and/or the brokerage house involved.

mark (marking) time: the condition of a commodity or security market where no trend or direction appears to be indicated by the prices of various transactions.

markup

(1) *general:* an increase, in dollars or percentage, between cost and selling price.

(2) *finance:* increasing the value of assets (i.e., securities) to show an improvement in their market value.

marshaling of assets: a rule for the distribution by a court of equity of a debtor's property among his or her creditors, requiring that each creditor so exhaust his or her right as to permit all others to be paid if possible.

Maryland Savings-Share Insurance Corporation: a state-chartered mutual corporation in Maryland that insures the savings deposits held by member savings associations and serves as a central credit facility. [59]

Massachusetts rule: a term frequently applied to a rule for the investment of trust funds enunciated by the Supreme Judicial Court of Massachusetts in 1830; now commonly referred to as the prudent man rule. see *prudent man rule*. [32]

Massachusetts trust: see *business trust*.

master budget: comprised of all the departmental budgets in a bank or financial institution.

master card: a card that contains fixed or indicative information for a group of punched cards. It is usually the first card of the group.

master file

(1) a file composed of records having similar characteristics or containing data of a relatively permanent nature. A cardholder master file would contain such information as account numbers, names, addresses, credit limits, expiration dates, and number of cards issued as minimum data.

(2) the updated record of the closing balance in each account at a bank, as produced by the combination of the previous day's tape with the daily transactions tape. [105]

master in chancery: an official appointed by a court to assist by taking testimony, calculating interest, projecting damage costs, determining liens, and so on, as requested by the court. cf. *referee.*

master lease: an original lease.

master notes: paper issued by big credit-worthy companies. Unlike commercial paper, which may be sold to another company, these notes are issued only to banks. cf. *commercial paper.*

master policy

(1) *general:* a policy issued to cover the interest of a lender or lessor of property in the possession of others.

(2) *banking:* a policy issued to an insured to cover property at more than one location. If locations are in more than one state, it is customary to issue underlying policies to meet the states' legal requirements.

master tariff: a tariff controlling the use of other tariffs.

master trust: an arrangement designating the custodianship and accounting for all employee benefit assets of a corporation or a controlled group of corporations to a single trustee, facilitating uniform administration of the assets of multiple plans and multiple investment managers. [105]

Mat.

(1) see *matured.*

(2) see *maturity.*

matched and lost: when two bids of the same stock are made on the trading floors simultaneously, and each bid is equal to or larger than the amount of stock offered, both bids are considered to be of an equal basis. The two bidders then flip a coin to decide who buys the stock. Also applies to *offers to sell.* [20]

matched orders

(1) manipulation by a person entering an order to purchase a specific security with one broker and simultaneously, an order to sell the identical security with a second broker. This practice is prohibited as a means of trying to either increase or decrease security prices.

(2) a specialist in a particular stock who buys and sells a security purporting to arrange an opening price that is reasonably close to the previous day's close.

matched sale-purchase agreements: when the Federal Reserve makes a matched sale-purchase agreement, it sells a security outright for immediate delivery to a dealer or foreign central bank, with an agreement to buy the security back on a specific date (usually within seven days) at the same price. The reverse of repurchase agreements, matched sale-purchase agreements allow the Federal Reserve to absorb reserves on a temporary basis. [1]

matched sales: Federal Reserve action to absorb reserve temporarily by selling securities with an agreement to purchase them back within a specified period (up to 15 days) at a stated price. synonymous with *reverse repos, reverse repurchase agreements.* [90]

matching: the process of equating assets and liabilities, either by time or currency.

materialmen's lien: see *mechanic's lien.*

matured: fully paid up, fully carried out as to terms, completed as to time or as to contract. [28]

matured bonds payable: see *bonds payable, matured.*

mature economy: describing the conditions of a nation's economy with a declining rate of population growth and a decrease in the proportion of national income utilized for new capital investment accompanied by a relative increase of national income used in purchasing consumer goods. cf. *underdeveloped country.*

maturity

(1) *finance:* the date on which a note, time draft, bill of exchange, bond, or other negotiable instrument becomes due and payable. A note, time draft, or bill of exchange drawn for a future date has a maturity date that is set starting with the date of the loan or acceptance and runs the specified number of days from date of loan or acceptance of maturity. Presentation and request for payment of the instrument are made on the maturity date.

(2) *law:* the completion of a contract, as with an insurance policy.

maturity basis: the ratio of the dollars of interest payable on a bond to the maturity value, ignoring any premium or discount at the time of acquisition. cf. *yield to maturity*.

maturity date: the date on which a financial obligation becomes due for payment and/or an obligation or contract expires.

maturity distribution of loans and securities: shows the amounts of loans, holdings of acceptances, and government securities that mature or are payable within the various periods specified. [40]

maturity gap exposure: the risk created by having an asset and liability of the same size and in the same currency but of different maturity.

maturity index: synonymous with *maturity tickler*.

maturity tickler: a form made and used in the loan department of a bank. The maturity tickler is usually a copy of the "note notice" and contains all information as to the amount, due date, maker, address, collateral, and so on. It is filed according to the due date of the note. This permits ready access to the number and total value of all notes maturing on any day. The maturity ticklers are generally used by bank officials and the loan committee in daily meetings when the maturing notes are under review and discussion for official reference and action. synonymous with *maturity index*. [10]

maturity value: the money that is to be paid when a financial obligation or other contract becomes due.

maximum and minimum tariff: a tariff providing maximum and minimum rates used to for the purpose of negotiating with foreign countries as to the tariff to apply.

MB

(1)   see *bond, municipal*.

(2)   see *merchant bank*.

MBA: see *Mortgage Bankers Association of America*.

MBO (management by objectives): a type of management in which superiors and those who report to them jointly establish objectives over a specified time frame, meeting periodically to evaluate their progress in meeting these goals.

MC: see *margin call*.

MCCD: message cryptographic check digits.

McFadden Act of 1927: federal statute that banned interstate banking. Recently, new legislation has been proposed to encourage competition in banking by permitting interstate banking as a way to stimulate competition for consumer loans. see also *Douglas amendment*.

McIntyre bill: legislation introduced in 1974 to establish an "Electronic Funds Transfer System Commission." The purpose of the bill was to concentrate on the need to preserve competition and maintain consumer privacy while considering all other impacts and implications of EFTS. [105]

McLean-Platt Act: superseded by the Edge Act. See *Edge Act*.

MD: see *maturity date*.

Md: the demand for nominal money. [81]

MDT: see *merchant deposit transmittal*.

measure of value: a function of money that gives the standard for identifying the results of production using the monetary unit as the common denominator.

mechanic's lien: the legal, enforceable claim of a person who has performed work on or provided materials for a given property. Such claims are permitted by law in certain states as a claim against the title to the property. A mechanics' lien may also grant the claimant a degree of preference in case of liquidation of an estate or business. cf. *particular lien.*

medium of exchange: any commodity (commonly money) which is widely accepted in payment for goods and services and in settlement of debts, and is accepted without reference to the standing of the person who offers it in payment. [39]

medium other than cash: checks, notes, credit.

meeting bond interest and principal: an expression indicating that payments are being made when due. [67]

megabuck: slang, $1 million dollars.

melon:
(1) slang, unusually large profits that have not been dispersed to eligible persons. see *cutting a melon.*
(2) slang, the profits gained from any business venture.

member: an organization that is a participant in a specific bank card plan. [105]

member bank: a commercial bank that is a member of the Federal Reserve System. All national banks are automatically members of the system, while state banks may be admitted. By law, member banks must hold reserves (consisting of their own vault cash and deposits with their Federal Reserve Bank) equal to a percentage of their customer's deposits. [7]

member-bank reserves: currency maintained by banks who are members of the Federal Reserve System, in addition to their deposits at Federal Reserve Banks.

member corporation: a securities brokerage firm, organized as a corporation, having at least one person who is a member of a stock exchange as a director and a holder of voting stock in the corporation.

member firm: a securities brokerage firm organized as a partnership and having at least one general partner who is a member of a stock exchange.

membership corporation: a corporation that does not issue stock but which members join by paying a membership fee.

membership dues: an annual fee paid to an exchange by members, as distinguished from an initiation fee.

member's rate: the amount of commission charged a member of an exchange who is not a member of the clearing association. This amount is less than the regular charge paid by the average customer.

memo entry: miscellaneous change to an individual cardholder account record. [105]

memo post: see *account inquiry.*

memorandum account: the record of an account maintained by a bank which is not included in its assets or liabilities. An example is the record of a bad debt written off, on which subsequent recoveries are anticipated. [10]

memorandum check: a check drawn by a borrower in favor of the creditor to be used to reduce a loan if the loan is not paid at the due date; the check is thus postdated.

memory: computer storage; a device into which a unit of information can be copied, held, and retrieved at another time. see *random access.*

mercantile agency: an organization that supplies to its subscribers credit data on individuals and firms. In addition, some mercantile agencies gather statistical information and serve as collection depositories of past-due accounts. see *Dun and Bradstreet.*

mercantile paper: commercial paper, that is, notes, bills, and acceptances that originate from wholesalers, retailers, or jobbers.

mercantile rate of return: the ratio, expressed in percentages, between the figure showing on the contemporary income statement and the figure appearing on the contemporary balance sheet.

mercantilism: the economic policy under which nations measure their power by the amount of precious metal they have acquired. see *kameralism.*

merchandise balance: see *retail balance.*

merchant: an individual who takes title to goods by buying them, for the purpose of resale.

merchantable title: that condition of title which is acceptable in the market. [44]

merchant accounting: the recording by a bank of the number and dollar value of all sales drafts and credit slips submitted by each merchant. [105]

merchant affiliate: an affiliate who receives paper from a merchant. [105]

merchant agreement: a written agreement between a merchant and a bank containing their respective rights, duties, and warranties with respect to acceptance of the bank card and related matters. [105]

merchant application: a request form prepared at the time the merchant signs up with a bank card plan. The application contains basic data about the merchant, such as type of business, number of locations, and bank references. [105]

merchant bank: used in Great Britain for an organization that underwrites securities for corporations, advises such clients on mergers, and is involved in the ownership of commercial ventures (i.e., Rothschild's, Hambro's).

merchant base: total number of merchants who have signed merchant agreements with a bank card plan. May be expressed in terms of number of agreements or number of merchant locations. [105]

merchant call report: form used by bank card sales personnel to record the results of each merchant's sales or service call. [105]

merchant collusion: the situation in which a merchant has cooperated with an individual using a fraudulent bank card for the purpose of defrauding a bank credit card plan. see *merchant fraud.* [105]

merchant depository account: a demand deposit account established by a merchant with a bank for the purpose of receiving payment for sales drafts submitted to the bank card plan. [105]

merchant deposit transmittal (MDT): form used by merchants to deposit sales drafts and credit vouchers. [105]

merchant directory: a consolidated listing of all merchants participating in a bank card plan. [105]

merchant discount

(1) the percentage of each retail sale a merchant pays when accepting a credit or debit card in lieu of cash at the time of purchase. The percentage is withheld, generally on a monthly basis from the total sales deposited by the merchant's bank. The rate of the discount is set by the merchant's bank

based on (a) card processor fees and/ or percentage of total sales retained, (b) competition, and (c) total relationship with the banks. Rates may vary by as much as 4 or 5 percent in different parts of the country.

(2) compensation received by a bank from a merchant for processing and accepting the credit risk on credit card sales. [105]

merchant file: a computer record of information on all merchants services by a card issuer. [105]

merchant fraud: the process by which a merchant has submitted and received payment for sales drafts imprinted with a lost, stolen, or revoked credit card, knowing that the bank card was invalid. [105]

merchant identification card: an embossed card supplied to each merchant to be used in imprinting a merchant summary slip which is included in the sales draft envelope. Minimum embossed data include merchant account number, name and location, and checking account number. [105]

merchanting: the process whereby an operator in country A purchases items in country B and ships them direct from B to C without bringing them to A; a third-country trade.

merchant member: the member with which a merchant has signed an agreement to accept blue, white, and gold bank cards. [105]

merchant membership fee: the amount charged to merchants for the privilege of affiliating with a bank card plan. [105]

merchant number: a series or group of digits that numerically identify each merchant to the merchant signing bank for account and billing purposes. [105]

merchant operating guide: a document provided by the bank to each merchant location describing the basic operating procedures that merchants must observe in handling bank card transactions and deposits. [105]

merchant-oriented data entry (MODE): a Chicago-based point-of-sale system. [105]

merchant outlet: a merchant location. [105]

merchant penetration: the total number of merchant outlets affiliated with a bank card plan, expressed as a percentage of total merchant outlets in the market area served by the plan. [105]

merchant plastic: see *merchant identification card.*

merchant rebate: the retroactive downward adjustment of merchant discounts paid by those merchants whose volume or average ticket size exceeds a predetermined amount over a stipulated period of time. [105]

merchant solicitation: the process of calling on merchants for the purpose of seeking their affiliation in a bank card plan. [105]

merchant's rule: a rule for partial payments of delinquent interest-bearing debts under which repayments are considered to earn interest until final settlement and not considered as applied to past-due interest.

merchant statement: a summary produced and mailed at specified intervals, usually monthly. [105]

merchant summary slip: a multipart format used to total daily merchant sales, imprinted with the merchant identification card and submitted to the bank together with sales drafts. [105]

merchant volume: total amount of transactions at a bank's merchant outlet(s). [105]

merge
(1) *general:* to combine two or more into one.
(2) *computers:* to combine items from two or more similarly ordered sets into one set that is arranged in a specified order.

merger: the combining of two or more entities through the direct acquisition by one of the net assets of the other. A merger differs from a consolidation in that no new entity is created by a merger, whereas in consolidation a new organization comes into being and acquires the new assets of all the combining units. see *conglomerate;* cf. *takeover.*

merger conversion: where mutual institution's depositors can vote on a merger but are not given any cash or stock by the acquirer. They do stand first to buy the acquirer's stock, in an offering equal to the mutual's market value, as appraised by, for example, an investment banker.

merit increase (pay): an individual wage increase in recognition of superior performance or service, commonly specified as negotiable in a contract between union and management. cf. *incentive pay.*

message: a communication containing one or more transactions. [105]

message amount: the sum of the transaction amounts of a message. [105]

message status indicators: information supplied by the sending bank or wire service defining special circum-stances pertaining to the transmission of this message (e.g., suspected/possible duplicate). [105]

metered mail: any class of mail with postage printed by a U.S. Postal Service-approved meter. The same privileges and conditions apply as to all material to which stamps have been affixed. [24]

metes and bounds: real property boundary lines.

methods study: the analysis of the flow of work; in particular, the utilization of materials to permit more efficient use of workers.

methods-time measurement (MTM): the listing of basic human movements, and the assignment of time values to each. MTM is used in establishing time standards for varying tasks.

MF: see *mutual fund.*

MFN: see *most favored nation (clause).*

Mgmt.: see *management.*

MI: see *minority interest.*

Michigan roll: slang, a wad of paper money, usually, smaller denomination notes wrapped by larger value ones.

MICR: see *magnetic ink character recognition.*

microeconomics: the examination of the economic behavior of individual units in the economy, such as households or corporations.

micro-hedge: a hedge designed to reduce the risk of holding a particular asset or liability. cf. *macro-hedge.* [107]

middle management: management personnel who report directly to top management; a level of management responsible for carrying out the directives of top management.

middle-of-the-road stand: to be non-committal about the future movement of security prices, that is, neither optimistic nor pessimistic.

middle way: synonymous with *mixed economy*.

Midwest Stock Exchange: formed in 1949 with the merger of the Cleveland, Minneapolis–St. Paul, and St. Louis Stock Exchanges with the Chicago Stock Exchange (1882). In trading volume, this exchange is the second largest among the "regional" securities exchanges.

milking: slang, management's attempt to squeeze the last remaining profits from the firm without, for example, leaving sufficient reserves for improvements preparing for a downturn period.

mill base system: a pricing system in which prices are quoted for delivery at the point of production with the buyer to pay freight from that point. cf. *basing point*.

milling: the corrugated edge found on a coin.

minibranch: a retail location consisting mainly of ATMs with very few desk people present. [105]

minimum balance: the amount of money required to be on deposit in a specific account in order to qualify the depositor for special services or to waive a service charge. [105]

minimum charge (rate): the lowest rate a public utility company charges for a commodity or service, even though on a per unit, per hour basis the amount of the charge would be less (e.g., there is a minimum monthly charge for your telephone, regardless of the frequency of telephone calls made).

minimum lending rate (MLR): a bank lending rate for its customers below which the financial institution will re-frain from loaning money. MLRs have been popularized by the Bank of England.

minimum payment: the smallest monthly payment a cardholder can make and remain in compliance with the terms and conditions of the cardholder agreement. [105]

minimum premium: the smallest premium an insurance company may charge under the manual rules for writing a particular policy or bond for a designated period. It is calculated to allow the defraying of the necessary expenses of the insurance transaction and to leave an adequate amount to contribute to the payment of losses.

minimum property standards: FHA regulations establishing minimum acceptable building standards for properties to be covered by FHA mortgage insurance. [105]

minimum rate: the lowest rate, set by regulatory commissions, that a public utility company is allowed to charge for a specific commodity or service.

minimum subscription: the figure given in a firm's prospectus identifying the minimum that must be raised for the organization to become operational.

minimum wage: the lowest allowable rate, by union contract, or by federal or state law, for a given job. The term is most widely used, however, in reference to the federal Wage and Hour Law (Fair Labor Standards Act), which sets a minimum hourly rate for all workers to which it applies, and to supplementary state and municipal statutes. see *union rate*.

minimum yield: the lesser of yield to call and yield to maturity.

minor coins: U.S. penny and 5-cent coins.

minority interest: the part of the net worth of a subsidiary relating to shares not owned by the controlling company or other members of the combined group.

minority investment: retaining less than 50 percent of a corporation's voting stock.

minority stockholder: a shareholder with less that 50 percent of a corporation's stock, individually or collectively.

minor trend: day-to-day shifts in security prices as contrasted to the longer intermediate and primary trends.

mint: where metallic money is coined or manufactured.

mintage: the charge made by a government for converting bullion into coins.

mint mark: the small letter found on a coin, or a similar device, showing at which mint the coin was produced.

mint par of exchange: the figure derived by dividing the pure gold or silver weight of the monetary unit of one country by the pure similar metal weight of the monetary unit of another country.

mint price of gold: the price for gold which the government will pay upon delivery to the mint.

mint ratio: the ratio of the weight of one metal to another, and their equivalent in terms of the national unit of currency, such as the dollar (e.g., x grains of silver = x grains of gold = $1).

MINTS: see *Mutual Institutions National Transfer System, Inc.*

minus asset: the amount that must be subtracted from the original value of an asset in order that the present value of the asset may be known. [73]

minus tick: synonymous with *down tick*.

minute book: an official record of a corporation's scheduled meetings (stockholders' gathering, board of director's meeting, etc.).

MIP: see *mortgage insurance premium.*

MIS: see *management information system.*

miscellaneous charges: any charges other than advice charges germane to the transfer. [105]

miscellaneous chattel mortgage: a chattel mortgage taken on items other than household goods or a licensed automobile or truck. [55]

Miscellaneous Revenue Act of 1980: federal legislation that lets companies write off, over a period of 60 months, new business startup costs that heretofore had to be capitalized.

miscellaneous stock: a security that does not properly belong to any particular industrial grouping.

misdemeanor: a criminal offense, less than a felony, not punishable by imprisonment or death.

misencoded card: a valid card on which erroneous information has been encoded or otherwise inadvertently applied (e.g., name and/or account number and/or expiration date). [105]

misencoded payment: the encoded dollar amount does not agree with the written dollar amount. [105]

misfeasance: illegal or improper exercise of a legal responsibility; failure to properly perform a lawful act, or the performing of an action without proper notice of those involved. cf. *nonfeasance.*

mismatch: when assets and liabilities in a foreign currency fail to balance, the imbalance being either in maturity or size.

misposting: an error that causes a monetary transaction to be posted to the wrong account. [105]

misrepresentation: the giving of a positive statement or the claim to an alleged fact that is not true, thus leading to a false conclusion.

missent item: an item that has been sent in error to another bank.

missing payment: payment made that has not been posted to the appropriate account. [105]

missing sales slip: a condition where the number of sales drafts posted to an account during the billing process does not agree with the physical count of sales drafts accompanying the monthly statement. [105]

missort: generally, a check drawn by a depositor which is wrongly sorted to a "book" or bank other than that in which the account is kept. [31]

miss the market: allowing a particular advantage to buy or sell a good or service to slip by.

MIT: see *market-if-touched order.*

mixed account: the balance in these accounts contains both a real and a nominal element. For example, expense or income accounts requiring adjustment for deferred expenses or income; or the sales account, the real element being cost of goods sold or decrease in merchandise, and the nominal element being profit or loss on sales.

mixed collateral: different forms of securities that are pledged against the payment of borrowed funds.

mixed currency: a currency consisting of (a) precious metals and notes, or (b) various kinds of precious metals.

mixed economy: an economic system in which features of both capitalism and socialism in addition to some control and regulation by a central government appears. synonymous with *middle way.*

mixed property: property having characteristics of both personal and real property (e.g., house fixtures).

mixing rates: used in the foreign exchange rate system, the use of varying rates of exchange for specific categories of overseas traded goods.

MJSD: March, June, September, December (quarterly interest payments or dividends).

Mkr.: see *maker.*

Mkt.: see *market.*

MLR: see *minimum lending rate.*

MM: see entries under *money market.*

MMC: see *money market certificate.*

MMDA: money market deposit accounts. see *Garnet St. Germain Depository Institutions Act of 1982.*

MMF: see *money market fund.*

M&N: May and November (semi annual interest payments or dividends).

MO
(1) see *mail order.*
(2) see *money order.*

mobile home: a movable, portable dwelling without permanent foundation, designed for year-round living. [59]

Mobile Home Certificates: lesser known variations of the Ginnie Mae. They are fully guaranteed pass-through securities consisting of mobile home mortgages carrying shorter maturities.

mobile home loan: a nonmortgage loan to an individual for the purchase of a mobile home, secured by the lender's claim on the mobile home. [59]

MODE: see *merchant-oriented data entry*.

modeling: the identification of the fixed and variable components in a system, assigning them numerical or economic values and relating them to one another in a logical fashion so that solutions to operational problems can be obtained.

model savings association act: a model for a code of state law providing for the organization, operation, and supervision of state thrift and home-financing institutions. [59]

modification agreement: any agreement between the association and borrower that alters permanently one or more of the terms—interest rate, number of years allowed for retirement, monthly payment amount and the like—of an existing mortgage loan. [59]

modified accrual basis: the basis of accounting under which expenditures other than accrued interest on general long-term debt are recorded at the time liabilities are incurred and revenues are recorded when received in cash, except for material and/or available revenues which should be accrued to reflect properly the taxes levied and the revenues earned. [49]

modified cash refund annuity: a form of annuity in which, if death of the annuitant occurs before he has received annuity payments equal to the amount of his own contributions at date of retirement, his designated beneficiary, or his estate, will receive the remainder in a single sum. [52]

MOD 10: see *modulus 10 check digit*.

modulus 10 check digit (MOD 10): a method of proofing an account number that has been entered into a computer system. It is used on a formula that, if the number was entered correctly, will result in a number called the *check digit*. [105]

momentum: the rate of acceleration in price or volume expansion, best noted by developing gaps in velocity figures, or gaps in an on-balance volume series. Upside momentum is greatest just short of price maturity, and downside momentum tends to reach a peak at or near an important bottom.

monetarism: the body of theory related to the quantity theory of money. Its basic precept is that the quantity and changes in the money supply have the primary effect on a nation's economy. [105]

monetarist: a believer in the concept that balanced economy depends on the supply of money. cf. *archmonetarist*.

monetary: a country's currency and/or coinage.

Monetary Accord of 1951: an agreement between the Federal Reserve System and the Treasury which permitted monetary policy to react to objectives, other than the interest-rate peg. The accord terminated the interest-rate peg. see *interest-rate peg*.

Monetary and Payments System (MAPS) Planning Committee: a committee established by the American Bankers Association in 1969 to conduct extensive research and planning efforts related to the nation's payments system. The four task forces of the committee produced detailed recommendations which were consolidated into a summary report by the committee, stressing the importance of preauthorized payments and bank charge cards as building blocks in a future electronic payments system. [36]

monetary asset: money or a claim to receive a sum of money, the amount of which is fixed or determinable without reference to future prices of specific goods or services. see *monetary liability.* [80]

monetary base: a monetary aggregate composed of funds retained by banks, by the public, and including member-bank deposits at the various Federal Reserve Banks. Measures "high powered money"—bank reserves and currency, serving as a guide to potential money creation. Issued each Thursday for the week that ended the day before.

monetary commission: specialists in banking and financial matters appointed by government action to prepare an analysis and recommendation for changes in existing legislation.

Monetary Control Act: requires that all banks and all institutions that accept deposits from the public make periodic reports to the Federal Reserve System. Starting in September 1981, the Fed charged banks for a range of services that it had provided free in the past, including check clearing, wire transfer of funds, and the use of automated clearinghouse facilities. see *Depository Institutions Deregulation and Monetary Control Act.*

monetary indemnity: the specified amount benefit, as contrasted to expense reimbursement.

monetary liability: the promise to pay a claim against a specified quantity of money, the amount of which is unaffected by inflation or deflation. see *monetary asset.*

monetary multiplier: a number show-

ing the anticipated change in income-per-unit change in the money supply.

monetary policy: a policy of the Federal Reserve System that attempts to affect the terms on which credit can be obtained in private markets; its purpose is to regulate the nation's sales level, level of employment, and prices. see *discretionary policy, Operation Twist (Nudge)*; cf. *fiscal policy.*

monetary reserve: the amount of bullion held by the government or banks as security for fiduciary or credit money in circulation. see *reserve.*

monetary sovereignty: a nation's right to safeguard its fiscal system against severe deflation, unemployment, or imbalance of its foreign payments, despite pledges of cooperation which may have given to such organizations as the International Monetary Fund.

monetary standard: the basis upon which a money is issued, that is, the principles that determine the quantity of money.

monetary system: all policies and practices affecting a nation's money.

monetary transaction: any transaction posted to an account which has a dollar value. [105]

monetary unit: the unit of money of a nation. The monetary unit may or may not be defined in terms of a commodity into which it is convertible.

monetary working capital: items that are related to operations and not, for example, liquid assets that are surplus to operating requirements. [80]

monetize: to convert assets into money.

monetizing the debt: money growth induced by attempts to moderate the effects of rapidly growing government debt on interest rates. [108]

money: any denomination of coin or paper currency of legal tender that passes freely as a medium of exchange; anything that is accepted in exchange for other things (e.g., precious metals). Major characteristics of money include easy recognition, uniformity in quality, easy divisibility, and a relatively high value within a small area. cf. *currency.*

money broker: a person or institution serving as a go-between for borrowers and lenders of money.

money-center bank: any large bank engaged in a wide range of services, primarily for corporate clients.

moneyed corporation: a financial organization such as a bank, trust company, or insurance firm and as such subject to the banking or insurance code.

money functions: there are four generally accepted functions of money; as a unit of account, a medium of exchange, a store of value, and a standard of deferred payment.

money funds: a type of mutual fund. Though they have been marketed practically as bank accounts, the individual owns shares in a fund. The value is usually $1 per share, to make the accounting simple. The purchaser doesn't actually have a cash balance. The shares owned purchased prior to March 14, 1980 were free from new Federal Restrictions. see *mutual fund.*

money illusion: perceived when an increase in all prices and incomes by the same proportion produces an increase in consumption, although real incomes remain the same.

money in circulation: the total amount of currency and coin outside the Treasury and the Federal Reserve Banks.

money income: the amount of money received for work performed.

money management: financial planning with the aim of gratifying long-range as well as immediate needs and of maintaining a sound relationship among income, savings, and spending. [55]

money market (brokers): all financial organizations that handle the purchase, sale, and transfer of short-term credit instruments and notes.

money market certificate (MMC): six-month Federal Home Loan Bank Board certificate at federally insured savings and loan associations.

money market deposit accounts: see *Garnet St. Germain Depository Institutions Act of 1982.*

money market fund (MMF)

(1) *banking:* many investment banking firms sponsor money-market mutual funds, which invest in such short-term credit instruments as Treasury bills. Customers earn high interest rates on the accounts and can write checks against their investment. Commercial banks contend that these accounts are offering traditional commercial banking services without the restrictions that apply to commercial banks, such as reserve requirements on deposits. see *Glass-Steagall Act of 1933, reserve requirements.*

(2) *finance:* an investment vehicle whose primary objective is to make higher-interest securities available to the average investor who wants immediate income and high investment safety. This is accomplished through the purchase of high-yield money market instruments, such as U.S. government securities, bank certificates of

deposit, and commercial paper. synonymous with *liquid assets.*

money market instruments: private and government obligations with a maturity of one year or less. These include U.S. Treasury bills, bankers acceptances, commercial paper, finance paper, and short-term tax-exempts. [105]

money market rates: current interest rates on various money market instruments. The rates reflect the relative liquidity, security of investment, size of investment, term of investment, and general economic factors. [105]

money markets: markets where short-term debt instruments are traded.

money market securities: high-quality and generally accepted senior securities whose market prices expressed on a yield basis relate more closely to the prevailing interest rate for money than to the risks in a company's operations or in general business conditions. [67]

money multiplier: see *M-1A.*

money of account: the unit in which monetary records are kept (i.e., U.S. entries in dollars and cents).

money order (MO): postal money orders and bank money orders are instruments commonly purchased for a fee by people who do not maintain checking accounts and wish to send money to others. The names of the purchaser and the payee are shown on the face of the money order. An advantage of the money order over checks is that presentation to their original place of purchase for payment, is not required. A disadvantage is that a bank or other financial institution may charge for the service of supplying a money order.

money pinch: see *pinch.*

money price: the number of money units that must be sacrificed to purchase a particular commodity.

money rates: interest rates that lenders charge their borrowers.

money stock: see *M-1A, M2, M3.*

money supply: the total sum of currency circulating in a country. see *price;* see also *money supply (Federal Reserve).*

money supply (Federal Reserve): measures several variants in the amount of money in the economy, issued each Thursday for the week that ended eight days earlier. It has been criticized as very erratic, subject to frequent revision.

money talks: slang, money is power and can therefore buy anything.

money wage: the amount of wages in money.

monger: any trader or seller; often used in a derogatory fashion.

monometallism: a monetary system: the monetary component is defined in terms of only one metal that is accepted in unlimited quantities for producing coins. see *real money;* cf. *bimetallism.*

monopolistic competition: the existing condition in a market when the activities of one or a few purchasers or sellers significantly alter the market price.

monopoly

(1) *general:* ownership of the source of a commodity or the domination of its distribution. see *competition, engross.*

(2) *finance:* exclusive dominance of the supply and price of a commodity that is acquired by a franchise or government patent. cf. *bilateral monopoly, legal monopoly, natural monopoly,*

partial monopoly, perfect (pure) monopoly, strategic resource monopoly.

monopsony: a market situation in which there is only one buyer for an item. cf. *duopsony, oligopsony.*

monthly investment plan (MIP): a pay-as-you-go method of buying odd lots of exchange listed shares on a regular payment plan for as little as $40 a month or every three months, and up to $1000 per payment. Under MIP the investor buys a stock designated by a securities broker by the dollar's worth. If the price advances, he or she gets fewer shares; if it declines, more shares. The investor may discontinue purchases at any time without penalty. cf. *investment company.*

monthly payment bonus account: a savings account that pays bonus earnings if the customer makes a specified number of fixed monthly deposits. [59]

monthly payment loan: a consumer or mortgage loan requiring a payment each month. [105]

monthly statement: in securities, an account issued by a brokerage house to its clients, stating the date, amount, prices, and so on, of any transaction for the month; plus a listing of dividends, interest, securities received or delivered, and the existing debit or credit balance.

mooch: slang, a person lured into purchasing securities with hopes of significant profits, without first making a careful investigation.

Moody's Bond Ratings and Stock Quality Groups

(a) bonds

Aaa: best quality, generally referred to as "gilt edge."

Aa: high quality by all standards; generally known as high-grade bonds.

A: possessing many favorable investment attributes and considered as high-medium-grade obligations.

Baa: considered as lower-medium-grade obligations—that is, neither highly protected nor poorly secured. Such bonds lack outstanding investment characteristics as well.

(b) preferred and common stocks

high quality: high quality by all standards.

good quality: possesses many favorable high-grade investment attributes.

medium quality: medium-grade equity securities. [3]

Moody's Bond Yield (Annual Averages of Monthly Yield): represents the average yield on 40 operating utility companies' bonds (10 each of Class Aaa, Aa, A, and Baa) as determined and rated by Moody's Investors Service. This "yield" is the arithmetical average of 12 months and is calculated on the basis of market price, coupon rate, and on being "held to maturity." [3]

Moody's Investor's Service: a subsidiary of Dun & Bradstreet founded in 1900 by John Moody, who was the first analyst to rate the investment quality and nature of bonds.

moola (moolah): slang, money.

moonlight: slang, working at a second job, usually to supplement the income from a permanent position.

moot: in law, not covered, debatable, or made clear by earlier cases or decisions of the court (e.g., there is no uniform or clear-cut opinion on a moot point).

MOP: see *margin of profit.*

moral hazard: the possibility of loss being caused by or aggravated by dishonesty or carelessness of the insured, his or her agents, or employees, it arises from the character and circumstances of the insured, as distinguished from the inherent nature of the property covered, or its location.

moral obligation: a debt or responsibility whose payment or fulfillment is not based on legal rights or action. [28]

moral suasion: Federal Reserve System pressure exerted on U.S. banking, unaccompanied by an effort to compel compliance with the suggested action. see also *jawboning.*

moratorium: the arrangement whereby a borrower states his or her inability to repay some or all of his or her outstanding debts. cf. *default, rescheduling.*

morning loan: bank loans to stockbrokers on an unsecured basis enabling the broker to handle stock deliveries until reimbursed by the customer.

mortality: the expectancy of an asset or class of aspects to expire or depreciate by use or the passage of time.

mortgage
(1) *general:* a written conveyance of title to property, but not possession, to obtain the payment of a debt or the performance of some obligation, under the condition that the conveyance is to be void upon final payment.
(2) *finance:* property pledged as security for payment of a debt. see *chattel mortgage;* cf. *conventional loan.*

mortgage administration: the part of a mortgage banker's service involving all clerical and supervisory functions necessary to ensure prompt repayment of mortgage loans, and to protect and enforce all rights of investors thereunder. [22]

mortgage-backed certificates: sev-eral banks, notably the Bank of America, have issued certificates covering pools of conventional mortgages insured by private mortgage insurance companies. These certificates are issued in big denominations, so the market is limited mainly to institutions.

mortgage-backed securities: bond-type investment securities representing an interest in a pool of mortgages or trust deeds. Income from the underlying mortgages is used to make investor payments. [105]

mortgage banker: a banker who specializes in mortgage financing; an operator of a mortgage financing company. Mortgage financing companies are mortgagees themselves, as well as being mortgage agents for other large mortgages.

Mortgage Bankers Association of America (MBA): the professional and business organization of persons operating under the correspondency system whose major purpose is continuing improvement in the quality of service to investors. [22]

mortgage banking: the packaging of mortgage loans secured by real property to be sold to a permanent investor with servicing retained by the seller for the life of the loan in exchange for a fee. The origination, sale, and servicing of mortgage loans by a firm or individual. [105]

mortgage banking company: specialist in purchase and sale of government-backed mortgages. [105]

mortgage bond: see *bond, mortgage.*

mortgage broker: a firm or individual that brings the borrower and lender together, receiving a commission. A mortgage broker does not retain servicing. [105]

mortgage certificate: an interest in a mortgage evidenced by the instrument, generally a fractional portion of the mortgage, which certifies as to the agreement between the mortgagees who hold the certificates and the mortgagor as to such terms as principal, amount, date of payment, and place of payment. Such certificates are not obligations to pay money, as in a bond or note, but are merely a certification by the holder of the mortgage, generally a corporate depository, that he or she holds such mortgage for the beneficial and undivided interest of all the certificate holders. The certificate itself generally sets forth a full agreement between the holder and the depository, although in some cases a more lengthy document, known as a *depository agreement*, is executed. [62]

mortgage chattel: a mortgage on personal property. [105]

mortgage clause: see *mortgagee clause*.

mortgage company: mortgage financing companies are mortgages themselves, as well as being mortgage agents for other large mortgagees. Serving as mortgage agents, these mortgage bankers collect payments, maintain complete mortgage records, and make remittances to the mortgagees for a set fee or service charge. [10]

mortgage constant: synonymous with *constant ratio*.

mortgage credit: money that is owed for the acquisition of land or buildings (frequently of a home) and which is paid back over an extended period of time; hence, long-term debt. [55]

mortgaged deed: see *deed, mortgaged.*

mortgage debenture: a mortgage bond. see *bond, mortgage.*

mortgage debt: an indebtedness created by a mortgage and secured by the property mortgaged. A mortgage debt is made evident by a note or bond.

mortgage department: a department in banks, building and loan, savings and loan associations, and trust companies, where mortgage counselors, mortgage loan officers, and mortgage recording personnel handle all phases of mortgage work for mortgagors. This department may also act as "escrow agents" for mortgagors, in that they collect in the monthly payment from the mortgagor a portion of the real estate taxes, assessments on real estate, and hazard insurance. They hold these in escrow funds until payable, and then disburse the funds for the benefit of the mortgagor, and also the mortgagee, to prevent the development of liens against the property. In some states, they administer escrow funds in connection with closing mortgages, whereas in other states mortgage closings are required to be handled by attorneys-at-law. [10]

mortgagee: the creditor or lender, to whom a mortgage is made. The mortgagor retains possession and use of the property during the term of the mortgage (e.g., the bank holds the mortgage on your house).

mortgagee clause: a clause in an insurance contract making the proceeds payable to a named mortgagee, as his or her interest may appear, and stating the terms of the contract between the insurer and the mortgagee. This is preferable usage but the same as *mortgage clause*. [53]

Mortgage Guarantee Insurance Corporation: see *magic mortgage*.

mortgage guarantee policy: a policy issued on a guaranteed mortgage. [62]

mortgage in possession: a mortgagee creditor who takes over the income from the mortgaged property upon default of the mortgage by the debtor.

mortgage insurance policy: issued by a title insurance firm to a mortgage holder, resulting in a title policy.

mortgage insurance premium (MIP): the consideration paid by a mortgagor for mortgage insurance—either to FHA or to a private mortgage insurer (MIC). [105]

mortgage investment trust: a specialized form of real estate investment trust that invests in long-term mortgages, usually Federal Housing Administration-insured or Veterans Administration-guaranteed, and makes short-term construction and development loans. [59]

mortgage lien: in a mortgage given as security for a debt, serving as a lien on the property after the mortgage is recorded.

mortgage life insurance: insurance on the life of the borrower that pays off a specified debt if he dies. synonymous with *credit life insurance*. [59]

mortgage loan: a loan made by a lender, called the mortgagee, to a borrower, called the mortgagor, for the financing of a parcel of real estate. The loan is evidenced by a mortgage. The mortgage sets forth the conditions of the loan, the manner of repayment or liquidation of the loan, and reserves the right of foreclosure or repossession to the mortgagee. In case the mortgagor defaults in the payment of interest and principal, or if he permits a lien to be placed against the real estate mortgaged due to failure to pay the taxes and assessments levied against the property, the right of foreclosure can be exercised. [10]

mortgage loan commitment: written statement by lender to grant a specific loan amount, at a given rate, for a certain term, secured by a specific property, if the real property transaction is closed before the expiration date. [78]

mortgage loan ledger record: a document that contains a complete record of all transactions—payments of principal and interest, special disbursements, fees, charges, and the like—on a particular mortgage loan. [59]

mortgage loan report: an updated report that requires the same kind of information as the full report plus a statement certifying that all Federal Housing Administration or Veterans Administration specifications, including public record items have been met. [76]

mortgage note: a note that offers a mortgage as proof of an indebtedness and describes the manner in which the mortgage is to be paid. This note is the actual amount of debt that the mortgage obtains, and it renders the mortgagor personally responsible for repayment.

mortgage origination: the part of a mortgage banker's service involving performance of all details concerned with the making of a real estate loan. [22]

mortgage pattern: the arrangement or design of payments and other terms established by a mortgage contract. [44]

mortgage portfolio: the aggregate of

mortgage loans or obligations held by a bank as assets. [44]

mortgage premium: an additional bank fee charged for the giving of a mortgage when the legal interest rate is less than the prevailing mortgage market rate and there is a shortage of mortgage money.

mortgager(or): a debtor or borrower who gives or makes a mortgage to a lender, on property owned by the mortgagor.

mortgage risk: the hazard of loss of principal or of anticipated interest inherent in an advance of funds on the security of a mortgage. [44]

mortgage securities: see *Freddie Macs, Gennie Mae trusts, Government National Mortgage Association, mortgage-backed certificates.*

mortgaging future income: pledging income not yet earned. [28]

mortgagor: see *mortgager.*

Mos.: months

MOS: see *margin of safety.*

MOSS: market oversight surveillance system; proposed by the chairman of the Securities and Exchange Commission, a $12 million computerized surveillance network capable of monitoring every facet of securities trading in the country.

most favored nation (clause): in international business treaties, a provision against tariff discrimination between two or more nations. It provides that each participant will automatically extend to other signatories all tariff reductions that are offered to nonmember nations. see *retaliatory duty.* cf. *open door policy.*

mother hubbard clause: a mortgage provision permitting the lender, upon default of the conditions of the mort-

gage, to foreclose on the overdue mortgage. Courts around the country have questioned the legality of this clause.

MOUs: memorandums of understanding.

movable exchange: instruments quoted in the currency of the nation in which payment is to be made rather than that in which the instrument is drawn.

movement: an increase or decrease in the price of a specific stock.

moving average: a technique for correcting small fluctuations of the stock market indicator to yield a general market trend.

MP: see *market price.*

MPC: see *marginal propensity to consume.*

MPI: see *marginal propensity to invest.*

MPS: see *marginal propensity to save.*

MS

(1) see *majority stockholders.*

(2) March, September (semiannual interest payments or dividends).

(3) see *margin of safety.*

(4) see *minority stockholder.*

(5) see *money supply.*

M^s: the supply of nominal money, composed of checkable deposits and currency. [81]

M&S: March and September (semiannual interest payments or dividends).

MSB: see *mutual savings bank.*

MSE: see *Midwest Stock Exchange.*

Mtg.: see *mortgage.*

Mthly.: monthly.

MTM: see *methods-time measurement.*

MTN: see *multilateral trade negotiations.*

MTS: manned teller system.

multicompany: diverse organizations

or a variety of firms under a single management.

multicurrency loan: a loan in which several currencies are involved.

multiemployer plan: for purposes of ERISA, a pension plan maintained pursuant to one or more collective bargaining agreements to which more than one employer is required to contribute. [105]

multi-industry: the management of firms involved in different activities.

multilateralism: an international policy having as its object the freeing of international trade from the restrictions involved in bilateralism in an effort to permit nations to specialize in production and exchange in accordance with the principle of comparative advantage.

multilateral trade negotiations (MTN): trade negotiations conducted between many nations; often referred to as a *round*.

multilinear tariff: synonymous with *multiple tariff system*.

multilingual notes: paper money issued with a legend in two or more languages, as in India, Belgium, or Cyprus. [27]

multinational corporation: a corporation that participates in international business activities. A firm that produces, markets, and finances its operations throughout various nations of the world. cf. *production sharing.*

multiple banking: the offering of all types of banking services to a bank's customers, as distinguished from specialization in a few services as offered by savings and loan associations, and other banking institutions. Often referred to as department store banking. cf. *full-service bank.*

multiple budget: a budget extending two or more periods of time into the future and extended as each time period elapses.

multiple capital structure company: a company having more than one class of outstanding securities. [105]

multiple-commodity reserve dollar: a scheme to maintain a constant value ratio between gold and other commodities in terms of dollars, purporting to set a reserve of selected items. Money is redeemed in either gold or in these reserve goods, and gold and the reserve goods can always be exchanged for dollars. A constant ratio should be maintained between the value of the commodities, the gold, and the dollar.

multiple currency practice: arises when two or more effective exchange rates exist simultaneously, at least one of which, as the result of official action, is more than 1 percent higher or lower than the par value. Such practices are usually to be found where a dual exchange market exists or where the monetary authorities set different exchange rates for imports, exports, current invisibles, and capital. They often result from taxes or subsidies on specified exchange transactions. [42]

multiple currency securities: securities, mostly bonds, payable in more than one currency at the election of the holder. In the event of devaluation of a currency, the holder can elect to be paid in the currency of a nation that has not devalued its currency.

multiple currency system: a means of controlling foreign exchange where domestic currency can be exchanged for foreign currency only through a government unit or controlled bank.

multiple exchange: three or more

principals involved with various pieces of property. [62]

multiple expansion of bank deposits: occurs when a loan made by one bank is used to finance business transactions and becomes a deposit in another bank. A portion of this loan can be used by the second bank as a required reserve, and the remainder can be loaned out for business use, so that it is eventually deposited in a third bank.

multiple management: a description of worker participation in a firm's management by assisting in the development and execution of policy.

multiple ownership: ownership by two or more parties. synonymous with *co-ownership*. [59]

multiple tariff system: a system of differential customs duties, that is, a tariff which applies duties at differing rates on the same imported commodity, the level of duty set by the importing nation. synonymous with *multilinear tariff*.

multiplier principle: the reciprocal of the marginal propensity to save. The multiplier is a figure that identifies the changes in investment and spending to alterations in aggregate incomes. see *Keynesian economics*.

multiprocessing
(1) *computers:* using several computers to logically divide jobs or processes, and to execute programs simultaneously.
(2) *systems:* loosely, parallel processing.
(3) *systems:* two or more processors in a system configuration.

multiprogramming: pertaining to the concurrent execution of two or more programs by a computer.

multivariate analysis, participation, and structure: see *MAPS*.

muni: a *municipal bond*.

Munic.: municipal.

municipal bond: see *bond, municipal*.

municipal improvement certificates: certificates issued in lieu of bonds for the financing of special improvements. [49]

municipal revenue bond: see *bond, municipal revenue*.

municipals: a popular word for the securities of a governmental unit.

munifunds: synonymous with *mutual funds*. see *investment company*.

muniment of title
(1) *general:* anything that protects or enforces; written proof that enables an owner to defend his or her title to property.
(2) *law:* deeds and contracts that show conclusive proof of ownership (e.g., warranty deed).

munis: Wall Street slang for municipal bonds. see *bond, municipal*.

mutilated currency: coin and paper currency that is not in an adequate condition for further circulation and can be withdrawn. When the mutilation is less than three-fifths of the paper bill present, it is not redeemed at face value without an affidavit from the holder that he or she certifies that the missing parts have been destroyed.

mutual assent: agreement by all parties to a contract to the same thing. Each must know what the other wishes.

mutual association: a savings association that issues no capital stock, but is owned and controlled solely by its savers and borrowers, who are called members. Members do not share in profits, because a mutual institution operates in such a way that it makes no "profit," but they exercise other ownership rights. [59]

mutual company: a corporation without capital stock (e.g., mutual savings bank): the profits, after deductions, are distributed among the owner-customers in proportion to the business activity carried with the corporation.

mutual fund: an investment company which ordinarily stands ready to buy back (redeem) its shares at their current net asset value; the value of the shares depends on the market value of the fund's portfolio securities at the time. Also, mutual funds generally continuously offer new shares to investors. see also *investment company, money funds.* [23]

Mutual Institutions National Transfer System, Inc. (MINTS): an organization affiliated with the National Association of Mutual Savings Banks (NAMSB). The MINTS Money Transfer Card is intended to become part of a future nationwide Mutual Savings Bank EFT system. [36]

mutual investment: see *unit trust.*

mutual investment fund: synonymous with *mutual fund.*

mutualism: the argument developed by Proudhon (1809–1865) that services exchanged for each other would be mutually equal if rent, interest, and profits were eliminated.

mutuality: equality of status and opportunity among members of a savings association. [59]

mutual mortgage insurance fund: one of four FHA insurance funds into which all mortgage insurance premiums and other specified revenue of the FHA are paid and from which losses are met. [105]

mutual savings bank: a banking organization without capital stock, operating under law for the mutual benefit of the depositors. The depositor is encouraged to practice thrift, and the savings of these small depositors are invested in very high grade securities and some first-class mortgages. Dividends from these investments are mutually distributed after deduction of expenses of the association and reserves for a guaranty fund for depositors. The principal idea of a mutual savings bank is to perform a social service for small depositors who cannot invest their savings at high yield. see also *mutual company.*

Mutual Savings Foundation of America, The: based in Washington, D.C., this nonprofit organization was established in 1961 as a vehicle to enable savings bankers to promote and improve education in the field of economics. The foundation assists educational institutions with grants-in-aid, gifts and loans to support research, and also grants scholarships, fellowships, and loans to students in the field of economics. It also provides aid to developing nations to assist them in accumulating domestic savings. Contributions to the foundation qualify as charitable contributions for federal income tax purposes. [8]

mutual wills: a common arrangement executed pursuant to an agreement in which the husband and wife leave everything to each other.

MV: see *market value.*

N

N: see *note.*

NA

  (1) see *net assets.*

  (2) see *no account.*

  (3) no approval required (full discretion).

  (4) see *nostro account.*

NACHA: National Automated Clearing House Association.

NACIS: National Credit Information Service.

NACM: National Association of Credit Management.

naird: monetary unit of Nigeria.

naked calls: the selling of options on stock that is not owned by a customer.

"naked" reserve: an adjusted reserve of each of the Federal Reserve Banks showing the true reserve position of the bank. see *reserve requirements.*

name

  (1) as in a street name, used for easing security transfers.

  (2) shorthand in foreign exchange markets referring to other participants (e.g., "I can't do the name," meaning "I am not allowed to trade with that institution").

  (3) in Great Britain, a marking name. synonymous with *street name.*

name day: see *settlement day.*

named insured: any person or firm or corporation or any of its members, specially designated by name as insured(s) in a policy, as distinguished from others who, although unnamed, are protected under some circumstances.

named schedule bond: see *bond, named schedule.*

NAMSB: see *National Association of Mutual Savings Banks.*

narrow market: a condition that exists when the demand for a security is so limited that small alterations in supply or demand will create major fluctuations in the market price.

NASD: see *National Association of Security Dealers and Investment Managers.*

NASDAQ: see *National Association of Securities Dealers Automated Quotations.*

NASDIM: see *National Association of Security Dealers and Investment Managers.*

National Advisory Council on International Monetary and Financial Problems: comprised of the Secretary of State, the Secretary of the Treasury, the Secretary of Commerce, and chairpersons of the Board of Governors of the Federal Reserve System and the Export-Import Bank. Its function is to coordinate the policies of the United States in the World Bank and the International Monetary Fund.

National Association of Mutual Savings Banks (NAMSB): exists to serve its member banks. It provides services to individual member banks which they would find impractical to provide for themselves, and it serves the savings bank industry as a whole, through national-level programs and activities to further industry goals and objectives and to meet needs common to all savings banks. [8]

National Association of Securities Dealers (NASD): see *National Association of Security Dealers and Investment Managers.*

National Association of Security Dealers and Investment Managers (NASDIM): the Maloney Act, passed in 1938, which amended the Securities Exchange Act of 1934, provides for self-regulation of the over-the-counter securities market by associations registered with the SEC. The NASD (National Association of Security Dealers) became the only association so registered, and most companies offering variable annuities became NASD members. On January 1, 1984, the National Association of Security Dealers and Investment Managers was awarded official government recognition as a self-regulatory body. NASDIM represents the efforts of a number of

licensed securities dealers and its members no longer are required to apply for an annual license to deal in securities.

National Association of Securities Dealers Automated Quotations (NASDAQ): an automated information network that provides brokers and dealers with price quotations on securities traded over the counter.

national bank: a commercial bank organized with the consent and approval of the Comptroller of the Currency and operated under the supervision of the federal government. National banks are required to be members of the Federal Reserve System and must purchase stock in the Federal Reserve Bank in their district.

National Bank Act of 1863: the act of Congress providing for the incorporation of banks under federal supervision. Such national banks are now under the supervision of the Federal Reserve System.

national bank association: synonymous with *national bank.*

national bank call: the report, submitted four times each year, to the Comptroller of the Currency on the well-being of the bank's commercial department.

national bank examination: all national banks each year are subject to a minimum of two examinations by the staff of a national bank examiner to check records to make certain that the bank is fulfilling the requirements of the National Bank Act.

national bank examiner: an employee of the Comptroller of the Currency whose function is to examine or audit banks periodically. Such an examination is done to determine the strength of a bank's financial position, the security of its deposits, and to verify that procedures are maintained consistent with federal regulations. [105]

national bank note: a type of currency issued in the United States. National bank notes are backed by two types of U.S. government bonds—2 percent consols of 1930, and the 2 percent Panama Canal bonds of 1916–1936 and 1918–1938. These bonds were called for redemption by the Bank Act of 1935, and no further issuance of national bank notes was authorized. They are being retired from circulation. National bank notes are in denominations of $5, $10, $20, $50, and $100, and each has a brown seal and the issuing bank's charter number on its face. [10]

national bank report: see *national bank call.*

National Bankruptcy Act of 1898: federal law stating the conditions under which an individual or business may declare bankruptcy, and the procedures for declaration. see *reorganization.*

National Bank Surveillance System (NBSS): a computer-based data collection and monitoring system maintained by the Office of the Comptroller of the Currency. NBSS is used to detect significantly changed circumstances within a specific bank or within the national banking system as a whole. [105]

National Commission on EFT: a commission authorized by a 1974 Act of Congress to conduct a two-year investigation into electronic funds transfer system policy and planning issues, concluding with reports and recommendations for congressional action. [36]

National Consumer Cooperative

Bank: federal legislation signed by President Carter in 1978 creating a national bank to provide credit for consumer cooperatives.

National Credit Union Administration (NCUA): the federal government agency that supervises, charters, and insures federal credit unions. NCUA also insures state-chartered credit unions that apply and qualify for insurance. As of October 1979, the NCUA also operates a credit facility for member credit unions. [1]

national currency: all Federal Reserve Bank notes and national bank notes that are now retired.

national debt: the debt owed by the federal government.

National Farm Loan Association: an agricultural cooperative of local operation created as a result of the Federal Farm Loan Act. Upon subscription to shares of the Federal Land Bank in its area, the association can secure financing for farm mortgages.

National Housing Act of 1934: created the Federal Housing Administration to insure home mortgage, low-income housing project, and home improvement loans made by private lenders; established the Federal Savings and Loan Insurance Corporation to insure savings accounts at member savings associations up to $5000. [51]

national income: the total of the incomes received by all the people of a country over a stated period. It is equal to the gross national product minus depreciation minus sales taxes and other small items.

national income and product accounts: accounts prepared and published by the U.S. Department of Commerce showing various aspects of the total output of the economy and of the total income received in the economy.

nationalization: takeover by the government, with or without compensation, of a public or private activity. cf. *confiscation, eminent domain.*

national liquidity: a nation's monetary situation as determined by its rates of interest on all loans and deposits.

National Monetary Commission: a body of banking and financial specialists reporting to Congress on the state of the banking structure and recommends changes. The Commission was formed in 1908.

National Mortgage Association: see *Federal National Mortgage Association.*

National Numerical System: see *transit number.*

National Quotation Bureau: the primary quotation source for securities traded over the counter.

National Security Exchange: not to be confused with the National Stock Exchange; any exchange labeled by the SEC. Included are most of the larger exchanges. Only a few smaller exchanges are not designated as National Security Exchanges.

National Stock Exchange: the third stock exchange of New York City, established in 1960.

national wealth: the combined monetary value of all the material economic products owned by all the people.

nationwide loan: a conventional loan made or purchased upon improved real estate located outside the insured institution's normal lending territory but within any state of the United States. [59]

Natl.: national.

natural business year: a 12-month period usually selected to end when inventory or business activity is at a low point.

natural capital: land that is used as a factor of production.

natural financing
(1) a real estate transaction requiring no outside financing, as is demanded in cash sales.
(2) the selling of properties that do not call for a third party.

Natural Gas Policy Act: federal legislation passed in October 1978 which created whole new categories for natural gas and raised ceiling prices on some of them.

natural interest rate: the interest rate at which the demand for loanable funds just equals the supply of savings. The interest rate that keeps the flow of money incomes constant rather than the interest rate, which keeps the price level constant.

natural monopoly
(1) *general:* a monopoly due to natural conditions (e.g., a crop that demands special climate is subject to monopolization by a grower in the area having that climate.
(2) *finance:* among industries that experience economies of scale, the cost per unit is lowest when there is only one company in the industry.

natural resources: all materials furnished by nature (minerals, timber, water, etc.).

NAV: see *net asset value.*

navicert: an official document released by a belligerent country authorizing specified items to be transported overseas by a neutral nation through a blockade to a named neutral port of entry.

NBA

(1)   see *National Bank Act of 1863.*

(2)   see *National Bankruptcy Act of 1898.*

NBI: National BankAmericard Incorporated, now known as Visa U.S.A., Incorporated. [105]

NBR: nonborrowed reserve, total reserve of depository institutions less depository institutions' borrowing from the Federal Reserve. [81]

NBS: National Bureau of Standards.

NBSS: see *National Bank Surveillance System.*

NC

(1)   see *net capital.*

(2)   see *net cost.*

NCB: see *bond, noncallable.*

NCCB: see *National Consumer Cooperative Bank.*

NCF: see *net cash flow.*

NCS: see *noncallable securities.*

NCUA: see *National Credit Union Administration.*

ND: see *net debt.*

NE: see *net earnings.*

nearby delivery: the closest active month of delivery, as stated in a commodity futures agreement.

near money: highly liquid assets (e.g., government securities) other than official currency.

near-term: short term as opposed to long term (i.e., the near future or less than two months usually).

negative amortizer: when a home buyer gets a bank mortgage below the going rate and the difference is added to the principal. Payments are low to start but much higher later.

negative authorization list: a list of accounts requiring exception authorization handling. [105]

negative carry: the cost incurred in ex-

cess of income when borrowing to finance the holding of securities. [105]

negative coverage: a property financed by a mortgage with a debt service that tops its earnings.

negative factor (or value):   a factor (such as advanced age) given an unfavorable or negative weight in a credit decision. [105]

negative file: an authorized system file containing a simple list of accounts for which credit, check cashing, and other privileges, should be denied. cf. *positive file.*

negative float: see *float.*

negative income tax: proposed by some to provide financial aid to individuals with incomes below a certain minimum. Rulings of the Internal Revenue Service would be followed, but the procedure would be to distribute rather than collect revenue.

negative interest: where a depositor is required to pay interest rather than receive it. [91]

negative investment: see *disinvestment.*

negatively sloping yield curve: a yield curve where interest rates in the shorter dates are above those in the longer dates.

negative pledge clause: a covenant in an indenture to the effect that the corporation will not pledge any of its assets unless the notes or debentures outstanding under the particular indenture are at least equally secured by such pledge. synonymous with *covenant of equal coverage.* [37]

negative verification: many banks have a legend printed on the statement form going to the depositor to the effect that "if no difference is reported within 10 days, the account will be considered correct." If the bank does not hear from the depositor, it assumes that the depositor finds no discrepancies between its statement and his or her records.

Negb.: see *negotiable.*

Neg. Inst.: see *negotiable instrument.*

Negl.: see *negligence.*

negligence: failure to do that which an ordinary, reasonable, prudent person would do, or the doing of some act that an ordinary, prudent person would not do. Reference is made of the situation, circumstances, and awareness of the parties involved.

negotiability: the quality of a bank check, promissory note, or other legal instrument of value that allows legal title to it to be transferred from one individual to another by endorsement and delivery, or by delivery without endorsement.

negotiable

(1) *general:* anything that can be sold or transferred to another for money or as payment of an debt.

(2) *investments:* a security, title to which is transferable by delivery. [20]

negotiable check: a check payable to "to order" or "to bearer." A negotiable check in order form can be made nonnegotiable by a restrictive indorsement.

negotiable instrument: the Uniform Negotiable Instruments Act states: "An instrument, to be negotiable, must conform to the following requirements: (a) it must be in writing and signed by the maker or drawer; (b) it must contain an unconditional promise or order to pay a certain sum in money; (c) it must be payable on demand, or at a fixed or determinable future time; (d) it must be payable to order or to bearer; and (e) where the instrument is addressed to a drawee, he must be named or otherwise indicated therein with reasonable certainty."

negotiable order of withdrawal: see *NOW account.*

negotiable paper: negotiable instruments that are used in the borrowing of money on a short-term period for business objectives.

negotiable securities: bearer instruments that result in the transfer of title by assignment or delivery. Bearer bonds, bearer notes, bearer warrants, stock certificates, and coupons can be negotiated, as distinguished from registered securities.

negotiable warehouse receipt: a certificate issued by an approved warehouse that guarantees the existence and the grade of a commodity held in store.

negotiate: in finance, to transfer a written obligation such as a note or bond. To handle successfully.

negotiated plan: a pension, profit-sharing, or other employee benefit plan that has been bargained for with an employer by a group of employees, usually through a union as bargaining agent. [105]

negotiated price: the result obtained by a purchaser who desires something different from what is available or is powerful enough to force the seller to accept prices lower than those usually charged.

negotiated purchase: the process of preparation of a security issue by the issuing company by negotiation with the underwriting investment banking firms. cf. *competitive bid.*

negotiated sale: a private arrangement between two or more parties to finance the sale of securities by an issuer, without competitive public bidding. [105]

negotiation

(1) *finance:* the act by which a negotiable instrument is placed into circulation, by being physically passed from the original holder to another person.

(2) *labor relations:* the deliberation or discussion by representatives of labor and management to set conditions of work (e.g., wages, hours, benefits, working conditions, machinery for handling grievances); the bargaining that goes on between these parties.

negotiation credit: a credit instrument under which the beneficiary draws his or her drafts in a foreign currency either on the opening bank or on a designated foreign bank. The beneficiary may then sell the drafts either to the local advising bank or to any other bank in his or her area that is willing to buy the drafts as foreign exchange. [105]

neoclassical economics: an economic approach developed between 1870 and 1918, utilizing mathematics in the analysis of data and models. Neoclassicists were primarily concerned with refining the concepts of price and allocation theory, marginalism, and the theory of capital.

neo-Keynesian: a follower of concepts dealing with tax adjustment and government spending as primary forces of economic expansion. see *Keynesian economics.*

nest egg: slang, money saved, often deposited in a savings bank in preparation for retirement.

net: that which remains after certain designated deductions have been made from the gross amount.

net assets: the property of a business, corporation, organization, or estate, remaining after all obligations have been met.

net asset value: it is common practice for investment companies to compute assets daily, or even twice daily, by totaling the market value of all securities owned. All liabilities are deducted; the balance is divided by the number of shares outstanding. The resulting figure is the net asset value per share.

net avails: the funds given to a borrower in the discounting of a note. It is equal to the face value of the note minus the discount.

net balance: the amount due at a particular time, after all refunds have been calculated. Often called the *payoff balance* or *net payoff.* [55]

net bonded debt: gross bonded debt less applicable cash or other assets. [49]

net borrowed reserves: borrowings less excess reserves.

net capital: a firm's net worth (assets minus liabilities) minus certain deductions, for assets that may not be easily converted into cash at their full value. In the securities industry, net capital is used to determine whether a brokerage house can be considered solvent and capable of operating.

net cash flow: the net cash consumed or produced in a period by an activity or product during a unit of time, including all revenue and expenses except noncash items such as depreciation.

net change: the change in the price of a security between the closing price on one day and the closing price on the following day on which the stock is traded. The net change is ordinarily the last figure on the stock price list. The mark $+1\frac{1}{4}$ means "up $1.250 a share from the last sale on the previous day the stock had been traded."

net charge-offs as percent of average net loans: loan charge-offs less recoveries as percent of net average loans outstanding. Net loans are gross loans outstanding minus unearned income and the valuation portion of loan loss reserves on an average daily basis for the year. A minus sign indicates that recoveries exceeded charge-offs.

net cost

(1) *general:* the true cost of an item. The net cost is determined by subtracting all income or financial gain from the gross cost.

(2) *banking:* the total premiums paid on a policy less any dividends, and the surrender value as of the time the net cost is determined.

net current monetary assets: equals monetary assets less monetary liabilities. The main difference between net current monetary assets and working capital is that the former definition of funds excludes inventory. see *working capital.* [80]

net debt: the sum of fixed and existing liabilities less the sinking fund and other assets that are earmarked for payment of the liabilities.

net demand deposits: the excess of demand deposits, including deposits, due to other banks and the U.S. government, over demand balances due from other domestic banks, with the exception of Federal Reserve Banks, foreign banks or branches, foreign branches of domestic and private banks, and cash items that are in the process of being collected.

net earnings: the excess of gross operating income over gross operating expenses is referred to as "operating

earnings before taxes." Income taxes applicable to operating earnings are deducted, to arrive at "net earnings" or "net operating earnings."

net estate: the part of an estate remaining after all expenses to manage it have been taken out.

net export of goods and services: the excess of exports of goods and services (domestic output sold abroad, and the production abroad credit to U.S.-owned resources) over imports (U.S. purchases of foreign output, domestic production credit to foreign-owned resources, and net private cash remittances to creditors abroad).

net federal funds borrowed as percent of average net loans outstanding: net federal funds borrowed are the bank-calculated average federal funds purchased and securities sold under agreements to repurchase, less the bank-calculated average federal funds sold and securities purchased under agreements to resell. A minus sign indicates that the bank was a net seller of federal funds. see *net charge-offs as percent of average net loans.*

net for common stock: net income less dividends on preferred stock applicable to the period on an accrual basis. [3]

net foreign investment: the net change in the nation's foreign assets and liabilities, including the monetary gold stocks, arising out of current trade, income on foreign investment, and cash gifts and contributions. It measures the excess of (a) exports over imports, (b) income on U.S. public and private investment abroad over payments on foreign investment in the U.S., and (c) cash gifts and contributions of the U.S. (public and private) to foreigners over cash gifts and contributions received from abroad. [70]

net free (or net borrowed) reserves: excess reserves less member-bank borrowings from Federal Reserve Banks. The resulting difference is called net free when positive and net borrowed when negative. [72]

net ground lease: see *lease ground*.

net income: the remains from earnings and profits after all costs, expenses, and allowances for depreciation and probable loss have been deducted.

net income after dividends: net income less dividends on preferred stock applicable to the period and dividends declared on common stock during the period. [3]

net income multiplier: a figure which, times the net income of a property, produces an estimate of value of that property. It is obtained by dividing the selling price by the monthly net rent (net income). [52]

net indebtedness: see *net debt.*

net interest: measures the excess of interest payments made by the domestic business sector over its interest receipts from other sectors, plus net interest received from abroad. Interest paid by one business firm to another business firm is a transaction within the business sector and has no effect on the overall interest payments or receipts of the sector. The same is true of interest payments within other sectors as from one individual to another, or one government agency to another. [73]

net interest cost: the average rate of interest over the life of a bond which an issuer must pay to borrow funds. [105]

net investment income per share: the net amount of dividends and inter-

est earned during an accounting period on an investment company's portfolio securities (after deduction of operating expenses) divided by the number of shares outstanding. [23]

net lease: a lease stating that the landlord will incur all maintenance costs, taxes, insurance, and other expenses usually paid by the owner.

net line: the amount of liability retained on a property by a company for its own account. [54]

net listing: the broker receives as commission all monies received above minimum sales price agreed to by owners and broker. [62]

net long-term debt: total long-term debt, less cash and investment assets of sinking funds and other reserve funds specially held for redemption of long-term debt.

net loss: the excess of expenses and losses during a specified period over revenues and gains in the same time frame.

net national debt: the total national debt less that part held by the government in various trust funds.

net national product: gross national product minus capital consumption (depreciation). The market value of the net output of goods and services produced by the nation's economy.

net-net income: the repetition of the word "net" emphasizes the actual profit, resulting in usable cash, after all expenses have been paid.

net new savings: see *net savings inflow.*

net operating earnings: see *net earnings.*

net operating income: net current operating income after minority interest and taxes but before securities gains and losses and preferred dividends for the year ending on December 31.

net option: a written instrument granting the right to buy a property at a specified price to the owner.

net payoff: see *net balance.*

net position: the difference between the open contracts long and the open contracts short held in any one commodity by an individual or group. [11]

net present value: sum of the present values of all cash flows, positives and negatives.

net price: the price after deductions, allowances, and discounts have been made.

net profit: the excess of all revenues over all costs and expenses incurred to obtain the income in a given enterprise during a given period of time. If the total expenses exceed the income, such amount is known as the net loss. synonymous with *net revenue.*

net profit on net sales: obtained by dividing the net earnings of the business, after taxes, by net sales (the dollar volume less returns, allowances, and cash discounts). This is an important yardstick in measuring profitability. [4]

net profits on net working capital: net working capital represents the equity of the owners in the current assets, as obtained by subtracting total current debt from total current assets. This equity, or margin, represents the cushion available to the business for carrying inventories and receivables, and for financing day-to-day operations. To illustrate how net working capital is computed: if a concern has current assets of $1,000,000 and current debt of $400,000, its net working capital is $600,000. [4]

net profits on tangible net worth: tangible net worth is the equity of stockholders in the business, as obtained by subtracting total liabilities from total assets, and then deducting intangibles. The ratio is obtained by dividing net profits after taxes by tangible net worth. The tendency is to look increasingly to this ratio as a final criterion of profitability. Generally, a relationship of at least 10 percent is regarded as a desirable objective for providing dividends plus funds for future growth. [4]

net realized capital gain per share: the amount of net capital gains realized on the sale of portfolio securities during an accounting period after deducting losses realized, divided by the number of shares outstanding. [23]

net registered tonnage: gross registered tonnage of a vessel, calculated on cubic capacity at 100 cubic feet per ton, less engine room, navigation, light, air, locker room spaces, and so on; represents the actual carrying capacity.

net revenue: see *net income.*

net revenue available for debt service: gross operating revenues of an enterprise less operating and maintenance expenses but exclusive of depreciation and bond interest. "Net revenue" as thus defined is used to compute "coverage" on revenue bond issues. [49]

net sales: gross sales, minus returns and allowances, over a stated period.

net sales to inventory: obtained by dividing annual net sales by merchandise inventory as carried on the balance sheet. This quotient does not yield an actual physical turnover. It provides a yardstick for comparing stock-to-sales ratios of one concern with another or with those for the industry. [4]

net sales to net working capital: net sales are divided by net working capital. This provides a guide as to the extent the company is turning its working capital and the margin of operating funds. [4]

net sales to tangible net worth: obtained by dividing net sales by tangible net worth. The result gives a measure of the relative turnover of capital. If capital is turned over too rapidly, liabilities build up excessively, as amounts owed to creditors become a substitute for permanent capital. And if capital is turned too slowly, funds become stagnant, and profitability suffers. [4]

net savings gain: synonymous with *net savings inflow*.

net savings inflow: the change in an association's savings account balances over a given period, determined by subtracting withdrawals during the period; also called net savings gain or net savings receipts. When interest credited to accounts during the period is excluded, the resulting figure is customarily referred to as *net new savings*. synonymous with *net savings gain* and *net savings receipts*. [59]

net savings receipts: synonymous with *net savings inflow*.

net surplus: the earnings or profits remaining to a corporation after all operating expenses, taxes, interests, insurance, and dividends have been paid out. The surplus is determined before deducting dividends while the net surplus is determined following the deduction of dividends.

net working capital: the excess of existing assets over present liabilities.

net worth

(1) *general:* the owner's equity in a given business, represented by the excess of the total assets over the total amounts owing to outside creditors at a given moment of time.

(2) *finance:* the *net worth* of an individual, as determined by deducting the amount of all his or her personal liabilities for the total value of personal assets.

net yield: the return from an investment following subtractions for costs and losses incurred in operating the investment.

net yield to redemption: the gross yield to redemption on a security, adjusted to take account of taxation.

neutral money: a system under which the dollar would be convertible into commodities at a fixed price with the object of stabilizing the price level.

neutral spread: an investment strategy, since on the downside it is impossible to lose more than commission costs. It involves buying a call option on a stock for a specific time period and selling two call options on the same stock for the same period, but at a higher exercise price. The idea is to pick a stock whose options at the high exercise price are trading at about half the price, or premium, of the option bought. The out-of-pocket costs are just the commissions on doing the deal. synonymous with *ratio bull spread, twofer.*

never used: designates a cardholder account that has never been active. [105]

new balance: the new balance owing after payments and credits have been deducted from the previous balance and the new purchases and finance charges have been added. [105]

new business department: a section

within the bank that obtains new accounts.

new business venture group: a separate company unit with a mandate to develop one or more new businesses or items that fall outside the natural charter of the firm's existing activities.

new cedi: monetary unit of Ghana.

new credit extended: amount of new credit the center has extended to a cardholder during the past billing period. [105]

new cruzeiro: monetary unit of Brazil.

New Economics: economic thought, initially developed by John Maynard Keynes in the 1930s, which states that an economy may be in equilibrium at any level of employment. Appropriate government fiscal and monetary policies are required to maintain full employment and keep economic growth with minimal inflation. see *Keynesian economics.*

New England NOW Accounts: a 1979 federal law that expanded NOW account authority to federally chartered associations in Connecticut, Maine, Rhode Island, and Vermont. see also *NOW account.* [51]

new high: usually, the highest price that a security has attained since its exchange listing.

new housing authority bond: see *bond, new housing authority.*

new issue: a stock or bond sold by a corporation for the first time. Proceeds may be issued to retire outstanding securities of the company to finance new plant or equipment, or to secure additional working capital.

new issue market: the market for new issues of securities (as opposed to the secondary market on securities already issued). [52]

new money: the amount by which a replacement issue of securities exceeds the original issue. cf. *pay-down.*

new rupiah: monetary unit of Indonesia.

New York Clearing House: the oldest and largest check-clearing facility in the United States. see also *clearinghouse.*

New York Clearing House Association (NYCHA): eleven banks of the NYCHA were the first to make use of an automated clearinghouse at the New York Federal Reserve Bank. [105]

New York Coffee and Sugar Exchange: founded in 1882, when it was originally known as the New York Coffee Exchange, it is the principal U.S. exchange for the trading of coffee and sugar futures contracts. see *Commodities Exchange Center.*

New York Curb Exchange: former name for the American Stock Exchange.

New York Dollars: synonymous with *New York Exchange.*

New York Exchange: any check drawn on a commercial bank in New York City. synonymous with *New York Dollars* and *New York Funds.*

New York Funds: synonymous with *New York Exchange.*

New York Futures Exchange: created in 1980, resulting from the absorption of the Amex Commodities Exchange (ACE). The new exchange began with trading futures in Treasury bonds, and contracts in five foreign currencies: British pounds, Canadian dollars, Japanese yen, Swiss francs and West German marks.

New York Insurance Exchange: opened in March 1980, allows insurance brokers to place large business orders with a variety of underwriters on one exchange floor.

New York interest: interest computed by the exact days in a month rather than by use of a 30-day month or other. cf. *Boston interest.*

New York Mercantile Exchange: founded in 1872 as a market for cheese, butter, and eggs, its principal commodities include potatoes, silver coins, and platinum. see *Commodities Exchange Center.*

New York NOW accounts: legislation passed in 1978 permitting FSLIC-insured institutions in New York State to offer NOW accounts. see *NOW account.* [51]

New York plan: an equipment trust arrangement using a conditional sale as the legal device. cf. *Philadelphia plan.*

New York Stock Exchange (NYSE): the largest, most prestigious security exchange in the world, reorganized under its existing name in 1863. In 1817, the New York Stock and Exchange Board moved indoors to a second-floor room at 40 Wall Street in New York City. On January 2, 1863, the title was changed to the New York Stock Exchange, and on the next day, the first subsidiary, the New York Stock Exchange Building Company, was created. see also *NYSE Common Stock Index.*

New York Stock Exchange Averages: a general market indicator comprised of the prices of 25 industrial and railroad stocks. [105]

New York Stock Exchange Composite Index: a weighted average of the prices of all NYSE common stocks. It is followed as a general indication of stock market trends or conditions. [105]

New York Stock Exchange Volume: a measure of the total of all shares traded in a single day on the NYSE. [105]

next day funds: in EFTS, significant funds available for transfer today in like funds, and available for the next business day for same-day funds transfer or withdrawal in cash subject to the settlement of the transaction through the payment mechanism used. [105]

next friend: one who, although not regularly appointed a guardian, acts for the benefit of a minor or incompetent person or, in some instances, a married woman or for any person who, for some legal reason, cannot appear for himself. [37]

next of kin: the person or persons in the nearest degree of blood relationship to the decedent. As the term is usually employed, those entitled by law to the personal property of a person who has died without leaving a valid will (such persons do not include the surviving husband and wife except where specifically so provided by statute); to be distinguished from the heirs, who take the real property. [37]

nexus: a relationship used in tax laws to express a connection between a tax and the activities of the individual or group being taxed. see *tax incidence.*

NF: see *no funds.*

NG: an expression used to designate a check as not good because of insufficient funds. [105]

NGPA: see *Natural Gas Policy Act.*

ngultrum: monetary unit of Bhutan.

NH: see *new high.*

NI
(1) see *national income.*
(2) see *negotiable instrument.*
(3) see *net income.*

(4) see *net interest*.

NIBOR: the New York interbank official rate.

NICs: newly industrializing countries (e.g., Mexico, South Korea, Brazil, and Taiwan).

night depository: a small vault located on the inside of a bank, but accessible to the streetside of the bank. To use this vault, depositors are given a pass-key to the outer door of the night depository vault. When this door is opened, the package of money properly identified by the depositor is dropped down a chute into the night depository vault. This convenience is used by merchants who do not wish the day's receipts to remain in their place of business, and so have this means of protecting their deposits after the regular business hours of the bank. The vault is opened by a bank attendant, and the deposits properly counted and credited to the depositor's account. [10]

NIL: negotiable instruments law. see *negotiable instrument*.

ninety-day savings account: an account paying interest usually equivalent to that paid on 90-day deposits in savings certificates. The account is a passbook account and is subject to substantial interest penalties if funds are withdrawn prior to the end of the 90-day period. If funds are left on deposit after 90 days, the pledge is automatically renewed for an additional period. [105]

NINOW's: non-interest-bearing NOW accounts.

NL

(1) see *net loss*.

(2) see *no-load funds*.

NLF: see *no-load funds*.

NLO: see *no-limit order*.

N&M: November and May (semiannual interest payments or dividends).

NM: see *narrow market*.

NMF: see *nonmember firm*.

NNI: see *net-net income*.

No.: number.

N/O: registered in name of.

No. AC: see *no account*.

no account: a situation when the drawer of a check fails to possess an account in the drawee bank and the drawee returns the check to the presenting bank for credit with a statement reading "no account."

no-book transactions: a transaction that is processed without being entered into the customer's passbook, but for which a temporary receipt is issued. [105]

no funds: a situation when the drawer of a check fails to possess needed funds in the drawee bank and the drawee returns the check to the presenting bank for credit with a statement reading "no funds."

no lien affidavit: a written document by a property owner that the work has been finished on an identified property and that no liens or mortgages encumber it. cf. *lien affidavit*.

no-limit order: a request to buy or sell a security without any stipulation about price. cf. *limited order, market order*.

no-litigation certificate: a statement issued by the bond attorney that there are no legal suits pending (and that as far as he or she knows none is being planned) that might result in an impairment of the validity of the bonds. [105]

no-load funds: mutual funds that are not sold by a salesperson. They do not involve extensive marketing schemes and contain no sales charge or load.

nolo contendere: "I will not contest [it]" (Latin). In a criminal case, a form of guilty plea on the basis of which a sentence may be passed. By pleading, the defendant admits to the facts of the case without admitting his formal guilt of a crime. The plea is most often used when a guilty plea would affect other interests (e.g., a contract, insurance).

nominal
(1) the face value of a bond.
(2) the probable level of a market, but that level is not based on actual transactions.

nominal account: an account established to analyze the changes in the surplus account. These include expense and income accounts which are closed into surplus at the end of each fiscal period. cf. *real accounts*.

nominal asset: an asset whose value is inconsiderable, to be questioned, or difficult to evaluate such as claims or judgments in reorganization. Accounting tradition suggests that nominal assets be written down and carried as some token value, usually one dollar. Copyrights, goodwill and other such assets can be considered nominal assets.

nominal capital: the par value of issued shares of a corporation, as differentiated from the book or market value.

nominal cost: cost measured in monetary units at the time it was incurred, that is, ignoring changes in the purchasing power of money. cf. *real costs*.

nominal effective exchange rate: an effective exchange rate that has not been adjusted for relative inflation differentials. [103]

nominal exchange rate: the mint par of exchange.

nominal income: the dollar value of income. Shifts in nominal income arise from changes in either real income or in price levels.

nominal interest rate: the contractual interest rate shown on the face and in the body of a bond and representing the amount of interest to be paid, in contrast with the effective interest rate. see *coupon rate.* [49]

nominalist: a person who believes that money is the standard money defined by a government.

nominally issued: capital stock, funded debt, and other securities when they are signed and sealed or certified and placed with the proper officer for sale and delivery, or pledged or placed in some special fund of the issuing corporation. [18]

nominally outstanding: securities reacquired by or for the issuing corporation under each circumstance as requires them to be considered as held alive, and not canceled or retired. see *actually outstanding.* [18]

nominal partner: an individual who lends his or her name to a business organization but is not a true partner because he or she may not have given sufficient financial backing or he or she does not take a full share of the profit.

nominal price
(1) *finance:* an amount of money so small in relation to the item purchased that it hardly justifies the use of the word "price." cf. *relative price*.
(2) *investments:* an estimated price for a security or commodity that is not traded often enough to warrant the setting of a definite market price.

nominal quote: the probable price of a security, based on an evaluation of previous prices of a security or similar securities.

nominal rate of exchange: the post rate of exchange, allowing a person to have a sound idea of what the foreign exchange rate is and which is used for small foreign exchange transactions.

nominal value: used in the United Kingdom for face value, or par value. In the United States, this term is equivalent to *par value.* see *par value.* [43]

nominal yield: the rate of return stated on a security calculated on its par or face value.

nomination: the naming or proposal of a person for an office, position, or duty; to be distinguished from appointment. Thus the testator nominates but the court appoints the executor under a will. [32]

nominee: an official of a bank or trust company, or an appointed agent into whose name securities or other funds are transferred by agreement. This is done to facilitate the purchase or sale of securities, when it may be inconvenient to obtain the signature of the principal to make such transfers. It also facilitates the collection and distribution of income from securities when these securities are held in the name of a nominee. Nominee arrangements also apply to custodianships. [10]

nominee (company) name: for purposes of concealment, a stock holding registered in the name of a firm whose sole purpose is to hold stocks.

no more credit: instruction to authorizers that no further credit be allowed a particular customer. [41]

nonaccrual asset: an asset, such as a loan, that has been questioned on bank examination is known to be a "slow" or "doubtful" (of payment) loan.

A reserve is set up or applied on this type of loan, and it is excluded from the earning or accrual assets.

nonassented securities: securities whose holders have not agreed to some change in the terms or status of a defaulted security. cf. *assented securities.*

nonassessable stock: most securities; stock whose owners cannot be assessed in the event of failure or insolvency. cf. *limited liability.*

nonassignable: synonymous with *inalienable.*

nonbank bank loophole: an interpretation of federal law allowing nonbanking companies to open banking offices and commercial banks to open limited service branches across state lines, despite the statutory ban on interstate banking. see also *Garnet St. Germain Depository Institutions Act of 1982.*

nonborrowed reserves: total reserves less member-bank borrowings from reserve banks. [72]

noncallable bond: see *bond, noncallable.*

noncallable securities: stocks that cannot be redeemed prior to maturity, even if the issuing company can afford to do so. They are not subject to call.

noncash charges: accounting allocation costs that are tax deductible but involve no actual cash outlay.

noncash item: any instrument that a bank declines to accept as a cash item, and therefore handles on a collection basis. The customer's account is not credited until settlement for the item takes place. [105]

nonclearinghouse stock: securities that do not clear through the New York Stock Exchange Clearing Corporation, including stocks traded on other exchanges or over the counter.

noncompetitive tender: the submission to a bank when wishing to purchase Treasury bills directly from a Federal Reserve Bank, indicating the willingness to pay the average price of all the competitive offers from large institutions that buy millions of Treasury bills each week. The minimum purchase is $10,000, with multiples of $5000 above that.

non compos mentis: describing an individual not possessing sufficient understanding to comprehend the nature, extent, and meaning of his or her obligations or contracts.

noncontingent preference stock: cumulative preferred stock.

noncontributory: describing a group insurance plan under which the policyholder (employee) pays the entire cost.

Non. Cum.: see *noncumulative.*

noncumulative: a preferred stock on which unpaid dividends do not accrue. Omitted dividends are, as a rule, gone forever. [20]

noncumulative quantity discount: a price reduction that is given based on the size of the individual order placed.

noncupative will: see *nuncupative will.*

noncurrency: the situation that exists when two or more policies provide differing coverages on the same risk. see *double insurance.*

noncurrent: that which is due more than one year after the date of issuance.

noncurrent liabilities: claims against the assets of an entity that will become due a year or more later.

no near bid-offer: where the highest bid or lowest offer is relatively far below or above the price of the previous sale.

nonexempt: a bond exempt from redemption for stated period of time.

nonexpendable disbursements: disbursements that are not chargeable as expenditures; for example, a disbursement made for the purpose of paying off an account payable previously recorded on the books. [49]

nonexpendable fund: the principal, and sometimes also the earnings, of which may not be expended. [49]

nonexpenditure disbursements: disbursements that are not chargeable as expenditures; for example, a disbursement made for the purpose of paying off an account payable previously recorded on the books. [49]

nonfeasance: failure to perform a legal duty. cf. *malfeasance.*

nonfiling insurance: insurance purchased by a lender to protect against any loss that may result from a loan on collateral without properly filing or recording any lien on the collateral. [105]

nonforfeiture options: privileges allowed under terms of a life insurance contract after cash values have been created. Four privileges exist: (a) surrender for full cash value; (b) loans up to the full amount of the cash value; (c) paid-up policy for the amount of insurance that cash value, as a single premium, will buy at net rates; and (d) term insurance for full face amount of the original policy for as long as the cash value will last to pay necessary premiums.

nonguaranteed debt: debt payable solely from pledged specific sources which does not constitute an obligation on any other resources of the government if the pledged sources are insufficient. [70]

nonindexed bond: see *bond, nonindexed.*

noninstallment credit: credit granted, with payment to be made in a lump sum, at a future date.

noninsured fund: pension or other fund invested through channels other than deposit with an insurance company. [22]

non-interest-bearing note: a note whose maker does not have to pay any interest.

noninvestment property: property that will not yield income.

nonledger asset: assets not carried in the general ledger, such as accrued dividends, uncollected and deferred premiums, and excess of market value of securities over book value. [42]

nonlegal investment: an investment that is outside the classes designated by statute or by some governmental agency as proper for the investment of trust funds. [37]

nonlegals: securities that do not conform to the requirements of the statutes, in certain states, concerning investments for savings banks and for trust funds; opposed to *legals*. see *legal list.* [67]

nonmarketable liabilities of U.S. goverment (including medium-term securities): other medium-term securities include foreign holdings of nonmarketable, medium-term U.S. government securities, payable before maturity only under special conditions. Examples of these are nonconvertible "Roosa Bonds" issued by the Treasury, and Certificates of Participation representing Export-Import Bank loans sold mainly to foreign governments and central banks. [73]

nonmember bank: U.S. banks that are not members of the Federal Reserve System. These institutions are either state or private banks.

nonmember firm: any brokerage firm that is not a member of the New York Stock Exchange. Usually such houses sell securities in the third market, often at lower fees than those charged by New York Stock Exchange members. see *member firm.*

nonmerchantable title: an unmarketable title that is legally unsound because it shows property defects. see *cloud on title.*

nonmonetary transactions: any transaction posted to an account which does not have a dollar value affecting the account balance. Changes to cardholder master file records, such as name changes, address changes, and changes of credit limit are nonmonetary transactions. [105]

nonmortgage loan: an advance of funds not secured by a real estate mortgage. [59]

nonnegotiable: wanting in one of the requirements of a negotiable instrument, and as a consequence not entitled to the benefits of negotiability, such as freedom from many defenses that could otherwise be raised by the maker (e.g., fraudulent inducement). A nonnegotiable document is transferable by assignment. To prevent transfer, the label "nontransferable" should be used.

nonnegotiable title: a title that cannot be transferred by delivery or by endorsement.

nonnotification loan: a loan made by a bank or commercial finance company on the security of accounts receivable. The original debtor is not notified that the account has been pledged; the loan is made with recourse, that is, if an account receivable is not paid, the borrower still remains liable for the amount loaned against the receivable.

nonnotification plan
(1) an indirect lending arrangement where a dealer's customer is not informed that his or her installment sales contract has been sold to the bank and the customer continues to make payments to the dealer.
(2) the act of pledging accounts receivable as loan security without notifying the account customers. [105]

nonoperating expense: the outlays and losses of a savings association that are nonrecurring in nature and that do not result from the ordinary savings and lending operations of the institution, such as the expense of maintaining real estate owned or a loss taken on the sale of a nonmortgage investment. [59]

nonoperating income: the receipts and profits of a savings association that are nonrecurring in nature and that do not result from the ordinary savings and lending operations of the institution, such as a profit on the sale of a nonmortgage investment. synonymous with *nonrecurring income*. [59]

non-par bank: see *non-par item*.

non-par item: a check that cannot be collected at the par or face value when presented by another bank. All checks drawn on member banks of the Federal Reserve System, and nonmember banks that have met the requirements of the Federal Reserve System, are collectible at par. Some nonmember banks in certain regions of the United States levy an exchange charge against the check presented for collection and payment. These banks are called non-par banks, and deduct the exchange charge when remitting the payment to the bank requesting collection and payment. see *par list.* [10]

nonpayment: the failure to pay as agreed. [28]

nonperformance: the failure of a contracting party to provide goods or services according to an agreement.

nonperformer: a nonperforming loan.

nonperforming loans: loans that are in trouble; loans where the lender's management judges that the borrower fails to have the ability to fulfill the original contractual terms of the loan or where payments of interest or principal are overdue by 90 days or more. cf. *default*.

nonpossessory estate: see *future estate*.

nonprice competition: applied to markets in which a seller maneuvers for influence on the basis of special aspects of the items to be sold, promotion, or marketing strategy. Most larger organizations avoid price competition by emphasizing nonprice marketing forces.

nonprofit corporation: see *not-for-profit*.

nonrecourse loan: the type of loan that the government makes to farmers under its price-support program. In the event the farmer defaults on the loan, the government has no recourse against the farmer if the security the farmer has put up (his or her crop) fails to bring the amount of the loan when sold.

nonrecurring charge: any cost, expense, or involuntary loss that will not, it is felt, be likely to occur again.

nonrecurring income: synonymous with *nonoperating income.*

nonrefundable: bonds ineligible, during a given period, for redemption with funds raised through the sale of an issue having a lower interest cost.

nonresidential mortgage loan: a mortgage loan secured by nonresidential property such as an office building, store, factory, or church. [59]

nonresident-owned (NRO) funds: open-end investment companies, notably in Canada, the shares of which are sold to U.S. investors.

nonrevenue receipts: collections, other than revenue, such as receipts from loans where the liability is recorded in the fund in which the proceeds are placed and receipts on account of recoverable expenditures. see also *revenue receipts.* [49]

nonstandard payment: any amount of payment other than the exact contract payment. see *standard payment.* [55]

nonstarred card: generally indicates that purchases under $50 do not require an authorization. [105]

nonstock corporation: one type of nonprofit corporation in which the members hold no stock. Among these are religious, charitable, mutual insurance, and municipal corporations.

nonstock money corporation: any corporation operating either under the banking law or the insurance law which does not issue stock (e.g., mutual savings banks, credit unions, mutual insurance companies).

nonsufficient funds: a term indicating that a check or item drawn against an account is in excess of the account balance. [105]

nonsuit: a court judgment against the plaintiff when he or she is unable to prove the case or for failure to continue with the trial once it has commenced.

nontariff barriers (NTB): factors, other than tariffs, inhibiting international trade (e.g., customs, advance deposits on import payments).

nontaxable income: incomes that are not liable to income tax.

nontaxable securities: securities having some tax-exempt features, the most common being the exemption for holders of municipal securities when filing their income taxes.

nonvalidating stamp: the stamp that banks place on the back of domestic drafts accompanying bills of lading which removes the bank from certain liability. The stamp words state that the bank is not responsible, nor does it guaranty the documents stamped.

nonvoting stock: securities of any class within a firm other than voting stock. They cannot be listed by the New York Stock Exchange. see *listing requirements.*

no-par value: having no face value.

no-par-value stock: stock of a corporation without designated par value.

no-passbook savings: the same as a regular passbook savings account, except that no passbook is used. Deposits and withdrawal slips are receipted by the teller, with a copy returned to the depositor for personal records. A periodic statement is rendered in place of a passbook. Withdrawals must be made by the depositor personally.

no protest: instructions given by one bank to another collecting bank not to object to items in case of nonpayment. The sending bank stamps on the face of the item the letters "NP." If the item cannot be collected, the collecting bank returns the item without objecting.

no record: the report given to a credit grantor by a credit bureau when no record exists in the bureau files regarding a particular customer. [41]

normal good: an item whose consumption changes directly with money income, where prices remain constant (e.g., consumer goods). synonymous with *superior good*.

normal lending territory: synonymous with *regular lending area*.

normal price: the price to which the market price tends to return following fluctuations up or down.

normal profit: the lowest price that an entrepreneur will accept as compensation for his or her activity. It is part of an organization's total economic costs, since it is a payment that must be received by the owner to keep him from withdrawing capital and effort that might have to be used in another way.

normal return: the income on a specific investment, computed at a standard interest rate. [105]

normal sale: a transaction that pleases both the seller and buyer of property and in which no unforessen or abnormal situations surface.

normal value: the price or a property commanded on the open market.

nostro account: "our" account; an account maintained by a bank with a bank in a foreign country. Nostro accounts are kept in foreign currencies of the country in which the monies are held, with the equivalent dollar value listed in another column. cf. *vostro account*.

nostro overdraft: part of the bank's statement indicating that it has sold more foreign bills of exchange than it has bought, resulting in the domestic bank's owing currencies to foreign banks in the amount of the nostro (our) overdraft.

not a delivery: when an instrument or document does not meet the requirements of an exchange and contains a fault.

notarial acknowledgment: the acknowledgment of the due execution of a legal instrument before a notary public. The statement of the notary public as to the face and date of the acknowledgment, with the notary public's signature and seal of office and date of expiration of commission to serve as notary public. [37]

notarial certificate: the certificate of the notary public as to the due acknowledgment of the instrument. [37]

notarial protest certificate: see *notice of dishonor (protest jacket).*

notarized draft: a withdrawal order signed and acknowledged before a notary public, who affirms that the person who signed the draft personally appeared before him or her, was known to be the person indicated, and executed the draft for the purpose indicated. [39]

notary public: a person commissioned by a state for a stipulated period (with the privilege of renewal) to administer certain oaths and to attest and certify documents, thus authorizing him or her to take affidavits and depositions. A notary is also authorized to "protest" negotiable instruments for nonpayment or nonacceptance. see *notice of dishonor (protest jacket).*

notch problem: the situation arising when tax rates increase progressively and a single rate is applied to the entire taxable amount. This problem is avoided by the bracket system applying different rates to different ranges rather than to the total.

note: an instrument, such as a promissory note, which is the recognized legal evidence of a debt. A note is signed by the maker, called the borrower, promising to pay a certain sum of money on a specified date at a certain place of business, to a certain business, individual, or bank, called the lender.

note broker: see *bill broker*.

note liability: the liability that a Federal Reserve Bank has for the notes it has outstanding.

note loan: the classification of an unsecured loan. [55]

note notice: a form made and used by the loan department of a bank. The note notice contains all information as to the amount: due date, maker's name and address, securities pledged, if any, and so on. It is mailed to the borrower several days before the maturity of the note, as a reminder of the due date of the note. If the bank is posting the "liability ledger" by machine, the "loans made register," customer's liability ledger card, note notice, and maturity tickler are all created in one posting operation. [10]

note of hand: any promissory note.

note payable: a liability, evidenced by a formal written promise to pay a specified sum at a fixed future date. Notes may be either short (one year or less) or long term.

note payable register: a special book where detailed records of all notes and acceptances payable are recorded.

note receivable: a promissory note collected by a business from a customer.

note receivable register: a special book where detailed records of all notes and acceptances receivable are recorded.

note teller: synonymous with *loan teller.*

not-for-profit: describes an activity of an organization established with the sole goal of providing service for society rather than for the purpose of making a profit. see *eleemosynary*.

not held: a customer's instructions accompanying a market order to a broker, giving the broker some discretion over the execution and relieving him or her of any responsibility if he or she temporarily misses the market.

notice account: a passbook savings account on which the customer agrees to give the association specified notice before making a withdrawal. As long as he gives the agreed notice, his funds earn at a higher interest rate than that paid on passbook accounts; insufficient notice for a withdrawal may incur a penalty. [59]

notice day: the day on which notices of intention to deliver may be issued.

notice of dishonor (protest jacket): when a "holder in due course" presents an instrument for payment or acceptance by a drawee, and the maker or drawee fails to honor the instrument, the holder in due course gives it to a notary public. The notary public also presents the instrument to the maker or drawee as a legal formality. If the maker or drawee again dishonors the instrument by refusing to pay for or to accept it, the notary public prepares a "notice of dishonor," or in the terminology of some states, a "mandate of protest" or a "notarial protest certificate." cf. *acceptance for honor.*

notice of intention to deliver: a certificate supplied by a short seller indicating his or her intention to fulfill his or her contract obligation by delivering the actual commodity.

notice of protest: a declaration made and witnessed by a notary public, stating that a check, bill of exchange, or note has been presented and payment has been refused. [105]

notice of withdrawal: a notice that may be required by a mutual savings bank or other recipient of savings deposits before a withdrawal of funds is permitted. The length of time required before the notice becomes effective varies in the several states. [39]

notice price: the fixed price at which futures deliveries are invoiced.

notice to creditors: the notice in writing by posting in public places or by notice in newspapers to creditors of an estate to present their claims for what the executor or administrator owes them; it usually is also a notice to debtors to come in and pay what they owe the estate. [37]

no-ticket savings plan: a variation of the "unit-savings plan" whereby the normal savings account transaction, either deposit or withdrawal, is accomplished without the use of either a deposit ticket or a withdrawal slip. A deposit is recorded just as in the unit-savings plan, but the depositor is not required to make out a deposit ticket under this machine-printed entry plan. In place of a withdrawal slip, the depositor merely writes his or her signature on the same line as the machine-printed entry of withdrawal. As in the unit savings plan, the passbook, ledger card, and lock-protected audit tape are posted in original printing in one operation directly in front of the depositor, who is the "auditor" of the transaction. [10]

notification plan: the act of pledging accounts receivable as loan security, and notifying the customers maintaining the accounts receivable of such action. The payments on the accounts are then usually sent directly to the party making the loan. [105]

noting a bill: the notation on a bill of exchange by a notary public after presentation of the bill protesting its nonpayment. The notation consists of the date, notary's initials, reason for nonpayment, and the notary's charges.

not subject to call: those bonds or notes that cannot be paid off and retired prior to their maturity date. cf. *callable.*

novation

(1) *general:* the replacement of a new debt or obligation for an older one. see *open-end mortgage;* cf. *renewal, standstill agreement.*

(2) *finance:* the replacement of a new creditor or debtor for a former creditor (or debtor).

NOW (negotiable order of withdrawal) account: a savings account from which the account holder can withdraw funds by writing a negotiable order of withdrawal (NOW) payable to a third party. [59] Until January 1, 1980 NOW accounts were available only in New England, New York, and New Jersey. Effective with new federal regulations, all savings and loans as well as banks, for the first time nationally, are allowed to offer interest-bearing checking accounts (NOW accounts). see also *super-NOW.*

NP

(1) see *net position*.

(2) see *net profit*.

(3) see *no protest*.

(4) see *notary public*.

(5) see *note payable*.

NPVS: see *no-par-value stock*.

NR: see *note receivable*.

NRO funds: see *nonresident-owned funds*.

NS: see *net surplus*.

NSE: see *National Stock Exchange*.

NSF: not sufficient funds.

NTB: see *nontariff barriers*.

NT Dollar: monetary unit of China (Taiwan).

nudge: see *Operation Twist (Nudge)*.

nudum pactum: "an empty promise" (Latin); a statement for which no consideration has been given.

nuisance tax

(1) *government:* any tax the revenue from which does not justify the inconvenience to a person subject to the tax.

(2) *government:* a tax that yields a low return following deduction of the costs of handling and administration.

nullification of agreement: setting aside the terms of an agreement. cf. *repudiation*.

numbered account: a bank account where the owner is identified only by a number so as to preserve anonymity.

numéraire: in dealing with multiple exchange and to avoid the special problems raised by the peculiar characteristics of money (such as liquidity), the particular commodity chosen as a standard of value.

numerical control: programming equipment by means of coded num-bers, stored on magnetic tapes or cards, according to the needs of different items.

numerical transit system: see *American Bankers Association number*.

numeric character: any allowable digit in a machine's number system.

numismatic: pertaining to coins and the collection of coins and medals.

nuncupative will: a will given orally before witnesses, which is reduced to writing at a later time.

nursery finance: institutional loans to profitable organizations that plan to go public shortly. see *adventure, risk capital, venture capital*.

NVS: see *nonvoting stock*.

NW: see *net worth*.

NWC: see *net working capital*.

NY: see *net yield*.

NYCE: see *New York Curb Exchange*.

NYCHA: see *New York Clearing House Association*.

NYFE: see *New York Futures Exchange*.

NYSE: see *New York Stock Exchange*.

NYSE Common Stock Index: a composite index covering price movements of all common stocks listed on the "Big Board." It is based on the close of the market December 31, 1965, as 50.00 and is weighted according to the number of shares listed for each issue. The index is computed continuously and printed on the ticker tape each half-hour. Point changes in the index are converted to dollars and cents, to provide a meaningful measure of changes in the average price of listed stocks. The composite index is supplemented by separate indices for four industry groups: industrials, transportation, utilities, and finances. cf. *Dow Jones averages*. [20]

O&A: October and April (semiannual interest payments or dividends).

OA
(1) see *open account.*
(2) see *operational analysis.*

OAPEC: see *Organization of Arab Petroleum Exporting Countries.*

OASI: see *old-age and survivors' insurance.*

OB
(1) see *bond, obligation.*
(2) see *operating budget.*

object: as used in expenditure classification, this term applies to the article purchased or the service obtained (as distinguished from the results obtained from expenditures). Examples are personal services, contractual services, materials, and supplies. [49]

object classification: a grouping of expenditures on the basis of goods or services purchased; for example, personal services, materials, supplies, and equipment. [49]

objection to title: a weakness in a title for property, requiring adjustment. see *cloud on title.*

objective indicators: an attempt to find factors affecting changes in the exchange rate—to date unsuccessful. [105]

objective value: the price that an economic good can command in terms of other goods in the market. [44]

objects of expenditure: see *object.*

Oblg.: see *obligation.*

Oblig.: see *obligation.*

obligation: the legal responsibility and duty of the debtor (the obligor) to pay a debt when due, and the legal right of the creditor (the obligee) to enforce payment in the event of default.

obligational authority: legal authorization of an administrative agency to make commitments to spend. The actual funds to be expended must be separately authorized.

obligation bond: see *bond, obligation.*

obligator: synonymous with *obligor.*

obligatory maturity: the compulsory maturity of any bond or note, as distinguished from optional maturity dates or early redemption dates.

475

obligee: a creditor or promisee.

obligor: a debtor or promisor; principal.

OBR: see *Overseas Business Reports.*

obsolete securities: abandoned or defunct corporation securities. Any bond that has matured or been withdrawn.

OBU: see *offshore banking unit.*

obverse: the front or face of a note, as opposed to the reverse or back. It usually bears the value of the note, its date, and the principal vignette. [27]

OC
(1) Office of Commissioner.
(2) see *operating company.*
(3) see *organizational chart.*

OCC: see *Options Clearing Corporation.*

occupational analysis: a descriptive approach for determining the jobs that have common activities, to permit grouping them under a common occupation.

occupational information: information resulting from analysis of questionnaires and other materials (e.g., *Dictionary of Occupational Titles*) that describe the functions and characteristics of specific occupations.

Occupational Safety and Health Act of 1970: federal legislation providing for health and safety standards for individuals in the performance of their labors; created the Occupational Safety and Health Administration (OSHA) of the Department of Labor to set the rules and enforce the laws. OSHA also administers training and education programs on occupational safety and health standards for employers and workers, supervises regional inspections, and issues citations to employers not meeting federal standards.

occupation currency: military cur-

rency introduced to a country by occupying forces. [27]

OCO: see *one-cancels-the-other order.*

OCR: see *optical character recognition.*

Od.
(1) see *overdraft.*
(2) see *overdraw.*
(3) see *overdue.*

OD
(1) see *on demand.*
(2) see *organizational development.*

ODC: see *on-line data capture.*

odd-days' interest: interest earned in closed-end credit transactions which accrues with respect to days that are not part of a regular payment schedule. "Odd days" generally arise in connection with dealer paper (retail installment sales contracts assigned to the bank) when the period before the first payment is either longer or shorter than the interval between the remainder of the payments. [105]

odd lot: an amount of stock less than the established 100-share unit or 10-share unit of trading: from 1 to 99 shares for the greatest majority of issues, 1 to 9 for so-called inactive stocks. see *inactive stock (bond), round lot.* synonymous with *uneven lot.* [20]

odd-lot dealer: a member firm of an exchange that buys and sells odd lots of stock—1 to 9 shares in the case of stocks traded in 10-share units and 1 to 99 shares for 100-share units. The odd-lot dealer's customers are commission brokers acting on behalf of their customers.

odd-lot differential: compensation for an odd-lot broker's services amounting to $1/8$ point ($12^1/2$ cents) per share on securities selling below $55, and ¼ point (25 cents) per share on securities selling above $55. The differential is added to the price of the effective round-lot sale on purchase orders and subtracted from the price of each share on sell orders.

odd-lot house: a brokerage company specializing as a dealer in handling orders from investors for amounts less than 100 shares (round lots). The broker takes positions in the market and draws on his or her own inventory to satisfy demand for stocks.

odd-lot index: a measurement determined by dividing total odd-lot sales by odd-lot purchases on a 10-day moving average. When sales outnumber purchases, this is judged as unfavorable because the public is hesitant to buy. When purchases outnumber sales, the reverse is true.

odd-lot orders: any purchase or sale of stock not in 100-share units. cf. *full lot.*

odd-lot trader: a person who purchases and sells securities in less than 100-share lots, as contrasted by professional investors and others of considerable means who deal in larger, more economical amounts.

OE: see *operating expense.*

OECD: see *Organization for Economic Cooperation and Development.*

OEEC: see *Organization for Economic Cooperation and Development.*

OEF: see *open-end funds.*

OEIC: see *open-end investment company.*

OEIT: see *open-end investment trust.*

OF: see *offshore funds.*

OFCC: see *Federal Contract Compliance Office.*

Ofd.: see *offer(ed).*

off: describes a given day on which the prices of stocks and commodities drop. see also *on.*

off-balance sheet financing: financing that is not clearly displayed on the balance sheet (i.e., some leasing).

off-board: describes over-the-counter transactions in unlisted securities, or a transaction involving listed shares that was not executed on a national securities exchange.

off-budget programs: a miscellany of government programs or agencies whose outlays are by law accounted for outside the budget.

offer(ed)
(1) *general:* to present for acceptance or refusal.
(2) *investments:* the price at which a person is ready to sell. Opposed to bid, the price at which one is ready to buy. [20]

offered ahead: a situation created when an individual who has placed an order to sell at a given price finds that other or lower offers have been given earlier on the same security; these obviously take precedence over his offer.

offered down: securities that are offered for sale at levels lower than the last sale or quoted price of the same stock.

offered firm: a firm offer to sell a stated amount of something at a stated price for a stated time period.

offeree: one to whom an offer has been made.

offering: used to indicate an issue of securities or bonds offered for sale to the public. see *secondary offering, special offering.*

offering book: see *offering list.*

offering list: a document showing the price, amount, and description of the item printed by a seller or dealer.

offering price: the price per share at which investment shares are offered to the public. The offering price usually consists of the net asset value per share plus a sales charge. synonymous with *asked (asking) price.*

offering sheet: see *offering list.*

offering telex: in Euromarkets, a telex sent out to banks offering participation in a bond issue or sometimes a credit.

offeror: one who makes an offer.

offers to sell: see *matched and lost.*

offer wanted: a request made by a buyer for a security for which no apparent market exists. Such a potential buyer is seeking a potential seller. see *bid wanted.*

off-exchange: commodity firms registered with the Commodity Futures Trading Commission that are not members of any of the 10 regulated futures exchanges that keep an eye on the daily operations of their members. In fact, these "off-exchange" houses, in practice, are barely regulated.

off-host: an operating mode in which the terminals do not have access to a positive file at the card-issuing bank. On-line/off-host implies connection to negative files stored in the front-end processor of the card-issuing bank. [105]

Office of Federal Contract Compliance Programs: see *Federal Contract Compliance Office.*

Office of Management and Budget (OMB): a federal agency that prepares the president's budget; with the Council of Economic Advisers and Treasury Department, develops the government's fiscal program; oversees the administration of the federal budget.

Office of the Comptroller of the Currency: the office within the U.S. Treasury Department having the responsibility for overall supervision and examination of national banks. [105]

office paper: see *finance bill.*

officer

(1) *general:* any principal executive of a corporation to whom authority has been delegated, usually by the board of directors.

(2) *banking:* a manager of a primary bank function.

officer's check: synonymous with *cashier's check.*

official check: synonymous with *cashier's check.*

official exchange rate: the ratio that is applied by the monetary authority of one nation in exchanging its money for that of another nation.

off-line computer system: a computer system that processes previously collected data in batches rather than at the time the data are produced. [59]

offset

(1) *general:* either of two equivalent entries on both sides of an account.

(2) *banking:* the right accruing to a bank to take possession of any balances that a guarantor or debtor may have in the bank to cover a loan in default. cf. *garnishment.*

(3) *banking:* a depositor who has both a deposit credit balance and a loan balance is denied the right of offset if the bank becomes insolvent and closes.

offsets to long-term debt: cash and investment assets of sinking funds, bond reserve, and other reserve funds held specifically for the redemption of long-term debt, and assets of credit funds that are pledged to redeem debt incurred to finance loan activities of such funds.

offsets to savings: ways of using liquid savings or creating expenditures that are equal to such use.

offshore banking unit (OBU): a bank in Bahrain, or any other center with similar organizations; not allowed to conduct business in the domestic market, only with other OBUs or with foreign institutions.

offshore funds: as they affect U.S. citizens, mutual funds that have their headquarters outside this country or off its shores. Usually, such funds are not available to Americans but are sold to investors in other parts of the world.

offshore profit centers: branches of major international banks and multinational corporations in Nassau, Bermuda, the Cayman Islands, and other low-tax banking centers as a way of lessening taxes.

off the board: a transaction made over the counter or involving a block of listed securities that were not executed on an organized exchange. synonymous with *off-board*; see *secondary distribution, third market.*

off time: describing a computer that is not scheduled for use, maintenance, alteration, or repair.

of record: as shown by the record; usually employed in such entries as "attorney of record," showing that the one named is the recognized representative of the party at interest. [37]

Ohio Deposit Guarantee Fund: a state-chartered mutual institution in Ohio that insures the savings accounts held by member savings associations and serves as a central credit facility. [59]

OI
(1) see *operating income.*
(2) see *ordinary interest.*

oil drafts: sales drafts used by oil companies. [105]

OJAJ: October, January, April, July (quarterly interest payments or dividends).

OJT: see *on-the-job training.*

ok: correct.

ok packages: a list or package of checks that has been processed in a branch office, proved for accuracy, checked for date and endorsement, and considered OK by the branch office. The total on the package is used at the main office for the final consolidation of totals without the main office having to rerun the items in the package. [10]

OL
(1) see *odd lot.*
(2) see *operating losses.*

old-age and survivors' insurance (OASI): the source of retirement income and other payments made to survivors of those eligible under Social Security legislation.

old and new balance proof: a method of proof used in a bank, especially in savings departments, to prove the correct pickup of old balances, and to establish the net amount of increase or decrease to ledger controls. An adding machine tape, or a columnar journal sheet is used as a permanent record of this proof. All affected ledger cards are sorted by account number, and then run on an adding machine. Generally, the new balances are run in the first column. In the next column, the old balances are run so that the old balances appear opposite the new balances and the old balances must equal the difference in the totals of the deposits and the withdrawals. If these two differences agree, it is proof that the old balance was picked up correctly on every account affected in the day's business. [10]

Old Lady of Threadneedle Street: a popular name for the Bank of England.

oligopoly: an industry in which a small number of producers sell identical products. cf. *monopoly.*

oligopoly price: a price that develops when there is a market of numerous buyers and few sellers, thus resulting in the sellers having the greatest power.

oligopsony: control by a number of buyers, who attempt to influence the demand for a specific commodity.

oligopsony price: a price that develops when there is a market of few buyers and numerous sellers, thus resulting in the buyers having the greatest power.

OLTT: on-line teller terminal.

OM
(1) see *on margin.*
(2) see *open market.*

OMB: see *Office of Management and Budget.*

omnibus account: an account carried by one futures commission merchant with another in which the transactions of two or more persons are combined rather than designated separately and the identity of individual accounts is not disclosed. [2]

Omnibus Banking Bill of 1984: New York State legislation designed to halt mortgage loan losses by state banks and to improve the business climate for New York banking institutions. Also repeals a 20 percent limit on out-of-state lending by state-chartered savings and loan associations.

Omnibus Reconciliation Act of 1980: federal legislation; imposed restrictions on use of mortgage subsidy bonds plus other miscellaneous tax changes.

on: the number of points that a cash commodity is higher than a specified futures month. see also *off.*

on account
(1) *general:* describes a payment made toward the settlement of an account.
(2) *finance:* a purchase or sale made on *open account.*

on a scale: in buying or selling securities: the customer purchases or sells equal amounts of a stock at prices that are spaced by a constant interval, as the market price rises or drops.

on balance
(1) *general:* the net effect or result.
(2) *investments:* the difference between offsetting sales and purchases; for example, if an investor sells 1000 shares of securities, then purchases 2200 shares of the same security, he has purchased 1200 shares on balance.

on-balance volume: an indicator that attempts to pinpoint where futures contracts are being accumulated or bought, and when they are being distributed or sold by controlling market forces, the hedgers, and large traders.

on bid (or offer): a method that an odd-lot trader transacts in a listed stock without waiting for an actual round-lot trade in the security to occur. A transaction is made by selling at the bid price or purchasing at the offering price.

on consignment: items sent to an agent with payment to be made after the sale is made.

on demand: describing a bill of exchange that is payable on presentation. see *demand note.*

one-bank holding company: a corporation that owns control of one commercial bank.

one-cancels-the-other order (OCO): a contingency order in which one part is automatically canceled as soon as the other part is filled.

one-day certificates: authorized by Congress in 1971, the Federal Reserve Banks buy and sell guaranteed obligations of the government directly from or to the United States. By law, these certificates cannot exceed $5 billion.

one-day loans: see *day loan.*

one hundred percent reserve: a banking system that can be substituted for the fractional reserve system. Commercial banks can be required to hold reserves for the full amount of their deposits and would not be able to make loans with any funds except those available from paid-in capital and surplus.

one hundred percent statement: a statement showing the conversion of all the individual items in a balance sheet to a percentage of the total assets.

one-name paper: single-name paper, straight paper. An instrument signed by only one party, individual, or firm, as contrasted with obligations having two or more obligors.

one-stop banking: provided by a bank whose clients can do all banking business at that bank. cf. *full-service bank.*

on-host: an operating mode in which the terminals do have access to a positive file at the card-issuing bank. On-line/ on-host implies connection to positive files stored in the bank's files. [105]

on-line computer system: a computer system that is available at all times for receiving data and making calculations. [59]

on-line data capture (ODC): an input system for bank card dollar entries. [105]

on-line off-host: an operating mode where financial service terminals are accessing only the front-end processor and do not have access to the central computer system containing the data base. Authorization is limited to the files contained in the processor. [105]

on-line on-host: an operating mode where financial service terminals are on-line, with the central computer system interfacing with a front-end processor. [105]

on margin: describes securities purchased when the buyer has borrowed part of the purchase price from the broker.

on opening: used to specify execution of an order during the opening call. [11]

on-the-job training (OJT): using the actual work site as a proper setting to instruct workers while at the same time engaging in productive work.

on-the-spot loan: an extension of funds on a preapproved credit line or credit card. [105]

on-us check: any depositor's check drawn on and payable at the bank wherein the account is carried is termed an "on us" check when presented for payment to the drawee bank. [10]

OO: see *open order.*

ooftish (offtish): slang, money, usually to be used for speculation.

OP

(1) see *offering price.*

(2) see *opening price.*

(3) see *opening purchase.*

(4) see *operating profit.*

Op. D.: delayed opening.

OPEC: see *Organization of Petroleum Exporting Countries.*

open account: credit extended that is not supported by a note, mortgage, or other formal written evidence of indebtedness (e.g., merchandise for which a buyer is billed later). synonymous with *book account.*

open book account: see *open account.*

open charge account: see *charge account.*

open contracts: contracts that have been bought or sold without the transaction having been completed by subsequent sale or repurchase or actual delivery or receipt of the commodity. [11]

open credit: credit that is allowed without immediate proof of a customer's credit worthiness.

open door policy: a condition where citizens and products of foreign countries receive the same treatment as domestic citizens and products. cf. *most favored nation (clause).*

open economy: an economy free of trade restrictions.

open-end bond: see *bond, open-end.*

open-end clause: an optional mortgage clause, used in states that recognize its validity, which provides that the pledge of real estate will cover additional advances of funds that the borrower may request and the lender agrees to grant at unknown times in the

future. Under the terms of this clause, all subsequent advances represent a claim on the property dating from the time of recording of the original mortgage. [59]

open-end credit: a line of credit that may be used repeatedly up to a certain limit. synonymous with *charge account* or *revolving credit.* [1]

open-end funds: mutual funds where new shares of the fund are sold whenever there is a request, with the expectation that the seller will eventually request to buy back the shares, at no additional charge. see *investment company.*

open-end investment company: an investment firm that sells and reclaims its capital stock continuously, selling it at book value, adding a sales charge, and redeeming it at a slight discount or at book value.

open-end investment trust: an investment trust in which the trustee, by the terms of the trust, is authorized to invest in shares of stock other than those in the trust at the time of the inception of the trust or of the participation in the trust. [37]

open-end lease: a lease that may involve an additional payment based on the value of property when returned. [78]

open-end mortgage: a mortgage that permits the borrower to reborrow money paid on the principal up to the original amount.

open fund: an open-end investment firm of mutual fund, so identified because it does not have fixed capitalization. Money is raised by selling its own stock to the public and investing the proceeds in other securities.

open indent: an importer's purchase

order to an exporter, which may be filled with goods from any manufacturer or firm provided that the goods meet specifications. cf. *closed indent.*

open inflation: the situation wherein there is no control of prices and there is an increase in money demand for goods relative to the supply of goods. Shortages are adjusted then by a rise in prices.

opening entry
(1) the entry made to begin a set of books; the entry debiting all existing assets and crediting liabilities, reserves, and capital accounts.
(2) the first entry in an account.

opening price
(1) *general:* the first price given in an auction or sales marketplace.
(2) *investments:* the initial price at which a transaction in a security takes place on every day; the first quoted price of a new stock issue.

opening purchase: a transaction in which an investor becomes the holder of a security or an option.

opening range: commodities, unlike securities, are often traded at several prices at the opening or close of the market. Buying or selling orders at the opening might be filled at any point in such a price range for the commodity. [2]

opening sale: a transaction in which an investor becomes the writer of an option. [5]

open interest: the number of outstanding contracts in the exchange market, or in a particular class or series. synonymous with *indicated interest.*

open letter of credit: an open letter with no restrictions on the presentation of documents such as bills of lading against drafts and is paid simply on a valid draft. see also *letter of credit.*

open market: a general term describing a condition of trading that is not limited to any area or persons.

open-market committee: a committee composed of the Board of Governors of the Federal Reserve System plus the presidents of five of the Federal Reserve District Banks. see *open-market operations.*

open-market credit: short-term financing enabling commercial paper houses to purchase notes and resell them in the open market.

open-market operations: operations carried out by the Federal Reserve System, in which it buys or sells government bonds in the same market other institutional investors use.

open-market paper: bills of exchange or notes drawn by one with high credit standing, made payable to himself or herself and indorsed in blank. These are sold to financial institutions other than banks.

open-market rates: the money rates set for classes of paper in the open market, as distinguished from banks rates offered to customers, and rates for advances and rediscounts set by Federal Reserve Banks for all member banks.

open mortgage: a mortgage that can be paid off, without penalty, at any period prior to its maturity.

open order: an order to buy or sell securities that has not yet been executed. Orders may be placed at market price or at a fixed price. synonymous with *good-'til-canceled order.*

open outcry: see *outcry market.*

open position: a dealer's aggregate assets and liabilities in a currency.

open price association: a trade association that gathers and distributes information about prices and quantities sold.

open price system: the practice of one or more firms in an industry of informing other producers about the prices and trends of their products.

open prospectus: a brochure that aims to obtain financial backing and does not clearly identify the use to be made of the investment.

open to buy: the currently unused portion of a total dollar credit line agreed upon. [28]

open trade: any transaction that has not yet been closed.

operating assets: those assets that contribute to the regular income from the operations of a business. Thus stocks and bonds owned, unused real estate, loans to officers, and so on, are excluded from operating assets.

operating budget: a budget that applies to all outlays other than capital outlays. see *budget.* [49]

operating capital: funds available for use in financing the day-to-day activities of a business. [105]

operating company: a company whose officers direct the business of transportation and whose books contain operating as well as financial accounts. [18]

operating costs: costs of maintenance, utilities, office equipment, salaries, and such required to keep a business operational.

operating earnings before taxes: see *net earnings.*

operating expense

(1) *general:* actual expense incurred in the maintenance of property (e.g., management, repairs, taxes, in-

surance); not included as operating expenses are mortgage payments, depreciation, and interest paid out.

(2) *finance:* any expense incurred in the normal operation of a business. This is to be distinguished from expenditures, which are disbursements that are capitalized and depreciate over a period of years. see *margin of profit.*

operating income

(1) *general:* income to a business produced by its earning assets and by fees for services rendered.

(2) *finance:* rental monies obtained from the operation of a business or from property.

operating income as percent of net interest income: net operating income before securities gains and losses, divided by total interest income, minus total interest expense, minus provision for loan losses.

operating lease: a lease where the asset is not wholly amortized during the obligatory period of the lease, and where the lessor does not rely for his or her profit on the rentals in the obligatory period.

operating losses: losses incurred in the normal (i.e., nonnegligent) operation of a business.

operating officer: the officer who heads up an operating department in a large bank. He or she is in complete charge of the operations of his or her department. A distinction is to be made between an operating officer and the other officials, such as the vice-presidents, who are specialists in their fields. The cashier of the bank can be considered the senior operating officer in charge of the overall operations of the bank in its routine work. The vice-presidents are specialists in the fields of loans, credits, investments, and trusts. In smaller banks, it is not uncommon for vice-presidents to be in charge of certain operations as well as being specialists in their field. Any decision regarding the operation of a department is usually left to the operating officer in charge of the department. His or her recommendations regarding personnel requirements, equipment purchases, type and quantity of supplies used, and so on, carry great weight with higher officials. [10]

operating profit: profit arising from the regular operation of an enterprise engaged in performing physical services (e.g., public utilities), excluding income from other sources and excluding expenses other than those of direct operation. [62]

operating profit (for purposes of marketing): gross margin (gross profit), less operating expenses (including salaries of managers, whether proprietors or employees), fixed plant and equipment cost, and sometimes interest on invested capital. [13]

operating profit ratio: the ratio of a firm's operating profit to its net sales. see *turnover ratio.*

operating ratio: total of expenses of operation divided by total of operating revenues. Usually, this includes only the ratio of (a) cost of goods sold plus selling, administrative, and general expenses to (b) net sales.

operating reserves: a group of balance sheet accounts reflecting the net accumulated balances provided for property insurance, injuries and damages, pensions and benefits, and amortization. [3]

operating return: operating income before income taxes and depreciation and amortization expense. [3]

operating statement: a statement providing net sales, costs, expenses, and the net operating profit or loss for a fixed period.

operating surplus: the remaining profit after deducting all operating costs of the business over a given time period. Items such as interest on capital and indebtedness are not deducted prior to determining the operating surplus.

operating system: software that controls the execution of computer programs and that may provide scheduling, debugging, input/output control, accounting, compilation, storage assignment, data management, and related services. [34]

operation

(1) *general:* any process or action that is part of a series in work.

(2) *computer:* the act specified by a single computer instruction.

(3) *computer:* a defined action of obtaining a result from one or more operands in accordance with a rule that completely specifies the result for any permissible combination of operands.

operational analysis (OA): a form of industrial engineering that separates work into activities and designs the work flow to construct the most efficiently scheduled sequences of output. synonymous with *operations research.* cf. *MAPS.*

operational control: the influence by management over the inputs and activities in the daily performances in a firm.

operations analysis: a system of analyzing specific savings association operations in order to establish norms, appraise efficiency, improve operations, and reduce costs accrued. [59]

operations manager: individual responsible for the operational phases of a bank card plan, including accounting, sales draft auditing, and statement preparation. [105]

operations research (OR): the application of scientific methods, techniques, and tools to problems involving the operation of a system, to provide those in control of the system with optimum solutions to the problems. see *cost-benefit analysis*; cf. *organizational analysis and planning.*

Operation Twist (Nudge): in 1961 the Federal Reserve and the U.S. Treasury attempted to raise short-term interest rates relative to long-term rates to harmonize domestic and foreign objectives. Bank time-deposit interest rates were increased, and funds were redirected from short- to long-term goals.

operator: slang, any person who makes a career in speculation on the prices of securities or commodities.

OPIC: see *Overseas Private Investment Corporation.*

opinion of title: legal opinion stating that title to property is clear and marketable; serves the same purpose as a certificate of title. [62]

OPM
(1) operations per minute.
(2) other people's money.

opportunity cost: a maximum alternative profit that could have been obtained if the productive good, service, or capacity had been applied to some other use.

opportunity cost of capital: the expected rate of return from effectively employing funds in the company.

Opt.: see *option.*

optical character recognition (OCR): the machine identification of printed characters through the use of light-sensitive devices. cf. *magnetic ink character recognition.*

optical reader: a device that interprets handwritten or machine-printed symbols into a computing system.

optical scanner: a device that scans optically and usually generates an analog or digital signal.

optimum capacity: the quantity of output that permits the minimum cost per unit to be incurred.

option
(1) *general:* a privilege to buy or sell, receive, or deliver property, given in accordance with the terms stated, with a consideration for price. This privilege may or may not be exercised at the option holder's discretion. Failure to exercise the option leads to forfeiture.
(2) *banking:* the right of an insured or a beneficiary to select the form of payment of the proceeds of an insurance contract.
(3) *investments:* an agreement, often for a consideration, to buy or sell a security or commodity within a stipulated time in accordance with the agreement. see *puts and calls*; cf. *covered option, straddle.*

option account: a charge account in which the consumer may choose either to pay at the end of 30 days or to spread payments over a longer period of time. If he or she chooses to spread payments beyond 30 days, he or she pays a service charge. [40]

optional bond: see *bond, callable.*

optional (revolving) credit: a regular open or 30-day charge account to which the customer has requested to have the "option" added. That is, he may pay the whole balance within 15 or 20 days of receipt of his bill (when there will be no credit service charge) or may pay any portion of it that is convenient. Then on any amount not paid by the time the next bill is made out (which would be after the 15- to 20-day period following the first bill), a charge of 1 percent, of $1\frac{1}{2}$ percent, or the like is added. As in other revolving credit plans, this charge would not be applied to purchases or additions in the then-current month but just to the sum left unpaid from the last billing. [28]

optional date: the date at which a municipality or corporation has the right to redeem its obligations under certain conditions.

optional dividend: the stockholder has the choice of receiving either a stock dividend or a cash dividend.

optional payment bond: see *bond, optional payment.*

optional valuation date: the date on which the size of an individual's estate is computed for purposes of tax payment. It can be set at the date of death or as of six months following death, provided the assets are not disposed of in the interim.

option contract
(1) a contract in foreign exchange to deal in foreign exchange, wherein the date of completion of the deal, but not its existence, is at the customer's choice with a specified period.
(2) in the securities market, buying an option that gives the choice of dealing in the securities at a certain price prior to a certain date. This differs from the foreign exchange option in that the deal itself, rather than its date, is optional.

option day: the specified date when an option expires unless exercised.

optionee: the holder of an option; a prospective buyer.

optioner: any property owner.

option income fund: the investment objective of these funds is to seek a high current return by investing primarily in dividend-paying common stocks on which call options are traded on national securities exchanges. Current return generally consists of dividends, premiums from expired call options, net short-term gains from sales of portfolio securities on exercises of options or otherwise, and any profits from closing purchase transactions. [23]

Options Clearing Corporation: the issuer of all options contracts on the American Stock Exchange. [5]

option spreading: the simultaneous purchase and sale of options within the same class. The options may be either at the same striking prices with different expiration months, or at different striking prices with the same or different expiration months. The spread is the dollar difference between the buy and sell premiums.

option writer: see *puts and calls.*

OR
(1) see *operating reserves.*
(2) see *operations research.*

oral will: see *nuncupative will.*

order
(1) *general:* a request to deliver, sell, receive, or purchase goods or services.
(2) *finance:* identifying the one to whom payment should be made: "Made to the order of."
(3) *investments:* a request to buy

or sell. see *buy, day order, discretionary order, limited order, open order, stop order.*

order bill of lading: a negotiable bill of lading stating that goods are to be delivered to the person named on the bill or to his or her order upon indorsement. cf. *straight bill of lading.*

ordering bank: the bank that instructs the sender to execute the transaction. [105]

ordering bank identifier: a code that uniquely identifies the ordering bank. [105]

ordering bank identifier type: a code that specifies the type of ordering bank identifier used. [105]

ordering bank name and addresss: identifies the ordering bank by name and, optionally, the ordering bank's postal address. [105]

order instrument: a negotiable instrument containing the words "pay to the order of . . ." or "pay to (the name of payee) or order," requiring endorsement and delivery prior to negotiation.

order of distribution: an order by a probate or other court having jurisdiction of an estate directing distribution of estate property to persons or others entitled thereto. [37]

order paper: in dealing with negotiable instruments, an instrument is called *order paper* when it is in such form as to require indorsement by the payee or indorsee. *Order paper* can be converted to *bearer paper* by a blank indorsement. cf. *bearer paper.*

order party: party instructing the sender to execute the transaction. [105]

order room: the department of a brokerage house responsible for transmitting buy and sell orders to and receiving reports of executions from the stock exchange trading floor.

orders
(1) *general:* requests made for the delivery of goods or services.
(2) *investments:* instructions to a broker to buy or sell shares.

orders good until a specified time: a market or limited price order that is to be represented in the "trading crowd" until a specified time, after which such order or the portion not executed is treated as canceled. cf. *good-'til-canceled order.* [20]

ordinary asset: an asset that is bought and sold as a regular component of a continuing business activity. What may be an ordinary asset to one firm may be a capital asset to another. A real estate broker selling property would be selling an ordinary asset, whereas a retailer would be selling a capital asset if he sold land.

ordinary discount: the difference between the value at maturity and the present value which at an assumed rate of interest will accumulate to the value of maturity.

ordinary gain (or loss): gain or loss realized from the sale or exchange of property that is not a capital asset, such as inventory.

ordinary income: in income tax filing, reportable income that does not qualify as capital gains.

ordinary interest: interest that is calculated based on 360 days to the year.

ordinary life: a type of insurance policy continuing in force throughout the policyholder's lifetime and payable on his or her death or when he or she attains a specified age. synonymous with *straight life* and *whole life insurance.*

ordinary shares: British term for the

junior stock issue of a corporation, similar to common stock in the United States.

ordinary stock: common or equity stock.

ordinary voting: the stockholder under this principle is entitled to one vote for each voting share and directors are elected one at a time. cf. *cumlative voting.*

organic structure: an organization design characterized by a decentralized hierarchy, flexible work procedures, and democratic leadership, with informal and open communications. cf. *organization, formal.*

organization: any structured system of roles and functional relationships designed to carry out a firm's policies, or more precisely, the programs such policies inspire.

organization, formal: a highly structured organization with little flexibility in the delegation of authority and assignment of tasks and responsibilities.

organization, informal: a flexibly structured organization, free of rigid rules for governing its activity and authority. synonymous with *organic structure.*

organizational analysis and planning: the study of the objectives, the surroundings, and the human, physical, and financial assets of a business to determine the most effective design for using the creative ideas and power generated by the firm's ultimate authority toward the accomplishment of its stated goals.

organizational chart: a graphic presentation of the relationships and interrelationships within an organization, identifying lines of authority and responsibility.

organizational climate: a set of properties of the work environment perceived by employees and assumed to be a major factor in influencing their behavior.

organizational development (OD): a planned process of reeducation and training designed by administrative personnel to facilitate adaption to demands placed on the environment of the company. see *multiple management.*

organization certificate: in the formation of a bank, one of the statements that must be filed, usually with the Comptroller of the Currency.

organization expense: direct costs when forming a new corporation (incorporation fees, taxes, legal fees, etc.).

Organization for Economic Cooperation and Development (OECD): created in 1948, an organization of 17 European nations (including the German Federal Republic) and known until 1960 as the Organization for European Economic Cooperation. Initially, OEEC developed and implemented economic recovery programs following World War II. It was enlarged to 24 members, including the United States, Canada, and Japan, with the changing of its name to OECD. Headquartered in Paris, it promotes the economic growth of member nations, the expansion of world investment and trade, and the economic development of emerging countries.

Organization for European Economic Cooperation (OEEC): see *Organization for Economic Cooperation and Development.*

Organization of Arab Petroleum Exporting Countries (OAPEC): includes members of OPEC less

Ecuador, Gabon, Indonesia, Iran, Nigeria, and Venezuela, plus Bahrain, Egypt, and Syria; aids in setting international oil prices and acts as liaison between the Arab oil states and other Arab nations, see also *Organization of Petroleum Exporting Countries.*

Organization of Petroleum Exporting Countries (OPEC): the group's 13 members are concentrated in the Middle East but also include countries in Africa, South America, and the Far East. By virtue of their large exports, Saudi Arabia and Iran have been the most powerful influences. see also *petrodollars.*

organized exchange: the place where goods or property rights are bought and sold according to recognized rules. Examples are stock and bond exchange, grain, butter, sugar, and other exchanges.

organized market: a group of traders, operating under recognized rules, for the purpose of buying and selling a single commodity or a small number of related commodities—for example, the Chicago Board of Trade. [13]

original asset: stocks, bonds, or other property received in a trust at the time of its creation, or an estate at the time of appointment of the executor or administrator. [37]

original balance: the beginning debt or obligation before any payment has been made on it to reduce it. [28]

original cost: the actual cost of construction or acquisition, or, in other words, the actual original cost of property to the carrier at the time of its dedication to public use. [18]

original investment: an investment received by the trustee as part of the de-

cedent's estate or from the settlor of a living trust. [32]

original issue discount: debt instruments that are originally sold at less than par but which return par at maturity, with the interest paid being equal to the discount.

original (originally) issue (issued) stock: securities initially issued at the time the corporation was established and which are part of the starting capitalization.

original margin: margin required at the onset of a transaction. [11]

original-package doctrine: a Supreme Court ruling that commodities in foreign or interstate commerce which were not removed from the containers in which they had been imported or shipped interstate were not subject to the taxing power or police regulations of the states. The doctrine has been modified pertaining to alcoholic beverages and items made by convict labor.

originating bank: a bank that receives paperless entries from participating business entries in an automated clearinghouse system and which forwards the entries to the Automated Clearing House. [105]

origination fee: a charge made for initiating and processing a mortgage loan.

originator: the banking house or individual investment banker who is the first to promote a proposed new issue for a corporation.

originator identifier: a code that uniquely identifies the originator to the originator's bank. [105]

originator identifier type: a code that specifies the type of identifier used in the originator identifier field. [105]

originator name and address: identifies the originator by name and, optionally, the originator's postal address. [105]

originator's bank: a bank that acts as the financial agent for the originator of a transfer. [105]

originator's reference: originator's transaction reference which identifies the original transaction in a transfer. [105]

originator to beneficiary information: information conveyed from the originator to the beneficiary. [105]

orphan's court: in many states the court that has jurisdiction over matters pertaining to the settlement of estates and sometimes over guardianships and trusts. [37]

O&S: see *over and short account.*

OS: see *option spreading.*

OS&D: see *over, short, and damaged.*

OSHA: see *Occupational Safety and Health Act of 1970.*

ostensible partner: a person openly recognized by the public as a partner.

OTB: see *off the board.*

OTC: see *over the counter.*

other income: a general heading on the income statement under which are grouped revenues from miscellaneous operations, income from the lease of road and equipment, miscellaneous rent income, income from nonoperating property, profit from separately operated properties, dividend income, interest income, income from sinking and other reserve funds, release of premiums on funded debt, contributions from other companies, miscellaneous income, and delayed income credits. [18]

other liabilities and accrued dividends: miscellaneous liabilities plus dividends accrued but unpaid on Fed-

eral Reserve Bank stock owned by the member banks. [40]

other loans: mostly loans to individuals, except farmers, for consumption purposes. [40]

other loans for purchasing or carrying securities: loans to other than brokers and dealers for the purpose of purchasing or carrying securities.

other long-term debt: long-term debt other than mortgage bonds and debentures. This includes serial notes and notes payable to banks with original maturity of more than one year. [3]

other real estate: synonymous with *owned real estate.*

other securities: all securities other than U.S. government obligations—that is, state, municipal, and corporate bonds. (Member banks are generally not permitted to invest in stocks other than Federal Reserve bank stock). [40]

ouguiya: monetary unit of Mauritania.

"our" account

(1) a term used by bank personnel in reference to their due from (nostro) account. see also *nostro account.*

(2) in EFTS, when used in funds transfer messages, the account "due to" the sending bank.

outbid: to offer a higher price for an item than that offered by other bidders.

out card: a card substituted for a ledger card when the latter is removed from the file. The out card should contain the balance, the date the ledger card was removed, by whose authority, and the person in whose possession the ledger card is held. There are occasions when ledger cards must be removed from the ledger trays for reference—for example, when a borrower who is already borrowing funds from the bank requests a large loan.

The ledger card is the record that must be used to review the borrower's use of credit, how the loans in the past were liquidated, and when the customer last completely liquidated his borrowings. This information supplements other available credit information held by the bank and is used by the loan committee in arriving at decisions. [10]

outcry market: commodity tradings by private contract that must be shouted out, as on the floor of an exchange, in order that the agreement be recorded. synonymous with *open outcry*.

outgo: slang, any expense or other cost in running a business.

outgoing interchange: transactions deposited with an acquiring bank and sent to an issuing bank. [105]

outlawed: promissory note debarred by the statute of limitations of actions. [105]

outlays
(1) *general:* any expenditures.
(2) *government:* disbursements or spending either for the government as a whole or for a particular department or function, such as health care.

out-of-area card: synonymous with *foreign card.*

out of line: a stock whose price is determined to be either too low or too high. This is often determined by noting the corporation's price-earnings ratio.

out-of-plan: a bank card issued by another bank or to a transaction originating at a merchant affiliated with another bank or bank card association [105]

out-of-plan card: synonymous with *foreign card.*

out-of-pocket expense: a cost incurred by an individual, often when on a business trip; the item or service is paid for in cash or by check or charge account, and the employee expects reimbursement from the company.

out of the money: a situation in which the striking price is above the market price of the underlying stock for a call, or the striking price is below the market price of the underlying stock for a put. [5]

out-of-town item: see *foreign items, transit letter.*

output
(1) *general:* the quantity yielded in any operation.
(2) *computers:* information transferred from the internal storage of a computer to output devices or external storage.
(3) *finance:* the average dollar gross domestic product produced in a stated period.

output costs: in public utilities, the costs that vary with the output of service consumed by a particular customer.

output rate: in public utilities, the part of the rate charge based on output costs.

outright transaction: a purchase sale or forward exchange without a corresponding transaction spot.

outside borrowing: borrowing funds from sources other than a Federal Home Loan Bank or a state-chartered central reserve institution.

outside broker: not a member of a regular stock exchange; a dealer in unlisted stocks.

outside collector: a person employed by a store or firm to make personal calls on debtors for the purpose of securing payment or a promise of payment. [41]

outside directors: directors of a corporation who enjoy no appreciable stock ownership and have no office in the corporation.

outside financing: the process of raising funds for a business expansion through the sale of securities, as opposed to the use of retained earnings. [105]

outside market: an over-the-counter market, or a market where unlisted securities are handled.

outsiders: the general investing public.

outside security: any security not listed or quoted on a major local exchange. For example, a security for the City of Los Angeles not traded on the Pacific Stock Exchange.

outstanding

(1) *general:* any unpaid or uncollected debt.

(2) *investments:* stock in the hands of stockholders, as distinguished from stock that has not yet been issued or, if issued, has not been released by the corporation. cf. *absorbed.*

outstanding checks: issued checks by a depositor that have not yet been paid by the bank.

Outstg.: see *outstanding.*

out the window: a new issue of securities or bonds that moves out rapidly or is sold quickly to investors.

outward collection: in Great Britain, the collection of payment on a bill of exchange from a firm overseas.

overage

(1) *general:* items additional to those shown on a bill of lading.

(2) *government:* created by a spending program that exceeds a specified budget target during a specified time period.

(3) see *shortfall.*

overall coverage: the relationship of income available or payments on corporate obligations divided by the amount of such annual charges. The better the coverage over a time period, the sounder the issue.

overall market price coverage: the ratio of net assets to the sum of all prior obligations at liquidating value plus the issue in question taken at market price. [30]

over and short account: an account carried in the general ledger. Overages and shortages from all sources, and their nature, are posted to this account, which is also termed a "suspense" or "differences" account in banks. At the end of the fiscal period, this account is closed out to profit and loss and becomes either an increase or a decrease to the undivided profits account in the general ledger. In larger banks, a subsidiary ledger is carried on this account so that the overages and shortages of all departments are carried as separate accounts. In this way, the frequency of any differences can be localized to a department and this department brought under control. [10]

overapplied overhead: the excess of amount of overhead cost applied to a product over the amount of overhead cost incurred.

overbought: reflecting an opinion about price levels. May refer to a security that has had a sharp rise, or to the market as a whole after a period of vigorous buying, which some are arguing, has left prices "too high."

overbought market: see *oversold market.*

overcapitalize

(1) *general:* to provide an excessive amount of capital to a business. see *capitalize, watered stock.*

(2) *banking:* to set too high a value on property.

(3) *finance:* to place too high a value on the nominal capital of a company.

overcarriage: carriage of goods, beyond the initially intended destination, usually resulting from the goods being refused at the destination.

overcertification: a rarely used certification by the bank of a customer's check where the collected balance in the person's account is less than the amount recorded on the check.

overcheck: a check drawn against an uncollected or insufficient balances; an overdraft.

overcommitment: synonymous with *over extension.*

overdraft: when a depositor draws a check for more than the balance on deposit with a bank and the bank honors that check, he or she is said to be "overdrawn." The bank can either return the check to the bank from which it came or to the person who presented it for payment, marked "insufficient funds." The bank can also elect to render the customer a service and pay the check.

overdraft banking: a service offered to demand deposit customers whereby a line of credit is associated with an individual's account. Checks drawn on insufficient funds are not returned to the presenter but are paid from funds from the credit line. [105]

overdraft checking account: a line of credit that allows a person to write checks for more than the actual balance, with a finance charge on the overdraft. [1]

overdraw: to write a bank check for an amount exceeding the deposit in the bank on which the check is drawn. see *cushion checking (credit), kite (kiting), overdraft.*

overdue: a payment that has not been made at the time it was due.

overextension

(1) *general:* the expansion by a business concern of buildings, equipment, and so on, in excess of the company's present or prospective future needs. synonymous with *overcommitment.*

(2) *finance:* credit received or extended beyond the debtor's ability to pay.

(3) *investments:* the condition of a dealer in securities who becomes obligated for an amount beyond his or her borrowing power or ability to pay.

overflow accounts: synonymous with *sweep accounts.*

overhead: a general term for costs or materials and services not directly adding to or readily identifiable with the product or service of the entity. see *conversion costs*; cf. *direct overhead, factory overhead.*

overhead expenses: applied to certain costs that do not vary much, regardless of business conditions, sales, and so on, such as rent, heat, the salaries of office clerks and company officers—as contrasted to the wages of those who are paid for what they make or sell. [28]

overheating: excessive price or money activity that some economists believe will lead to inflation.

overinvestment theory: a business cycle concept which holds that economic variations are a function of too much investment in the economy as business managers try to measure increasing demands during an upswing, and of major cutbacks in investment during a downswing when they realize that they expanded too much in the previous prosperity. synonymous with *oversaving theory.*

overissue: the release of stock in excess of the authorized or ordered amount. see *registrar, undigested securities.*

overlapping debt: the proportionate share of the debts of local government units located wholly or in part within the limits of the reporting government which must be borne by property within each governmental unit. [49]

overlay: an amount included in the tax levy on general property to cover abatements and taxes that will probably not be collected. [105]

overlimit account: an account in which the assigned dollar limit has been exceeded. [105]

overlining: under federal regulations, a bank cannot make loans to any one borrower that amounts to more than 10 percent of its capital. One way around that restriction is for a small bank to parcel out shares in proposed large loans deals to more important banks. This practice is called *overlining.*

overlying bond: see *bond, overlying.*

overlying mortgage: a junior mortgage subject to the claim of a senior mortgage, which has a claim prior to the junior mortgage. cf. *equal dignity.*

over on bill: additional freight described on the bill of lading.

overplus: synonymous with *surplus.*

overprints: official marks on a current paper money issue for the reason indicated: for purposes of revaluation, cancellation, and so on. [27]

override: a commission paid to managers that is added to their salary.

oversaving: when planned saving exceeds planned investment, oversaving is said to occur, and the quantity of cash removed from income movement exceeds the amount returned to it, resulting in the decline of income. cf. *marginal propensity to invest, saving.*

oversaving theory: synonymous with *overinvestment theory.*

Overseas Business Reports (OBR): a publication of the U.S. Department of Commerce providing basic background data for businesspeople who are evaluating various export markets or are considering entering new areas. [61]

Overseas Private Investment Corporation (OPIC): a federal agency that insures U.S. companies against seizure of their overseas property by foreign governments, damage to property from acts of war, or conditions under which they are unable to take their profits out of the foreign country. see *nationalization, seizure.*

overseas sterling area: see *sterling area.*

over, short, and damaged (OS&D): the discrepancy between the amount and/or condition of cargo on hand and that shown on the bill. cf. *clean bill of lading.*

oversold

(1) *general:* the situation of a manufacturer who has become obligated to deliver more than he or she is able to supply within the stated period.

(2) *investments:* an opinion—the reverse of overbought. A single security or a market that is believed to have declined to an unreasonable level. [20]

oversold market: when the speculative long interest has been drastically reduced and the speculative short interest increases, actually or relatively, a market is said to be oversold. At such times, sharp rallies often materialize. On the other hand, when the speculative short interest decreases sharply, a market is said to be overbought. At such times, the market is often in a position to decline sharply. [2]

overspeculation: a market situation wherein activity is abnormally high, caused not by the normal needs of legitimate buyers and sellers, but by speculators.

overstay the market: holding a position in stocks for too long a period of time—for example, a sustained advance when the market appears overbought and about to have a price correction.

oversubscribed: a situation in which, for a given issue of shares, more orders have been received than can be filled. cf. *undigested securities.*

overt act: an act done openly in pursuance of an avowed interest or design; in contradistinction to a threat without any act to carry it out. [37]

over the counter (OTC): securities not listed or traded on any of the regular exchanges. Such securities are traded through dealers in unlisted stocks. Sales or purchases are arranged by these dealers or through a chain of them until the desired securities and prices are obtained. However, members of regular stock exchanges also handle trades in unlisted securities, but not through the exchange. see *National Association of Securities Dealers Automated Quotations*; cf. *offboard*; see also *third market.* synonymous with *unlisted.*

over-the-counter market: a securities market conducted by dealers throughout the country through negotiation rather than through the use of an auction system as represented by a stock exchange. [26]

overtrading: the activity of a firm that even with high profitability cannot pay its own way for lack of working capital and finds itself in a liquidity crisis.

overturn: synonymous with *turnover.*

over without bill: freight without its bill of lading.

OWC: see *owner will carry.*

owe: to be obliged to pay something to someone for something received; an indebtedness.

owl: slang, any business activity that operates during the evening hours.

owned real estate: real estate acquired by a bank through foreclosure of a mortgage or through a deed in lieu of foreclosure or in settlement of any other obligation to the bank. synonymous with *other real estate.* [105]

owner: a person possessing title to property.

owner financing: a creative home-financing approach where the potential buyer bypasses the bank and borrows money directly from the person selling the house. Owners often find that this type of financing is the only way they can sell their houses because so many potential buyers cannot qualify for bank loans. The buyer, for example, might borrow half the needed money from the owner at 8 percent interest and the rest from a bank at 14 percent.

owner of record: a person or organization whose name appears on a corporation's transfer agent's book as the proper owner of securities in that firm as of a specified date. This name is identified to be entitled to receive any benefits or dividends declared.

ownership: the right to services and/or benefits provided by an asset. Ownership is usually shown by the possession of legal title or by a beneficial interest in the title. [105]

ownership certificate: a form required by the government and furnished by the Collector of Internal Revenue which discloses the real owner of stocks registered in the name of a nominee. Such a form must also accompany coupons presented for collection on bonds belonging to nonresident aliens, or partially tax-free corporate bonds issued prior to January 1, 1934. [37]

owner's paper: all forms of mortgage debt, including second mortgages, held by the seller of a house, rather than a bank.

owner will carry (OWC): mortgages at below-market rates wherein a good bargainer can knock costs down further.

P
- (1) see *partnership.*
- (2) see *payee.*
- (3) see *peso.*
- (4) see *private trust.*
- (5) see *purchaser.*

PA
- (1) see *paying agent.*
- (2) see *per annum.*
- (3) see *power of attorney.*

pa'anga: monetary unit of the Tonga Islands.

Pacific Coast Stock Exchange: formed in January 1957, by a consolidation of the San Francisco Stock Exchange (1882) and the Los Angeles Stock Exchange (1899), it is the most active U.S. securities exchange outside New York City.

package mortgage: a home-financing mortgage covering appliances and other household items (e.g., air conditioners, refrigerators, dryers).

package pay: used particularly with reference to executive compensation where other components of pay loom large in comparison with salary, stock options, increased pensions, profit-sharing and bonus arrangements, and similar devices.

packet: a London Stock Exchange term for *block,* as in a block purchase of securities.

paid check: a check that has been canceled and paid.

paid-in capital: capital contributed by stockholders and assigned to accounts other than capital stock.

paid-in surplus: excesses of a business arising from sources other than profits; the surplus from the sale of capital stock at a premium.

paid-up capital: the total of par value stock and the given value of no-par securities for which full consideration is received by a corporation.

paid-up insurance: a policy on which no further premium payments need to be made; the company will be held liable for any benefits claimed under terms of the contract.

paid-up shares: see *paid-up stock.*

paid-up stock: capital stock on which the initial buyer has paid in services, goods, or funds an amount at least equal to the par value.

painting the tape

(1) *investments:* creating an interest in a particular stock by trading constantly in it, thus causing it to appear on the ticker tape at frequent intervals.

(2) *investments:* unusual public interest in a specific security.

PAL: preapproved loan.

Palmer rule: the Rule of 1832 (after Palmer, governor of the Bank of England at that time) which sought to make fluctuations in English currency conform to what would occur under purely metallic currency by keeping bank-owned paper at a constant level.

PAN: see *Primary Account Number.*

P & L: profit and loss.

panic: a sudden, spreading fear of the collapse of business or the nation's economy, resulting in widespread withdrawal of bank deposits, stock sales, and similar transactions. A depression may but does not always follow a panic.

PAN-PIN pair: an account number and its corresponding secret code. [105]

PAP: prearranged payments.

paper: a loan contract; commercial paper, short-term evidence of a debt.

paper basis: indicating that a nation does not employ a metallic basis for its currency. see *paper money.*

paper gain or loss: an expression for unrealized capital gains or losses on securities in a portfolio, based on comparison of current market quotations and the original costs. [67]

paper gold: see *special drawing rights.*

paper hanger: slang, an individual who attempts to pass or forge worthless checks on a nonexistent bank account.

paper lease: a transaction permitted by the Treasury Department, allowing a company that faces the possibility of bankruptcy to arrange a lease as long as its secured creditors agree to honor the lease if they take possession of the leased property. Originally, the Treasury's rules called for the lease to end unless the bankruptcy trustee agreed to honor it.

paperless item processing system (PIPS): an electronic funds transit system that is capable of performing transit functions by establishing accounting transactions by which bank funds are shifted from one ledger or subledger to another.

paper money: currency on which a value is printed, although unlike coins, the bills have no value in themselves; usually represents bullion held in government vaults. cf. *fiat money.*

paper profit: an unrealized profit on a security still held. Paper profits become realized profits only when the security is sold. see *short sale.* [20]

paper standard: a monetary system, based on paper money, that is not convertible into gold or any other item of intrinsic value.

paper title: a written document that appears to convey proof of ownership but may not in fact show proper title. cf. *cloud on title.*

paper truncation: the act terminating the flow of paper in a transaction-processing system. For example, in an Electronic Funds Transfer system, once pertinent data from checks or credit card sales drafts are captured electronically, the paper records would be stored and would not be required in subsequent system operations. Paper truncation mandates a descriptive statement in lieu of the return to the customer of individual records of each transaction. [36]

paper wars: attempting to drown the other side in motions, interrogatories, depositions, pleadings, cross-claims and countersuits, using every conceivable procedure to attempt to avoid or delay trial on the merits. Often used in complex antitrust cases.

par: when the exchangeable value of an instrument is equal to that expressed on its face without consideration of any premium or discount. see also *face value.*

parachutes: see *golden parachutes.*

paradox of thrift: a concept of John Maynard Keynes that any effort by society to raise its savings rate can lead to a reduction in the amount it can really save.

parallel loans: see *back-to-back.*

parallel standard: a monetary standard; two or more metals are coined and authorized unconditionally as legal tender. cf. *bimetallism.*

paramount title: the foremost title, a title that is superior to all others. Often the original title used to prepare later ones.

parastatal: agencies with a quasi-government standing, such as highway authorities, nationalized industries, and so on. Usually, is applicable to agencies with more than 50 percent government control.

par bond: see *bond, par.*

par clearance: any check that clears at par as contrasted with a check that is non par. see *par.*

par collection: the process of check collections as stated in the "par collection requirements" of the Federal Reserve Act. see *par.*

parent company: a controlling organi-

zation that owns or manages business properties. synonymous with *proprietary company.*

Pareto optimality: distribution of resources that will make at least one person better off and no one else worse off. synonymous with *economic efficiency.*

Pareto's law: the theory of Vilfredo Pareto, Italian sociologist and economist, that income tends to become distributed in the same proportion among consumers throughout the world, regardless of differing forms of taxation.

par exchange rate: the free market price of one country's money in terms of the currency of another.

pari delicto: fault or blame that is equally shared.

Paris Bourse: the national stock exchange of France, established in 1724.

Paris Club: an informal grouping of governments meeting on an ad hoc basis to find agreement on measures to be taken when a nation is unable to repay its foreign borrowings on time. [91]

par item: any item that can be collected at its par or face value upon presentation.

parity
(1) *finance:* the equivalence established between the wage schedules of some categories of employees.
(2) *government:* a farm policy established to keep the purchasing power of a unit of farm output equal to the purchasing power of the units of production bought by a farmer in the same ratio that existed during a chosen period. see *farm subsidies;* cf. *Brannan plan.*
(3) *investments:* the state or quality of being equal or equivalent; equiva-

lence of a commodity price expressed in one currency to its price expressed in another.

(4) *investments:* equality of purchase power established by law between different kinds of money at a given ratio.

parity check: a summation check in which the binary digits in a character or word are added and the sum checked against a single previously computed parity digit (i.e., a check to test whether the necessary number of ones and zeros are encoded in the computer to represent a number or word correctly). [105]

parity clause: a mortgage clause by virtue of which all notes obtained by the mortgage have "equal dignity"; that is, none has priority.

par list: a Federal Reserve System list of banks that will remit in full for items that are payable to the system.

par of exchange: the market price of money in one national currency that is exchanged at the official rate for a specific amount in another national currency, or another commodity of value (gold, silver, etc.).

parol evidence: oral testimony or evidence, as contrasted with written or documentary evidence. [37]

Part.: see *participation.*

partial audit: see *limited audit.*

partial equilibrium analysis: an inquiry that looks at only one market of an economy under the assumption that solutions in other markets will not be altered by a change in the market examined.

partially amortized mortgage: a mortgage partly repaid by amortization during the life of the mortgage and partly repaid at the end of the term.

partial monopoly: exists when there are so few sellers of an item or service that each may alter the price and market. cf. *perfect (pure) monopoly.*

partial payment: a payment that is not equal to the full amount owed and is not intended to constitute the full payment.

partial release: the giving up of a claim to a portion of the property held as security for the payment of a debt. [51]

participant: a bank, brokerage house, or investment firm that has agreed to sell a stock issue to the public as part of a syndicate.

participating bond: see *bond, participating.*

participating certificate

(1) an instrument that specifies a partial owner interest in a stock.

(2) a federal security sold in multiples of $5000 and guaranteed by the Federal National Mortgage Association.

(3) see also *participation certificate.*

participating life insurance: insurance on which the policyholder is entitled to receive policy dividends reflecting the difference between the premium charged and actual experience. The premium is calculated to provide some margin over the anticipated cost of the insurance protection. [58]

participating preferred: describing a preferred stock that is entitled to its stated dividend and, also, to additional dividends on a specified basis (i.e., with respect to the plan participated in) on payment of dividends on the common stock.

participation: an ownership interest in a mortgage. [51]

participation agreement: an understanding, the terms of which are usually specified in writing between institutional investors, to buy or sell partial ownership interests in mortgages. [51]

participation certificate
(1) a certificate representing a beneficial interest in a pool of federal agency mortgages or loans; a formal credit instrument carrying a contractual interest obligation on a specified principal.
(2) a document showing participation in a syndicated Eurocredit; usually in negotiable form so that it can legally be sold to another bank.
(3) see also *participating certificate*.

participation dividends: earnings of a cooperative that are distributed to every member in direct proportion to the amount of business that he or she has done with the cooperative during the fiscal period.

participation fee: in the Euromarket, a bank's fee for participating in a loan.

participation loan: a loan having two or more banks as creditors. Laws prohibit banks from lending more than a fixed percentage of their capital and surplus to any one borrower. Thus banks invite other banks to participate in making large loans.

particular lien: a right to keep something valuable that belongs to another person as compensation for labor, supplies, or money spent in his or her behalf. synonymous with *special lien*. cf. *factor's lien, general lien, mechanic's lien;* see also *voluntary conveyance or deed*.

particular operating expenses: those expenses that vary directly with the amount of business done (e.g., in running a particular train, the coal and the wages of the crew).

partisan issues: paper money for limited circulation issued by partisans fighting the forces occupying their country. [27]

partly paid: in securities, those stocks held in a margin account (i.e., a balance is owed by an investor to his or her broker on the full amount of the stock bought).

partner: a person who is a member of a partnership; usually for the purpose of operating a business.

partnership: a contractual relationship between two or more people in a joint enterprise, who agree to share, not necessarily equally, in the profits and losses of the organization. cf. *joint venture*.

partnership certificate: a certificate filed with a bank showing the interest of each partner in a business enterprise operating as a partnership. This certificate also shows the limited partners (partners who specify a maximum amount for which they may be held responsible in settlement of obligations incurred by the partnership), and also "silent partners" (partners who have invested funds in the partnership, but who, for certain reasons, do not wish to be publicly known as partners). [10]

party at interest: individual or group of individuals having a vested interest in a commercial enterprise.

par value: face value; the par value of stocks on the date of issuance is the principal.

par value (of currency): the value of a currency in terms of gold as formally proposed to the International Monetary Fund, normally subject to fund concurrence. The fund's Articles of Agreement envisage that each member country shall have an effective par value, i.e., a unitary, fixed exchange rate for spot transactions that is established and maintained in accordance with the provisions of the Articles. [42]

pass(ing) a dividend: a corporation's decision to omit the declaration of an expected dividend.

passbook: a book record prepared by a bank for a depositor, listing date and amount of deposits, with an initial or identifying symbol indicating the teller who received the deposit. In the case of savings accounts, the passbook lists deposits, withdrawals, interest paid by the bank, dates of all transactions, each new balance, and the initial or identifying symbol of the teller handling each transaction. The passbook shows the depositor's name or names and account number. cf. *no-passbook savings.*

passbook account: a savings account that normally requires no minimum balance, no minimum term, no specified deposits, and no notice or penalty for withdrawals. [59]

passbook loan: see *savings account loan.*

passbook savings: a savings account that uses a passbook, in which the bank records transactions. [105]

passed dividend: a regular or scheduled dividend that has been omitted.

passing title: synonymous with *closing title.* see *closing (or passing) title.*

passive bond: see *bond, passive.*

passive trade balance: synonymous with *unfavorable balance of trade.*

passive trust: one whose trustee has no tasks to perform and merely retains title to the trust property.

pass no more: see *no more credit.*

pass-through certificates: certificates guaranteed by the Government National Mortgage Association.

past due: an account on which payment has not been made according to agreement and owes a given amount which is in arrears. [41]

past-due item: any note, acceptance, or other time instrument of indebtedness that has not been paid on the due date.

past service benefit: credit toward a pension, provided by the employer, for all or part of a participant's years of service with the company before the adoption of a pension plan. [105]

PAT: prearranged transfers.

pataca: monetary unit of Macao.

pawn: the pledge to pay a debt.

pawnbroker: a business manager who lends items that are pledged as security for the loan.

pawned stock: see *hypothecated stock.*

pay

(1) to pay a check in cash, as when a check is paid by the paying teller.

(2) to charge a check against a customer's account, as in the case of a check coming through the clearings. [50]

(3) slang, currency of denomination of a bond.

payable in exchange: the requirement that a negotiable instrument be paid in the funds of the place from which it was originally issued.

payables: a bookkeeping term for any and all accounts or notes payable total. cf. *receivables.*

pay-as-you-go accounts: a variation of "special checking accounts" or "special fee accounts." Under the pay-as-you-go plan, the special-checking-account depositor purchases a checkbook, usually at the rate of 5 or 10 cents per check. The fee or service charge is therefore prepaid to the bank, and the depositor can control the cost of his checking account by the number of checks he writes. In this plan, no service charge is posted as checks are posted against the account. [10]

payback period: the period of time that passes before the incoming cash equals the outgoing cash on a specific project, order, or other effort.

pay-by-phone: a service enabling customers to instruct their financial institution via telephone to initiate one or more payments from their accounts. [33]

pay date: see *PDate.*

pay-down: the sum by which the principal amount of securities maturing exceeds the amount of new securities issued to replace them. cf. *new money.*

payee: the person or organization to whom a check or draft or note is made payble. The payee's name follows the expression "pay to the order of." [7]

payer: the party primarily responsible for the payment of the amount owed as evidenced by a given negotiable instrument.

pay-in: a monetary contribution or deposit in a fund or account, usually on a periodic basis.

paying agent: an agent to receive funds from an obligor to pay maturing bonds and coupons, or from a corporation for the payment of dividends. [37]

paying bank: a bank upon which a check is drawn and pays a check or other draft to the holder and/or collecting bank.

paying teller: a representative of the bank who is responsible for the proper paying or cashing of checks presented at the window. see *unit teller system.* [50]

pay-in warrant: see *deposit warrant.*

payload: that part of the total load yielding revenue.

pay loans: computing and counting out the currency (and/or issuing the checks) to be paid out to a customer in closing his loan. [55]

payment: total sum of money borrowed, plus all finance charges, divided by the number of months in the term of the loan. [78]

payment bill: a bill of exchange presented for payment instead of acceptance.

payment bond: see *bond, contract.*

payment coupon: the section of the billing statement containing payment information and which should be returned by the customer with the payment. [105]

payment date: the date on which a customer has agreed to make his payment each month. synonymous with *due date.* [55]

payment for honor: paying a bill by another other than the one on whom it is drawn, when the latter has defaulted, to save the reputation or credit of the original drawee.

payment-in-kind (PIK) program: created in 1983, producers who have reduced acreage by the 20 percent of base stipulated by the reduced acreage program (RAP) may idle up to an additional 30 percent of base acreage under PIK. PIK attempts to remove more land from production than has been possible under existing programs. On the other hand, the distribution of reserve grain to farmers will reduce surplus stocks. see also *farmer-owned reserve.* [99]

payment order: an order given to a bank to pay or transfer an amount of money to a third party, for the account of the third party or the account of another. [105]

payment record: a record of a customer's past payment pattern on installment cash loans and other credit transactions. [105]

payments balance: see *balance of payments.*

payments deficit: the excess of the value of a nation's imports over its exports.

payments mechanism: systems designed for the movement of funds, payments, and money between financial institutions throughout the nation. The Federal Reserve plays a major role in the nation's payments mechanism through distribution of currency and coin, check processing, wire transfers, and automated clearinghouses. Various private associations also perform many payments mechanism operations. [1]

payments surplus: the excess of the value of a nation's exports over its imports.

payments system: a system (composed of people, machines, and procedures) used to transfer value from one party to another. [36]

payment stopped: a negotiable instrument such as a check upon which a "stop payment" has been issued. see *stop payment.*

payment supra protest: payment after protest. An indorser liable on a dishonored negotiable instrument that has been protested receives a right to reimbursement from the drawer for paying the instrument.

payment voucher: usually the upper part of a customer's monthly statement presented or mailed together with remittance. Becomes the posting medium for the accounts receivable bookkeeper. [41]

payoff

(1) *banking:* the complete repayment of loan principal, interest, and any other sums due; payoff occurs either over the full term of the loan or through prepayments. [59]

(2) *finance:* money given for an unethical or illegal service.

(3) *systems:* the result of a decision problem transformed to represent its true utility to the decision maker.

payoff balance: see *net balance.*

payoff statement: a formal statement prepared when a loan payoff is contemplated, showing the current status of the loan account, all sums due, and the daily rate of interest. synonymous with *letter of demand.* [59]

payola: slang, any gift or other valuable item offered to people who have the potential for using their influence in the promotion or sale of a product or service.

payor: a person who makes, or is to make, a payment. [59]

pay-out ratio: the ratio of dividends paid to earnings in a given period.

payroll

(1) *general:* the wages or salary earned by a firm's employees for a certain period of time. Various deductions for withholding tax, health benefits insurance, and so on, are identified on the employee's record affixed to his or her payroll check.

(2) *general:* a list of employees receiving pay during a wage period.

payroll deduction plan (mutual fund): an arrangement whereby an employee may accumulate shares in a mutual fund by authorizing his employer to deduct and transfer to a fund a specified amount from his salary at stated times. [23]

payroll deductions: sums withheld from an employee's gross pay for federal and state income taxes, social security, or other governmental levies; may include, on authorization of employees, deductions for union dues and assessments, premiums for group insurance, contribution for pension plan, and so on.

payroll savings plan: a plan whereby an employee authorizes his employer to deduct from his wages or salary each pay period a specified amount and to forward that amount to his savings association for deposit to his savings account. [59]

payroll tax: used to finance an employer's contribution to the Social Security program, a tax levied on a company's payroll. see *Federal Insurance Contributions Act.*

Payt.: see *payment.*

pay to: indicates that the receiver should provide the specified funds to the designated payee. [105]

pay to bearer: see *bearer instrument.*

pay to order: a negotiable instrument having such words is negotiable by endorsement of the within named payee and his or her delivery to another.

pay-up: the loss of cash following the sale of one block of funds and the purchase of another block at a higher cost.

PB: see *Paris Bourse.*

PBWSE: see *Philadelphia-Baltimore-Washington Stock Exchange.*

P&C: see *puts and calls.*

PC: see *petty cash.*

PCS: see *preferred capital stock.*

Pd.: paid.

PD
(1) see *past due.*
(2) see *per diem.*

PDA: personal deposit account.

PDate (pay date): the date on which the beneficiary is to be credited or paid. It is conventional in the United States not to recognize any payment dates other than value date. [105]

PE: see *price-earnings ratio.*

peak: an exceptionally busy period in a business.

peculation: the embezzlement of funds or goods, especially public funds or goods, by an individual in whose care they have been entrusted. see *defalcation.*

pecuniary exchange: any trade using money.

pecuniary legacy: a gift of money by will. [37]

peer group: in the National Bank Surveillance System, national bank statistics are classified into 20 peer groups, based on asset size and other characteristics. [105]

peg (pegging): to fix or stabilize the price of something (e.g., stock, currency, commodity) by manipulating or regulating the market. For example, the government may peg the price of gold by purchasing all that is available at a stated price. see also *adjustable peg, crawling peg.*

pegged price
(1) the agreed, customary, or legal price at which any commodity has been fixed.
(2) price level for a specific stock at which buying support nearly always evolves and prevents a decline—thus "pegging" the price. see also *peg (pegging).*

peg point: the pay rate of a key operation that serves as the base from which rates of pay for other activities are calculated.

penal bond: see *bond, penal.*

penalty: see *liquidated damages.*

penalty clause
(1) a clause in a promissory note specifying a penalty for late payments. (2) a clause in a savings certificate specifying a penalty for premature withdrawal from such an account. [59]

penalty rate: the rate charged a member bank by the Federal Reserve Bank for a deficiency in the legal reserves required to be held against the deposits of that member bank.

pendente lite: Latin, pending during the progress of a suit at law. see also *lis pendens.*

pending claim: a claim submitted to a company by a policyholder which is in the process of consideration of preparation for payment. [12]

penetration pricing: strategy of using a low initial price means to capture a large share of the market as early as possible. [105]

Pennsylvania Rule: a rule that requires credit of extraordinary dividends received in trust on the basis of the source of such dividends; to income if declared from earnings of the corporation during the life of the trust, and to principal if from earnings accumulated before commencement of the trust. [37]

penny ante: slang, involving an insignificant amount of cash.

penny stocks: low-priced issues, often highly speculative, selling at less than $1 a share. Frequently a term of disparagement, although a few penny stocks have developed into investment-caliber issues. [20]

pension: French for a money market borrowing against securities held in pension by the lender until repayment.

Pension Benefit Guaranty Corporation: see *Employee Retirement Income Security Act of 1974.*

pension fund: a fund out of which pensions are to be paid either to those entitled thereto under specific agreement or to those who may be selected by persons in control of the fund. [49]

pension plan: a method used by a firm or union to pay annuities or pensions to retired and/or disabled employees. Sections 401 and 404 of the Internal Revenue Code identify conditions enabling an organization to establish a pension plan. see *Employee Retirement Income Security Act of 1974, trust agreement (trust instrument).*

pension reserve: an actuarial computation of the financial obligation for future payments to be made on account of a pension or retirement allowance or benefit. [52]

pension trust: a trust established by an employer (commonly a corporation) to provide benefits for incapacitated, retired, or superannuated employees, with or without any contributions made by the employees. [37]

people's capitalism: the full range of income levels in the population of a community is represented in the ownership of the business.

PEP: paperless electronic payment.

Pepper-McFadden Act: see *McFadden Act of 1927.*

PER
(1) see *par exchange rate.*
(2) see *price-earnings ratio.*

per annum: by the year.

Per. Cap.: per capita.

per capita: by the individual.

per capita output: the gross national product of a nation divided by its population; often used to identify a country's standard of living.

per capita tax: by the individual; a tax based on the result of dividing stated sums of money by a specified group of people to show the amount to be paid by each person.

percentage lease: a lease providing for payment of rent based on a percentage of the gross sales or the sales over a fixed amount. [37]

percentage order: either a market or a limited price order to buy (or sell) a stated amount of a specified stock after a fixed number of shares of such stock have traded.

per cent per month: the method of computing loan interest in which the charge is specified as a monthly percentage of the outstanding balance, as "1 percent per month on the unpaid balance." The effective yield to the lender is 12 times the monthly rate. [59]

percent return on investment: profit received from the firm as compared to the money and property invested in the firm.

per centum: by the hundred.

per contra item: a balance in one account that is offset by a balance from another account.

per curiam: a full court's decision (e.g., to remand), when no opinion is given.

per diem: for each day.

perfect competition: a description for an industry or market unit consisting of a large number of purchasers and sellers all involved in the buying and selling of a homogeneous good, with awareness of prices and volume, no discrimination in buying and selling, and a mobility of resources.

perfected lien: a security interest in an asset that is properly documented and has been filed with the appropriate legal authority. Thus the claim of the creditor has been protected. [105]

perfectly elastic demand (or supply): the situation in which a small price change results in an unlimited increase in the quantity bought (or offered for sale).

perfectly inelastic demand (or supply): the situation in which a small price change results in no change in the quantity bought (or offered for sale).

perfect (pure) monopoly: one person or organization has total control over the manufacture and marketing of an item. see *monopoly, oligopoly.*

perfect title

(1) *general:* property displaying total right of ownership.

(2) *law:* a title that is not open to dispute or challenge because it is complete in every detail, and has no legal defects. see also *marketable title, muniment of title, quiet title suit, warranty deed*; cf. *cloud on title.*

performance: the fulfillment or accomplishment of a promise, contract, or other obligation according to its terms. [105]

performance appraisal: a methodical review of an employee's performance on the job to evaluate the effectiveness or adequacy of the person's work.

performance bond: see *bond, contract.*

performance budgeting: grouping of budget accounts into categories related to a specific product or service that is produced and the evolution of product-cost measurements of these activities.

performance fee: fees charged by some mutual fund managers when their purchasing and selling for the fund portfolio helps it to outperform certain market averages over a stated time period. synonymous with *incentive fee.*

performance fund: a mutual fund that places more of its monies into speculative risky investments, such as some common stocks, rather than more conservative investments, such as bonds.

performance report: a comparison of actual results against those anticipated in a stated budget.

peril point: the greatest reduction in U.S. import duty that could be made for a stated item without creating a major hardship to domestic manufacturers or to makers of a closely related item.

period analysis: in monetary theory, the effort to analyze the cumulative effects as regards income, price level, employment, and so on, of changes in investment, expenditures, hoarding, and so on, over time by breaking time into periods with changes taking place discontinuously between periods and not continuously within a period.

period cost: see *fixed cost (or expense).*

periodic payment plan: see *contractual plan.*

periodic rate: an amount of finance charge expressed as a percentage that is to be applied to an appropriate balance for a specified period, usually monthly, provided that there is a balance which is subject to a finance charge. [105]

periodic statement: the billing sum-

mary produced and mailed at specified intervals, usually monthly. [105]

period of digestion: a time immediately following the release of a new or large security offering, during which sales are made primarily to regular investment customers.

period of redemption: the length of time during which a mortgagor may reclaim the title and possession of his property by paying the debt it secured. [51]

peripheral equipment: any of the units of computer equipment, distinct from the central processing unit, that provide outside communication. Not all systems have peripheral equipment. see *auxiliary operation.*

perjury: knowingly false testimony delivered under an oath that has been properly administered in a judicial proceeding.

perks: compensations given by corporations to executives (e.g., home repairs, company owned cars) that are not considered as taxable income. short for *perquisites.*

permanent accounts: see *real accounts.*

permanent asset: any fixed or capital asset.

permanent capital: common and preferred stock as well as retained earnings that do not have to be paid back.

permanent certificate: a certificate engraved for the purpose of making counterfeiting more difficult and to fulfill the rules of most security exchanges. cf. *temporary receipt.*

permanent financing: a long-term mortgage, amortized over 15, 20, or more years at a fixed rate of interest.

permanent income: the average income anticipated to be received over a number of years.

permanent life insurance: a phrase used to cover any form of life insurance except term; generally insurance that accrues cash value, such as whole life or endowment. [58]

permanent stock association: see *stock association.*

permissible nonbank activities: financial activities closely related to banking that may be engaged in by bank holding companies, either directly or through nonbank subsidiaries. Examples are owning finance companies and engaging in mortgage banking. The Federal Reserve Board determines which activities are closely related to banking. Before making such activities permissible, the board must also determine that their performance by bank holding companies is in the public interest. [1]

permit bond: see *bond, permit.*

permit mail: mail with printed indicia in lieu of a stamp, showing that postage was paid by the sender. [24]

perpetual bond: see *bond, perpetual.*

perpetuity

(1) *general:* endless; the quality of going on forever (e.g., an estate willed in perpetuity).

(2) *finance:* anything that is removed from the ordinary channel of commerce by limiting its capacity to be sold for a period longer than that of a life or lives in being and 21 years thereafter, plus the period of development, is said to be *removed in perpetuity.* see *consol(s), emphyteutic lease.*

per procuration: the signature of a principal made by his or her agent, who has limited authority instead of having power of attorney.

perquisites: see *perks.*

personal account: an account carried in the name of a person or firm.

personal asset: an asset that is owned for personal use. [73]

personal check: a check drawn by someone as an individual (i.e., not acting as an employer or in a fiduciary capacity).

personal consumption expenditures: the sum of money and imputed expenditures made by consumers (individuals, not-for-profit institutions such as hospitals, etc.) for goods and services. It excludes purchases of dwellings (included in gross private domestic investment) but includes rental value of owner-occupied houses.

personal credit: a credit that a person possesses as differentiated from credit of a company, corporation, or partnership.

personal distribution of income: the distribution of natural income among individuals or households.

personal estate: synonymous with *personal property.*

personal finance company: a business that lends small sums of money to people, usually for personal needs, at relatively high interest rates. Most states require these organizations to be licensed.

personal financial statement: an account of an individual's personal resources and obligations. A personal financial statement is comparable to a balance sheet for a business. [105]

personal holding company: a holding company which under income tax law derives at least 80 percent of its gross income from royalties, dividends, interest, annuities, and sale of securities, and in which over 50 percent of the outstanding stock is owned by not more than five persons.

Personal Identification Number (PIN): the PIN, generally a four-digit number or word, is the secret number given to a plastic cardholder either by selection by the cardholder (customer-selected PIN) or randomly assigned by the card processor. The PIN is to be used in conjunction with the plastic card to effect any kind of transfer, withdrawal, deposit, or inquiry. It is intended to prevent unauthorized use of the card while accessing a financial service terminal. [105]

personal income: national income less various kinds of income not actually received by individuals, nonprofit institutions, and so on (e.g., undistributed corporate profits, corporate taxes, employer contributions for social insurance), plus certain receipts that do not arise from production (i.e., transfer payments and government interest).

personal installment loan: funds, borrowed by an individual for personal needs, which are repaid in regular monthly installments over a specified period.

personalized sales draft: sales drafts that have been especially printed for a merchant to provide stronger identification than would be the case if a standard form were used. [105]

personal liability: the sum owed by a natural person.

personal line of credit: synonymous with *reserve checking/overdraft checking.*

personal loan: a type of loan generally obtained by individual borrowers in small amounts, usually less than $1000. A personal loan is often se-

cured for the purpose of consolidating debts, or paying taxes, insurance premiums, or hospital bills.

personal outlays: made up of personal consumption expenditures, interest paid by consumers, and personal transfer payments to foreigners. They represent the disbursements made by individuals of that portion of personal income available after payment of personal taxes. The residual is personal saving. [73]

personal property: the rights, powers, and privileges an individual has in movable things such as chattels, and choses in action. synonymous with *personal estate.*

personal representative: a general term applicable to both executor and administrator. [37]

personal saving: the difference between disposable personal income and personal consumption expenditures; includes the changes in cash and deposits, security holdings, indebtedness, reserves of life insurance companies and mutual savings institutions, the net investment of unincorporated enterprises, and the acquisition of real property net of depreciation.

personal security: an unsecured accommodation in which the net worth and the stature of the business borrower are relied on rather than some collateral which is pledged.

personal surety: surety provided by an individual as contrasted with surety provided by an insurance company.

personal trust: see *trust, personal.*

personalty: personal property.

personnel psychology: a subdivision of applied psychology that treats an individual's psychological qualities in relation to his or her job. It deals with employment procedures, selection, placement, training, promotion, supervision, morale, and other personal aspects of job attitude and behavior.

PERT: see *program evaluation and review technique.*

PERT/COST: a modified PERT system that in addition to time, deadlines, and schedules, includes all cost considerations.

pertinent element of creditworthiness: in relation to a judgmental system of evaluating applicants, any information about applicants that a creditor obtains and considers and that has a demonstrable relationship to a determination of creditworthiness. [105]

peseta: monetary unit of Andorra, Balearic Island, Canary Islands, and Spain.

peso: monetary unit of Bolivia, Chile, Colombia, Cuba, Dominican Republic, Mexico, Republic of the Philippines, and Uruguay.

pet bank: applied to banks in which government deposits were made after the expiration of the second U.S. Bank in 1836.

petition in bankruptcy: the form used for declaring voluntary bankruptcy. see *bankruptcy.*

petitioning on creditors' bond: see *bond, petitioning on creditors'.*

petrobonds: instruments that are backed by a specific number of barrels of oil. Since 1977, the Mexican government has been raising money by selling these bonds that trade in direct relations to the rapidly rising official price of Mexico's crude oil. see also *petrodollars.*

petrodollars: huge sums of money from oil-producing nations other than the United States or Great Britain. These funds are initially converted into Eurocurrency and deposited with international banks to be used for future investment and for paying debts. These banks traditionally set limits on the sum they will accept from any one country. see *Organization of Petroleum Exporting Countries.*

petty cash: cash kept on hand for the payment of minor items. [59]

Pfd.: preferred.

phantom stock: used in executive compensation programs, the executive is granted a number of shares of the company; each shares entitles the executive to the amount, if any, by which the market price of the stock at some future time exceeds the current market price.

Philadelphia—Baltimore—Washington Stock Exchange: in 1919, the Philadelphia Stock Exchange became the Philadelphia-Baltimore Stock Exchange. In July 1953, the Washington Stock Exchange merged with the PBSE and in 1969, the Pittsburgh Stock Exchange consolidated with the Philadelphia-Baltimore-Washington Stock Exchange.

Philadelphia bank roll: slang, a $10 or $20 bill wrapped around a roll of $1 bills.

Philadelphia plan: an equipment trust arrangement using a lease as the legal device. cf. *New York plan.*

Phillips curve: a correlation between the unemployment level and the rate of wage changes. The curve shows that it is possible to lower unemployment only at the expense of a climbing price level, thereby making it necessary to trade off between lowering unemployment and maintaining the price level stable.

phony dividends: rather than paying dividends from stock earnings, dividends that are paid immediately from a portion of the money that comes in from the public's purchasing of that stock. This is an illegal activity.

photo card: a bank credit card containing a picture of the cardholder. [105]

physical value: erroneously used to designate an estimate of reproduction or replacement cost, or the estimated value of physical assets as distinct from nonphysical assets. [62]

PI: see *prime interest (rate).*

pickup: the gain in yield resulting from the sale of one block of bonds and the purchase of another block with a higher yield.

pickup card: an instruction to an authorizer or a merchant directing him or her to take possession of the cardholder bank card and return it to the issuing bank. [105]

piece-of-the-action financing: a lending arrangement in which the mortgagee receives, besides regular loan interest, a negotiated percentage of the gross income of an income property, of increases in rentals over a stated period of the life of an income property, or the gross or net profit of a commercial or industrial enterprise. [59]

piece rate (wage): the amount of money received for each unit of output; when wages are so determined, an incentive wage system is in operation.

piggyback item: when one document attaches itself to or overlaps another during processing, causing the item to be missing from its assigned pocket in the sorter and to be sorted "free" to an unidentified pocket. [105]

pig on port: British for *accommodation paper.*

Pigou effect concept: a theoretical countercyclical force which, under an extreme condition, might provide some stimulus to an economy in a depression. synonymous with *wealth effect.*

PIK: see *payment-in-kind program.*

pilgrims' receipts: currency on which an overprint indicated that the notes were for use by pilgrims in another country. Pakistan, for example, overprinted some notes "for use in Saudi Arabia by pilgrims only." [27]

PIN: see *Personal Identification Number.*

pinch

(1) *general:* a bind or tight situation.

(2) *finance:* a sudden, unanticipated rise in prices; when money rates go up suddenly, it is called a *money pinch.*

pink sheets: price quotations of many over-the-counter stocks that are published on pink sheets. synonymous with *"sheets,"* the.

pip: foreign exchange dealers' term for 0.00001 of a unit.

PIPS: see *paperless item processing system.*

pit: a circular area in the middle of the floor of a stock exchange; steps lead down into the pit, giving greater visibility to the trading action occurring there. synonymous with *ring.* see *floor, open order, outcry market.*

PITI: common abbreviation for principal, interest, taxes, and insurance, used when describing the monthly carrying charges on a mortgage.

Pittsfield Project: This EFTS project in Pittsfield, Massachusetts, involves banks, savings and loans, credit unions, and many merchants in the Pittsfield area. The system involves direct payroll depositing by the employers, and a card-activated point-of-sale retail system which records transaction data for next-day funds transfer processing. [105]

pivotal stock: a stock that is accepted as the leader of its group and often influences the activity of other stocks.

P&L: see *profit and loss statement (operating statement).*

PL: see *place.*

place: to locate a market for a security; to sell it to an investor.

placement: negotiating for the sale of a new securities issue, or the arranging of a long-term loan.

placement memorandum: a document prepared by the lead manager of a syndicate in the Eurocredit market; seeks to provide information to other potential leaders to assist them in deciding whether to participate in the credit.

placing power: the ability of a bank or broker to sell securities to investors (i.e., to place the securities).

plain bond: see *bond, plain.*

plaintiff: a complaining party or the person who begins a legal action against another person or organization, seeking a court remedy.

PLAM: see *price-level-adjusted mortgage.*

planholder: a pension plan shareholder.

plan manager: an individual responsible for all bank credit card activities. [105]

planning—programming—budgeting (PPB): mainly in government accounting, a system of administration for federal agencies. Concepts included are (a) long- and short-range planning of objectives and end products, (b) realistic cost estimates, (c) a search for greater efficiency, (d) budgetary projections of outputs in terms of goods and services, and (e) reports on current and prospective outlays, designed to service management controls and to supply information on budgetary administration for all levels of government.

plastic: any type of plastic card used by a consumer as a payments mechanism. The types of cards in use are generally described as credit cards, debit cards, and cash cards. [105]

plate numbers: figures in extremely small print on the side of some notes, to identify the printing plate from which they were made. [27]

platform: that portion of a bank's lobby where officers and new accounts personnel are located. [105]

Plcy.: see *policy.*

please advise fate: see *fate (inquiry).*

pledge

(1) *general:* the act of transferring personal property to a trustee or creditor as security on a debt.

(2) *lending:* bailment of goods to a creditor by a pledgor (bailor) to a creditor (bailee/pledgee) as security for some debt or engagement. [105]

pledged-account mortgage: a variation on graduated-payment mortgages, where a portion of the borrower's down payment is used to fund a pledged savings account, which is drawn on to supplement the monthly payment during the first years of the loan. The net effect to the borrower is lower payments at first. Payments gradually rise to slightly above those on conventional mortgages. see also *flexible-payment mortgage, graduated-payment mortgage, reverse-annuity mortgage, rollover mortgage, variable-rate mortgage.*

pledged assets: securities owned by a bank, generally U.S. government bonds and obligations, specified by law, which must be pledged as collateral security for funds deposited by the U.S. government, or state or municipal governments.

pledged loan: a mortgage loan that has been pledged as security for a borrowing; particularly, one that has been pledged as security for a Federal Home Loan Bank advance. [59]

pledged securities: securities issued or assumed by the accounting company that have been pledged as collateral security for any of its long-term debt or short-term loans. [18]

pledgee: the person or firm to whom the security for a loan is pledged.

pledging: the offering by a borrower of his or her assets as security for the repayment of a debt. cf. *distrain, hypothecation.*

pledging receivables: obtaining a short-term loan with receivables as collateral.

pledgor: the person or firm that makes a pledge of real or personal property as the collateral for a loan.

plow back: to put earnings from sales back into the business operation.

plum: slang, extra profits or additional stock dividends.

plunge: reckless speculation.

plunger: an individual speculator who takes great risks, resulting in substantial profits or losses.

plunk down: slang, to make a payment in cash.

plus tick: synonymous with *up tick.*

PM
(1) see *primary market.*
(2) see *purchase money.*
(3) see *push money.*

PMM: see *purchase-money mortgage.*

PN: see *promissory note.*

PO
(1) see *preauthorization order.*
(2) see *public offering.*
(3) see *purchase order.*

POA: see *power of attorney.*

POB: point of business.

POC: see *preservation of capital.*

Poincare franc: gold franc.

point
(1) in shares of stock, a point means $1.
(2) a loan discount, which is a one-time charge, used to adjust the yield on the loan to what market conditions demand. Each point equals one percent of the principal amount. [78]
(3) the minimum unit in which changes in futures price may be expressed ($1/_{000}$ cent, equivalent to $3.00). [11]

point of sale (POS): systems that permit bank customers to effect transfers of funds from their bank accounts and other financial transactions at retail points of sale. [33]

point-of-sale terminal (POST): a communication and data capture terminal located where goods or services are paid for. POST terminals may serve merchant accounting needs and may assist in processing financial transactions. In the latter case, the terminal may operate as part of an authorization/verification system or initiate direct exchanges of value among merchants, customers, and financial institutions. [36]

"poison pen": special corporate warrants that deny shareholders the right to consider tender offers for their shares and that transfer that right to the board.

Pol.: see *policy.*

policy

(1) *general:* any plan of action.

(2) *banking:* a written contract of insurance.

policy dividend: a refund of part of the premium on a participating life insurance policy reflecting the difference between the premium charged and actual experience. [58]

policyholder: a person or company protected by an insurance contract. synonymous with "the insured."

policy loan: funds borrowed from a life insurance organization, usually at low interest rates, using as security the cash value of the holder's policy.

policy reserves: see *reserve.*

policy value: the amount of money available to the insured upon the maturity of the policy.

polymetallism: a theoretical monetary system where more than two metals are made standard money and coined in a definite ratio one to another in the matter of weight and fineness.

polyopsony: the market situation in which the number of buyers is so few that their actions materially affect the market price, yet large enough that each buyer cannot with confidence judge the effect of his or her actions on the conduct of other buyers in the market.

polypoly: the market situation in which the number of sellers is so few that their actions materially affect the market price, yet large enough that each seller cannot with confidence judge the effect of his or her actions on the conduct of the others sellers in the market.

pool

(1) *general:* any combination of resources of funds, and so on, for some common purpose or benefit.

(2) *finance:* an agreement between two or more companies to curtail output, divide sales areas, or in any other way avoid competition.

(3) *finance:* firms joined to share business over a fixed time.

(4) *investments:* a combination of persons (brokers, traders) organized for the purpose of exploiting stocks. The SEC prohibits pool operations. see *SEC.*

pooled income fund: a fund to which several donors transfer property, retaining an income interest, and giving the remainder to a single charity. [105]

pooling of interests: a method of accounting for business combinations under which the net assets are accounted for in the combined corporation's financial statements at their book value as recorded in the combining corporations, and comparative figures are restated on a combined basis. [43]

pooling of wealth: placing together the money of different individuals so that a sufficient amount will be available for a special purpose.

pooling operation: a business similar to an investment trust or syndicate, which solicits, accepts, or receives from others funds for the purpose of trading in any commodity for futures delivery. see *pool.*

poor debtor's oath: in some states, an impoverished debtor may summon a creditor before a judge, and by taking a *poor debtor's oath,* be absolved from paying that particular debt. A poor person's method of bankruptcy.

poor merchant description: error in the printout of merchant name and location on the descriptive statement. [105]

portability: a characteristic of valuables that allows them to be carried easily (e.g., diamonds or stamps are more portable than bullion).

port differential: the difference in freight charges on the same item from a point of origin to two or more competing ports.

portfolio: holdings of securities by an individual or institution. A portfolio may contain bonds, preferred stocks, and common stocks of enterprises of various types.

portfolio selection theory: a concept developed by Nobel laureate James Tobin, enabling economists to trace the effects of monetary policies, interest rates, and inflation on investment decisions. Tobin showed that investors tend not just to seek a good return but to balance their holdings in accordance with the overall risks involved.

port of entry: in the United States, a place where a customs officer is stationed and responsible for administering customs regulations and collect duties on imported items.

POS: see *point of sale.*

POSDCORB: the seven functions of administration: planning, organizing, staffing, directing, coordinating, reporting, and budgeting.

position
(1) *general:* a job; an employment situation.
(2) *investments:* a stake in the market. see *technical position.*

position evaluation: the process of measuring the relative internal value of each position in the bank. [105]

position-schedule bond: see *bond, position-schedule.*

position sheet: an accounting statement, indicating the bank or foreign exchange firm's commitment in overseas currencies.

position traders: traders who take the long-term approach to the commodity markets, meaning anywhere from six months to a year or more.

positive authorization: authorization procedure whereby every account on file in the computer system can be accessed to determine its status before an authorization is granted or declined. [105]

positive carry: a condition where the yield on a security is greater than the interest cost on funds borrowed to finance its retention. [105]

positive file: an authorization system file that contains information about every account holder and is capable of providing a variety of data to be evaluated in responding to a request for authorization of credit, check cashing, or other privileges. see *ratio of accounts payable to purchases;* cf. *negative file.*

positively sloping yield curve: a yield curve where interest rates in the shorter periods are below those in the longer.

positive verification: see *direct verification.*

post
(1) *general:* to record onto detailed subsidiary records (ledgers) amounts that were recorded in chronological records of original entry. see also *suspense account.*
(2) *investments:* the horseshoe-shaped fixture on the New York Stock

Exchange trading floor where 100-share unit stocks and active 10-share unit stocks are bought and sold.

(3) see *point-of-sale terminal*.

postage currency: U.S. fractional currency issued in 1862 and 1863, deriving its name from the facsimile of a postage stamp on the reverse. Not to be confused with stamp money. [27]

postal money order: a checklike instrument sold by U.S. post offices for payment of a specified sum of money to the individual or firm designated by the purchaser. [59]

postaudit: an audit made after the transactions to be audited have taken place and have been recorded or have been approved for recording by designated officials, if such approval is required. see *preaudit*. [49]

postdate: dating an instrument a time after that on which it is made. see also *posting date*.

postdated check: a check bearing a date that has not yet arrived. Such a check cannot be paid by a bank before the date shown and must be returned to the maker or to the person attempting to use it. If presented on or after the date shown, the same check will be honored if the account contains sufficient funds.

POS terminal: device placed in a merchant location which is connected to the bank's system via telephone lines and is designed to authorize, record, and forward by electronic means each sale as it is taking place. [105]

posting: the act of transferring to an account in a ledger the data, either detailed or summarized, contained in a book or document of original entry. [49]

posting date

(1) *banking:* date a transaction is charged or credited to a cardholder account.

(2) *EFTS:* date on which entries are made on the books of the receiving bank. [105]

postlist: used generally in the book-keeping department of banks. Many banks use a posting plan whereby the old balances are listed *after* a posting run to prove the correct pickup of old balances, and to catch any "high posting" (posting over or above the last previous balance). When this type of proof is used, the bookkeeper is said to create a postlist of the previous old balances. The total of the postlist is the total of all old balances of accounts affected by the posting run. [10]

postmortem: pertaining to the analysis of an operation after its completion. [34]

postpurchase feelings: customer attitudes developed toward the bank and its various products based on experience and information which strongly influence future behavior. [105]

Post 30: the trading post at the New York Stock Exchange where usually inactive issues are traded in 10-share units rather than the normal roundlots of 100 shares. No odd-lot differential is involved on sales or purchases. Post 30 is located in the Exchange's annex, popularly referred to as the *garage*. see *garage*; see also *inactive post*.

pot: that part of a security issue set aside by a syndicate manager for distribution to dealers or institutions. see *pot protection*.

potentially dilutive: see *dilution*.

potential output (potential gross national product): the value of the final output of goods and services produced in a year if all resources (land, labor, and capital) are fully utilized. [57]

potential stock: the difference between the total authorized capital stock and the actually issued one.

potential value: a loose term signifying a value that would or will exist if and when future probabilities become actualities. [62]

pot protection: an arrangement guaranteeing that an institution receives a specified amount of stocks or bonds from a *pot*.

pound (pound sterling): monetary unit of Great Britain. Also the currency of Bermuda, Cyprus, Eygpt, Fiji Islands, Gibraltar, Grand Cayman Island, Ireland (Republic), Lebanon, Malta, Sudan, and Syria.

pourover: referring to the transfer of property from an estate or trust to another estate or trust upon the happening of an event as provided in the instrument. [37]

POW: pay order of withdrawal.

power: the authority or right to do or to refrain from doing a particular act, as a trustee's power of sale or power to withhold income. [37]

power in trust: a power that the donee (the trustee) is under a duty to exercise in favor of the beneficiary of the trust. [37]

power of alienation: the power to assign, transfer, or otherwise dispose of property. [37]

power of appointment: the equivalent of total ownership of part or all of a trust, since the individual having this power can identify the ultimate recipients of the trust's assets.

power of attorney: a written statement identifying a person as the agent for another with powers stated in the docu-ment. Full power may be granted, or the authority may be limited to certain functions, such as making deposits and withdrawals from a checking account. The statement must be executed before a notary and the signature of the agent is then placed on file with the bank. [29]

power of retention: the power expressed or implied in will or trust agreement permitting the trustee to retain certain or all of the investments comprising the trust property at inception, even though they may not be of a type suitable for new investments made by the trustee. [37]

power of sale: a clause included in a mortgage giving the holder or trustee the right to seize and sell the pledged property upon default in payments or upon the occurrence of any other violation of the conditions in the mortgage. see *shortcut foreclosure.*

POW money: paper money issued during World War II, valid for circulation in specified prisoner-of-war camps. [27]

pp
(1) see *paper profit.*
(2) see *partial payment.*
(3) see *purchase price.*

PPB: see *planning-programming-budgeting.*

PPBS: programming, planning, and budgeting systems; see *planning-programming budgeting.*

PPP: see *purchasing power parity theory.*

PPS: see *prior preferred (stock).*

Pr.
(1) preferred.
(2) see *principal.*

PR: see *pro rata.*

praecipium: in the Euromarket, the manager of a credit or bond who negotiates a fee payable by the borrower. From this the manager deducts a specified amount for itself—the praecipium before dividing the balance of the fee between the rest of the management group. [104]

PRD: see *payroll deductions.*

preaudit: the examination of a creditor's invoices, payrolls, claims, and expected reimbursements before actual payment, or the verification of sales transactions before delivery.

preauthorization order (PO): an agreement that permits the cardholder to effect a transaction, after signing an authorization with a merchant for such purchases, to be made from the merchant at a future date or dates without any need for the cardholder executing the resulting sales drafts or slips. [105]

preauthorized electronic fund transfer: an electronic funds transfer authorized in advance to recur at substantially regular intervals. [105]

preauthorized payment: a service that enables a debtor to request funds to be transferred from the customer's deposit account to the account of a creditor.

Prec.: precedent.

precatory words: expressions in a will praying or requesting (but not directing) that a thing be done or not done. [37]

precautionary liquidity balance: cash and securities held for use in emergencies.

precedence of order: the priority that one security has over another for buying or selling. When bids arrive, a priority exists to determine whose buy or sell order is accepted first.

preclusive purchasing
(1) *finance:* buying materials with the expectation of denying their use to a competitor.
(2) *government:* the activity of a belligerent country, aimed at preventing neutrals from selling the items purchased to an enemy. cf. *blockade.*

precomp: precomputation or precomputed loan. [55]

preconstruction affidavit: an affidavit, required by the lender on a construction loan, in which the borrower and contractor affirm that up to a specific date no work has been started on the lot and no materials delivered, prepared for use, or used.

predatory pricing: when a company attempts to damage or destroy a competitor by cutting the price of a product below cost (later, it can push prices back up). In a variation it can charge higher prices on some products to subsidize such below-cost sales. Or a big national company can cut prices on a product below cost in just one area to wipe out a small local competitor.

preemption
(1) in foreign trade, the right of a government to seize goods and sell them at the value declared by the importer if suspicion exists that the value declared is too low.
(2) as to public lands, the securing of the prior right to such lands by the party first taking possession and recording a claim together with nominal payment. This statutory right was repealed in 1891 and the Homestead Law substituted.

preemptive right: the privilege of a stockholder to buy a portion of a new issue of stock equal to his or her existing percentage holding.

preexamination: the process of analysis and review undertaken by the examiner in advance of the examination to establish objectives, determine the scope of the examination, and identify key activities of the bank. The examiner coordinates data and personnel needs with the bank during this phase, which may begin up to 60 days prior to the actual examination. [105]

Pref.: preference.

preference as to assets: in the event of dissolution of a firm, before disbursement of a declared dividend, stockholders holding preferred shares are entitled to claim payments before payments are made to common stockholders.

preference bond: see *bond, preference.*

preference shares (preferred stock): shares that receive a dividend at a stated rate prior to the paying out of any dividend on the firm's common shares.

preferential duty: synonymous with *differential duty.*

preferential tariff: a tariff that grants lower rates of duty on goods imported from certain "preferred" countries than on the same goods from other nations. cf. *most favored nation (clause).*

preferred capital stock: capital stock to which preferences or special rights are attached (i.e., preferred as to dividends and/or proceeds in liquidation) as compared to another class of stock issued by the same company.

preferred creditor: a creditor whose claim takes legal preference over the claim of another (such as government taxes over the amount owed to an individual). [10]

preferred debt
(1) *banking:* a first mortgage.

(2) *finance:* a debt that takes precedence over others.

preferred dividend charge: a financial ratio calculated as

$$\frac{\text{net income after taxes and interest}}{\text{annual preferred dividends payable}}$$

preferred dividends payable: an account containing a record of the amount owed to the preferred stockholders for dividends.

preferred lender banks: banks with more autonomy than other banks in approving loans.

preferred shares: a portion of the capital stock of a corporation which ranks after all bonds or other debt but has certain preferences over common stock. see *preferred stock.* [26]

preferred stock: corporate stock whose owners have some preference as to assets, earnings, and so on, not granted to the owners of common stock of the same corporation. see also *adjustment preferred securities, Class A stock, cumulative preferred (stock), effective par, guaranteed stock, privileged issue, voting right (stock).*

preferred stock, cumulative: see *cumulative preferred (stock).*

preferred stock, noncumulative: see *noncumulative.*

preferred stock, participating: see *participating preferred.*

preferred stock, prior: ranks ahead of any other preferred and common in claim on dividends and assets. [68]

preferred stock ratio: the stated or par value of preferred stock divided by the total value of bonds, preferred stock, common stock, reserves, and surplus.

preferring creditors: a solvent debtor may prefer his or her creditors (i.e., pay them as he or she sees fit). An insolvent debtor who has within four months before bankruptcy paid creditors who did not at the time of payment give full consideration is presumed to have preferred them, and the payment may be recalled unless it can be shown that the payment did not defraud the other creditors. Even payments prior to four months may be proven to be fraudulent preferences, but the burden of so proving is on the party claiming fraud.

prelegal section: the component of a bank card operation responsible for collection effort on accounts in an advanced stage of delinquency, prior to the necessity for legal action. [105]

preliminary expenses: expenses incurred in the establishment of an organization (e.g., costs for developing and circulating a prospectus).

preliminary prospectus: an advance report giving the details of a planned offering of corporate stock. The issue is still in the process of being registered by the SEC and cannot be sold until clearance is received. synonymous with *red herring*; see also *open prospectus.*

preliminary title report: the results of a title search by a title company prior to issuing a title binder or commitment to insure. [105]

prelist: used generally in bookkeeping in a bank as a part of the bank's posting plan. After offsetting the ledger sheets to be affected by a posting run, the bookkeeper makes a prelist run of the balances, thus creating a total of all balances that will be affected by the run to be made. This is the opposite of *postlist*, but has the same effect in the proof of pickup of old balances. [10]

Prem.: see *premium.*

premium

   (1) ***banking:*** the sum paid for a pol-

icy, not to be confused with premiums. An earned premium is the portion of the written premium covering the part of the policy term that is included in the time period. The pure premium is found by dividing losses by a hazard or contingency, and to which no operating expenses of the firm has been added (e.g., commissions, taxes).

   (2) ***finance:*** the amount by which one form of funds exceeds another in buying power.

   (3) ***investments:*** the amount by which a preferred stock or bond may sell above its par value. In the case of a new issue of bonds or stocks, a premium is the amount the market price rises over the original selling price.

   (4) ***investments:*** a charge sometimes made when a stock is borrowed to make delivery on a short sale.

   (5) ***investments:*** the redemption price of a bond or preferred stock, if this price is higher than face value.

   (6) ***investments:*** the price of a put or call determined through the auction process. [5]

premium audit: an examination by a representative of the insurer of the insured's records, insofar as they relate to the policies or coverages under consideration. see *audit.*

premium bond: see *bond, premium.*

premium card: a bank or credit card issued at a greater cost than that of an ordinary card but having greater buying power or associated features for its holder. cf. *debit card.*

premium currency: see *currency.*

premium finance: a facility that allowed an insured to finance his or her payment over a specified period within the term of the policy.

premium for risk: the actual yield on

an investment minus the basic yield prevailing at the time.

premium loan: a policy loan made for the purpose of paying premiums. [58]

premium of initial servicing fee: see *loan fee.*

premium on bonds: the amount or percentage by which bonds are purchased, sold, or redeemed for more than their face value.

premium on capital stock: the excess of the cash or cash value of the consideration received from the sale of capital stock (excluding accrued dividends) over the par or stated value of such stock. [3]

premium on funded debt: the excess of the actual cash value of the consideration received for funded debt securities (of whatever kind) issued or assumed over the par value of such securities and the accrued interest thereon. [18]

premium on securities: the amount by which a security (a bond or a share of stock) is bought or sold for more than its face or par value; opposed to discount on securities. [37]

premium over conversion value: the difference between the price of the convertible and its conversion value, often expressed in percentages. If the conversion value is $400 and the convertible is selling at $500, then the premium is 25 percent.

premium pay: a wage rate higher than straight time, payable for overtime work, work on holidays, or scheduled days off, or for work on evening shifts.

premium raids: the unannounced, lightning-quick buying sprees that several companies have mounted to build up large stakes in other companies by offering a bonus over the prevailing stock market share price.

premium recapture: the time it takes for the convertible's yield advantage (the difference between what the bond pays in interest yearly and what the underlying common would pay in dividends) to recoup the premium paid over the conversion value. The shorter, the better. Anything less than two years is considered good.

premiums on bonds: the amount or percentage by which bonds are bought, sold, or redeemed for more than their face value. [37]

premium stock
(1) a stock that lends at a premium (i.e., an amount charged for loaning it to a person who borrowed it to make delivery on a short sale).
(2) an average, superior stock; any confirmed leader.

prenuptial agreement: a contract made before marriage; each future spouse forfeits any interest in the other's estate.

prepaid: indicating that shipping charges have already been paid or are to be paid at the point of delivery. see *franco delivery.*

prepaid charge plan: see *contractual plan.*

prepaid expense: payment for items not yet received; a charge deferred for a period of time until the benefit for which payment has been made occurs (e.g., rent paid for future months). cf. *accrued liabilities.*

prepay: to pay before or in advance of receipt of goods or services.

prepayment: the payment of a debt before it actually becomes due.

prepayment clause
(1) *general:* the privilege of repay-

ing part or all of a loan in advance of date or dates stated in a contract.

(2) *banking:* a clause in a mortgage allowing the mortgagor to pay off part or all of the unpaid debt before it becomes due. This affords a saving for the mortgagor.

prepayment fee: see *prepayment penalty.*

prepayment of taxes: the deposit of money with a governmental unit on condition that the amount deposited is to be applied against the tax liability of a designated taxpayer after the taxes have been levied and such liability has been established. [49]

prepayment penalty: a penalty placed on a mortgagor for paying the mortgage before its due date. This applies when there is no prepayment clause to offset the penalty.

prepayment privilege: an optional clause in a mortgage which gives the mortgagor the right to pay all or part of a debt prior to its maturity. [105]

prepurchase activity: period during which the individual becomes sensitive to cues which may satisfy a need. This is the period during which the customer is most open to and aware of promotions. [105]

prerefunding: an exchange by holders of securities maturing in less than one year for securities of longer original maturity, usually due within 10 years. [71]

prerogatives: the rights, powers, privileges (e.g., diplomatic immunity) of an individual that others do not possess.

Pres.: see *president.*

prescription: title to property or means of obtaining title based on uninterrupted possession.

presentation: a legal term used in con-

nection with negotiable instruments. The act of presentation technically means the actual delivery of a negotiable instrument by a holder in due course to the drawee for acceptance, or to the maker for payment. Upon presentation, the holder in due course requests acceptance of a draft, or requests payment of the instrument from the maker of a note, check, or whatever. see *negotiable.* [10]

present beneficiary: synonymous with *immediate beneficiary.* [32]

present capital: proprietorship at the conclusion of a fiscal period.

presenting bank: the bank that forwards an item to another bank for payment. [105]

presentment: synonymous with *presentation.*

present value: the discounted value of a certain sum due and payable at a certain specified future date.

present value of expected cash flow: the net cash that a company expects to realize or pay out from holding an asset or liability, discounted by an appropriate rate of interest.

preservation of capital: a form of investment, with the objective of preserving capital by way of avoiding high-risk situations. cf. *go-go fund.*

Preservation of Consumer Claims and Defenses Rule: see *Holder in Due Course Rule.*

preshipment finance: finance covering an exporter's costs prior to despatch of the items.

president: the highest ranking executive responsible for the policy decisions of an organization; the president reports to a board of directors.

prestige card: a plastic identification card issued by savings and loan associations to their customers to be used in electronic funds transfer systems.

presumptive tax: a tax based on some circumstance of living, such as a hearth tax, a window tax, or a carriage tax, on the presumption that such a tax indicates ability to pay and economic or social status.

presumptive title: possession of property that leads others to presume ownership, where in fact ownership may not exist. cf. *cloud on title.*

pretax earnings: income which is subject to federal income tax.

pretermitted child: a child to whom the parent's will leaves no share of his or her estate without affirmative provision in the will showing an intention to omit. It frequently is an after-born child, a posthumous child, a child erroneously believed to be dead or unintentionally omitted. [37]

pretermitted heir: an heir not included in the descent or devolution of the parent's estate. [37]

previous balance: the cardholder account balances as of the last billing period. [105]

previous balance method: method used for calculating finance charges on accounts that have not converted to average daily balance. Calculated by subtracting payments and credits posted during the billing period from the previous balance. [105]

price: the amount of money the seller receives for goods or services at the factory or place of business. Price is not what the seller asks for the product, but what is actually received.

price auction: see *auction.*

price clearing: the settlement price at which a clearinghouse clears all the buy and sell orders for the day, or at which an exchange settles unliquidated contracts.

price control
(1) *finance:* the result of the demand by a manufacturer that the buyer for resale not be able to determine a resale price for the goods.
(2) *government:* regulation of the prices of goods and services with the intent to reduce increases in the cost of living, to fight inflation, or during emergencies. see *rollback.*

priced out of the market: a market situation wherein the asked-for price of an item eliminates possible buyers, leading to a decline in sales volume.

price-earnings (P/E) ratio: the price of a share of stock divided by earnings per share for a 12-month period. For example, a stock selling for $50 a share and earning $5 a share is said to be selling at a price-earnings ratio of 10:1. [20]

price elasticity: reflected in a reduction in sales when the price of an item is raised.

price fixing: an agreement by competing organizations to avoid competitive pricing by charging identical prices or by changing prices at the same time. Price fixing is in violation of the Sherman Antitrust Act. cf. *price stabilization.*

price index: a measure used to illustrate the changes in the average level of prices. see *purchasing power of the dollar, wholesale price index.*

price leadership: a situation in which prices can be determined by one major manufacturer in an industry, thus influencing others to accept the prices as determined. see *administered price.*

price level: a relative position in the

scale of prices as determined by a comparison of prices (of labor, materials, capital, etc.) with prices as of other times. [62]

price-level-adjusted mortgage (PLAM): a unique mortgage plan in which the outstanding loan balance is indexed. The interest rate is a rate net of any inflation premium. The payments on a PLAM are based on this real rate, and at the end of each year, the then outstanding balance is adjusted by an inflation factor. The principal benefit of a PLAM is the much lower initial payment than either a GPM, GPAM, or a shared appreciation mortgage. see *graduated-payment adjustable mortgage, graduated-payment mortgage, shared-appreciation mortgage.*

price limit: the price that is entered on the trading floor of an exchange for placing an order to buy or sell. see *limited order, market order.*

price loco: the price at the place where a purchase occurs.

price range: the area bound by the highest and lowest prices of a stock under discussion, or the general market, over a specified time frame such as a day, week, and so on.

price rigidity: long-term insensitivity of prices of raw or manufactured items to the inflationary influences of a recession or depression.

price rule: requires that the monetary authority attempt to maintain a chosen price index at a particular level by varying the stock of money. The sole function of policy is to prevent the price index from deviating substantially from a predetermined level. This is equivalent to keeping the relevant inflation rate at zero. [99]

price-special flow theory: a theory stating that imports of precious metals increase the supply of funds and therefore advance the price level of items using these metals.

price-specie-flow mechanism: the theory that when trade and gold are free to move internationally in settlement of balances of trade, a country receiving gold because of an excess of exports over imports will find its price level rising because of the increase in its money supply. As a result the country will experience less exports. Conversely, because of higher prices at home its imports will grow. This will require the export of gold, and the price level of imports will rise enough to produce equilibrium of trade. Opposite events occur in the nation from which the gold was first shipped.

price spreading: the simultaneous purchase and sale of options in the same class with the same expiration date but with different striking prices. see *spread.*

price stabilization: keeping prices at a stated level. Primarily a government strategy, especially during wartime or periods of rapid inflation, but illegal when practiced by private companies. see *Sherman Antitrust Act of 1980;* cf. *price fixing.*

price support: subsidy or financial aid offered to specific growers, producers, or distributors, in accordance with governmental regulations to keep market prices from dropping below a certain minimum level. see *farm subsidies;* cf. *Brannan plan.*

price taker: a relatively small purchaser or seller who has no impact on the market price.

pricing out the market: a price structure so high that goods fail to sell in their traditional market.

prima facie: at first view; that which appears to be true until contrary evidence is given.

Primary Account Number (PAN): the embossed and/or encoded number, consisting of the major industry identifier, issuer identifier, individual account identifier, and check digit which identifies the card issuer to which the transaction is to be routed and the account to which the transaction is to be applied unless specific instructions, with a transaction message, indicate otherwise. [105]

primary bank reserve: the total of legal reserves plus working reserves. This total is shown on bank statements with the title "cash and due from bank."

primary beneficiary: synonymous with *immediate beneficiary.*

primary boycott: see *boycott.*

primary commodity: a commodity that has not undergone any significant amount of processing (i.e., raw wool, crude oil).

primary data: information obtained from original sources for the specific purpose of the study being conducted, such as a survey of corporate accounts to determine their degree of satisfaction with the bank's performance. [105]

primary deposits: cash deposits in a bank.

primary distribution: the original sale of a company's securities. synonymous with *primary offering.* [20]

primary insurance: see *excess insurance.*

primary market
(1) *general:* the initial market for any item or service.

(2) *investments:* the initial market for a new stock issue.

(3) *investments:* a firm, trading market held in a security by a trader who performs the activities of a specialist by being ready to execute orders in that stock.

primary money: standard money.

primary movement: synonymous with *major trend.*

primary offering: synonymous with *primary distribution.*

primary points: primary trading centers for agricultural commodities (e.g., Chicago, Kansas City).

primary producer: a nation producing a primary commodity.

primary receipts: the amount of a commodity received at a primary trading center for the commodity during a fixed period or agricultural marketing season.

primary reserves: a bank's legal reserves of cash and demand deposits with the Federal Reserve Bank and other banks.

primary trend: the direction in stock values that last for many months and usually for years.

prime: a very high grade or quality.

prime bill of exchange: a draft or trade acceptance which states on the face of the instrument that it was created through a business transaction inolving the movement of goods. Bankers' acceptances are considered prime bills of exchange, although smaller banks must generally have the endorsement without recourse of a large bank enjoying high financial recognition in order to give the instrument "prime status." Prime bills of exchange are acceptable for rediscount with the Federal Reserve Bank, and therefore can be construed as a "secondary reserve" for banks. [10]

prime cost: the sum of direct labor expenditures plus direct materials cost that are identified with a product. see also *loading*.

prime interest (rate): the rate of interest charged by a bank for loans made to its most credit-worthy business and industrial customers; it is the lowest interest rate charged by the bank. The prime rate level is determined by how much banks have to pay for the supply of money from which they make loans. see also *discount rate*.

prime investment

(1) *general:* quality, first-class investment.

(2) *investments:* a high-grade investment, considered so safe and sound that dividends or interest payments are assumed.

prime maker: the party (or parties) signing a negotiable instrument and becoming the original party responsible for its ultimate payment. see *liabilities*.

prime merchant category: a classification of merchants which historical data show are good producers of credit card volume and are most likely to affiliate with a bank card plan. [105]

prime rate: see *prime interest (rate)*.

prime status: see *prime bill of exchange*.

primogeniture: under common law, the right of the eldest child to inherit all real property of the parent; the estate usually passes to the son, but daughters are increasingly inheriting under this right. cf. *entail*.

Prin.: see *principal*.

principal

(1) *general:* one of the major parties to a transaction; either the seller or purchaser.

(2) *banking:* the original amount of a deposit, loan, or other amount of money on which interest is earned or paid. see also *billed principal*.

(3) *finance:* the face value of an instrument, which becomes the obligation of the maker or drawee to pay to a holder in due course. Interest is charged on the principal amount.

(4) *investments:* the person for whom a broker executes an order, or a dealer buying or selling for his or her own account.

principal balance: the outstanding total of a mortgage or other debt, excluding interest or premium.

principal beneficiary: synonymous with *ultimate beneficiary*.

principal only: an account on which payment is being credited to principal; that is, interest is no longer being charged on remaining balance. [55]

principal sum: the amount specified under a life insurance policy, such as the death benefit.

principal underwriter: synonymous with *managing underwriter*.

prior deductions method: an improper method of determining bond interest or preferred dividend coverage: the requirements of senior obligations are first deducted from earnings and the balance is applied to the requirements of the junior issue.

prior lien: a mortgage that ranks ahead of another.

prior-lien bond: see *bond, prior-lien*.

prior preferred (stock): see *preferred stock, prior*.

prior redemption: an obligation that a debtor has paid prior to stated maturity.

prior redemption privilege: a privilege frequently extended by a debtor to the holders of called bonds permitting them to redeem their holdings prior to the call date or maturity. There are chiefly three types of offers prior redemption: (1) with interest in full to the call date; (2) with interest in full to the call date less a bank discount (usually $1/4$ percent per annum) based on the period from the date of collection to the date of call; and (3) with interest to the date of collection only. [37]

prior sale: when the supply of an item or commodity is limited, the owner or his or her broker can offer it, at a price subject to the fact that more than one buyer may wish the item. Thus the first bid for the item will purchase it. The public is told that bids after the first may not be effective because of some prior sale.

prior stock: any preferred stock.

prior years' tax levies: taxes levied for fiscal periods preceding the current one. [49]

private bank: a bank chartered by the state in which it operates, subject to state laws and regulations, and subject to examinations by the state banking authorities. The principal distinction between private banks and other state banks is that the private bank may arise from a partnership, in which there is no capital stock.

private corporation: a corporation created to conduct enterprises for private profit.

private debt: the monetary amount owed by the public and firms of a country and not including the amount owed by various levels of government.

private enterprise: the organization of production in which the business is owned and operated by people taking

risks and motivated by the wish to make a profit. see *capitalist;* cf. *people's capitalism.*

Private Export Funding Corporation: a U.S. company owned primarily by U.S. commercial banks and industrial firms.

private financing: the raising of capital for a business venture via private rather than public placement, resulting in the sale of securities to a relatively few number of investors. Such investments do not have to be registered with the SEC since no public offering is involved. synonymous with *private placement.*

private lender: an individual who lends money from institutional funds (insurance companies, banks, etc.).

private mortgage insurance: insurance offered by a private company that protects an association against loss up to policy limits (customarily 20 to 25 percent of the loan amount) on a defaulted mortgage loan. Its use is usually limited to loans with a high loan-to-value ratio; the borrower pays the premiums. [59]

private notes: paper money issued by merchants, shopkeepers or anyone other than the legally authorized government agency. [27]

private placement: synonymous with *private financing.*

private property: all land not owned by the government.

private rate of return
(1) *general:* the financial rate of return anticipated by business-people prior to investing their monies.
(2) *finance:* the expected net profit after taxes and all costs, including depreciation, expressed as a percentage annual return on the total cost of an

effort or the net worth of the stock-holder owners. see *ROI*.

private remittances: represent transfers or transmissions of cash and goods by individuals and by charitable and nonprofit institutions to individuals or groups residing abroad. Personal remittances include all noncommercial transfers of funds to be sent abroad by means of customary bank drafts and money orders. [73]

private sector: the segment of the total economy composed of businesses and households, but excluding government. cf. *public sector.*

private trust
(1) a trust created for the benefit of a designated beneficiary or designated beneficiaries; as, a trust for the benefit of the settlor's or the testator's wife and children; opposed to a charitable (or public) trust.
(2) a trust created under a declaration of trust or under a trust agreement; as, a living trust or an insurance trust; opposed to a trust coming under the immediate supervision of a court. see *court trust.* [32]

private trust fund: a trust fund that will ordinarily revert to private individuals or will be used for private purposes. For example, a fund that consists of guarantee deposits. [49]

private wire firm: brokerage companies that are sufficiently large to allow them to rent telegraph wires for their own branch office communications.

privilege: see *spread, straddle*. see also *privilege dealer.*

privilege broker: see *privilege dealer.*

privileged bond: see *bond, privileged.*

privilege dealer: a broker or dealer in the business of selling puts and calls

and variations of such options, which are also referred to as *privileges.*

privilege issue: a preferred stock or bond having a conversion or participating right, or having a stock purchase warrant on it.

privileges: options such as puts, calls, and straddles.

Pro.: see *protest.*

probate
(1) *general:* the right or jurisdiction of hearing and determining questions or issues in matters concerning a will.
(2) *law:* the action or process of proving before a court of law that a document offered for official recognition as the last will and testament of a deceased person is genuine.

probate court: the court that has jurisdiction with respect to wills and intestacies and sometimes guardianships and adoptions; also called *court of probate, ordinary court, orphan's court, perfect's court,* and *surrogate's court.* [37]

probate in solemn form: the probate of a will in a formal proceeding after notice to the interested parties; opposed to probate in common form, which is an informal proceeding without such notice. [37]

probate of will: presentation of proof before the proper officer or court that the instrument offered is the last will of the decedent. [37]

problem bank: a bank, watched by a government agency, in danger of failure or bankruptcy.

Proc.: procedure.

proceeding: any transaction; a measure or action taken in a business.

proceeds
(1) *finance:* the actual amount of funds given to a borrower, following de-

ductions for interest charges, fees, and so on.

(2) *finance:* the funds received by a seller after deductions for the payment of commissions, as with proceeds from a sale.

process effects: the increase in consumer spending and private investment created by the spending on a public-works project.

processing: the preparation of a mortgage loan application and supporting documents for consideration by a lender or insurer. [105]

processing date: the date on which the transaction is processed by the acquiring bank. [105]

process method of cost accounting: a system of accumulating manufacturing costs by process (or by department or cost center). These accumulated costs are allocated on some averaging basis to the units of the product flowing through the process. This system is usable where there is mass production of homogenous units, as opposed to the production of individual or special jobs. cf. *job method of cost accounting.*

procuration: the authority given to another to sign instruments and to act on behalf of the person giving the procuration.

produce exchange
(1) a spot market for perishable agricultural products.
(2) a contract market where futures contracts are transacted for agricultural products.

producer prices: the successor to the wholesale price index, this measure contains data on prices by stage of processing, sector, industry, and commodity. Bureau of Labor Statistics

measure issued the first week of the month for the previous month.

product: goods and services made available to consumers. The total of benefits offered.

production costs: factory costs plus administrative expenses.

production loan: a loan, the proceeds of which are used for the purpose of producing goods or services.

production unit method of depreciation: taking the initial cost of a capital asset, deducting the expected salvage value at the time it is discarded, and spreading the difference on the basis of actual units produced in a period as a percentage of the total number of units that the asset will produce in its expected life.

product item: a specific version of a product (e.g., a one-year certificate of deposit). [105]

productivity: a measurement of the efficiency of production: a ratio of output to input (e.g., 10 units per man-hour).

product line: a group of products that are closely related (e.g., the entire group of savings accounts offered). [105]

product payback: trade financing where an import is financed with some of the exports it helps to produce.

professional: in the securities business, a student of the market or a person who makes a living buying and selling securities. A professional may direct the investments of a pension fund or other institution, or be a member of a brokerage firm who advises or acts for his firm's clients. [20]

profit
(1) *general:* the excess of the selling price over all costs and expenses incurred in making a sale.

(2) **banking:** the monies remaining after a business has paid all its bills. see also *contribution profit.*

(3) **finance:** the reward to the entrepreneur for the risks assumed by him or her in the establishment, operation, and management of a given enterprise or undertaking.

profitability: a firm's ability to earn a profit and the potential for future earnings.

profitability index: present value of future cash flow benefits divided by the initial investment.

profitability ratios: ratios indicating how efficiently a firm is being managed. [105]

profit and loss account: an account transferred from accounts receivable to a separate ledger. An amount deducted from the accounts receivable balance. An account deemed to be uncollectable, or a certain number of months past due, becomes eligible for transfer to the "profit and loss account" ledger. [41]

profit and loss reserve: an amount set aside by a firm to provide for anticipated "P & L accounts" during the fiscal period. Usually calculated as given percentage of the total "accounts receivable." [41]

profit and loss statement (operating statement; P & L): the summary listing of a firm's total revenues and expenses within a specified time period. synonymous with *income and expense statement.*

profit and loss summary account: an account to which balances of all the income and all the expense accounts are transferred at the conclusion of the fiscal period.

profit break-even point: assuming a

plant organized for a given ideal volume of output, units of output are put on one axis and total dollars on the other axis. The profit break-even point is the intersection of the total income curve (including accruals) and the total cost curve (including accruals).

profit center: a segment of a business that is responsible for both revenues and expenses.

profit margin: the ratio of sales less all operating expenses divided by the number of sales.

profit on fixed assets: the profit resulting when the book value of a fixed asset is less than the actual value at the time the asset is sold.

profit on net worth ratio: a profitability ratio (net profit after taxes divided by net worth) indicating how well invested funds are used. [105]

profit sharing: an arrangement under which employees share in company profits, based on company successes, according to a plan. This compensation is paid in addition to wages. There are cash plans (giving a share of profits in cash) and deferred plans (setting up a trust for payment upon retirement, death, or disability). see *employee stock ownership plans, Lincoln Incentive Management Plan.*

profit-sharing bond: see *bond, profit-sharing.*

profit-sharing securities: participating bonds or participating preferred stock.

profit-sharing trust: a trust established by an employer (usually a corporation) as a means of having the employees share in the profits of the enterprise. [37]

profit squeeze: profit shrinkage resulting from stable prices and increasing costs.

profits tax: a tax on business profits, excluding income taxes.

profit taking: the sale of stock that has appreciated in value since purchase, in order to realize the profit that has been made possible. This activity is often cited to explain a downturn in the market following a period of rising prices. cf. *unloading.*

pro forma invoice: a preliminary invoice indicating the value of the items listed and informing the recipient that all have been sent. It is not a demand for money.

pro forma statements: financial statements projected or predicted to occur given certain assumptions about future economic events.

program
(1) a set of step-by-step instructions that prepares a computer to perform an operation; also, the operation itself, performed upon the date for which it is designed.
(2) to prepare instructions for a specific operation or to enter these instructions into the computer. [59]

program budgeting: a long-range approach to budgetary decision making that relates future expenditures to broadly defined objectives of the organization.

program evaluation and review technique (PERT): an approach to facilitate planning and to give management tools for the control of specific programs. Original PERT programs were developed by the U.S. Navy. cf. *critical path method, PERT/COST.*

programmer: a person who designs, writes, and tests computer programs. see *analyst, program.*

programming: the art of reducing the plan for a solution to a problem to instructions that can be fed to a computer. see *programmer.*

progressive tax: an income tax that rises as income increases. The rate of increase varies. see *ability to pay, degressive taxation, graduated tax;* cf. *regressive taxes.*

progress payment plan: a method of construction loan payouts in which the contractor presents to the association all bills and lien waivers from time to time as construction progresses. [59]

prohibited basis: the Equal Credit Opportunity Act provides that consumer credit cannot be denied on a prohibited basis, including race, color, religion, national origin, sex, marital status, or age (provided that the applicant has the capacity to enter into a binding contract); the fact that all or part of the applicant's income derives from any public assistance program; or the fact that the applicant has in good faith exercised any right under the Consumer Credit Protection Act. [105]

project budget: a budget separate from the general budget of a business and containing estimates for a contemplated activity, such as a new product.

project line: a line of credit made available to finance a specific project; used in export credits financing.

Project Link: a huge econometric model of the global economy that generates consistent forecasts for individual economies while considering the feedback effects among countries. The popularizer of this concept is the 1980 Nobel Prize winner in economics, Dr. Lawrence R. Klein, of the University of Pennsylvania.

promisor: a firm or person responsible

in keeping a promise such as an acceptor or maker of a bill or note.

promissory note: any written promise to pay; a negotiable instrument that is evidence of a debt contracted by a borrower from a creditor, known as a lender of funds. If the instrument does not have all the qualities of a negotiable instrument, it cannot legally be transferred see *accommodation paper, note.*

promoter: one who acts as a middleman in business in order to bring together those with money to risk and those who have a business proposition. His or her duties may include securing new funds for old or new business ventures, discovering new ventures, or merging established businesses.

prompt date: on the London Metal Exchange, the date on which a metal has to be delivered to fulfill the terms of the purchase contract.

proof

(1) an operation for testing the accuracy of a previous operation—for example, relisting the checks and adding their amounts to determine the accuracy of the total shown on a deposit slip.

(2) applied to the proof sheet, the record on which the test is made.

(3) describes the method by which a type of transaction is proved, as in transit proof. Proof is generally affected when a total agrees with another total of the same items arrived at in a different manner; it is then said to be in balance. [32]

proof department: a department of a bank charged with the duties of sorting, distributing, and proving all transactions arising from the commercial operations of the bank. The proof function involves the creation of adequate records of all transactions, showing the proper distribution of all items going to other departments for further processing, and proof of the correctness of all transactions passing through the bank. The records created by the proof department are of vital importance, since examination of these records may be made months after a transaction occurs, in order to substantiate the accuracy of deposits made by customers and to establish legally that deposits were made by certain individual depositors. [10]

proof machine: equipment that simultaneously sorts items, records the dollar amount for each sorted group, and balances the total to the original input amount. [105]

proofs: the final design of an issue prepared by a printing company as a sample for the issuing authority, but not of course intended for circulation. Proofs are always printed on a different type of paper from that used for the final issue, whereas specimen notes are always on the same paper. [27]

Prop.: see *property.*

propensity to consume (average): the ratio between consumption and income (for an individual or a nation). cf. *marginal propensity to consume.*

propensity to invest (average): the ratio between new capital formation and nation income. cf. *marginal propensity to invest.*

propensity to save (average): the ratio between the income not spent on consumption and national income, or in the case of an individual, the ratio of income not spent on consumption to income. cf. *marginal propensity to save.*

property

(1) *general:* the exclusive right or interest of a person in his or her belongings.

(2) *law:* that which is legally owned by a person or persons and may be used and disposed of as the owner(s) see fit.

property assessment: the valuation of real property for tax purposes. [59]

property capital: stocks, bonds, mortgages, and notes are examples, but currency and bank deposits are not.

property dividends: dividends paid by one corporation in the form of stocks of another corporation, which the former may have acquired by purchase or received from the sale of property.

property search report: a type of credit bureau report that deals specifically with details of real property owned by a subject of inquiry. Frequently involves a search of country courthouse records for details of purchase, title, mortgage, or other encumbrance on property. [41]

property tax: synonymous with *land tax.*

proportional tax: a tax whose percentage rate stays constant as the tax base increases, resulting in the amount of paid tax being proportional to the tax base (e.g., property tax).

proprietary accounts: those accounts which show actual financial condition and operations such as actual assets, liabilities, reserves, surplus, revenues, and expenditures, as distinguished from budgetary accounts. [49]

proprietary card: a plastic card designed and for the exclusive benefit of customers of the issuing institution.

Some EFT systems will allow proprietary cards to access a shared system without compromising proprietary features. [105]

proprietary company: a nonfunctioning parent company of a nonfunctioning controlling company, formed for the purpose of investing in the securities of other companies, and for controlling these companies through such holdings. synonymous with *holding company* and *parent company.*

proprietor: a person who has an exclusive right or interest in property or in a business.

proprietorship: a business owned by one person. The individual owner has all the rights to profits from the business as well as all the liabilities and losses. synonymous with *individual proprietorship.*

proprietorship certificate: a certificate filed with a bank showing the ownership of a privately owned business enterprise.

pro rata: "according to the rate" (Latin); in proportion to a total amount. For example, if a contract is terminated prior to the end of the period for which payment has been given, a pro rata return of the payment is made, in proportion to the unused period of time remaining.

pro rata rate: a premium rate charged for a short term at the same proportion of the rate for a longer term as the short term bears to the longer term. see *short-rate cancellation.* [53]

pro rata sinking fund: a sinking fund that allocates redemption payments according to a formula established by the issuer.

prorate: to redistribute a portion of a cost to a department or product in accordance with an agreed-upon formula.

pro rate cancellation: the termination of an insurance contract or bond, with the premium charge being adjusted in proportion to the exact time the protection has been in force. cf. *flat cancellation, short-rate cancellation.*

prospect: a potential customer. see *qualified prospect.*

prospectus

(1) *general:* a plan of a proposed enterprise.

(2) *banking:* a description of property for sale or lease.

(3) *investments:* a written offer to sell a security; it provides information about the quality of the stock that is regulated by the SEC. cf. open *prospectus, red herring.*

prosperity: the uppermost phase of a business cycle. cf. *depression.*

protected check: a check that is prepared in such a manner as to prevent alterations. For example: *machine protection*—perforating the paper with pressure and indelible ink. *Paper protection*—any erasure of matter written in ink, by rubber eraser, knife, or chemical eradicator will remove the sensitive color and show instantly that an alteration has been attempted. *Machine printing protection*—the machine automatically prints stars or asterisks between the dollar sign and first digit of the amount. An indelible ink ribbon is used, or a ribbon treated with a acid that eats into the paper. [10]

protection

(1) *banking:* synonymous with *coverage.*

(2) *government:* the imposition of high (i.e., protective) tariffs on imports that are presumed to compete with do-

mestic items, with the objective of giving the domestic manufacturer an advantage. see *infant industry argument.*

protectionists: people who favor high tariffs and other import restrictions to enable domestic items to compete more favorably with foreign items.

protective committee: a committee formed to represent security holders in negotiations on defaulted securities. [39]

protective stocks: synonymous with *defensive stocks.*

protective tariff: a tax on imported goods designed to give domestic manufacturers an economic shield against price competition from abroad. cf. *revenue tariffs.*

protest: a written statement by a notary public, or other authorized person, under seal for the purpose of giving formal notice to parties secondarily liable that an instrument has been dishonored, either by refusal to accept or by refusal to make payment. [50]

protest fee: a charge made by a notary public for protesting a negotiable instrument which has failed to be honored.

protest jacket: synonymous with *notice of dishonor (protest jacket).*

prove: in banking, the act of creating a record, to show by a list or run of the items, the accuracy of a list or deposit created by another person. The list shows that each item is listed correctly as to amount, and that the amounts listed add up to an exact total. The two lists, one made by the bank as a record, and the other created by another person, such as a depositor, must agree in total to be *in proof.* [10]

proving cash: determining that the

cash on hand is equal to the original balance plus the receipts minus payments.

provision: a charge for an estimated expense or liability or for the diminution in the cost or value of an asset. [43]

provision for loan loss: a charge for anticipated loan losses, which appears on the bank's income statement as an operating expense.

proximate clause: defining the cause that directly produces a loss.

proximo: in the following month. cf. *instant (inst.)*.

proxy: a power of attorney given by a stockholder to an individual or individuals to exercise the stockholder's rights to vote at corporate meetings.

proxy statement: printed information required by the SEC to be given to potential holders of securities traded on a national exchange, supplying minimum descriptions of the stock, timing of the proposed sale, and so on.

prudent investment-cost standard: a means of defining the value of an organization by subtracting the costs of unwise, inappropriate, or wasteful investments from the original costs of the assets.

prudent man rule: an investment standard. In some states, the law requires that a fiduciary, such as a trustee, may invest the fund's money only in a list of securities designated by the state—the so-called legal list. In other states, the trustee may invest in a security if it is one that would be bought by a prudent person of discretion and intelligence, who is seeking a reasonable income and preservation of capital.

P&S: see *purchase and sale statement*.

PS
(1) see *penny stocks*.
(2) see *pink sheets*.
(3) see *preferred stock*.
(4) see *price spreading*.
(5) see *profit sharing*.

PSE: see *Pacific Coast Stock Exchange*.

PST: see *profit-sharing trust*.

psychological theory of the cycle: emphasis is placed in this theory on waves of optimism or pessimism as causing the business cycle through the consequent buying or hoarding. Many causes are recognized as possible reasons for the optimism or pessimism.

PT
(1) see *paper title*.
(2) see *passing title*.
(3) see *perfect title*.
(4) see *profit taking*.

Ptas.: see *peseta*.

PTE: see *pretax earnings*.

P. Tr.: see *private trust*.

public administrator: in many states, a county officer whose main duty is to settle the estates of persons who die intestate, when there is no member of the family, creditor, or other person having a prior right of administration who is able to administer the estate. [32]

public bond: see *bond, public*.

public corporation: a corporation created by government for a partly specific public purpose.

public credit: the capacity of political units to acquire funds in return for their promise to pay. Represented by government, municipal, and other public agencies' bonds and notes.

public debt: the debt of the federal

government. Sometimes includes the debt of state and local governments.

public debt transaction: see *back-door financing.*

public deposits: any bank deposit made by a federal, state, or municipal government.

public domain

(1) lands over which a government exercises proprietary rights. synonymous with *public lands.*

(2) the condition when a copyright or patent right expires, and the process or concept identified may then be exploited by anyone.

public finance: see *finance.*

public funds: accounts established for any government, agency, or authority of government, or political subdivision. [105]

public lands: see *public domain.*

Public Law 94-455: see *Tax Reform Act of 1976.*

publicly owned corporation

(1) a company owned by some unspecified number of people who have purchased shares of its capital stock.

(2) a company whose shares are traded on the open market. [105]

public offering: new or subsequent issues of stocks sold to the general public. cf. *private financing (private placement).*

public official bond: see *bond, public official.*

public ownership: ownership by the public of the common or other equity stock of a New York Stock Exchange firm.

public relations department: a department within a bank or other business institution created and maintained to promote and encourage better harmony and relationships between

that particular institution and the general public by offering a wide variety of services—educational and other—to the public without cost to the recipient. Such departments operate under a variety of names such as "courtesy," "customer's service," "public aid," and "public service." [10]

public revenue: income received by a governmental agency (taxes, tariffs, customs, etc.).

public sector: a segment of the total economy including all levels of government and excluding businesses and households. cf. *private sector.*

public trust: synonymous with *charitable trust*; opposed to a *private trust.* [37]

public trust fund: a trust fund whose principal, earnings, or both, must be used for a public purpose—for example, a pension or retirement fund. [49]

public utility: a business organization that performs an essential service for the public. Usually the state grants it a monopoly in its particular territory and in return exerts strict supervision or regulation of the company's rates and business practices.

public warehouse: see *warehouse, public.*

PUDs: abbreviation for the bonds of a public utility district.

PUHCA: Public Utility Holding Company Act. Passed by Congress in 1935 to regulate public utility holding companies. For the principal provisions, see *"death sentence."*

pula: monetary unit of Botswana.

pull: raising the offering price, or lowering the bid price of a stock, or if neither, then to cancel completely.

pull down: slang, the sum of money

earned from working (e.g., one's weekly salary).

pull order: a method used to withhold a card from being mailed at reissue. This usually results from the account being in a past-due or overlimit status at the time of reissue. [105]

pull statement: process whereby a cardholder's statement is segregated from regular mailing procedures and routed to the requesting department. [105]

pull the plug on the market: removing or canceling supporting bids which had earlier been entered just below the market prices prevailing for certain leading stocks.

pump priming: the theory that money incomes can be increased in a depression mostly through government expenditures, on the assumption that a given expenditure by the government will induce additional expenditures through turnover of the money. If, however, the psychological reaction of the people to the process is fear, the exact opposite result may occur; a lesser velocity of circulation.

punch card check: a check that has perforations either in the body of the check or around a portion of its border. These perforations are used to re-sort and correlate the checks after they have been canceled and returned with the bank statement. This type of check must be canceled in some special manner agreed upon by the banker and the depositor. Punch card checks are used to correlate the checks by number or some other coding; thus facilitating the reconcilement of the depositor's bank statement. [10]

punched card: a card punched with a pattern of holes to represent data.

punched tape: a tape on which a pattern of holes or cuts is used to represent data.

punt: slang, shares that will rarely turn out to be profitable.

pup: slang, a low-priced, inactive security.

Pur.: purchase.

purchase: any and every method of acquiring property except by descent. [105]

purchase and sale statement: a statement sent by a commission merchant to a customer when his or her futures position has been reduced or closed out. It shows the amount involved, the price at which the position was acquired and reduced or closed out, respectively, the gross profits or loss, the commission charged, and the net profit or loss on the transaction. Frequently referred to as a P&S. [11]

purchased funds: large-denomination certificates of deposits held by banks.

purchased paper: as distinguished from paper that has been discounted, any commercial paper that has been bought outright.

purchase group: in security underwriting, the group of investment banking firms that buys an entire issue of securities from the issuing company, each member of the group buying a stated amount. The part each member of the group cannot sell is then turned over to a syndicate manager, who sells the remaining securities to the members of the selling group. cf. *competitive bid.*

purchase money: monies paid to obtain ownership of property.

purchase-money bond: see *bond, purchase-money.*

purchase-money mortgage: for those who put their homes on the market and find that, to sell their property, they must act as the lender themselves. The mortgage is actually a short-term instrument, that runs no more than five years and often only a year or two. In most cases, a purchase-money mortgage is a second mortgage, supplementing the buyer's partial bank financing.

purchase option: fair market; an option given to a lessee to buy equipment at the end of a lease.

purchase order: a document that authorizes the delivery of specified merchandise or the rendering of certain services and the making of a charge for them. [49]

purchase outright: to pay the full amount in cash for purchased stocks.

purchase price

(1) *general:* the amount for which any item is bought.

(2) *banking:* the combination of monies and mortgages given to obtain a property.

purchaser: a buyer; a person who obtains title to or an interest in property by the act of purchase.

purchasing power: the value of money measured by the items it can buy. cf. *money, real value of money, wages.*

purchasing power of the dollar: a measurement of the quantity of goods and services that a dollar will buy in a specified market compared with the amount it could buy in some base period. It is obtained by taking the reciprocal of an appropriate price index. see *money, wage.*

purchasing power parity (PPP) theory: a theory to explain the rate of exchange between currencies not on a metallic standard. According to the the-

ory, a rate of exchange will be established which equates the domestic purchasing power of the two currencies.

purchasing power risk: in investments, used in contradistinction to financial risk and interest rate risk to refer to the risk that the price level may move, thus affecting the market value of bonds, for example, relative to common stocks. synonymous with *purchasing power uncertainties.*

purchasing power uncertainties: synonymous with *purchasng power risk.*

pure competition: the market situation in which no individual buyers or sellers are large enough to influence the market.

pure interest: the price paid for the use of capital, not to include monies for risk and all other costs incurred because of the loan. synonymous with *net interest* or *true interest.*

pure market economy: a competitive economic system of numerous buyers and sellers, where prices are determined by the free interaction of supply and demand. see *free enterprise.*

pure monopoly: see *perfect (pure) monopoly.*

pure premium: premium arrived at by dividing losses by exposure, and to which no loading has been added for commission, taxes, and expenses.

pure profit: see *economic profit.*

purpose clause: a clause in a Euromarket borrowing stating the purpose for which the borrowing is made. [104]

purpose statement: the signed affadavit required by Federal Reserve Regulation U. The borrower of a loan must indicate the use to which any loan secured by stock is to be put. see *Regulation U*. [105]

push money (PM):   paid to retail clerks during special sales as an incentive to dispose of slow-moving items.

put: an option contract that entitles the holder to sell a number of shares of the underlying stock at a stated price on or before a fixed expiration date. [5] see *puts and calls.*

put and call broker: a broker who deals in options or privileges, which are contracts to exercise some right or privilege during a specified time period. Put and call brokers are not allowed on a stock exchange floor.

put bond option: gives the owner the right, but not the obligation, to sell the underlying bond futures at a fixed price.

put out a line: the selling short of a considerable amount of the stock of one or more firms over a period of time with the hope of falling prices. cf. *take on a line;* see *short sale.*

puts and calls: options that give the right to buy or sell a fixed amount of certain stock at a specified price within a specified time. A put gives the holder the right to sell the stock; a call conveys the right to buy the stock. Puts are purchased by those who think a stock may go down. A put obligates the seller of the contract, commonly known as the option writer, to take delivery of the stock and to pay the specified price to the owner of the option within the time limits of the contract. The price specified in a put or call is usually close to the market price of the stock at the time the contract is made. Calls are purchased by those who think a stock may rise. A call gives the holder the right to buy the stock from the writer at the specified price within a fixed period of time. Put and call contracts are written for 30, 60, or 90 days, or longer. Six months and 10 days is the most common term. If the purchaser of a put or call does not wish to exercise the option, the price paid for the option becomes a loss. see *spread.*

PV

(1)   see *par value.*

(2)   see *present value.*

PY: prior year.

Pymt.:   see *payment.*

pyramiding: employing profits of open or unliquidated positions to add to the holder's original position; buying additional stocks or commodities by offering unrealized paper profits as additional margin. Used with commodities; rarely with stocks.

pyramid ratio: a tool used in the analysis of management and income ratio between profits and capital.

pyramid selling (schemes):   business opportunity frauds, usually promoted through advertisement for job opportunities guaranteed to yield enormous or quick profits—requiring little education or demanding a minimal personal investment. There are government regulations against certain pyramid schemes. The pyramider induces people to buy his products, which they are to resell at a higher price. For example, if 10 people buy 50 units each and sell only 15 each, the pyramider is still ahead because he has sold 500 units. see *fraud.*

Q
   (1) in receivership or bankruptcy proceedings.
   (2) quarterly.
   (3) see *Regulation Q*.

QA: see *quick assets*.

QC: see *quasi-contract*.

QP: see *quoted price*.

QPC: see *quasi-public company*.

Q-ratio: developed in the early 1960s by Yale University economist James Tobin, a way of explaining how the level of stock market prices affects capital spending—and thus the overall economy—even though the vast majority of firms never consider raising fresh equity capital. The Q-ratio relates the market value of a company's physical assets to the cost of replacing those assets. A ratio greater than 1 means that the stock market values a dollar of a company's assets at more than a dollar. Conversely, if Q is less than 1, the assets are being valued at less than dollar for dollar.

QS: see *quality stock*.

QT: see *quotation ticker*.

Qtly.: quarterly.

Qtr.: quarter.

qualification
   (1) a statement in an auditor's report directing attention to any limitation to the examination, or any doubt concerning a reported item in a company's financial statements.
   (2) the operation of inscribing data fields to prepare them for automatic sorting and processing by a MICR sorter-reader. [105]

qualified acceptance: any counteroffer.

qualified endorsement: an endorsement by which the endorser seeks to avoid the usual liabilities inherent in his act. "Without recourse" is the most common example. If the instrument is not honored, the endorser does not want to become responsible for it. cf. *recourse*.

qualified plan (or trust): an employer's trust or plan that qualifies under the Internal Revenue Code of 1954 for the exclusive benefit of his or her employees or their beneficiaries in such manner and form as to entitle the employer who makes the payments to the plan or trust to the deductions and income tax benefits as set forth in that Code. [37]

qualified prospect: a potential customer who is able to buy a product or service and has the authority to make a decision to purchase. This conclusion is often arrived at following a check on the individual's credit.

qualified retirement plan: a private retirement plan that meets the rules and regulations of the Internal Revenue Service. Contributions to a qualified retirement plan are in almost all cases tax deductible, and earnings on such contributions are always tax sheltered until retirement. [23]

qualified stock option: synonymous with *restricted stock option*.

qualifying distribution: with regard to a private foundation, any amount paid out to accomplish a legitimate eleemosynary purpose (as well as the administrative expenses which are incident thereto) or paid out to acquire an asset used directly in carrying out such purpose. [105]

qualifying dividends: dividends from taxable U.S. corporations, $100 of which can be excluded from an individual's income, $200 for married taxpayers filing a joint return.

qualifying period: see *waiting period.*

qualitative forecasting: predictions on the future activity of bank products or services based on human judgment. [105]

quality of estate: the form in which an estate is to be owned, including type of possession and time. No indication of property value or physical characteristics is given.

quality stock: a stock of high grade, of superior merit. synonymous with *blue chip stock.* see *blue chip.*

quantity discount: a reduction given for volume buying.

quantity theory: a theory stating that a special relationship exists between the quantity of money and money income. People spend excess money holdings irrespective of the interest rate and the manner in which the new money holdings were received. cf. *Gresham's law, liquid trap, marginal propensity to invest, marginal propensity to save.*

quantum meruit: "as much as he deserved" (Latin); a principle of business law providing that when a service is given without a written estimate of price, there is an implied promise by the purchaser of the service to pay for the work as much as it is worth.

Quar.: quarter.

quarter stock: stock with a par value of $25 for each share.

quasi: as if; that which resembles.

quasi-arbitrage: see *arbitrage.*

quasi-contract: an obligation similar in character to that of a contract, but which arises not from an agreement between the parties but from some relationship between them or from a voluntary act by one or more of them—for example, the management of the affairs of another without authority or the management of a common property without authority. [37]

quasi-corporation: any political subdivision of an organization or group (e.g., an unincorporated town).

quasi-money: assets that have properties similar to those of money in the strict sense, namely notes and icon plus bank deposits payable at sight.

quasi-public company: a corporation operated privately in which the public has a special interest (e.g., eleemosynary institutions).

quasi-rent: the yield on an investment in capital goods (sunk cost). If there is no alternative use, the total yield, and if there is an alternative use, the yield over the alternative. The capital good is not a determinant of the price of the product since it will continue to be used as long as the price is greater than the average variable cost. Thus any return on such goods is similar to a rent.

quasi-reorganization: a restructuring that does not lead to the formation of a new company, undertaken for purposes of absorbing a deficit, avoiding bankruptcy, and affording an opportunity to begin again.

query: to extract, from a file, records based on requested criterion. For example, listing all the customers in a title whose balance is greater than 1000. [105]

quetzal: monetary unit of Guatemala.

queue: a line or group of items or people in a bank waiting for service.

quick assets

(1) *general:* assets that in the ordinary course of business, will be converted into cash within a reasonably short time.

(2) *finance:* assets that can be readily converted into cash without appreciable loss. see *liquidity.*

quick (quickie) buck: slang, money made rapidly; a windfall.

quick ratio: the ratio between existing liabilities and quick assets; shows a firm's ability to pay off its liabilities rapidly with available funds.

quick turn: any quick buy and sale transaction over a brief time period, often within hours. see *day trading.*

quid pro quo: "something for some-thing" (Latin): a mutual consideration; securing an advantage or receiving a concession in return for a similar favor.

quiet title suit: a legal action to remove a defect or any questionable claim against the title to property. cf. *cloud on title.*

quit claim: synonymous with *remise.*

quitclaim deed: see *deed, quitclaim.*

quit rent: the last rental payment made by a tenant before leaving the property.

quota

(1) a restriction on imports that specifies a quantity limitation.

(2) assigned to each member of the International Monetary Fund, determines the voting power and subscription of that member and the normal quantitative limitations on its use of the fund's reserves. [105]

quota agreement: an agreement between members of a cartel assigning each firm a fixed proportion of the total production of the cartel.

quota share treaty: treaty reinsurance providing for a fixed proportion of all the risks of a given class of insurance as a whole to be ceded to the reinsurer, along with the same proportion of the premium, less commission.

quotation: the highest bid to buy and the lowest offer to sell a security in a given market at a given time. For example, if you ask a broker for a "quote" on a stock, the reply may be something like "45¼ to 45½." This means that $45.25 is the highest price any buyer wanted to pay at the time the quote was given on the floor of a stock exchange, and $45.50 was the lowest price any seller would take at the same time. The word is often shortened to *quote.* synonymous with *bid and asked.*

quotation board: an electrically operated board on the wall of a brokerage house or other financial institution, showing stock price ranges, dividends payments, and transactions. cf. *quotation ticker*.

quotation ticker: the ticker of an exchange carrying prices of actual transactions.

quote: see *quotation*.

quoted price: the stated price of a security or commodity.

quote wire: the direct wire from a brokerage house to the quotation department of the New York Stock Exchange by which a firm can learn the highest bid and lowest offer for a listed security. A quotation can be obtained during regular business hours by dialing the number assigned to the stock.

quo warranto: Latin for "by what authority." A suit to test the authority of a person in office or of a corporation to its franchise or charter.

R

(1) see *range*.

(2) see *rate of interest*.

(3) see *right*.

RA

(1) see *restricted account*.

(2) see *Revenue Act of 1962, Revenue Act of 1964, Revenue Act of 1971, Revenue Act of 1976, Revenue Act of 1978*.

rack: used to describe the "rack department," which sorts, distributes, and proves items in the commercial operations of the bank.

racket: slang, a dishonest business activity. synonymous with *swindle*.

rack rent: an unusually high rent in an amount equal to or nearly equal to the total value of the items produced on the rented property. cf. *economic rent*.

rag money: American term for *paper money*. [27]

raid: a deliberate attempt by professionals, traders, and others to depress the market price of a stock.

raise

(1) *general:* any increase in value or amount (e.g., wages or prices).

(2) *investments:* a fraudulent increase in the face value of a negotiable instrument.

raised bills: the denomination of paper money that has been illegally raised.

raised check: a check on which the amount has been illegally increased.

raised notes: those on which there is an overprint indicating that the denomination has been increased as a result of government revalidation. [27]

raise (raising) funds: acquiring money, financing, or credit from surplus earnings of the firm, to stockholders, the public, creditors, customers, or employees.

rally: a brisk rise following a decline in the general price level of the market, or in an individual stock. [20]

RAM: random-access memory; cf. *ROM*. see *reserve adjustment magnitude*.

rand: monetary unit of Lesotho, Republic of South Africa, and South-West Africa.

random access: a quality of a computer's memory device allowing data to be written in or read from the memory through direct locating rather than locating through reference to other data in the memory. synonymous with *direct access*.

random walk: name given to the theory that price movements have no memory and occur at random.

range: the difference between the high and low price of the future during a given period. [11]

rank

(1) *general:* a title or position in an organization.

(2) *computers:* to arrange in an ascending or descending series according to importance.

(3) *investments:* see *restricted shares*.

RANs: see *revenue-anticipation notes*.

rapid amortization: a program that permits owners of facilities to write off all or a part of their cost for income tax purposes in a short space of time, usually five years. see also *amortization*.

rapid-payoff mortgage: synonymous with *growing equity mortgage*.

ratable distribution: the proportionate distribution of an estate according to a percentage. For example, if all the legacies cannot be paid in full and each of them is reduced by the same percentage, there is ratable distribution. [37]

rate

(1) *general:* to categorize and rank in terms of special qualities or properties.

(2) *banking:* the cost of a unit of insurance. cf. *premium*.

(3) *finance:* a charge, fee, or price.

rate base: the value established by a regulatory authority, upon which a utility is permitted to earn a specified rate of return. [3]

rate basis: the formula of the specific

factors that control the construction of a rate.

rate discrimination: charging different prices for almost identical services. When this action tends to lessen competition, it may be illegal under antitrust laws.

rate-making line: a transportation line that controls the making of rates between points because of geographical location.

rate of estimated depreciation: annual depreciation of a fixed asset expressed as a percentage of the cost price; obtained by dividing the annual depreciation of a fixed asset by the original cost.

rate of exchange (ROE): the amount of funds of one nation that can be bought, at a specific date, for a sum of currency of another country. Rates fluctuate often because of economic, political, and other forces.

rate of inflation: the average percentage rate of increase of the price of money, weighted and stated in annual terms.

rate of interest: the charge for borrowing money.

rate of return (ROR)

(1) the yield obtainable on a security based on its purchase price or its current market price. This may be the amortized yield to maturity on a bond or the current income return.

(2) the income earned by a public utility company on its property or capital investment, expressed as a percentage. [67]

(rate of) return on investment (capital): see *ROI*.

rate regulation: the determination by a commission or public service agency of the maximum, and at times the minimum, charge that public utility corporations may demand for their services. see *fair rate of return, utility.*

rate-sensitive assets: bank loans. see *liability hedge.*

rate-sensitive liabilities: bank deposits and borrowings. see *liability hedge.*

rate setting: the establishment of rates by agreement between labor and management or by an employer alone.

rate structure: the charges made to customers for their use of bank funds, specified in terms of annual percentage rates. [105]

rate variance: in accounting procedures, the difference between actual wages paid and the standard wage rate, multiplied by the total actual hours of direct labor used.

rate war: a negative form of competition; sellers drop their prices below their costs for purposes of putting the competition out of business.

rating

(1) ***general:***   evaluation of the moral or other risk of an individual or company.

(2) ***investments:***   a system of rating that provides the investor with a simple system of gradation by which the relative investment qualities of stocks and bonds are indicated.

ratio

(1) ***general:***   a number relationship between two things (i.e., ratio of births to deaths).

(2) ***finance:***   any relationship that can be used in measuring the rating or financial position of a firm (e.g., the relationship of a company's earnings to the firm's market price for its stock).

(3) ***finance:***   one of the various analyses made by a money-lending or credit agency, of the financial state-

ments of a given individual, company, or other business enterprise seeking credit, to determine the desirability of granting the requested credit.

(4) ***finance:***   the relative values of silver and gold in a monetary system based on both. see *bimetallism.*

ratio analysis: analysis of the relationships of items in financial statements. see listings under *ratio.*

ratio bull spread: see *neutral spread.*

rational expectations theory: see *theory of rational expectations.*

rationalization: especially as applied to Germany after World War I, to describe a conscious and determined effort to obtain the economies that vertical and horizontal combinations have to offer. This may be achieved by market sharing, quotas, and similar devices.

rationing: any arrangement, usually under governmental regulation, limiting the quantity of product that can be purchased by a given class of buyers.

rationing of exchange: governmental control of foreign exchange through the forced surrender of exchange by exporters for domestic currency at the government rate, and the subsequent allocation of such exchange to importers according to a government ration schedule.

ratio of accounts payable to purchases: this ratio, determined for the present period and compared with a similar ratio for previous periods, indicates the trend toward or from prompt payment of current obligations.

ratio of capital to fixed assets: this ratio is usually determined for a number of years to ascertain whether there is a trend toward converting the investment of the owners into fixed assets, thereby indicating a possible reliance on creditors for furnishing the required working capital.

ratio of collateral to debt: a measure for determining how effectively stock margin is achieved. It is shown as a fraction with full collateral value as the numerator and the total securities margin as the denominator.

ratio of finished goods inventory to the cost of goods sold: this ratio is determined by dividing the cost of goods sold by the average finished goods inventory. The resulting figure is the number of times the investment in the finished goods inventory has turned over during the period under consideration. The present ratio is compared with a similar ratio for several previous periods, since it tends to portray the stability and trend of sales, or the possible overstated or expanded inventory.

ratio of fixed assets to fixed liabilities: this ratio tends to indicate the margin of safety to the present mortgage and bond holders, if any. Failure of the ratio to meet the minimum requirement frequently suggests that additional funds should be raised from the owners rather than by mortgaging fixed assets.

ratio of notes payable to accounts payable: three quantitative factors are frequently considered when determining whether the resulting ratio (notes payable/accounts payable) is desirable: (a) notes issued in payment of merchandise, (b) notes issued to banks and brokers, and (c) notes issued to others. If a relatively large amount of the outstanding notes was issued to merchandise creditors, this might indicate that the firm is unable to take advantage of the cash discounts offered in the trade, and, also, that other lending agencies might consider the firm's credit unfavorably.

ratio of notes receivable to accounts receivable: if a financial statement discloses a large ratio of notes receivable to accounts receivable, as compared with other firms in a similar line of business, the firm with the high ratio may have a lax credit policy, or it may be extending credit to customers whose ability to pay promptly is dubious.

ratio of owned capital to borrowed capital: this ratio is considered to be important in determining the advisability of extending additional long-term credit to an applicant. If this ratio is not considered favorable, it frequently suggests that the funds desired should be raised from the owners of the business (i.e., the applicants themselves) rather than through the additional pledging of any assets.

ratio of raw materials inventory to cost of manufacture: this ratio is determined by dividing the cost of goods manufactured by the average raw materials inventory. The resulting figure is the number of times the investment in the raw materials inventory has turned over during the period under consideration. When the present ratio is compared with a similar ratio for previous periods, it tends to portray the trend and steadiness of production, or to indicate an overstated or overexpanded inventory.

Ravenswood plan: the combination of a checking account with a bank repurchase agreement. A high-yielding checking account first developed by the Bank of Ravenswood on Chicago's North Side.

RB

(1)   see *bond, redeemable.*

(2)   see *bond, revenue.*

RC

(1)   see *recurring charges.*

(2)   see *register(ed) check.*

(3)   see *reserve currency.*

(4)   see *risk capital.*

Rcd.:   received.

RCPC: see *Regional Check Processing Center.*

Rcpt.:   see *receipt.*

Rct.:   see *receipt.*

R&D: see *research and development.*

RE

(1)   see *rate of exchange.*

(2)   see *real estate.*

reacquired   securities: securities, once outstanding, that have been acquired by the issuing corporation and are legally available for reissue or resale (in some states these securities cannot be reissued without approval of regulatory authorities). [3]

reaction: a drop in securities prices following a sustained period of increasing prices.

reader

(1)   ***computers:***   a device that converts information in one form of storage to information in another form of storage.

(2)   ***computers:***   a   part   of   the scheduler   that   transfers   an   input stream into the system.

readiness-to-serve   costs: synonymous with *capacity costs, demand costs.*

read(ing) the tape: a technique for judging the performance of various stocks by following their price changes as given on the ticker tape.

readjustment plan: a voluntary program worked out by creditors and a debtor firm outside the framework of the bankruptcy courts for the purpose of avoiding going through a formal bankruptcy.

real   accounts: those   accounts—asset, liability, reserve and capital—whose balances are not canceled out at the end of an accounting period but are carried over to the next period. These accounts appear on the postclosing trial balance and the statement of condition. Sometimes called *permanent accounts.* [59]

real bills doctrine: the principle that if only "real" bills (i.e., bills growing out of trade transactions) are discounted, the expansion of bank money will be in proportion to the needs of trade. Expansion and contraction would thus be automatic.

real costs

(1)   costs measured in dollars of constant purchasing power or adjusted by some index serving the same purpose. cf. *nominal cost.*

(2)   costs that involve effort or sacrifice.

real earnings: earnings adjusted to exclude the effects of price change.

real effective exchange rate: an effective exchange rate adjusted for inflation differentials between the nation whose exchange rate is being measured, and other nations making up the group against which the exchange rate is calculated. [103]

real estate: tangible land and all physical property. Includes all physical substances below, upon, or attached to land; thus houses, trees, and fences are classified as real estate. All else is personal property.

real estate bond: see *bond, real estate.*

Real Estate Investment Trust (REIT): an organization, usually corporate, established for the accumulation of funds for investing in real estate holdings, or the extension of credit to others engaged in construction. These funds are usually accumulated by the sale of share of ownership in the trust.

real estate loans: loans secured by real estate, regardless of the purpose. see *mortgage*. [40]

real estate owned: all real estate directly owned by a bank, usually not including real estate taken to satisfy a debt. [44]

Real Estate Settlement Procedures Act: federal legislation of 1974, this act provided comprehensive guidelines for loan closing costs and settlement practices; effective in June 1975. see *Real Estate Settlement Procedures Act amendments*. [51]

Real Estate Settlement Procedures Act amendments: federal legislation of 1976 which eased the requirement of the Real Estate Settlement Procedures Act by permitting lenders to disclose good faith estimates of closing costs instead of actual charges, and by tying disclosure timing to receipt of the application instead of the date of closing; also eliminated disclosure of the property's previous selling price. see *Real Estate Settlement Procedures Act*. [51]

real estate sold on contract: real estate that has been sold for which the buyer does not have sufficient down payment to warrant the seller giving title; the contract generally provides that when the contract balance is reduced to a certain amount, the buyer may refinance the contract to get title to the property. [59]

real estate tax: a pecuniary charge laid upon real property for public purposes. [62]

real income: the sum total of the purchasing power of a nation or individual.

real interest rate: the rate at which a person earns future purchasing power on monetary assets. It equals the money rate minus the rate of inflation.

real investment: an expenditure that establishes a new capital asset, thus creating a new capital formation.

realization (realize)
(1) *finance:* the act or process of converting into cash an asset, or the total assets, of an individual or business.
(2) *investments:* receiving a profit from selling a security following an increase in its price.

realization account: an account established to summarize and adjust the accounts of a business being liquidated. The account reflects the item-by-item realization of the assets through reduction to cash or application to the reduction of liabilities.

realization value: the amount received from the sale of an item as differentiated from other types of value, such as par, book, and so on.

realized profit (or loss): a profit or loss resulting from the sale or other disposal of a security, as distinguished from a paper profit or loss. [67]

realized value: under the Consumer Leasing Act, includes (a) the price received by the lessor for the leased property at disposition, (b) the highest offer for disposition, or (c) the fair market value at the end of the lease term. [105]

realized yield: the return a bond earns over a stated time period, based on the purchase price and on the assumption that the incoming cash is reinvested at a stated rate.

realizing: when a profit is realized either by a liquidating sale or the repurchase of a short sale. [11]

realizing sale: a sale to convert a paper profit into an actual profit.

reallowance: the maximum part of the selling concession that an underwriter gives up or "reallow" to another NASD member, who need not be a syndicate member. Reallowance is specified at the time of pricing.

real money: money containing one or more metals having intrinsic value, as distinguished from representative money such as currency issued by a realm, and checks, drafts, and so on, issued by legal entities. see *bimetallism, monometallism;* cf. *fiat money.*

real-money balances: the amount of goods and services that can be bought from a given stock of money retained by individuals. Shifts in real-money balances are computed by adjusting changes in the amount of money held for changes in the level of prices.

real national income: the national income measured in terms of unchanging purchasing power. Usually measured by dividing national income in current dollars by a price index.

real price: the price of goods and services measured by the quantity of labor needed to earn sufficient money to purchase the goods or services.

real property: the property that is devised by will to a party known as the devisee; or all fixed, permanent, immovable property, such as land and tenements.

real property transaction: an extension of credit in connection with which a security interest is or will be retained or acquired in real property, as defined by the law of the state in which it is located. [105]

real spendable earnings: a U.S. Bureau of Labor Statistics measure of the economy; successor to the wholesale price index. It contains a wealth of data on prices by stage of processing, sector, industry, and commodity. This index is issued the first week of the month for the previous month.

real stock: as contrasted with stock that is sold short, any long stock.

real time

(1) *computers:* the actual time during which a physical process transpires.

(2) *systems:* "in real time" refers to the performance of a computation during the same time that the related physical process transpires, allowing the results of the computation to be used in guiding the physical process.

realtor: a real estate broker or an associate holding active membership in a local real estate board affiliated with the National Association of Realtors. [105]

realty: synonym for *real estate.*

real value of money: the price of money measured in terms of goods. cf. *purchasing power.*

real wages: the cost of items and services that can be purchased with money wages. It is useful for comparing changes in the standard of living by eliminating the effect of changes in the general price level.

reappraisal: the term applied when property is appraised a second time.

reasonable value: a value placed on property that parallels the existing market value.

reassessment: the result of a change in the assessed value of property or reappraisal of property.

rebate

(1) *finance:* unearned interest that may be returned to a borrower if his or her loan is paid off before the maturity date.

(2) *finance:* any deduction made from a payment or charge. As contrasted with a discount, the rebate is not deducted in advance but is returned to the consumer following payment of the full amount (e.g., a General Electric appliance costs $24 with a rebate of $5 after the consumer has mailed in a coupon from the appliance package). cf. *discount.*

rebated acceptance: an anticipated acceptance; an acceptance paid prior to its due date.

rebating: the illegal and unethical practice of selling a policy at less than the legal rate, or allowing the insured a refund of the premium, or giving him or her the goods of any value, thus avoiding payment of the full legal premium.

Rec.: see *receipt.*

recap: an abbreviated term for "recapitulation" (or assembling) of totals taken from "batch proof" sheets or from proof machines which must be assembled in proper order so as to build up control totals for the various departments charged with the items. Recap sheets may be used in all departments of the bank, and all recap sheets assembled into a final recap sheet for the settlement of the entire bank. see also *settlement clerk.* [10]

recapitalization: altering the capital structure of a firm by increasing or decreasing its capital stock.

recapitalization surplus: the surplus resulting upon a recapitalization, which usually arises from reduction in the par value of stocks and the exchange of bonds for securities of lesser value.

recapitulation: see *recap.*

recap sheet: see *settlement clerk.*

recapture clause: a clause in an agreement providing for retaking or recovering possession. As used in percentage leases, to take a portion of earnings or profits above a fixed amount of rent. [62]

recast: see *recomputation.*

recasting a mortgage: reconstructing an existing mortgage by increasing its amount, interest rate, or time period.

Recd.: received.

recede: any drop in prices.

receipt: any written acknowledgment of value received.

receipt book: a bound book of blank receipt stubs with detachable blank receipts.

receipts outstanding for funded debt: receipts for payments on account of subscriptions to funded debt. [18]

receipts outstanding for installments paid: receipts for payments on account of subscriptions to capital stock. [18]

receivables: accounts receivable owned by a business. These may be pledged as collateral for a loan secured from a bank or other financial institution.

receivables turnover: a computation done to evaluate the quality of a company's accounts receivable. Receivables turnover is calculated as the ratio of net sales to current value of receivables. The resulting figure gives an indication of the average length of time for which the firm's receivables remain outstanding. [105]

receive (advice to): an advance notice to an account-maintaining bank that it will receive funds to be credited to the sender of the message. [105]

receiver: a court-appointed, neutral party named to handle property under litigation or the affairs of a bankrupt person. The receiver is required to maintain the property and its assets for the benefit of those having equity in it until a court decision as to its disposition is made. see also *bailee, interim receiver, remaindermen, sequestered account.*

receivers' and trustees' securities: evidences of indebtedness (other than equipment securities or obligations) issued by a receiver or trustee acting under orders of a court. [18]

receiver's certificate: a note issued by a receiver to obtain working capital to keep a distressed company in operation. The note is usually a short-term obligation and is given a priority over other open book accounts, with the precise priority determined by authority of the court.

receiver's correspondent bank: a bank with which the receiver of a transfer has an account relationship and which may act as a reimbursement bank in a transfer of funds. [105]

receivership: the state of being under the care or administration of a receiver.

receiving bank
(1) a bank that receives paperless entries from the ACH following their entry by an originating bank.
(2) the bank to whom the service transmits the message. [105]

receiving bank identifier: a code that uniquely identifies the bank that is to receive the message. Constitutes the routing code or address by which the destination bank is known to the wire service handling the message. [105]

receiving bank name: names the bank that receives the message from the service. [105]

receiving bank output sequence number: a consecutive sequence number that allows for output message control between the service and the receiving bank. [105]

receiving bank terminal identifier: a code uniquely identifying the terminal or station within the destination bank to which the message is sent. Augments and further qualifies the address of the destination bank. [105]

receiving bank time and date: time and date that the message was delivered to the receiving bank by the service. [105]

receiving teller: a bank employee assigned to the duties of accepting deposits from depositors. This teller is responsible for counting all cash received, and for verification of the count to the customer's deposit. The teller should also see that all checks deposited are properly endorsed by the depositor. The receiving teller enters the amount of the deposit in the depositor's passbook, or issues a receipt from a teller's machine for the depositor's record. [10]

recession: a phase of the business cycle that shows a downswing or contraction of the economy.

recession (growth): period of sluggish growth in output—up to 2.5 or 3 percent without six months of actual decline.

reciprocal business: a business favor where a request to purchase or sell stocks by one person is expected from another in return for a similar order.

reciprocal demurrage: a demurrage system which assesses shippers for car detention and charges carriers for failure to furnish cars as ordered.

reciprocal statutes: similar statutes in two or more states providing mutual provisions or reciprocal treatment within the states affected concerning the subjects treated in such statutes; for example, similar provisions with regard to corporations or inheritance taxes, a trust institution, bank, or business in another state. [37]

reciprocal trade agreement: an international agreement between two or more countries to establish mutual trade concessions that are expected to be of equal value.

reciprocal trust: a trust created by one person in consideration of the creation by the beneficiary of a similar trust for him or her. [105]

reciprocity principle: the granting of trade, tariff, or other concessions by one country in return for equivalent treatment from the grantee.

recission: cancellation of a contract without penalty. [105]

reclamation
(1) *general:* a business term to describe the act of obtaining useful materials from waste products.
(2) *banking:* a sum of money due or owing by a bank resulting from an error in the listing of the amount of a check on a clearinghouse balance.

reclassification of stock: a change or modification of the capital structure of an organization.

recognizance: acknowledgment of a former debt upon the record. [105]

recognized quotations: statements regarding the highest bid and lowest offer prevailing for a specific stock listed on an exchange.

recompense: a payment or award made to anyone to make amends for a loss or damage. see *compensation.*

recomputation: to refigure and reapply, on a simple interest basis, all payments made on a precomputed loan. see *acceleration.* [55]

reconciliation: a process for determining the differences between two items of an account so as to bring them into agreement (e.g., a bank statement and an up-to-date checkbook). see *adjustment.*

reconditioning property: improving a property's value by repairing it or making changes to enhance it.

reconveyance: the transfer of title of property back to a former owner.

recordation: the public acknowledgment in written form that a lien exists against a specific property that is identified in a mortgage. see *lien affidavit.*

record date: the date on which a person must be registered as a shareholder on the stock book of a company in order to receive a declared dividend, or among other things, to vote on company affairs. cf. *ex-dividend.*

recording fee: cost of recording necessary documents with the appropriate state or county administrative office. [78]

records of original entry: the general journal, the cash receipts record, and the cash disbursement record. All transactions must first be analyzed and recorded in one of these records before posting to the general ledger accounts. [59]

recourse: the rights of a holder in due course of a negotiable instrument to force prior endorsers on the instrument to meet their legal obligations by making good the payment of the instrument if dishonored by the maker or acceptor. The holder in due course must have met the legal requirements of presentation and delivery of the instrument to the maker of a note or acceptor of a draft, and must have found that this legal entity has refused to pay for, or defaulted in payment of the instrument. see also *notice of dishonor (protest jacket)*. [10]

recoverable expenditure: an expenditure made for or on behalf of another governmental unit, fund, or department, or for a private individual, firm, or corporation which will subsequently be recovered in cash or its equivalent. [49]

recovery
(1) *finance:* the period of the business cycle that follows a depression.
(2) *investments:* following a period of declining prices, the rise in stock prices. synonymous with *expansion*.

Recovery Act: see *Economic Recovery Tax Act of 1981*.

Rect.: see *receipt*.

recurring charges: those financial obligations of a recurring nature that a potential borrower must pay or has obligated himself to pay, including taxes, debt repayments, legal obligations such as alimony, and other items. [59]

red, in the: slang, losing money from operating a business.

red clause: a clause, printed in red, on a letter of credit, authorizing a negotiating banker to make advances to a beneficiary so that he or she can buy the items, and deliver them for shipment. [85]

redeem: to buy back.

redeemable bond: *bond, redeemable*.

redeemable preferred stock: see *capital stock*.

redeemable rent: payments of rent that can be recovered (i.e., with a rental agreement containing the option to buy the property). When such an option is exercised, the purchaser receives all or a portion of the rents, or the monies may be applied to the sales price.

redeemable stock: a preferred stock that can be called in, at the option of the issuing company. see *redemption price*.

Redem.: see *redemption*.

redemise: to renew a lease.

redemption
(1) *finance:* the liquidation of an indebtedness, on or before maturity, such as the retirement of a bond issue prior to its maturity date.
(2) *banking:* purchasing back; a debtor redeems his mortgaged property when he has paid his debt in full.

redemption agent: synonymous with *clearinghouse agent*.

redemption bond: see *bond, redemption*.

redemption fund: a fund created for the purpose of retiring an obligation.

redemption notice: information mailed to concerned stockholders whose securities are being redeemed or which is printed in financial periodicals according to requirements of the indenture of the issue. The notice provides the time and terms of the redemption.

redemption period: the time in which a mortgagor may buy back property by paying the amount owed (with principal and interest) on a foreclosed mortgage. The specific time is subject to state law. [105]

redemption price

(1) the price (usually at its par value) at which a bond may be redeemed before maturity, when retired at the option of the issuing company.

(2) the amount a company must pay to call in certain types of preferred stock.

redemption right: a defaulted mortgagor's right to redeem his property after default and court judgment, both before and after its sale. see also *equitable right of redemption.* [59]

redemptions: cash-ins made of investment company shares.

redemption value

(1) the price at which bonds can be redeemed; old bond issues were often redeemable at par value.

(2) the cash-in value of investment company shares.

redemption value bond: see *bond, redemption value.*

red herring: synonymous with *preliminary prospectus.* see *open prospectus.*

Redi Check Plan: the customer arranges a top credit limit with the bank. He is issued a book of special checks (usually of a type prepared for automated bookkeeping). It is his privilege to write checks as he wishes, up to the total of his line of credit, which may be for $300, $500, $1000, and at times as high as $5000. Each month he receives a statement which records all of his checks that have "cleared" the bank. A service charge may be added but usually is not if he makes a deposit to cover the statement within 10, 15, or 20 days; except perhaps 25 cents for each check that has been drawn, to cover the bookkeeping. [28]

Redisc.: see *rediscount.*

rediscount

(1) *banking:* a negotiable instrument that has been discounted by a bank and subsequently discounted a second time by a Federal Reserve bank or another bank for the benefit of the bank that originally discounted the instrument. see *bank credit.*

(2) *finance:* to discount for the second time.

rediscounting: see *bank of discount.*

rediscount rate: the rate set by the Federal Reserve Bank for discounting a second time monies offered by their district member banks; the interest rate charged for discounting a negotiable instrument that has already been discounted.

redlining: the alleged practice of certain lending institutions of making it almost impossible to obtain mortgages, improvement loans, and insurance by homeowners, apartment house landlords, and businesses in neighborhoods outlined in red on a map, usually areas that are deteriorating or considered by the lending institution as poor investments. cf. *greenlining.*

redraft: when a check or other bill of exchange that has been presented for payment is dishonored and consequently protested, the instrument holder can draw a bill of exchange for the original amount of the obligation plus the cost of the notary and other protest expenses. This new instrument is called a *redraft* or *cross bill.*

reduced rate average: see *coinsurance.*

reentry: a landlord's right to reacquire leased property if terms in the lease, such as the making of rent payments, are not satisfied. A reentry clause must be inserted by the landlord in the original lease. cf. *landlord's warrant.*

reexchange: the charge by the drawer of a redraft for his or her expense due to the default on the original draft.

reexport: to export already imported items without duty charges, in basically similar form, to a third country.

Ref.

(1) see *referee.*

(2) see *refunding.*

refer authorizer: a person in a credit office with the authority to approve or disapprove credit transactions which need special attention. The person is usually a section supervisor. [41]

referee: when a case is pending in court, the presiding officer requests an individual (the referee) to receive testimony from the parties and present the information to the court. When appropriate, the referee can accept foreclosed property and make a deed. see *bankruptcy, foreclose (foreclosure)*; cf. *master in chancery.*

referee's foreclosure deed: a deed made by a court official that forecloses the mortgage on a property and passes the title on to the referee.

referee's partition deed: a deed made by a referee, conveying title to property when co-owners choose to divide their interest.

reference currency: a currency used in making payments to a bondholder.

reference number

(1) number assigned to each monetary transaction in a descriptive billing system. Each reference number is printed on the monthly statement to aid in retrieval of the document, should it be questioned by the cardholder.

(2) a numeric or other symbolic

means of identifying a particular transaction. [105]

referral: request for an authorization referred to a security or credit officer. [105]

refinance

(1) *banking:* to extend existing financing or to acquire new monies. Usually done when a mortgage is withdrawn so that a larger one can be placed on the property. see *refunding mortgage.*

(2) *finance:* to revise a payment timetable and, frequently, to modify interest charges on the obligation.

refinanced loan: a loan that has had an addition to the principal balance. Such increases are usually for property improvements such as an added room. Normally the term and/or payment amount is also affected.

refinancing: synonymous with *refunding.*

reflation: upon recovering from a depression or a recession, the period during which prices are returned to the level they had attained during a period of prosperity by lowering the purchasing power of money.

refreshing: synonymous with *buffering.*

refund

(1) an amount paid back of credit allowed because of an overcollection or on account of the return of an object sold.

(2) to pay back or allow credit for an amount because of an overcollection or because of the return of an object sold.

(3) to provide for the payment of a loan through cash or credit secured by a new loan.

(4) to replace one bond issue with an-

other, usually in order to extend the maturity, to reduce the interest rate, or to consolidate several issues. [49]

refundable interest: the unearned portion of interest previously charged that will be returned to the debtor (maker of a note) if the indebtedness is liquidated prior to maturity.

refund check

(1) *general:* a check or other instrument of currency that is repayment of money for any reason. see *rebate.*

(2) *finance:* a statement for a customer's purchase that is returned.

(3) *taxes:* a check from a governmental tax agency.

refunding

(1) *investments:* replacing an old bond issue with a new issue, either before or at maturity of the older one. It is often done to change the interest rate on the debt.

(2) *finance:* the act of returning a portion of money to the giver from an amount already paid out. see *debt.*

refunding bond: see *bond, refunding.*

refunding certificates: U.S. $10 certificates of deposit, which had an interest of 4 percent for an indefinite period of time. They were issued in 1879 and intended to induce people not to redeem them but to keep them in circulation. [27]

refunding mortgage: refinancing a mortgage with monies derived from a new loan.

refund slip: synonymous with *credit slip.*

Reg.

(1) see *register.*

(2) see *registrar.*

regional bank: one of the 12 Federal Reserve District or Regional Banks around the United States.

Regional Check Processing Center (RCPC): a Federal Reserve facility in which check-processing operations are performed. These centers serve a group of banks located within a specified area of a Federal Reserve District. They expedite collection and settlement of checks within the area on an overnight basis. [7]

regional differential: among broad geographical subdivisions, the difference in prevailing wages for equal work.

regional exchange: any organized securities exchange found outside New York City. All regional exchanges together account for less than 10 percent of all stock transactions.

register

(1) *general:* the making of a permanent record of events.

(2) *computers:* a device capable of storing a specified amount of data (e.g., one word).

(3) *finance:* a written document prepared by a customs official allowing a ship to engage in foreign trade.

(4) *systems:* a unit or machine for temporarily storing information while or until it is used.

register(ed) check: the title given to a check prepared by a teller, using funds recorded and placed aside in a special register, for the convenience of members of the general public who may wish to make a payment by check, but who do not maintain a checking account. The check has two stubs: one is for the purchaser and the other is used by the bank for record keeping. It is actually a money order, prepared in the form of a check, and the bank usually charges a small fee for each registered check sold.

registered as to principal: a term applied to a coupon bond, the name of the owner of which is registered on the bond and on the books of the company. Such bonds are not negotiable and cannot be sold without an assignment. [37]

registered bond: see *bond, registered.*

registered check: see *register(ed) check.*

registered exchange: a registered security exchange that subscribes to the regulation of the SEC or a commodity exchange which has registered and subscribed to the regulation of the Commodity Exchange Commission.

registered form: an instrument that is issued in the name of the owner and payable only to the owner. [105]

registered investment company: an investment company which has filed a registration statement with the SEC, fulfilling the requirements of the Investment Company Act of 1940. [30]

registered mail: mail recorded in a U.S. Post Office at the mailing and at each successive point of transmission, to guarantee special care in delivery. Registered mail can be insured to guarantee indemnity in case of loss, fire, or damage. cf. *certified mail.*

registered representative (trader): present name for "customer's man," a full-time employee of a stock exchange member organization who has met the requirements of the exchange with respect to background and knowledge of the securities business. Also known as an *account executive* or *customer's broker.*

registered warrant: a warrant registered by the paying officer for future payment on account of present lack of funds and which is to be paid in the order of its registration. In some cases, such warrants are registered when issued; in others, when first presented to the paying officer by the holders. see also *warrant.* [49]

register of wills: in some states (Delaware, for example), the name of the officer before whom wills are offered for probate and who grants letters testamentary and letters of administration. [32]

registrar: an agency, usually a trust company or a bank, charged with the responsibility of preventing the issuance of more stock that has been authorized by a company. The registrar's primary function is to authenticate the issuing of securities. see *overissue.* see also *Torrens certificate.*

registration: before a public offering may be made of new securities by a company, or of outstanding securities by controlling stockholders, the securities must be registered under the Securities Act of 1933. A registration statement is filed with the SEC by the issuer, disclosing pertinent information relating to company's operations, securities, management, and purpose of the public offering. On security offerings involving less than $300,000, the information required is less detailed.

registry: a public recording of documents or information.

regressive supply: when the price of an item drops, a greater quantity of the item is offered.

regressive supply curve: the graphic showing of the condition when a commodity is offered in increasing amounts as a market price drops.

regressive taxes: rates in a tax system that decrease as the base amount taxed increases (a rate of 5 percent applied to a base of $500, 4 percent applied to a base of $2000, etc.). A sales tax is a regressive tax. cf. *progressive tax.*

regs: slang, regulations.

regular dating: referring to terms of a sale under which the period for discount and the date on which payment is required are determined from the date of the invoice. cf. *ROG dating.*

regular delivery: in govenment securities market, delivery of a security made on the business day following purchase or sale. cf. *cash delivery.*

regular dividend: the established rate of dividend set by a firm on its stock which is usually paid every three or six months.

regularity of dividends: the pattern of constant payment of dividends by a corporation. Confidence by the public is often related to a firm's regularity of dividends.

regular lending area: the geographical boundaries within which a security property must be located in order for a savings association to invest in a mortgage loan secured by the property, without the loan and the association being subject to special limitations set by regulatory and supervisory agencies. synonymous with *normal lending territory.* [59]

regular lot: the unit of trading on a specific stock or commodity exchange; the full or board lot.

regular mortgage: the legal document used in most states to pledge real estate as security for the repayment of a debt. [59]

regular savings account: a savings account to which additions or withdrawals may be made in any amount at any time; earnings typically are credited directly to the account at the appropriate earnings distributions times rather than mailed to the account holder. [59]

regular serial bond: see *bond, regular serial.*

regular warehouse: a government-authorized warehouse for commodity deliveries under futures contracts.

regular-way delivery: unless otherwise specified, securities (other than government) sold on the New York Stock Exchange are to be delivered to the buying broker by the selling broker and payment made to the selling broker by the buying broker on the fourth business day after the transaction. Regular-way delivery for government bonds is the following business day. see *delivery, transfer.* [20]

regular-way sale: any securities transaction that is not a short sale.

regulated commodities: those commodities over which the Commodity Exchange Authority has supervision are known as "regulated." This does not means that the prices are controlled. The CEA simply concerns itself with the orderly operation of the futures market and, at times, investigates abnormal price movements. Under the Commodity Exchange Act, approved June 15, 1936, definite regulations are established providing for the safeguarding of customers' money deposited as margin. Commodities currently supervised by the CEA are wheat, cotton, corn, rice, oats, barley, rye, flaxseed, grain sorghums, bran, shorts, middlings, butter, eggs, potatoes, onions, wool tops, wool futures, lard, tallow, soybean oil, cottonseed meal, cottonseed, peanuts, soybeans, and soybean meal. [2]

regulated investment companies: investment companies that can avoid income tax on its ordinary income and capital gains by distributing profits as dividends and by conforming to other statutory rules.

Regulation A: establishes the conditions and means by which Federal Reserve Banks extend credit to member banks and others. Credit extended to member banks is usually in the form of an advance on the bank's promissory note secured by U.S. government and federal agency securities; eligible commercial, agricultural, or construction paper; or banker acceptances. The credit cannot be extended for speculative purposes, and paper offered as collateral must be acceptable for discount or purchase under criteria specified in the regulation. [105]

Regulation B: prohibits discrimination by lenders on the basis of age, race, color, religion, national origin, sex, marital status, or receipt of income from public assistance programs. It establishes guidelines for gathering and evaluating credit information, and requires written notification to the applicant in cases where credit is denied. [105]

Regulation C: requires depository institutions making federally related mortgage loans to make annual public disclosure of the locations of certain residential loans. This is done to carry out the Home Mortgage Disclosure Act of 1935 and applies to most commercial banks, savings and loan associations, building and loan associations, homestead associations, and credit

unions that make federally related mortgage loans. [105]

Regulation D: the regulation of the Federal Reserve Board which defines and prescribes legal reserve requirements of member banks. [36]

Regulation E: for financial institutions, implementing the Electronic Fund Transfer Act, which covers the limits of consumer liability and rules on the issuance of cards; adopted in March 1979. In January 1980, the Federal Reserve Board adopted additional amendments to its Regulation E proposals to become effective in May 1980. The more recent actions deal with documentation of transfers, preauthorized credits, and procedures for processing errors. see *Electronic Fund Transfer Act.* [14]

Regulation F: a regulation issued by the Board of Governors of the Federal Reserve System under authority of Section 11(k) of the Federal Reserve Act, as amended, relating to the conduct of fiduciary business by national banks. The full title of the regulation is Regulation F—Trust Powers of National Banks. [37]

Regulation G: Federal Reserve Board rule regulating lenders other than commercial banks, brokers, or dealers who, in the ordinary course of business, extend credit to people to buy or carry securities.

Regulation H: defines membership requirements and other conditions required of state-chartered banks. It also stipulates the necessary procedures to be followed when requesting approval to establish branches, and for requesting voluntary withdrawal from membership. [105]

Regulation I: requires banks joining

the Federal Reserve System to subscribe to the stock of the Federal Reserve Bank in its district. The amount of stock ownership required is a percentage of the member bank's capital plus surplus. Ownership of Federal Reserve stock must be adjusted with fluctuations in the member bank's capitalization. [105]

Regulation J: the regulation of the Federal Reserve Board containing the terms and conditions governing collection of checks and other items by Federal Reserve Banks. [36]

Regulation L: discourages noncompetitive practices among member banks by restricting the relationships a director, officer, or employee of one bank can have with another banking institution. [105]

Regulation M: governs the foreign activities of member banks. Regulation M covers the requirements for establishing a foreign branch, the reserve requirements imposed on transactions by foreign branches, and determines permissible foreign banking activities. [105]

Regulation Nine (9): a regulation issued by the Comptroller of the Currency under authority of Section 1(j) of the act of September 28, 1962 (76 Stat. 668, 12 U.S.C. 92a) relating to the conduct of fiduciary business by national banks. The full title of the regulation is Regulation 9—Fiduciary Powers of National Banks and Collective Investment Funds. [37]

Regulation O: stipulates the conditions under which a member bank may loan funds to its own executive officers. [105]

Regulation Q: as established by the Federal Reserve Board, a formula it uses to determine the maximum interest that can be paid by commercial banks to their customers on time deposits.

Regulation T: the Federal Reserve Board criterion governing the amount of credit that may be advanced by brokers and dealers to customers for the purchase of securities. see *margin.*

Regulation U: the Federal Reserve Board criterion governing the amount of credit that may be advanced by a bank to its customers for the purchase of listed stocks when the requested loan is to be secured by listed stocks.

Regulation Z: this so-called truth-in-lending regulation was adopted, effective July 1, 1969, by the Board of Governors of the Federal Reserve System to implement Title I (Truth in Lending Act) and Title V (General Provisions) of the Consumer Protection Act. Dealing with the information customers of consumer credit should be given, it specifies, among other things, that they must be told the exact dollar amount of the finance charge and the annual percentage rate computed on the unpaid balance of the loan. [33]

regulatory taxation: the use of taxation not only for purposes of public revenue but to control by restricting economic development along any given line.

rehypothecate: to pledge a second time.

rehypothecation: using collateral pledged as security for a loan by an original lender, who in turn uses it as collateral for a loan. Stockbrokers secure the approval of their customers to rehypothecate securities left as collateral on margin accounts.

Reichsbank: German for "imperial

bank." The central bank of Germany, which receives and disburses state funds.

reimbursement: cash or other assets received as a repayment of the cost of work or services performed or of other expenditures, made for or on behalf of another governmental unit, or department, or for an individual, firm, or corporation. [49]

reimbursement arrangement: an arrangement by which a foreign correspondent bank is reimbursed for payments made according to the instructions of the bank issuing credit. [105]

reimbursement bank: the bank providing cover as a result of a funds transfer. [105]

reimbursement letter of credit: an arrangement by which a foreign correspondent bank is reimbursed for payments made according to the instructions of the bank issuing credit by drawing on another correspondent bank. [105]

reimbursement method: instructions specifying how the receiver is to obtain reimbursement for the payment requested by the sender. With prior agreements this instruction may specify a debit party other than the sender. [105]

reindustrialization: often used for resuscitating industries and modernizing factories, in part by marshaling capital for new businesses. Amitai Etzioni is credited with having coined the term, which was later popularized by President Carter.

reinstatement: the payment of a claim reduces the principal amount of the policy by the amount of the claim. Provision is usually made for reestablish-

ing the policy to its original amount. Depending on policy conditions, it may be done automatically, either with or without premium consideration, or it may be done at the request of the insured.

reinsurance: the assumption by one insurance company of all or part of a risk undertaken by another.

reinvestment: using proceeds of dividends, interest, or sale of stocks to buy other securities. One popular feature of some securities of investment companies is that the proceeds can be reinvested at favorable terms.

reinvestment privilege: the automatic investment of dividends from holdings in a mutual fund in additional shares of the fund, at times without a sales charge.

reissue month: the month the customer's cards are sent out. The cycle number correlates with the reissue month. [105]

reissues: issues replaced into circulation after a specific lapse of time and usually with an overprint. [27]

REIT: see *real estate investment trust.*

reject: to refuse or decline a risk. [12]

related funds: funds of a similar character which are brought together for administrative and reporting purposes; for example, sinking fund. [49]

relationship banking: a strategy to attract investors, where a customer deals with just one officer who can handle all services—and who becomes a salesperson in the process.

relative income concept: the hypothesis that spending is a function of a family's relative place in the income distribution of similar family units (i.e., people who earn the same tend to spend the same amount of money).

relative price: expresses the cost of a good in terms of other goods, not in terms of money. That is, if a book's nominal price is $2, the relative price of a newspaper—relative to a book—is $1/8$ ($0.25 ÷ $2.00 = $1/8$). This shows that the newspaper is worth one-eighth of a book. cf. *normal price*. [100]

relative price of energy: measured by the producer price index for "fuels and related products and power" divided by the business sector deflator. [108]

relative priority: a principle of reorganization under which each group of creditors and stockholders, based on seniority, survives the reorganization, but the losses of each group are inversely proportional to its seniority.

release

(1) *general:* the written statement of a claim's settlement.

(2) *banking:* the discharge of property from a mortgage lien; a written statement that an obligation has been satisfied.

(3) *law:* the cancellation or resolution of a claim against another person. [59]

release clause: a clause in a mortgage permitting payment of a part of the debt in order that a proportionate part of the property can be freed.

release date and time: date and time the sender authorizes the service to forward the instructions to the receiver. [105]

released rate: with respect to a commodity varying greatly in value, a released rate is an agreement by the shipper to set a limit to the value of the shipment in return for a concession in the rate. Now illegal under the Interstate Commerce Act except for bag-gage, special livestock, and specific exemptions by the Commission.

release of liability: agreement in which a lender terminates the personal obligation of a mortgagor for the payment of a debt. [105]

release of lien: an instrument discharging secured property from a lien. [105]

release of mortgage: dropping a claim against property established by a mortgage.

release of premiums on funded debt: a credit to income each fiscal period of a proportion of the premium realized at the sale of funded securities, based on the ratio of such fiscal period to the remaining life of the securities. [18]

reloader: slang, an individual who is clever in selling further securities to a person who has just purchased a small amount of the same stock.

Rem.: see *remittance*.

remainder: upon completion of a life estate, the property reverts to the owner or goes to an heir. If the owner does not take the property back, a remainder estate is created by the same instrument. This estate begins upon the termination of the temporary estate (i.e., the life estate) that preceded it.

remainder beneficiary: the beneficiary of a trust who is entitled to the principal outright after the prior life beneficiary or other prior beneficiary has died or his or her interest has been terminated. [32]

remainder estate: an estate in property created simultaneously with other estates by a single grant and consisting of the rights and interest contingent upon and remaining after the termination of the other estates. [58]

remainder interest: a future interest

which will become an interest in possession after the termination of a prior interest created at the same time and by the same instrument as the future interest. For example, H leaves his estate in trust with income to be paid to W, and on her death the trust is to terminate and the property is to be delivered to C. C has a remainder interest. [37]

remaindermen: those persons who receive the proceeds from the final distribution of a trust or estate. [25]

remainder notes: unissued and unsigned notes of a bank which either closed down or changed its design, leaving a supply of unwanted notes. With few exceptions, these should be in absolutely perfect condition. [27]

remand: the action of an appellate court in sending a cause back to the lower court that sought the appeal, accompanied by the instructions of the higher court.

remargining: placing added margin against a loan. Remargining is one option when brokers require additional cash or collateral when their securities have lost some of their value.

reminder letter: the first in a series of collection letters, sent by a creditor to a debtor, where the latter has neglected to make a payment on time. [105]

remise: to give or grant back; to discharge or release. synonymous with *quit claim.*

Remitt.: see *remittance.*

remittance: funds forwarded from one person to another as payment for bought items or services.

remittance letter: a transit letter containing a list of checks sent for collection and payment by a sending bank to a receiving bank. The sending bank does not maintain an account with the receiving bank, and hence requests the latter to remit payment for the items sent. The receiving bank pays for the checks by remitting a bank draft to the sending bank. This is to be distinguished from a cash letter of credit, in which case the receiving bank credits the account of the sending bank in its "due to banks" ledger. [10]

remittance payment: payment sent by mail to center for processing. [105]

remitter: the party who is the source of funds to the receiver. [105]

remitter advice charges: information specifying who to charge for advising the remitter and how to apply these charges. [105]

remitter advice identifier: information used in contacting the remitter in order to send an advice (e.g., phone number, cable address). [105]

remitter advice instructions: additional information that pertains to notification of the remitter (e.g., bank's/person's name, hours of availability). [105]

remitter advice method: a code that specifies the method to be used to notify the remitter that the account has been credited or that funds are available (e.g., phone, letter, wire). [105]

remitter identifier: a code that uniquely identifies the remitter. [105]

remitter identifier type: a code that specifies the type of identifier used for the remitter. [105]

remitter name and address: identifies the remitter by name and, optionally, the remitter's postal address. [105]

remitting: paying, as in remitting a payment; also canceling, as in remitting a debt. [28]

remonetization: the reinstatement of a

coin as standard money after it has been demonetized.

remote electronic banking: electronic funds transfer systems through which bank customers conduct banking business at a location other than a bank office, for example, point-of-sale or CBCT. [33]

remoteness of vesting: see *rule against perpetuities.* [37]

remote service unit: the terminology used by savings and loan associations that corresponds to the customer-bank communication terminal (CBCT) that may be employed by banks. see *customer-bank communication terminal.* [36]

removed in perpetuity: see *perpetuity.*

remuneration: wages and other financial benefits received from employment.

rendu price: an import delivered price. The price of imported goods, including all charges for tariff and freight.

renege: to go back on a promise; to pull out of an agreement. see also *repudiation.*

renegotiable-rate mortgage (RRM): authorized by the Federal Home Loan Bank Board, requires home buyers to renegotiate the terms of the loan every three to five years—a distinct advantage if interest rates drop but a poor hedge against inflation if they go up. cf. *variable-rate mortgage*; sometimes called the *rollover mortgage.*

renewable term insurance: insurance that offers a guaranteed option to renew without a health examination up to retirement age and sometimes beyond.

renewal: extending the maturity of an existing loan obligation, or other document of relationship. cf. *novation.*

renewal certificate: an insurance policy is sometimes renewed by issuing a certificate rather than writing out a new policy. The certificate refers to the policy but does not enumerate all its items.

renounce

(1) an act by which an individual or trust institution named under a will as executor or trustee declines to accept such appointment.

(2) the act of a surviving husband or wife under the decedent's state law declining to take the provision made for him or her under the other's will and taking his or her share of the estate had the other died without a will.

(3) any action by which the beneficiary of any interest in real or personal property therewith refuses to accept such interest. [37]

rent: income received from leasing real estate.

rentes: the annual interest payable on the bonded debt of France, Austria, Italy, and a few other countries. The term is also applied to the bonds themselves.

rentier: a person living on income received from fixed investments.

renunciation: giving up a right or claim, without any reservation, or without naming the person who is to assume the title.

REOP: reopening after a halt in trading.

reorganization: the altering of a firm's capital structure, often resulting from a merger, that affects the rights and responsibilities of the owners. The objectives of a reorganization are to eliminate the cause of failure, settle with creditors, and allow the firm to remain in business. see *National Bank-ruptcy Act of 1898*; cf. *quasi-reorganization.*

reorganization bond: see *bond, reor-ganization.*

reorganization committee: a commit-tee representing investors or creditors which develops plans for the reorgani-zation of a distressed corporation. The National Bankruptcy Act sets strict conditions under which such groups operate.

reparations: money, goods, or ser-vices paid by one country to another as compensation for damages incurred in war.

repatriated earnings: a U.S. Depart-ment of Commerce definition in ser-vices (not manufacturing, agriculture, or raw materials) where most of the dollar total in the service group is attrib-utable to investment income earned on American-owned assets and enter-prises abroad.

repatriation: the liquidation of over-seas investments and the return of the proceeds to the country of the investor.

repayments: see *loan repayments.*

replacement-cost standard: the cost of replacing equipment with new equip-ment for tasks identical to those per-formed by worn or obsolete equipment; it provides a way of determining a firm's value.

replacement demand: demand for capital items or durable consumer goods created because of obsoles-cence or depreciation.

replacement notes: those which do not run in serial sequence and which have been issued to replace a dam-aged or misprinted note. They usually bear an indicative symbol of some sort,

such as the asterisk used in the United States as part of the serial number. [27]

repledge: synonymous with *rehy-pothecate.*

replenishment deposit: a payment that increases the balance of the origi-nator's account with the receiver main-taining correspondent balances. [105]

replevin: a statute remedy for the re-covery of the possession of a chattel. The right of possession can be tried only in such action. cf. *seisin (seizin).*

REPO: see *repurchase agreement.*

report (or certificate): the report (or certificate) of an independent accoun-tant (or auditor) is a document in which he indicates the nature and scope of the examination (or audit) that he has made and expresses the opinion that he has formed in respect of the finan-cial statements. [77]

reporter: person employed by a credit bureau. Makes reports on credit inqui-ries. [41]

repossession: the reclaiming or taking back of items that were bought on an installment sales contract on which the buyer has fallen behind in payments.

representations and warrants: the promise or pledge by a seller made prior to or in connection with a sale to induce the buyer to purchase. Also the guarantees the seller gives the guaran-tees the seller gives to the purchaser of its installment notes, relating to such matters as signatures, validity of obli-gation, and legal sufficiency of the notes. [55]

representative
(1) a general term designating either an executor or an administrator.
(2) the person who acts or speaks for another under his or her authority. [37]

representative goods: evidences of

ownership of wealth, such as notes, bonds, stocks, and money, are examples of representative goods.

representative money
(1) *finance:* paper money secured by monetary metal (i.e., gold or silver certificates) deposited in the treasury of a country.
(2) *investments:* funds that are backed in full by a commodity.

repressed inflation: the situation where there is limited control of prices and wages accompanied by an increase in money demand for goods relative to the supply of goods after the economy is at full employment.

repressive tax: a tax purporting to discourage production and thereby reduce potential tax income.

reproduction-cost standard: the cost of reproducing a firm's assets minus an allowance for depreciation for the period during which the existing assets have been in use. see also *valuation*.

reproduction value: the sum of money which would be required to reproduce a building less an allowance for depreciation of that building. [44]

repudiation: the intentional and willful refusal to pay a debt in whole or in part. The term usually refers to the willful act of a government or a subdivision thereof. cf. *nullification of agreement*.

repurchase agreement (REPO): an arrangement allowing the owner of debt securities (usually Treasury bills) to borrow money by selling the securities to a buyer while promising to repurchase them at a fixed price on a specified date. see also *retail repo*.

repurchase plan: type of dealer financing plan in which the responsibility is shared between a dealer and a bank in case of consumer default, and which

usually provides for the sale of contracts to a bank without recourse regarding a customer's obligation to pay; the dealer, however, agrees to repurchase, for the net unpaid balance, those goods repossessed by the bank and delivered to the dealer's place of business within a specified number of days after maturity of the oldest unpaid installment. [105]

repurchases: in closed-end companies, refers to voluntary open market purchases by investment companies of their own securities, usually for retirement. In open-end funds, the term represents stock taken back at approximate liquidating value. [30]

request for a report: a request on the status of a security order made through the order room of a brokerage house to the broker concerned on the stock exchange floor.

request for conditional commitment to guarantee loan: the bank's request to FmHA to indicate its willingness to guarantee a loan on the terms spelled out by the bank in its Application for Guaranteed Loan. [105]

request for contract of guarantee: a bank's request to FmHA to issue a guarantee on the bank's loan as presented in the bank's Application for Guaranteed Loan. [105]

request for proposal (RFP): the official document requesting from prospective contractors a detailed description of the manner in which they plan to achieve the goals specified by the RFP were they awarded a contract to do so. The plan usually includes the proposer's estimate of total cost and required schedule.

required rate of return: rate of return that investors feel constitutes an appropriate discount of the cash flow of a particular investment.

required reserves: liquid assets that state-chartered banks must hold in accordance with regulations of state banking agencies and Federal Reserve officials.

required return: the lowest return of profit needed to justify an investment.

Res.: see *reserve.*

res: in the phrase trust res, the same as trust property. The corpus of the trust. [37]

res adjudicata: Latin; the principle according to which a controversy that has once been decided is deemed to be settled forever; that is, the courts will not hear claims to which the issue adjudicated applies.

rescheduling: the renegotiation of the terms of existing debt. [91]

rescind: see *right of rescission.*

rescission: making void or annulling (e.g., the rescission of a law or judgment). see *right of rescission.*

rescript: a duplicate of a document.

research and development
(1) *general:* applying the findings of science and technology to create a firm's products or services.
(2) *investments:* the dollar amount spent on company-sponsored research and development for the year as reported to the SEC. The total excludes any expenditures for research and development performed under contract for others, such as U.S. government agencies.

reservation price: the highest offered price at which a seller will continue to hold back from selling. The seller will, however, sell at any offer above the reservation price.

reserve
(1) *finance:* a portion of the profits allocated to various reserve accounts to protect any depreciation in asset values. The reserves are taken from profits before any declaration of dividends by the board of directors.
(2) *banking:* assets in the form of cash maintained in a bank's own vault. see *reserve requirements.*
(3) *banking:* funds earmarked for specific purposes. For example, reserves for unearned premiums and reserves for losses in process of adjustment. cf. *legal reserve.*

reserve adjustment magnitude (RAM): measures the impact of changes in reserve requirements by simply subtracting the current period's required reserves from those that would have been required if some base period's reserve requirements were, instead, in effect. The purpose of a RAM is to capture in the adjusted monetary base those total reserve changes that arise from changes in reserve requirements by the Federal Reserve. [79]

reserve bank: any one of the 12 Federal Reserve Banks. see *banker's bank, Federal Reserve Bank.*

reserve bank credit: credit extended to member banks by the Federal Reserve Bank through rediscounting member bank loans, purchasing acceptances, or direct loans on various security. In addition, all deposits made by a member bank qualify.

reserve checking/overdraft checking: a combination of a checking account and a preauthorized personal loan. synonymous with *personal line of credit.* [105]

reserve city bank: a member bank of the Federal Reserve System located in cities identified by the Federal Reserve Act as amended as reserve cities. These banks are divided for reserve requirements by the act into reserve city banks and country banks.

reserve clause: a Eurocurrency credit clause allowing a lender to pass on to a borrower any further costs resulting from the imposition on the lender of new reserve requirements. [83]

reserve currency: foreign funds retained by a nation's central bank as a vehicle for settling international financial obligations. The U.S. dollar and the pound sterling are the dominant reserve currencies today.

reserve depository: an authorized bank serving as depository for part of the legal reserves against deposits other banks must hold, under law.

reserve for bad debts: a reserve account to which bad debt losses are charged. Under federal tax laws, savings associations are allowed to build up such reserves by making tax-deductible allocations of earnings according to a specified formula. synonymous with *allowance for bad debts.* [59]

reserve for encumbrances: a reserve representing the segregation of a portion of a fund balance to provide for unliquidated encumbrances. see also *reserve.* [49]

reserve for retirement of sinking fund bonds: a reserve that indicates the amount of cash and other resources that should have been accumulated at a certain date in order eventually to redeem bonds outstanding. [49]

reserve for revenue bond contingency: a reserve in an enterprise fund which represents the segregation of a portion of retained earnings equal to current assets that are restricted for meeting various contingencies as may be specified and defined in the revenue bond indenture. [49]

reserve for revenue-bond-debt-service: a reserve in an enterprise fund which represents the segregation of a portion of retained earnings equal to current assets that are restricted to current servicing of revenue bonds in accordance with the terms of a bond indenture. [49]

reserve for uncollected taxes: a reserve representing the segregation of a portion of a fund balance equal to the amount of taxes receivable by a fund. [49]

reserve fund: any asset such as cash or highly liquid securities created to meet some expense.

reserve ratio (requirement): see *reserve requirements.*

reserve requirements: percentage of customer deposits that banks must set aside in the form of reserves. The reserve requirement ratio determines the expansion of deposits that can be supported by each additional dollar of reserves. The Board of Governors can raise or lower reserve requirements for member banks within limits specified by law. Reserve requirements act as lending controls (lowering reserve requirements allows more bank lending; raising requirements, less lending). [1]

reserves: see *reserve.*

reserve split: reduction in the number of shares of a class of capital stock, with no reduction in the total dollar amount of the class, but with an increase in the par or stated value of the shares. This is achieved by substituting one new share for so many outstanding shares. [43]

reserves with Federal Reserve Banks:

deposits of reporting member banks with the Federal Reserve Banks. Members banks are required by law to hold an amount equal to a percentage of their deposits as reserve (a deposit) in the Reserve Banks. [40]

residence
(1) the place where one resides, whether temporarily or permanently. see *domicile*.
(2) as used in Regulation Z, any real property in which the customer lives or expects to live. Important in real estate transactions because when an interest to secure an obligation is taken in a customer's principal residence, notice of the right of rescission must be given to the customer. [105]

residential mortgage: a loan extended for which real estate is given as collateral. The collateral is usually a single owner-occupied home or a small number of dwelling units. [105]

residential real property: improved real property used or intended to be used for residential purposes, including single-family homes, dwellings for from two to four families, and individual units of condominiums and cooperatives. [105]

residual cost (or value): the difference between the cost of a particular asset and any amortized or expensed account. see also *book value*. [105]

residual legacy: see *legacy*.

residual ownership: what is left following claims.

residual securities: stocks that derive most of their value from conversion rights. see *conversion price, conversion ratio*.

residuary bequest: the part of a will that gives instruction for the disposal of any portion of an estate remaining after

payments of debts and other obligations.

residuary clause: the provision in the will or trust agreement that disposes of all of the decedent's property remaining after the payment of all taxes, debts, expenses, and charges and the satisfaction of all other gifts in the will or trust agreement. [37]

residuary devise: a gift by will of the real property remaining after all specific devices have been made. [37]

residuary devisee: a recipient by will of any real property after all other claimants to the estate have received payment.

residuary estate: what remains in an estate after all claims to the estate have been properly disposed of.

residuary legatee: a person to whom is given the remainder of a testator's personal property after all other legacies have been satisfied. [37]

residuary trust: a trust composed of the property of the testator that remains in the estate after the payment of all taxes, debts, expenses, charges, and the satisfaction of all other gifts under the will. [37]

residue: (rest, residue, and remainder); that portion of a decedent estate remaining after the payment of all debts, expenses, and charges and the satisfaction of all legacies and devises. [37]

resistance points: points or areas of price fluctuation at which a security or security average comes to a resistance or stop before moving in a direction.

resolution: a formal document expressing the intention of a board of directors of a corporation. [37]

resources: the bank's title for assets owned. The resources of a bank are offset by the liabilities and capital accounts as listed on the daily statement of condition. The major resources of a bank are cash on hand and due from banks; investments held; loans and discounts; and buildings, furniture, fixtures, and equipment. [10]

RESPA: see *Real Estate Settlement Procedures Act.*

respondentia: under conditions of hypothecation, the security offered against a loan (e.g., the goods on a truck).

responsibility costing: a system by which individuals are responsible for expenditures under their control. Costs are identified with individuals rather than with products or procedures. [105]

resting order: an order that can remain open or good until canceled when (a) an order to purchase securities is limited to a price lower than the market, or (b) an order to sell is limited to a price above the market.

restitution: the enforced payment of money, or its equivalent, to its rightful owner as established by law. cf. *replevin.*

restoration premium: the premium charged to restore a policy or bond to its original value after payment of a loss.

restraining order: a court order in aid of a suit to maintain the status quo until all parties can be heard from. see also *injunction.*

restraint of trade: the effect of any contract, combination, or agreement (e.g., a monopoly) that impedes free competition. see *Robinson-Patman Act of 1936. Sherman Antitrust Act of 1890.*

restraint on alienation of property: a limitation on the right of a person to transfer title to property or property rights. [37]

restricted account: any margin account where the debit balance exceeds the maximum loan value of stocks retained in that account.

restricted assets: money or other resources, the use of which is restricted by legal or contractual requirements. The most common examples of restricted assets in governmental accounting are those arising out of revenue bond indentures in enterprise funds. synonymous with *restricted funds*, but this terminology is not preferred. [49]

restricted card list: a listing of cardholder accounts, in either alphabetic or numeric sequence, on which transactions are restricted and not to be completed by merchants without authorization. see *hot card*. [105]

restricted funds: synonymous with *restricted assets*. See *restricted assets.*

restricted retained earnings: see *retained earnings, restricted.*

restricted securities: see *restricted shares.*

restricted shares: common stock shares released under an agreement whereby they do not rank for dividends until some event has taken place— usually the attainment of certain levels of earnings. Any unregistered stock acquired in private transactions as employment bonuses and the like.

restricted stock option: a privilege granted to an employee of a corporation to purchase during a specified period, at the market price at the date of the option, a specified number of shares of its capital stock. synonymous with *qualified stock option*. [43]

restricted surplus: that portion of retained earnings which is not regarded as available for dividends. This may be because of legal requirements or loan agreements. [43]

restrictive covenants: written agreements limiting the use of property.

restrictive endorsement: an endorsement that limits the negotiability of an instrument, or contains a definite condition as to payment; it purports to preclude the endorsee from making any further transfer of the instrument. [59]

resulting trust: a trust that arises in law from the acts of the parties, regardless of whether they actually intend to create a trust—as when a person disposes of property under circumstances that raise an inference that he or she does not intend that the person taking or holding the property shall have the beneficial interest in it; to be distinguished from an *express trust* and a *constructive trust*. [32]

retail balance: that portion of the total balance reflecting purchase of goods or services as opposed to cash advances; sometimes referred to as *merchandise balance*. [105]

retail banking: banking services offered to the general public, including commercial enterprises, consumers, and small business. [105]

retail credit: charge accounts, credit cards, or installment loans extended to consumers by merchants. [105]

retail credit bureaus: a center of local consumer credit information. Its primary function is to furnish reports on consumers desiring to obtain money. [105]

retail lending: loans to individuals, including home mortgages and consumer installment loans. [105]

retail money: see *wholesale money*.

retail repo: arrangements in which a lender lends the bank cash for a flexible period—usually a week to 89 days, and the bank promises to return the principal to the lender, plus interest. They are more liquid than bank savings certificates because there are usually no penalties for early withdrawal. The interest rate is competitive with money market mutual funds and much higher than the rate on passbook savings. The minimum denomination is typically $1000. However, a retail repo is an investment, not a deposit, and the money is not insured. see also *repurchase agreement*.

retail sales (index): a U.S. Bureau of the Census measure of sales of all types of retail establishments. It is issued around the 10th of the month for the previous month.

retained earnings: net income key by firm's management and reinvested on common stockholders' behalf rather than paid as dividends.

retained earnings, appropriated: the net accumulated balance reflecting reservations of retained earnings bring held for a special purpose, and not available for dividends. [3]

retained earnings, restricted: retained earnings restricted, usually against payment of dividends, by corporate indentures and other covenants and/or by orders of regulatory authorities. [3]

retained earnings, unappropriated: formerly earned surplus; accumulated net income less distribution to stockholders and transfers to other capital accounts. It is the connecting link between the income account and the balance sheet and represents the excess of the book value of the depreciated assets (and other debits) over the sum of long-term debt, current and accured liabilities, deferred credits, operating reserves, contributions in aid of construction, accumulated deferred income taxes (when used by the company), and proprietary capital other than retained earnings. [3]

retainer: payment to cover future services and advice, submitted in advance to the individual expected to render service.

retaliatory duty: a differential duty designed to penalize foreign nations for alleged discriminatory commerce activity or to force them into making trade concessions. see *tariff war;* cf. *most favored nation (clause).*

retention: the percentage of a syndicate member's underwriting participation retained for his or her own retail sales.

retirement: the paying off of a debt prior to or at maturity.

retirement fund: monies set aside by an organization; the fund builds up value over the year to provide income for employees eligible to retire and receive income from it.

retirement income: a stipulated amount of income starting at a selected retirement age. This is derived by exercising one of the settlement options available against the policy or annuity cash value. see also *Individual Retirement Accounts.*

retirement plan trusts: trusts established to enable the employees on retirement to receive a pension from funds created out of payments made by the employees, their employers, or both. [37]

retiring a bill: paying a bill of exchange

on its due date or beforehand, at a discount.

retreat: any drop in the price level of securities or commodities.

retrieval: see *information retrieval.*

retroactive restoration: a provision in a policy or bond whereby, after payment of a loss, the original amount of coverage is automatically restored to take care of prior undiscovered losses as well as future losses.

return: a statement of financial and related information required by government tax agencies (e.g., tax return). see *yield.*

returned check: a check the bank refused to accept and returned unpaid. [55]

return item: a negotiable instrument, principally a check, that has been sent to one bank for collection and payment and is returned unpaid to the sending bank.

return on assets (ROA): a profitability ratio defined as net income divided by total assets.

return on equity (ROE): a profitability ratio defined as net income divided by equity.

return on investment: see *ROI.*

return on investment ratio: a profitability ratio (net profit divided by total assets) representing the total investment in a firm. [105]

return on net worth: the ratio of an organization's net profit following taxes to its net worth, providing a measure of the rate of return on a shareholder's investment.

return on total assets: the ratio of an organization's net profit following taxes to its total assets, providing a measure of the rate of return on, or productivity of, total assets.

return premium: the amount due the insured if a policy is reduced in amount, canceled, or—if subject to audit—the audit yields a finding of less exposure(s) than the original estimate(s).

revalidated notes: paper money bearing an official overprint, stamp, or other mark to indicate its renewed status as legal tender, despite the invalidity of the original note. [27]

revaluation (revalorization): the restoration (by lowering the request for, or raising the supply of foreign currencies by restricting imports and promoting exports) of the value of a depreciated national currency that has previously been devalued.

revenue: the grand total of all resources received from the sale of a firm's product or service during a stated period. Not to be confused with *general revenue.* cf. *gross revenue;* see also *government revenue.*

Revenue Act of 1962: federal legislation; provided investment tax credit of 7 percent on new and used property other than buildings. see also *Revenue Act of 1964, Revenue Act of 1971, Revenue Act of 1978, Revenue Adjustment Act of 1975.*

Revenue Act of 1964: federal legislation; provided for two-stage cut in personal income tax liabilities and corporate-profits tax liabilities in 1964 and 1965. see also *Revenue Act of 1962, Revenue Act of 1971, Revenue Act of 1978, Revenue Adjustment Act of 1975.*

Revenue Act of 1971: federal legislation; accelerated by one year scheduled increases in personal exemptions and standard deduction. Repealed automobile excise tax retroactive to Au-

gust 15, 1971; on small trucks and buses to September 22, 1971. Reinstated 7 percent investment tax credit and incorporated depreciation range guidelines.

Revenue Act of 1976: much of this act was revised by the Revenue Act of 1978. see *Revenue Act of 1978.*

Revenue Act of 1978: federal legislation affecting the following areas.

(a) *Individual and corporate tax cuts:* lowers tax rates and widens brackets so that raises will not bring people so quickly into higher tax levels; the personal exemption deduction goes to $1000 beginning with 1979; the top corporate rate will be 46 percent in 1979 and after, with new graduated rates for lower income corporations.

(b) *Capital gains:* sellers of capital assets held more than a year can exclude 60 percent of the gain for sales on or after November 1, 1978. Capital gains have no adverse impact on the maximum tax on earned income on or after that date; nor are they subject to the add-on 15 percent preference tax in 1979 and later.

(c) *New alternative tax on capital gains:* the excluded portion of capital gains and adjusted itemized deductions are no longer subject to the regular add-on preference tax to be replaced by a new alternative minimum tax. If a person has heavy capital gains or itemized deductions, he or she must now figure two taxes—regular taxes and an alternative tax, which is at graduated rates (25 percent maximum) above an exclusion base of $20,000; the individual pays whichever is higher.

(d) *Homeowners:* personal residence sales will no longer produce gains subject to the old add-on minimum tax or to the new alternative minimum tax described above. There is also the right to exclude all gain up to $100,000 if the individual is 55 years of age or over. Both changes apply to home sales after July 26, 1978.

(e) *Tax shelter rules:* these are broader, causing more entities to be subject to the "at risk" rules that keep people from deducting more than their equity investment. Entertainment facilities such as hunting lodges and yachts are no longer to be accepted as business deductions. Partnerships face more stringent reporting requirements, with stiff new penalties if partnership returns are not sent in on time.

(f) *Carryover basis rules postponed:* a stepped-up basis for inherited property is back. The carryover basis rules enacted in 1976 did not apply until 1980. Refund possibilities abound for those who have reported gains using carryover basis for assets inherited from someone who died in 1977 or 1978.

(g) *Other provisions:* there are changes on deductions and credits— for example, there is a new targeted jobs credit, and the investment credit is set permanently at 10 percent. The new law also contains important changes for employee benefits. See *Tax Reform Act of 1976;* see also *Energy Tax Act of 1978.*

Revenue Adjustment Act of 1975: federal legislation; provided extensive redrafting of tax laws. Restricted use of tax shelter investments and made changes in taxing of gifts and estates. Increased taxes on very wealthy. Continued tax cuts passed in 1975.

Revenue and Expenditure Control Act of 1968: federal legislation; levied 10 percent surtax on personal income taxes effective April 1, 1968, and on corporate taxes effective January 1, 1968. Postponed reduction in excise tax rates on automobiles and telephone service.

revenue-anticipation notes (RANs): short-term municipal borrowings that fund current operations and are to be funded by revenues other than taxes, especially federal aid.

revenue application notes: short-term notes sold in anticipation of receipt of revenues and payable from the proceeds of those revenues. [105]

revenue bond: see *bond; revenue.*

revenue bonds payable: a liability account which represents the face value of revenue bonds issued and outstanding. [49]

revenue expenditure: see *expenditure.*

revenue from own sources: total revenue consisting of taxes and charges and miscellaneous revenues, and revenue from utility, liquor stores (where applicable), and insurance trust.

revenue receipts: a term used synonymously with "revenue" by some governmental units which account for their revenues on a "cash basis." see also *nonrevenue receipts.* [49]

Revenue Reconciliation Act of 1980: grants a credit of up to $1000 for the windfall profits tax imposed on oil royalty holders.

revenues collected in advance: a liability account which represents revenues collected before they become due. [49]

revenue sharing: the return by a larger unit of government, with greater taxing powers, of a part of its revenue to a smaller component of government. see *highway trust fund, intergovernmental expenditures, shared revenue*; cf. *grants-in-aid.*

revenue stamps: documentary stamps; adhesive stamps issued by the federal or state government, which must be purchased and affixed, in amounts provided by law, to documents or instruments representing original issues, sales, and transfers of stocks and bonds, deeds of conveyances, and certain types of foreign insurance policies. [37]

revenue tariffs: duties placed on imports with the goal of increasing revenues rather than protecting domestic industries.

reverse: the back of a note. see *obverse.* [27]

reverse-annuity mortgage: designed for retirees and other fixed-income homeowners who owe little or nothing on their houses. Typically, it permits them to use some or all of the equity already in the home as supplemental income, while retaining ownership. In effect, they are borrowing against the value of the house on a monthly basis. The longer they borrow, of course, the less equity they retain in the house. The loan becomes due either on a specific date or when a specified event occurs such as the sale of the property or death of the borrower. see also *flexible-payment mortgage, graduated-payment mortgage, pledge-account mortgage, rollover mortgage, variable-rate mortgage. synonymous with equity conversion.*

reverse money transfer: a debit transfer in which the credit party is the sender. [105]

reverse mortgage: a loan against the value of a house.

reverse repos: synonymous with *matched sales.*

reverse repurchase agreements: synonymous with *matched sales.*

reverse repurchases: where a lender purchases securities with a commitment to resell them at the same price plus a specified interest charge. [90]

reverse split: the number of outstanding shares of a corporation reduced and the market price of remaining shares is increased. opposite of *stock split*; synonymous with *split down.*

reverse stock split: the reduction of the number of outstanding shares. see *stock split down.*

reverse yield gap: a situation where fixed-interest securities yield more than industrial shares.

reversible term insurance: insurance that is generally the cheapest policy for healthy people who gamble on continuing to stay healthy. However, it is not automatically renewable. In later years a person who becomes sick would not be able to renew at the cheap rate and might have to pay a higher rate, sometimes much higher.

reversing entries: an accounting procedure by which equal and opposite entries are made to an account to adjust the financial records of an association. This normally occurs after closing procedures. [59]

reversion: the interest in an estate remaining in the grantor after a particular interest, less than the whole estate, has been granted by the owner to another person; to be distinguished from remainder. The reversion remains in the grantor; the remainder goes to some grantee. [37]

reversionary interest: a claim or interest that an individual can keep to property or income that has been assigned to someone else. cf. *estate in reversion, remainder.*

reversionary right: the right to receive possession and use of property upon termination or defeat of an estate bearing the rights of possession and use and vested in another.

reverter: the interest which the grantor retains in property in which he has conveyed an interest less than the whole to another party. If the grantor makes the conveyance subject to a condition which may or may not be broken sometime in the future, he retains a possibility of reverter. [37]

revocable beneficiary: a beneficiary whose rights in the policy are subject to the insured's right of change. see *beneficiary.*

revocable letter of credit: any letter of credit that may be canceled.

revocable living trust: the income from such a trust is paid to the grantor during his or her lifetime, and to the family following the grantor's death. It can be canceled by the person granting or initiating the trust.

revocable trust with consent or approval: a trust which may be terminated by the settlor or by another person but only with the consent or approval of one or more other persons. For example, A creates for his son B a trust which may be revoked by B with C's consent (in this case C may be B's mother). To be distinguished from an *irrevocable trust.* [37]

revocation: the act of annulling or making inoperative a will or a trust instrument. [37]

revolver: see *revolving credit line.*

revolving account: a line of credit that may be used repeatedly up to a certain specified limit. [78]

revolving credit
(1) see *open-end credit.*
(2) see *optional (revolving) credit.*

revolving credit line: a guaranteed standby credit arrangement whereby the firm can borrow from the bank when needed up to a certain limit.

revolving fund: money that is renewed as it is used, either by additional appropriations or by income from the programs it finances; thus the fund retains a balance at all times.

revolving letter of credit: a letter of credit issued for a specific amount that is automatically renewed for the same amount over a given period. Usually the unused renewable portion of the credit is cumulative, as long as drafts are drawn before the expiration of the credit.

revolving loan: a loan that is automatically renewed (upon maturity) without additional negotiation.

reward account: a type of checking account that gives no-charge checking to anybody with a minimum (e.g., $2000) savings account.

RF: see *revolving fund.*

RFC: Reconstruction Finance Corporation (defunct).

Rfg.: see *refunding.*

RFP: see *request for proposal.*

RFQ: request for quotation. synonymous with *request for proposal.*

RH: see *red herring.*

rial: monetary unit of Iran, Oman, and Yemen.

rialto: slang, a stock exchange or other financial center.

rich: an expression applied to security prices when the current market quotation appears to be high (or the income return low) in comparison with either the past price record of the individual security or the current prices of comparable securities. [67]

riel: monetary unit of Cambodia and Kampuchea.

rigged market: the situation that exists when purchases and sales are manipulated to distort a normal supply and demand price.

right

(1) the privilege attaching to a share of stock to subscribe to other securities in a fixed ratio.

(2) that which is reserved by a settlor, as the right of amendment or revocation; opposed to the power granted to the trustee. [37]

right-hand side: the rate at which a bank will buy foreign currencies. [105]

right of action: the right to enforce a claim in court.

right of curtesy: see *curtesy.*

right of dower: see *dower.*

right of election: the right of a surviving husband or wife, under the decedent's estate law, to take his or her intestate share in preference to the provision made in the deceased person's will. [37]

right of foreclosure: the right of the association to take over property and close out the mortgagor's interest in it if the mortgagor violates the provisions of the mortgage or note. [59]

right of offset: a clause in the loan contract that gives the lender the right to use the balances in any of the customer's accounts as payment for the loan in the event of default. [105]

right of redemption: the right to free a property from foreclosure by paying off all debts.

right of rescission (ROR): the privi-

lege, guaranteed by the Truth in Lending Act to cancel a contract under certain circumstances within three business days, without penalty and with full refund of all deposits submitted. see *voidable contract.*

right of survivorship: the right establishing a surviving joint owner as holder of the title to the property jointly owned. see *tenancy by the entirety*; cf. *tenancy in common.*

right of withdrawal: the privilege of an insured or beneficiary permitting withdrawal of funds placed on deposit. [12]

rights: when a company wants to raise more funds by issuing additional securities, it may give its stockholders the opportunity, ahead of others, to buy the new securities in proportion to the number of shares each owns. The piece of paper evidencing this privilege is called a right. Because the additional stock is usually offered to stockholders below the current market price, rights ordinarily have a market value of their own and are actively traded. In most cases they must be exercised within a relatively short period. Failure to exercise or sell rights may result in actual loss to the holder. see also *cum right.* [20]

rights off: synonymous with *ex-rights.*

rights on: when a security is selling at a price and on a basis including the privilege to purchase a pro rata amount of additional securities offered.

ring: synonymous with *pit.*

ringgit: monetary unit of Malaysia.

ringing out (or up): a practice of commodity brokers and commission merchants of settling existing futures contracts by exchanging sale and purchase contracts among themselves before the instruments mature and become deliverable. For example, A has agreed to purchase in the future from C and at the same time to sell the same item to C. In the meantime, B has agreed to sell the item to C. The ring is complete and the transaction can be approved. The ringing-out process permits incomplete ring participants to clear up their responsibilities and commitments.

rising bottoms: a bullish formation that reveals the ability of a futures contract to turn up above each preceding important low point. To be complete, however, there should also be an accompanying series of rising tops. Rising bottoms precede rising tops and are thus the first technical requirment that must be met if a situation is to be termed bullish.

risk: the possibility of loss; specifically chance of nonpayment of a debt. [59]

risk-adjusted discount rate: discount rate established by the inherent riskiness of the activity being evaluated.

risk analysis: an examination of the elements or sources of risk in a mortgage loan and of their efforts both separately and in combination. [44]

risk arbitrage: the trading of stocks in companies that are involved in mergers and acquisitions. see *arbitrage*.

risk assets: all bank assets, except cash and direct U.S. government obligations. [105]

risk capital
(1) *general:* capitalization that is not secured by a lien or mortgage.
(2) *finance:* long-term loans or capital invested in high-risk business activities.
(3) *investments:* common stock from a new enterprise.

risk category: a class or group into which related elements affecting mortgage risk are placed for purposes of convenience in analysis. [44]

risk feature: an item affecting mortgage risk. [105]

risk-free rate of return: rate of return on perfectly safe government securities.

risk premium: additional required rate of return due to extra risk incurred.

risk rating: a systematic process of analyzing mortgage risk that results in estimation, in precise relative terms, of the soundness of individual transactions. [105]

rival demand: see *composite demand*.

rival supply: see *composite supply*.

rivets: slang, money.

riyal: monetary unit of Oman, Saudi Arabia, and Yemen.

RL: see *round lot.*

Rmdr.: see *remainder.*

ROA: see *return on assets.*

Robinson-Patman Act of 1936: federal legislation amending the Clayton Antitrust Act of 1914. Price discrimination practices are more clearly identified. Quantity discounts in excess of the cost savings realized by selling in such quantities are declared illegal, as are false brokerage deals. Promotional allowances must be made to all buyers on a proportionately equal basis, and price discrimination is acceptable if made to meet a proper low price of a competitor so long as the price does not restrict competition.

rock: slang, any quantity of money.

rock bottom: slang, the lowest level that will be entertained in a business transaction (e.g., the rock-bottom price is the lowest price at which a seller will agree to sell his or her goods).

ROE

(1) see *rate of exchange.*

(2) see *return on equity.*

ROG dating: receipt-of-goods dating. Under this condition of sales, the date for payment and discount period are determined from the date when the buyer obtains shipment, rather than from the invoice date.

ROI: return on investment; the amount earned in direct proportion to the capital invested. see *private rate of return.*

rollback

(1) **computers:** a program returned to a prior point that has been verified.

(2) **government:** an effort to create, as the legal price, a price lower than the existing market price—that is, to return to a price that existed earlier.

rolled over: see *rollover mortgage.*

roll over: renewing a loan contract to extend the term. It is often used to put off payments of balloons. see *balloon, buy down.*

rollover CD: a certificate of deposit package with a maturity of three years, divided into 12 six-month periods for which CDs are issued. synonymous with *roly-poly CD.*

rollover mortgage: a short-term mortgage where the unpaid balance is refinanced, or "rolled over," every few years; at that time, the interest rate is adjusted up or down, depending on prevailing market conditions. Before the Depression of 1929, such loans were common, but since then the fixed-rate mortgage has generally been standard. During the early 1980s, the rollover mortgage again became popular. see also *flexible-payment mortgage, graduated-payment mortgage, pledged-account mortgage, reverse-annuity mortgage, variable-rate mortgage.* synonymous with *renegotiable-rate mortgage.*

roly-poly CD: synonymous with *rollover CD.*

rook: slang, to misrepresent, overcharge, or cheat another.

Roosa Bonds: see *nonmarketable liabilities of U.S. government.*

ROR

(1) see *rate of return.*

(2) see *right of rescission.*

Rouble: see *ruble.*

round: see *multilateral trade negotiations.*

round lot: this is a unit of trading. On the New York Stock Exchange, the unit is generally 100 shares. In some inactive stocks, the trading unit could be 10 shares. An amount of stock less than the established unit of trading is called an odd lot. [29]

round trip trade: any complete transaction, made up of a buy followed by a sale of the same stock, or vice versa. synonymous with *round turn.*

routing symbol: see *check-routing symbol.*

round turn: see *round trip trade.*

royalty: compensation for the use of a person's property based on an agreed percentage of the income arising from its use (e.g., to an author on sales of his book, to a manufacturer for use of his machinery in the factory of another person, to a composer or performer, etc.). It is a payment reserved by the grantor of a patent, lease, or similar right, while a residual payment is often made on properties that have not been patented or are not patentable. see also *syndicate.*

RPQ: request for price quotation.

RR

(1) see *rediscount rate.*

(2) see *registered representative (trader).*

(3) see *required reserves.*

(4) required reserves of depository institutions. [81]

RRM: see *renegotiable-rate mortgage.*

RS: see *redeemable stock.*

RSU: see *remote service unit.*

Rt.: see *right.*

RTA: see *reciprocal trade agreement.*

rubber check: slang, a check that bounces, that is returned for lack of sufficient bank funds.

ruble: monetary unit of Union of Soviet Socialist Republics.

rubricated account: any earmarked account.

rule against accumulations: the limitation imposed by common law or by statute upon the accumulation of income in the hands of a trustee. [37]

rule against perpetuities: a rule of common law that makes void any estate or interest in property so limited that it will not take effect or vest within a period measured by a life or lives in being at the time of the creation of the estate plus 21 years and the period of gestation. In many states the rule has been modified by statute. Sometimes it is known as the *rule against remoteness of vesting.* [37]

rule against remoteness of vesting: see *rule against perpetuities.*

rule in Shelly's case: a rule of law that nullifies a remainder interest in the heirs of the grantee. For example, A conveys Blackacre to B for life, the remainder to heirs of B. Under this rule, B's heirs received nothing and B took a fee-simple absolute interest in Blackacre. This rule has been abolished by statute or judicial decision in many states. [37]

rule of 78ths: see *factor, 78th.*

Rule of 72: a means for determining how long it will take for money to double at various interest rates. By dividing the rate of return into 72, the result is the number of years required to double money at that rate of interest, assuming annual compounding.

rules of the class: the terms and conditions, established by the association's board of directors and included in the savings account contract, applicable to each savings account classification, such as time and amount of deposit, rate of interest, penalty provisions, and the account designation. [59]

rumor: in securities, hearsay or unfounded gossip intended to create a rise or drop in security prices. Stock Exchange members are restricted fromcirculating any information detrimental to the well-being of the exchange.

run

(1) *general:* an action of a large number of people (e.g., a run on a bank occurs when a great many customers make massive withdrawals of funds).

(2) *computers:* one routine automatically connected to another form on an operating unit, during which manual interruptions are not normally required.

(3) *computers:* a single, continuous performance of a computer program or routine.

runaway: a cardholder account that has exceeded the excessive-number-of-purchases limitation and may have exceeded its credit limit, and on which charges continue to be received or otherwise is indicative of unauthorized use. [105]

runaway inflation: synonymous with *galloping inflation.*

runner: an employee of the bank who delivers items to other banks in the same community, and who in turn may receive and bring back to his bank the items that the other banks may wish delivered there. The runner's duties may involve all types of messenger service for his bank. [10]

running a book: one function of the individual who specializes in certain stocks on the trading floor of a stock exchange. A list of orders that are limited to a price other than that currently prevailing is kept in the book.

running costs: direct or indirect costs incurred when keeping an operation and/or machinery functioning. These costs include wages, rent, and taxes.

running days: consecutive days including Sundays, as distinguished from working days, which excludes Sundays.

running in the shorts: purchasing different securities where there is a substantial short position for the purpose of advancing the price so that those short will purchase their securities back, or cover their short selling contracts, and hence lead to an additional climb in price. see *short covering, short sale.*

running yield: see *current yield.*

runoff: the closing prices printed by the stock exchange ticker following the closing of the daily market. During a heavy trading session, the runoff may be hours late.

run on a bank: see *run.*

rupee: monetary unit of India, Maldives, Mauritius, Nepal, Pakistan, Seychelles, and Sri Lanka.

rupiah: monetary unit of Indonesia.

SA: see *savings account.*

S/A: in banking, survivorship agreement. see *survivorship account.*

saddle blankets: nickname for the large-size U.S. paper money before 1929. [27]

saddled: a situation describing an individual holding an undesirable security purchased at a price above the prevailing market price.

safe deposit box: a metal container that remains under lock and key in a section of a bank vault when the person who rents it is not handling or inspecting the jewelry, stock certificates, or other valuables it contains. The boxes are kept in small compartments, each with two separate locks. A box is rented with its compartment to a customer, not necessarily a depositor, for an annual fee.

safe deposit company: any financial warehouse, retaining securities, wills, and other documents.

safe deposit privilege: a plan by which customers rent compartments in a vault to keep valuable documents and possessions.

safe deposit vault: a section of the bank's vault set aside for the use of customers who may rent space in the vault for the safekeeping of valuable securities, papers, and small objects of value. see also *safe deposit box.* [10]

safekeeping: a service rendered by banks, especially banks in large metropolitan areas, where securities and valuables of all types and descriptions are protected in the vaults of the bank for the customer for a service fee. (These valuables may include securities, precious gems, valuable paintings, collection pieces of great value, silver and gold services, etc.) Many of these items are too large to be placed in safe deposit boxes. In the case of securities, some customers "buy" security counselor services of large banks, requesting the banks to handle their securities to the best advantage. The banks will buy and sell, collect dividends and interest, and credit the depositor's account with this income. Many clients of this type are foreign citizens, and wealthy Americans who spend a good portion of their time

585

abroad, traveling or living in foreign countries. Since they cannot have constant access to safe deposit boxes, they appoint banks to act as their fiscal agents to protect and control their holdings for them in their absence. [10]

safekeeping account: an agency account concerning which the duties of the agent are to receipt for, safekeep, and deliver the property in the account on demand of the principal or on his or her order; to be distinguished from a custody account and a managing agency account. [32]

safekeeping (deposit for): the receipt by a bank of custody of specific property to be returned, as contrasted with an ordinary deposit to be repaid in money and with a safe deposit box, rented to a customer, to which the renter rather than the bank has access. [50]

safe rate: see *capitalization rate(s), safe.*

safety factor: the ratio of the interest on a funded debt to the net income following the payment of the interest.

safety fund system: a system of bank insurance used in New York in the nineteenth century. The state treasurer held the fund derived from payments of 3 percent of each bank's capital stock. The fund guaranteed the bank notes issued by bank members of the system.

safety of principal: the major characteristic of a sound investment.

safety stock: inventory maintained to avoid stockouts.

sag: a minimal drop or price weakness of shares, usually resulting from a weak demand for the securities.

sale
(1) *banking:* the transfer of title for

a sum of money and conditions, for the change of ownership of property.
(2) *finance:* the transfer of title to an item or items or the agreement to perform a service in return for cash or the expectation of cash payment.

sale and lease-back: a transaction where used equipment is bought from a firm by a lessor, with title passing from the user to the lessor. The lessor then leases the equipment back to the firm, which now becomes the lessee.

sale and servicing agreement: in secondary-market transactions, a contract under which the seller-servicer agrees to supply, and the buyer to purchase, loans from time to time; the contract sets forth the conditions for the transactions, and the rights and responsibilities of both parties. [59]

sale on approval: a contract under which title does not pass to the buyer until he or she indicates an approval (or fails to disapprove within a stated time). Unless otherwise specified, risk of loss stays with the seller until approval is indicated.

sale or return: a contract under which there is a sale and title immediately passes to the buyer, who has the right to revest title in the seller by returning the goods. The buyer takes risk of loss, however, while the goods are in his or her hands.

sales
(1) *general:* the sum of the income received when goods and services are sold.
(2) *finance:* revenue received from the sale of goods.

sales agreement: a written document by which a seller agrees to convey property to a buyer for a stipulated price under specified conditions. [44]

sales audit: verification of the proper preparation and acceptability of bank card sales drafts, credit slips, merchant summaries, and cash advances. [105]

sales authorization: the obtaining of approval by the merchant from the bank for sales in excess of preestablished floor limits. Authorization may also be required for reasons other than dollar amount. [105]

sales budget: an estimate of the probable dollar sales and probable expenses of selling and publicity for a specified period.

sales charge: the amount charged in connection with the issuance of shares of a mutual fund and their distribution to the public. It is added to the net asset value per share in determining of the offering price. [23]

sales draft: an instrument arising from the usage of a bank card which shows an obligation on the part of the cardholder to pay money to the card issues. synonymous with *sales slip.*

sales draft clearing: in interchange arrangements, exchange of bank card items between merchant banks and cardholder banks. [105]

sales draft envelope: see *deposit envelope.*

sales finance company: synonymous with *commercial credit company* and *discount house.*

sales literature: literature used by an issuer, underwriter, or dealer to inform prospective purchasers concerning an investment company the shares of which are offered for sale. Such literature is governed by the SEC's Statement of Policy and various regulations issued by the state. [23]

sales slip: synonymous with *sales draft.*

sales tax: a tax placed by a state or municipality on items at the time of their purchase. It may be a tax on the sale of an item every time it changes hands, or only upon its transfer of ownership at one specific time. The sales of manufacturers are taxed when the items are considered to be completed goods; the sales of wholesalers are taxed when their goods are sold to retailers; and retail sales are taxed when the goods are purchased by consumers. see *tax.*

Sallie Mae: see *Student Loan Marketing Association.*

salt-down stock: buying securities and keeping them over a long time period, disregarding paper profits that evolve.

salvage: the attempt to get repayment of some portion of a loan obligation which has already been written off the bank's books. [105]

salvage value: market salvage value of an asset, net of disposal costs.

same-day funds
(1) funds placed in an account which are immediately available for Federal Reserve transfer or withdrawal in cash.
(2) signifies funds available for transfer today in like funds or withdrawal in cash, subject to the settlement of the transaction through the payment mechanism used. [105]

same-day settlement: where banks routinely receive the equivalent of cash payments on the same day that they make payments on behalf of foreign banks.

sampling
(1) *general:* choosing a representative portion of a population to characterize a larger population.
(2) *computers:* a random method

of checking and controlling the use of data by obtaining the values of a function for regularly or irregularly spaced, discrete values.

(3) **computers:** a method of communication control in which messages are selected by a computer that chooses only those for which processing is needed.

SAN: see *subsidiary account number.*

sanction

(1) **finance:** a coercive measure, usually undertaken by several nations, to force another country to cease violation of a treaty or international agreement. see *embargo.*

(2) **law:** a penalty for the breach of a rule of law.

sandwich lease: a leasehold in which the interest of the sublessor is inserted between the fee owner and the user of the property. The owner A of a fee simple leases to B, who in turn leases to C. The interest of A may be called the leased fee; that of B the sandwich lease, and that of C the leasehold. [62]

San Francisco Stock Exchange: see *Pacific Coast Stock Exchange.*

SARs: see *stock-appreciation rights.*

satellite office: a convenience facility of fewer than four teller stations where any business of a federal association can be transacted; such an office must be located in retail stores, or, in the case of a fully automated satellite, in office buildings, shopping centers, or transportation centers. [59]

satellite processor: a processor that is under the control of another processing piece of equipment and performs subsidiary operations. The function of this unit is to process programs which are subsidiary to the main work of the system.

satisfaction of judgment: the legal procedure followed when a debtor pays the amount of judgment, together with interest and costs. "Satisfaction of judgment" is then entered on records of the court of record. [41]

satisfaction of mortgage: a document issued by mortgagee when a mortgage is paid off. [62]

satisfaction piece: an instrument acknowledging payment of an indebtedness due under a mortgage.

satisfactory account: in credit references, indicating that the terms of the account have been met as agreed. [105]

saturation: a market condition where the supply of a commodity or stock is so large that price reductions are needed to absorb any additional offerings. see also *saturation point.*

saturation point: the time when the supply of stocks for purchase starts to exceed the public demand. see *distribution, undigested securities.*

Saturday night special: a direct tender offer, made without any forewarning, that expires in one week. Such offerings were made possible by the Williams Act of 1968, which permits tender offers to run as short as seven days and does not require the bidder to tip his hand in advance with any notification.

Sav.: see *saving.*

saver's surplus: the differences between the amount of interest that savers actually get and the amount of interest for which they would have been willing to lend if the demand for loans (quantity demanded) had been less.

saving: the amount of existing income that is not spent on consumption.

savings account: money that is deposited in a bank, usually in small amounts periodically over a long period, and not subject to withdrawal by check. Savings accounts usually bear interest and some banks levy a service charge for excess withdrawal activity on an account.

savings account contract: the contractual relationship encompassing all the terms and conditions to which the customer and the association are subject when the customer opens a savings account. [59]

savings account ledger card: the association's complete record of account transactions on a particular savings account. [59]

savings account loan: a loan secured by the pledging of savings funds on deposit with the association. [59]

savings and investment theory: developed by John Maynard Keynes and D. H. Robertson: business cycles occur because people save either more or less than the amounts invested in new capital. cf. *veil of money theory.*

savings and loan association: a mutual, cooperative quasi-public financial institution, owned by its members (depositors), and chartered by a state or by the federal government. The association receives the savings of its members and uses these funds to finance long-term amortized mortgage loans to its members and to the general public. Such an association may also be organized as a corporation owned by stockholders. see *Cincotta-Conklin Bill of 1976.*

savings bank: a banking association whose purpose is to promote thrift and savings habits in a community. It may be either a stock organization (a bank with a capital stock structure) or a "mutual savings bank." Until passage of the Cincotta-Conklin Bill in New York State or other similar bills, a savings bank had no power to perform commercial functions, but specialized in interest-bearing savings accounts, investing these savings in long-term bonds, mortgage loans, and other investment opportunities for the benefit of all depositors. see *NOW accounts.*

Savings Bank Life Insurance (SBLI): insurance written in several states through savings banks. Characterized by having no agents selling the insurance. It is bought over the counter and is available in statutory limited amounts in the form of whole life, limited-payment life, endowment, term, and annuities on a participating basis.

Savings Bank Life Insurance Council: a voluntary association of issuing savings banks formed in 1939 in Massachusetts. It supplies mutual savings banks and their policyholders with various services.

Savings Bond: see *Bond, Savings (U.S.).*

savings certificate: evidence of the ownership of a savings account typically representing a fixed amount of funds deposited for a fixed term. [59]

savings deposits: a deposit of funds to the credit of one or more individuals or to a nonprofit institution which may be subject to 30 days written notice prior to withdrawal. In practice, commercial banks have not required this notice. [69]

savings liability: the aggregate amount of savings accounts of an association's members, including earnings credited to such accounts, less redemptions or withdrawals. [59]

savings rate: a ratio showing the portion of income saved to income earned.

sawbuck: slang, a $10 bill.

Say's law of markets: formulated by Jean Baptiste Say (1767–1832), the law holds that aggregate demand price of output as a whole is equal to its aggregate supply price for all volumes of output. It emphasises that there can never be general overproduction because every supply generates equivalent demand. The law assumes that liquidity preferences do not change.

SBA: see *Small Business Administration.*

SBIC: see *Small Business Investment Company.*

SBLI: see *Savings Bank Life Insurance.*

SC

(1) see *silver certificates.*

(2) see *stock certificate.*

scale buying: synonymous with *buying on scale.* see *scaling.*

scale order: an order to buy (or sell) a security specifying the total amount to be bought (or sold) and the amount to be bought (or sold) at specified price variations. [20]

scaling: trading in securities by placing orders for purchase or sale at intervals of price instead of giving the order in full at the market or at a stated price.

scalper: a speculator who constantly sells his or her shares at fractional profit or at one or two points profit per share.

scalping: a speculative attempt to derive a quick profit by the purchase of a security at an initial offering price with the hope that the issue being oversubscribed will then advance in price at this time the security can then be sold. Scalping is also found on commodity exchanges where a scalper purchases and sells during the trading day in equal amounts so that at the end of the trading time he or she has no position either long or short.

Scanlon plan: designed by Joseph Scanlon of MIT; a management incentive scheme created to achieve increased productivity with improved efficiency and the chance for accrued savings to be distributed among the employees.

scanner: see *optical scanner.*

scarce currency: in international finance, used to describe the situation where the demand for a particular nation's currency threatens to exhaust the available supply at the usual rates of exchange. When a currency becomes "scarce" in the International Monetary Fund, members of the fund are authorized to introduce exchange restrictions against that nation.

scarcity value: value created by a demand for an item, the supply of which cannot be raised (e.g., an antique clock).

scavenger sale: property taken over by the state as the result of nonpayment of taxes (e.g., failure of a state resident to pay state income taxes). After full notice, the state may hold a public sale of the property to recover monies entitled to it, and the excess of the sale beyond the taxes and penalties due the state are returned to the resident.

SCC: see *Stock Clearing Corporation.*

schedule: a systematic plan for future operations over a given period.

schedule bond: see *bond, schedule.*

schedule demand: see *demand.*

scheduled items: an FSLIC regulatory category in which every insured association is required to include the total amount of its slow loans, real estate owned as a result of foreclosure, and real estate sold on contract or financed at a high loan-to-value ratio. [59]

scheduled payment: a payment promised at a particular time, or one of several payments scheduled as to due date. [28]

schedule of charges: a schedule showing the rate charged by an international department for handling various transactions. [105]

schedule of distribution: a form of accounting which sets forth in detail the estate property contained in each share to be distributed. [37]

schedule supply: see *supply.*

schilling: monetary unit of Austria.

school bond: see *bond, school.*

school savings: a plan designed to promote the lesson of thrift in children in schools. A bank representative will call at the school one day a week, and assist teachers in accepting deposits in any small amount for the account of the pupil. [10]

Schuman Plan: see *European Coal and Steel Community.*

scienter: awareness by a defrauding party of the falsity of a representation.

scientific management: a term popularized in the work of Frederick W. Taylor, this theory proposes approaches for increased efficiency, cost reductions, and maximum utilization of human and material resources.

scientific tariff: a duty to cover foreign and domestic manufacturing costs.

scoop
(1) *general:* to beat out a rival.
(2) *finance:* a considerable profit following a transaction that is likely to involve advance notice over, or exclusion of competitors.

scratch: slang, available money.

scrip: any temporary document that entitles the holder or bearer to receive stock or a fractional share of stock in a corporation, cash, or some other article of value upon demand, or at some specified future date. Some industries issue scrip to their employees as a supplement to salary for use in company-owned stores.

scrip certificate: a certificate showing ownership of a fractional share of stock that can be converted into a full share when presented in amounts equal to a full share.

scrip dividend: a type of dividend issued by a corporation to its stockholders, entitling the holder or bearer to receive cash, stock, or a fractional share of stock, or one or more units of the product manufactured, upon presentation or at a specified future date.

scrivener's error: a typographical error introduced when reducing an oral agreement to writing or when an agreement is typed or printed in final form.

SCT: see *service counter terminals.*

SD
(1) see *secondary distribution.*
(2) see *sight draft.*
(3) see *stock dividend.*

SD. CO.: see *safe deposit company.*

SDMJ: September, December, March, June (quarterly interest payments or dividends).

SDR: see *special drawing rights.*

SE: see *stock exchanges.*

sealing: concealed bids that are simultaneously revealed; the most attractive one is accepted on the spot, without further bidding.

search

(1) *general:* the process of recruiting executive talent for a specific organization.

(2) *banking:* in the consideration of property transfer, the examination of records for evidence of encumbrances (unpaid taxes, mortgages, etc.) against the property. synonymous with *title search.*

(3) *computers:* to locate a desired word or record in a set of words or records. cf. *dump.*

seasonal unemployment: unemployment created by seasonal changes in the volume of production of some industries, such as clothing and construction.

seasoned issues: securities from well-established corporations that have been favorably known to the investment population over time, including good and bad periods.

seasoned loan: a loan that has been on the association's books long enough to demonstrate that the borrower's credit is sound. [59]

seasoned mortgage: periodic payments of a mortgage that are made over a long span based on the borrower's payment structure.

seasoned security: a security possessing a fine performance record in the paying of dividends or interest; one that has been listed for a considerable period of time and sells at a relatively stable price.

seat: a traditional figure of speech designating a membership on an exchange. Price and admission requirements vary. [20]

SEC: the Securities and Exchange Commission, established by Congress to protect investors. The SEC adminis-ters the Securities Act of 1933, the Securities Exchange Act of 1934, the Trust Indenture Act, the Investment Company Act, and the Public Utility Holding Company Act. The principal provisions of these acts are: (a) the Securities and Exchange Commission, created in 1934, administers the federal laws applying to securities; (b) corporations issuing securities and investment bankers selling them must make "full disclosure" of the character of the securities (i.e., they must state all relevant facts in registration statements to the SEC and in prospectuses submitted to the public). see also *waiting period;* (c) any omission of fact or insertion of false information makes all persons (bankers, lawyers, accountants, etc.) whose names appear on the prospectus and the registration statement liable to the purchasers of the securities for any losses suffered; (d) the organization of people (brokers, traders, etc.) to manipulate the price of securities is forbidden. see *pool;* (e) dealings by corporation officers in securities of their own corporations are restricted; (f) the Board of Governors of the Federal Reserve System is given power to fix margin requirements on loans secured by bonds and stocks. see also *National Association of Securities Dealers, unlisted trading privileges.*

secondaries: slang, for smaller companies to which investors are attracted. They usually involve considerable risk but offer the opportunity for possible large gains.

secondary bank reserve: high-grade securities that are readily convertible into money.

secondary beneficiary: a beneficiary

whose interest in a trust is postponed or is subordinate to that of the primary beneficiary. [37]

secondary boycott: see *boycott.*

secondary distribution: the redistribution of a block of stock sometime after it has been sold by the issuing company. The sale is handled off the exchange by a securities firm or group of firms, and the shares are usually offered at a fixed price that is related to the current market price.

secondary financing: see *junior mortgage.*

secondary market: the market, referred to as the aftermarket, that exists for a new stock issue following distribution to the public. see *primary market.*

secondary mortgage market: an informally constituted market that includes all activity in buying, selling and trading mortgages among originators and purchasers of whole loans and interests in blocks of loans. [59]

secondary movement: security price movements consisting of sharp rallies in a bear market and sharp reaction in a primary bull market; part of Dow theory.

secondary offering: the selling by a large stockholder of a large block of shares. Such a sale is frequently made on an exchange, to minimize the impact on the general market. synonymous with *secondary distribution.*

secondary rental: a lease determined in part by the landlord's costs. As the landlord's costs (taxes, fuel, etc.) increase, proportionate rent increases are demanded.

secondary reserves: assets other than primary reserves retained by banks and capable of being rapidly converted into cash. Government

bonds are a prime example of these assets.

second-generation computer: a computer utilizing solid-state components.

second lien: a lien that ranks following the first lien and is to be fulfilled next.

second mortgage: a mortgage on real property that already possesses a first mortgage.

second-mortgage bond: see *bond, second-mortgage.*

second partner: an active partner in an organization whose capacity as a partner is not known to the public. cf. *silent partner.*

second preferred stocks: a series of preferred security issues that rank behind first preferred stock but in front of any third preferred issue or common stock in dividends or assets.

secretary: an officer of a trust company whose signature is necessary on all official documents. In large trust companies where a secretary's duties are too numerous, the board of directors may appoint assistant secretaries to perform specific duties in connection with his official functions. [10]

secret partner: a firm's member not known to the public, who may play a significant role in the firm's operations.

Section 403(b) plan: Section 403(b) of the Internal Revenue Code permits employees of certain charitable organizations and public school systems to establish tax-sheltered retirement programs which may be funded with annuities and mutual fund shares. [23]

secular inflation: the most serious economic problem of the late 1960s and the 1970s. In contrast to cyclical inflation, which moves in and out of the economic system roughly every two years, secular inflation is primarily a long-term social phenomenon. see *cyclical inflation.*

secular stagnation: a low level of economic movement measured over an extended time period.

secular trend: a long-term trend as distinguished from a seasonal variation or business cycle movement.

secured: guaranteed as to payment by the pledge of something valuable. [28]

secured account: an account against which collateral or other security is held. [105]

secured bond: see *bond, secured.*

secured creditor: a creditor whose obligation is made safe or backed by a pledge or collateral. see *collateral.*

secured debt: any debt for which some form of acceptable collateral has been pledged see *hypothecation.*

secured deposits: bank deposits of state or local government funds which, under the laws of certain jurisdictions, are secured by the pledge of acceptable securities or by a surety contract (known as a depository bond) for the direct protection of these funds. [67]

secured liability: an obligation that has been guaranteed by the pledge of some asset or collateral. In the event of default or inability to liquidate the liability, title of the pledged asset will pass to the creditor. [105]

secured loan: a loan that is made safe, or backed, by marketable securities or other marketable values.

secured note: a note containing a provision that, upon default, certain pledged property may be claimed by the lender as payment of a debt. [78]

securities: any documents that identify legal ownership of a physical commodity or legal claims to another's wealth.

Securities Act of 1933: federal legislation dealing with full disclosure of material facts and antifraud. see also *SEC.*

Securities and Exchange Commission: see *SEC.*

securities company: an organization that relies for its income on other firms' securities, which it retains for investment. It may also issue stocks and bonds of its own. synonymous with *investment company*; see *holding company.*

securities depository: a physical location or organization where securities certificates are deposited and transferred by bookkeeping entry. [25]

Securities Exchange Act: see *SEC.*

Securities Investor Protection Corporation: see *SIPC.*

securities trading: anyone who sells or buys securities through recognized channels is said to engage in securities trading; also applies to the operations of brokers in the various exchanges.

security

(1) *general:* property pledged as collateral.

(2) *investments:* stocks and bonds placed by a debtor with a creditor, with authority to sell for the creditor's account if the debt is not paid.

(3) *law:* any evidence of debt or right to a property.

(4) *law:* an individual who agrees to make good the failure of another to pay.

security agreement: an agreement between the seller and the buyer stating that the seller will have a security interest in the goods. [105]

security analysis: the application of comprehensive examination of the factors concerning a security, including variables of growth of sales and earnings, ratio analysis of financial statements, and evaluation of trends that affect a security.

security audit: in operations, an examination of EDP security procedures and measures for evaluating their adequacy and compliance with established policy. [105]

security capital: low-risk capital (e.g., government bonds, mortgages).

security data: a set of characters on a bank card which controls its use and limits fund withdrawals in off-line terminals. It may also contain an encyphered form of the cardholder PIN. [105]

security department: the component of a credit card operation responsible for the investigation, apprehension, and prosecution of individuals perpetrating fraud against the bank; may also be responsible for physical security of the bank card center. [105]

security dollars: synonymous with *investment dollar.*

security element: the property that will secure a loan. [59]

security exchange: see *stock exchanges.*

security instrument: the mortgage or trust deed evidencing the pledge of real estate as security for the repayment of the mortgage note. [105]

security interest: an interest that a lender has in the borrower's property to assure repayment. [78]

security loan: any loan secured by the pledge of securities collateral.

security market: the places for sale and purchase of stocks and bonds; on the organized exchange and in the unorganized market.

security price level: the existing price level for a specified stock, any group of stocks, or the general securities market at a given period.

security ratings: ratings placed on securities according to the degree of investment risk incurred by the purchaser. [3]

security record: applied to any accounting record relative to the custody of securities, whether it be for safekeeping, collateral, or trust ownership. [10]

seed funds: funds run by former operations executives who specialize in taking raw ideas and packaging them into feasible business proposals that will be passed on to other venture capital firms for funding.

segmentation: a bank marketing strategy involving figuring out who the richest and biggest customers are, showering them with favors, freebies, and other inducements to open or increase their accounts and, if necessary, as it often is, raising rates and fees among the less affluent to pay for it all.

segregated account: used to describe funds segregated to meet obligations which the bank has assumed for a customer. Usually it applies to cash set aside to meet drafts drawn under a letter of credit issued by the bank. It may also apply to funds set aside to honor checks certified by the bank. It is a *liability account.* [10]

segregation: separating from an operating or holding firm one or more of its subsidiaries or operating divisions, effected by distributing stock of the subsidiary to the parent company's shareholders.

seignorage: a government's profit from issuing coins at a face value higher than the metal's intrinsic worth. It is the difference between the bullion price and the face value of the coins made from it. see *brassage.*

seisin (seizin): taking legal possession of real estate. The rightful owner seizes the property. cf. *disseisin, replevin.*

seizure: the act of taking possession of property, see *condemnation.*

selection check: a check, usually automatic, to verify that the correct register or other device has been selected in the performance of an instruction. [21]

self-check: a check deposited in a bank for credit, or one presented for payment in the banking institution on which it was drawn.

self-employed: the gainfully occupied part of the work force whose members work for themselves, as opposed to salaried or commissioned workers who are the employees of others.

Self-Employed Retirement Plan: see *Keogh plan.*

self-insurance: a system whereby a firm or individual, by setting aside an amount of monies, provides for the occurrence of any losses that could ordinarily be covered under an insurance program. The monies that would normally be used for premium payments are added to this special fund for payment of losses incurred.

self-liquidating: describing an asset that can be converted into cash or subject to the total recovery of invested money, over a period of time.

self-liquidating bond: see *bond, self-liquidating.*

self-liquidating loan: a short-term commercial loan, usually supported by a lien on a given product or on the sale of the product or commodities.

self-reducing clause: a life insurance statement that has the effect of lowering an obligation or mortgage: the amount of insurance automatically drops during the term of the policy, matching the lowering amount of the debt involved.

self-supporting (self-liquidating) debt: debt obligations whose principal and interest are payable primarily or solely from the earnings of the municipal utility or enterprise for the construction or improvement of which they were originally issued. [49]

sell and leaseback agreement: an arrangement whereby a business owning and occupying improved real estate sells it to an investor, (e.g., an insurance company) and takes back a long-term lease on the property and usually an option to buy it, at the termination of the lease. cf. *repurchase agreement.*

sell (or buy) at the close: an order to be executed at the market (best price obtainable) at the close of the market on the day the order is entered.

sell (or buy) at the opening: an order to be executed at the market (best price obtainable) immediately after a stock exchange opens for business.

sell-down: where a security or syndicated borrowing is offered to other possible participants outside the syndicate that is underwriting the deal, the proportion which these outsiders take.

seller's call: the buying of a commodity of a given quality identified in a contract that freezes the future price.

seller's market: a descriptive term: demand is greater than supply in this type of market, resulting in seller's setting the prices and terms of sale. It is a market characterized by rising or high prices.

seller's option: a special transaction on an exchange: the seller holding the option can deliver the stocks or bonds at any time within a specified period, ranging from not less than 6 business days to not more than 60 days.

seller's put: see *put* and *puts and calls.*

seller's seven sale: an agreed-upon delay of several or more days for the delivery of a security. see *settlement day.*

seller's surplus: the difference between the price a seller acutally receives and the lowest price that he or she would accept.

seller's 30: a security contract giving the seller an option of delivering a security which has been sold at any time within 30 days of the date of sale.

selling against the box: see *short sale.*

selling below the market: an expression indicating that a security is currently quoted for less than similar securities of comparable quality and acceptance. [67]

selling charge: see *load.*

selling climax: the unsystematic dumping of stocks; a burst of panic selling indicating the termination of a declining period, as in a bear market. The rebounding rally after this climax is often short-lived, but strong. see *blowing off.*

selling flat: when a purchaser of securities is not required to pay an additional sum beyond the purchase price of the principal of a bond. This added sum is the payment for accrued interest that the issuer pays the holder. The bonds that typically sell flat are bonds in default or income bonds.

selling group: syndicated dealers of an underwriting company that operates in the public sale of an issue of securities.

selling group pot: a percentage of an offering set aside for a selling group.

selling hedges: synonymous with *short hedges.*

selling off: descending prices of an issue, group of stocks, or the general market. When there are fewer offers to purchase stock at the time that more stocks are being offered for sale, prices usually drop and the market is said to be selling off.

selling on balance: the period of time, such as a day or week, when a broker of commodities or securities processes more selling orders than buying orders.

selling on scale: see *scaling.*

selling period: the period allotted to a selling group of an issue to complete its goal.

selling price: the cash price that a customer must pay for purchased items.

selling rate: the rate of exchange used by the seller of a currency. [105]

selling short: a technique employed with the expectation of a drop in the market with the expectation of a drop in the market price of the security. A temporarily borrowed stock is sold to effect delivery. If the price drops, the trader can purchase the security for less than he or she sold it, pay the borrowing cost, and clear a profit. see *bear position, loaned flat.*

selling the intermarket spread: buying a futures contract in bank CDs and selling Treasury bill futures short. see *intermarket spread*; cf. *buying the intermarket spread.*

sell out

(1) *general:* to betray a person, organization, or cause, usually for profit or special treatment.

(2) *investments:* to close out a customer's account by selling held securities or commodities.

sell-out notice (notification): an urgent notice sometimes sent by a brokerage house to a client stating that an amount due must be immediately paid or the house will be obliged to sell enough of the client's stocks to satisfy the liability. This final warning is usually made when a client fails to pay for stocks bought, or needs to deposit cash or securities to maintain sufficient margin in his or her account.

sender's correspondent bank: a bank with which the sender of a transfer has an account, which may act as a reimbursement bank in a transfer of funds. [105]

sending bank: an entity that inputs the message to the service. [105]

sending bank identifier: a code that identifies the bank that inputs the message to the service. [105]

sending bank input sequence number: a consecutive sequence number that allows for input message control between sending bank and service. [105]

sending bank name: names the bank that inputs the message to the service. [105]

sending bank terminal identifier: a code identifying the terminal or station within the sending bank from which the message was input to the service. [105]

sending bank time and date: time and date that the sending bank message was accepted by the service. [105]

sending bank transaction reference: reference assigned by the sending bank which should uniquely identify the transaction. [105]

send money: funds set aside to commence an activity.

senior: a debt ranking ahead of other debts. cf. *subordinated.*

senior bond: see *bond, senior.*

senior equity: preferred stock that ranks before junior equity (common stock) in the event of the liquidation and distribution of assets of the issuing company. [105]

senior interest: a participation senior or ahead of another participation.

senior issue: a security having a prior claim before another security issue.

senior obligations: synonymous with *senior securities.*

senior refunding: an exchange by holders of securities maturing within 5 to 12 years for issues with original maturities of 15 years or longer. [17]

senior securities: preferred securities and bonds that receive consideration before common stock when a firm is at the point of being dissolved or actually fails. synonymous with *senior obligations.* see also *junior securities.*

sensitive market: characterized by fluctuations determined by the announcement of favorable or unfavorable news.

SEP: see *Simplified Employee Pension.*

separate property: property that is owned individually and is not jointly held.

sequence analysis: the study of the causal connection of the economic events of one period with the economic events of the succeeding period or periods.

sequential computer: a computer in which events occur in time sequence, with little or no simultaneity or overlap of events. see also *serial computer.*

sequestered account: an account that has been impounded under due process of law. Since disbursement of such an account is subject to court order, the account is usually set up in a separate control. see *frozen account, receiver.*

sequestration: legal appropriation of property by a third party until there is a settlement of a stated dispute.

Ser.: see *serial.*

serial

(1) *general:* one after the other.

(2) *computers:* the sequential or consecutive occurrence of two or more related activities in a single device or channel.

serial annuity bond: see *bond, serial annuity.*

serial bond: see *bond, serial.*

serial bond issue: bonds of a single issue which mature on staggered dates rather than all at one time. The purpose of a serial bond issue is to enable the issuer to retire the bonds in small quantities over a long period. [105]

serial bonds payable: a liability account that records the face value of general obligation serial bonds issued and outstanding. [49]

serial computer: a computer having a single unit that performs arithmetic and logic functions.

serial issue: a bond issue with a staggered maturity, usually due in equal annual amounts over a period of successive years. [67]

serial letters and numbers: the system of numbering notes assists the checking of quantities put into circulation as well as guarding against counterfeits and forgeries. Misprints whereby different serial numbers appear on the same note are often collected as curiosity items, as are particular combinations of serial numbers. [27]

series: options of the same class having the same exercise price and expiration time. [5]

service charge: a payment by a financial institution against an individual or organization for services rendered or are about to be rendered.

service corporation: a corporation, owned by one or more savings associations, that performs services and engages in certain activities for its owners, such as originating, holding, selling, and servicing mortgages; performing appraisal, brokerage, clerical, escrow, research, and other services; and acquiring, developing, or renovating, and holding real estate for investment purposes. [59]

service counter terminals (SCTs): a device for handling information, located in retail stores and similar places, through which individuals can obtain access to funds and possible credit at their disposal, for purposes of making deposits and withdrawals, and for making third party payments. see *electronic funds transfer system(s), Hinky Dinky.*

service credit: a credit arrangement allowing bills to be paid at month-end for services provided during the month. Utility companies and medical professionals extend this type of credit. [78]

service life: the anticipated time of usefulness of an asset.

Servicemen's Readjustment Act of 1944: (The GI Bill of Rights) established a program of loan guarantees under Veterans Administration auspices to encourage private lending on generous terms to veterans of the armed forces. [51]

service value: the difference between the ledger value of a unit of property and its salvage value. [18]

servicing: in mortgage financing, the performance by the mortgagee or his or her agent of the many services which must be taken care of while the mortgage is held by the institution, such as title search, billing, collection of interest and principal payments, reinspections and reappraisals of the real property, readjustment of the terms of the mortgage contract when necessary, and tax follow-up work.

servicing contract: in secondary-market transactions, a document that details servicing requirements and legally binds the servicing institution to perform them. Such a contract refers to the seller of mortgage participations, binding it to continue accepting loan payments. see also *loan servicing*. [59]

session: in securities, the period of trading activity which usually coincides with a stock exchange's hours of business (e.g., volume was 100 million shares in today's session).

setback: a reversal or partial loss in an activity.

settlement
(1) the winding up and distribution of an estate by an executor or an administrator; to be distinguished from the administration of an estate by a trustee or a guardian.
(2) a property arrangement, as between a husband and wife or a parent and child, frequently involving a trust. [37]

settlement check: a memorandum issued by the manager of a clearinghouse association to settle the results of a clearinghouse exchange between the member banks. This memorandum is sent to the local Federal Reserve Bank, which adjusts the accounts of the clearinghouse banks to settle the debits and credits, or "wins and losses" in the exchange each day. The term may also be used with reference to checks and drafts received in payment of items sent for collection under remittance letters. [10]

settlement clerk: a senior clerk in the proof department of a bank who is responsible for assembling totals obtained in the proof department. These totals, showing all credits and charges to all departments, are assembled and written on a "settlement sheet," or recap sheet of the proof department. It is from this source that the proof department shows a settlement of the day's work. The settlement sheet then becomes a subsidiary record for the general ledger, and the general ledger bookkeeper may use all final totals shown on this record. [10]

settlement day: the deadline by which a purchaser of stock must pay for what has been bought and the seller must deliver the certificates for the securities that have been sold. The settlement day is usually the fifth business day following the execution of an order. cf. *shave.*

settlement options: provisions in a life policy or annuity contract for alternative methods of settlement in place of lump-sum payments.

settlement price: the daily price at which the clearinghouse clears all the day's trades. It may also refer to the price established by the exchange to settle contracts unliquidated because of acts of God, such as floods or other causes. [2]

settlements bank: see *Bank for International Settlements.*

settlement sheet: see *settlement clerk.*

settlor: one who finalizes a property settlement (e.g., creator of a trust).

78th: see *factor, 78th.*

severable contract: a contract whose performance is divisible into parts particularly as regards the price for each part.

severalty: property owned by one person only. see *singular property title, sole owner.*

severance damage: see *consequential damage.*

S/F: see *statute of frauds.*

SF: see *sinking fund.*

SH.: see *stockholder.*

shade: a small reduction in price or terms.

shading: giving a small reduction in a price or terms of a sale.

shadow price: considering the market price as a "real" price, the "equilibrium" price is a "shadow" price—the price that would prevail under equilibrium conditions.

shake out

(1) *finance:* a trend or shift in a industry that forces weaker members toward bankruptcy.

(2) *investments:* any shift in activity that forces speculators to sell their shares.

share: synonymous with *stock.*

share account: see *savings account.*

Sharebuilder Investment Plan (SIP): developed by Merrill Lynch and Chase Manhattan Bank, a plan whereby a depositor's account is debited automatically on a prescribed date and the money transferred to a special sharebuilder account at Chase. The broker buys stock for the depositor the next morning. Chase and Merrill Lynch split the commissions on sales of the plan. There is a three-way split if a correspondent institution makes the sale. Customers benefit from rates discounted from the standard Merrill Lynch schedule, and they can buy stock with weekly or monthly installments too small to cover investments made through normal channels.

share capital: the total direct ownership in a corporation. When all stock to be issued by a firm is ordered and paid for, the funds collected constitute the share capital of the corporation.

share certificate: a certificate of deposit issued by a credit union.

shared-appreciation mortgage: a home-financing technique whereby the borrower receives a mortgage rate that is one-third lower than the prevailing level. But the borrower must agree to give the lender one-third of the profits from the eventual sale of the house. A shared-appreciation mortgage has payments that are based on a long amortization schedule, but the loan becomes due and payable no later than at the end of 10 years. It has an interest rate below that on a conventional mortgage. It has a contingent interest feature, whereby at either the sale or transfer of the property or the refinancing or maturity of the loan, the borrower must pay the lender a share of the appreciation of the property securing the loan.

share draft: an order by a credit union member to pay a third party against funds on deposit with the credit union and cleared through a commercial bank.

shared revenue: payments to the states and localities of a portion of the proceeds from the sale of certain federal property, products, and services, and payments to the territories of certain federal tax collections derived within their boundaries or from transactions affecting them. synonymous with *intergovernmental revenue,* cf. *revenue sharing.*

shareholder: the possessor of shares or stocks in an organization (company, corporation, etc.).

share loan: a simple interest loan secured by funds on deposits at a credit union or a savings and loan institution. One purpose of a share loan is to preserve dividends due on deposits by not withdrawing the funds until the date on which the dividend payment is due.

share of stocks: units of ownership in a firm.

share register: the records of a corporation indicating ownership of shares of that firm by the public. A share register is required by law for every corporation.

shares: equal interests into which the capital stock of a corporation is divided, the ownership being evidenced by certificates called stock certificates. see also *capital stock.*

shares outstanding: the shares issued by a corporation, excluding treasury stock.

share turnover: see *volume.*

sharing: the establishment of EFT systems as a joint enterprise by an organization of depository institutions. Sharing allows the participating depository institutions to divide the responsibilities (risks, costs) of establishing and maintaining POS and ATM systems. The four types of sharing are mandatory sharing, permissive/non-discriminatory sharing, permissive sharing, and pro-competitive sharing. Detailed descriptions of the four types of sharing are included in *EFT and the Public Interest: A Report of the National Commission of Electronic Fund Transfers.* [105]

sharing the market: any scheme by which sellers limit their individual efforts to given parts of the total market for a product or service (e.g., the "sharing" may be on a geographical basis).

shark repellent: a state statute that demands strict notification and disclosure of tender offers for companies incorporated or transacting business within its boundaries.

shave

(1) *finance:* a charge that is higher than the accepted rate, made for the handling of a note or other instrument of low quality or when the seller will take a smaller amount for any other reason.

(2) *investments:* the additional charge (premium) made for the right to extend the delivery time on a security.

sheared: an unsuccessful trader of securities or commodities.

"sheep": see *fleece.*

"sheets;" the: synonymous with *pink sheets.*

shekel: the official currency of Israel, resurrected from Biblical times, that replaced the pound in 1980.

shelf distribution: a method of selling securities. Stocks, owned by stockholders, are placed on the shelf for sale at a later time. To be contrasted with the usual public offering of stocks to when all are sold at one time at a fixed price through underwriters.

shelf registration: a Securities and Exchange Commission ruling effective March 1983 permitting an issuer to register one big issue of bonds with the SEC. Instead of selling the bonds all at once, issuers will put at least some of them aside—on the shelf—to be sold piecemeal whenever they see a need for funds, find favorable market conditions, or receive a call from a trader or institution offering attractive terms. see also *shelf distribution.*

shell firm: an organization that is incorporated but does not function or produce any goods or services.

shelter trust: see *spendthrift provision.*

sheriff's deed: an instrument drawn under order or court to convey title to property sold to satisfy a judgment at law. [62]

Sherman Antitrust Act of 1890: federal legislation aimed at the prevention of business monopoly. Some courts, however, applied the sanctions of the law against strikes, and unions where fined triple damages for acts that were considered to be in restraint of trade. New legislation (see *Clayton Antitrust Act of 1914*) was required to protect the unions against further such misinterpretations since in the absence of legislative action, antiunion rulings would continue to be sustained under the principle of res adjudicata. see *res adjudicata.*

Sherman Silver Purchase Act: passed by Congress in 1890, requiring the Secretary of the Treasury to purchase $4\frac{1}{2}$ million ounces of silver monthly and issue in payment Treasury Notes redeemable in gold or silver. Repealed in 1893.

sheriff indemnity bond: see *bond, sheriff indemnity.*

shift differential: additional pay for working more than one shift.

shifting loan: the act of securing funds from other lending banks for assistance at the time banks ask their borrowers to pay their loans.

shifting tax: a tax whose burden is transferred from the original taxpayer (individual or organization) to another.

shift premium: extra compensation given to a shift worker for the inconvenience of altering his daily working hours. see *shift differential.*

shilling: monetary unit of Kenya, Somalia, Tanzania, and Uganda.

shinplaster

(1) *general:* any money made worthless either by inflation or by inadequate security.

(2) *banking:* a pre-Civil War term used to deprecate the value of paper money.

(3) *finance:* paper money, usually of less than one dollar face value, once used by some private financial institutions.

ship broker: a person who, for a fee, secures cargoes for vessels and obtains freight space on ships for shippers.

shipping: preparing and sending the complete package of mortgage documents to the investor. [105]

shock loss: a loss larger than expected.

shoestring: slang, a tiny amount of money.

shoestring trading: existing on minimal, barely adequate margin.

short: an individual who sells a futures

contract in anticipation of purchasing it back at a lower cost. see *short hedges, short interest, short sale.*

short account: the account of a company or person who is short.

short against the box: see *short sale.*

shortage: deficiency in quantity.

short and intermediate term credit: debt repaid over a relatively short span of time. [55]

short bill: a bill of exchange payable upon request, at sight, or within a brief period, usually less than 10 days.

short certificate: a certificate by the proper officer of a court as to the appointment and authority of a fiduciary, as distinguished from a full certified copy of letters testamentary, administration, or trusteeship. [37]

short covering: buying a stock to return stock previously borrowed to make delivery on a short sale. [20]

shortcut foreclosure: a method of foreclosure in which a power of sale clause in the mortgage allows the lender to sell a property if it goes into default. The borrower must be informed, but the issuing of a public statement need not be carried out. Upon property foreclosure, the junior mortgage holders' positions are wiped out, unless the sale yields more than the outstanding first mortgage.

short dates: usually periods up to one week, but sometimes periods up to a month.

shortfall: spending, usually in a governmental agency, that falls sharply below projections, thus contributing to an economic sluggishness. cf. *overage.*

short-form credit report: a type of credit bureau report, usually combining certain features of an oral report and a written report in abbreviated form. [14]

short-form mortgage clause: a mortgage clause permitting the buyer to take over the mortgage, subject to and not assuming liability for its payment.

short-funded: where banks buy short-term money at high rates of interest, in the expectation that rates would soon fall and that they subsequently could obtain lendable funds more cheaply.

short hedges: sales of futures created as hedges against holdings of the spot commodity or product. see *hedge.* synonymous with *selling hedges.*

short interest: the sum of the short sales outstanding in a security or commodity or on an exchange.

short of exchange: the position of a foreign exchange trader who has sold more foreign bills than the quantity of bills he or she has in possession to cover sales.

short of the basis: said of a person or firm who has sold cash or spot goods and has hedged them with purchases of futures. He has therefore sold at a certain "basis" and expects to buy back at a better basis for a profit. [2]

short of the market: holding a short position in stock with the expectation that lower prices will occur. see *short sale.*

short position

(1) stocks sold short and not covered as of a particular date. On an exchange, a tabulation is usually issued once a month listing all issues on the exchange in which there was a short position of 5000 or more shares and issues in which the short position had changed by 2000 or more shares in the preceding month.

(2) the total amount of stock an indi-

vidual has sold short and has covered, as of a particular date.

short purchase: buying a stock to cover an earlier short sale of the same stock.

short-rate cancellation: describes the charge required for insurance or bonds taken for less than one year. Also in some cases, it denotes the earned premium for insurance or bonds canceled by the insured before the end of the policy period or term of bond. cf. *pro rate cancellation.*

short run

(1) *general:* a one-time job.

(2) *finance:* the time during which a firm can alter the price or output of its goods but not change the size of its plant or close down operations.

shorts

(1) bear traders on the short side. see *short sale.*

(2) in Great Britain, gilt-edged securities with less than five years to maturity.

short sale: a transaction made by a person who believes a stock will decline and places a sell order, though he or she does not own any of these shares. Stock exchange and federal regulations govern and limit the conditions under which a short sale may be made. Sometimes a person will sell short a stock already owned to protect a paper profit. This is known as *selling against the box.*

short seller: a securities pessimist, that is, bearish on the trend of securities prices and substantiates this feeling by selling short.

short selling: selling a stock and purchasing it at a lower price to receive a profit.

short side: pessimists who sell short as contrasted with being on the long side. see *short sale.*

short squeeze: a sharp runup of prices that forces shorts to make offsetting purchases in order to avoid larger losses. A short squeeze occurs when people who have sold borrowed shares, in anticipation of replacing them at lower prices, are forced to cover those borrowed shares by buying shares, even at higher price. When a confluence of short covering occurs, price tend to jump because of the increased demand.

short stock: securities that have been sold short and not yet covered. see *short covering, short sale.*

short-term debt: an obligation that is usually due within the year.

short-term funds: money borrowed from 30 days up to one year.

short-term savings account: ordinarily, an account that is to be withdrawn within less than 24 months from the date the account is opened. [59]

short-term securities: securities payable on demand or which mature not more than one year from date of issue. [18]

short-term trust: an irrevocable trust running for a period of 10 years longer, in which the income is payable to a person other than the settlor, and established under the provisions of the Revenue Act of 1954. The income from a trust of this kind is taxable to the income beneficiary and not to the settlor. The agreement may provide that on the date fixed for the termination of the trust, or on the prior death of the income beneficiary, the assets of the trust shall be returned to the settlor. [37]

Shr.: see *share.*

shrinking stocks: stocks of corporations that are bought by the firms of their own shares, thus drastically reducing the number of shares outstanding. These corporations feel that they can earn a higher return on the money spent for their stock than on investing in new business schemes.

shut-off rates: high mortgage rates that are designed to turn away prospective buyers.

SI: see *simple interest.*

SIBOR: Singapore Interbank Offered Rate.

SIC
(1) see *split investment company.*
(2) see *Standard Industrial Classification System.*

sick market: in securities, a weak, tremulous market, giving an appearance of being sick.

side collateral: security for a loan that is less than the required margin, less than the principal amount of the loan or not to be held for the full term of the loan. A loan secured only by side collateral is classified as unsecured. [105]

sideliner: any person who withdraws temporarily from an active role in the market after closing out his long and/or short position.

Sig.: signature.

Sig. Cd.: see *signature card.*

sight bill of exchange: any bill of exchange that becomes due and payable when presented by the holder to the party on whom it is drawn. see also *short bill.*

sight credit: popular designation for a sight letter of credit.

sight draft: a draft payable upon delivery and presentation to the drawee, or *upon sight.*

sight rate: the exchange rate tied to a demand draft or check. synonymous with *check rate.*

signature book: a book containing facsimiles of the signatures of the authorized officers of a bank who may commit that bank. Such books are exchanged by banks establishing a correspondent relationship. [105]

signature card: a card signed by each depositor and customer of the bank. The signature card is technically a contract between the bank and its customer, in that it recites the obligations of both in their relationship with each other. The principal use of the signature card is that of identification of the depositor. Signature cards are made out in at least two sets, one for the signature file department, where all signatures are kept for ready reference, and the other for the file at the teller's window where the depositor will most frequently transact his business. [10]

signature field: the individual or department within the sending bank that created the message. [105]

signature file department: this department is the custodian for all signature cards. The employees of this department issue daily reports on all accounts opened and all accounts closed. As a part of the public relations and "new business" work, the signature file department may write "thank you" letters to new depositors. [10]

signature guaranteed: a securities industry requirement to have a registered owner of a security have a brokerage firm or a bank guarantee his or her signature so that a good delivery or transfer of the stock can be made.

signature panel: a small elongated

rectangular strip, affixed to either side of a bank card during manufacture, which permits the cardholder to write his or her signature on the card. [105]

signed instrument: any legal agreement, or note which is written and signed. [28]

silent partner: an individual who gives funds for a business partnership but takes no part in the management of the firm.

silver certificates: U.S. paper money since 1873 issued as receipts for the stated amount of silver in the U.S. Treasury. The redemption privilege was revoked by Congress in 1968. [27]

silver dollar: coined since 1792, containing 371¼ grains of silver (77.34 percent of an ounce) and 41¼ grains of alloy. Total weight is 412½ grains. Based on the Spanish dollar.

Silver Purchase Act of 1934: authorized and directed the Secretary of the Treasury to purchase silver at home and abroad until the proportion of silver in the combined stocks of gold and silver of the United States is one-fourth of the total monetary value of such stocks or until the price of silver is $1.29½ an ounce. No time limit is set for the achievement of a 3:1 ratio between gold and silver.

silver standard: that monetary system under which money is convertible into silver at a specified rate, and vice versa, and free shipment of silver internationally is permitted. cf. *gold standard, paper standard.*

Silver Thursday: March 27, 1980, when the commodity industry and the entire financial community was imperiled after a major brokerage house, Bache Halsey Stuart Shields, was momentarily unable to get a commodity

customer, the billionaire Hunt brothers, to cover a margin call for $100 million.

silver wing: slang, a half-dollar (50 cents).

simple arbitrage: arbitrage achieved by using only three markets. cf. *compound arbitrage.*

simple interest: interest calculated on a principal sum and not on any interest that has been earned by that sum. cf. *compounded interest.*

simple trust: used only in tax laws to describe a trust that is required to distribute all of its income currently and that does not provide for any charitable distribution; opposed to *complex trust.* [37]

Simplified Employee Pension (SEP): made possible by the Revenue Act of 1978; a retirement plan that increases the limit on yearly contributions to $7500 an employee. This plan combined element of both Keogh plans and Individual Retirement Accounts. The SEP option permits an employee to establish an IRA whether or not the worker is covered by a company pension plan. An SEP also increases the amount that can be contributed annually to an IRA from the usual $1500 to $7500. Earnings from investments are tax-free until after age 59½. Upon the death of the person, any undistributed funds can escape the estate tax by going to the heirs in installments over at least 36 months.

simulation: the process of imposing various hypothetical conditions on a model in order to observe their effects on certain variables. [57]

simultaneous inflation and unemployment (inflump): a situation calling for a value judgment of whether inflation or unemployment is the more serious problem and whether the economy is moving toward worse inflation or worse unemployment.

sinecure: a position of limited or non-existent responsibility demanding little or no labor or service.

single capital structure company: company having only one class of security outstanding. [30]

single debit reporting: normal method used by mortgage bankers for reporting the current status of its mortgages when making a regular remittance to an investor. [22]

single debt: a system of mortgage accounting by which a servicer reports current installments as a lump sum. A detailed payment analysis is given only on uncollected and unscheduled payments. [105]

single entry: a bookkeeping approach in which each transaction is entered only once on the account books. The single-entry system is primarily used by small businesses. cf. *double entry.*

single-family dwelling: a housing unit designed for ownership and occupancy by one individual or family. [59]

single-interest insurance: this installment loan insurance is only for the bank's interest in the collateral with the owner/borrower subject to the loss of equity. synonymous with *ultimate loss insurance.* [105]

single liability: the situation in which the stockholder is liable for the corporation's losses only to the extent of his or her investment.

single-lump-sum credit: a closed-end credit arrangement whereby the total outstanding balance is due on a specified date. [78]

single-name account: an account having only one owner. [105]

single-name paper: a note for which only one legal entity—the maker—is obligated to make payment at maturity. A legal distinction exists in single-name paper, in that if the obligation is incurred for one purpose, or one common interest, the paper may have more than one maker or endorser, and still be termed single-name paper. Such a case would be two or more partners making a note for a loan to the common partnership or a subsidiary company making a note endorsed by the parent company. Single-name paper is also frequently termed *straight paper.* [10]

single option: as contrasted from a spread or straddle, any put or call. see *option.*

single-payment loan: a loan whose entire principal is due on one maturity date.

single-posting system: a plan of posting used in the bookkeeping department of a bank. Single posting generally means the posting of a depositor's statement only. The ledger record may be either a carbonized ledger created with the posting of the statement, or a photographed record of the statement (under the unit-photographic plan) made on microfilm. This posting plan is to be distinguished from the *dual plan* where the statement is posted in one run and the ledger is posted in another. [10]

single proprietorship: ownership of a business by one person.

single-schedule tariff: a tariff that has the same rate for a commodity regardless of the country of origin.

single standard: monometallism, where one metal, usually gold, is given free and unlimited coinage.

single tax: a proposal by Henry

George that the government appropriate all the unearned increment of land by means of a tax, and that this tax alone would yield revenues large enough so that the government could abolish all other taxes.

singular property title: property title granted to only one person. see *severalty.*

sinkers: synonymous with *sinking fund bonds.* see *bond, sinking fund.*

sinking fund: a fund used to accumulate the cash needed to pay off a bond or other security. By accumulating cash in a sinking fund, the firm is in a better position to pay its securities when due, and the risk is therefore reduced to the security holder.

sinking fund bond: see *bond, sinking fund.*

sinking fund depreciation: a system for calculating depreciation: the yearly amount is presumed to be deposited in a sinking fund that will also increase as a result of earnings from the fund investment.

sinking fund requirements: the amount by which a sinking fund must be increased periodically through contributions and earnings so that the accumulation thereof will be sufficient to redeem sinking fund bonds as they mature. [49]

sinking fund reserve: see *reserve for retirement of sinking fund bonds.*

SIP: see *Sharebuilder Investment Plan.*

SIPC: Securities Investor Protection Corporation; provides funds for use, if necessary, to protect customers' cash and securities which may be on deposit with an SIPC member firm in the event the firm fails and is liquidated under the provision of the SIPC Act. SIPC is not a government agency. It is a nonprofit membership corporation created, however, by an act of Congress. [20]

situs: Latin, a place or situation where a thing is located. An owner's home is the situs of his personal property.

six and seven nations of (economic) Europe: see *European Economic Community, European Free Trade Association.*

six bits: the equivalent of 75 cents.

sixty-day notice: notice required to be given to the Internal Revenue Service in those cases where the decedent's gross taxable estate exceeds or may exceed the exemption under the federal estate tax law. [37]

sixty-five-day election: in the case of distribution made during the first 65 days following the close of a complex trust's taxable year, a fiduciary of a complex trust may elect to treat part or all of the distribution as having been made on the last day of the preceding taxable year. [105]

size of the market: the number of round lots bid for at the highest price showing on the specialist's book and the total number being offered for sale simultaneously at the lowest price quoted, at any specified time.

Sk.: see *safekeeping.*

skate: slang, avoidance of a creditor; the attempt to avoid payment.

Skg.: see *safekeeping.*

skimming: an unauthorized method of duplicating the magnetically encoded data on plastic identification cards. Skimming can be accomplished by covering the magnetic stripe of a card with a piece of recording tape and applying heat. The tape can then be applied to a blank card with another application of heat, thus transferring data from one card to another. It is possible to duplicate cards with this technique without serious degradation in information recording quality. New production methods allow for easy detection of any tampering with the magnetic stripe. [105]

skimming prices: a high introductory price followed by a series of price reductions, designed to get all the trade the market will bear at one price level before lowering the price, as well as to appeal to the more price-conscious consumer.

skip: person owing money who has moved leaving no forwarding address. [41]

skip account: a cardholder with a balance owing whose whereabouts are unknown. [105]

skip insurance: insurance to protect a lender from conversion, embezzlement, secretion, or misappropriation of collateral. [105]

skip-payment privilege: a privilege provided in certain mortgage contracts that allows the borrower to skip monthly payments at any time the loan is paid ahead of schedule as long as the loan is prepaid. [59]

skunk: slang, to fail to pay a debt.

skyrocketing: slang, a sharp rise in stock prices within a relatively short time period.

S & L Assn.: see *savings and loan association.*

slack
(1) the time in which a minor operation can be completed in advance of the next major operation that depends on it.
(2) a dull or inactive business period, a "slack season."

slander: an oral utterance that tends to harm the reputation of another.

slaughter: slang, the indiscriminate selling of securities at very low levels, often unnecessarily low.

Sld.: sold.

sleeper: a slow-moving security that has a sound potential for growth.

slice: slang, having a portion or interest in a business venture or activity.

slide: a posting error by which an amount is wrongly recorded by a bookkeeper who unintentionally places the decimal one or more digits to the right or left of the true decimal position.

sliding parity: see *crawling peg.*

sliding-scale tariff: the varying of tariff duties according to the current prices of the imported items. In general, duties are lowered as prices rise, and advance the duties as prices fall.

slid off: a drop in the price of stocks.

slipping: slang, a downward movement in the prices of securities or commodities which is not severe.

slow asset: an asset that can be converted into cash, near its book value, usually after a lengthy passage of time.

slow loan: a Federal Savings and Loan Insurance Corporation regulatory category in which every insured savings association is required to list its delinquent loans. The regulations spell out what constitutes a slow loan in terms of the loan's age and length of delinquency. Loans less than one year old are slow when 60 days delinquent, those between one and seven years old are slow when 90 days delinquent, and so on. [59]

sluggish market: a slow-moving, inactive securities trading where volume is unusually low. Few stocks are traded with only minimal price fluctuations.

slump: a short-lived decline in the activity of a business or economy.

slush fund: slang, monies given for political purposes with the expectation that it will influence the receiver to favor the giver.

S & M: September and March (semi-annual interest payments or dividends).

SM

(1) see *secondary market.*

(2) see *second mortgage.*

small bread: slang, a small amount of money.

Small Business Administration (SBA): a federal agency established in 1953 solely to advise and assist the nation's small businesses. The SBA provides loans, loan guarantees, and offers loans to victims of floods, riots, and other catastrophes and to those who have suffered economic harm as a result of federal programs. The SBA also conducts research on conditions affecting small businesses.

Small Business Investment Company (SBIC): a federal agency that provides capital to small businesses, licensed and regulated by the Small Business Administration as authorized by Congress in 1958. The SBICs may make long-term loans or buy convertible debentures or stock in small enterprises, as defined as having less than $5 million in assets, net worth less than $2½ million, and average net income following taxes the previous two years not exceeding $250,000.

small loan: sometimes used to designate a personal cash loan. [41]

small loan law: a regulatory code covering cash installment loans, administered by the state, and protecting both the borrower and the lender. [55]

small potatoes: slang, a small amount of money.

small-saver certificates: certificates issued in denominations of less than $100,000 with maturities of 2.5 years or more.

small-size notes: American paper money since 1928, characterized by new designs and a smaller size. [27]

"smart" credit cards: originally developed in France, a credit card that deducts charges from a customer's bank balance at point of sale. For banks and stores, the advantage of "smart" credit cards is increased automation and expected lower costs. A unique feature is that such cards can have information placed on them and altered with ease. see *carte à mémoire.*

smart money: experienced and professional security traders who exploit inside information to make profits at the expense of other investors.

smash: a severe drop in the market, approaching a panic.

Smithsonian Agreements (1971): a reassessment (upward) of the value of foreign currencies in relation to the dollar. [105]

smuggling: conveying goods or persons, without permission, across the borders of a country or other political entities (e.g., cigarette smuggling across state lines).

snake system: an international agreement between Belgium, The Netherlands, Luxembourg, Denmark, Sweden, Norway, and West Germany, linking the currencies of these countries together in an exchange rate system. The signatories have agreed to limit fluctuations in exchange rates among their currencies to 2.25 percent above or below set median rates. The snake was designed to be the first stage in forming a uniform Common Market currency. Members maintain fairly even exchange rates among themselves by buying or selling their currencies when the rates threaten to drop or rise beyond the 2.25 percent limits specified. see *European Economic Community, European Free Trade Association, swap.*

snowballing: resulting transaction following stop orders that become market orders, during periods of either advance or decline. see *touch off the stops.*

SO

(1) see *seller's option.*

(2) see *standing order.*

(3) see *stock option.*

Social Security: the combination of social insurance plans sponsored by the federal government, and including old age and survivors' insurance and unemployment insurance. Wage and payroll deductions are made to finance these programs. Federal employees are exempt from having to contribute to the costs of such coverage.

Social Security Act of 1935: resulted in a national social insurance program providing old age and survivor benefits, public assistance to the aged, the blind, and needy children, unemployment insurance, and disability benefits.

Social Security Payment Program: a cooperative effort between the Social Security Administration and the U.S. Treasury Department devoted to planning and implementing a system for direct deposits of Social Security benefit payments to individuals, initially by distributing checks directly to recipients' banks, to be followed by gradual conversion from checks to tape. [36]

Society for Worldwide Interbank Financial Telecommunications (SWIFT): an organization developing a system for the electronic transfer of funds among participating banks in Europe and North America. [36]

Society of Savings and Loan Controllers: formed in 1950 under the sponsorship of the American Savings and Loan Institute as a professional organization, the society is devoted to improving the professional status of accounting and auditing officers through the development of better accounting methods and new aids to management. The society presently exists as a separate organization closely allied to institute activities and interests. This organization consists of more than 1500 of the principal accounting and chief auditing officers in savings associations. The society's technical publications are available on a subscription basis to nonmembers. [51]

SOE: see *short of exchange.*

soft: a security or general market that moves toward a lower price level.

soft arbitrage: arbitrage between public-sector and private paper.

soft currency: the funds of a country that are controlled by exchange procedures, thereby having limited convertibility into gold and other currencies.

soft landing: when an economy slows down from a period of unsustainable growth to a slower but more manageable growth rate, and does so without a recession.

soft loan: a loan whose terms of repayment are generous, at times holding a low rate of interest.

soft market: a condition in which the

market prices are falling or the relative number of buyers is decreasing.

soft money: paper currency, as contrasted with coinage (hard money).

soft spot: while the general securities market is holding or even moving ahead, the sudden decline in specific stocks or groupings of securities.

software

(1) *computers:* a set of programs or procedures concerned with the operation of a data-processing system.

(2) *computers:* a set of coded instructions prepared to simplify programming and computer operations.

(3) *computers:* applied to computer operations that include compilers, assemblers, executive routines, and input and output libraries.

soil bank: a farm program established by the government to pay farmers for removing land from cultivation.

sol: monetary unit of Peru.

sola: any overseas bill of exchange or check made up on one document instead of a check or bill drawn together.

solde: French for *balance.*

sold loan: a mortgage loan that has been sold to another institution but is still serviced by the seller. [59]

sold-out market: a market in which liquidations of weakly held contracts has largely been completed and offerings have become scarce. [2]

sole owner: the only person holding the title to a specific property or business. see *severalty.*

sole proprietorship: a proprietorship in which all equity lies with one individual.

solicit: to offer additional credit to a customer. [55]

solid-state computer: a computer that uses solid-state, or semiconductor,

components; a second-generation computer.

solvency: exists when liabilities, other than those of ownership, amount to less than the total assets; the ability to pay debts.

solvent: the condition of an individual who is able to pay his or her debts.

solvent debtor section: a part of the Bankruptcy Tax Act of 1980 whereby a company that buys back its own bonds at a discount price must pay income tax on the spread between the face value of the bonds, or the original sales price, and the discount repurchase price.

Sonnie Mae: synonymous with the "New York State Mortgage Authority."

SOP: see *statement of policy.*

SOR: see *stockholder of record.*

So. shilling: monetary unit of Somalia.

source document: a record used by the association of the initial recording of a transaction. [59]

source of shifts analysis: a means of assessing the effects of new accounts on the monetary aggregates. [98]

sovereign risk limit: a bank's limit on the amount of money in the Euromarkets that it is prepared to lend to one government.

SP

(1) see *selling price.*

(2) see *short position.*

(3) see *spot price.*

(4) see *stop payment.*

special administrator: an administrator appointed by the court to take over and safeguard an estate pending the appointment of an executor or administrator; sometimes known as *temporary administrator.* [37]

special assessment: a compulsory levy made by a local government against certain properties to defray part or all of the cost of a specific improvement or service which is presumed to be of general benefit to the public and of special benefit to such properties. [49]

special assessment bond: see *bond, special assessment.*

special assessment fund: in governmental accounting, a fund established to account for financing improvements or services from special charges levied against the properties or persons benefited.

special assessment liens: claims which governmental units have upon properties until special assessments levied against them have been paid. [49]

special assessment roll: the official list showing the amount of special assessments levied against such property presumed to be benefited by an improvement or service. [49]

special assistance bond: see *bond, special assistance.*

special bank credit plans: lines of credit extended to borrowers by banks. Based upon a prearranged limit, the borrower may use all or part of the credit by writing a check. Interest charges are based on the amount of credit used during the month and the total amount outstanding. [78]

special bid: a method of filling an order to buy a large block of stock on the exchange floor. The bidder for the block of stock pays a special commission to the broker who represents him or her in making the purchase. The seller does not pay a commission. The special bid is made on the floor of the exchange at a fixed price, which may not be below the last sale of the secur-

ity or the current bid in the regular market, whichever is higher. Member firms may sell this stock for customers directly to the buyer's broker during trading hours. [20]

special checking account: see *pay-as-you-go accounts.*

special deposit: a fund established for the payment of interest, dividends, or other debts, or to insure the performance of contracts, and other deposits of a special nature; as distinguished from *sinking fund.* [18]

special depository: any bank authorized by the U.S. Treasury to receive as deposits the proceeds of sales of government bonds.

special devise: a gift, by will, of a specific parcel of real property. [32]

special district bond: see *bond, special district.*

special dividend: in addition to the regular corporation dividend, a further dividend in stock or money. synonymous with *extra dividend.*

special drawing rights (SDRs): the amount by which each country is permitted to have its international checking account with the International Monetary Fund go negative before the nation must ask for additional loans. SDRs were established at the Rio de Janeiro conference of 1967. cf. *collective reserve unit.*

special endorsement: an endorsement that transfers title to a negotiable instrument to a party specified in the endorsement. [59]

special fee account: see *pay-as-you-go accounts.*

special fund: any fund that must be devoted to some special use in accordance with specific regulations and restrictions. Generally, the term applies to all funds other than the general fund.

special guardian: a guardian appointed by a court for a particular purpose connected with the affairs of a minor or an incompetent person; sometimes a guardian ad litem is known as a special guardian. see *guardian ad litem.* [37]

special handling code: indicates that the customer's statement requires special treatment by the mailroom or that the statement is to be routed to a specific department. [105]

special indorsement: see *special endorsement.*

special interest account: used by commercial banks to describe a savings account. Some states do not permit a commercial bank to accept savings accounts. However, deposits may be accepted on which interest is paid and under the same interest-bearing rates as a savings bank, but another name, such as *special interest accounts*, must be used.

special issues: securities issued by the U.S. Treasury for investment of reserves of government trust funds and for certain payments to veterans.

specialist: a member of an exchange who has two functions: to maintain an orderly market, insofar as is reasonably practicable, in the stocks in which he or she is registered by an exchange as a specialist; and to act as a broker's broker.

specialist block purchase: purchase by the specialist for his or her own account of a large block of stock outside the regular market on the exchange. Such purchases may be made only when the sale of the block could not be made in the regular market within a reasonable time and at reasonable prices, and when the purchase by the specialist would aid him or her in maintaining a fair and orderly market. [20]

specialist block sale: opposite of *specialist block purchase*. Under exceptional circumstances, the specialist may sell a block of stock outside the regular market on the exchange for his or her own account at a price above the prevailing market. The price is negotiated between the specialist and the broker for the buyer. [20]

specialist's book: the "book"; composed of orders that have come to the specialist in a security on the stock exchange floor at prices limited to other than the prevailing market price. Orders are kept in a book, to be executed at such time as the market price reaches their limitations.

specialized capital good: a capital good used for only one purpose or for a limited number of purposes.

specialized examination: examination performed twice in a two-year period between general exams, which focus on specific departments and review of directors' and committee minutes, and regulatory reports. [105]

specialized management trust: an investment firm whose investment policy is limited to securities of businesses found in one industry, such as oils, chemicals, or electronics.

special lien: see *particular lien.*

special lien bond: see *bond, special lien.*

special loan: a loan involving unusual collateral; consequently, a higher rate of interest is often required. Over-the-counter securities are usually classified in this category.

special offering: occasionally a large

block of stock that becomes available for sale requires special handling because of its size and the market in that particular issue. A notice is printed on the ticker tape announcing that the stock will be offered for sale on the exchange floor at a fixed price. Member firms may buy this stock for customers directly from the seller's broker during trading hours. The price is usually based on the last transaction in the regular auction market. Only the seller pays a commission on a special offering. Special offerings must be approved by the SEC.

special partner: a partner in a financial organization whose liability is limited to the interest he or she has in the company and is not active in the management. see *active partner, general partner, limited partnership, silent partner.*

special power of appointment: see *limited power of appointment, power of appointment.*

special-privilege monopoly
(1) a monopoly emanating from government enactments or special favors granted by private firms.
(2) a special grant of the government to a firm or group of private persons, giving them an exclusive trading or other valuable franchise.

special-purpose computer: a computer that is designed to handle a restricted class of problems.

special-purpose funds: mutual funds that invest exclusively in securities from one industry. see *investment company.*

special security: effective September 1981, banks and savings and loan associations are able to take the deposits resulting from their new tax-exempt

savings certificates and reinvest the money in securities offered by the Federal National Mortgage Association. see *All-Saver certificates.*

special situation: usually describes a venture capital type of investment, but may also refer to a conservative but relatively unknown investment or to heavy commitments in investments which, in the opinion of the management, are temporarily undervalued by the market. [30]

special supervisory examination: examination of banks with problems and conditions requiring more than two reviews in one year. [105]

special tax bond: see *bond, special tax.*

specialty (specialized) fund: investment company concentrating its holdings in specific industry groups (insurance, oil, aviation stocks, etc.). [30]

specialty stock: a security from a particular industry or grouping.

special warranty deed: see *deed, special warranty.*

specie: money in coin.

specie payment: payment in coin rather than with paper money.

specific address: synonymous with *machine address.*

specifications: in foreign exchange, the conditions and terms used with bills of exchange drawn under letters of credit.

specific coding: synonymous with *absolute code.*

specific commodity sales tax: in effect, the same as an excise tax. Examples are the taxes on gasoline, drugs, and the like.

specific deposit: a deposit made for a specific purpose, for example, bond coupons deposited for collection purpose only. Not a general deposit. The bank becomes only the agent or bailee of the depositor, not the debtor. The distinction is important in the case of bankruptcy or failure to follow instructions.

specific devise: a gift, by will, of a specific parcel of real property. [37]

specific duty: a customs duty based on weight, quantity, or other physical characteristics of imported items. cf. *ad valorem*.

specific issue market: a subsector of the repurchase agreement market. A reverse repurchase agreement is made in respect of a specific security issue whose price is expected by the dealer to drop. [90]

specific legacy: see *legacy*.

specific performance: the actual accomplishment of a contract by the party bound to fulfill it. An action to compel the performance of a contract according to its terms—that is, to do the thing contracted for, usually brought where the payment of money damages would not adequately compensate the aggrieved party. [37]

specific subsidy: the per unit subsidy on a commodity.

specific tariff: a tariff based on the number of units, weight, or other specific measure but not value. cf. *ad valorem*.

specific tax: the per unit tax on a commodity.

speculate: investing in securities with the expectation of making a profit over a relatively short period.

speculation: the employment of funds by a speculator. Safety of principal is a factor secondary to increasing capital.

see *letter stock;* cf. *defensive investment, digested securities*.

speculative market: an organized exchange where speculative buying and selling regularly occurs.

speculative position: an open position held by a trader that is unhedged.

speculative purchasing: buying items when prices appear lowest, with the expectation that there will be a future price increase, making possible a profit.

speculative securities: a classification for securities that have a relatively sizable risk.

speculator: one who is willing to assume a relatively large risk in the hope of gain. His or her principal concern is to increase capital rather than dividend income. Speculators may buy and sell the same day, or may invest in enterprises they do not expect to be profitable for years.

spendable earnings: net earnings after deductions for taxes. Often referred to as take-home pay, or the amount available for spending.

spendthrift provision: a provision in a trust instrument which limits the right of the beneficiary to dispose of his interest, as by assignment, and the right of his creditors to reach it, as by attachment. [32]

spendthrift trust: see *spendthrift provision*.

spilling stock: disposing of securities out of necessity, throwing the stocks on the market for sale.

spillovers: synonymous with *externalities*.

spillover trust: type of trust which by its terms is merged with or added to another trust or estate upon the occurrence of a certain event. see *pourover*. [37]

spinoff: with respect to federal income taxes, a transfer by a firm of a portion of its assets to a newly formed organization in exchange for the latter's capital stock, which is thereupon distributed as a property dividend to the stockholders of the initial corporation.

split: the division of the outstanding shares of a corporation into a larger number of shares. A 3-for-1 split by a company with 1 million shares outstanding would result in 3 million shares outstanding. Each holder of 100 shares before the 3-for-1 split would have 300 shares. Of course his or her proportionate equity in the company would remain the same, since 100 parts of 1 million is the equivalent of 300 parts of 3 million. Ordinarily, a split must be voted by directors and approved by shareholders. Such action by a corporation does not alter the total contributed capital but merely increases the number of shares issued and outstanding and the par value per share. cf. *stock split-down*.

split close: variations in price; for example, the Dow Jones shows a higher closing price for the industrial averages, but a lower closing price for the utility average.

split commission: sharing a commission with someone else who has assisted in procuring the business for the broker, agent, or counselor. see *give-up*.

split deposit: the act of simultaneously cashing a check and depositing some portion of it in a bank account. [105]

split down: where the number of outstanding shares is reduced and the market price is increased. synonymous

with *reverse split*; the opposite of *stock split*.

split funding: a program which combines the purchase of mutual fund shares with the purchase of life insurance contracts or other products. [23]

split gift: a gift made by a husband or wife to a third person may be treated as having been made one-half by each if the other spouse consents to the gift. [105]

split investment company: a closed-end investment firm issuing two types of capital stock. The first (income shares) receives dividends from investments; the second (capital shares) receives dividends from the appreciation of investments. synonymous with *dual-purpose fund*.

split-off: the exchange of stock by the shareholders of a parent (controlling) corporation in return for stock in a subsidiary corporation. cf. *spinoff*.

split-off point: see *joint product method of cost accounting*.

split opening: a situation where a security or commodity has simultaneous opening prices which are spread or different. This occurs when a number of traders at a trading post break up into groups and the sales occur in two groups at the same time but at differing prices.

split order: a large order that is separated into smaller units that are sold over a period of time. When purchasing or selling a security or commodity, a very large transaction could cause substantial price fluctuation which splitting may prevent.

split quotation: a quotation expressed in a different unit than the adopted standard quotation (e.g., a quote at $1/16$ of a point).

split-rate account: a passbook savings account that pays increasing rate of interest, up to regulatory maximums, for increasing account balances. [59]

split-schedule loan: a mortgage that establishes interest for only a few years and then a complete amortization schedule. The loan is usually accomplished through split amortization schedules on the loan.

split stock: new outstanding securities of a corporation resulting from a stock split.

split-up: the issuance of two or more stock shares replacing each outstanding share, used for financial and tax purposes. This increase, although lowering the value per share, does not alter the total liability of the issuing firm for the outstanding capital stock. see *split.*

Sp. Off.: see *special offering.*

sponsor: to take an interest in a security issue and protect the market in it.

sponsored nonrecourse plan: an indirect lending arrangement without recourse, but with the agreement that a dealer will repurchase from a bank either a defaulted contract or the repossessed goods. [105]

sponsorship: the banking institution holding an interest in the selling price of a specific securities issue.

spooks: see *fictitious paper.*

spot: in commodities and foreign exchange, denoting something that can be delivered readily.

spot against forward: a central bank's limit to control the extent to which banks can hold net current assets in foreign currency against net forward liabilities. The purpose is to prevent a buildup of foreign currency assets outside the official reserves.

spot cash: immediate cash payment as distinguished from payment at a later date.

spot commodity: see *cash commodity.*

spot delivery: immediate delivery.

spot delivery month: the nearest delivery month among all those traded at any point in time. The actual contract month represented by the spot delivery month is constantly changing throughout the calendar year as each contract month reaches its last trading day.

spot exchange rate: the price of one country's currency in terms of another country's currency that is effective for immediate (today) delivery.

spot exchange transaction: a purchase or sale of foreign currency for ready delivery. In practice, market usage normally prescribes settlement within two working days. For purposes of the International Monetary Fund's Articles of Agreement, the term excludes transactions in banknotes or coins. [42]

spot/fortnight: see *spot/next.*

spot grain: synonymous with *cash grain.*

spot market: a market where commodities are sold for cash and quickly delivered. see *fixing the price.*

spot news: any type of sudden news or condition that can temporarily impact on the general market action.

spot/next: a purchase of currency on Monday for settlement on Thursday is transacted at the exchange rate for spot delivery plus an adjustment for the extra day. The adjustment is referred to as the *spot/next. Spot/week* refers to delivery a week after spot; *spot/fortnight* refers to delivery a fortnight after spot.

spot price: the price at which the spot commodity is selling. [11]

spot sale: the sale of a product for cash and current delivery rather than for at a future date.

spot stock: a stock of goods shipped by a producer to a public warehouse as his or her property with the intention of disposing of the goods to a distinct market.

spotted market: a market condition characterized by small price movement either upward or downward and no general price trend or movement is observable.

spot trading: cash sales for immediate delivery.

spot/week: see *spot/next*.

spousal IRA: an IRA for the nonworking spouse.

SPP: see *stock purchase plan*.

spraying trusts: synonymous with *sprinkling trusts*.

spread

(1) *finance:* two prices given instead of one.

(2) *finance:* the difference between two prices.

(3) *investments:* two different options, a put (price below the prevailing market), and a call (price above the prevailing market), with both options pertaining to the same stock and expiring on the same day. Thus the trader is guaranteed a sale not lower than the put price if the market drops and a buy at a price not higher than the call price if the market increases. see also *butterfly spread, straddle*.

(4) *investments:* the differences between the bid and asked prices of securities.

sprinkling trusts: trusts in which the income or principal is distributed among the members of a designated class in amounts and proportions as may be determined in the discretion of the trustee. synonymous with *spraying trusts*. [37]

SPS: see *second preferred stocks*.

spurt: any short, but considerable climb in prices.

square: a position in a currency, security, or commodity which is balanced (i.e., neither long nor short).

Square Mile, the: see *City*.

squeeze

(1) *finance:* when interest rates are high and money is difficult to borrow.

(2) *investments:* results when people who have sold stocks short in a climbing market are obligated to buy back their securities at a loss in order to fulfill their short-selling contract obligations. see *short covering, short sale*.

SS

(1) see *selling short*.

(2) see *senior securities*.

(3) see *short sale*.

(4) see *shrinking stocks*.

(5) see *Social Security*.

SSD: see *stock split-down*.

ST

(1) see *sales tax*.

(2) see *stock transfer*.

stabilization fund: a 1934 fund created as a result of the dollar devaluation with $2 billion to stabilize exchange values of the U.S. dollar for dealing in foreign exchange and gold and to invest in direct government obligations. Under the Bretton Woods Agreement much of the assets of the Fund were used to contribute to the international Bank for Reconstruction and Development and the International Monetary Fund.

stabilization policy: the efforts of government to use fiscal and monetary means to eliminate inflation, unemployment, or both. see *wage stabilization.*

stabilized dollar: a plan to provide constant purchasing power for the U.S. dollar by making it into a commodity standard by means of altering the weight of the gold content of the dollar to compensate for changing prices.

stabilizing bid: a bid that the managers of an issue make for the bonds which have been issued to prevent the price of the security from going below the issue price for a certain period after the issue.

stable money: currency that remains constant in terms of the items and services it can purchase.

stag: an individual speculator who rapidly buys and then sells shares for profit, having had no intention of retaining the securities for any length of time. cf. *digested securities.*

stagflation: inflation coexisting with economic stagnation. Prices increase during a period of minimal capital investment in equipment, research and development, and so on.

Staggers Rail Act of 1980: gives the railroads greater freedom to set freight-hauling rates and greater authority to enter into long-term agreements with their customers, the freight shippers. It also makes it easier for railroads to eliminate unprofitable routes, although they will remain subject to control by the Interstate Commerce Commission.

stagger system: a practice whereby only a portion of a board of directors is elected in any one year.

stagnation: conditions of minimal growth rate, or growth increasing at a rate lower than expected.

stake: slang, a rather substantial amount of money.

stale: a bill of exchange payable on demand, or a check, which appears on the face of it to have been in circulation for an unreasonable time period.

stale check: any check dated 90 days prior to presentation for payment.

stamped bond: see *bond, stamped.*

stamped notes: paper money issued with revenue stamps on it to add to the value. [27]

stamped security: a stock that has been stamped to show any alteration made on it since it was first released—for example, a change in the date of maturity.

stamp tax: a government tax collected through the sale of stamps that are affixed to certain products (e.g., liquor, tobacco, stock certificates, or title deeds). see *transfer tax.*

Standard & Poor's 500-Composite-Stock Index: an index of stock prices composed of 400 industrials, 40 utilities, 40 financial firms, and 25 transportations. cf. *Dow Jones Averages.*

standard bullion: bullion containing the same proportions of metals and the same degree of purity as the standard gold and silver coins and, thereby, making the bullion ready for coinage without further refining.

standard cost: the predetermined cost of performing an operation or producing a product when labor, materials, and equipment are utilized efficiently under reasonable and normal conditions. [49]

standard deviation: a statistical measure of dispersion.

Standard Industrial Classification System (SIC): a numerical system developed by the U.S. Bureau of the Budget to classify establishments by type of activity for purposes of facilitating the collection, tabulation, presentation, and analysis of data relating to such establishments and for promoting uniformity within U.S. agencies. cf. *Dictionary of Occupational Titles.*

standard money: the money or unit of money on which a particular nation's monetary system is based.

standard of living: the level of material affluence of a nation as measured by per capita output. see *per capita output.*

standard payment: a customer's exact contract payment amount. see *nonstandard payment.* [55]

standards of practice: formulated for the guidance of commercial banks operating in the installment credit field, sets forth certain standards that should be followed at all times. [105]

standard stocks: securities of established and well-known firms.

standard underwriting: the purchase pursuant to agreement by investment banking firms of the unsold portion of an issue offered by the issuing company directly to its own security holders or some other restricted group.

standby commitment: commitment for a limited period made, for a fee, as security for a construction lender by an investor who stands ready to make or purchase the committed loan at above-market terms in the event that a takeout commitment cannot be obtained on market terms. [22]

standby controls: government credit, commodity, or other restraints that are legal and authorized but held in abeyance by authorities pending conditions that warrant their invocation.

standby credit

(1) an International Monetary Fund arrangement where a member receives assurance that, during a fixed time period, requests for drawing on the IMF will be permitted on the member's representation as to need.

(2) an arrangement with a bank or group of banks whereby they agree to make a certain amount of funds available to a borrower for a specified time period.

standby letter of credit: a letter of credit that can be drawn against only if another business transaction is not performed. [105]

standby offering: an offering of rights by a firm where an underwriter offers to stand-by to purchase any of the rights the firm is unable to sell.

standing authorization: an authorization that is executed once between a customer and a company to cover all paperless entries generated by the company for the customer's account thereafter of the same amount and for the same purpose. This contrasts with a single-entry authorization, which covers only a single paperless entry. [105]

standing mortgage: a loan in which interest is paid at specified intervals, but no principal payments are made; the entire loan falls due at maturity.

standing order: an authority given by the customer for the bank to regularly pay funds, usually a fixed dollar amount, from his or her demand deposit account.

standstill agreement: an arrangement between a debtor and a creditor under which exist new limits and conditions for the loan. Typically, a postponement of obligation payment is the result. cf. *novation.*

staple: cotton and other major commodities; also, the length of cotton fibre.

star notes: U.S. replacement notes. Also the name given to some interest-bearing notes issued in 1837 by the Treasury of Texas. [27]

starred card: generally indicates that purchases under $100 do not require an authorization. [105]

state bank: a bank that is organized according to the laws of a state and is chartered by the state in which it is located to operate as a banking business. The various states have different laws governing the operation of banks.

state banking department: the organization in each state which supervises the operations and affairs of state banking institutions. The chief officer of this department is designated superintendent of banks or commissioner of banks or is given some comparable title. [39]

state bank notes: an American term referring to issues by banks which are subject to the laws in the state, as opposed to federal laws. [27]

state bond: see *bond, state.*

state bonded warehouse: see *warehouse, state bonded.*

stated capital: the sum of capital amounts contributed by stockholders.

stated value: in the case of no-par shares of stock of a corporation, the stated value of a share is the dollar amount per share set aside by resolution of the board of directors or by the charter as capital and therefore unavailable for dividends until the stated value is reduced. cf. *par value.*

stateless: slang, currency deposited in banks outside the country of original issue and used by the banks like any other exchange medium.

statement

(1) *banking:* a record prepared by a bank for a depositor listing all checks drawn and deposits made together with the new balance after each posting.

(2) *computers:* an instruction to perform some sequence of operations.

(3) *finance:* a summary of transactions between a creditor and his or her debts or a presentation of names and amounts of accounts to show a financial condition (e.g., an IRS statement).

statement analysis: applying such ratios as a current ratio, turnover ratio, and other accounting and credit measuring the devices for the purpose of reaching a decision on the outlook of a firm or security.

statement balance: that dollar amount representing the sum of the previous balance due plus cash advances and merchandise purchases for the billing period less credit for payments and/or merchandise returns plus any appropriate finance charges and service charge. [105]

statement clerk: an employee in the bookkeeping department of a bank. This title has two different meanings as applied to the duties of the clerk. In some banks the statement clerk posts the statements for depositors' checking accounts under the dual system. In other banks this title is used in describing an employee who is responsible for verification of all paid checks listed on a depositor's statement to see that the statement is complete before it is mailed to the depositor. [10]

statement film: photocopy of the actual billing statement [105]

statement of changes in financial position: a report summarizing the flow of funds within an organization during a designated period of time. The statement should disclose all important aspects of the organization's financing and investing activities regardless of whether cash or other elements of working capital are directly affected. [43]

statement of condition: a detailed listing of a bank's resources, liabilities, and capital accounts showing its conditions on a given date. On requests (calls) by supervisory authorities several times a year, banks are required to submit sworn statements of condition. In general accounting, this type of financial report is known as a *balance sheet*. [50]

statement of liability: an expression of a cardholder's responsibilities stated on the reverse side of credit cards, cardholder agreements, or on other printed documents. [105]

statement of loan: a statement itemizing all details of a loan transaction which must be given to the borrower at the time the loan is negotiated. [55]

statement of operations: a summary of the financial operations during a given period showing the sources of income and its allocation to the payment of operating expenses, dividends to holders of savings accounts, and allocations to reserves for the protection of savers. [51]

statement of policy: a guide issued by the SEC to assist issuers, underwriters, dealers, and salespersons in complying with statutory disclosure standards as applied to sales literature, reports to shareholders, and other communications "addressed to or in-

tended for distribution to prospective investors." [30]

statement savings: a savings account in which a periodic statement replaces the passbook. [105]

statement savings account: a savings account for which the customer records his or her own balance and transactions information. A periodic balance statement is received from the bank. The balance statement is reconciled to the customer's records. [105]

statement stub: the portion of a cardholder statement which is returned with the payment. [105]

state notes: issued by an American state, now forbidden. [27]

State Street: Boston's financial area.

statewide banking: the establishment of bank branches throughout a state. [105]

static economy: an economy at equilibrium, where the forces of supply and demand are equated by price and where little change in production or demand is established.

station
(1) *general:* a worker's assigned post or place of activity.
(2) *computers:* one of the input or output points of a system that uses communication facilities.
(3) *investments:* the place where a specialist on an exchange transacts orders.

statism: any indication of increased government intervention in a nation's economic activity, with primary focus on movement toward greater control over major industries. see *controlled economy*.

statistical accounting: the application of probability theory and statistical sampling approaches to the evolution of prime accounting information and/or verification, authentication, and audit of accounting data prepared by other means.

status code: an alphanumeric code assigned to an account either through manual input or generated by the computer system, indicating that the account is in a restricted condition or requires special attention or handling. see *blocked accounts*. [105]

"statused" account: a cardholder record to which a status code has been posted, indicating a condition under which the cardholder may not use his account. see *blocked accounts*. [105]

status report: a hard-copy record of the status of all cardholder accounts or group of accounts on which there has been activity. [105]

statute of frauds: a law that requires certain contracts, such as agreements of sale, to be in writing in order to be enforceable. [62]

statute of limitations: see *limitations of actions (statutes of)*.

statutes of distribution: laws, rules, or statutes governing the distribution of personal property under intestacy. [37]

statutory exemptions: specified articles of personal property and a specified amount of cash left by a decedent which are set apart for his or her immediate family and which may not be subjected to the claims of creditors. [37]

statutory fee: the administrative cost of closing a loan. [78]

statutory investment: an investment which a trustee is specifically authorized to make under the terms of the statutes of the state having jurisdiction of the trust. [37]

statutory warranty deed: a warranty deed form prescribed by state statutes. [62]

steady: showing that market prices are barely moving in any direction.

stepped costs: costs that climb by increments with increased volumes of activity.

sterilizing gold: a strategy for preventing newly imported gold from expanding the credit base of a nation. One method is to have the U.S. Treasury pay for the gold with a draft on a commercial bank in which it has an account rather than drawing upon the Federal Reserve System and then issuing gold certificates. cf. *desterilizing gold*.

sterling: the currency of Great Britain. The unit is the pound sterling. May also represent bills of exchange that are drawn in terms of British currency. Sterling silver is silver of at least 222 parts out of 240 of pure silver, and no more than 18 parts of an alloy.

sterling area: an association of countries involving trade preferences between the members and pooling of their holdings of certain currencies, particularly American dollars, for maximum mutual benefit. The group was formed in 1939, upon the opening of World War II, and included Egypt, Eire, Iceland, Iran, and the entire British Empire with the dominions (except Canada), all under British leadership.

sterling balances: sums held in sterling by a foreign nations and private persons.

sterling bloc: those nations whose trade is heavily with England and whose monetary program and currencies were kept at parity with the English pound through monetary reserves deposited in London. The bloc included the Scandinavian countries, Uruguay, Bolivia, the countries of the British Empire, and to an extent Argentina and Japan. The bloc came into existence when England left the gold standard in 1931 and the block was replaced by the sterling area in 1939.

sterling bond: see *bond, sterling.*

sterling credit: a letter of credit denominated in British pounds sterling.

sterling exchange: a check or bill denominated in pounds sterling and payable through a bank in the United Kingdom.

Stg.: see *sterling.*

sticky prices: prices that do not change readily. The opposite is flexible prices.

Stk.: see *stock.*

Stk. Ex.: see *stock exchanges.*

St. Louis equation: introduced in 1968 to investigate the relative impact of monetary and fiscal actions on economic activity. [100]

stock: the legal capital of a corporation divided into shares. see *assented securities, authorized stock, blue chip, callable, capital stock, common stock, convertible, cumulative preferred (stock), deferred stock, float, growth stock, guaranteed stock, inactive stock (bond), issue, listed securities (stocks), nonassessable stock, noncumulative, no-par-value stock, ordinary stock, outstanding, over the counter, paid-up stock, participating preferred, par value, penny stocks, preferred stock, prior preferred (stock), redeemable stock, treasury stock, unissued stock, unlisted, voting right (stock), watered stock.*

stock ahead: describing a situation when an investor who has entered an order to buy or sell a stock at a certain price sees transactions at that price reported on the ticker tape before his or her own order has been executed. This may have occurred because other buy and sell orders at the same price came in to a trading specialist earlier and had priority.

stock allotment: the quantity of stock set aside by the manager of an underwriting syndicate as the portion for a member of the syndicate to distribute.

stock-appreciation rights (SARs): privileges that can be attached to a nonqualified option. With an SAR, an executive can ignore the option and take a bonus equal to the value of the stock's appreciation over a span of time. An SEC rule permits an SAR bonus to be paid in cash, rather than in company shares. The SAR can be acted on at any time during the 10-year term of the attached nonqualified stock option.

stock assessment: a levy made upon a stockholder to make up a capital deficiency created by adverse economic developments in the corporation's activities.

stock association: a savings association organized as a capital stock corporation, with investors providing operating capital by purchasing an ownership interest in the institution, represented by shares of stock. Their stock holdings entitle them to virtually the same rights as stockholders in any other corporation, including a share of the profits. Stock associations operate in 23 states. [59]

stock-bonus trust: a trust established by a corporation to enable its employees to receive benefits in the form of the corporation's own stock as a reward for meritorious service or as a means of sharing in the profits of the enterprise. [37]

stock borrowed: securities borrowed by one broker from another to result in delivery. These stocks are subject to going interest and premium rates. see *short sale.*

stockbroker: an individual who acts as a middleman between buyers and sellers of stock. cf. *specialist.*

stock certificate: written evidence of ownership of a company's shares, indicating the number of shares registered in the name of the owner, the corporation issuing the capital stock, and whether the stock is a par value or a non-par-value stock.

stock certificate book: a book of blank stock certificates.

stock clearing agency: an organization that periodically balances and clears accounts among trading members of an exchange, settles their debit cash balances, and aids them in distributing stocks and other securities which were bought and sold. see *Stock Clearing Corporation.*

Stock Clearing Corporation: the New York Stock Exchange's clearinghouse. Major responsibilities include the clearing and settling of money balances between members, the clearing of purchases and sales transaction, and the delivery of stock.

stock company: a company in which stockholders contribute all the capital, pay all the losses, and share in the profits. [12]

stock discount: the excess of par value of a stock over the paid-in capital. [105]

stock dividend: a portion of the net earnings of a corporation payable (in shares of fractional shares of desig-nated stock of a given corporation) to the stockholders of record of the corporation. It is paid in securities rather than cash, and it may be additional shares of the issuing company or shares of another company held by the corporation.

stock exchanges: organizations that provide a market for the trading of bonds and stocks. Regulations for the admission of securities for trading on the stock exchanges are very stringent.

stock exchange seat: membership in a stock exchange.

stockholder: the legal owner of at least one share of security in a corporation.

stockholder of record: a stockholder whose name is registered on the books of the issuing corporation. see *voting right (stock).* [20]

stockholders annual report: report compiled annually for stockholders showing financial position and progress during the fiscal year. [18]

stockholder's ledger: a subsidiary ledger containing detailed data about the stock owned by each stockholder.

stockholders' list: a list of stockholders of a corporation entitled to vote in the affairs of the corporation. Each name appears alphabetically with corresponding address and the number of shares owned.

stock insurance company: an insurance company with stockholders who get the profit or suffer the loss of the insurance business rather than having the gain or loss distributed among the people insured.

stock-in-trade

(1) *general:* equipment used to carry on a trade or business; by exten-

sion, the usual activity of a trade or business.

(2) *investments:* quantity of securities held.

stock jobber: an English term for commission broker. In England, the stock jobber sells to the public and buys from a floor trader.

stock jobbing: irresponsible or dishonest manipulation of the price of securities.

stock market: the buying and selling of stock for the purpose of profit for both buyers and sellers of the security. see *market.*

stock option: an arrangement for compensating top management, in addition to salary, with an opportunity to buy a certain amount of company stock, often under the market price. see *Tax Reform Act of 1976.*

stock option contract: a negotiable instrument that provides the purchaser the right to buy (call) or sell (put) the number of shares of stock designated in the contract at a fixed price within a stated period of time. synonymous with *paper.*

stock power: a power of attorney permitting a person other than the owner of stock to legally transfer the title of ownership to a third party. Stock powers are usually given when stock is pledged as collateral to loans.

stock purchase plan: a company plan for the purchase of stock by employees, with or without a contribution from the employer at terms usually below the market price.

stock purchase trust: a trust under which a surviving stockholder of a close corporation can purchase the stock of a deceased stockholder; usu-

ally, but not necessarily, as an insurance trust.

stock quotation: the price of a stock, usually given in terms of a round lot and expressed in eighths or units of $12\frac{1}{2}$ cents.

stock quotation instrument: the original name for the *stock ticker.*

stock registrar: a bank, financial institution, or person permitted to serve in a fiduciary position, to certify that a corporation's issued shares have not exceeded the approved amount.

stock repurchase agreement: an agreement by a corporation at the time the stock is issued to repurchase the stock on demand. Particularly used in the utility field for sales to employees or customers. Also used as an incentive which allows employees to own the stock during the period of employment but requires them to resell the stock to the employers upon termination of employment.

stock rights: shareholder's privileges to buy shares of a new issue of a corporation's stock at a stipulated price, in quantities limited to a proportion of their existing holdings. These rights are usually defined by an instrument known as a *stock warrant.*

stock savings bank: a bank established under state law as a profit-making organization with customary capital stock and shareholders that can accept time deposits for the purpose of saving. Most of these banks now provide expanded services and are indistinguishable from traditional commercial banks.

stock split: see *split.*

stock split-down: the reverse of stock split; the total number of shares outstanding is lowered without reducing the total value of the issue, by issuing a new stock share to replace each of two or more shares presently in circulation. The motivation is to increase the market price of a stock. synonymous with *reverse stock split.*

stock subscription: an agreement to purchase the stock of a corporation from the corporation.

stock ticker: see *stock quotation instrument.*

stock transfer: the act of canceling a stock certificate submitted for transfer, issuing a new certificate in the name of the designated transferee, and recording the change in ownership on the records of a corporation's stock transfer book. see *stock-transfer tax.*

stock-transfer agent: the agent of a corporation appointed for the purpose of effecting transfers of stock from one stockholder to another by the actual cancellation of the surrendered certificates and the issuance of new certificates in the name of the new stockholder. [37]

stock transfer book: a special journal used to record transfers of securities. Its entries are posted to the stockholders' ledger.

stock-transfer tax: a tax levied by some states on the transfer of securities from one owner to another, either when purchased or given as a gift. see *stock transfer.*

stock trust certificate: issued in exchange for stock of competing firms entering the trust form of combination, deposited with trustees, who issue in exchange trust certificates under the deposit agreement, and who control the firm's activities by reason of their power. synonymous with *trust certificate.*

stock turnover: see *turnover.*

stock warrant: the document evidencing a stock right.

stock watering: see *watered stock.*

stock yield: the rate of return on a stock based upon its market value as of a particular date and the dividend being currently paid by the company. [37]

stolen card: a bank card that has been stolen either through the mail or directly from the cardholder of receipt. [105]

stone broke: slang, penniless.

stop: the lowest rate the central bank charges dealers who temporarily tender their government securities for cash in these operations.

stop limit order: a stop order that becomes a limit order after the specified stop price has been reached. see *limited order, stop order.* [20]

stop loss: a guarantee from one company (the reinsurer) to another (the reinsured) that losses over and above an agreed upon amount will be paid by the reinsuring company.

stop order: an order to buy at a price above or sell at a price below the current market. Stop buy orders are generally used to limit loss or to protect unrealized profits on a short sale. Stop sell orders are generally used to protect unrealized profits or to limit loss on a holding. A stop order becomes a market order when the stock sells at or beyond the specified price and thus may not necessarily be executed at that price. [20]

stop-out price: the lowest accepted price for Treasury bills at the regular weekly auction. [88]

stop payment: the order given to a bank by a depositor who wishes to prevent payment on a check he or she has issued. The depositor requests the bank to stop payment of the item in writing, or telephones the instructions and confirms them in writing.

stopped at: a price for a security that is often guaranteed to a purchaser or a seller by the specialist in it.

stop price: the price at which a customer's stop order to his broker becomes a market order.

store credit: credit extended by means of a charge account covering item purchased.

straddle

(1) *investments:* the purchase or sale of an equivalent number of puts and calls on a given underlying stock with the same exercise price and expiration date. [5]

(2) *investments:* an option allowing the trader to buy or sell securities at an agreed-upon price within a given period. see also *butterfly spread, spread.*

straight: a bond with unquestioned right to repayment of principal at a specified future date, unquestioned right to set interest payments on given dates, and no right to any additional interest, principal, or conversion privilege.

straight amortization plan: an amortization plan that provides for the payment of a fixed amount of principal at specified intervals, with interest payable on the remaining balance of the loan. [44]

straight bankruptcy: a proceeding by which an individual files for release from his debts after a court arranges for his creditors to divide whatever assets he has. [76]

straight bill of lading: a bill of lading that cannot be negotiated, identifying the individual who is to receive goods.

straight credit: a credit instrument under which the beneficiary is paid by a bank in his or her area that has been designated by the bank opening the credit. The drafts are usually drawn in the currency of the exporter. The paying bank debits the payment to the account of the opening bank on the books of the paying bank. [105]

straight investment: a preferred stock or bond, limited in interest or dividend rate, that is bought because of its income return and not for expectation of any rise in value. see *investment.*

straight lease: a lease describing regular rental payments (e.g., monthly, quarterly). synonymous with *flat lease.*

straight letter of credit: a letter of credit in which the insurer (e.g., a bank) recognizes only the person named (e.g., an exporter) as authorized to draw drafts under the letter for advances to the named person for whose benefit the letter is issued.

straight life: synonymous with *ordinary life.*

straight-line depreciation: the simplest method of depreciation. Amortization of capital cost in uniform periodic amounts over the anticipated life of the asset.

straight-line interest: a method of computing interest payments which takes a straight percentage of the unpaid balance on an annual basis. [105]

straight loan: a loan to an individual or other legal entity; the basis for granting credit is the debtor's general ability to pay, unsupported by any form of collateral security.

straight mortgage: a mortgage under which the borrower is obligated to pay interest during the term of the mortgage with the full amount of the principal to become due at the end of the mortgage term.

straight paper: all unsecured notes, bills of exchange, and acceptances.

straight-reduction plan: an amortization plan that provides for the payment of a fixed amount of principal at specified intervals, with interest payable on the remaining balance of the loan. [105]

straight serial bond: see *bond, straight serial.*

straight-term mortgage loan: a mortgage loan granted for a fixed term of years, the entire loan becoming due at the end of that time. [44]

straight-term plan: an amortization plan that provides for the payment of a fixed amount of principal at specified intervals, with interest payable on the remaining balance of the loan. [105]

strap: a stock option contract made up of two calls and one put. see *strip.*

strategic resource monopoly: an organization having a monopoly by virtue of controlling a vital input to a production process (e.g., DeBeers of South Africa owns most of the world's diamond mines).

strategics: slang, for investments made in precious metals, including, for example, chromium, manganese, germanium, titanium, nickel, and cobalt.

straw: untrue, valueless, or financially irresponsible. See *straw bid*.

straw bid: a bid whose maker is unable to fulfill the requirements for acquisition.

straw man: a person who purchases property for another without identifying the valid buyer. The result is that the *straw man* maintains a naked title on the property and is a dummy buyer.

Street: the New York financial community; the lower Manhattan (i.e., Wall Street) area.

street broker: an over-the-counter broker, as distinguished from a broker who is a member of an exchange.

street certificate: a stock certificate with a blank indorsement by an owner whose signature is guaranteed so that the stock can be transferred by delivery without the formality of transfer on the books of the corporation.

street loan: see *call loan.*

street name: any stock certificate in the name of a broker who trades in securities and is a member of an exchange is said to be in *street name.* This stock is never considered to be part of the broker's personal wealth.

street orders: form of order used by the representative of one carrier to secure tickets of another carrier's issue, settlement of which is made directly or through accounting office. [18]

street practice: any unwritten practice used by the financial community.

street price: in securities trading, the price for a stock delivered outside the stock exchange process.

stretching the payables: deferring payments on accounts payable beyond the due date.

stretch the float: keeping cash in a high-interest account as long as possible before using it to pay bills.

strict foreclosure: a legal proceeding in which the association brings court action against the borrower and the court sets a date by which the borrower must redeem his or her debt in full, or the title will pass automatically to the association without public sale. [59]

strike from the list: occurs when a stock exchange prevents, by canceling, any transactions in that particular stock. The stock is suspended. see *delist.*

strike suit: in corporation finance, designating a law suit by a minority stockholder whose main purpose is to be bought out (at a high price) by the management in order to get rid of his or her objections.

striking price: synonymous with *exercise price.*

stringency: a money market condition in which it is hard to obtain credit, accompanied by an increase in the rates of interest.

string of coconuts: slang, money, especially a large number of bills.

strip: a stock option contract made up of two puts and one call. see *strap.*

strip bond: see *bond, strip.*

stripped Treasury obligations: an artificial equivalent of zero-coupon bonds, featuring Treasury issues, with the safety of government debt. Represents a call on interest payments of U.S. government obligations, with maturities from three months to 29 years.

"strips": see *bond, strip.*

strong (or weak) hands: holders of securities held for investment purposes over a period of time are *strong hands. Weak hands* include investors who will sell at the slightest chance of profit or sell out during reactions, and include the general public, traders, and other speculators.

strong market: a greater demand for purchasing than there is for selling.

structural inflation: increasing prices are caused by an uneven upward de-

mand or cost pressures in a key industry, even when total demand remains in balance with total supply for the economy as a whole.

stuck (with): slang, having bought a poor or worthless good or service; overcharged.

Student Loan Marketing Association: a government-sponsored private corporation created to increase the flow of funds into student loans by facilitating the purchase of student loans in the secondary market; commonly called *Sallie Mae.*

Sub.: see *subordination.*

subchapter M: the sections of the Internal Revenue Code which provide special tax treatment for organizations known as *regulated investment companies.* [30]

Subchapter S corporation: an election available to a corporation to be treated as a partnership for income tax purposes. To be eligible to make the election, a corporation must meet certain requirements as to kind and number of shareholders, classes of stock, and sources of income. [105]

subject bid: a bid that is negotiable, rather than firm.

subject offer: an offer that is not firm but instead exploratory, in the expectation that it might induce a bid permitting additional negotiation on price.

subject premium: the insurance premium of the ceding firm to which the reinsurance premium rate is applied in order to produce the reinsurance premium.

subject to call: see *subject to redemption.*

subject to check: any payable-on-demand check where the customer need not inform the bank of his desire to withdraw funds. All commercial checking accounts are subject to check.

subject to collection: although a bank has accepted a deposit for immediate credit to an account, funds that the bank is not able to collect for some reason will be charged back to the account. [105]

subject to confirmation
(1) a price quotation that is not firm.
(2) a word for potential buyers that all securities have provisionally been sold but that depending on subsequent availability, the buyer's order may be filled.

subject to count: a deposit that has been credited to an account is subject to adjustment if later counting shows a discrepancy. [105]

subject to prior sale: a condition existing when, because the market is strong and the supply of securities is limited, there may be more buy orders than stock. At times such a statement may serve as a stimulant for submitting early bids.

subject to redemption: stocks that can be called (redeemed) with advance notice to the shareholders.

subject to sale: when property has been offered for sale, a "subject to sale" stipulation provides for the automatic withdrawal of the offer if the property is sold before the party to whom the stipulation was made has accepted the offer.

subject to verification: although a particular deposit has been accepted for immediate credit to an account, if mathematical verification of the amount of the deposit differs from that shown on the deposit ticket, the appropriate adjustment will be made to the account. [105]

sublease: the letting of premises to a third party with the original tenant retaining an interest in the property. All or part of the leased property may be subleased. If the tenant gives up his or her entire interest, the transaction becomes an assignment of lease. synonymous with *underlease.*

submission: mortgage banker's offering of mortgages for purchase by an investor. [22]

submittal notice: a broker's notification to a property owner stating that the owner's property has been offered for sale; offering price and prospect's name and address are included.

submortgage: the result of a pledge by a lender of a mortgage in his or her possession as collateral to obtain a loan for himself or herself.

subordinated: a promise to pay which cannot legally be fulfilled until payments on certain other obligations have been made and any other conditions, defined in the indenture, are met. cf. *senior.*

subordinated debenture: a special debenture whose bearer has a chance for payment lower than that for other creditors. As it holds a higher yield, it is considered a risky bond.

subordinated exchangeable variable-rate note: competing with bank loans, this note has the flexibility that it offers a company to raise money at prevailing short-term rates while providing the built-in option to fix the rate for longer periods.

subordinated interest: an interest in property that is inferior to another interest (e.g., a second mortgage that is inferior to the first mortgage). cf. *equal dignity.*

subordinated securities: securities

whose asset claims are secondary to claims of specified superior securities.

subordination: acknowledgment by a creditor in writing that the debt due him from a specified debtor shall have a status inferior or subordinate to the debt which the debtor owes another creditor. [44]

subordination agreement: where more than one legal entity has an interest or claim upon the assets of a prospective borrower, a bank may require that the other interested parties sign subordination agreements before a loan will be granted. The subordination agreement is an agreement in which another interested party grants the bank a priority claim or preference to the assets of the borrower ahead of any claim that he or she may have. [10]

subpoena: a process by a court requiring the attendance of a witness, usually at a trial. Failure to comply can result in a penalty. In addition to trials, a subpoena can compel a witness to appear at proceedings of a grand jury and at other investigations.

subrogation: substitution of one person for another, either as a creditor or the owner of any lawful right, in order that the substituted individual succeed to the rights, remedies, or proceeds of the claim.

subscribed capital: the total capital stock contracted for. When paid for, it becomes *paid-in capital.*

subscriber: one who agrees in writing to purchase a certain offering—for example, a certain number of shares of designated stock of a given corporation or a certain number of bonds of a given stipulated face value.

subscribing witness: one who sees a document signed or hears the signa-ture acknowledged by the signer and who signs his own name to the document, such as the subscribing witness to a will; to be distinguished from an *attesting witness.* [37]

subscription: an agreement to purchase a security; a solicitation of subscribers.

subscription cash record: a memorandum cash record of down payments and installment payments received from subscribers to capital stock.

subscription list: a subscriber signed agreement showing the amount of stock that each subscriber has agreed to buy.

subscription price: see *subscription rights.*

subscription rights: a privilege to the stockholders of a corporation to purchase proportionate amounts of a new issue of securities, at an established price, usually below the current market price; also, the negotiable certificate evidencing such privilege. [3]

subscriptions receivable: a current asset account showing the amount to be collected from subscribers to capital stock in a corporation.

subscription warrant: a document for the shareholder of record indicating his or her right to subscribe to new shares under stated terms and conditions as to price, time, and quantity.

subsidiary: any organization more than 50 percent of whose voting stock is owned by another firm.

subsidiary account: one of group of related accounts which support in detail the debit and credit summaries recorded in a control account. An example is the individual property taxpayers' accounts for taxes receivable in the general ledger. see also *control account, subsidiary ledger.* [49]

Subsidiary Account Number (SAN): the encoded number identifying an individual account other than the primary account. [105]

subsidiary coins: coins with a denomination of less than one dollar, including minor coins such as pennies or cents.

subsidiary firm: a business whose activities are subject to the control of another company.

subsidiary ledger: individual records of mortgage loan accounts, savings accounts, loans in process, and other accounts whose total appear in the general ledger. [59]

subsidy: a sum of money granted by the state to assist in the establishment or support of an enterprise or program which is considered to be of some advantage to the public.

subsistence theory of wages: an economic theory of the late eighteenth and early nineteenth centuries claiming that wages per employee tend to equal what the worker needs to maintain himself and his family. see *standard of living.*

substandard: describing conditions making a risk less desirable than normal for its class.

substituted trustee: a trustee appointed by the court (not named or provided for in the trust instrument) to serve in the place of the original trustee or of a prior trustee; to be distinguished from a *successor trustee.* [32]

substitution: see *subrogation.*

Substitution Account: a plan of the International Monetary Fund that would allow dollar holders to exchange them for assets denominated in a bas-

ket of currencies known as special drawing rights (SDRs). The objective of the plan is to reduce the $500 billion to $1 trillion floating around the world, and thus cut the gyrations of the international financial markets. see *special drawing rights.*

substitution effect: the effect of a change in the price of a commodity upon the demand schedule for that commodity resulting from a change in the price of that good relative to other goods. cf. *income effect.*

substitution of collateral: exchanging or replacing one portion of collateral, such as a block of stock, with another block of stock or notes.

subtenant: a tenant who leases a premises from another tenant; a sublessee. see *sublease.*

subvene: a grant, such as a subsidy.

subvention: financial aid or support, usually a grant from a government.

Suby.: see *subsidiary.*

succession
(1) *general:* following another in an office, estate, and so on.
(2) *law:* the transfer of all the rights and obligations of a deceased person to those who are entitled to inherit.

succession tax: a tax on the privilege of receiving property, either by descent or by will. It is not a burden on property.

successive beneficiaries
(1) beneficiaries who receive one after another by succession. Thus, under a will in which property is left to A for life, then to B for life, and then to C outright, B and C are successive beneficiaries.
(2) the inheritance of property by descent or transmission to the next in a succession—as from parent to child and so on down the direct line. [37]

successor trustee: a trustee following the original or a prior trustee the appointment of whom is provided for in the trust instrument; to be distinguished from a *substituted trustee.* [32]

sucre: monetary unit of Equador.

Suffolk bank system: a Massachusetts plan started in 1837, under which participating banks agreed to accept only the notes of such out-of-town banks as maintained a sufficient redemption account in the system. This held the notes of participating banks at par.

suit: any proceeding at law for the purpose of obtaining a legal decision.

sum at disposal: an amount of money held available in cash at the office of a bank for a beneficiary at the instructions of another. [105]

summarizing entry: an entry in journal form written below the footings in a columnar journal showing the debits and credits to be equal.

summary deposit ticket: a special deposit ticket used by customers with large numbers of deposit items. [105]

summons: a court writ directing the sheriff to notify the defendant that the plaintiff claims to have a cause of action against the defendant, who is expected to appear in court. A summons does not strictly compel the defendant to appear but merely puts him on notice that if he fails to appear, judgment is taken by default and the action will be decided against him.

sumptuary laws: laws that attempt to minimize the consumption of items believed to be harmful to individuals or society in general.

sunk costs: costs already incurred and not relevant to decision making.

sunrise industries: high-risk ventures in advanced technology with promising potential for growth and export.

sunset: termination or the end of a time period.

supercheck: generic term for *multiple-bill-payment system.* [105]

superintendent of banking: see *state banking department.*

superior good: synonymous with *normal good.*

super-NOW: accounts offered by banks and thrifts on January 5, 1983, permitting unlimited monthly transactions with a minimum balance of $2,500. The Super-NOW pays a near-market rate of interest, with a yield somewhat lower than that on the money market deposit account because banks have to post a reserve of 12 percent against the super-NOWS.

superprime instrument: a 10-day, nonrenewable note priced only a fraction above what a bank itself pays for funds.

superseded suretyship rider: a continuity of coverage clause in the form of a rider attached to a new fidelity bond, taking the place of another bond and agreeing to pay losses that would be recoverable under the first bond except that the discovery period has expired. Losses caused by dishonest employees frequently have been found to have occurred at various times stretching over a period of years. This may involve a chain of several bonds, each one superseding a prior obligation. These losses will be covered if the chain of bonds is unbroken and each has included the superseded suretyship rider. [54]

supervised lender: according to the Veterans Administration classification, any lender subject to examination and supervision by a state or federal agency. [59]

supervisory merger: a move in the banking industry, where an institution in serious danger is forced to merge with a stronger one. To encourage this movement, loans are provided by the government-managed Federal Savings and Loan Insurance Corporation.

supplemental agreement: an amendment to an agreement setting forth additional terms to the agreement. [37]

supplementary cost: see *fixed cost.*

supplementary special deposits: see *corset.*

supplier credit: export finance available to a supplier of items, as distinct from credits to the overseas purchaser under buyer credit.

supply: the amount of a good that sellers are ready to sell at each specified price in a given market at a given time. Sometimes used to mean quantity forthcoming at one specified price. synonymous with *supply schedule.*

supply and demand: economic forces that influence changes in business performance and strategy.

supply area: the price area on a security or market average chart indicating a resistance level, or a place where earlier advances have been extinguished.

supply curve: a graphical presentation of supply with dollars on the vertical axis and quantity of product on the horizontal axis. Then the curve connecting the different quantities of product that sellers will offer at different prices is a *supply curve.*

supply price: the lowest price needed to produce a specified output. It is the lowest price a seller will accept for the

act of supplying a given quantity of a commodity.

supply schedule: a stabular arrangement showing the quantities of product that sellers will offer at different prices.

supply-side economics: a concept that shifts the emphasis from aggregate demand economics (which Keynes considered the most important economic variable) to investment and production. It lays great stress on the repressive role of taxes, and it leads logically to a strong endorsement of tax cuts designed to encourage investment.

support: action by a person, organization, or government agency such as the Federal Reserve Banks in buying government securities in the open market or of the Department of Agriculture in purchasing agricultural commodities in the market. This practice tends to push prices of the products or items upward.

supporting orders: orders entered to support the price of a specific security.

supporting schedules: additional lists of facts or financial reports used with a balance sheet or profit and loss statement as supplementary reports.

supporting the market: placing purchasing orders at or somewhat below the prevailing market level for the purpose of maintaining and balancing existing prices and to encourage a price rise.

support level: an area of repeated demand on the price chart for a security or market average; often stops price declines and encourages rallies.

support point: the point when a central bank is obliged to intervene to support its currency.

suppressed inflation: the situation

where prices and wages are controlled by the law and there is an increase in money demand for goods relative to the supply of goods after the economy is at full employment. Shortages are adjusted then by rationing or priorities.

supreme court of finance: popular name for the seven-member Federal Reserve Board.

Sur.: see *surplus.*

surcharge: an added charge to a tax or other cost or account.

surety

(1) *finance:* a bond, guaranty, or other security that protects a person, corporation, or other legal entity in cases of another's default in the payment of a given obligation, improper performance of a given contract, malfeasance of office, and so on.

(2) *law:* an individual who agrees, usually in writing, to be responsible for the performance of another on a contract, or for a certain debt or debts of another individual.

surety bond: see *bond, surety.*

suretyship: obligations to pay the debt or default of another; the function of being a *surety.*

sur mortgage: a document that demands that a person who has defaulted on mortgage payments show cause why the mortgage should not foreclose.

surplus

(1) *general:* anything remaining or left over.

(2) *banking:* the surplus account is a part of the capital structure of a bank, and is carried in the general ledger. Before a bank can open for business as a national bank, it must have a beginning surplus equal to 20 percent of the paid-in capital stock. A state bank must conform to whatever the laws of the state require as pertaining to surplus. After a bank has opened, the surplus account is made up of all past earnings less the dividends declared and paid from the profits. National banks are required to carry a minimum of 10 percent of each previous six months' earnings to their surplus account before the Comptroller of the Currency will approve the payment of a dividend. State laws deal with surplus requirements in various ways. The surplus is a part of the net worth or ownership of the bank, and in case of liquidation, any remaining portion of surplus after all creditors have been satisfied will be divided in the same related percent as the capital stock held by the stockholders. [10]

(3) *finance:* excess of assets over the total liabilities and capital.

surplus equity: the amount of difference between the market value of securities and the amount required to satisfy margin requirements of a brokerage account.

surplus fund: see *guaranty fund.*

surplus reserves: an amount of surplus or net worth set up as a reserve to indicate that it is considered not available for withdrawal in dividends.

surplus value: in Marxian philosophy, the profit derived from the amount above labor costs.

surrender of lease: a mutual agreement between landlord and tenant to terminate all aspects of a lease before its normal expiration date.

surrender value (cash surrender value): designating the amount of the total life insurance in force that will be paid to the policyholder after a certain stipulated number of premiums have been paid, if the policyholder elects to surrender the policy and receive such proportionate part. The cash surrender value of a policy is also the amount used to determine how much will be loaned against the policy.

surrogate's court: synonymous with *probate court.*

surtax: the extra tax applied to corporations when their net taxable income has exceeded a certain amount. For example, a surtax is demanded at the rate of 26 percent for all corporate income over $25,000. see *Tax Reform Act of 1969.*

survivorship account: an account in the names of two or more persons, each signature alone being sufficient authority for the withdrawal of funds, the balance in the account belonging to the survivor or survivors on the death of the other or others. see *alternate account, joint account.* [50]

survivorship annuity: an annuity paid to a beneficiary following the death of the individual providing for such annuity.

suspended trading: a binding stock exchange decision to cease trading resulting from an unusual occurrence, such as an unexpected jump in buy or sell orders on all or several securities. Sometimes, suspended trading may be brought about by equipment failure or other unexpected emergencies.

suspense account: an account in the general ledger used to hold over unposted items so that the business day can be closed in a state of balance.

suspense fund: a fund established to account separately for certain receipts pending the distribution or disposal thereof. [49]

suspension
(1) *general:* disciplinary layoff of a worker without pay.
(2) *banking:* a temporary closing of a bank.
(3) *investments:* a decision made by a stock exchange board of directors prohibiting a securities firm or broker from conducting business for a period. see *under the rule.*

swag: slang, stolen items or money.

swap
(1) *general:* to exchange or barter.
(2) *banking:* an arrangement between the central banks of two countries for standby credit to facilitate the exchange of each other's currencies. see *credit, swap network;* see also *bond swap.*
(3) *computers:* to write the main storage aspects of a job to auxiliary storage and read the image of another job into main storage.
(4) *investments:* a process by which portfolios are adjusted to lengthen or shorten maturities or raise or lower coupon rates to wring out the last bit of revenue.

swap contract: an agreement between two parties for the exchange of a series of cash flows, one representing a fixed rate and the other a floating rate. see also *interest rate swap.*

swap credits: standby credits established on a reciprocal basis from time to time among major central banks and the Bank for International Settlements enabling the central bank of a nation to settle a debit balance in its international account with another participating nation by using the latter nation's currency in place of having to resort to foreign or gold exchange.

swap fund: a fund into which many investors put their own investments and receive a share in the pooled investment portfolio. The purpose of this exchange of investments is to obtain a diversified portfolio without selling stock and paying capital gains taxes.

swap line: a mutual credit facility whereby a government buys a foreign currency from a foreign central bank, uses the foreign currency held by foreigners, and agrees to sell the foreign currency back to the foreign central bank at the end of three or six months. [105]

swap network: to finance U.S. interventions in the foreign exchange market, a series of short-term reciprocal credit lines between foreign banks under which the Federal Reserve System exchanges dollars for the currencies of other nations within the group, thereby allowing the Fed to buy dollars in the foreign exchange market. see *swap.*

sweat equity: equity created by the labor of a purchaser or borrower that increases the value of the property. [62]

sweating: to lower the metallic content of gold coins so that the coin can eventually be used and the gold dust can be recovered.

Swedish budget: a governmental budget which is balanced over a period of years rather than for each particular year.

sweep accounts: where banks automatically transfer checking account deposits into a money market fund once they exceed a certain, generally high threshold, and just as automatically transfers the money back into the checking account when the checking balance falls too low. synonymous with *overflow accounts.*

sweetening a loan: slang, to add more securities on deposit to margin a loan following the drop in security values so as to maintain the margin or to improve the condition of the margin.

SWIFT: see *Society for Worldwide Interbank Financial Telecommunications.*

swimming market: a healthy, active market.

swindle: slang, a deceptive business activity.

swindlers: unscrupulous people who distort facts and deal in worthless and doubtful securities.

swindle sheet: slang, an account ledger organized by a businessman itemizing expenses in order that he will be reimbursed by his company.

swindling: the selling of worthless shares through misrepresentation.

swing: the price movement of a security, either up or down.

swingers: financial managers with considerable business transactions.

swing loan: a loan extended to enable the borrower to purchase real estate where the proceeds of sale of another property will be used to repay the loan. synonymous with *bridge loan.* [105]

switch: the sale of an already existing long position and the simultaneous purchase of another position, or vice versa.

switching: selling one security and buying another. see *switch (contingent) order.*

switching and processing center (SPC): a facility that would link point-of-sale transaction terminals to depository and credit-granting institutions in order to accomplish instantaneous authorizations and funds transfers. [36]

switch (contingent) order: an order

for the purchase (sale) of one stock and the sale (purchase) of another stock at a stipulated price difference. [20]

syli: monetary unit of Guinea.

symbol

(1) *general:* the single capital letter or combination of letters acquired by a corporation when it is to be listed on an exchange: International Business Machines is IBM; American Telephone and Telegraph is T.

(2) *computers:* a representation of something by reason of relationship, association, or convention.

(3) *investments:* the letters used to identify traded securities on a ticker tape, exchange board, or newspaper listing.

symmetallism

(1) a monetary system where paper currency is redeemable in two or more metals which are paid in a fixed and proportionate combination.

(2) a standard coin combining two or more precious metals.

syndicate

(1) *general:* the association of two or more individuals, established to carry out a business activity. Members share in all profits or losses, in proportion to their contribution to the resources of the syndicate. cf. *joint venture, partnership.*

(2) *finance:* a group of investment bankers and securities dealers who, by agreement among themselves, have joined together for the purpose of distributing a new issue of securities for a corporation.

syndicate agreement: a document used for joining together members of an underwriting or loan syndicate.

syndicated loan: a loan in which a

number of banks around the world participate.

syndicate manager: synonymous with *managing underwriter.*

syndicate member: an investment banker, brokerage house, or bank which joins with others under the guidance of a syndicate manager in the underwriting and distribution of a security issue.

syndicate restrictions: contractual obligations placed on an underwriting group for a security relating to distribution; price limitations, and market transactions. see *syndicate termination.*

syndicate termination (release): the point when syndicate restrictions are terminated; occurs when a security involved in trading or expected to trade at or over its initial offering price. This does not necessarily apply in the Eurobond market.

synthetic fixed-rate loan: a concept for the financial community; for borrowers, these loans would provide the security of fixed interest costs, and for lenders, it would have all the advantages of floating rates.

system

(1) *computers:* a collection of operations and procedures by which an activity is carried on.

(2) *systems:* an assembly of methods, procedures, or techniques united by regulated interaction to form an organized whole. see *systems theory.*

systems analysis: the analysis of any business activity to determine precisely what must be accomplished and how to accomplish it. see *operations research.*

systems theory: an analysis that stresses the necessity for maintaining the basic elements of input-process-output and for adapting to the larger environment that sustains the organization.

T: see *testator.*

TA

(1)   see *tangible assets.*

(2)   see *tax abatement.*

tab: slang, an unpaid bill.

tables, annual investment accumulation: shows amounts to be invested yearly at a given rate of interest which will accumulate to $1000 in a given number of years. [12]

tables, discount: tables showing the present value of a unit of money due at the end of various periods of time, or the present value of one unit per period for various periods of time at various rates. [12]

tables, interest: see *interest table.*

tabular standard of value: a theoretical monetary standard in which a price index of representative commodities are used and the unit of value represented by a given quantity of each of the component commodities.

tabulating equipment: machines and equipment that use punched cards. synonymous with *electronic accounting machine.*

tacking: a process of adding a junior claim to a senior one in order to create some gain. Used in a mortgage, as when a third mortgage holder adds the first mortgage and tacks them to assume a superior position over the second mortgage holder. cf. *equal dignity.*

Taft-Hartley Act: the Labor-Management Relations Act of 1947, amending the Wagner-Connery Act of 1935. Major provisions are: (a) the closed shop is forbidden; (b) the government is authorized to seek an injunction preventing any work stoppage for 80 days when a strike threatens the nation's welfare and health; (c) unions cannot use union monies in connection with national elections (see also *Hatch Act*); (d) officers of unions must swear that they are not members of the Communist Party before the union can be certified (amended by the Landrum-Griffin Act); (e) unions must file financial reports with the U.S. Department of Labor along with a membership list; and (f) the states are permitted to pass right-to-work laws. Certain unfair labor practices are also identified.

643

T. Agt.: see *transfer agent.*

taha: monetary unit of Bangladesh.

tail

(1) in U.S. Treasury cash auctions, the difference between the average issuing price and the stop-out price.

(2) in the repurchase agreement market, when a dealer deliberately makes a reverse repurchase agreement for longer than the repurchase agreement in the hope that in the interim interest rates will drop. [90]

take

(1) *law:* to lay hold of, seize, or have in possession. see *seisin (seizin).*

(2) *slang:* any profit from a business activity, usually one of a suspicious nature.

take a bath: to have a substantial financial loss.

take a flier: purchasing securities without thought, planning, and/or advice, with the expectation of making a large profit. Of course, a significant loss may also occur.

take-and-pay contract: in project finance, a guarantee to purchase an agreed amount of a product or service, provided that it is delivered. cf. *take-or-pay contract.*

take a position: an expression for the actions of a principal or a dealer (sometimes a broker serving as a principal) in buying a block of a specific security as inventory in the expectation of resale at a profit.

take back: the recapture of shares or bonds, by the syndicate of a new issue, that have been allotted for the retention of the selling group or the underwriters.

take down: the number of shares or bonds alloted to underwriters or any allotment to members of a selling group of a new issue.

take-home pay: see *spendable earnings.*

take it: used by brokers on the floor of an exchange to show their willingness to purchase a specific security at a stipulated price.

take on a line: purchasing a significant quantity of stock of one or more corporations over a set time period, in anticipation of climbing prices. cf. *put out a line.*

take-or-pay contract: in project finance, an unconditional guarantee to purchase an agreed amount of a product or service whether or not it is delivered. cf. *take-and-pay contract.*

takeout loan: permanent loan on real property which takes out the interim, construction lender. [22]

takeover: the acquisition of an on-going organization by another through the purchase of the firm and/or exchange of capital stock. cf. *consolidation, merger.*

take profits: realizing a capital gain by selling a stock.

taker: a borrower.

take-up

(1) paying for stock, originally bought on margin, in cash.

(2) an underwriters' term showing that they will handle specific securities for direct sale.

tala: monetary unit of Samoa.

tale: contracts detailing payment of metallic monies, where there is a request *by tale,* that is, by count, as contrasted with payment based on weight.

talon

(1) *general:* a special coupon (e.g., a voucher stub).

(2) *finance:* that part of a debt instrument remaining on an unmatured bond after the interest coupons that

were formerly attached have been presented.

TAN: see *tax-anticipation note.*

tandem plan: a method of keeping home financing active by the purchase of mortgages by GNMA for resale to FNMA at a discount. [105]

tangible assets: physical and material (perceptible to touch) assets, as distinguished from intangible assets, which are imperceptible to touch. Examples of tangible assets are cash, land, and buildings.

tangible net worth
(1) ordinarily, the total capital accounts (owned capital) less miscellaneous assets (intangibles). synonymous with *total net worth.*
(2) the difference between a company's equity and the valuation of any intangible assets. [105]

tangible property: property in physical form. It can be touched, such as a house or land.

tap: slang, to ask a person or a lending organization for money.

tap CD: a certificate of deposit issued by a bank on an as-required basis with a minimum denomination of $25,000 and for a minimum of one month in dollars.

tape
(1) the narrow tape or slip of paper or plastic carrying quotations of prices of securities or commodities; represents the telegraphed quotations from an exchange floor.
(2) the broad tape or wider slip of paper that Dow Jones uses to release news on the economy to subscribing brokers.

tape price: the last sale of a stock as shown on the ticker tape.

tape reading: using only the price, vol-ume, activity, and other factors indicated on the ticker tape to project the price movement of securities.

tape-to-tape merchants: merchants who record their draft information onto magnetic computerized tapes for processing. The sales drafts are retained at the individual merchant outlets. [105]

tap out: slang, to lose one's money.

target company: a firm selected by another company as being attractive for takeover or acquisition.

tariff
(1) *finance:* any list of prices, charges, duties, and so on.
(2) *government:* a schedule of taxes on items imported or exported. In the United States the imposition of tariffs is made on imported goods only.

tariff for revenue only: a system of tariff duties intended to protect domestic industry but only to yield revenue for the government.

tariff union: see *customs union.*

tariff war: a form of competition between nations as shown by tariff discrimination of various forms. see *retaliatory duty.*

taux d'intérêt: French for *interest rate.*

taw: slang, sufficient funds to fully finance a business venture.

tax: a charge levied by government against the income of an individual, corporation, or other profit-making center of activity.

tax abatement: a decrease or rebate of a tax or burden improperly made. At times a tax abatement may reflect only an acknowledgment of a changed situation.

taxable distribution: in general, any distribution that is reported as taxable income to the recipient. As it relates to a generation-skipping trust, any distribution that is not out of income to a beneficiary in a generation younger than the settler's and whose generation is younger than that of any other younger-generation beneficiary. [105]

taxable equivalent yield: the yield on a bond producing taxable income which would be required to match the yield on a tax-exempt bond.

taxable estate: as defined by a state, the gross estate of a citizen or resident less allowable administrative and funeral expenses; indebtedness; taxes; losses; transfer for public, charitable, and religious uses; transfer to a surviving spouse; and a specific exemption. see *marital deduction.*

taxable gifts: property transferred by giver to the extent that its value exceeds allowable exemptions, exclusions, and deductions. [105]

taxable income: the amount of income remaining after all permitted deductions and exemptions have been subtracted; thus the income that is subject to taxation.

taxable value: an assessed value utilized for taxing property, items, or income.

tax act of 1981: see *Economic Recovery Tax Act of 1981.*

Tax Adjustment Act of 1966: federal legislation; restored excise tax rates on transportation equipment and telephone service to rates in effect prior to January 1966. Introduced graduated withholding on personal tax collections.

tax anticipation note (TAN): any short-term, interest-bearing obligation created to be bought by businesses with monies assembled as a reserve in order to pay taxes. These notes are sold by government agencies to increase revenue.

tax anticipation warrant: see *tax anticipation note.*

tax avoidance: taking advantage of deductions and other provisions of tax law to reduce one's taxes. see *tax shelter;* cf. *tax dodge.*

tax base: the commodity, income, or service on which a tax is levied; the part of the value of an item that can be taxed.

tax-based income policy (TIP): a surcharge placed on the corporate income of a firm's tax if it grants its employees wage increases in excess of some government-set standard. Likewise, by holding their average wage increases below the standard, companies become eligible for a government tax reduction.

tax capitalization: to the extent that a tax is not shifted, it can be capitalized at an assumed rate of interest by dividing the tax (or change in tax) by the rate of interest and subtracting this amount from the value of the asset before the tax change. Most commonly done with the property tax.

tax carryback and carryover: a provision which is often in American corporation income and excess profits taxes to the effect that losses (or in the case of an excess profits tax, unused credits) can be carried over to apply against a preceding or following year's income. The effect is to level income over the years for tax purposes.

tax certificate: a certificate issued by a governmental unit as evidence of the conditional transfer of title to tax delinquent property from the original owner to the holder of the certificate. If the owner does not pay the amount of the tax arrearage and other charges required by law during the specified period of redemption, the holder can foreclose to obtain title. Also called, in some jurisdictions, *tax lien certificate*, or *tax sale certificate*. see also *tax deed*. [49]

tax cost: the figure used as the starting point under which gain or loss on a sale or exchange of property is determined. In the usual case, this gain or loss is simply the difference between the amount that a taxpayer paid for property (adjusted for depreciation) and the amount received when the taxpayer sells it. [37]

Tax Court of the United States: a special federal court that hears appeals from the decisions of the Bureau of Internal Revenue about almost all federal taxes (except tariffs). Formerly called the U.S. Board of Tax Appeals. Appeals from this court go to the U.S. Court of Appeals.

tax credit: a 100 percent offset against tax liability; a deduction provides a tax benefit equal only to the individual's tax rate times the deducted amount.

tax deed: a deed issued to the buyer of property that is sold because of nonpayment of taxes.

tax dodge: an activity (e.g., moving out of the country) that constitutes an illegal attempt to avoid paying taxes. see *tax exile (expatriate)*.

tax effect: the result in output change caused by the tax change. cf. *tax shifting*.

Tax Equity and Fiscal Responsibility Act of 1982 (TEFRA): federal legislation designed (a) to raise revenues to narrow anticipated budget deficits; (b) to ensure that both individual and business taxpayers pay their fair share of the total tax burden; (c) to reduce distortions in economic behavior resulting from the present tax system; and (d) to charge groups benefiting from specific government programs with the costs of those programs. Aside from the fundamental objective of increasing government revenues, TEFRA is intended to curtail perceived abuses and unintended benefits in the present tax system, assure better compliance with existing tax laws, and impose increase excise taxes on selected products and services.

tax equivalent: the payment by a municipally (or federally) owned utility made to other units of government in lieu of taxes because of tax exemptions of the governmentally owned utility.

tax evasion: unlawful attempts to avoid payment of a tax (e.g., not properly reporting all earned income).

tax-exempt bond: see *bond, tax-exempt*.

tax-exempt securities: the interest on securities of the federal government is immune from state and local government taxation, and the interest on the securities of state and local governments is exempt from federal taxation. This immunity does not extend as between states or between the states and local governments.

tax exemption: a right, secured by law, permitting freedom from a charge of taxes (e.g., on income that constitutes primary support of a child).

tax exile (expatriate): an individual choosing to leave his country rather than pay taxes.

tax foreclosure: the taking of property because of unpaid taxes.

tax-free rollover: provision whereby

an individual receiving a lump-sum distribution from a qualified pension or profit sharing plan can preserve the tax-deferred status of these funds by a "rollover" into an IRA or another qualified plan if rolled over within 60 days of receipt. [105]

tax haven: a nation offering low tax rates and other incentives for corporations of other countries. see *flight of capital.*

tax incidence: the business and/or persons on whom a tax finally comes to rest. see *nexus.*

tax lease: a long-term lease issued to the buyer of tax-delinquent property when the law prevents an outright sale.

tax lien: a lien by the government against real property for unpaid taxes. see also *tax certificate.*

tax lien certificate: synonymous with *tax certificate.*

tax liens receivable: legal claims against property which have been exercised because of nonpayment of delinquent taxes, interest, and penalties. The account includes delinquent taxes, interest, and penalties receivable up to the date the lien becomes effective and the cost of holding the sale. [49]

tax limit: a legislative decision that limits the tax ceiling that can be imposed by an appropriate authority.

tax loophole: an obvious discrimination or exemption from tax.

tax-managed funds: where income from stocks in a fund's portfolio is constantly reinvested. The portfolio manager's only goal is to increase the fund's net asset value per share. Because there are no distributions to shareholders, the investor in a tax-managed fund does not pay any current taxes.

tax note: see *tax anticipation note.*

tax offset: a form of tax cancellation or exemption. A tax is levied, but it is remitted in whole or in part usually on the basis of another tax paid.

tax on net investment income: an excise tax of 4 percent imposed on the net investment income of all tax-exempt private foundations, including operating foundations, for each taxable year beginning after December 31, 1969. Net investment income is the amount by which the sum of gross investment income and the net capital gain exceeds certain allowable deductions. [105]

taxpayer
(1) *general:* a small building or store.
(2) *finance:* an owner of property who pays taxes.
(3) *government:* any person who payes taxes.

tax penalty: forfeiture of a sum because of nonpayment of taxes. [62]

tax policy: the policy whereby a government structures the tax rates. see entries under *tax.*

tax preference item: specified items that provide special tax allowances. In some cases, these items precipitate an increased tax liability under the alternative minimum tax.

tax pyramiding: the situation in which a tax imposed on one is added to his or her cost and the customary markup is applied to this total. Thus a markup is taken on the tax.

tax rate: the amount of tax applied per unit of tax base, expressed as a percentage; a tax of $5 on a base of $100, for example, represents a tax rate of 5 percent.

tax rate limit: the maximum rate at

which a governmental unit may levy a tax. The limit may apply to taxes raised for a particular purpose, or to taxes imposed for all purposes, and may apply to a single government, to a class of governments, or to all governmental units operating in a particular area. Overall tax rate limits usually restrict levies for all purposes and of all governments, state and local, having jurisdiction in a given area. [49]

tax receivership: the office or function of a receiver appointed by a court or under a statute upon default of taxes. [62]

Tax Reduction Act of 1975: federal legislation; provided for 10 percent rebate on 1974 taxes up to maximum of $200 for individuals. Provided tax cuts retroactive to January 1975 for both individuals and corporations. For individuals it was in the form of increased standard deductions, a $30 exemption credit, and an earned income credit for low-income families. Reduced corporate income tax and increased investment surtax exemption. Increased investment tax credit to 10 percent.

Tax Reduction and Simplification Act of 1977: legislation signed by President Carter for a $34 billion tax cut, giving credit to industry to create jobs and attempting to simplify tax-filing procedures.

Tax Reform Act of 1969: federal legislation removing major benefits from controlled corporations. Multiple surtax exemptions and multiple accumulated earnings credits were withdrawn by 1975, and the incentives for establishing additional corporations within a controlled group ceased at the end of 1974. The law provided for the accumulation of capital losses to the three preceding years prior to the loss of revenue for a corporation, with no change in the future five-year advance provision for capital losses. Restrictions are given on employee benefit plans. see *Tax Reform Act of 1976, Tax Reform Act of 1984.*

Tax Reform Act of 1976: federal legislation affecting income, estate, and gift taxes. The holding period to qualify for long-term capital gains was increased from 6 to 12 months. Also placed new restrictions on tax shelters. see also *Tax Reform Act of 1969, Tax Reform Act of 1984.*

Tax Reform Act of 1984: federal legislation enacted by Congress as part of the Deficit Reduction Act of 1984 to reduce the federal budget deficit without resorting to repeal of across-the-board cuts in marginal tax rates adopted in the Economic Recovery Tax Act of 1981. Two major features of the Act are: (a) shortened the minimum holding period for assets to qualify for long-term capital gains treatment from one year to six months, but only for assets acquired after June 22, 1984; (b) permitted contributions to be made to an Individual Retirement Account no later than April 15 after the tax year for which an IRA benefit is sought. see also *Economic Recovery Tax Act of 1981, Tax Reform Act of 1976, Tax Reform Act of 1969.*

tax roll: an official statement describing property taxed, including the names of the taxpayers and the amount of their tax.

tax sale: sale of property in default because of nonpayment of taxes. see *scavenger sale. see tax certificate.*

tax sale certificate: synonymous with *tax certificate.*

tax-saving retirement plan: see *Keogh plan*.

tax search: a determination by searching official records to determine whether there are any unpaid property taxes.

tax selling: reducing or offsetting the tax liability on capital gains by selling off stocks that show a loss. It is sometimes done to realize profits.

tax service contract: an agreement between a title company and an association under which the title company is responsible for notifying the lender of all tax and improvement lien payments as they come due. [59]

tax sharing: see *revenue sharing, shared revenue*.

tax shelter: a means of legal avoidance of paying a portion of one's income taxes by careful interpretation of tax regulations and adjustment of one's finances to take advantage of IRS rulings. The Tax Reform Act of 1976 placed new restrictions on tax shelters.

tax shield: the amount of depreciation charged against income, thus protecting that amount from tax; a depreciation deduction of $10,000 produces a tax shield of $3600 when the tax rate is 36 percent.

tax shifting: the process of passing the tax from the one who pays the tax to a person forward such as to the one who buys or uses the taxed article or service (e.g., adding the gasoline tax to the price of the gasoline or the admissions tax to the price of admissions). A tax may also be shifted backward to the producer of the taxed good in the form of a lower revenue after taxes for the product or service purchased. cf. *tax effect*.

tax swap: see *swap, swap fund, tax shifting*.

tax title: title to property acquired by purchasing land that was sold as the result of unpaid taxes.

tax waiver: a written consent of the state tax department permitting the withdrawal of property belonging to the estate of a decedent by the executor or administrator, in order to permit the assembling of assets and to permit distribution. [37]

Taylorism: the work of Frederick W. Taylor (1856–1915), who outlined the concepts of scientific management and work efficiency.

T bill: see *Treasury bill*.

T bond: see *bond, treasury*.

TC
(1) see *tax certificate*.
(2) see *time certificates of deposit*.

TD
(1) see *time deposit (open account)*.
(2) *Department of the Treasury, U.S.*
(3) time and savings deposits of depository institutions. [81]

TDOA: see *time deposit (open account)*.

T&E: see *travel and entertainment credit card*.

Technical Corrections Act of 1979: passed in April 1980, created a possible refund opportunity for holders of "section 1244" stock.

technical decline (drop): the fall in price of a security or commodity resulting from market conditions and not attributed to external forces of supply and demand.

technical divergence: part of the Dow theory, an existing condition when one of the market averages fails to follow, or confirm to, the action of the other.

technical market action: the market's

overall price performance affected by technical factors, such as volume, short interest, odd-lot transactions, and the movement of individual stocks.

technical position: applied to the various internal factors affecting the market; opposed to external forces, such as earnings, dividends, and general economic conditions. Some internal factors are the size of the short-term interest, whether the market has had a sustained advance or decline without interruption, and the amount of credit in use in the market.

technical rally: the increase in the price of a security or commodity resulting from conditions within the market itself and not attributed to external supply and demand forces.

technical research: analysis of the market and stocks based on supply and demand. The technician studies price movements, volume, and trends and patterns which are revealed by charting these factors and attempts to assess the possible effect of current market action on future supply and demand for securities and individual issues. see *fundamental research.* [20]

technician: synonymous with *chartist.*

Tee.: see *trustee.*

TEFRA: see *Tax Equity and Fiscal Responsibility Act of 1982.*

telegraphic transfer (T/T): the use of cable or telegraph to remit funds. Physical money does not move, but instead the order is wired to the cashier of a firm to make payment to an identified person or firm.

telephone bill paying: a service that permits a customer to pay a bill(s) without writing a check. The customer gives authorization to debit his or her checking account for a specific bill pay-

ment amount. The bank extracts these paperless entries for its own customers by debiting their account. At the same time the offsetting credit may be sent through the ACH, as an originating entry, to the merchant/retailer depositing bank. The ACH processes the entries and makes settlement between the originating and receiving banks. The receiving bank posts the entries and reflects them on periodic statements to the merchant/retailer. [105]

telephone order (TO): a direction received by a merchant, by telephone from a cardholder, wishing to charge the purchase amount to his or her bank card account without executing the resulting sales draft. [105]

teller: an employee of a bank who is assigned the duty of waiting on depositors and customers of the bank. The teller's principal responsibility is to handle cash for the depositor and the bank and to serve the depositor or the customer as far as his or her duties will permit. The teller is the "personal" contact between the customer and the bank. see also *head teller, loan teller, paying teller, receiving teller.* [10]

teller proof: a system of individual teller control whereby the teller balances and settles his own cash position daily. If the teller is using a bank teller's machine, this proof is very simple, because the machine will carry totals for cash received and cash paid out. Otherwise, the teller will maintain his own cash settlement sheet, listing all cash taken in and all checks cashed. Teller proof consists of using the teller's starting cash total, adding his cash received, and subtracting his cash paid out, to arrive at his cash on hand. The cash counted must agree with this cash ending total for proof. [10]

teller's check: a check drawn by a bank on another (drawee) bank and signed by a teller or tellers of the drawer bank. Tellers' checks are used in payment of withdrawal orders and, in lieu of savings bank money orders, are sometimes sold to depositors in exchange for cash. [39]

teller's stamp: a rubber stamp, usually showing the teller's number or initials and the bank's name or transit number, which the teller uses to identify deposits, cashed checks, or other posting media that he or she handles. [10]

teller terminal: an input-output unit of a computer system that replaces the teller's window posting machine in a computerized association. [59]

temporal distribution: synonymous with *time series*.

temporary administrator: an individual or a trust institution appointed by a court to take over and safeguard an estate during a suit over an alleged will, or over the right of appointment of an executor or administrator, or during the period that probate is delayed for any reason, such as difficulty in finding or citing missing heirs. [32]

temporary admission: admitting goods to a nation for eventual export; no customs duty is paid on such items and hence no drawback is claimed. see *drawback*.

temporary bond: see *bond, temporary*.

temporary certificate: see *temporary receipt*.

temporary loans: short-term obligations representing amounts borrowed for short periods of time and usually evidenced by notes payable or warrants payable. They may be unsecured, or secured by specific revenues to be collected. see *tax anticipation note*. [49]

temporary receipt: the printed or lithographed acknowledgment used until the engraved certificate is ready to be released and which is then exchanged for the definitive security by the holder of the temporary receipt. cf. *permanent certificate*.

tenancy: the holding of real property by any form of title. [37]

tenancy at sufferance: a tenancy in which the tenant comes into possession of real property under a lawful title or interest and continues to hold the property even after his title or interest has terminated. [37]

tenancy at will: that estate which may be terminated by either the lessor or the lessee at any time. [62]

tenancy by the entirety: tenancy by a husband and wife in such a manner that, except in concert with the other, neither husband nor wife has a disposable interest in the property during the lifetime of the other. Upon the death of either, the property goes to the survivor. To be distinguished from *joint tenancy* and *tenancy in common*. [37]

tenancy for years: a tenancy for a definite period of time—for example, a year or 99 years. It cannot be terminated by either party alone except at the expiration of the time agreed upon. [32]

tenancy in common: ownership of property by two or more persons, each holding a separate interest. No right of survivorship exists. see *undivided right*.

tenancy in common account
(1) a savings account that is owned

by two or more persons, each of whom has a separate interest; when one owner dies, his or her shares passes to his or her heirs, not to the remaining owner(s). [59]

(2) a type of checking account, often requiring that both parties sign checks, notes, and so on; in other words, one individual cannot act independently of the other.

(3) stock certificates that are issued to "tenants in common."

tenant: one who holds or possesses real property. [37]

tenant in dower: a wife who has survived her husband and in most states receives one-third of his inherited estate for the remainder of her life.

tendency: the inclination for a stock or market average to shift in a specific direction, either up, down, or sideways over a period of time.

tender

(1) *investments:* a corporation's offer of securities by asking for bids for them, at prices above a minimum.

(2) *law:* the offering of money in satisfaction of a debt by producing the money and stating to the creditor a desire to pay.

tenderable: a commodity fulfilling the standard of quality set by the commodity exchange or exchanges as well as the requirements as to time and place of delivery.

tender offer

(1) a bid by an outsider to purchase some or all of a firm's outstanding shares, usually for the purpose of obtaining effective control.

(2) an offer by a company to purchase its own shares or other types of securities such as bonds or debentures. [43]

ten-forty: a U.S. bond that is redeemable after 10 years, and due and payable after 40 years.

10-K report: a version of an annual report that all U.S. corporations must file with the Securities and Exchange Commission. Since 1974, it has also been required that this report, which generally contains more information than the annual report to stockholders, be made available to any interested stockholders. [105]

1099: the Internal Revenue Service form for reporting the payment of interest, dividends, and miscellaneous fees to individuals.

tenor: the period between the formation of a debt and the date of expected payment.

ten-spot: slang, a $10 bill.

ten-year trust: see *Clifford trust.*

term bond: see *bond, term.*

term bonds payable: a liability account which records the face value of general obligation term bonds issued and outstanding. [49]

terme sec: French term meaning *outright transaction* in forward foreign exchange.

terminable bond: see *bond, terminable.*

terminable interest: an interest that will terminate or fail on the lapse of time, on the occurrence of a contingency, or on the failure to occur of a contingency. [105]

terminal: a device connected to a computer system, used for the input and/or output of data. Technically, a terminal may be as simple as a telephone; as complex as a small computer. [36]

terminal bond: see *bond, terminal.*

terminal market: a market (i.e., a commodity market) that deals in futures.

terminal reserve: the reserve of an insurance policy at the end of the policy year.

termination of offer: an offer can be ended by acceptance, counteroffer, expiration of time, insanity, or death of the offeror or offeree, refusal to accept, or revocation of the offer.

term issue: a bond issue maturing as a whole in a single future year.

term life insurance: life insurance protection during a certain number of years, but usually expiring without policy cash value if the insured survives the stated period. see *extended term insurance, family income rider.*

term loan: usually a long-term loan running up to 10 years. Such loans are generally made by the larger commercial banks and insurance companies to large, well-established business enterprises for capital expenditures such as plant improvements and purchases of equipment.

term mortgage: a mortgage with a fixed time period, usually less than five years, in which only interest is paid. Following termination of the mortgage, the total principal is demanded.

term plan: a life insurance policy where the company agrees to pay a stipulated sum of money upon the death of the insured if death occurs within the term fixed by the policy, usually 5 or 10 years.

term rider: term life insurance added to a "whole life" policy when purchased or at a later date.

terms: the details, specifications, and conditions of a loan.

terms of trade: the relations of export and import prices. Terms of trade become most favorable if the prices of imported goods fall in relation to prices of exported goods.

territorial bond: see *bond, insular.*

tertiary movement: insignificant daily shifts in price caused by trifling developments; part of Dow theory.

testament: the declaration of an individual's intentions for the disposition he or she wishes to be made of property following death. synonymous with *will.*

testamentary account: a category of savings accounts recognized by the Federal Savings and Loan Insurance Corporation as separately insurable, and including funds owned by an individual and invested in a revocable trust account, tentative or Totten trust account, payable-on-death account, or similar account evidencing an intention that on his or her death the funds shall belong to a specified member of the owner's family. see *Totten trust.* [59]

testamentary disposition: the disposition of property by deed, will, or otherwise in such a manner that it shall not take effect unless or until the grantor dies. [37]

testamentary guardian: a guardian of a minor or an incompetent person named in the decedent's will. [37]

testamentary trust: see *trust under will.*

testate: having completed and left an acceptable will.

testator: a deceased male who left a will setting forth the disposition of his wealth (total assets).

testatrix: a deceased female who left a will setting forth the disposition of her wealth (total assets).

test period: see *dry run.*

THA: see *Taft-Hartley Act.*

theory of rational expectations:

based on the premise that market participants construct forecast of the future in a manner that fully reflects the relevant information available to them. Because wealth-maximizing individuals will not make forecasts that are continually wrong in the same direction, the rational expectations approach suggests that forecasts of economic phenomena should be unbiased. [100]

thin corporation: a corporation owing a large number of debts relative to its equity position.

thin margin: a condition where the owner of an item, such as a security, commodity, or other property, has a very small equity. Consequently, any small drop in the price or value of the item will result in a condition in which the debtor owes more than the value of the collateral put up for the loan.

thin market: a market in which there are comparatively few bids to buy or offers to sell or both. The phrase may apply to a single security or to the entire stock market. In a thin market, price fluctuations between transactions are usually larger than they are when the market is liquid. A thin market in a particular stock may reflect lack of interest or a lack of demand for stock.

third-generation computer: a computer utilizing tiny circuits and components to replace vacuum tubes, increase accuracy, and speed up the processing of work.

third market: listed stocks not traded on a securities exchange; over-the counter trading in listed securities.

third mortgage: a mortgage that is junior to both the first and second mortgages.

third-party check: a check which is given by one party to another, the recipient of which offers it to still another (third) party. [55]

third-party credit transfers: automatic deposits, or credits, to a checking, savings, or NOW account from a third party. Examples include payroll credits, Social Security payments or other federal recurring retirement benefits. cf. *third-party debit transfers.* see *electronic fund transfers.*

third-party debit transfers: automatic withdrawals, or debits, from a checking, savings or NOW account and payable to a third party (e.g., periodic deductions for insurance premium payments). cf. *third-party credit transfers.* see *electronic fund transfers.*

third-party payment service: a payment plan whereby a financial institution transfers a depositor's funds to a third party or to the account of the third party upon the negotiable or nonnegotiable order of the depositor. A checking account is one type of third-party payment service. [59]

third-party transaction: a three-way business activity involving a buyer, a seller, and a source of consumer credit.

third-party transfer: a nonnegotiable order to a savings association, issued by an account holder, to pay a specified sum of money to a third party. [59]

thirty days after date: an amount due for payment on a time draft 30 days following the date of the draft.

this transaction only: synonymous with *accommodation charge.*

thou: slang, $1000.

Threadneedle Street: the financial area of London.

threat monitoring: the analysis, assessment, and review of audit trails and other data collected for searching out system events which may constitute security violations. [105]

360-day year—365-day year: the base used for calculations of daily interest to be paid on certain interest-bearing accounts. The difference in income as computed by the two methods will be material when large sums of money are involved. [105]

three-party paper: sales contracts purchased from retail merchants by banks and other lenders. [105]

threshold companies: companies on the threshold of corporate maturity in that they are not yet managed by professionals but are run intuitively by a handful of entrepreneurs. This concept was developed by Donald Clifford, Jr.

thrift account: synonymous with *savings account* or *special interest account.* see *savings account, special interest account, thrifts.*

thrift institution: the general term for mutual savings banks, savings and loan associations, and credit unions. see *thrifts.* [1]

thrifts: there are two types of thrifts, the savings banks and savings and loan industries. Today they are both engaged in basically the same business—taking in consumer deposits and reinvesting them in mortgages. Together they hold almost $800 billion (1981) in assets, more than any financial industry except commercial banks, whose assets amount to $1.5 trillion (1981). Savings banks, which theoretically are owned by their depositors, were established by philanthropists to promote savings among the poor. The founders gave ultimate power to self-perpetuating boards of trustees. Thus, unlike depositors in S&Ls, savings bank depositors do not have the right to elect their trustees. Several savings banks are trying to convert to federal from state charters. Under federal rules, their depositors would gain voting rights within their respective organizations. Savings and loans originally were formed by community members to finance housing, not to promote savings. Initially, they existed for limited periods, long enough for each member to buy a home. The members chipped in to raise enough money to finance home construction. Lots were drawn to determine which member would be the first to get a house. The modern version of the savings and loan association got its start in the early 1930s. The industry boomed after World War II, when 11 million returning veterans needed housing.

through bill of lading: a bill of lading covering items moving from the origin point to a final location, even if they are moved from one carrier to another.

through the market: a situation when a new bond offering has come to market and the yield to maturity is lower than comparable bonds outstanding.

throwback rule: distribution by a trust (with some exceptions) of previously accumulated income are taxed in theoretically the same way as the distributions would have been taxed if made when the income was earned by the trust (i.e., "thrown back" to the year earned). [105]

TI: see *taxable income.*

ticker: the instrument that prints prices and volume of security transactions in cities and towns throughout the United States and Canada within minutes of each trade on any listed exchange.

ticker symbol: stock abbreviations listed on an exchange.

tickler: an index for maturity dates of notes, bonds, acceptances, and so on, serving as a reminder to banks and financial institutions that these instruments will at some future time period be approaching maturity.

tied-in sale: see *tie-in sale*.

tied loan: a foreign loan limiting the borrower to spending the proceeds only in the nation making the loan. cf. *counterpart monies.*

tie-in sale: a sale made with a stipulation that some article other than the one bought must also be purchased. see also *tying contract.*

tight credit: synonymous with *tight money.*

tight money: high interest rates demanded in the borrowing of money. synonymous with *tight credit.*

tight money market: a condition when the supply of money is less than the demand for it, with a resulting tendency for a firming of interest rates. see also *easy money.*

till money: funds kept at a front desk or register, as distinguished from monies held in a bank.

time adjusted rate of return: the rate of interest at which the existing value of anticipated cash inflows from a particular project equals the present value of expected cash outflow of the same activity.

time-and-a-half pay: compensation at the rate of one and one-half times the worker's regular pay. The Fair Labor Standards Act of 1938 made this rate mandatory for work performed beyond 40 hours a week by workers employed by firms engaged in interstate commerce.

time bargain: struck when a seller and a purchaser of securities consent to exchange a specific stock at a stated price at a stated future time.

time bill: a bill of exchange having a fixed or determinable date of payment. cf. *demand bill, sight bill of exchange.*

time certificates of deposit: a time deposit evidenced by a negotiable or nonnegotiable instrument specifying an amount and a maturity. Savings bonds and savings certificates are merely forms of nonnegotiable time certificates of deposits. [69]

time deposit: a deposit from which a customer has the right to withdraw funds at a specified date 30 or more days following the date of deposit, or from which, if the bank requires, the customer can withdraw funds only by giving the bank written notice 30 days or more in advance of the planned withdrawal.

time deposit (open account) (TDOA) (golden passbook): funds deposited under agreement. They bear interest from the date of deposit, although the agreement usually requires that such funds remain on deposit for at least 30 days. The agreement stipulates a fixed maturity date or number of days after which payment will be made, or it is stipulated that payment will be made after a given period following notice by the depositor of intention to withdraw. see *Regulation Q.*

time draft: a draft payable a specified number of days (30, 60, or 90 days, for example) after its date of issuance or acceptance. [10]

time loan: a loan made for a specified period. The maturity date generally is 30, 60, 90, or 120 days after the date of the loan. Interest is usually collected in advance, at the time the loan is made, as a *discount*.

time lock: a device on safes and vaults preventing the safe door from opening until a certain time has passed.

time money: funds loaned out for a specified time period.

time of the note: the number of days or months from date of issue to date of maturity.

time open accounts: a time deposit evidenced by a written contract specifying a maturity but leaving open the amount involved. [69]

time order: an order that becomes a market or limited price order at a specified time. [20]

time plan loans: a type of loan in which interest and payment are made in fixed regular amounts at monthly intervals. [105]

time policy: an insurance policy valid for a specified time period.

time preference theory of interest: an explanation of interest as the price people are willing to pay for immediate possession of goods as opposed to future possession.

time sale financing: a form of indirect loan. This is an arrangement where a lender (usually a bank) purchases a loan contract from a retailer. The contract is an installment loan agreement between the retailer and the purchaser of a good. The borrower makes payment to the bank or other indirect creditor. [105]

time series: statistical data arranged according to periods of time, usually months or years. synonymous with *temporal distribution*.

time-sharing: a method of using a computing system that allows a number of users to execute programs on the same hardware and to interact with the programs during execution.

times interest and preferred dividend earned: a common measure of the "earnings protection" which a preferred stock has. The figure is computed by dividing the net earnings per year (after taxes) by the sum of the interest and preferred dividend requirements.

times interest earned: a common measure of the "earnings protection" of a bond. The figure is computed by dividing the net earnings per year (without deducting the interest of the specific issues but after taxes) by the interest requirements of the specific issue for that year.

times preferred dividend earned: a common measure of "earnings protection" of a preferred stock. The figure is computed by dividing the net earnings per year (after taxes, interest, and any prior dividends) by the preferred dividend requirements of that issue for that year.

time warrant: a negotiable obligation of a governmental unit having a term shorter than bonds and frequently tendered to individuals and firms in exchange for contractual services, capital acquisitions, or equipment purchases. [49]

time warrants payable: the amount of time warrants outstanding and unpaid. [49]

timing: the skill in choosing the proper time to purchase or sell securities. Good timing results in selling before a decline and buying prior to an advance.

timing of notes: the function of calculating and marking the maturity date on notes and other evidences of debt. Also the number of days that a loan must run until maturity for interest calculations. [10]

TIP: see *tax-based income policy.*

tips

(1) *finance:* monies offered to encourage or ensure promptness; monies given for services rendered (e.g., 15 percent of a restaurant bill constitutes the waiter's tip).

(2) *investments:* supposedly *inside information* on corporation affairs; a subjective recommendation to buy or sell a particular stock.

tipster: people who say that they have inside information on where you should invest your money.

tipster sheet: an unofficial list of stocks that are recommended to customers.

title: proper and rightful ownership.

title company: see *title guaranty company.*

title deed: a legal document indicating proof of an individual's ownership of a piece of land.

title defect: a fact or circumstance that challenges property ownership. see *cloud on title.*

title exception: a specified item appearing in a title policy against which the title company does not insure. [105]

title guaranty company: a business firm created to examine real estate files (i.e., to conduct title searches) to determine the legal status of the property and to find any evidence of encumbrances, faults, or other title defects. Once a search has been completed and the property found sound, the company receives a fee from the property purchaser who needed to determine that his or her title was clear and good. The property purchaser receives an abstract of the prepared title, and the title is verified by an attorney of the

company who gives an opinion but does not guarantee the accuracy of the title. The company agrees to indemnify the owner against any loss that may be experienced resulting from a subsequent defect. A title guaranty policy is evidence of the title insurance, with costs based on the value of the property and the risk involved as determined by the condition of the title. see also *title insurance.*

title guaranty policy: title insurance furnished by the owner, provided as an alternative for an abstract of title. synonymous with *Torrens certificate.* see also *title guaranty company.* [62]

title insurance: an insurance contract from a title guaranty company presented to owners of property, indemnifying them against having a defective or unsalable title while they possess the property. This contract is considered to be a true indemnity for loss actually sustained by reason of the defects or encumbrances against which the insurer agrees to indemnify. Title insurance includes a thorough examination of the evidences of title by the insurer. see *title guaranty company.*

title insurance company: see *title guaranty company.*

title 1: the section of the FHA Insurance Program for home improvements and mobile homes. [105]

title report: the report issued by the title company prior to settlement of a real estate purchase. The report provides a legal description of the property and lists all restrictions and liens against the property.

title search: see *search, title guaranty company, title insurance.*

title theory: a system in which the

mortgagee has legal title to the mortgaged property and the mortgagor has equitable title. [62]

Title VII: see *Civil Rights Act of 1964, Title VII.*

TL

(1) see *time loan.*

(2) see *trading limit.*

TLI: see *term life insurance.*

TM: see *third market.*

TMS: see *Transmatic Money Service.*

TN: see *transferable notice.*

T note: see *Treasury note.*

To.: see *turnover.*

TO

(1) see *telephone order.*

(2) see *Treasury obligations.*

to arrive: the portion of a sales contract defining how the price of a commodity is computed following its reaching a stated destination.

to arrive price: in foreign trade, the price quoted by a seller for goods already in transit.

to come–to go: the exact number of shares in a transaction which are to be sold but still remain (to go); or the number in a buying transaction which are yet to be purchased (to come).

to credit: in the context of a payment order, this is an instruction to credit an account on the books of the paying bank, as distinct from actually paying or remitting. [105]

to debit: an instruction to charge an account on the books of a bank. [105]

token coin: see *token money.*

token money: an object, usually coins, whose value as money is greater than the market value of the materials of which it is composed.

Tokyo Round: international trade negotiations begun in Tokyo in 1973. see *Dillon Round, Kennedy Round.*

tombstone: an advertisement placed by an underwriting syndicate outlining a public sale. A listing of the syndicate members is given.

tom/next: from tomorrow to the next business day.

tonnage

(1) in a ship, the cubical contents expressed in units of 100 cubic feet.

(2) a tax on ships, based on their capacity.

tontine: any scheme in which payments are made by a large number of persons with eventual distribution to those who survive after a time interval.

took a bath: see *take a bath.*

top credit: ready credit.

topheavy: the condition of a price series such as one of securities or commodities in which the series, while being high compared with some other period, is considered to be vulnerable for a reaction downward.

topheavy market: technical conditions showing that the market appears too high and is likely to fall.

topping out: employed to denote loss of upside energy at the top after a long price run-up.

toppy: slang, topheaviness in a market, or stock, indicating a possible decline.

Torrens certificate: a document, issued by the proper public authority called a *registrar* acting under the provision of the Torrens law, indicating in whom title resides. [62]

tort: a wrongful act committed by a person against another person or his or her property.

tortfeasor: a person committing a tort.

total assets: all money, machinery, other equipment, real estate, and credits owned by a business.

total asset turnover: the ratio obtained by dividing total assets into sales but more correctly, dividing total operating assets into sales since funds devoted to outside investments do not affect sales but produce an independent income.

total cost: the sum of a firm's total fixed costs and total variable costs.

total debt: all long-term obligations of the government and its agencies and all interest-bearing short-term credit obligations. Long-term obligations are those repayable more than one year after issue.

total debt to tangible net worth: obtained by dividing total current plus long-term debts by tangible net worth. When this relationship exceeds 100 percent, the equity of creditors in the assets of the business exceeds that of owners. [4]

total fixed costs: the costs that do not change with an organization's output (e.g., payments on rent, property taxes).

total net worth: synonymous with *tangible net worth*.

total of payments: the total of all installments scheduled to be made in the repayment of a loan or sales contract; face of note; the sum of the amount financed and the finance charges. [55]

total reserves: member bank deposits with Federal Reserve Banks plus member bank vault cash. The sum of required and excess reserves. [72]

total revenue: total receipts of a company. It is equal to the price per unit times the number of units sold.

total variable costs: costs that change directly with the firm's output, increasing as output rises over the total range of production (i.e., labor, fuel).

Totten trust: a trust created by the deposit of one's own money in his own name as trustee for another. Title is vested in the record owner (trustee), who during his life holds it on a revocable trust for the named beneficiary. At the death of the depositor, a presumption arises that an absolute trust was created as to the balance on hand at the death of the depositor. see *testamentary account.* [37]

touch: asking for a loan of a sum of money from an acquaintance or friend.

touch off the stops: when stop orders become market orders because the price at which the stop orders were placed has been attained. A situation described as *snowballing* results should prices continue to drop and successive stop orders are hit or touched off (i.e., become market orders and creating even more selling pressure).

tough buck: slang, wages earned from a difficult or hard job.

TPIN (True Pin): The Personal Identification Number used as reference, as opposed to the code remembered by the cardholder. (The TPIN is related to the PIN by the offset on the card.) [105]

TPS: see *trigger-price system.*

TPT: see *third-party transaction.*

Tr.: see *trust.*

TR
(1) see *tax rate.*
(2) see *Treasury Receipt.*
(3) see *trust receipt.*

TRA: see *Tax Reform Act of 1969, Tax Reform Act of 1976.*

trace
(1) *general:* the record of a series of events.
(2) *banking:* to record a policyholder's record of premium payment.

trade: the purchasing, selling or exchanging of commodities either by wholesale or by retail, within a country or between countries.

trade acceptance: a bill of exchange that is drawn by the seller of goods or materials at the time of the purchase and which is accepted by the purchaser. [10]

trade agreement: a trade or commercial treaty.

trade balance: see *balance of trade*.

trade barrier: interference with the free exchange of goods or services among different political jurisdictions. The most typical trade barriers are customs duties and import quotas.

trade bill: a bill of exchange drawn by the seller of goods on the buyer and covering payment of the goods.

trade bloc: two or more nations which have agreed to a common policy on customs duties and trade regulations applicable to other nations and which apply preferentialy policies to trade among themselves on a reciprocal basis, such preferential agreements not extended to other nations.

trade credit: accounts payable and accounts receivable.

trade creditor: a person or firm that is owed on an open account basis as a result of a transaction by a trade debtor.

trade deficit: synonymous with *unfavorable balance of trade*.

trade discount: a deduction from the agreed price, usually expressed as a percentage or a series of percentages, that is used in commerce to encourage prompt payment of bills. Trade discount should not be entered in the books of account, nor should it be considered to be a type of earnings.

trade dollar: a special silver coin minted by the United States from 1873 to 1885 with more silver content than the standard silver dollar and intended for trade with the Orient.

traded option: an option sold to someone else.

Trade Expansion Act of 1962: federal legislation permitting the president to negotiate additional tariff reductions, eliminate or reduce tariffs on items of the European Common Market, reduce tariffs on the basis of reciprocal trade agreements, and grant technical and financial assistance to employers whose business is adversely affected by tariff reductions. see also *Dillon Round, Kennedy Round*.

trade house: a firm that buys and sells futures and actuals for the accounts of customers as well as for its own account. [11]

trademark: a distinctive identification of a manufactured product or of a service taking the form of a name, logo, motto, and so on; a trademarked brand has legal protection and only the owner can use the mark. Organizations that file an application at the U.S. Patent Office and use the brand for five years may be granted a trademark. A firm may lose a trademark that has become generic. Generic names are those which consumers use to identify the product, rather than to specify a particular brand (e.g., escalator, aspirin, and nylon).

trade monopoly: special-privilege monopoly created by a government allowing a private trading firm to monopolize business between that nation and another area, usually a colony.

trade name: the name under which an organization conducts business, or by which the business or its goods and services are identified. It may or may not be registered as a trademark.

trade paper: short-term negotiable instrument such as an acceptance, bill, or note that originated out of the purchase of goods.

trader

(1) *general:* anyone who is engaged in trade or commerce.

(2) *investments:* one who buys and sells for his or her own account for short-term profit. [20]

trade reference: a person or firm to which a seller is referred for credit data on a potential customer.

trader's market: an advantageous market for active trading whereby shifts are relatively narrow without extended movements.

trading difference: a difference of a fraction of a point in the charged price for securities bought and sold in an odd-lot transaction, which is in excess of the price at which the security would be traded in traditional round lots.

trading flat: see *flat.*

trading floor: see *floor.*

trading limit

(1) the price limit above or below which trading in commodities is not allowed during a given day.

(2) as specified by the Commodity Exchange Act, the number of contracts a person may legally retain.

trading market: a condition where the primary volume of transactions is attributed to professional traders as contrasted from transactions attributed to the general public. As a result, volume is down and off with only narrow fluctuations in prices.

trading post: one of many trading locations on the floor of stock exchanges at which stocks assigned to that loca-

tion are bought and sold. see *floor, specialist.*

trading profits: profits made in the course of a trade; profits made by a securities dealers from buying and selling securities. [90]

trading range: the amount that futures prices can fluctuate during one trading session; essentially, the price distance between limit up and limit down.

trading unit: the unit adopted by an association or exchange where transactions are regularly expressed. The unit varies with the exchange and can vary between the spot or futures market, as well as by the commodity.

traditio: delivery and transfer of possession of property by an owner.

transaction: any agreement between two or more parties, establishing a legal obligation.

transaction amount: the stated funds transferred between two parties without consideration of charges. [105]

transaction card: see *debit card.*

transaction code: a code encoded or keypunched into a document prior to computer processing to indicate the type of transaction being entered into the system. [105]

transaction date: the date on which a transaction occurs. see *posting date.* [105]

transaction document

(1) a form that contains information pertaining to a transaction generated by a bank card and which shows a transaction.

(2) a check guaranteed by a bank card. Sales slips, refund slips, and cash advance/withdrawal slips are transaction documents.

transaction file: a file containing relatively transient data to be processed in combination with a master file. For example, in payroll application, a transaction file indicating hours worked might be processed with a master file containing employee name and rate of pay. [105]

transactions balances: cash and securities kept to facilitate the ongoing requirement to pay bills as they arise in the normal course of business.

transactions tax: a tax on turnover; a sales tax on both retail and wholesale sales.

transaction-type code: a code that further defines the purpose of the transaction, such as deposit, federal funds sold, draw-down. [105]

transaction velocity of money: the ratio of the total of all money transactions in a time period to the quantity of money. cf. *income velocity of money*.

transcript: a recap of account activity for a designated period of time. [105]

transfer

(1) *general:* the shifting of an employee from one job to another within the same organization.

(2) *computers:* to move information from one storage device to another or from one part of memory to another.

(3) *investments:* see *stock transfer*.

transferability: the ability to transfer ownership or title. Transferability can be restricted by so stating in a contract. The usual word is *nonassignable*.

transferable letter of credit: a documentary credit under which a beneficiary has the right to give instructions to the paying or accepting bank or to any bank entitled to effect negotiations, to make the credit available to one or more third parties.

transferable notice: a written announcement issued by a seller signifying his intention of making delivery in fulfillment of a futures contract. The recipient of the notice may make a sale of the futures contract and transfer the notice within a specified time to another party, on some exchanges directly, and on others through the clearing association. The last recipient takes delivery of the commodity tendered. Notices on some exchanges are not transferable. [2]

transfer agent: a transfer agent keeps a record of the name of each registered shareowner, his or her address, and the number of shares owned; it is the agent's responsibility to see that certificates presented to the office for transfer are properly canceled and that new certificates are issued correctly in the name of the transferee. [20]

transfer costs: the costs that a department accepts for items supplied by other departments. see *transfer price*.

transferee: the person or corporation to which property has been transferred. [37]

transfer fees: fees collected from buyers and/or sellers of property to defray governmental charges for changing and maintaining public records. [105]

transfer income: income received without service rendered by the person receiving it. The major transfer incomes are old-age pensions, unemployment relief, and Social Security. Government bond interest gets special treatment.

transfer in contemplation of death: a transfer of property by gift made in apprehension of death arising from some existing bodily condition or impending peril and not the general expectation of eventual decease commonly held by all persons. [37]

transfer journal: a book kept by a corporation to show stock certificates issued, transferred, and canceled.

transfer of title: the change of property title from one person to another. synonymous with *voluntary alienation.*

transfer of value: a banking concept that offers the consumer a variety of ways to pay for what he or she wants without cash.

transferor: the person or corporation which conveys or transfers property. [37]

transfer payment: in government statistics, money transactions among people, government, and business for which no services are performed; there is no addition to the national product.

transfer price: the price charged by one segment of an organization for a product or service it supplies to another part of the same firm. see *transfer costs.*

transferred account: a cardholder account that has been transferred from one processing center to another, from one area to another within a processing center, or from one associate to another in the same bank card plan. [105]

transfers (mail, wire, cable): *mail transfer* is the remittance of money by a bank to be paid to a party in another town or city. The instruction to pay such funds is transmitted by regular mail, hence the term "mail transfer." *Wire transfer* is used to designate a transfer of funds from one point to another by wire or telegraph. *Cable transfer* is used to designate a transfer of funds to a city or town located outside the United States by cable. Commis-

sions or fees are charged for all types of transfers. When transfers are made by wire or cable, the cost of transmitting the instructions to pay by wire or cable is charged to the remitter in addition to the commission. [10]

transfer service fee: service fee for instant cash transaction. [105]

transfer tax: a tax imposed by the federal or some state governments when a security is sold or transferred from one person to another. The tax is paid by the seller. There is no tax on transfers of bonds. The transfer tax is usually collected as a stamp tax.

transfer voucher: a voucher authorizing transfers of cash or other resources between funds. [49]

transit department: a department of a bank whose function is the processing of all out-of-city items. The transit department writes all transit letters, both cash letters and remittance letters and forwards these letters to the Federal Reserve Bank, correspondent banks, and other banks for collection and payment. [10]

transit items: cash items payable outside the town or city of the bank receiving them for credit to customers' accounts. [50]

transit letter: a letter or form of deposit slip on which a bank lists and describes transit items. [50]

transit machine: a machine designed to write transit letters. [105]

transit number: the identification of a bank on its checks under the national numerical system. The number has three parts, the first designating the location of the bank, the second the bank's name, and the third (below the line) the Federal Reserve district and area within the district. These numbers facilitate routing out-of-town checks.

translation (of foreign currencies): the expression of an amount denominated in one currency in terms of another currency by use of an exchange rate between the two currencies. [43]

trans-lux: an electrical unit used to project the quotations of a commodity or security exchange on a screen in a board room of a brokerage house.

Transmatic: the trade name of a franchised, preauthorized payment system for savings associations. [59]

Transmatic Money Service (TMS): an EFTS service first offered in the winter of 1974 by First Federal Savings and Loan of Lincoln, Nebraska. [105]

transmittal letter: a letter accompanying a shipment of securities, documents, or other property usually containing a brief description of the securities, documents, or property being forwarded and an explanation of the transaction. [37]

travel and entertainment credit card (T&E card): a credit card issued for use primarily for the purchase of meals, lodging, and transportation. Major American cards are American Express, Carte Blanche, and Diner's Club.

travel department: a department in a bank established to render service to the bank's customers in any matter relative to travel or foreign transactions. In the larger coastal banks, all foreign transactions are handled by the foreign department of the bank. In interior banks, the travel department deals directly with their coastal bank correspondents in handling foreign transactions. The travel department will arrange accommodations for do-

mestic or foreign travel, plan vacation trips, and handle foreign transactions for its customers. [10]

travelers check: a form of check especially designed for travelers, including persons on vacation and business trips. These checks are usually preprinted in denominations of $10, $20, $50, and $100, and can be cashed and used to purchase goods and services in places of business that accept them.

travelers cheque: see *travelers check*.

traveler's letter of credit: a letter of credit is issued by a bank to a customer preparing for an extended trip. The customer pays for the letter of credit, which is issued for a specified period of time in the amount purchased. The bank furnishes a list of correspondent banks or its own foreign branches at which drafts drawn against the letter of credit will be honored. see *guaranteed letter of credit, letter of indication*.

Tr. Co.: see *trust company*.

Treas.
(1) see *treasurer*.
(2) treasury.

treasurer: the person who is responsible for the financial transactions of an organization.

Treasurer of the United States: the cabinet-rank executive who heads the Treasury Department.

treasurer's check: see *cashier's check*.

treasureship: the functions of management holding responsibility for the custody and investment of money, the granting of credit and collection of accounts, capital provision, maintenance of a market for the firm's securities, and so on.

Treasury bill: a U.S. government

short-term security sold to the public each week, maturing in 91 to 182 days.

Treasury bond: see *bond, Treasury.*

Treasury bonds and notes: interest-bearing certificates showing indebtedness of the U.S. government. Notes have maturities of between one and seven years, whereas bonds are longer term. [105]

treasury cash holdings: currency and coin held by the Treasury. [40]

Treasury certificates: U.S. government short-term securities, sold to the public and maturing in one year.

Treasury currency: U.S. notes, paper money, silver certificates, silver coins, nickels, and cents issued by the U.S. Treasury Department. [105]

Treasury currency outstanding: currency such as U.S. notes and silver certificates, and coin in the hands of the public for which the Treasury is responsible. [40]

Treasury note: a U.S. government long-term security, sold to the public and having a maturity of one to five years.

Treasury obligations: see *bond, Treasury; Treasury bill; Treasury certificates; Treasury note.*

Treasury Receipt (TR): zero-coupon bonds of U.S. Treasury-backed certificates available from brokerage and investment banking concerns.

treasury securities: interest-bearing obligations of the U.S. government issued by the Treasury as a means of borrowing money to meet government expenditures not covered by tax revenues. Marketable Treasury securities fall into three categories: bills, notes, and bonds. The Federal Reserve System holds more than $100 billion of these obligations, acquired through open market operations. [1]

treasury stock: the title to previously issued stock of a corporation that has been reacquired by that corporation by purchase, gift, donation, inheritance, or other means. The value of such stock should be considered to be a deduction from the value of outstanding stock of similar type rather than as an asset of the issuing corporation.

Treasury Tax and Loan Account (TTSL): an account held by the Treasury with a commercial bank.

Treasury warrant: an order on the U.S. Treasury in ordinary bank check form. It is the instrument by which all treasury disbursements are made.

trend: the direction that prices are taking.

Trf.: transfer.

trial balance: a list of the balances of the accounts in a ledger kept by double entry with the debit and credit balances shown in separate columns. If these are equal or their net balance agrees with a controlling account, the ledger from which the figures are taken is said to be *in balance.* [49]

triangular arbitrage: arbitrage between the exchange rates of three foreign currencies. see *arbitrage.*

triangular trade: trade between three countries, in which an attempt is made to create a favorable balance for each.

trick: a special low coupon at a high yield on a long maturity of a municipal bond issue, which enables a bidder to lower the net interest cost (NIC) to the issuer in the hopes of making a winning bid on the bonds. [105]

trickle down: the process by which federal funds flowing into the national economy stimulate growth through being distributed into organizations, as opposed to stimulating growth by direct payments (e.g., welfare).

triggering: see *trigger-price system*.

trigger-price system: a federal system for identifying all cut-rate steel *dumped* in the United States. It sets minimum prices below which imported steel cannot be sold in this country without *triggering* an investigation by the Treasury Department. If the agency determines that the steel has been sold at unfairly low prices, bonds and ultimately antidumping duties can be imposed on the products.

triple tax free: an investment free from federal, state, and local taxes.

triple (bottom) top: the point, high or low, reached by the market or a particular security, duplicating a level attained on two earlier occasions. To the market specialist, the three levels establish a triple top (bottom) and show that a major wall of price support (overhead resistance) has been established.

troc (troquer): French for *swap*.

troubleshoot: synonymous with *debug*.

trough: the lowest point of economic activity.

TRSA: see *Tax Reduction and Simplification Act of 1977*.

true annual rate of interest: synonymous with *annual percentage rate*.

true cost banking: an efficient way of providing money to borrowers, a policy requiring consumers and corporations to pay higher borrowing costs. see *Depository Institutions Deregulation and Monetary Control Act*.

true discount rate: an installment finance method by which the rate is calculated on the total note, by deducting

the charge at the time the loan is created.

true interest: see *pure interest*.

True PIN: see *TPIN*.

truncation: a banking industry term for check safekeeping. The electronic sorting out of charges and transmitting them back to the issuer banks, which send payment back the same way.

trust

(1) *general:* a fiduciary relationship between persons: one holds property for the benefit and use of another.

(2) *investments:* a combination of corporations, usually in the same industry; stockholders relinquish their stock to a board of trustees, who then issue certificates and dividends. The purposes of creating a trust include controlling costs of production, increasing profits, and reducing competition. see *monopoly*.

trust, corporate: the name applied to the division of a bank that handles the trust and agency business of corporations.

trust, personal: that branch of a trust company whose function is connected with the handling of trusts for individuals. Some of the functions performed are those of executorship of estates, administration of trust funds, investment services, and guardianships. Detailed records are maintained and statements mailed to beneficiaries of every transaction affecting a trust. [10]

trust account: a general term to cover all types of accounts in a trust department, including estates, guardianships, and agencies as well as trusts proper. [37]

trust administrator: a person in the employment of a trust institution who handles trust accounts in the sense of having direct contacts and dealings with trust customers and beneficiaries. [37]

trust agreement (trust instrument): an agreement between an employer and a trustee used in connection with a pension plan. It defines the trustee's powers and duties, and tells how the funds of the pension plan shall be invested and how payments shall be made to those who benefit under the plan. A trust agreement is usually used in connection with self-administered pension plans and individual policy pension plans.

trust and agency fund: in governmental accounting, a fund established to account for assets held by the government as trustee or agent (e.g., the government is trustee of a fund bequeathed to it under a will for loaning for stated purposes, but agent of a fund to account for taxes collected for other governmental units).

trust authority: the legal right of a corporation to engage in trust business. [32]

trust business: a trust company, or a trust department of a bank, which settles estates, administers trusts, and performs agency functions for individuals, corporations, governments, associations, and public or educational or related institutions is said to engage in the trust business. [10]

trust by declaration: see *declaration of trust*.

trust by order of court: a trust created by an order of a court of competent jurisdiction. [37]

trust certificate: see *stock trust certificate*.

trust charges: the charges made by a trust institution for its trust and agency services. see *commission, fee*. [32]

trust committee: a committee of directors or officers or both of a trust institution charged with general or specific duties relating to its trust business. [37]

trust company: an institution, usually state supervised, that engages in the trust business, and usually in all commercial banking activities.

trust costs: the costs to a trust institution of rendering trust and agency services; opposed to trust charges, which are the costs to trust institution customers or beneficiaries for obtaining trust and agency services. [32]

trust deed: see *deed, trust*.

trust department: the department of a bank that provides trust and agency services. The trust department by regulation must have books and assets separate from those of commercial banking activities. [25]

trust deposit: a deposit made by a trustee under a trustee account agreement.

trustee: a person to whom the title to property has been conveyed for the benefit of another.

trustee deed: see *deed, trustee*.

trusteed fund: any accumulation of capital held in trust for retirement, religious, educational, research, profit-sharing, or other purposes. [22]

trusteed pension plan: a pension plan in which the corporation's contributions to the plan are placed in a trust for investment and reinvestment, as distinguished from a plan in which the benefits are secured by life insurance. [37]

trustee in bankruptcy: the individual appointed by a court or by creditors to carry out the responsibilities of trust in a bankruptcy proceeding.

trustee shares: in an investment company formed under the business organization form of a Massachusetts trust, the certificates of beneficial interest.

trusteeship: the status of a carrier's property while in the charge of trustees appointed under Section 77 of the Bankruptcy Act, approved March 3, 1933. A reorganization proceeding under trustees differs from a receivership equity proceeding chiefly in the fact that the former may be instituted by a railroad as well as by creditors and must follow a detailed prescribed procedure in regard to the presentation, consideration, and adoption of plans of reorganization, involving participation by the Interstate Commerce Commission as well as by the court. [18]

trust estate: an estate held in trust by one individual for the welfare of another.

trust for support: a trust which provides that the trustee shall pay or apply only so much of the income or principal as in its judgment is necessary for the support, including education, of the beneficiary. [37]

trust function: the fiduciary capacity in which an individual or a trust institution may act, such as executor, administrator, guardian, or trustee. [37]

trust fund: the funds held by a trustee for the benefit of another person.

trust funds, federal: trust funds established to account for receipts that are held in trust by the government for use in carrying out specific purposes and programs in accordance with a trust agreement or a statute.

trust indenture: an instrument in writing that contains a description of all property originally placed in the trust, the agreement with respect to the duties of the trustee in administering the property, the rights of all beneficiaries named, along with their proportionate shares in the trust, the duration of the trusteeship, the distribution of income from the trust principal to the life tenants, and the distribution of the trust property to the remaindermen at the termination of the trust.

Trust Indenture Act: passed by Congress in 1939, this law regulates some of the terms and conditions of trust arrangements in connection with corporate security issues.

trust institution: a trust company, state bank, national bank, or other corporation engaged in the trust business under authority of law. A corporation is a trust institution if any of its department is engaged in trust business, although other departments may be engaged otherwise. [37]

trust instrument: see *trust agreement*.

trust instrument committee: a committee of directors or officers (or both) of a trust institution charged with specific duties relating to trust investments; duties other than those relating to investments may be imposed by the board of directors. [37]

trust inter vivos: synonymous with *living trust* and *voluntary trust*.

trust investments: the property in which trust funds are invested; a broad term that includes all kinds of property, not securities alone. [37]

trust officer: the administrative officer of a trust company, or of the trust department of a bank. He is responsible for the proper administration of trusts, the investment of trust funds, and the administration of agencies for trust clients. [10]

trustor: an individual who establishes a trust. synonymous with *settlor.*

trust or commission clause: a clause extending the coverage of the insurance contract to the insured's interest in a legal liability for property belonging to others and held by the insured in trust, on commission, on storage, for repairs, or otherwise held. [53]

trust powers: as used in the Federal Reserve Act, authority to engage in the trust business; to be distinguished from the powers of a trustee. [37]

trust property: see *res.*

trust receipt: a receipt in the form of an agreement by which the party signing the receipt promises to hold the property received, in the name of the bank delivering the property. It further agrees that the property shall be maintained in a form that can be readily identified. If the property is further fabricated in a manufacturing process, it must be properly identified on the trust receipt. Trust receipts are used mostly to permit importers to obtain possession of merchandise for resale. Arrangements for this type of financing are usually completed before the issuance of letters of credit. The trust receipt is used as collateral security for the advance of funds by the bank to meet the acceptances arising out of the letter of credit. Under the terms of the agreement, the importer is required to pay to the bank proceeds from the sale of merchandise as soon as they are received. The importer is also required to keep the merchandise insured, and the bank may take possession of the merchandise at any time without due process of law. Federal Reserve

Banks do not recognize trust receipts as good collateral, and the legal status of the trust receipt has not been clearly defined by the courts. [10]

trust relationship: when an individual or other legal entity takes over legal title to certain property to hold it in trust for another individual or other legal entity as specified in the trust indenture, a trust or fiduciary relationship is established. The legal entity taking possession of the property is the trustee; the legal entity who will benefit from the relationship is the beneficiary. The beneficiary has an equitable title to the property, and may bring suit in courts of equity to maintain his or her rights as set forth in the trust agreement, and to prevent mishandling of the property by the trustee. [10]

trust under agreement: a trust evidenced by an agreement between the settlor and the trustee. synonymous with *trust inter vivos* or *living trust.* [32]

trust under decree: a trust evidenced by a decree of a court of equity. [37]

trust under deed: a trust evidenced by a deed of conveyance, as distinguished from an agreement; originally confined to real property but now frequently applied to personal property as well. [37]

trust under will: a trust created by a valid will, to become operative only on the death of the testator; opposed to a *living trust* and the same as *testamentary trust.* [37]

Truth-in-Lending Act of 1968: officially, the Consumer Credit Protection Act of 1968, it requires most categories of lenders to disclose the true annual interest rate on virtually all types of loans and credit sales as well as the total dollar cost and other terms of a loan. see *Fair Credit Billing Act, Regulation Z, right of rescission.*

TS

(1) see *tax shelter.*

(2) see *treasury stock.*

T/T: see *telegraphic transfer.*

TTSL: see *Treasury Tax and Loan Account.*

tub, in the: slang, in bankruptcy.

tughrik: monetary unit of Mongolia.

turkey

(1) *general:* any poor or unprofitable venture.

(2) *finance:* any investment that initially appeared attractive but suddenly became unattractive.

(3) *investments:* a stock that suddenly, without reason, drops in value.

turn: a description of the full cycle in the buying and selling of a security or a commodity.

Turnkey program: any one of several U.S. Department of Housing and Urban Development programs for public housing whereby, under contract to a local housing authority, a private developer builds public housing with private loan funds and, upon completion of the project, turns over to the housing authority the keys to the property. [59]

turnover

(1) *general:* the rate at which workers move into and out of employment, usually expressed as the number of accessions and separations during a fixed period for every 100 employees. The Bureau of Labor Statistics computes turnover rates by industry on a monthly basis.

(2) *investments:* the volume of business in a security or the entire market. If turnover on the exchange is reported at 15 million shares on a particular day, this means that 15,000,000 shares changed hands. Odd-lot turnover is tabulated separately and ordinarily is not included in reported volume.

turnover ratio: a measure of capital activity, or another factor of business (e.g., where the portfolio of securities is altered, or turned over, within one year). see *operating profit ratio.*

turnover tax: a form of sales tax employed in the Soviet Union.

turn (turning) the corner: a change in the prevailing direction of a business index or time series, either upward or downward.

tutor: under civil law, a person legally appointed to care for the person and the property of a minor; the equivalent of a *guardian.* [37]

twenty-four-hour banking: the availability for customer transactions that is provided by the presence of automated teller machines. Customers using these machines can access their accounts at any time. [105]

twenty percent rule: where a customer wishing to borrow funds from a bank must maintain an average deposit balance equal to at least twenty percent of the proposed borrowing.

twisting: the practice of inducing a policyholder to allow to lapse or cancel a policy for the purpose of replacing it with another, to the detriment of the policyholder. This practice is both unethical and illegal.

two bits: slang, a quarter, 25 cents.

two-case note: a $2 bill.

two-dollar brokers: members on the floor of the exchange who execute orders for other brokers having more business at that time than they can handle themselves, or for firms who do not have their exchange members on the floor. The term recalls the time when these independent brokers received $2 per hundred shares for executing such orders. see *give-up.*

twofer: see *neutral spread.*

two-name paper: a short-term negotiable instrument wherein two people guarantee payment.

two-tier gold price: a 1968 agreement among central bank members of the Gold Pool, the International Monetary Fund, and the Bank for International Settlements, to suspend the pool's sale of gold on the free market at the U.S. price of $35 per troy ounce.

two-tier markets: an exchange rate re-gime which insulates a nation from the balance-of-payments impact of capital flow while it maintains a stable exchange rate for current account transactions.

tycoon: an extremely wealthy and potentially influential business person.

tying contract: an agreement to sell items or lease property which contains clauses requiring the purchaser or lessee to abstain from using goods of competing sellers or lessers in connection with the items or property purchased or leased. Legislation, specifically the Clayton Act, prohibit tying clauses in contracts.

UCC: see *Uniform Commercial Code.*

UCCC: see *Uniform Consumer Credit Code.*

ULCC: see *ultra-large crude carrier.*

ultimate beneficiary: a beneficiary of a trust who is entitled to receive the principal of the trust property in final distribution; synonymous with *principal beneficiary;* opposed to *immediate beneficiary* and *income beneficiary.* [37]

ultimate loss insurance: synonymous with *single-interest insurance.*

ultimo: the month prior to the existing one.

ultra-large crude carrier (ULCC): a tanker able to carry from 450,000 to 500,000 deadweight tons of crude oil.

ultra vires: "beyond power" (Latin). Acts of a corporation are ultra vires when they exceed the power or capability of the corporation as granted by the state in its charter.

unaccrued: income resulting when payments are received but not yet due, as in the case of one receiving a rent payment before the due date.

unadjusted rate of return: an expression of the utility of a given project as the ratio of the increase in future average annual net income to the initial increase in needed investment.

unallotted balance of appropriation: an appropriation balance available for allotment. [49]

unamortized bond discount: the portion of the original bond discount that has not been charged off against earnings.

unamortized discounts on bonds sold: that portion of the excess of the face value of bonds over the amount received from their sale which remains to be written off periodically over the life of the bonds. [49]

unamortized discounts on investments (credit): that portion of the excess of the face value of securities over the amount paid for them which has not yet been written off. [49]

unamortized premiums on bonds sold: an account which represents that portion of the excess of bond proceeds over par value and which remains to be amortized over the remaining life of such bonds. [49]

unamortized premiums on investments: that portion of the excess of the amount paid for securities over their face value which has not yet been amortized. [49]

unappropriated profits: that portion of a firm's profit which has not been paid out in dividends or allocated for any special purpose.

unappropriated retained earnings: see *retained earnings, unappropriated.*

unassented securities: those stocks or bonds which a corporation wishes to alter but which have not been approved of for change by the stockholders.

unattended banking terminal (automated teller, cash dispenser): an electronic machine usually activated by a magnetically striped plastic card, capable of dispensing cash in stipulated amounts or performing other teller-type functions, such as the transfer of funds from checking to savings; may be remote and free standing or affixed to a banking building. [105]

unauthorized growth: capital investment that grows at different rates in different areas of an economy.

unauthorized investment: a trust investment that is not authorized by the trust instrument; to be distinguished from a *nonlegal investment.* [37]

unbilled accounts receivable: an account that designates the estimated amount of accounts receivable for services or commodities sold but not billed. For example, if a utility bills its customer bimonthly but prepares monthly financial statements, the amount of services rendered or commodities sold during the first month of the bimonthly period would be re-

flected in the balance sheet under this account title.

uncalled capital: that portion of the issued share capital of a corporation which has not yet been called up.

unclaimed balances: the balances of the accounts for funds on deposit that have remained inactive for a period designated by the bank. Eventually these unclaimed balances are handed over to the U.S. Comptroller of the Currency.

uncollected cash items: checks in the process of collection for which payment has not yet been received from the banks on which the checks are drawn. [40]

uncollected funds: a portion of a deposit balance that has not yet been collected by the depository bank. That is, sufficient time has not elapsed to permit checks drawn on other banks to have been returned for nonpayment. see *float.*

unconditional call money: Japanese term for funds lent for an initial period of two days which can then be called for repayment upon one day's notice.

unconfirmed documentary credit: a documentary credit where an advising bank informs the beneficiary of the terms and conditions of the credit without adding its undertaking that it will honor drawings on the credited, provided that documents are presented in order and in conformity with the terms of the credit.

unconfirmed letter of credit: a letter of credit in which the issuing bank has processed all the needed documents and advised the financial organization upon which the letter is drawn but the organization has not confirmed acknowledgment and accepted the advice of the letter. see *letter of credit.*

uncontrollable expense: an expense not under the direct control of the authority who will ultimately be charged with it. For example, the foreman has no control over the amount of rent, taxes, or depreciation charged to his department. Generally speaking, uncontrollable expenses are fixed. see *fixed cost or expense.* [38]

uncovered interest arbitrage: where an investment is made in a foreign currency asset to benefit from a more attractive rate of interest without simultaneously taking out forward exchange cover to protect an investor against the risk of intervening exchange rate changes.

uncovered money: irredeemable paper money; money only partially, or not at all, supported by a specie reserve.

uncover the stops: depressing the price of a security to a point where many stop orders are created. synonymous with *gather in the stops.*

undercapitalized: a business with insufficient ownership funds for the scale of operations it is carrying on.

undercharge: to charge less than the legal amount.

underdeveloped country: a nation in which per capita real income is proportionately low when contrasted with the per capita real income of nations where industry flourishes. see also *less developed country;* cf. *mature economy.*

underlease: a tenant's lease of property to a third party; a sublease.

underlying bond: see *bond, underlying.*

underlying company: synonymous with *subsidiary.*

underlying lien: a claim that has prior-

ity over another claim which is junior to it.

underlying mortgage: a mortgage senior to a larger one (e.g., a building first mortgage of $100,000 that has a prior claim over a second one of $200,000). cf. *equal dignity.*

underlying movement: synonymous with *primary movement.*

underlying stock: the stock subject to purchase upon exercise of the option. [15]

underlying syndicate: to the original members of the underwriters of a new issue of securities as distinguished from a distributing syndicate which can include some members of the underlying syndicate and also additional brokerage houses.

under protest: a payment made under compulsion with the payer using these words to negate any implication from the act of payment that he or she is waiving whatever rights he or she may have.

under the rule: an action of selling or buying by stock exchange officers to complete a transaction entered into by a delinquent member of the exchange, who is charged with any difference in price that occurs.

undertone: the technical basis of the market—strong or weak.

underwrite: the designing, preparing, bringing forth, and guaranteeing the sale of a new issue of stock. see *investment banker, syndicate.*

underwriter

(1) *general:* an individual or organization that assumes a risk for a fee.

(2) *investments:* an individual or party that agrees to underwrite a securities issue. cf. *letter stock.*

underwriter's spread: compensation

to investment bankers for helping the firm issue securities; expressed as the difference between gross and net security sales as a percent of gross sales.

underwriting

(1) assumption of a risk, particularly an investment or insurance risk. Insurance underwriting involves guaranteeing a cash payment in the event of a loss or casualty. Investment underwriting involves guaranteeing the sale of a securities issue.

(2) the analysis of risk and the settling of an appropriate rate and term for a mortgage on a given property for given borrowers. [105]

underwriting fee: a percentage of the spread that accrues only to members of the syndicate, in proportion to the amount of the issue underwritten.

underwriting syndicate: a combination of underwriters joined together in a joint venture to undertake the resale of securities which are to be purchased from the corporation issuing the securities (or from an intermediary). The syndicate operates under a contract setting out the terms of their responsibilities.

undesignated city: a city not designated by the Federal Reserve System as one of its reserve cities.

undigested securities: securities that are issued beyond the need for or ability of the public to absorb them. see *overissue;* cf. *float, oversubscribed.*

undisclosed earnings: synonymous with *equity earnings.*

undistributed net income (UNI): the amount by which the distributable net income for the year exceeds the sum of any amount of income for the year required to be distributed currently; any other amounts properly paid, credited, or required to be distributed for such year; and the amount of taxes properly allocable to the undistributed portion of the distributable net income. [105]

undistributed profit: the profit of a partnership, syndicate, or joint venture prior to division among the individuals concerned.

undistributed profits tax: a tax designed to supplement the income tax. By holding profits in a corporation and not paying dividends, stockholders can delay the income tax that would personally be due if dividends were paid. Letting such earnings accrue, stockholders can get the earnings out by selling part of their stock and paying only a capital gains tax. Section 102 of the Internal Revenue Code imposes a heavy tax on earnings kept in a corporation without a good business reason.

undivided interests: see *joint tenancy, tenancy by the entirety, tenancy in common.*

undivided profits: undistributed earnings available for dividends and for the writing off of bad debts or special losses. [50]

undivided right: a part owner's right that cannot be excluded from the other owner's rights. This right exists in tenancy in common and in joint tenancy.

undo: to reverse a transaction.

undue influence: the influence that one person exerts over another person to the point where the latter is prevented from exercising his own free will. [37]

unearned discount: interest received but not yet earned.

unearned income: income that has been collected in advance of the performance of a contract; income derived from investment dividends, property rentals, and other sources not involving the individual's personal efforts. cf. *earned income.*

unearned increment: the increase in the value of property that can be attributed to changing social or economic conditions beyond the control of the title holder, as distinguished from an increase in value that can be attributed to the improvements made or additions made by the labor or investment of the title holder.

unearned interest: interest on a loan that has already been collected but has not yet been earned because the principal has not been outstanding long enough. [59]

unemployment compensation: a system of insuring workers against hardship during periods of unemployment. The Unemployment Insurance Act of 1935, as part of the Social Security program, is administered by the states individually, allowing for variations in rates, duration of payments, and eligibility. Costs are borne by the employers, who get allowances in the form of tax credits.

unencumbered property: real estate free and clear of any mortgages, liens, or debts of any type. see *perfect title.*

uneven lot: synonymous with *odd lot.*

uneven market: a market with widely fluctuating prices.

unexpired cost: any asset.

unfavorable balance of trade: in international trade, a condition of a nation when the money value of its goods imported exceeds the money value of its items exported over a specified time period. synonymous with *passive trade balance* and *trade deficit.*

unfunded debt: any short-term or floating debt; any indebtedness not covered by a bond.

unfunded insurance trust: an insurance trust in which the premiums on the policies are to be paid by the insured or by some third person and not by the trustee; to be distinguished from a *funded insurance trust.* [37]

UNI: see *undistributed net income.*

unified bond: see *bond, consolidated.*

unified credit: a dollar amount allocated to each taxpayer which can be applied against the gift tax, the estate tax, and under certain circumstances, the generation-skipping tax. [105]

uniform accounting system: a system of accounts that is common to similar organizations. This includes those promoted by a trade association for a particular industry or those promulgated by federal and state regulatory bodies. [105]

uniform acts: a series of acts drafted by the National Conference of Commissioners on Uniform State Laws and suggested for passage in the various states with a view toward making the laws in the states uniform as to the particular subjects covered. [37]

uniform cash flows: cash flows that are the same for every year.

Uniform Commercial Code: a set of statutes purporting to provide some consistency among states' commercial laws. It includes uniform laws dealing with bills of lading, negotiable instruments, sales, stock transfers, trust receipts, and warehouse receipts.

Uniform Consumer Credit Code (UCCC): a consumer protection act which contains one uniform set of regulations for all major credit grantors.

Uniform Customs and Practice: standardized code of practice issued by the

International Chamber of Commerce in Paris covering Documentary Credits.

uniform delivered price: a pricing system under which a product is sold at the same price and delivered anywhere within a given area without additional charge for the delivery.

Uniform Gifts to Minors Act: an act adopted by most states providing for a means of transferring property to a minor, wherein the designated custodian of the property has the legal right to act on behalf of the minor without the necessity of a guardianship. [105]

Uniform Negotiable Instrument Act: see *negotiable instrument.*

Uniform Small Loan Law: passed on a state level, this law specifies requirements relating to the interest rate charged, maximum size of loan, and licensing and supervision of small loan companies. [105]

uninsurable title: property that a title insurance company will not insure.

union rate: the minimum hourly wage rate, accepted by a union for a specific type of activity and employed in negotiations.

unissued stock: part of the authorized capital stock of a corporation that is not issued or outstanding. It is not part of the corporation's capital stock and receives no dividends, although it must be shown on the firm's balance sheet even though it is neither an asset nor a liability. see *when issued.*

unitary: a Savings and Loan subsidiary.

unitary investment fund: instead of being governed by an elected board that selects an investment adviser with considerable latitude to make investment decisions, the funds are operated only by an adviser.

unitary tax: a state tax method that calculates a local company's tax as a percentage of its total, worldwide profits, not simply on the profits of the subsidiary situated within the state.

unit bank: a single independent bank that conducts all its operations at one office. [50]

unit banking: the type of banking in which an individual bank is separate and distinct from every other bank with regard to operation, management, and control. [50]

unit cost: the total cost of a single item or unit of service which includes the variable cost, plus a proportionate share of the fixed cost.

United States: see entries under *U.S.*

unit investment trusts: an investment vehicle that buys and holds a portfolio of securities—most commonly municipal bonds—and then sells shares to investors. The investor then receives a prorated share of interest and principal payments. Bond mutual funds are similar but are able to manage their portfolios actively, which may allow for better protection of capital in periods of volatile interest rates.

unit of account: an artificial concept providing a consistent reference value against varying exchange rates.

unit of trading: the lowest amount established by a stock exchange in which the market in a specific security may be made. see *odd lot, round lot.*

unit posting plan for checking accounts: a system used in a bank's commercial bookkeeping department whereby the ledger, original statement, and original journal are posted simultaneously. [105]

unit savings plan: a plan whereby savings deposits and withdrawals are posted by machine to the depositor's passbook, the bank's ledger card, and the auditor's detailed audit tape, all in original printing in one simultaneous operation. The ledger card is posted at the teller's window by the teller in the same machine operation that posts the entry in the depositor's passbook. The entry must be identical, because of the simultaneous machine printing. This assures complete protection to the depositor (who can "audit" his or her account at the window), the bank teller, and the bank. see also *dual savings plan, no-ticket savings plan.* [10]

unit system: an accounting system in which the records of the customer and the association are posted simultaneously. [59]

unit teller: an employee of a bank who is charged with the duties of both a paying and receiving teller. This teller may receive deposits or pay out funds to depositors. His cash balance at the end of the business day will be the net of his cash received, less his cash paid out. see *paying teller, receiving teller.* [10]

unit teller system: an arrangement for the convenience of customers who wish to make deposits and withdrawals at the same time. When this system is in use, the bank representative at each window is responsible for handling both receiving and paying operations. [50]

unit trust

(1) corporate and municipal bonds; a mix of corporate issues and closed-end trusts, some designed for investors in a single state.

(2) a British term for *mutual investment*; a *mutual fund.*

(3) an inflexible investment. A trust managers buys a stated portfolio of securities and deposits them with a trustee. After the deposit date, no new securities are added, and with rare exceptions, none are sold. As a result, the return, or yield, is fixed and predictable.

universal life policies: a variation of whole life, appears to offer excellent interest rates on the savings portion; provides greater variation of premium payment and amount of insurance to meet changing needs. Premiums are put to work in money markets or other high-yielding investments. In addition, the policyholder is regularly notified about the gross rate of return on the investment, management costs, and other fees.

universal numerical system: a system of numbering checks with a code showing the city, state, and bank, aiding in rapid sorting of checks.

universal teller: a teller who is capable of handling all bank transactions without being assisted or having to leave the teller window. [105]

unlawful: see *illegal.*

unlimited accounts: large or reputable businesses that are eligible for any amount of credit.

unlimited liability: the right of creditors to attach and seize any assets of a debtor to the extent of the indebtedness held against a business. A characteristic of the partnership and the individual proprietorship.

unlimited mortgage: any open-end mortgage; a mortgage not limited to a fixed amount.

unlimited tax bond: see *bond, unlimited tax.*

unliquidated claim: where debtor honestly disputes the amount owing on the claim. [105]

unliquidated encumbrances: encumbrances outstanding. see also *encumbrance.* [49]

unlisted: synonymous with *over the counter.*

unlisted market: a market created by person-to-person transactions, usually between brokers, for stocks not listed on an organized stock exchange.

unlisted trading privileges: on some exchanges a stock may be traded at the request of a member without any prior application by the company itself. The company has no agreement to conform with standards of the exchange. Companies admitted to unlisted trading privileges prior to enactment of the Securities Exchange Act of 1934 are not subject to the rules and regulations under that act. Today, admission of a stock to unlisted trading privileges requires SEC approval of an application filed by the exchange. The information in the application must be made available by the exchange to the public. No unlisted stocks are traded on the New York Stock Exchange. see *listed securities (stocks).* [20]

unloading
(1) *finance:* selling goods at a relatively low price.
(2) *investments:* the sale of stocks and commodities to avoid a loss during a period of a falling market. cf. *profit taking.*
(3) synonymous with *dumping.*

unpaid balance: on a credit purchase, the difference between the purchase price and the down payment or the value of a trade-in. With a cash loan, it is the difference between the total loan and the amount that is still owed.

unpaid dividend: a dividend declared but not yet distributed.

unparted bullion: bullion containing base metals in addition to the precious metal.

Unpd.: unpaid.

unrealized profits: paper profits that are not made actual until the firm's securities have been sold.

unrealized revenue: revenue that is attributed to a completed business transaction but accompanied by the receipt of a noncurrent asset (e.g., an installment sale). [105]

unrecovered cost
(1) that portion of an original investment not amortized through depreciation or depletion.
(2) uninsured losses from extraordinary obsolescence, fire, theft, or market fluctuations. [105]

unregistered stock: a security that is not tradable and not easily converted into a cash position. It is usually sold in private transactions that are exempt from the SEC registration requirements, often at a discounted price. synonymous with *letter stock.*

unreported earnings: synonymous with *equity earnings.*

unsatisfactory account
(1) an indication, for credit references, that a customer has not met the terms of his or her contract.
(2) the irregular payment of a loan or frequent overdrawing of a checking account. [105]

unseasoned securities: the opposite of seasoned securities. see *seasoned security.* [67]

unsecured: see *side collateral.*

unsecured bond: see *bond, unsecured.*

unsecured creditor: a lender whose

loan or debt is not secured by any collateral or mortgage. cf. *secured creditor.*

unsecured debt: a debt for which no collateral has been pledged.

unsecured loan: a loan made by a bank based on credit information about the borrower and his or her ability to repay the obligation. The loan is not secured by collateral but is made on the signature of the borrower. A person's spouse may be asked to sign such a note. see *comaker, debenture.*

unsecured note: a loan granted on the basis of a borrower's credit worthiness and signature; not secured by collateral. [78]

unstable market: a market in which forces of disequilibrium are reinforced so that movements away from equilibrium are not reversible.

unsteady market: a market where prices fluctuate rapidly but no identifiable trend is noted.

unvalued stock: stock having no par or stated value. The term is a misnomer since it must have value to be purchased and sold, but the unvalued reference is to the value at which the issuer of the stock carries it on the books; usually taxed as if it had a value of $100 par.

UOT: see *unit of trading.*

up: slang, any potential buyer.

UP: see *unrealized profits.*

UPC: Universal Product Code.

upgrade: an increase in the credit limit. [105]

upon sight: see *sight draft.*

upset price: a previously fixed starting price in the auctioning of a piece of real estate. The prospective seller will not entertain a bid below that figure.

upside gap: the open space on a se-curity chart when the highest price of one day is lower than the lowest price of the next day.

upside momentum: see *momentum.*

upstream loan: a holding company with poor credit using its subsidiaries as a source of funds. Such lending by the subsidiary to a parent will not appear on a consolidated statement of the parent and the subsidiaries.

up tick: a transaction made at a price higher than the preceding transaction. A stock may be sold short only on an up tick, (i.e., a transaction at the same price as the preceding trade but higher than the preceding different price). synonymous with *plus tick.*

urbank: first proposed by Professor Charles Haar, in 1968, as an urban development bank controlled by a federal agency to assist communities to build needed facilities. The urbank would be a federally financed institution, making long-term loans at favorable interest rates to employers willing to return to or upgrade plants in cities.

US
(1) see *underlying stock.*
(2) United States.
(3) see *unregistered stock.*

usance: the period of time allowed by law or commercial practice for the payment of a bill of exchange.

U.S. Customs bonded warehouse: see *warehouse, U.S. Customs bonded.*

use: as a noun, the beneficial ownership of property the legal title to which is in another; the forerunner of the present-day trust. [32]

use data: the set of characters in bank cards used in off-line terminals, recording the most recent use of the card. [105]

used mortgage: synonymous with *assumable mortgage.*

user cost: depreciation defined in unit cost on the basis of the amount that the discounted expected future earnings of the capital equipment has been lowered because of producing that unit.

use tax: a device to protect the sales tax from wholesale evasion. A state having a sales tax places a similar tax on the use of all articles on which no sales tax has been paid so that people are not encouraged to go out of the state to make tax-free purchases which they can then bring home.

use value: the value placed on a good or service, not for its possible exchange, but for its usefulness to the individual directly.

U.S. government deposits: all deposits in reporting member banks held for the account of the U.S. government or one of its departments or bureaus. [40]

U.S. Internal Revenue warehouse: see *warehouse, U.S. Internal Revenue.*

U.S. rule: a method traditionally employed in first-mortgage real estate financing where payments are applied first to accrued interest and then to the reduction of principal. [41]

U.S. Savings Bond: see *Bond, U.S. Savings.*

usuance
(1) *general:* employment.
(2) *finance:* interest or income.
(3) *finance:* the period allowed for payment of a foreign obligation.

usufructuary right: a right to appropriate use and pleasure from property owned by another.

usurious: describing a contract when made for a loan of money at a rate of interest in excess of that authorized by the statute.

usurious rate of interest: the maximum rate of interest which the law allows cf. *legal rate of interest.*

usury: the rate of interest paid for the use of another's money, or for credit extended, which exceeds the legal limit allowed for that type of transaction by the state whose laws govern the legality of the transaction. see *legal interest.*

usury rate: see *usurious rate of interest.*

U/T: under trust.

utility
(1) *general:* the capability or power of an item to satisfy a need as determined by the satisfaction that one receives from consuming something.
(2) *finance:* a publicly owned facility, such as an electric power plant.

utter a check: to give a check to another in payment of an obligation.

Uw.: see *underwriter.*

V: five.

VA: see *Veterans Administration.*

vacation club account: funds deposited in a financial institution to accumulate money for a vacation period. Deposits are generally made weekly in small amounts. [105]

VA guaranteed loan: see *Veterans Administration loan.*

Val.: see *value.*

valeurs: French for *securities.*

valid: that which is sufficient to satisfy the requirement of the law; a fact.

validation: proof or confirmation; an instrument or other evidence to confirm or give legal support to a claim or contract (e.g., factual data from an experiment).

valid date: a date expressed as month and year before which a bank card is not valid. The valid date may appear on the face of the card in embossed characters or in a magnetic strip. [105]

valorization: governmental action leading to the establishment of a price or value for an item or service.

valuation: the fixing of value to anything. synonymous with *appraising.*

valuation account (or reserve): an account that relates to one or more other accounts, either partly or wholly offsetting it (e.g., reserve for depreciation, unamortized debt discount). The valuation reserve is deducted from the stated value of the asset, giving its net value. [105]

valuation reserves

(1) *finance:* reserves established to provide for a drop in the existing value of the assets to which they pertain. see *appraisal.*

(2) *finance:* reserves established to provide for a reasonably probable failure to achieve full value.

value: the worth of property, goods, services, and so on. see *book value, purchasing power.*

value added: that part of the value of produced goods developed in a company. It is determined by subtracting from sales the costs of materials and supplies, energy costs, contract work, and so on, and it includes labor expenses, administrative and sales costs, and other operating profits.

value-added tax (VAT): a government tax on the value added; a tax on the selling price of manufactured items less the cost of the materials and expenses used in their production.

value asset: *per common share,* a company's net resources (after deduction of all liabilities, preferred stocks' liquidating value, and accrued dividends, if any), divided by the number of common shares outstanding; *per preferred share* (another way of showing asset coverage), a company's net resources (after deduction of all liabilities, any prior preferred stocks' liquidating value, and accrued dividends, if any), divided by the number of preferred shares outstanding. [3]

value compensated: describing a purchase or sale of foreign exchange to be executed by cable; the purchaser reimburses the seller for the earlier value of the data of actual payment abroad of the foreign currency, theoretically resulting in no loss of interest to either party.

value date: the date on which a bank deposit becomes effective. The date is fixed based on the time required to collect a payment on the item deposited from another bank. see *collection.*

value of money: its purchasing power. The amount of goods and services it will buy at any given time.

VA mortgage: mortgage made in conformity with requirements of the Servicemen's Readjustment Act, and guaranteed to an amount specified in the act by the Veterans Administration. [22]

"vanilla" transactions: where a company either sold pieces of itself as shares of stock or issued bonds to borrow money for up to 30 years at a set interest rate.

variable: a quantity that may assume a succession of values, which need not be distinct. [57]

variable amount note: note evidencing the amount the trust department lends to a borrower from cash held in various fiduciary accounts; the amount of the loan outstanding fluctuates depending on the amount of cash on hand. [105]

variable annuity: an annuity contract providing lifetime retirement payments that vary in amount with the results of investment in a separate account portfolio.

variable cost: a cost that is uniform per unit but changes in total in direct proportion to changes in the related total activity or volume.

variable cost ratio: variable costs divided by sales.

variable interest plus (VIP): an innovative certificate of deposit. First attempted by Western Savings Bank, the second largest in Philadelphia; under the plan, the interest rate on the six-month certificate would be tied to the prevailing rate at the weekly auction of six-month Treasury bills. The primary motivation behind this new variable-interest-rate certificate was to stop the flow of funds out of the bank and into higher-yielding instruments, particularly money-market mutual funds. Under terms of the VIP, a depositor also could borrow as much as $9900 against the certificate at an interest rate of 1 percent above the weekly rate being earned. Bank regulators stopped this proposal in 1981.

variable interest rate U.S Savings Bond: see *Bond, Savings (U.S).*

variable life insurance: a relatively new form of coverage; the death benefit is based on the performance of the stock market, or more specifically, on the performance of stocks in the insurer's portfolio. The better the market performs over the life of the policy (i.e., a lifetime), the more cash the benefit will receive. If the market should collapse, a specified minimum death benefit will be paid nonetheless. A variable life insurance policy costs a little less than a standard whole life policy that pays dividends on its investments, but somewhat more than one that pays no dividends.

variable rate: offered by many major lenders, monthly bank payments that are tied to prevailing rates. The advantage is to the buyer when rates slide, and to the seller when they soar.

variable-rate account: a passbook savings account that pays extra earnings if the customer leaves a specified amount on deposit for a specified term. [59]

variable-rate CDs: introduced in 1975, a certificate of deposit with a normal minimum maturity of 360 days. The interest rate is pegged by an issuing bank at a specified spread over the bank's current rate on 90-day CDs and is adjusted every 90 days.

variable-rate certificate: a savings certificate on which the rate of interest payable varies, depending on the term for which the money is pledged. The interest rate is set by government regulatory agencies. [105]

variable-rate mortgage: a type of mortgage, initially available in California, and now authorized nationally, which permits the interest charges on the loan to rise or fall automatically in accordance with a predetermined index, for instance, an index of banks' cost-of-funds. The interest rate can fluctuate every six months, but cannot be raised by more than $2\frac{1}{2}$ percentage points over the life of the mortgage. In addition, banks must offer customers a choice between variable-rate and conventional mortgages. see also *flexible mortgage, renegotiable-rate mortgage, Wachovia adjustable mortgage.*

variable-ratio plan: an investment plan under which funds are divided at a time considered normal into two equal parts: a stock fund to purchase diversified common stocks and a cash fund to be held in liquid form. When prices rise, shares are sold to maintain the ratio of the stock fund value and the cash fund, and vice versa when prices fall. This assumes fluctuations about normal which may be readjusted periodically to take a long-term trend into account.

variance: a statistical measure of dispersion.

variation margin: additional margin needed on commodities resulting from variations in price.

VAT: see *value-added tax.*

vault: a large room or rooms in a bank or financial institution, where the cash on hand is stored, and safe deposit boxes are located.

vault cash: that portion of the cash on hand which is not required for immediate use and is left in the vault of the bank as an immediate reserve. The remainder of the cash on hand is carried in the cash busses and cash tills under the custodianship of the tellers. [10]

VC: see *venture capital.*

VCF: see *venture capital funds.*

VD: see *volume discount.*

veil of money theory: the idea that money is neutral and does not reflect a nation's true economic condition but is merely a cosmetic for other social and financial forces and activity. cf. *savings and investment theory.*

velocity: the rate at which money is spent on goods and services within a given period (usually measured as the ratio of GNP to the money stock). Greater velocity means that a given quantity of money is used for greater dollar volume of transactions. [1]

velocity of circulation: the rate at which money supply is spent for a stated time period, usually one year.

velocity of money: see *velocity of circulation.*

velocity shop: where mortgages are sold by banks to secondary lending markets so that it can quickly get back funds to make even more mortgages.

velvet: slang, an unearned income or profit.

vend: any offer to sell something.

vendee: the party who purchases or agrees to purchase property owned by another.

vendor: a manufacturer, wholesaler, or importer from whom goods are purchased.

vendor's lien: an unpaid seller's right to take possession of property until the purchase price has been recovered. see *general lien.*

venture: a business activity or undertaking involving some or considerable risk.

venture capital
(1) *finance:* funds invested in enterprises that do not usually have access to conventional sources of capital (banks, stock market, etc.).

(2) *investments:* funds available from the issue of new stock.

(3) *investments:* reinvested monies from stockholders.

venture capital funds: mutual funds invested in securities of firms that are little known and often not yet registered with the SEC.

venue: the place or county where a suit is brought. [76]

verification: the auditing process by which a customer is contacted regarding the status of an account or loan, to confirm the bank's records. [105]

verification factor: a numeric factor used to prove balance pickups or account selection. [105]

vertical expansion: expansion of a business by gaining control of all the operations involved in the production and sale of its output, from securing raw materials through marketing.

vertical merger: merger between firms in a supplier-customer relationship.

vest: as a verb, to confer an immediate, fixed right of immediate or future possession and enjoyment of property. [37]

vested: giving the rights of absolute ownership, although enjoyment can be postponed.

vested estate: an interest in property holding present and future rights, but with the existing interest able to be transferred.

vested interest: an immediate, fixed interest in real or personal property although the right of possession and enjoyment may be postponed until some future date or until the happening of some event; to be distinguished from a *contingent interest.* [37]

vested remainder: a fixed interest in real property, with the right of possession and enjoyment postponed until the termination of the prior estate; to be distinguished from a *contingent remainder*. [37]

vested renewals: future commissions for business placed to become due to a soliciting agent or general agency if the business remains in force. [12]

vested rights: provisions in a pension program ensuring that if a worker leaves the firm for any reason, he or she can retain the pension rights acquired while employed by the company offering the plan. see *fully vested*.

vesting: the right of an employee under a retirement plan to retain part or all of the annuities purchased by the employer's contributions on his or her behalf; or, in some plans, the right to receive a cash payment of equivalent value on termination of employment after certain qualifying conditions have been met. see *contingent interest*.

Veterans Administration (VA): established as an independent agency on July 21, 1930, to coordinate and consolidate federal agencies concerned with the administration of laws providing benefits for veterans. The VA helps veterans purchase homes. see *VA mortgage*. [33]

Veterans Administration loan: loaned funds, guaranteed by the Veterans Administration. These are usually housing and education loans. [105]

Veterans Administration Mortgage Guarantees: home mortgage guarantees issued by the VA under the Servicemen's Readjustment Act, to eligible applicants for any of the following purposes: (1) the purchase or construction of an owner-occupied home by the veteran; (2) the construction of a farm residence on land owned by a veteran; (3) the repair, alteration, or improvement of an owner-occupied farm or home by the veteran. Interest is set by the Veterans Administration. [66]

VI: see *vested interest.*

VIP: see *variable interest plus.*

virtuous cycle: a concept describing the kinds of actions some bankers think governments should take to minimize the impact of currency fluctuations. The virtuous cycle approach produces a series of sound economic policies to set off a chain of events in which improved economic performance produces sound currencies, which, in turn, further improves economic performance.

visible items of trade: exports and imports of item and specie. cf. *invisible items of trade.*

visibles: trade in items (i.e., items imported and exported) as opposed to invisibles (i.e., trade in services).

visible supply: usually refers to supplies of a commodity in licensed warehouses. [11]

visible trade: that portion of commerce between nations that is shown by records of transactions involving the exchange of tangible items.

V loans: pursuant to Regulation V of the Federal Reserve System, defense production loans guaranteed by the Board of Governors.

void: that which has no legal effect.

voidable contract: an agreement that can be rescinded by either of the parties in the event of fraud, incompetence, or other sufficient cause.

volatility: a measure of a stock's tendency to move up and down in price, based on its daily price history over the latest 12 months. Stocks with higher volatilities tend to exhibit greater price fluctuation than those with lower volatility values. A volatility of 20 percent would indicate the stock has, over the last 12 months of trading activity, fluctuated about 20 percent above and below the average price for that period. [68]

volume: the total number of securities traded during a stated period of time. synonymous with *turnover.*

volume discount: institutional organizations that invest heavily are often given a commission discount when the order is significant, that is, $500,000 or more.

volume of trading (or sales): represents a simple addition of successive futures transactions. It is the total of the sales (or of the purchases), and not of the sum of both. [11]

voluntary alienation: transfer of title when the property assumes a new owner.

voluntary association: a group of individuals, joined together for a common economical, social, religious, political, professional, or similar purpose, who have not incorporated or otherwise regularized their group under state statutes. [59]

voluntary association account: a savings account held by a nonincorporated group, such as a women's club, baseball team, church, civic group, or charity; otherwise, generally similar to the corporation account. [59]

voluntary bankruptcy: see *bankruptcy.*

voluntary conveyance or deed: the instrument of transfer of an owner's title to property to the lien holder. Usually such conveyance serves to bypass a legal situation of a court judgment showing insufficient security to satisfy a debt, and occurs without transfer of a valuable consideration. see *particular lien.*

voluntary plan: a type of accumulation plan for investment on a regular basis but without any total time period or ultimate investment amount specified. The sales charge is applicable individually to each purchase made. [23]

voluntary trust: established by a deed of transfer of certain property made voluntarily by an individual or other legal entity to a trustee for a specified purpose.

vostro account: "your account"; used by a depository bank to describe an account maintained with it by a bank in a foreign country. cf. *nostro account.*

voting right (stock): the stockholder's right to vote his or her stock in the affairs of the company. Most common shares have one vote each. Preferred stock usually carries the right to vote when preferred dividends are in default for a specified period. The right to vote is usually delegated by proxy of the stockholder to another person. [20]

voting trust: an agreement whereby stockholders turn over their voting rights to a small group of people, who are called voting trustees.

voting trust certificate: see *voting trust.*

voucher: a written statement that bears witness or vouches for something (e.g., a voucher showing that services have been rendered or goods bought).

voucher audit: examination and approval by administrative authority of a proposed disbursement. [105]

voucher check: a form of check to

which is attached another form termed a voucher. The voucher portion of the check is used to describe or otherwise designate the purpose for which the check is drawn. When a voucher check is received from a buyer by a seller, the seller detaches the voucher from the check before presenting the check for payment. The voucher is then used as the posting medium to credit the accounts receivable ledger, thereby showing payment received from the buyer. Many businesses use copies of voucher checks as their record of invoices paid.

vouchers payable: liabilities for goods and services evidenced by vouchers which have been preaudited and approved for payment but have not been paid. [49]

voucher payment plan: a method of construction loan payouts in which the contractor or borrower completes lender forms requesting each payout when a particular, prespecified stage of construction is reached. [59]

voucher register: a book of original entry in which information is accumulated as to cash payments.

voucher system: a system which calls for the preparation of vouchers for transactions involving payments and for the recording of such vouchers in a special book of original entry known as a voucher register, in the order in which payment is approved. [49]

VR: see *vested rights.*

VRM: see *variable-rate mortgage.*

VT: see *voting trust.*

Vtg.: *voting.*

WA: see *Williams Act.*

Wachovia adjustable mortgage: a recent approach in mortgage lending, developed by this North Carolina bank. It works this way: a customer buys a home with a 30-year adjustable mortgage. The initial mortgage rate is tied to money market and local market rates. The interest rate is adjusted every quarter in line with bill rates. The monthly payment stays the same for five years, but the new rate determines how much will go for interest and how much for principal. Every five years the monthly payment is adjusted—up or down by up to 25 percent—so the loan will be paid off on time. After 25 years the monthly payment can be adjusted by more than 25 percent if there is a danger the loan will not be paid off on time. If after 30 years the loan has not been paid off, the borrower may refinance. see *renegotiable-rate mortgage; variable-rate mortgage.*

wad: slang, a roll of paper money.

wage: compensation of employees receiving a stated sum per piece, hour, day, or any other unit or period. Usually it is all compensation paid, including salaries. cf. *earnings, payroll, rate variance.*

Wage and Hour Law: see *Fair Labor Standards Act of 1938.*

wage and salary administration: a well-defined approach for establishing wages and salaries according to an organization's rule and policies, in line with the practice of other companies in the same industry and/or area of work.

wage assignment: an agreement permitting a lender to collect a certain portion of a borrower's salary from his or her employer if payment is not made as specified in the credit contract. [78]

Wage Earner Plan: formally called *adjustment of debt of an individual with regular income plan*; a plan whereby a debtor arranges to make periodic payments to a trustee of the bankruptcy court. The trustee disburses the money to the creditors. [76]

wage freeze: a limit, usually imposed by a government, on salary increases.

wage stabilization: a governmental program to keep wages for a particular industry or location from rapidly in-

691

creasing beyond existing levels. see *inflationary spiral, stabilization policy.*

Wagner-Connery Act: federal legislation that guarantees the right of workers to organize and bargain collectively for a contract and declares specific employer actions to be unfair labor practices. see *bargaining unit;* see also *Baby Wagner Acts,* which interfere with guaranteed rights. The law created the National Labor Relations Board to administer its functions.

waiting period

(1) *general:* the time between filing a claim for unemployment benefits or workmen's compensation and the beginning of such benefit payments.

(2) *investments:* the time, usually 20 days, that must pass between the application for listing a new security from the SEC and the date when the securities can be offered to the public.

waiver: the voluntary relinquishment of a right in a piece of property or to a claim against another's property that would be legally enforceable if the person waiving so elected.

waiver of citation: a document executed by an interested party in an accounting proceeding by which he relinquishes his right to the formal issue and service of a citation. [37]

waiver of demand: see *waiver of protest.*

waiver of premium: nearly all life insurance companies will add to their contracts, upon payment of a small additional premium, a clause providing that if the insured becomes totally and permanently disabled, his or her insurance policy will be continued in full force and the company will exempt the insured from paying further premiums during disability.

waiver of protest: a statement, signed by the endorser of a note, indicating that he or she will remain liable even if he or she is not notified that the note has not been paid when due.

Wall Street: popular name for the New York City business and financial district.

Wall Street Journal: one of America's leading newspapers, noted for its coverage of financial, corporate, and market news.

wanted for cash: appearing on the ticker tape showing that an individual is interested in purchasing a given quantity of shares designated and will pay for them the same day.

war babies (brides): securities of corporations involved in manufacturing materials for the U.S. Department of Defense.

ward: the infant or incompetent person who is the beneficiary of an estate of a deceased person. The ward is under the care of a guardian who is appointed by a court of law to administer the affairs of the ward with the sanction of the court having such jurisdiction, until some time as the court finds that the ward has reached majority or has become fully competent to handle his own affairs. [10]

warehouse, bonded: see *warehouse, state bonded; warehouse, U.S. Customs bonded.*

warehouse, captive: see *warehouse, private.*

warehouse, commodity: a warehouse storing commodity goods (cotton, wool, tobacco, and other grown items). see also *go-down.*

warehouse, company: see *warehouse, private.*

warehouse, private: a warehouse operated by an owner, which hold his goods. synonymous with *captive warehouse* and *company warehouse.*

warehouse, public: a warehouse that is rented out by the owner as a facility for the storing of goods.

warehouse, state bonded: a public warehouse, under government supervision, that has been licensed by a state prior to operation. Merchandise is stored there without the payment of duties or taxes until it is withdrawn from the warehouse.

warehouse, U.S. Customs bonded: a federal warehouse where goods remain until duty has been collected from the importer. Goods under bond are also kept here.

warehouse, U.S. Internal Revenue: a public warehouse; the owner of goods has posted a bond guaranteeing payment of internal revenue tax on U.S.-produced items.

warehouse customs bond: see *bond, warehouse customs.*

warehouse receipt: an instrument listing the goods or commodities deposited in a warehouse. It is a receipt for the commodities listed, and for which the warehouse is the bailee. Warehouse receipts may be either nonnegotiable or negotiable.

warehouse stock: goods held in quantity in a warehouse for reasons of economy.

warehousing: hypothecation of mortgage to a commercial bank as security for repayment of short-term loans. [22]

warehousing loan: a loan made on inventory held in warehouses.

war-profits tax: a tax on profits arising from war efforts. A distinction exists between this and excess-profits taxation, which reaches high profits whatever their cause.

Warr.: see *warrant.*

warrant
(1) *investments:* a certificate giving the holder the right to purchase securities at a stipulated price within a specified time limit or at any time. Sometimes offered with securities as an inducement to buy. [20]
(2) *law:* a written order in the name of the state and signed by a magistrate directing an officer to make an arrest.

warrants payable: the amount of warrants outstanding and unpaid. [49]

warranty
(1) *banking:* a statement in a policy of the existence of a fact or a condition of the subject of insurance which, if found to be untrue by misrepresentation, will void the policy.
(2) *law:* a statement, either written, expressed, or implied, that a certain statement identified in a contract is presently true or will be true.

warranty, implied: a warranty assumed to be a part of the insurance contract even though not expressly included. In connection with products liability insurance, the warranty is assumed to be made by one who sells a product that is fit for the purpose for which it is sold. [53]

warranty deed: see *deed, general warranty.*

wash sale: a false transaction of security or commodity sales that are purchased and sold by the same individual so as to create the impression of activity and/or volume of the item.

wasting assets: assets whose value is depleted and will eventually be exhausted by the continued operations of an extractive business (oil wells, mining claims, etc.). see *depletion allowance.*

wasting trust: a trust of property that is gradually being consumed.

watch filing: a procedure by which losses on small risks are referred to the underwriter for his or her attention.

watch (watching) my number: the request by a broker on an exchange floor to another broker to watch for the firm's broker's assigned number on the annunciator board should he or she be off the floor. If a broker's number is flashed on the board, it means that he or she is requested to go to his or her firm's booth on the edge of the floor.

watered capital: see *watered stock.*

watered stock: corporate stock issued by a corporation for property at an overvaluation, or stock released for which the corporation receives nothing in payment.

waybill: a document made out by the carrier at the point of origin which shows the point of origin, destination, route, consignor, consignee, description of shipment, and freight charge. cf. *bill of lading.*

WD
(1) see *deed, general warranty.*
(2) see *withdrawal.*

weak: a condition of declining prices for securities or commodities.

weak hands: see *strong (or weak) hands.*

weak holdings: stocks retained on margin by speculators who will use any reason to sell them.

weak market: a situation characterized by a greater demand for selling than there is for purchasing.

wealth: an economic term designating the value of one's total possessions and rights in property. cf. *national wealth.*

wealth effect: see *Pigou effect concept.*

wealth tax: an annual tax on a person's assets above a stated minimum, even those assets which do not yield any income.

Webb-Pomerene Act of 1918: federal legislation exempting exporters' associations from the antitrust regulations.

weed off: slang, to take money from a roll of bank notes.

weekend arbitrage: a now defunct maneuver by which banks lowered their reserve requirements by borrowing clearing house funds overseas on Friday which they did not have to cover until Monday.

weekly premium insurance: see *industrial insurance.*

week order: on the stock exchange, an order to buy or sell which automatically expires if it cannot be executed during the coming week.

weighted average
(1) an average of items in which the raw figures are multiplied by "weights," which vary, according to the relative importance of each component of the average.
(2) a method of inventory valuation. The average cost of a particular inventory item is calculated by dividing its total cost by the number of the items purchased. This average price is then assigned to all items of this class. Inventory value is computed by summing all items. [105]

weighted average cost of capital: the overall required rate of return the firm must pay to raise long-term capital from a composite of capital sources.

wellhead tax: a government proposal to tax domestic oil as it leaves the well; the amount of the tax is the difference between its current controlled price and the world market price imposed by the OPEC cartel.

went to the wall: any bankrupt or failing corporation or individual.

wheeler-dealer: slang, a scheming, clever person.

when, as, and if issued (WI): see *when issued.*

when issued (WI): a short form of *when, as, and if issued.* The term indicates a conditional transaction in a security authorized for issuance but not yet actually issued. All when-issued transactions are on a conditional basis, to be settled if and when the actual security is issued and the exchange or National Association of Securities Dealers rules that the transactions are to be settled. [20]

when-issued basis (WIB): quotations for securities that are traded before they are actually issued. The sources of this type of stock vary but usually result from corporate reorganizations, mergers, rights financing, and stock splits. [105]

whipsawed: to have experienced a substantial loss at both ends of a securities transaction.

white elephant: property that is so costly to maintain that it is virtually impossible to operate it at a profit; also property with respect to which a loss is certain.

white knight: in order to encourage a successful company takeover by another firm, a friendly suitor is brought in to put down another bidder. cf. *gray knight.*

whole coverage: any type of insurance that provides for payment from all losses without any deductions.

whole life insurance: synonymous with *ordinary life.*

whole loan: in the secondary market to indicate that the full amount of a loan is available for sale with no portion, or participation, retained by the seller. [105]

wholesale banking: the function of providing bank services, loan security, and loans to large corporate customers with strong financial statements. [105]

wholesale money: money borrowed in large amounts from banks, large firms or financial organizations, in contrast to *retail money* which is acquired by attracting deposits from individuals and small companies.

wholesale price index: a measure compiled by the U.S. Bureau of Labor Statistics, showing the average change in the price of approximately 2200 commodities at the primary market level (usually the level at which the commodity is first sold commercially in substantial volume), compared to the average level in selected base years.

wholesaler: an individual or firm selling its goods or services at a reduced or discounted rate; usually for large sales. synonymous with *distributor.*

Whous.: warehouse.

WI: see *when issued.*

WIB: see *when-issued basis.*

wide market

(1) a situation where price quotations are relatively far apart.

(2) a market where there are a relatively large number of investors.

widening of capital: increasing the quantity of capital employed through increasing the volume of goods produced but without changing the ratio of the amount of capital employed to a given quantity of goods.

wide opening: a securities situation characterized by a considerable difference in the bid and asked prices at the beginning of the market day.

widow-and-orphan stock: a high-income, noncyclical stock with security but which is in other ways unrewarding—that is, a slow market mover.

widow's allowance: the allowance of personal property made by the court or by statute to a widow for her immediate requirements after her husband's death. [37]

widow's exemption: the amount allowed as a deduction in computing the state inheritance tax on the widow's share of her husband's estate. [37]

wildcat bank: one of the unsound banks chartered by the states during the hectic banking years between 1816 and 1863. Most of these banks failed.

wildcat money: bank notes issued by wildcat banks.

wildcat scheme: a highly speculative venture with few signs for success.

will: a document in which an individual (the testator or testatrix) having full mental faculties sets forth his or her desires and bequests regarding the disposition of his total wealth after his death. cf. *nuncupative will.*

Williams Act: federal legislation of 1968, requiring that tender offers be made to all securities holders at the same price. see *Saturday night special.*

Wilmington Plan: a plan initiated by the Wilmington Savings Funds Society, a mutual savings bank, providing individual customers with a free checking account, a savings account and an agreement to permit the savings ac-

count to serve as security for an automatic short-term advance if the checking account is overdrawn. Direct payroll deposit, automatic bill paying, a cash-dispensing machine, and a percentage credit to the customer on purchases via direct debit from the customer's checking account are also available. [36]

windfall profit: an unexpected profit arising from causes not controlled by the recipient.

windfall profits tax: federal legislation passed in 1980; a tax designed to divert from the oil industry to the government a share of profits attributable to the president's decision to phase out price controls, earmarking the money for a variety of energy-producing and energy-saving programs. The Crude Oil Windfall Profits Tax act increased the dividend exclusion to $200 for single taxpayers and $400 for married taxpayers filing separately, and broadened exclusion to cover interest. But neither change was effective for 1980 returns. The act also increased the renewable-source energy credit to $4000 from $2200.

winding up: the process of liquidating a company.

window dressing: the practice of executing transactions shortly before the end of an accounting period to change artificially the items in the accounting statements of the period.

winning bid: the successful bid for a particular securities issue. This will generally be the bid that produces the lowest interest cost to a municipal borrower or the one offering the highest premium in the event of a single coupon bid. [105]

wins and losses: see *settlement check.*

wiped out

(1) *general:* the failing of a business.

(2) *investments:* when all available margin and cash are exhausted.

(3) *investments:* a considerable, irreversible investment loss.

wire-fate item: check or other item sent for collection or in transit letters to out-of-town banks, accompanied by instructions to notify the sending bank by wire as to whether the item is paid or not paid. This enables the sending bank to ascertain quickly whether or not the item is paid. [10]

wire house: a member firm of an exchange maintaining a communications network either linking its own branch offices to offices of correspondent firms, or linking some combination of such offices. [20]

wire off: telegraphic instructions to an agent to cancel a specific policy on receipt of the telegram.

wire transfer: see *transfer.*[50]

with all faults: without a guarantee, usually in real estate transactions; of the absence of imperfections; as is.

withdrawal: the manner in which funds on deposit in savings accounts may be paid out by the bank. The depositor must present his passbook and sign either a withdrawal slip or the ledger card (no-ticket savings plan) before the bank can pay out funds against the deposit account. The signature on the withdrawal slip or signed on the proper line of the ledger card should always agree with the signature on file in the bank to insure that the right person is receiving the withdrawn funds. [10]

withdrawal form: a source document and authorization for withdrawals from a savings account used by the customers and kept by the association for its records. [59]

withdrawal notice: the written notification of intent to remove funds from an account on or after a specified date. This is required on certain types of accounts. [105]

withdrawal plan: arrangement provided by certain open-end companies by which an investor can receive monthly or quarterly payments in a designated amount that may be more or less than actual investment income. [30]

withdrawal ratio: withdrawals expressed as a percentage of gross savings for a given period. [59]

withdrawal value: the amount credited to the savings account of a member, less deductions as shown on the records of the savings association. [59]

with exchange: a designation on a check or draft of payable with exchange indicating that any collection or exchange charges will be against the payer in the event that it is a check, or the drawee in the event that it is a draft.

with full recourse: in lending, a term in a written agreement that gives the buyer in a sale or other transaction the right to full reimbursement from the seller for any losses resulting from the loans or other items purchased. [59]

withholding tax: federal, state, or city taxes withheld by employers from the salaries of employees and paid directly to the taxing agency.

without dividend: see *ex-dividend.*

without interest: securities and other debt instruments in default sell on a flat or without interest basis where a purchaser does not make an additional payment for the accrued interest. Income bonds, although not in default, since the interest is not required to be paid unless earned, sell on a flat or without interest basis.

without recourse

(1) *finance:* used in endorsing a negotiable instrument where the endorser of a note is no longer responsible, should the obligation not be paid. see *qualified endorsement.*

(2) *law:* an agreement that the purchaser accepts all risks in the transaction, and gives up all rights to any recourse. see also *caveat emptor.*

with partial recourse: in lending, a term in a written agreement that gives the buyer in a sale or other transaction the right to reimbursement for an agreed-upon portion of any losses resulting from the loans or other items purchased. [59]

with recourse

(1) *finance:* used in endorsing a negotiable instrument where the endorser of a note continues to be responsible, should the obligation not be paid.

(2) *law:* an agreement that if the seller is unable to meet his or her obligations, the purchaser has the right to endorse a claim against the seller for sustained damages.

wolf: an experienced and often crafty speculator.

won: monetary unit of Korea.

worked off: a minute drop in the price of a security or commodity.

working asset: those assets invested in securities that can be expected to fluctuate more or less with common stock prices generally. Corrections may be made to eliminate an invest-

ment company's holdings of cash and high-grade senior securities and to give weight to holdings of junior issues. [3]

working capital: the excess of current assets over current liabilities representing the capital immediately available for the continued operation of a business.

working capital acceptance: a banker's acceptance that does not finance a specific trading transaction but finances a firm's general working capital needs. It is not eligible for rediscount at the Federal Reserve.

working capital fund: see *intragovernmental service fund.*

working capital loan: a short-term loan to provide money to purchase income-generating assets, such as inventory. [105]

working capital turnover: the ratio of sales to current assets.

working control: theoretically, ownership of 51 percent of a company's voting stock is necessary to exercise control. In practice—and this is particularly true in the case of a large corporation—effective (i.e., working) control sometimes can be exerted through ownership, individually or by a group acting in concert, of less than 50 percent of the stock.

working fund: the amount of money made available to a teller for the handling of routine transactions. [59]

working reserve (bank): consists of cash held in the bank, cash items in process of collection, and demand deposits with other individual banks, but not deposits with a Federal Reserve Bank.

work in process: the cost of partially completed products manufactured or processed, such as a partially completed printing job. Sometimes referred to as *work in progress.* *[49]*

work in progress: see *work in process.*

workmen's compensation: a system for compensating workers injured or disabled on the job. Workmen's compensation programs are established by state law and differ widely. Typically, benefits are paid under private insurance policies, but awards are determined by state boards. see *average weekly benefit.*

workout loan: a loan granted to a borrower in a distressed financial condition pursuant to a plan to "work out" of the difficulty. Accordingly, many restrictions are imposed to assure the achievement of the purpose.

work simplification: a reorganization of methods, equipment, resources, and working conditions to minimize worker fatigue and increase worker efficiency and output.

World Bank: see *International Bank for Reconstruction and Development.*

World Bank Group: collectively, the International Bank for Reconstruction and Development (World Bank) and its affiliates, the International Finance Corporation and the International Development Association.

worth: the total value of something, including an investment in a business. see *net worth.*

WOW: written order of withdrawal.

WP: see *windfall profit.*

WPA: see *Webb-Pomerene Act of 1918.*

WPT: see *windfall profits tax.*

WR: see *warehouse receipt.*

wraparound: see *wraparound mortgages.*

wraparound annuities: tax-deferral schemes allowing an individual to shelter current interest income on a bank savings certificate or shares in a mutual fund in a tax-deferred annuity administered by an insurance company.

wraparound mortgages: involves two lenders, a mortgage originator and a wraparound lender. Rather than providing an entirely new mortgage at current market rates to a home buyer, the wraparound lender agrees to continue to pay the monthly installments on the existing mortgage on the home to be bought, at the original contract interest rate of the mortgage, and also to make any additional payments needed to meet the purchase price of the home. As a result, the terms of the original mortgage continue to be satisfied, the seller is compensated for the sale of his or her investment, and the home buyer is able to purchase a home and share in the benefits of the below-market rate paid by the wraparound lender on a portion of the money financed.

writ: a written instrument, under a state's seal, issued from a court directing an officer of the court to do some act, or enjoining an individual to do or refrain from doing some act.

write-down: the book value to which an asset has been reduced to adjust for the capital that has been lost on the decline of the asset's value.

write-off: an asset that has been determined to be uncollectible and therefore has been charged off as a loss. Sometimes it is the debt itself. cf. *written-down value.*

writer: the seller of an option contract. *[5]*

write-up: an increase in an asset's book value not resulting from added costs or an adjustment of an asset account to correspond to an appraisal value.

writ of execution: a court order issued to an officer of law commanding him or her to take certain action. [76]

written-down value: an accounting term for the valuation or cost of any asset minus the written-off depreciation.

written off: see *write-off.*

Ws.: warrants, see *warrant.*

WS

  (1) see *Wall Street.*

  (2) see *watered stock.*

WSJ: see *Wall Street Journal.*

WT: see *wellhead tax.*

X: see *no protest.*

X-C: see *ex-coupon.*

X-Ch.: see *exchange.*

X-CL: excess current liabilities.

X-D: see *ex-dividend.*

X-Dis.: see *ex-distribution.*

X-Div.: see *ex-dividend.*

X-I: see *ex-interest.*

X-In.: see *ex-interest.*

X loan: loan made under a law other than a small loan law. [55]

X mark signature: when an individual is unable to sign his or her name because of injury or illiteracy, provision can be made for him or her to "sign" with an X. In this situation, his or her name is inserted by another person and the notation "his mark" or "her mark" is put next to the "X" and then witnessed by a person, who in addition signs the document with the notation that he or she witnessed the "X."

Xmas Club account: see *Christmas Club account.*

X-R: see *ex-rights.*

X-Rts.: see *ex-rights.*

X-Warr.: see *ex-warrants.*

XX: without securities or warrants.

Y: nominal gross national product. [81]

Yankee bond market: issues floated in the United States, in dollars, by reign governments and corporations.

Yankees: American securities on the London Stock Exchange.

yard: slang, a $100 bill, or $100.

yardstick rates: rates of one business used as a criterion for the basic regulation of rates charged by other companies.

year-end adjustment: a modification of a ledger account at the close of a fiscal period arising from an accrual, prepayment, physical inventory, reclassification, policy change, audit adjustment, or other entry, which can be done at discrete intervals. [105]

year-end dividend: an extra dividend paid at the end of the fiscal year in addition to the regular dividend.

yellow-back: slang, a bank note, specifically a gold certificate.

Yellow Book: the British Stock Exchange's listing of requirements for a London stock market quotation.

yen: monetary unit of Japan.

yield
(1) *general:* the profit or income created through an investment in property.
(2) *finance:* to give up possession; to pay.
(3) *government:* the net return of a tax.
(4) *investments:* the rate of return received from one's investment in a specific security or a specific piece of property; most commonly expressed in terms that designate the annual rate of return on the investment. see *ROI.*

yield auction: see *auction.*

yield curve: graphical relationship between yields and maturities of equally risky securities.

yield maintenance: the adjustment upon delivery of the price of a GNMA or other mortgage security purchased under a futures contract or standby commitment to provide the same yield to the purchaser as that which was specified in the original agreement.

yield spread: the difference in yields on varying stocks. A concept utilized by portfolio managers.

yield test: a measurement applied to bond investments in insurance firm portfolios. It is the relationship of the yield of bonds the insurance firm has in its portfolio individually to the yield of fully taxable U.S. government bonds of the same maturity.

yield to adjusted minimum maturity: a measure designed to give the yield to the shortest possible life of a bond.

yield to average life: the yield derived when the average maturity of a bond is substituted for the final maturity date of the issue.

yield to crash: see *yield to adjusted minimum maturity.*

yield to lessor: the internal rate of return generated from a lease transaction alone.

yield to maturity: the rate of return on an investment when it is retained until maturity, given as a percentage.

yield to put: the return a bond earns assuming that it is retained until a certain date and put (sold) to the issuing company at a specific price (the put price).

yield to worst: see *yield to adjusted minimum maturity.*

Y loan: loan made under a law other than a small loan or X loan law. [55]

young adult account: a limited amount of revolving credit which some retail establishments make available to young adults, primarily to give them direct experience in money management. [41]

younger-generation beneficiaries: for generation-skipping tax purposes, beneficiaries who are assigned to a generation younger than the grantor's generation. [105]

"your account": see *vostro account.*

yo-yo stocks: highly volatile securities; these stocks are high-priced specialty issues that fluctuate greatly in price.

Yr.: year

YS: see *yield spread.*

yuan: monetary unit of China.

YYS: see *yo-yo stocks.*

Z

zaire: monetary unit of Congo (Kinshasa) and Zaire.

ZBB: see *zero-base(d) budgeting.*

Z certificate: a certificate issued by the Bank of England to discount houses in lieu of stock certificates to facilitate their dealings in short-dated gilt-edged securities.

zebra plan: an employee benefits plan, known as a *zero-balance reimbursement account*, is a flexible-spending employee benefits plan that does not require participants to earmark a set amount in advance for benefits. Instead, the employee submits proof of eligible expenses and the plan makes a reimbursement in pretax dollars.

zero-balance account: an arrangement, agreed to in advance by a drawee bank, under which a customer issues checks on an account even though funds do not exist in that account to cover the items. When the checks are physically presented to the drawee and posted, creating a minus balance, the bank contacts the customer, reports the overdraft figure, and transfers funds from another account to eliminate it, thus restoring the account to a zero balance. Commonly used by corporations that have many disbursing points and by many agencies of government.

zero-balance reimbursement account: see *zebra plan.*

zero-base(d) budgeting (ZBB)
(1) *general:* a financial management technique to redirect funds from lower-priority current programs to higher ones, to pinpoint opportunities for improved efficiency and effectiveness, to reduce budgets while raising operating performance, and to improve profitability. see also *planning-programming-budgeting.*
(2) *government:* the approach of justifying the budget and its program for each year or two, instead of studying funding increases or decreases in the programs separately as the need arises.

zero basis: the condition occurring when a convertible bond is valued so highly by investors that they buy it at a premium high enough that interest received is canceled out by the premium paid to purchase the bond. The bond is said to be trading on a *zero basis*. [105]

zero bracket amount: the standard amount of income free from tax depending on a taxpayer's filing status. The tax tables already incorporate these amounts into their figures.

zero-coupon bond: see *bond, zero-coupon*.

zero-coupon Eurobonds: American company issues that pay no interest but are sold at a steep discount.

zero floor limit: see *floor limit*.

zero-minus (plus) tick: any sale that takes place at the same price of the previous sale, but at a price that is lower (higher) than the earlier, different price. see *up tick*.

zero-plus tick: see *up tick*.

zero proof: a mechanical method of posting records in a manner serving to prove that the previous balance on each line of posting was made correctly.

zero-rate and low-rate mortgage: a home mortgage appearing to be completely or almost interest free. Requires a large down payment and one-time finance charge, then the loan is repaid in fixed monthly payments over a short term.

zloty: monetary unit of Poland.

zone freight rate: one freight rate applicable to shipments from any of the points in one area or zone to any of the points in another.

zone pricing: a pricing system under which the seller divides the market into a number of zones, quoting different prices in different zones. Originally, a compromise between FOB, under which the seller pays all freight, and CIF, under which the buyer pays all freight. The term now extends beyond the freight question. cf. *basing point, delivery price*.

[1] Federal Reserve System, Board of Governors: *Glossary.*

[2] The Association of Commodity Commission Merchants: *Trading in Commodity Futures.*

[3] Edison Electric Institute: *Glossary of Electric Utility Terms.*

[4] Dun & Bradstreet, Inc.: *How Does Your Business Compare with Others in Your Line?*

[5] American Stock Exchange, Inc.: *Introducing Puts.*

[6] Society of Residential Appraisers: *Real Estate Appraisal Terminology.*

[7] Federal Reserve Bank of New York: *The Story of Checks.*

[8] National Association of Mutual Savings Banks: *This is NAMSB.*

[9] U.S. Department of Commerce: *Selected U.S. Marketing Terms and Definitions.*

[10] National Cash Register Corp.: *Financial Terminology.*

[11] Commodity Research Publication Co.: *Understanding the Cocoa Market.*

[12] Mutual of Omaha: *Terms and Definitions.*

[13] American Marketing Association: *Report on Definitions—SBA Aids, No. 127.*

[14] National Association of Mutual Savings Banks: *Annual Report, 1980.*

[15] American Stock Exchange, Inc.: *The Versatile Option.*

[16] World Bank: *Development Finance Companies.*

[17] National Foreign Trade Council: *Revised American Foreign Trade Definitions.*

[18] Association of American Railroads: *Railway Statistics Manual.*

[19] American Insurance Association: *National Building Code.*

[20] The New York Stock Exchange, Inc.: *The Language of Investing.*

[21] U.S. Office of Management and Budget: *American National Dictionary for Information Processing.*

[22] Mortgage Bankers Association of America: *Mortgages for Retirement and Endowment Funds.*

[23] Investment Company Institute: *Mutual Fund Fact Book, 1979, "Glossary."*

[24] U.S. Postal Service: *Glossary of Postal Terms.*

[25] American Bankers Association: *Trust Fact Book.*

[26] Securities Industry Association: *A Profile of Investment Banking.*

[27] Beresiner, Y. A.: *Collector's Guide to Paper Money.* New York: Stein & Day, 1977.

[28] National Foundation for Consumer Credit: *Using Credit Intelligently.*

[29] New York State Bankers Association: *What Every Woman and Man Should Know about Consumer Banking.*

[30] Wisenberger Investment Companies Service: *Investment Companies, 1979.*

[31] Burroughs Corp.: *Glossary of Financial and Data-Processing Terms.*

[32] American Institute of Banking: *Trust Department Service.*

[33] American Bankers Association: *Bank Fact Book.*

[34] International Business Machines Corp.: *Data Processing Glossary.*

[35] Small Business Administration: *SBIC Financing for Small Business.*

[36] National Science Foundation: *Consequences of Electronic Funds Transfer.*

[37] American Bankers Association: *Glossary of Fiduciary Terms.*

[38] National Cash Register Corp.: *Industrial Accounting Terminology.*

[39] American Institute of Banking: *Savings Banking.*

[40] Federal Reserve System: *Terms.*

[41] International Consumer Credit Association: *How to Use Consumer Credit Wisely.*

[42] International Monetary Fund: *Annual Report on Exchange Arrangements and Exchange Restrictions.*

[43] American Institute of Certified Public

Continued

Accountants: *Glossary for Accounting Terms.*

[44] American Institute of Banking: *Home Mortgage Lending.*

[45] UNIVAC: *Glossary of Computer Terms.*

[46] Conference Board: *Economic Almanac.*

[47] U.S. Department of Commerce, National Bureau of Standards: *Units and Systems of Weight and Measures, Their Origin, Development, and Present Status.*

[48] American Marketing Association: *A Glossary of Marketing Terms.*

[49] Municipal Finance Officers Association: *Governmental Accounting and Financial Reporting Principles.*

[50] American Institute of Banking: *Principles of Bank Operation.*

[51] United States League of Savings Associations: *Savings and Loan Fact Book.*

[52] Municipal Finance Officers Association: *Public Employee Retirement Administration—Terminology.*

[53] Chamber of Commerce of the U.S.: *Dictionary of Insurance Terms.*

[54] The Hartford: *Glossary—Terms and Phrases Commonly Used in Property, Casualty, and Life Insurance.*

[55] Household Finance Corporation: *General Glossary.*

[56] Employers Insurance of Wausau: *A Dictionary of Insurance Terms.*

[57] Federal Reserve Bank of Atlanta: *Econometric Models.*

[58] American Council of Life Insurance: *Life Insurance Fact Book.*

[59] Institute of Financial Education: *Glossary of Savings Association Terminology.*

[60] U.S. Department of Labor: *Glossary of Currently Used Wage Terms.*

[61] U.S. Department of Commerce: *A Basic Guide to Exporting.*

[62] Realtors National Marketing Institute: *Real Estate Handbook.*

[63] Retail Merchant Association: *Glossary—The Display Manual.*

[64] Association of Bank Holding Companies: *Bank Holding Companies Today.*

[65] Federal Reserve Bank of New York: *Definitions.*

[66] Federal Home Loan Bank Board: *Types of Mortgages-Fact Sheet.*

[67] American Institute of Banking: *Investments.*

[68] Pacific Coast Stock Exchange: *Directory of Securities, Options Stock Analysis.*

[69] Federal Reserve Bank of Boston: *Pandora's Box—Glossary of Terms.*

[70] Tax Foundation, Inc.: *Glossary—Facts and Figures on Government Finance,* 20th edition, 1979.

[71] Federal Reserve Bank of Cleveland: "Terms," *Economic Review,* January 1967

[72] Federal Reserve Bank of St. Louis: "Definitions," *Review.*

[73] U.S. Department of Commerce: *Dictionary of Economical and Statistical Terms.*

[74] Federal Reserve Bank of Chicago: *Definitions.*

[75] Federal Reserve Bank of Philadelphia: *What Are Federal Funds?*

[76] Associated Credit Bureaus, Inc.: *Glossary.*

[77] American Institute of Certified Public Accountants: *Accounting Research and Terminology.*

[78] Federal Reserve Bank of New York: *Consumer Credit Terminology Handbook.*

[79] Federal Reserve Bank of St. Louis: *Review,* December 1980.

[80] Financial Accounting Standards Board: *FASB Discussion Memorandum.*

[81] Federal Reserve Bank of St. Louis, *Review,* October 1982.

[82] IMF Staff Papers, *Effects of Devaluation on a Trade Balance,* Washington, D.C., 1952.

[83] *Borrowing by Developing Countries*

Continued

on the Euro-Currency Market, OECD, Paris, 1977.

[84] Exchange Control Notice EC1, Bank of England, 1976.

[85] Finance of International Trade, Institute of Bankers, London, 1976.

[86] Depositary Receipts, Morgan Guaranty Trust Company, New York, 1973.

[87] Eurocurrency Financing, Chase Manhattan Bank, N.A., New York, 1975.

[88] Federal Reserve Bank of Kansas City, Monthly Review, July—August 1977.

[89] Spotlight on the Term Loan, Bankers' Magazine, Boston, Summer 1976.

[90] Federal Reserve Bank of New York, Quarterly Review, Summer 1977.

[91] International Monetary Relations, Royal Institute of International Affairs, London, 1976.

[92] Development Co-operation: 1976 Review, OECD Development Assistance Committee, Paris, 1976.

[93] Federal Reserve Bank of Chicago, Economic Perspectives, March–April 1978.

[94] American Management Association, International Money Management, New York, 1973.

[95] International Chamber of Commerce Brochure, Incoterms, No.274, Paris, 1976.

[96] IMF, IMF Survey, Washington, D.C., March 1979.

[97] Japan Securities Research Institute, Securities Market in Japan, 1977.

[98] Federal Reserve Bank of St. Louis, Review, March 1983.

[99] Federal Reserve Bank of St. Louis, Review, February 1983.

[100] Federal Reserve Bank of St. Louis, Review, April 1983.

[101] Financing Accounting Standards Board, Statement of Financial Accounting Standards, No. 8, Connecticut, 1975.

[102] Euromoney, London, October 1976.

[103] Morgan Guaranty Trust Co., World Financial Markets, New York, May 1978.

[104] Euromoney, London, March 1977.

[105] The American Bankers Association, Banking Terminology, Washington, D.C., 1981.

[106] Federal Reserve Bank of St. Louis, Review, March 1984.

[107] Federal Reserve Bank of St. Louis, Review, October 1984.

[108] Federal Reserve Bank of St. Louis, Review, December 1984.